CONVERSION FACTORS

Energy	1 J	$= 9.478\,17 \cdot 10^{-4}$ Btu
		$= 2.388\,5 \cdot 10^{-4}$ kcal
Energy rate	1 W	$= 3.412\,14$ Btu/hr
Force	1 N	$= 0.224\,809$ lb_f
Heat flux	1 W/m^2	$= 0.317\,1$ Btu/(hr·ft^2)
Kinematic viscosity and diffusivities	1 m^2/s	$= 3.875 \cdot 10^4$ ft^2/hr
Length	1 m	$= 39.370$ in
		$= 3.280\,8$ ft
Mass	1 kg	$= 2.204\,6$ lb_m
Mass density	1 kg/m^3	$= 0.062\,428$ lb_m/ft^3
Mass flow rate	1 kg/s	$= 7\,936.6$ lb_m/hr
Pressure	Pa	$= 1$ N/m^2
		$= 0.020\,885\,4$ lb_f/ft^2
		$= 1.450\,4 \cdot 10^{-4}$ lb_f/in^2
		$= 4.015 \cdot 10^{-3}$ in water
	$1 \cdot 10^5$ N/m^2	$= 1$ bar
Specific heat	1 J/kg·K	$= 2.388\,6 \cdot 10^{-4}$ Btu/(lb_m·°F)
Temperature	K	$= (5/9)$°R
		$= (5/9)$ (°F $+ 459.67$)
		$=$ °C $+ 273.15$
Time	3600 s	$= 1$ hr

For accompanying disk, please ask at the issue desk.

AN INTRODUCTION TO COMBUSTION
Concepts and Applications

DATE DUE FOR RETURN

The loan period may be shortened if the item is requested.

McGraw-Hill Series in Mechanical Engineering

Consulting Editors

Jack P. Holman, Southern Methodist University
John R. Lloyd, Michigan State University

AN INTRODUCTION TO COMBUSTION
Concepts and Applications

Stephen R. Turns

Propulsion Engineering Research Center
and
Department of Mechanical Engineering
The Pennsylvania State University

McGraw-Hill, Inc.

New York   St. Louis   San Francisco   Auckland   Bogotá   Caracas   Lisbon
London   Madrid   Mexico City   Milan   Montreal   New Delhi
San Juan   Singapore   Sydney   Tokyo   Toronto

This book was set in Times Roman.
The editors were John J. Corrigan and John M. Morriss;
the production supervisor was Louise Karam.
The cover was designed by Anthony Farenga.
Project supervision was done by Keyword Publishing Services.
R. R. Donnelley & Sons Company was printer and binder.

1000692022

AN INTRODUCTION TO COMBUSTION
Concepts and Applications

This book is printed on acid-free paper.

1 2 3 4 5 6 7 8 9 0   DOC DOC   9 0 9 8 7 6 5

P/N 065531-6
PART OF
ISBN 0-07-911812-7

Library of Congress Cataloging-in-Publication Data

Turns, Stephen R.
   An introduction to combustion: concepts and applications
  Stephen R. Turns.
      p.   cm. — (McGraw-Hill series in mechanical engineering)
  Includes bibliographical references and index.
  ISBN 0-07-911812-7 (set)
   1. Combustion engineering.   I. Title.   II. Series.
TJ254.5.T88   1996
621.402′3—dc20   95-11905

ABOUT THE AUTHOR

Stephen R. Turns received degrees in mechanical engineering from The Pennsylvania State University (B.S., 1970), Wayne State University (M.S., 1974), and the University of Wisconsin at Madison (Ph.D., 1979). He was a research engineer at General Motors Research Laboratories from 1970 to 1975. He joined the Penn State faculty in 1979 and is currently Professor of Mechanical Engineering. Dr. Turns teaches a wide variety of courses in the thermal sciences and has received several awards for teaching excellence at Penn State. He is an active combustion researcher, publishing widely, and is an active member of The Combustion Institute, the American Society of Mechanical Engineers, and the Society of Automotive Engineers.

This Book Is Dedicated to
My Wife, Joan, and Our Sons,
Matthew and Michael

By contrast, the first fires flickering at a cave mouth are our own discovery, our own triumph, our grasp upon invisible chemical power. Fire contained, in that place of brutal darkness and leaping shadows, the crucible and the chemical retort, steam and industry. It contained the entire human future.

LOREN EISELEY
THE UNEXPECTED UNIVERSE

CONTENTS

14 Burning of Solids 443

15 Pollutant Emissions 472

PREFACE

High interest in combustion and combustion applications exists among many engineering students. Although undergraduate, senior-level courses in combustion and combustion-related areas are offered at many institutions, finding an appropriate textbook for such courses is difficult, at best. The need for an introductory text on combustion, specifically structured for an undergraduate readership, has served as the motivation for writing this book. The offering of an introductory course at Penn State and the development of an introductory textbook were conceived jointly, and this book is the result of those developments.

Although the primary audience is intended to be senior-level students in mechanical and related engineering majors, others may find the text useful as a bridge between the basic undergraduate thermal sciences and advanced treatments of combustion. Many examples and problems are presented to aid in understanding and to relate to practical applications. Thus, is it hoped that both first-year graduate students and practicing engineers can benefit from the material presented here.

In its organization, the text provides flexibility. The 15 chapters provide much more material than can be covered in a single-semester course; this overkill makes it easy for an instructor to tailor a course to a particular theme or set of topics, while allowing the theme to evolve or change from one course offering to another. For example, a one-semester course providing a general overview could cover Chapters 1–6, 15, 8, 9, and 14; while a course with some emphasis on spark-ignition engines could cover Chapters 1–6, 8, 11, 12, 15, and 9.

Located in Chapters 1–3 are topics considered essential for an undergraduate course. Chapter 1 defines combustion and the types of flames, and introduces the effects and control of combustion-generated air pollution, which is treated in greater detail in Chapter 15.

The thermochemistry needed for a study of combustion is presented in Chapter 2. This chapter emphasizes the importance of chemical equilibrium to combustion. Software provided with this book provides students with a simple means of calculating complex equilibria for combustion gases; this software can be put to good use in many interesting and pedogogically helpful projects. Chapter 3 introduces mass transfer. The approach taken here, and throughout the book, is to simplify theoretical developments by treating all mass transfer within the context of simple binary systems. Except for a brief mention in Chapter 7, the treatment of multi-component diffusion is left to more advanced texts. Such an approach allows students with no previous exposure to mass transfer to gain an appreciation of the subject without getting bogged down in its inherent complexities. Chapter 3 uses both the classical Stefan problem and simple droplet evaporation to illustrate mass transfer theory.

Onward to the subject of chemistry, Chapters 4 and 5 deal with chemical kinetics by presenting basic concepts (Chapter 4) and discussing chemical mechanisms of importance to combustion and combustion-generated air pollution (Chapter 5). In addition to showing the unavoidable complexity of hydrocarbon combustion chemistry, simple single- and multi-step kinetics are presented that can be used to incorporate chemical kinetic effects in simple analyses or models, recognizing, of course, the pitfalls of simplified kinetics.

The interrelation of chemical kinetics and thermodynamic modeling is the subject of Chapter 6. Here, models of constant-pressure and constant-volume reactors, and well-stirred and plug-flow reactors, are developed. These simple models allow a student to clearly grasp how chemical kinetics fits into the bigger picture. This chapter also offers many opportunities for projects involving reactor analysis and/or design. Both the usefulness and uniqueness of this chapter make it a lot of fun.

Having completed our study of thermochemistry, molecular transport, and chemical kinetics, Chapter 7 is devoted to the development of the simplified conservation equations for reacting systems used in subsequent chapters. The conserved-scalar concept is introduced here. This chapter is intended to provide a background from which more rigorous developments can be followed. For an undergraduate course, this chapter is clearly optional, and is probably best skipped; however, for an introductory graduate-level course, the chapter may be quite useful.

Elementary treatments of flames are presented in Chapters 8–13. Laminar premixed flames are discussed in Chapter 8, and laminar nonpremixed flames in Chapters 9 and 10; while turbulent flames are dealt with in Chapter 12 (premixed) and Chapter 13 (nonpremixed). Topics treated include flame propagation, ignition and quenching, and flame stabilization. Simplified analyses are presented wherever possible, and practical applications emphasized. In all cases, rigorous mathematical development is eschewed in favor of developing the most basic understanding. This approach has the shortcoming of not being able to deal with some phenomena at all, and others, incompletely at best. Usually in these areas, warnings are given and references cited to help the reader who seeks a more complete understanding. Because of the wealth of material in these chapters, one can conveniently choose to cover only laminar flames (Chapters 8, 9, and 10) or to focus only on premixed flames (Chapters 8, 11, and 12) or nonpremixed flames (Chapters 9, 10, and 13). Particular emphases on specific applications might suggest which topics to cover.

Linking droplet vaporization theory to practical devices is the subject of the second half of Chapter 10, where a model of a one-dimensional vaporization-controlled combustor is developed. The primary purposes of this section are to reinforce previous concepts of equilibrium and evaporation, help develop students' powers of analysis, and to provide ideas and concepts that can be used in applications-oriented projects. Design projects can easily be fitted into the framework of Chapter 10. Depending on course objectives, this section of Chapter 10 can be treated as optional.

In Chapter 14, burning of solids is introduced, using carbon combustion as the archetypical system. Again, simplified analyses are presented to illuminate heterogeneous combustion concepts and to introduce the ideas of diffusionally and kinetically controlled combustion. This chapter also acquaints the student with coal combustion and its applications.

Omitting a treatment of combustion-generated pollutants would be unthinkable in a modern book on combustion. Chapter 15 focuses on this topic. This chapter introduces the reader to the quantification of emissions as well as discussing the mechanisms of pollutant formation and their control. This chapter emphasizes applications and should be of particular interest to the intended readers of this book. The placement of this chapter does not suggest its relative importance. Depending on course objectives, the material here could be covered following Chapters 1–6.

Now, in summary, this book attempts to present an introduction to combustion at a level easily comprehended by students nearing the completion of an undergraduate study in mechanical engineering and related fields. Through the use of examples and homework problems, students can develop confidence in their understanding and go on to apply this to various projects and "real world" problems. It is hoped that this text will fit the needs of instructors, and others, desiring simplified and appropriately structured materials for an introductory study of the fascinating field of combustion.

Stephen R. Turns
University Park, PA

ACKNOWLEDGMENTS

It is a great pleasure to acknowledge the many people who contributed their support, time, and psychic energy to this project. First, I would like to thank the many reviewers of various drafts along the way: in particular, James F. Driscoll, The University of Michigan; Norm Laurendeau, Purdue University; John Lloyd, Michigan State University; Michel Louge, Cornell University; Jon Van Gerpen, Iowa State University; and Carl Wikstrom, University of Arkansas, all of whose comments on an early draft were extremely helpful in guiding my final efforts. Also, the detailed comments of Steve Goebel and Alan Feitelberg, who used a late draft of the book in teaching a course at Rensselaer Polytechnic Institute, were extremely valuable. My friend and colleague, Chuck Merkle, continually provided moral support and served as a sounding board for ideas on both content and pedagogy. Many students at Penn State contributed in various ways, and I want to acknowledge the particular contributions of Jeff Brown, Jonguen Lee, and Don Michael. Sankaran Venkateswaran deserves special thanks for providing the turbulent jet flame model calculations; and a major debt of thanks is owed to Donn Mueller, who painstakingly solved all of the end-of-chapter problems. John Corrigan at McGraw-Hill was an enthusiastic supporter of this project from the outset; his encouragement was always appreciated. The skillful efforts of Alan Hunt and the meticulous copyediting of Keyword Publishing Services are gratefully acknowledged. I would also like to thank the Gas Research Institute for their support of my research activities through the years, as it was these activities that provided the initial inspiration and impetus to write this book. Invaluable to my efforts throughout was the unflagging support of my family. They tolerated amazingly well the time spent writing on weekends and holiday breaks, time that I could have spent with them. My wife, Joan, also typed several sections of the first draft to speed the project along. I have reserved the last acknowledgment for Cheryl Adams. It is difficult to conceive how this project would have been carried out without her. She typed and word-processed the many drafts and created many of the line drawings appearing in the text. Being able to always count on Cheryl contributed greatly to making the writing of this book an enjoyable experience.

Stephen R. Turns

CHAPTER

1

INTRODUCTION

MOTIVATION TO STUDY COMBUSTION

Combustion and its control are essential to our existence on this planet as we know it. In 1989, approximately 89% of the energy used in the U.S. came from combustion sources [1] (Table 1.1). A quick glance around your local environment shows the importance of combustion in your daily life. More than likely, the heat for your room or home comes directly from combustion, either a gas- or oil-fired furnace or boiler, or indirectly, through electricity that was generated by burning a fossil fuel. Our nation's electrical needs are met primarily by combustion.

TABLE 1.1
U.S. energy consumption estimates by source and end-use sector, 1989[a]

Sources	Quadrillion BTU (%)	End-use sector	Quadrillion BTU (%)
Coal	18.970 (23.3)	Residential	16.630 (20.4)
Natural gas	19.384 (23.8)	Commercial	12.867 (15.8)
Petroleum	34.209 (42.1)	Industrial	29.463 (36.2)
Nuclear electric power	5.677 (7.0)	Transportation	22.382 (27.5)
Hydroelectric power	2.884 (3.5)		
Other[b]	0.217 (0.3)		
TOTAL[c]	81.342 (100)	TOTAL	81.342 (100)

[a]Data from Ref. [1].

[b]Electricity generated for distribution from wood and waste, geothermal, wind, photovoltaic, and solar thermal energy.

[c]Totals may not equal sum of components due to independent rounding.

TABLE 1.2
1990 U.S. electricity generation [2]

	(Million kW-hr)	%
Coal	1,557,498	55.5
Nuclear	576,784[a]	20.6
Hydro	279,893	10.0
Gas	263,452	9.4
Oil	117,062	4.2
Other	10,645	0.4
Total	2,805,334	100.0

[a]Up 9% from 1989.

Presently, only 30.6% of the electrical generating capability is nuclear or hydro-electric; while more than half is provided by burning coal, as shown in Table 1.2 [2]. Our transportation system relies almost entirely on combustion. In the United States in 1989, ground vehicles and aircraft burned 3991 million barrels of various petroleum products annually [1], or approximately two-thirds of all of the petroleum imported or produced in the U.S. Aircraft are entirely powered by on-board fuel burning, and most trains are diesel-engine powered. Recent times have also seen the rise of gasoline-engine driven appliances such as lawn mowers, leaf blowers, chain saws, weed-whackers, and the like.

Industrial processes rely heavily on combustion. Iron, steel, aluminum, and other metals refining industries employ furnaces for producing the raw product, while heat-treating and annealing furnaces or ovens are used downstream to add value to the raw material as it is converted into a finished product. Other industrial combustion devices include boilers, refinery and chemical fluid heaters, glass melters, solids dryers, surface coating curing and drying ovens, and organic fume incinerators [3], and many others. The cement manufacturing industry is a heavy user of heat energy delivered by combustion. Rotary kilns, in which the cement clinker is produced, use over 0.4 quads[1] of energy, or roughly 1.4% of the total industrial energy use in the U.S. in 1989. At present, rotary kilns are rather inefficient devices, and potentially great energy savings could be made by improving these devices [4].

In addition to helping us make products, combustion is used at the other end of the product life cycle as a means of waste disposal. Incineration of waste has been used for a long time, but it is receiving renewed interest because of the limited availability of landfill sites in densely populated areas. Also, incineration is attractive for its ability to safely dispose of toxic wastes. Currently, siting of incinerators is a politically controversial and sensitive issue.

Having briefly reviewed how combustion is beneficial, we now look at the downside issue associated with combustion—environmental pollution. The major

---

[1]quad = 1 quadrillion BTU = 10^{15} BTU.

TABLE 1.3
Typical pollutants of concern from selected sources

Source	Pollutants				
	Unburned hydrocarbons	Oxides of nitrogen	Carbon monoxide	Sulfur oxides	Particulate matter
Spark-ignition engines	+	+	+	–	–
Diesel engines	+	+	+	–	+
Gas-turbine engines	+	+	+	–	+
Coal-burning utility boilers	–	+	–	+	+
Gas-burning appliances	–	+	+	–	–

pollutants produced by combustion are unburned and partially burned hydro-carbons, nitrogen oxides (NO and NO_2), carbon monoxide, sulfur oxides (SO_2 and SO_3), and particulate matter in various forms. Table 1.3 shows which pollutants are typically associated with various combustion devices and, in most cases, subjected to legislated controls. Primary pollution concerns relate to specific health hazards, smogs, acid rain, global warming, and ozone depletion. National trends for pollutant emissions from 1940–1989, showing the contributions from various sources, are presented in Figs. 1.1–1.5 [5]. The impact of the Clean Air Act Amendments of 1970 can be clearly seen in these figures.

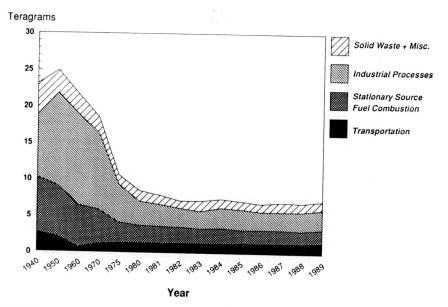

FIGURE 1.1
Trends in emissions of particulate matter for U.S., 1940–1989. (From Ref. [5].)

Teragrams

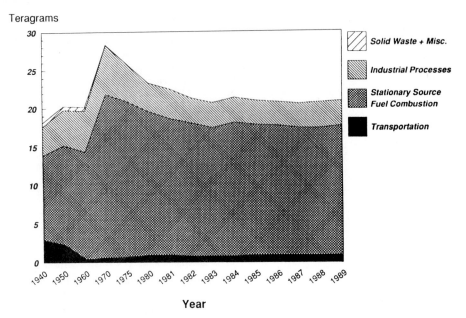

FIGURE 1.2
Trends in emissions of sulfur oxides for U.S., 1940–1989. (From Ref. [5].)

Teragrams

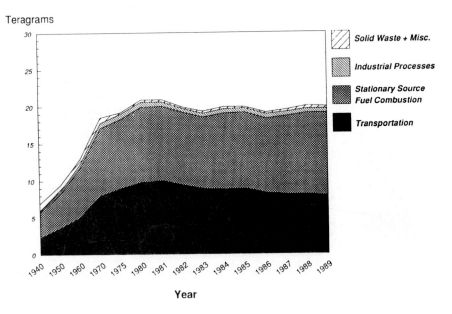

FIGURE 1.3
Trends in emissions of nitrogen oxides for U.S., 1940–1989. (From Ref. [5].)

Teragrams

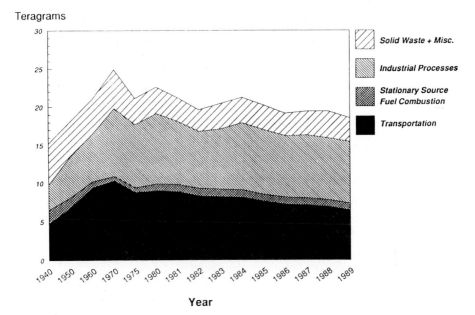

FIGURE 1.4
Trends in emissions of reactive volatile organic compounds for U.S., 1940–1989. (From Ref. [5].)

Teragrams

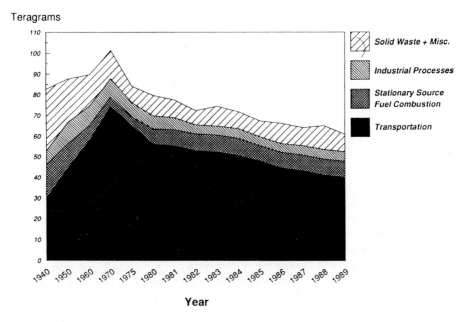

FIGURE 1.5
Trends in emissions of carbon monoxide for U.S., 1940–1989. (From Ref. [5].)

Considering the importance of combustion in our society, it is somewhat surprising that very few engineers have more than a cursory knowledge of combustion phenomena. However, with an already demanding curriculum, it is unrealistic to expect the subject to be given more attention than it presently receives. Therefore, engineers with some background in combustion may find many opportunities to use their expertise. Aside from the purely practical motivations for studying combustion, the subject is in itself intellectually stimulating in that it integrates all of the thermal sciences nicely, as well as bringing chemistry into the practical realm of engineering.

A DEFINITION OF COMBUSTION

Webster's Dictionary provides a useful starting point for a definition of **combustion** as *"rapid oxidation generating heat, or both light and heat; also, slow oxidation accompanied by relatively little heat and no light."* For our purposes, we will restrict the definition to include only the rapid oxidation portion, since most practical combustion devices belong in this realm.

This definition emphasizes the intrinsic importance of chemical reactions to combustion. It also emphasizes why combustion is so very important: combustion transforms energy stored in chemical bonds to heat that can be utilized in a variety of ways. Throughout this book, we illustrate the many practical applications of combustion.

COMBUSTION MODES AND FLAME TYPES

Combustion can occur in either a **flame** or **nonflame** mode, and flames in turn are categorized as being either **premixed flames** or **nonpremixed (diffusion) flames**. The difference between flame and nonflame modes of combustion can be illustrated by the processes occurring in a knocking spark-ignition engine (Fig. 1.6). In Fig. 1.6a, we see a thin zone of intense chemical reaction propagating through the unburned fuel–air mixture. The thin reaction zone is what we commonly refer to as a flame. Behind the flame are the hot products of combustion. As the flame moves across the combustion space, the temperature and pressure rise in the unburned gas. Under certain conditions (Fig. 1.6b), rapid oxidation reactions occur at many locations within the unburned gas, leading to very rapid combustion throughout the volume. This essentially volumetric heat release in an engine is called **autoignition**, and the very rapid pressure rise leads to the characteristic sound of engine knock. Knock is undesirable, and a recent challenge to engine designers has been how to minimize the occurrence of knock while operating with lead-free gasolines.[2] In compression-ignition or diesel engines, however, autoignition initiates the combustion process by design.

---

[2]The discovery that tetraethyl lead reduces knock, made by Thomas Midgley in 1921, allowed engine compression ratios to be increased, and thereby improved efficiency and power.

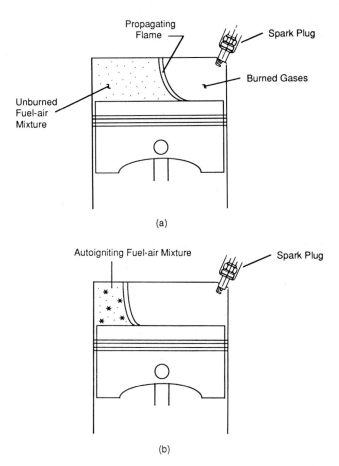

FIGURE 1.6
(a) Flame and (b) nonflame modes of combustion in a spark-ignition engine.

The two classes of flames, premixed and nonpremixed (or diffusion), are related to the state of mixedness of the reactants, as suggested by their names. In a premixed flame, the fuel and the oxidizer are mixed at the molecular level prior to the occurrence of any significant chemical reaction. The spark-ignition engine is an example where premixed flames occur. Contrarily, in a diffusion flame, the reactants are initially separated, and reaction occurs only at the interface between the fuel and oxidizer, where mixing and reaction both take place. An example of a diffusion flame is a simple candle. In practical devices, both types of flames may be present in various degrees. Diesel engine combustion is generally considered to have significant amounts of both premixed and nonpremixed or diffusion burning. The term "diffusion" applies strictly to the molecular diffusion of chemical species, i.e., fuel molecules diffuse toward the flame from one direction while oxidizer molecules diffuse toward the flame from the opposite direction. In turbulent nonpremixed flames, turbulent convection mixes the fuel and air together on a macroscopic basis. Molecular mixing at the small scales, i.e., molecular diffusion, then completes the mixing process so that chemical reactions can take place.

APPROACH TO OUR STUDY

We begin our study of combustion by investigating the key physical processes, or sciences, which form the fundamental framework of combustion science: **thermochemistry** in Chapter 2; **molecular transport of mass (and heat)** in Chapter 3; **chemical kinetics** in Chapters 4 and 5; and in Chapters 6 and 7, the coupling of all of these with **fluid mechanics**. In subsequent chapters, we apply these fundamentals to develop an understanding of laminar premixed flames (Chapter 8) and laminar diffusion flames (Chapters 9 and 10). In these laminar flames, it is relatively easy to see how basic conservation principles can be applied. Most practical combustion devices operate with turbulent flows, however, and the application of theoretical concepts to these is much more difficult. Chapters 11, 12, and 13 deal with turbulent flames and their practical applications. The final chapters concern the combustion of solids, as exemplified by carbon combustion (Chapter 14), and pollutant emissions (Chapter 15).

A major goal of this book is to provide a treatment of combustion that is sufficiently simple so that students with no prior introduction to the subject can appreciate both the fundamental and practical aspects. It is hoped, moreover, that as a result, some may be motivated to learn more about this fascinating field, either through more advanced study, or as a practicing engineer.

REFERENCES

1. U.S. Department of Energy, "State Energy Data Report, Consumption Estimates 1960–1989," DOE/EIA-0214(89), May 1991.
2. U.S. Council for Energy Awareness, Info, No. 262, March 1991.
3. Bluestein, J., "NO_x Controls for Gas-Fired Industrial Boilers and Combustion Equipment: A Survey of Current Practices," Gas Research Institute, GRI-92/0374, October 1992.
4. Tresouthick, S. W., "The SUBJET Process for Portland Cement Clinker Production," presented at the 1991 Air Products International Combustion Symposium, 24-27 March 1991.
5. U.S. Environmental Protection Agency, "National Air Pollutant Emission Estimates 1940–1989," EPA-450/4-91-004, March 1991.

CHAPTER 2

COMBUSTION AND THERMOCHEMISTRY

OVERVIEW

In this chapter, we examine several thermodynamic concepts that are important in the study of combustion. We first briefly review basic property relations for ideal gases and ideal-gas mixtures and the first law of thermodynamics. Although these concepts are likely to be familiar to you from a previous study of thermodynamics, we present them here since they are an integral part of our study of combustion. We next focus on thermodynamic topics related specifically to combustion and reacting systems: concepts and definitions related to element conservation; a definition of enthalpy that accounts for chemical bonds; and first-law concepts defining heat of reaction, heating values, etc., and adiabatic flame temperatures. Chemical equilibrium, a second-law concept, is developed and applied to combustion-product mixtures. We emphasize equilibrium because in many combustion devices, a knowledge of equilibrium states is sufficient to define many performance parameters of the device; for example, the temperature and major species at the outlet of a steady-flow combustor are likely to be governed by equilibrium considerations. Several examples are presented to illustrate these principles.

REVIEW OF PROPERTY RELATIONS

Extensive and Intensive Properties

The numerical value of an **extensive property** depends on the amount (mass or number of moles) of the substance considered. Extensive properties are usually denoted with capital letters; for example, V (m³) for volume, U (J) for internal energy, H (J) $(= U + PV)$ for enthalpy, etc. An **intensive property**, on the other hand, is expressed per unit mass (or per mole), and its numerical value is independent of the amount of substance present. Mass-based intensive properties are generally denoted with lower case letters; for example, v (m³/kg) for specific volume, u (J/kg) for specific internal energy, h (J/kg) $(= u + Pv)$ for specific enthalpy, etc. Important exceptions to this lower-case convention are the intensive properties temperature, T, and pressure, P. Molar-based intensive properties are indicated in this book with an overbar, e.g., $\bar{u}$ and $\bar{h}$ (J/kmol). Extensive properties are obtained simply from the corresponding intensive properties by multiplying the property value per unit mass (or mole) by the amount of mass (or number of moles), i.e.,

$$V = mv \,(\text{or } N\bar{v})$$
$$U = mu \,(\text{or } N\bar{u}) \qquad (2.1)$$
$$H = mh \,(\text{or } N\bar{h}), \text{ etc.}$$

In the following developments, we will use either mass- and molar-based intensive properties, depending on which is most appropriate to a particular situation.

Equation of State

An **equation of state** provides the relationship among the pressure, P, temperature, T, and volume V (or specific volume v) of a substance. For ideal-gas behavior, i.e., a gas that can be modeled by neglecting intermolecular forces and the volume of the molecules, the following equivalent forms of the equation of state apply:

$$PV = NR_u T, \qquad (2.2a)$$

$$PV = mRT, \qquad (2.2b)$$

$$Pv = RT, \qquad (2.2c)$$

or

$$P = \rho RT, \qquad (2.2d)$$

where the specific gas constant R is related to the universal gas constant R_u $(= 8315 \text{ J/kmol-K})$ and the gas molecular weight MW by

$$R = R_u/MW. \tag{2.3}$$

The density ρ in Eqn. 2.2d is the reciprocal of the specific volume $(\rho = 1/v = m/V)$. Throughout this book, we assume ideal-gas behavior for all gaseous species and gas mixtures. This assumption is appropriate for nearly all of the systems we wish to consider since the high temperatures associated with combustion generally result in sufficiently low densities for ideal-gas behavior to be a reasonable approximation.

Calorific Equations of State

Expressions relating internal energy (or enthalpy) to pressure and temperature are called **calorific equations of state**, i.e.,

$$u = u(T, v) \tag{2.4a}$$

$$h = h(T, P). \tag{2.4b}$$

The word "calorific" relates to expressing energy in units of calories, which has been superseded by the use of joules in the SI system.

General expressions for a differential change in u or h can be expressed by differentiating Eqns. 2.4a and b:

$$du = \left(\frac{\partial u}{\partial T}\right)_v dT + \left(\frac{\partial u}{\partial v}\right)_T dv \tag{2.5a}$$

$$dh = \left(\frac{\partial h}{\partial T}\right)_P dT + \left(\frac{\partial h}{\partial P}\right)_T dP \tag{2.5b}$$

In the above, we recognize the partial derivatives with respect to temperature to be the **constant-volume** and **constant-pressure specific heats**, respectively, i.e.,

$$c_v \equiv \left(\frac{\partial u}{\partial T}\right)_v, \tag{2.6a}$$

$$c_p \equiv \left(\frac{\partial h}{\partial T}\right)_P. \tag{2.6b}$$

For an ideal gas, the partial derivatives with respect to specific volume, $(\partial u/\partial v)_T$, and pressure, $(\partial h/\partial P)_T$, are zero. Using this knowledge, we integrate Eqn. 2.5, substituting Eqn. 2.6 to provide the following ideal-gas calorific equations of state:

$$u(T) - u_{\text{ref}} = \int_{T_{\text{ref}}}^{T} c_v \, dT \tag{2.7a}$$

$$h(T) - h_{\text{ref}} = \int_{T_{\text{ref}}}^{T} c_p \, dT. \tag{2.7b}$$

In a subsequent section, we will define an appropriate reference state that accounts for the different bond energies of various compounds.

For both real **and** ideal gases, the specific heats c_v and c_p are generally functions of temperature. This is a consequence of the internal energy of a molecule consisting of three components: translational, vibrational, and rotational; and the fact that, as a consequence of quantum theory, the vibrational and rotational energy storage modes become increasingly active as temperature increases. Figure 2.1 schematically illustrates these three energy storage modes by contrasting a monatomic species, whose internal energy consists solely of translational kinetic energy, and a diatomic molecule, which stores energy in a vibrating chemical bond, represented as a spring between the two nuclei, and by rotation about two orthogonal axes, as well as possessing kinetic energy from translation. With these simple models (Fig. 2.1), we would expect the specific heats of diatomic molecules to be greater than monatomic species. In general, the more complex the molecule, the greater its molar specific heat. This can be seen clearly in Fig. 2.2, where molar specific heats for a number of combustion product species are shown as functions of temperature. As a group, the triatomics have the greatest specific heats, followed by the diatomics, and, lastly, the monatomics. Note that the triatomic molecules also have a greater temperature dependence than the diatomics, a consequence of the greater number of vibrational and rotational modes that are available to become activated as temperature is increased. In comparison, the monatomic species have nearly constant specific heats over a

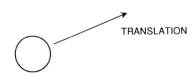

(a) MONATOMIC SPECIES

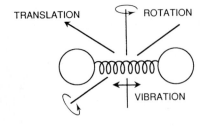

(b) DIATOMIC SPECIES

FIGURE 2.1
(a) The internal energy of monatomic species consists only of translational (kinetic) energy, while (b) a diatomic species' internal energy results from translation together with energy from vibration (potential and kinetic) and rotation (kinetic).

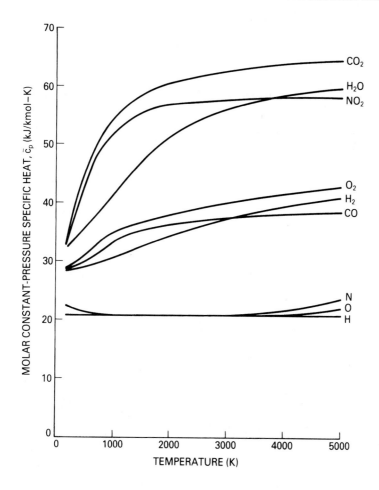

FIGURE 2.2
Molar constant-pressure specific heats as functions of temperature for monatomic (H, N, and O), diatomic (CO, H_2, and O_2), and triatomic (CO_2, H_2O, and NO_2) species. Values are from Appendix A.

wide range of temperatures; in fact, the H-atom specific heat is constant ($\bar{c}_p = 20.786$ kJ/kmol-K) from 200 K to 5000 K.

Constant-pressure molar specific heats are tabulated as a function of temperature for various species in Tables A.1–A.12 in Appendix A. Also provided in Appendix A are the curvefit coefficients, taken from the Chemkin thermodynamic data base [1], which were used to generate the tables. These coefficients can be easily used with spreadsheet software to obtain $\bar{c}_p$ values at any temperature within the given temperature range.

Ideal-Gas Mixtures

Two important and useful concepts used to characterize the composition of a mixture are the constituent mole fractions and mass fractions. Consider a multi-component mixture of gases composed of N_1 moles of species 1, N_2 moles of species 2, etc. The **mole fraction of species i**, χ_i, is defined as the fraction of the total number of moles in the system that are species i; i.e.,

$$\chi_i \equiv \frac{N_i}{N_1 + N_2 + \ldots N_i + \ldots} = \frac{N_i}{N_{\text{tot}}} \tag{2.8}$$

Similarly, the **mass fraction of species i**, Y_i, is the amount of mass of species i compared to the total mixture mass:

$$Y_i \equiv \frac{m_i}{m_1 + m_2 + \ldots m_i + \ldots} = \frac{m_i}{m_{\text{tot}}}. \tag{2.9}$$

Note that, by definition, the sum of all the constituent mole (or mass) fractions must be unity, i.e.,

$$\sum_i \chi_i = 1 \tag{2.10a}$$

$$\sum_i Y_i = 1 \tag{2.10b}$$

Mole fractions and mass fractions are readily converted from one to another using the molecular weights of the species of interest and of the mixture:

$$Y_i = \chi_i MW_i / MW_{\text{mix}}, \tag{2.11a}$$

$$\chi_i = Y_i MW_{\text{mix}} / MW_i. \tag{2.11b}$$

The **mixture molecular weight**, MW_{mix}, is easily calculated from a knowledge of either the species mole or mass fractions:

$$MW_{\text{mix}} = \sum_i \chi_i MW_i, \tag{2.12a}$$

$$MW_{\text{mix}} = \frac{1}{\sum_i (Y_i / MW_i)}. \tag{2.12b}$$

Species mole fractions are also used to determine corresponding species partial pressures. The **partial pressure of the ith species, P_i**, is the pressure of the ith species if it were isolated from the mixture at the same temperature and volume as the mixture. For ideal gases, the mixture pressure is the sum of the constituent partial pressures,

$$P = \sum_i P_i. \tag{2.13}$$

The partial pressure can be related to the mixture composition and total pressure as

$$P_i = \chi_i P. \qquad (2.14)$$

For ideal-gas mixtures, many **mass- (or molar-) specific mixture properties** are calculated simply as mass (or mole) fraction weighted sums of the individual species-specific properties. For example, mixture enthalpies are calculated as

$$h_{\text{mix}} = \sum_i Y_i h_i, \qquad (2.15a)$$

$$\bar{h}_{\text{mix}} = \sum_i \chi_i \bar{h}_i. \qquad (2.15b)$$

Other frequently used properties that can be treated in this same manner are internal energies, u and $\bar{u}$. Note that, with our ideal-gas assumption, neither the pure-species properties $(u_i, \bar{u}_i, h_i, \bar{h}_i,)$ nor the mixture properties depend on pressure.

The mixture entropy also is calculated as a weighted sum of the constituents,

$$s_{\text{mix}}(T, P) = \sum_i Y_i s_i(T, P_i) \qquad (2.16a)$$

$$\bar{s}_{\text{mix}}(T, P) = \sum_i \chi_i \bar{s}_i(T, P_i). \qquad (2.16b)$$

In this case, however, the pure-species entropies $(s_i$ and $\bar{s}_i)$ depend on the species partial pressures as indicated in Eqn. 2.16. The constituent entropies in Eqn. 2.16 can be evaluated from standard-state $(P_{\text{ref}} \equiv P^o = 1 \text{ atm})$ values as

$$s_i(T, P_i) = s_i(T, P_{\text{ref}}) - R \ln \frac{P_i}{P_{\text{ref}}}, \qquad (2.17a)$$

$$\bar{s}_i(T, P_i) = \bar{s}_i(T, P_{\text{ref}}) - R_u \ln \frac{P_i}{P_{\text{ref}}}. \qquad (2.17b)$$

Standard-state molar specific entropies are tabulated in Appendix A for many species of interest to combustion.

Latent Heat of Vaporization

In many combustion processes, a liquid–vapor phase change is important. For example, a liquid fuel droplet must first vaporize before it can burn; and, if cooled sufficiently, water vapor can condense from combustion products. Formally, we define the **latent heat of vaporization, h_{fg},** as the heat required in a constant-pressure process to completely vaporize a unit mass of liquid at a given temperature, i.e.,

$$h_{fg}(T, P) \equiv h_{\text{vapor}}(T, P) - h_{\text{liquid}}(T, P). \qquad (2.18)$$

The latent heat of vaporization is also known as the **enthalpy of vaporization**. Latent heats of vaporization for various fuels at their normal (1 atm) boiling points are tabulated in Table B.1 (Appendix B).

The latent heat of vaporization at a given saturation temperature and pressure is frequently used with the **Clausius–Clapeyron equation** to estimate saturation pressure variation with temperature:

$$\frac{dP_{sat}}{P_{sat}} = \frac{h_{fg}}{R} \frac{dT_{sat}}{T_{sat}^2}. \tag{2.19}$$

This equation assumes that the specific volume of the liquid phase is negligible compared to that of the vapor and that the vapor behaves as an ideal gas. Assuming h_{fg} is constant, Eqn. 2.19 can be integrated from $(P_{sat,1}, T_{sat,1})$ to $(P_{sat,2}, T_{sat,2})$ in order to permit, for example, $P_{sat,2}$ to be estimated from a knowledge of $P_{sat,1}$, $T_{sat,1}$, and $T_{sat,2}$. We will employ this approach in our discussion of droplet evaporation (Chapter 3) and combustion (Chapter 10).

FIRST LAW OF THERMODYNAMICS

First Law—Fixed Mass

Conservation of energy is the fundamental principle embodied in the first law of thermodynamics. For a **fixed mass**, i.e., a **system**, (Fig. 2.3a), energy conservation is expressed for a finite change between two states, 1 and 2, as

$$_1Q_2 \quad - \quad _1W_2 \quad = \quad \Delta E_{1\text{-}2}. \tag{2.20}$$

| Heat added to system in going from state 1 to state 2 | Work done by system on surroundings in going from state 1 to state 2 | Change in total system energy in going from state 1 to state 2 |

Both $_1Q_2$ and $_1W_2$ are path functions and occur only at the system boundaries. $\Delta E_{1\text{-}2} (\equiv E_2 - E_1)$ is the change in the total energy of the system, which is the sum of the internal, kinetic, and potential energies, i.e.,

$$E = m(\quad u \quad + \quad \tfrac{1}{2}v^2 \quad + \quad gz \quad). \tag{2.21}$$

| Mass-specific system internal energy | Mass-specific system kinetic energy | Mass-specific system potential energy |

The system energy is a state variable and, as such, ΔE does not depend on the path taken to execute a change in state. Equation 2.20 can be converted to unit mass basis or expressed to represent an instant in time. These forms are

$$_1q_2 - _1w_2 = \Delta e_{1\text{-}2} = e_2 - e_1 \tag{2.22}$$

and

$$\dot{Q} \quad - \quad \dot{W} \quad = \quad dE/dt, \tag{2.23}$$

| Instantaneous rate of heat transferred into system | Instantaneous rate of work done by system, or power | Instantaneous time rate of change of system energy |

or

$$\dot{q} - \dot{w} = de/dt, \qquad (2.24)$$

where lower case letters are used to denote mass-specific quantities, e.g., $e \equiv E/m$.

First Law—Control Volume

We next consider a control volume, illustrated in Fig. 2.3b, in which fluid may flow across the boundaries. The steady-state, steady-flow (SSSF\,) form of the first law is particularly useful for our purposes and should be reasonably familiar to you from previous studies of thermodynamics [2-4]. Because of its importance, however, we present a brief discussion here. The SSSF first law is expressed as

$$\dot{Q}_{cv} \quad - \quad \dot{W}_{cv} \quad = \quad \dot{m}e_o \quad - \quad \dot{m}e_i \quad + \quad \dot{m}(P_o v_o - P_i v_i)$$

| Rate of heat transferred across the control surface, from the surroundings, to the control volume | Rate of all work done by the control volume, including shaft work, but excluding flow work | Rate of energy flowing out of the control volume | Rate of energy flowing into the control volume | Net rate of work associated with pressure forces where fluid crosses the control surface, flow work |

$$(2.25)$$

where the subscripts o and i denote the outlet and inlet, respectively, and $\dot{m}$ is the mass flowrate. Before rewriting Eqn. 2.25 in a more convenient form, it is appropriate to list the principal assumptions embodied in this relation:

1. *The control volume is fixed relative to the coordinate system.* This eliminates any work interactions associated with a moving boundary, as well as eliminating the need to consider changes in the kinetic and potential energies of the control volume itself.

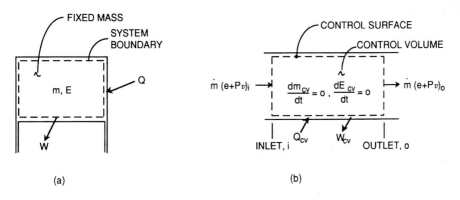

FIGURE 2.3
(a) Schematic of fixed-mass system with moving boundary above piston. (b) Control volume with fixed boundaries and steady flow.

2. *The properties of the fluid at each point within the control volume, or on the control surface, do not vary with time.* This assumption allows us to treat all processes as steady.

3. *Fluid properties are uniform over the inlet and outlet flow areas.* This allows us to use single values, rather than integrating over the area, for the inlet and exit stream properties.

4. *There is only one inlet and one exit stream.* This assumption is invoked to keep the final result in a simple form and can be easily relaxed to allow multiple inlet/exit streams.

The specific energy *e* of the inlet and outlet streams consists of the specific internal, kinetic, and potential energies, i.e.,

$$ \underset{\substack{\text{Total energy} \\ \text{per unit mass}}}{e} \quad = \quad \underset{\substack{\text{Internal energy} \\ \text{per unit mass}}}{u} \quad + \quad \underset{\substack{\text{Kinetic energy} \\ \text{per unit mass}}}{\tfrac{1}{2}v^2} \quad + \quad \underset{\substack{\text{Potential energy} \\ \text{per unit mass}}}{gz}, \qquad (2.26) $$

where v and z are the velocity and elevation, respectively, of the stream where it crosses the control surface.

The pressure–specific volume product terms associated with the flow work in Eqn. 2.25 can be combined with the specific internal energy of Eqn. 2.26, which we recognize as the useful property, enthalpy:

$$ h \equiv u + Pv = u + P/\rho. \qquad (2.27) $$

Combining Eqns. 2.25–2.27, and rearranging, yields our final form of energy conservation for a control volume:

$$ \dot{Q}_{cv} - \dot{W}_{cv} = \dot{m}\left[(h_o - h_i) + \tfrac{1}{2}\left(v_o^2 - v_i^2\right) + g(z_o - z_i)\right]. \qquad (2.28) $$

The first law can also be expressed on a mass-specific basis by dividing Eqn. 2.28 by the mass flowrate $\dot{m}$, i.e.,

$$ q_{cv} - w_{cv} = h_o - h_i + \tfrac{1}{2}\left(v_o^2 - v_i^2\right) + g(z_o - z_i). \qquad (2.29) $$

In Chapter 7, we present more complete expressions of energy conservation that are subsequently simplified for our objectives in this book. For the time being, however, Eqn. 2.28 suits our needs.

REACTANT AND PRODUCT MIXTURES

Stoichiometry

The **stoichiometric** quantity of oxidizer is just that amount needed to completely burn a quantity of fuel. If more than a stoichiometric quantity of oxidizer is supplied, the mixture is said to be fuel lean, or just **lean**; while supplying less than the stoichiometric oxidizer results in a fuel-rich, or **rich** mixture. The stoichiometric oxidizer– (or air–) fuel ratio (mass) is determined by writing simple atom balances, assuming that the fuel reacts to form an ideal set of products. For a hydrocarbon fuel given by C_xH_y, the stoichiometric relation can be expressed as

TABLE 2.1

Some combustion properties of methane, hydrogen, and solid carbon for reactants at 298 K

	Δh_R (kJ/kg$_{fuel}$)	Δh_R (kJ/kg$_{mix}$)	$(O/F)_{stoic}$ [a] (kg/kg)	$T_{ad,eq}$ (K)
CH$_4$ + air	$-55,528$	-3066	17.11	2226
H$_2$ + O$_2$	$-142,919$	$-15,880$	8.0	3079
C(s) + air	$-32,794$	-2645	11.4	2301

[a] O/F is the oxidizer–fuel ratio, where for combustion with air, the air is the oxidizer not just the oxygen in the air.

$$C_xH_y + a(O_2 + 3.76N_2) \rightarrow xCO_2 + (y/2)H_2O + 3.76\,a\,N_2, \qquad (2.30)$$

where

$$a = x + y/4. \qquad (2.31)$$

For simplicity, we assume throughout this book that the simplified composition for air is 21% O$_2$ and 79% N$_2$ (by volume), i.e., that for each mole of O$_2$ in air, there are 3.76 moles of N$_2$.

The **stoichiometric air–fuel ratio** can be found as

$$(A/F)_{stoic} = \left(\frac{m_{air}}{m_{fuel}}\right)_{stoic} = \frac{4.76a}{1}\frac{MW_{air}}{MW_{fuel}}, \qquad (2.32)$$

where MW_{air} and MW_{fuel} are the molecular weights of the air and fuel, respectively. Table 2.1 shows stoichiometric air–fuel ratios for methane and solid carbon. Also shown is the oxygen–fuel ratio for combustion of H$_2$ in pure O$_2$. For all of these systems, we see that there is many times more oxidizer than fuel.

The **equivalence ratio**, Φ, is commonly used to indicate quantitatively whether a fuel–oxidizer mixture is rich, lean, or stoichiometric. The equivalence ratio is defined as

$$\Phi = \frac{(A/F)_{stoic}}{(A/F)} = \frac{(F/A)}{(F/A)_{stoic}} \qquad (2.33a)$$

From this definition, we see that for fuel-rich mixtures, $\Phi > 1$, and for fuel-lean mixtures, $\Phi < 1$. For a stoichiometric mixture, Φ equals unity. In many combustion applications, the equivalence ratio is the single most important factor in determining a system's performance. Other parameters frequently used to define relative stoichiometry are **percent stoichiometric air**, which relates to the equivalence ratio as

$$\% \text{ stoichiometric air} = \frac{100\%}{\Phi} \qquad (2.33b)$$

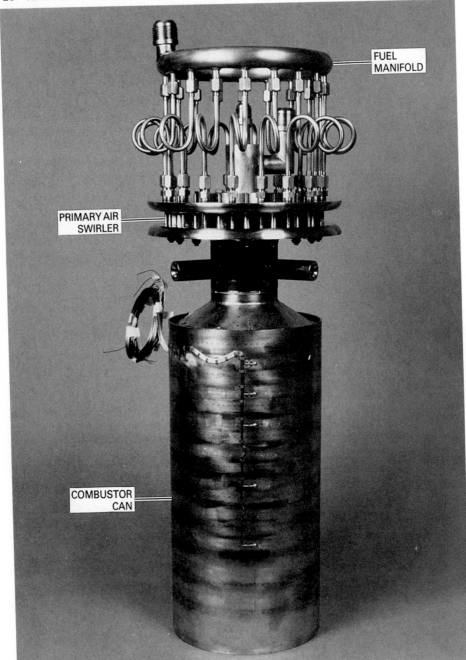

FIGURE 2.4
Experimental low-NO_x gas-turbine combustor can (left) and fuel and air mixing system (right). Eight cans are used in a 3950 kW engine. (Copyright © 1987 Electric Power Research Institute, EPRI AP-5347, *NO_x Reduction for Small Gas Turbine Power Plants*; reprinted with permission).

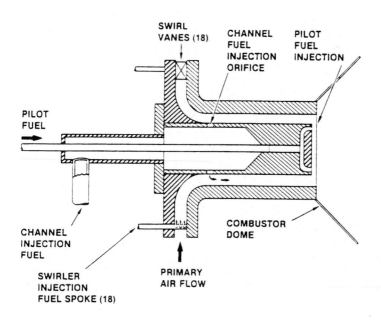

and **percent excess air**, or

$$\% \text{ excess air} = \frac{(1 - \Phi)}{\Phi} \cdot 100\%. \qquad (2.33c)$$

Example 2.1. A small, low-emission, stationary gas-turbine engine (see Fig. 2.4) operates at full load (3950 kW) at an equivalence ratio of 0.286 with an air flowrate of 15.9 kg/s. The equivalent composition of the fuel (natural gas) is $C_{1.16}H_{4.32}$. Determine the fuel mass flowrate and the operating air–fuel ratio for the engine.

Solution

Given: $\Phi = 0.286$ $MW_{air} = 28.85$
         $\dot{m}_{air} = 15.9$ kg/s $MW_{fuel} = 1.16 (12.01) + 4.32 (1.008) = 18.286$.
Find: $\dot{m}_{fuel}, (A/F)$.

We will proceed by first finding A/F and then $\dot{m}_{fuel}$. The solution requires only the application of definitions expressed in Eqns. 2.32 and 2.33, i.e.,

$$(A/F)_{stoic} = 4.76a \frac{MW_{air}}{MW_{fuel}},$$

where $a = x + y/4 = 1.16 + 4.32/4 = 2.24$.
Thus,

$$(A/F)_{stoic} = 4.76 (2.24) \frac{28.85}{18.286} = 16.82,$$

and from Eqn. 2.33,

$$\boxed{(A/F)} = \frac{(A/F)_{stoic}}{\Phi} = \frac{16.82}{0.286} = \boxed{58.8}.$$

Since (A/F) is the ratio of the air flowrate to the fuel flowrate,

$$\boxed{\dot{m}_{fuel}} = \frac{\dot{m}_{air}}{(A/F)} = \frac{15.9 \text{ kg/s}}{58.8} = \boxed{0.270 \text{ kg/s}}.$$

Comment. Note that even at full power, a large quantity of excess air is supplied to the engine.

Example 2.2. A natural-gas-fired industrial boiler (see Fig. 2.5) operates with an oxygen concentration of 3 mole percent in the flue gases. Determine the operating air–fuel ratio and the equivalence ratio. Treat the natural gas as methane.

Solution

Given: $\chi_{O_2} = 0.03$ $MW_{fuel} = 16.04$
                        $MW_{air} = 28.85$.

Find: $(A/F), \Phi$.

FIGURE 2.5
Two 10-MW (34 million BTU/hr) natural-gas burners fire into a boiler combustion chamber 3 m deep. Air enters the burners through the large vertical pipes, while the natural gas enters through the horizontal pipes on the left. (Courtesy of North American Manufacturing Co.)

We can use the given O_2 mole fraction to find the air–fuel ratio by writing an overall combustion equation assuming "complete combustion," i.e., no dissociation (all fuel C is found in CO_2 and all fuel H is found in H_2O):

$$CH_4 + a\,(O_2 + 3.76\,N_2) \rightarrow CO_2 + 2H_2O + b\,O_2 + 3.76\,a\,N_2$$

where a and b are related from conservation of O atoms

$$2a = 2 + 2 + 2b\,)$$

or

$$b = a - 2.$$

From the definition of a mole fraction (Eqn. 2.8),

$$\chi_{O_2} = \frac{N_{O_2}}{N_{mix}} = \frac{b}{1 + 2 + b + 3.76\,a} = \frac{a - 2}{1 + 4.76\,a}$$

Substituting the known value of $\chi_{O_2}(= 0.03)$ and then solving for a yields

$$0.03 = \frac{a - 2}{1 + 4.76\,a},$$

or

$$a = 2.368.$$

The mass air–fuel ratio, in general, is expressed,

$$(A/F) = \frac{N_{air}}{N_{fuel}} \frac{MW_{air}}{MW_{fuel}}$$

so

$$(A/F) = \frac{4.76\,a}{1} \frac{MW_{air}}{MW_{fuel}}$$

$$\boxed{(A/F)} = \frac{4.76(2.368)(28.85)}{16.04} = \boxed{20.3}.$$

To find Φ, we need to determine $(A/F)_{stoic}$. From Eqn. 2.31, $a = 2$; hence,

$$(A/F)_{stoic} = \frac{4.76(2)28.85}{16.04} = 17.1.$$

Applying the definition of Φ (Eqn. 2.33),

$$\boxed{\Phi} = \frac{(A/F)_{stoic}}{(A/F)} = \frac{17.1}{20.3} = \boxed{0.84}.$$

Comment. In the solution, we assumed that the O_2 mole fraction was on a "wet basis," i.e., moles of O_2 per moles of moisture-containing flue gases. Frequently in the measurement of exhaust species, moisture is removed to prevent condensation in the analyzers; thus, χ_{O_2} can also be reported on a "dry basis" (see Chapter 15).

Absolute (or Standardized) Enthalpy and Enthalpy of Formation

In dealing with chemically reacting systems, the concept of absolute enthalpies is extremely valuable. For any species, we can define an **absolute (or standardized) enthalpy** that is the sum of an enthalpy that takes into account the energy associated with chemical bonds (or lack thereof), the **enthalpy of formation, h_f,** and an enthalpy that is associated only with the temperature, the **sensible enthalpy change,** Δh_s. Thus, we can write the molar absolute enthalpy for species i as

$$\underset{\substack{\text{Absolute enthalpy} \\ \text{at temperature } T}}{\bar{h}_i(T)} = \underset{\substack{\text{Enthalpy of formation} \\ \text{at standard reference} \\ \text{state } (T_{ref}, P^o)}}{\bar{h}_{f,i}^o(T_{ref})} + \underset{\substack{\text{Sensible enthalpy} \\ \text{change in going from} \\ T_{ref} \text{ to } T}}{\Delta \bar{h}_{s,i}(T)} \qquad (2.34)$$

where $\Delta \bar{h}_{s,i} \equiv \bar{h}_i(T) - \bar{h}_{f,i}^o(T_{ref})$.

To make practical use of Eqn. 2.34, it is necessary to define a **standard reference state**. We employ a standard-state temperature, $T_{ref} = 25°C$ (298.15 K), and standard-state pressure, $P_{ref} = P^o = 1\,atm$ (101,325 Pa), consistent with the Chemkin [1] and NASA [5] thermodynamic data bases. Furthermore, we adopt the convention that enthalpies of formation are zero for the elements in their naturally occurring state at the reference state temperature and pressure. For example, at 25°C and 1 atm, oxygen exists as diatomic molecules; hence,

$$\left(\bar{h}^{o}_{f,O_2}\right)_{298} = 0,$$

where the superscript o is used to denote that the value is for the standard-state pressure.

To form oxygen atoms at the standard state requires the breaking of a rather strong chemical bond. The bond dissociation energy for O_2 at 298 K is 498,390 kJ/kmol-O_2. Breaking this bond creates two O atoms; thus, the enthalpy of formation for atomic oxygen is half the value of the O_2 bond dissociation energy, i.e.,

$$\left(\bar{h}^{o}_{f,O}\right) = 249,195 \text{ kJ/kmol-O}.$$

Thus, enthalpies of formation have a clear physical interpretation as the net change in enthalpy associated with breaking the chemical bonds of the standard state elements and forming new bonds to create the compound of interest.

Representing the absolute enthalpy graphically provides a useful way to understand and use this concept. In Fig. 2.6, the absolute enthalpies of atomic oxygen (O) and diatomic oxygen (O_2) are plotted versus temperature starting from absolute zero. At 298.15 K, we see $\bar{h}_{O_2}$ is zero (by definition of the standard-state reference condition) and the absolute enthalpy of atomic oxygen equals its enthalpy of formation, since the sensible enthalpy at 298.15 K is zero. At the

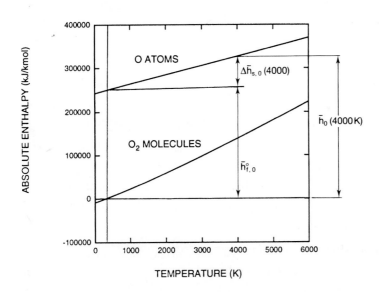

FIGURE 2.6
Graphical interpretation of absolute enthalpy, heat of formation, and sensible enthalpy.

temperature indicated (4000 K), we see the additional sensible enthalpy contribution to the absolute enthalpy. In Appendix A, enthalpies of formation at the reference state are given, and sensible enthalpies are tabulated as a function of temperature for a number of species of importance in combustion. Enthalpies of formation for reference temperatures other than the standard state 298.15 K are also tabulated.

Example 2.3. A gas stream at 1 atmosphere contains a mixture of CO, CO_2, and N_2 in which the CO mole fraction is 0.10 and the CO_2 mole fraction is 0.20. The gas-stream temperature is 1200 K. Determine the absolute enthalpy of the mixture on both a mole basis (kJ/kmol) and a mass basis (kJ/kg). Also determine the mass fractions of the three component gases.

Solution

$$\text{Given:} \quad \chi_{CO} = 0.10 \qquad T = 1200 \text{ K}$$
$$\chi_{CO_2} = 0.20 \qquad P = 1 \text{ atm.}$$
$$\text{Find:} \quad \bar{h}_{mix}, h_{mix}, Y_{CO}, Y_{CO_2}, \text{ and } Y_{N_2}.$$

Finding $\bar{h}_{mix}$ requires the straightforward application of the ideal-gas mixture law, Eqn. 2.15, and, to find χ_{N_2}, the knowledge that $\Sigma \chi_i = 1$ (Eqn. 2.10). Thus,

$$\chi_{N_2} = 1 - \chi_{CO} - \chi_{CO_2} = 0.70$$

and

$$\bar{h}_{mix} = \Sigma \chi_i \bar{h}_i$$

$$= \chi_{CO} \left[\bar{h}^o_{f,CO} + \left(\bar{h}(T) - \bar{h}^o_{f,298} \right)_{CO} \right]$$

$$+ \chi_{CO_2} \left[\bar{h}^o_{f,CO_2} + \left(\bar{h}(T) - \bar{h}^o_{f,298} \right)_{CO_2} \right]$$

$$+ \chi_{N_2} \left[\bar{h}^o_{f,N_2} + \left(\bar{h}(T) - \bar{h}^o_{f,298} \right)_{N_2} \right].$$

Substituting values from Appendix A (Table A.1 for CO, Table A.2 for CO_2, and Table A.7 for N_2):

$$\bar{h}_{mix} = 0.10[-110,541 + 28,440]$$

$$+ 0.20[-393,546 + 44,488]$$

$$+ 0.70[0 + 28,118] =$$

$$\boxed{\bar{h}_{mix} = -58,339.1 \text{ kJ/kmol}_{mix}}.$$

To find h_{mix}, we need to determine the molecular weight of the mixture:

$$MW_{mix} = \Sigma \chi_i MW_i$$

$$= 0.10(28.01) + 0.20(44.01) + 0.70(28.013).$$

$$MW_{mix} = 31.212$$

Then

$$\boxed{h_{mix}} = \frac{\bar{h}_{mix}}{MW_{mix}} = \frac{-58,339.1}{31.212} = \boxed{-1869.12 \, kJ/kg_{mix}} \, .$$

Since we have previously found MW_{mix}, calculation of the individual mass fractions follows simply from their definitions (Eqn. 2.11):

$$Y_{CO} = 0.10 \frac{28.01}{31.212} = 0.0897$$

$$Y_{CO_2} = 0.20 \frac{44.01}{31.212} = 0.2820$$

$$Y_{N_2} = 0.70 \frac{28.013}{31.212} = 0.6282$$

As a check, we see that $0.0897 + 0.2820 + 0.6282 = 1.000$, as required.

Comment. Both molar and mass units are frequently used in combustion. Because of this, you should be quite comfortable with their interconversions.

Enthalpy of Combustion and Heating Values

Knowing how to express the enthalpy for mixtures of reactants and mixtures of products allows us to define the enthalpy of reaction, or when dealing specifically with combustion reactions, the enthalpy of combustion. Consider the steady-flow reactor, shown in Fig. 2.7, in which a stoichiometric mixture of reactants enter and products exit, both at standard state conditions (25°C, 1 atm). The combustion process is assumed to be complete, i.e., all of the fuel carbon is converted to CO_2 and all of the fuel hydrogen is converted to H_2O. For the products to exit at the same temperature as the entering reactants, heat must be removed from the reactor. The amount of heat removed can be related to the reactant and product absolute enthalpies by applying the steady-flow form of the first law (Eqn. 2.29):

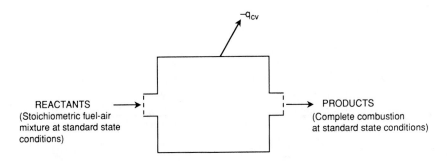

FIGURE 2.7
Steady-flow reactor used to determine enthalpy of combustion.

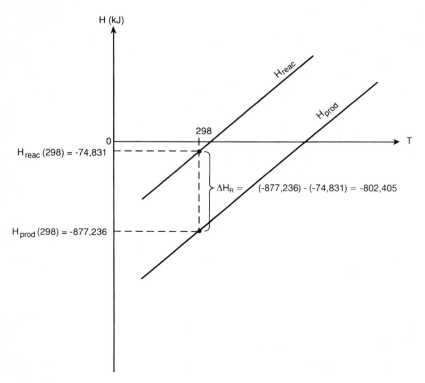

FIGURE 2.8
Enthalpy of reaction using representative values for a stoichiometric methane–air mixture. The water
in the products is assumed to be in the vapor state.

$$q_{cv} = h_o - h_i = h_{prod} - h_{reac}. \tag{2.35}$$

The definition of the **enthalpy of reaction**, or the **enthalpy of combustion**, Δh_R, (per
mass of mixture) is

$$\Delta h_R \equiv q_{cv} = h_{prod} - h_{reac}, \tag{2.36a}$$

or in terms of extensive properties,

$$\Delta H_R = H_{prod} - H_{reac}. \tag{2.36b}$$

The enthalpy of combustion can be illustrated graphically, as shown in Fig. 2.8.
Consistent with the heat transfer being negative, the absolute enthalpy of the
products lies below that of the reactants. For example, at 25°C and 1 atm, the
reactants enthalpy of a stoichiometric mixture of CH_4 and air, where 1 kmol of
fuel reacts, is −74,831 kJ. At the same conditions (25°C, 1 atm), the combustion
products have an absolute enthalpy of −877,236 kJ. Thus,

$$\Delta H_R = -877,236 - (-74,831) = -802,405 \text{ kJ}.$$

This value can be adjusted to a per-mass-of-fuel basis

$$\Delta h_R \left(\frac{kJ}{kg_{fuel}} \right) = \Delta h_R / MW_{fuel} \tag{2.37}$$

or

$$\Delta h_R \left(\frac{kJ}{kg_{fuel}} \right) = (-802{,}405/16.043) = -50{,}016.$$

This value can in turn be converted to a per-unit-mass-of-mixture basis

$$\Delta h_R \left(\frac{kJ}{kg_{mix}} \right) = \Delta h_R \left(\frac{kJ}{kg_{fuel}} \right) \frac{m_{fuel}}{m_{mix}} \tag{2.38}$$

where

$$\frac{m_{fuel}}{m_{mix}} = \frac{m_{fuel}}{m_{air} + m_{fuel}} = \frac{1}{(A/F) + 1}. \tag{2.39}$$

From Table 2.1, we see that the stoichiometric air–fuel ratio for CH_4 is 17.11, thus,

$$\Delta h_R \left(\frac{kJ}{kg_{mix}} \right) = \frac{-50{,}016}{17.11 + 1} = -2761.8.$$

Note that the value of the enthalpy of combustion depends on the temperature chosen for its evaluation since the enthalpies of both the reactants and products vary with temperature, i.e., the distance between the H_{prod} and H_{reac} lines in Fig. 2.8 is not constant.

The **heat of combustion, Δh_c,** (known also as the **heating value**) is numerically equal to the enthalpy of reaction, but with opposite sign. The **upper** or **higher heating value, HHV,** is the heat of combustion calculated assuming that all of the water in the products has condensed to liquid. This scenario liberates the most amount of energy, hence the designation "upper." The **lower heating value, LHV,** corresponds to the case where none of the water is assumed to condense. For CH_4, the upper heating value is approximately 11% larger than the lower. Standard-state heating values for a variety of hydrocarbon fuels are given in Appendix B.

Example 2.4

A. Determine the upper and lower heating values at 298 K of gaseous n-decane, $C_{10}H_{22}$, per kmol of fuel and per kg of fuel. The molecular weight of n-decane is 142.284.

B. If the enthalpy of vaporization of n-decane is 359 kJ/kg_{fuel} at 298 K, what are the upper and lower heating values of liquid n-decane?

Solution

A. For 1 mole of $C_{10}H_{22}$, the combustion equation can be written

$$C_{10}H_{22}(g) + 15.5(O_2 + 3.76N_2) \rightarrow 10CO_2 + 11H_2O(l\,or\,g) + 15.5(3.76)N_2.$$

For either the upper or lower heating value,

$$\Delta H_c = -\Delta H_R = H_{\text{reac}} - H_{\text{prod}},$$

where the numerical value of H_{prod} depends on whether the H_2O in the products is liquid (determining higher heating value) or gaseous (determining lower heating value). The sensible enthalpies for all species involved are zero since we desire ΔH_c at the reference state (298 K). Furthermore, the enthalpies of formation of the O_2 and N_2 are also zero at 298 K. Recognizing that

$$H_{\text{reac}} = \sum_{\text{reac}} N_i \bar{h}_i \quad \text{and} \quad H_{\text{prod}} = \sum_{\text{prod}} N_i \bar{h}_i,$$

we obtain

$$\Delta H_{c,H_2O(l)} = \text{HHV} = (1)\bar{h}^o_{f,C_{10}H_{22}} - \left[10\bar{h}^o_{f,CO_2} + 11\bar{h}^o_{f,H_2O(l)}\right].$$

Table A.6 (Appendix A) gives the enthalpy of formation for gaseous water and the enthalpy of vaporization. With these values, we can calculate the enthalpy of formation for the liquid water (Eqn. 2.18):

$$\bar{h}^o_{f,H_2O(l)} = \bar{h}^o_{f,H_2O(g)} - \bar{h}_{fg} = -241{,}847 - 44{,}010 = -285{,}857 \text{ kJ/kmol}.$$

Using this value, together with enthalpies of formation given in Appendices A and B, we obtain the higher heating value:

$$\Delta H_{c,H_2O,(l)} = (1)\left(-249{,}659\,\frac{\text{kJ}}{\text{kmol}}\right)$$
$$- \left[10\left(-393{,}546\,\frac{\text{kJ}}{\text{kmol}}\right) + 11\left(-285{,}857\,\frac{\text{kJ}}{\text{kmol}}\right)\right]$$
$$= 6{,}830{,}096 \text{ kJ}$$

and

$$\Delta \bar{h}_c = \frac{\Delta H_c}{N_{C_{10}H_{22}}} = \frac{6{,}830{,}096 \text{ kJ}}{1 \text{ kmol}} = 6{,}830{,}096 \text{ kJ/kmol}_{C_{10}H_{22}}$$

or

$$\Delta h_c = \frac{\Delta \bar{h}_c}{\text{MW}_{C_{10}H_{22}}} = \frac{6{,}830{,}096\,\frac{\text{kJ}}{\text{kmol}}}{142.284\,\frac{\text{kg}}{\text{kmol}}} = 48{,}003 \text{ kJ/kg}_{C_{10}H_{22}}.$$

For the lower heating value, we use $\bar{h}^o_{f,H_2O(g)} = -241{,}847 \text{ kJ/kmol}$ in place of $\bar{h}^o_{f,H_2O(l)} = -285{,}857 \text{ kg/kmol}$. Thus,

$$\Delta \bar{h}_c = 6{,}345{,}986 \text{ kJ/kmol}_{C_{10}H_{22}}$$

or

$$\Delta h = 44{,}601 \text{ kJ/kg}_{C_{10}H_{22}}.$$

B. For $C_{10}H_{22}$, in the liquid state,

$$H_{\text{reac}} = (1)\left(\bar{h}^o_{f,C_{10}H_{22}(g)} - \bar{h}_{fg}\right),$$

or

$$\Delta h_c \left(\frac{\text{liquid}}{\text{fuel}}\right) = \Delta h_c \left(\frac{\text{gaseous}}{\text{fuel}}\right) - h_{fg}.$$

Thus,

$$\Delta h_c \,(\text{higher}) = 48{,}003 - 359$$
$$= 47{,}644 \, \text{kJ}/\text{kg}_{C_{10}H_{22}}$$
$$\Delta h_c \,(\text{lower}) = 44{,}601 - 359$$
$$= 44{,}242 \, \text{kJ}/\text{kg}_{C_{10}H_{22}}$$

Comment. Graphical representations of the various definitions and/or thermodynamic processes are valuable aids in setting up problems or in checking their solutions. Figure 2.9 illustrates, on h–T coordinates, the important quantities used in this example. Note that the enthalpy of vaporization given for n-decane is for the standard state temperature (298.15 K), while the value given in Appendix B is at the boiling point (447.4 K).

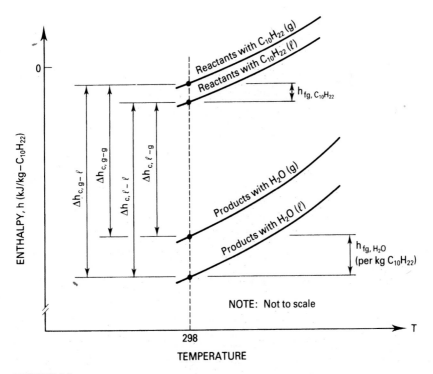

FIGURE 2.9
Enthalpy–temperature plot illustrating calculation of heating values in Example 2.4.

ADIABATIC FLAME TEMPERATURES

We define two adiabatic flame temperatures, one for constant-pressure combustion and one for constant-volume. If a fuel–air mixture burns adiabatically at constant pressure, the absolute enthalpy of the reactants at the initial state (say, $T = 298$ K, $P = 1$ atm) equals the absolute enthalpy of the products at the final state ($T = T_{ad}$, $P = 1$ atm), i.e., application of Eqn. 2.28 results in

$$H_{\text{react}}(T_i, P) = H_{\text{prod}}(T_{ad}, P), \qquad (2.40a)$$

or, equivalently, on a per-mass-of-mixture basis,

$$h_{\text{react}}(T_i, P) = h_{\text{prod}}(T_{ad}, P). \qquad (2.40b)$$

This first-law statement, Eqn. 2.40, defines what is called the **constant-pressure adiabatic flame temperature**. This definition is illustrated graphically in Fig. 2.10. Conceptually, the adiabatic flame temperature is simple; however, evaluating this quantity requires knowledge of the composition of the combustion products. At typical flame temperatures, the products dissociate and the mixture is comprised of many species. As shown in Table 2.1 and Table B.1 in Appendix B, flame

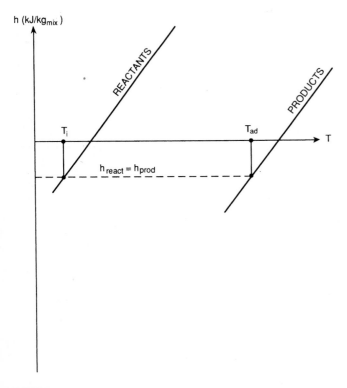

FIGURE 2.10
Illustration of constant-pressure adiabatic flame temperature on h–T coordinates.

temperatures are typically several thousand kelvins. Calculating the complex composition by invoking chemical equilibrium is the subject of the next section. The following example illustrates the fundamental concept of constant-pressure adiabatic flame temperatures, while making crude assumptions regarding the product mixture composition and evaluation of the product mixture enthalpy.

Example 2.5. Estimate the constant-pressure adiabatic flame temperature for the combustion of a stoichiometric CH_4-air mixture. The pressure is 1 atm and the initial reactant temperature is 298 K.

   Use the following assumptions:

1. "Complete combustion" (no dissociation), i.e., the product mixture consists only of CO_2, H_2O, and N_2.
2. The product mixture enthalpy is estimated using constant specific heats evaluated at 1200 K ($\approx 0.5(T_i + T_{ad})$, where T_{ad} is guessed to be about 2100 K).

Solution. Mixture composition:

$$CH_4 + 2(O_2 + 3.76N_2) \rightarrow 1\,CO_2 + 2H_2O + 7.52N_2$$

$$N_{CO_2} = 1, N_{H_2O} = 2, N_{N_2} = 7.52.$$

Properties (Appendices A and B):

Species	Enthalpy of formation @298 K $\bar{h}^o_{f,i}$ (kJ/kmol)	Specific heat @ 1200 K $\bar{c}_{p,i}$ (kJ/kmol-K)
CH_4	−74,831	—
CO_2	−393,546	56.21
H_2O	−241,845	43.87
N_2	0	33.71
O_2	0	—

First law (Eqn. 2.40):

$$H_{react} = \sum_{react} N_i \bar{h}_i = H_{prod} = \sum_{prod} N_i \bar{h}_i$$

$$H_{react} = (1)(-74{,}831) + 2(0) + 7.52(0)$$
$$= -74{,}831\,\text{kJ}$$

$$H_{prod} = \sum N_i[\bar{h}^o_{f,i} + \bar{c}_{p,i}(T_{ad} - 298)]$$
$$= (1)[-393{,}546 + 56.21(T_{ad} - 298)]$$
$$+ (2)[-241{,}845 + 43.87(T_{ad} - 298)]$$
$$+ (7.52)[0 + 33.71(T_{ad} - 298)].$$

Equating H_{react} to H_{prod} and solving for T_{ad} yields,

$$\boxed{T_{ad} = 2318\,\text{K}}.$$

Comments. Comparing the above result with the equilibrium-composition based computation shown in Table 2.1 ($T_{ad,eq} = 2226$ K) shows that the simplified approach overestimates T_{ad} by slightly less than 100 K. Considering the crudeness of the assumptions, this appears to be rather surprisingly good agreement. Removing assumption 2 and recalculating T_{ad} using variable specific heats, i.e.,

$$\bar{h} = \bar{h}_{fi}^o + \int_{298}^{T} \bar{c}_{p,i}\, dT,$$

yields $T_{ad} = 2328$ K (Note that Appendix A provides tabulations of these integrated quantities. Similar tabulations are found in the JANAF tables [6].) Since this result is quite close to our constant-c_p solution, we conclude that the ~ 100 K difference is the result of neglecting dissociation. Note that dissociation causes a lowering of T_{ad} since more energy is tied up in chemical bonds (enthalpies of formation) at the expense of the sensible enthalpy.

In the above, we dealt with a constant-pressure system, which would be appropriate in dealing with a gas-turbine combustor, or a furnace. Let us look now at **constant-volume adiabatic flame temperatures**, which we might require in an ideal Otto-cycle analysis, for example. The first law of thermodynamics (Eqn. 2.20) requires

$$U_{\text{react}}(T_{\text{init}}, P_{\text{init}}) = U_{\text{prod}}(T_{ad}, P_f) \tag{2.41}$$

where U is the absolute (or standardized) internal energy of the mixture. Graphically, Eqn. 2.41 resembles the sketch (Fig. 2.10) used to illustrate the constant-pressure adiabatic flame temperature, except the internal energy replaces the enthalpy. Since most compilations or calculations of thermodynamic properties provide values for H (or h) rather than U (or u) [1,6], we can rearrange Eqn. 2.41 to the following form:

$$H_{\text{react}} - H_{\text{prod}} - V(P_{\text{init}} - P_f) = 0. \tag{2.42}$$

We can apply the ideal-gas law to eliminate the PV terms,

$$P_{\text{init}}V = \sum_{\text{reac}} N_i R_u T_{\text{init}} = N_{\text{reac}} R_u T_{\text{init}},$$

$$P_f V = \sum_{\text{prod}} N_i R_u T_{ad} = N_{\text{prod}} R_u T_{ad}.$$

Thus,

$$H_{\text{react}} - H_{\text{prod}} - R_u(N_{\text{reac}} T_{\text{init}} - N_{\text{prod}} T_{ad}) = 0. \tag{2.43}$$

An alternative form of Eqn. 2.43, on a per-mass-of-mixture basis, can be obtained by dividing Eqn. 2.43 by the mass of mixture, m_{mix}, and recognizing that

$$m_{\text{mix}}/N_{\text{reac}} \equiv MW_{\text{reac}}$$

or

$$m_{\text{mix}}/N_{\text{prod}} \equiv MW_{\text{prod}}.$$

We thus obtain

$$h_{\text{react}} - h_{\text{prod}} - R_u\left(\frac{T_{\text{init}}}{MW_{\text{reac}}} - \frac{T_{ad}}{MW_{\text{prod}}}\right) = 0. \qquad (2.44)$$

Since the equilibrium composition of the product mixture depends upon both temperature and pressure, as we will see in the next section, utilizing Eqn. 2.43 or 2.44 with the ideal-gas law and appropriate calorific equations of state, e.g., $h = h(T, P) = h$ (T only, ideal gas), to find T_{ad} is straightforward, but nontrivial.

Example 2.6. Estimate the constant-volume adiabatic flame temperature for a stoichiometric CH_4–air mixture using the same assumptions as in Example 2.5. Initial conditions are $T_i = 298$ K, $P = 1$ atm ($= 101{,}325$ Pa).

Solution. The same composition and properties used in Example 2.5 apply here. We note, however, that the $c_{p,i}$ values should be evaluated at a temperature somewhat greater than 1200 K, since the constant-volume T_{ad} will be higher than the constant-pressure T_{ad}. Nonetheless, we will use the same values as before.
First law (Eqn. 2.43):

$$H_{\text{react}} - H_{\text{prod}} - R_u(N_{\text{reac}}T_{\text{init}} - N_{\text{prod}}T_{ad}) = 0$$

or

$$\sum_{\text{react}} N_i\bar{h}_i - \sum_{\text{prod}} N_i\bar{h}_i - R_u(N_{\text{reac}}T_{\text{init}} - N_{\text{prod}}T_{ad}) = 0.$$

Substituting numerical values, we have

$$\begin{aligned}
H_{\text{react}} &= (1)(-74{,}831) + 2(0) + 7.52(0) \\
&= -74{,}831 \text{ kJ.} \\
H_{\text{prod}} &= (1)[-393{,}546 + 56.21(T_{ad} - 298)] \\
&\quad + (2)[-241{,}845 + 43.87(T_{ad} - 298)] \\
&\quad + (7.52)[0 + 33.71(T_{ad} - 298)] \\
&= -877{,}236 + 397.5(T_{ad} - 298) \text{ kJ,}
\end{aligned}$$

and

$$R_u(N_{\text{reac}}T_{\text{init}} - N_{\text{prod}}T_{ad}) = 8.315(10.52)(298 - T_{ad})$$

where $N_{\text{reac}} = N_{\text{prod}} = 10.52$ kmol.
Reassembling Eqn. 2.43 and solving for T_{ad} yields,

$$\boxed{T_{ad} = 2889 \text{ K}}.$$

Comments. (i) For the same initial conditions, constant-volume combustion results in much higher temperatures (571 K higher in this example) than for constant-pressure combustion. This is a consequence of the pressure forces doing no work when the volume is fixed. (ii) Note, also, that the number of moles was conserved in going from the initial to final state. This is a fortuitous result for CH_4 and does not occur for other fuels. (iii) The final pressure is well above the initial pressure: $P_f = P_{\text{init}}(T_{ad}/T_{\text{init}}) = 9.69$ atm.

CHEMICAL EQUILIBRIUM

In high-temperature combustion processes, the products of combustion are not a simple mixture of ideal products, as may be suggested by the simple atom-balance used to determine stoichiometry (cf. Eqn. 2.30). Rather, the major species **dissociate**, producing a host of minor species. Under some conditions, what ordinarily might be considered a minor species is actually present in rather large quantities. For example, the ideal combustion products for burning a hydrocarbon with air are CO_2, H_2O, O_2, and N_2. Dissociation of these species and reactions among the dissociation products yields the following species: H_2, OH, CO, H, O, N, NO, and possibly others. The problem we address in this section is the calculation of the mole fractions of all of the product species at a given temperature and pressure, subject to the constraint of conserving the number of moles of each of the elements present in the initial mixture. This element constraint merely says that the number of C, H, O, and N atoms is constant, regardless of how they are combined in the various species.

There are several ways to approach the calculation of equilibrium composition. To be consistent with the treatment of equilibrium in most undergraduate thermodynamics courses, we focus on the equilibrium-constant approach and limit our discussion to the application of ideal gases. For descriptions of other methods, the interested reader is referred to the literature [5,7].

Second-Law Considerations

The concept of chemical equilibrium has its roots in the second law of thermodynamics. Consider a fixed-volume, adiabatic reaction vessel in which a fixed mass of reactants form products. As the reactions proceed, both the temperature and pressure rise until a final equilibrium condition is reached. This final state (temperature, pressure, and composition) is not governed solely by first-law considerations, but necessitates invoking the second law. Consider the combustion reaction

$$CO + \tfrac{1}{2}O_2 \rightarrow CO_2. \tag{2.45}$$

If the final temperature is high enough, the CO_2 will dissociate. Assuming the products to consist only of CO_2, CO, and O_2, we can write

$$\left[CO + \tfrac{1}{2}O_2\right]^{cold}_{reactants} \rightarrow \left[(1-\alpha)CO_2 + \alpha CO + \tfrac{\alpha}{2}O_2\right]^{hot}_{products} \tag{2.46}$$

where α is the fraction of the CO_2 dissociated. We can calculate the adiabatic flame temperature as a function of the dissociation fraction, α, using Eqn. 2.42. For example, with $\alpha = 1$, no heat is released and the mixture temperature, pressure, and composition remain unchanged; while with $\alpha = 0$, the maximum amount of heat release occurs and the temperature and pressure would be the

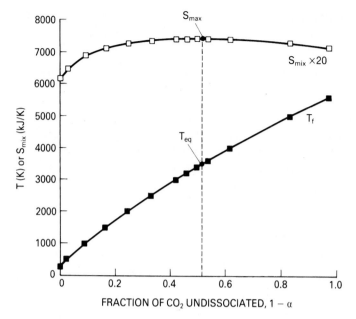

FIGURE 2.11
Illustration of chemical equilibrium for fixed-mass isolated system.

highest possible allowed by the first law. This variation in temperature with α is plotted in Fig. 2.11.

What constraints are imposed by the second law on this thought experiment where we vary α? The entropy of the product mixture can be calculated by summing the product species entropies, i.e.,

$$S_{\text{mix}}(T_f, P) = \sum_{i=1}^{3} N_i \bar{s}_i(T_f, P_i) = (1 - \alpha)\bar{s}_{CO_2} + \alpha\bar{s}_{CO} + \frac{\alpha}{2}\bar{s}_{O_2}, \qquad (2.47)$$

where N_i is the number of moles of species i in the mixture. The individual species entropies are obtained from

$$\bar{s}_i = \bar{s}_i^o(T_{\text{ref}}) + \int_{T_{\text{ref}}}^{T_f} \bar{c}_{p,i}\frac{dT}{T} - R_u \ln\frac{P_i}{P^o} \qquad (2.48)$$

where ideal-gas behavior is assumed, and P_i is the partial pressure of the ith species. Plotting the mixture entropy (Eqn. 2.47) as a function of the dissociation fraction, we see that a maximum value is reached at some intermediate value of α. For the reaction chosen, $CO + \frac{1}{2}O_2 \rightarrow CO_2$, the maximum entropy occurs near $1 - \alpha = 0.5$.

For our choice of conditions (constant U, V, and m, which implies no heat or work interactions), the second law requires that the entropy change internal to the system

$$dS \geq 0. \qquad (2.49)$$

Thus, we see that the composition of the system will spontaneously shift toward the point of maximum entropy when approaching from either side, since dS is positive. Once the maximum entropy is reached, no further change in composition is allowed, since this would require the system entropy to decrease in violation of the second law (Eqn. 2.49). Formally, the condition for equilibrium can be written

$$(dS)_{U,V,m} = 0. \qquad (2.50)$$

In summary, if we fix the internal energy, volume, and mass of an isolated system, the application of Eqn. 2.49 (second law), Eqn. 2.41 (first law), and Eqn. 2.2 (equation of state) define the equilibrium temperature, pressure, and chemical composition.

Gibbs Function

Although the foregoing was useful in illustrating how the second law comes into play in establishing chemical equilibrium, the use of an isolated (fixed-energy) system of fixed mass and volume is not particularly useful for many of the typical problems involving chemical equilibrium. For example, there is frequently a need to calculate the composition of a mixture at a given temperature, pressure, and stoichiometry. For this problem, the **Gibbs free energy**, G, replaces the entropy as the important thermodynamic property.

As you may recall from your previous study of thermodynamics, the Gibbs free energy is defined in terms of other thermodynamic properties as

$$G \equiv H - TS. \qquad (2.51)$$

The second law can then be expressed

$$(dG)_{T,P,m} \leq 0, \qquad (2.52)$$

which states that the Gibbs function always decreases for a spontaneous, isothermal, isobaric change of a fixed-mass system in the absence of all work effects except boundary (P–dV) work. This principle allows us to calculate the equilibrium composition of a mixture at a given temperature and pressure. The Gibbs function attains a minimum in equilibrium, in contrast to the maximum in entropy we saw for the fixed energy and volume case (Fig. 2.11). Thus, at equilibrium,

$$(dG)_{T,P,m} = 0. \qquad (2.53)$$

For a mixture of ideal gases, the Gibbs function for the ith species is given by

$$\bar{g}_{i,T} = \bar{g}^o_{i,T} + R_u T \ln(P_i/P^o) \tag{2.54}$$

where $\bar{g}^o_{i,T}$ is the Gibbs function of the pure species at the standard-state pressure (i.e., $P_i = P^o$) and P_i is the partial pressure. The standard-state pressure, P^o, by convention taken to be 1 atmosphere, appears in the denominator of the logarithm term. Values for $\bar{g}^o_{i,T}$ can be calculated in a manner similar to absolute enthalpies where $\bar{g}^o_{i,T}$ is the sum of a **Gibbs function of formation, $\bar{g}^o_{f,i}$**, and a sensible contribution, i.e.,

$$\bar{g}^o_{i,T} = \left(\bar{g}^o_{f,i}\right)_{T_{\text{ref}}} + \left[\bar{g}^o_i(T) - \bar{g}^o_i(T_{\text{ref}})\right]. \tag{2.55}$$

As with enthalpies, the Gibbs functions of formation of the naturally occurring elements are assigned values of zero at the reference state. Appendix A provides tabulations of Gibbs function of formation over a range of temperatures for selected species. Having tabulations of $\bar{g}^o_{f,i}(T_{\text{ref}})$ for reference temperatures other than the standard-state temperature of 298 K is quite useful. In later calculations, we will need to evaluate differences in $\bar{g}^o_{i,T}$ between different species at the same temperature. These differences can be obtained easily by using the Gibbs function of formation for the reference temperature equal to the temperature of interest ($T_{\text{ref}} = T$), which are provided in Appendix A. Tabulations for over 1000 species can be found in the JANAF tables [6].

The Gibbs function for a mixture of ideal gases can be expressed as

$$G_{\text{mix}} = \sum N_i \bar{g}_{i,T} = \sum N_i \left[\bar{g}^o_{i,T} + R_u T \ln(P_i/P^o)\right] \tag{2.56}$$

where N_i is the number of moles of the ith species.

For fixed temperature and pressure, the equilibrium condition becomes

$$dG_{\text{mix}} = 0 \tag{2.57}$$

or

$$\sum dN_i \left[\bar{g}^o_{i,T} + R_u T \ln(P_i/P^o)\right] + \sum N_i d\left[\bar{g}^o_{i,T} + R_u T \ln(P_i/P^o)\right] = 0. \tag{2.58}$$

The second term in Eqn. 2.58 can be shown to be zero by recognizing that $d(\ln P_i) = dP_i/P_i$ and that $\sum dP_i = 0$, since all changes in the partial pressures must sum to zero because the total pressure is constant. Thus,

$$dG_{\text{mix}} = 0 = \sum dN_i \left[\bar{g}^o_{i,T} + R_u T \ln(P_i/P^o)\right]. \tag{2.59}$$

For the general system, where

$$a\text{A} + b\text{B} + \ldots \Leftrightarrow e\text{E} + f\text{F} + \ldots, \tag{2.60}$$

the change in the number of moles of each species is directly proportional to its stoichiometric coefficient, i.e.,

$$dN_A = -\kappa a$$
$$dN_B = -\kappa b$$
$$\vdots \quad \vdots$$
$$dN_E = +\kappa e$$
$$dN_F = +\kappa f$$
$$\vdots \quad \vdots$$

(2.61)

Substituting Eqn. 2.61 into 2.59 and canceling the proportionality constant κ, we obtain

$$-a\left[\bar{g}^o_{A,T} + R_u T \ln(P_A/P^o)\right] - b\left[\bar{g}^o_{B,T} + R_u T \ln(P_B/P^o)\right] - \dots$$
$$+e\left[\bar{g}^o_{E,T} + R_u T \ln(P_E/P^o)\right] + f\left[\bar{g}^o_{F,T} + R_u T \ln(P_F/P^o)\right] + \dots = 0.$$

(2.62)

Equation 2.62 can be rearranged and the log terms grouped together to yield

$$-\left(e\bar{g}^o_{E,T} + f\bar{g}^o_{F,T} + \dots - a\bar{g}^o_{A,T} - b\bar{g}^o_{B,T} - \dots\right) = R_u T \ln \frac{(P_E/P^o)^e \cdot (P_F/P^o)^f \cdot \text{etc.}}{(P_A/P^o)^a \cdot (P_B/P^o)^b \cdot \text{etc.}}$$

(2.63)

The term in parentheses on the left-hand-side of Eqn. 2.63 is called the **standard-state Gibbs function change ΔG^o_T**, i.e.,

$$\Delta G^o_T = \left(e\bar{g}^o_{E,T} + f\bar{g}^o_{F,T} + \dots - a\bar{g}^o_{A,T} - b\bar{g}^o_{B,T} - \dots\right) \qquad (2.64a)$$

or, alternately,

$$\Delta G^o_T \equiv \left(e\bar{g}^o_{f,E} + f\bar{g}^o_{f,F} + \dots - a\bar{g}^o_{f,A} - b\bar{g}^o_{f,B} - \dots\right)_{T_{\text{ref}}=T}. \qquad (2.64b)$$

The argument of the natural logarithm is defined as the **equilibrium constant K_p** for the reaction expressed in Eqn. 2.60, i.e.,

$$K_p = \frac{(P_E/P^o)^e \cdot (P_F/P^o)^f \cdot \text{etc.}}{(P_A/P^o)^a \cdot (P_B/P^o)^b \cdot \text{etc.}}. \qquad (2.65)$$

With these definitions, Eqn. 2.63, our statement of chemical equilibrium at constant temperature and pressure, is given by

$$\Delta G^o_T = -R_u T \ln K_p, \qquad (2.66a)$$

or

$$K_p = \exp\left(-\Delta G^o_T/R_u T\right). \qquad (2.66b)$$

From the definition of K_p (Eqn. 2.65) and its relation to ΔG_T^o (Eqn. 2.66), we can obtain a qualitative indication of whether a particular reaction favors products (goes strongly to completion) or reactants (very little reaction occurs) at equilibrium. If ΔG_T^o is positive, reactants will be favored since $\ln K_p$ is negative, which requires that K_p itself is less than unity. Similarly, if ΔG_T^o is negative, the reaction tends to favor products. Physical insight to this behavior can be obtained by appealing to the definition of ΔG in terms of the enthalpy and entropy changes associated with the reaction. From Eqn. 2.51, we can write

$$\Delta G_T^o = \Delta H^o - T \Delta S^o,$$

which can be substituted into Eqn. 2.66b:

$$K_p = e^{-\Delta H^o / R_u T} \cdot e^{\Delta S^o / R_u}.$$

For K_p to be greater than unity, which favors products, the enthalpy change for the reaction, ΔH^o, should be negative, i.e., the reaction is exothermic and the system energy is lowered. Also, positive changes in entropy, which indicate greater molecular chaos, lead to values of $K_p > 1$.

Example 2.7. Consider the dissociation of CO_2 as a function of temperature and pressure,

$$CO_2 \Leftrightarrow CO + \tfrac{1}{2}O_2.$$

Find the composition of the mixture, i.e., the mole fractions of CO_2, CO, and O_2, that results from subjecting originally pure CO_2 to various temperatures ($T = 1500$, 2000, 2500, and 3000 K) and pressures (0.1, 1, 10, and 100 atm).

Solution. To find the three unknown mole fractions, χ_{CO_2}, χ_{CO}, and χ_{O_2}, we will need three equations. The first equation will be an equilibrium expression, Eqn. 2.66. The other two equations will come from element conservation expressions that state that the total amounts of C and O are constant, regardless of how they are distributed among the three species, since the original mixture was pure CO_2.

To implement Eqn. 2.66, we recognize that $a = 1, b = 1$, and $c = \tfrac{1}{2}$, since

$$(1)\,CO_2 \Leftrightarrow (1)\,CO + \left(\tfrac{1}{2}\right)O_2.$$

Thus, we can evaluate the standard-state Gibbs function change. For example, at $T = 2500$ K,

$$\Delta G_T^o = [(\tfrac{1}{2})\bar{g}_{f,O_2}^o + (1)\bar{g}_{f,CO}^o - (1)\bar{g}_{f,CO_2}^o]_{T_{ref}=2500}$$

$$= (\tfrac{1}{2})0 + (1)(-327{,}245) - (-396{,}152)$$

$$= 68{,}907 \text{ kJ/kmol}.$$

The values above are taken from Tables A.1, A.2, and A.11.

From the definition of K_p, we have

$$K_p = \frac{(P_{CO}/P^o)^1 (P_{O_2}/P^o)^{0.5}}{(P_{CO_2}/P^o)^1}.$$

We can rewrite K_p in terms of the mole fractions by recognizing that $P_i = \chi_i P$. Thus,

$$K_p = \frac{\chi_{CO}\chi_{O_2}^{0.5}}{\chi_{CO_2}} \cdot (P/P^o)^{0.5}$$

Substituting the above into Eqn. 2.66b, we have

$$\frac{\chi_{CO_2}\chi_{O_2}^{0.5}(P/P^o)^{0.5}}{\chi_{CO_2}} = \exp\left[\frac{-\Delta G_T^o}{R_u T}\right]$$

$$= \exp\left[\frac{-68,907}{(8.315)(2500)}\right] \quad\quad (I)$$

$$\frac{\chi_{CO}\chi_{O_2}^{0.5}(P/P^o)^{0.5}}{\chi_{CO_2}} = 0.03635.$$

We create a second equation to express **conservation of elements:**

$$\frac{\text{No. of carbon atoms}}{\text{No. of oxygen atoms}} = \frac{1}{2} = \frac{\chi_{CO} + \chi_{CO_2}}{\chi_{CO} + 2\chi_{CO_2} + 2\chi_{O_2}}$$

We can make the problem more general by defining the C/O ratio to be a parameter Z that can take on different values depending on the initial composition of the mixture:

$$Z = \frac{\chi_{CO} + \chi_{CO_2}}{\chi_{CO} + 2\chi_{CO_2} + 2\chi_{O_2}}$$

or

$$(Z - 1)\chi_{CO} + (2Z - 1)\chi_{CO_2} + 2Z\chi_{O_2} = 0. \quad\quad (II)$$

To obtain a third and final equation, overall mass (mole) conservation requires that all of the mole fractions must sum to unity, i.e.,

$$\sum_i \chi_i = 1$$

or

$$\chi_{CO} + \chi_{CO_2} + \chi_{O_2} = 1. \quad\quad (III)$$

Simultaneous solution of Eqns. I, II, and III for selected values of P, T, and Z yield values for the mole fractions χ_{CO}, χ_{CO_2}, and χ_{O_2}. Using Eqns. II and III to eliminate χ_{CO_2} and χ_{O_2}, Eqn. I becomes

$$\chi_{CO}(1 - 2Z + Z\chi_{CO})^{0.5}(P/P^o)^{0.5} - [2Z - (1 + Z)\chi_{CO}]\exp(-\Delta G_T^o/R_u T) = 0.$$

The above expression is easily solved for χ_{CO} by applying Newton–Raphson iteration, which can be implemented simply using spreadsheet software. The other unknowns, χ_{CO} and χ_{O_2}, are then recovered using Equations II and III.

TABLE 2.2
Equilibrium compositions at various temperatures and pressures for
$CO_2 \Leftrightarrow CO + \frac{1}{2}O_2$

	$P = 0.1$ atm	$P = 1$	$P = 10$	$P = 100$
	$T = 1500$ K, $\Delta G^o_T = 1.5268 \cdot 10^8$ J/kmol			
χ_{CO}	$7.755 \cdot 10^{-4}$	$3.601 \cdot 10^{-4}$	$1.672 \cdot 10^{-4}$	$7.76 \cdot 10^{-5}$
χ_{CO_2}	0.9988	0.9994	0.9997	0.9999
χ_{O_2}	$3.877 \cdot 10^{-4}$	$1.801 \cdot 10^{-4}$	$8.357 \cdot 10^{-5}$	$3.88 \cdot 10^{-5}$
	$T = 2000$ K, $\Delta G^o_T = 1.10462 \cdot 10^8$ J/kmol			
χ_{CO}	0.0315	0.0149	$6.96 \cdot 10^{-3}$	$3.243 \cdot 10^{-3}$
χ_{CO_2}	0.9527	0.9777	0.9895	0.9951
χ_{O_2}	0.0158	0.0074	$3.48 \cdot 10^{-3}$	$1.622 \cdot 10^{-3}$
	$T = 2500$ K, $\Delta G^o_T = 6.8907 \cdot 10^7$ J/kmol			
χ_{CO}	0.2260	0.1210	0.0602	0.0289
χ_{CO_2}	0.6610	0.8185	0.9096	0.9566
χ_{O_2}	0.1130	0.0605	0.0301	0.0145
	$T = 3000$ K, $\Delta G^o_T = 2.7878 \cdot 10^7$ J/kmol			
χ_{CO}	0.5038	0.3581	0.2144	0.1138
χ_{CO_2}	0.2443	0.4629	0.6783	0.8293
χ_{O_2}	0.2519	0.1790	0.1072	0.0569

Results are shown in Table 2.2 for four levels each of temperature and pressure. Figure 2.12 shows the CO mole fractions over the range of parameters investigated.

Comments. Two general observations concerning these results can be made. First, at any fixed temperature, increasing the pressure suppresses the dissociation of CO_2 into CO and O_2; second, increasing the temperature at a fixed pressure promotes the dissociation. Both of these trends are consistent with the **Principle of Le Châtelier** that states that any system initially in a state of equilibrium when subjected to a change (e.g., increasing pressure or temperature) will shift in composition in such a way as to minimize the change. For an increase in pressure, this translates to the equilibrium shifting in the direction to produce fewer moles. For the $CO_2 \Leftrightarrow CO + \frac{1}{2}O_2$ reaction, this means a shift to the left, to the CO_2 side. For equimolar reactions, pressure has no effect. When the temperature is increased, the composition shifts in the endothermic direction. Since heat is absorbed when CO_2 breaks down into CO and O_2, increasing the temperature produces a shift to the right, to the $CO + \frac{1}{2}O_2$ side.

Complex Systems

The preceding sections focused on simple situations involving a single equilibrium reaction; however, in most combustion systems, many species and several simultaneous equilibrium reactions are important. In principle, the previous example could be extended to include additional reactions. For example, the reaction

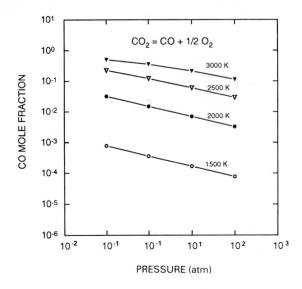

FIGURE 2.12

CO mole fractions resulting from dissociation of pure CO_2 at various pressures and temperatures.

$O_2 \Leftrightarrow 2O$ is likely to be important at the temperatures considered. Including this reaction introduces only one additional unknown, χ_O. We easily add an additional equation to account for the O_2 dissociation:

$$\left(\chi_O^2 / \chi_{O_2}\right) P / P^o = \exp\left(-\Delta G_T^{o\prime} / R_u T\right),$$

where $\Delta G_T^{o\prime}$ is the appropriate standard-state Gibbs function change for the $O_2 \Leftrightarrow 2O$ reaction. The element-conservation expression (Eqn. II) is modified to account for the additional O-containing species,

$$\frac{\text{No. of C atoms}}{\text{No. of O atoms}} = \frac{\chi_{CO} + \chi_{CO_2}}{\chi_{CO} + 2\chi_{CO_2} + 2\chi_{O_2} + \chi_O},$$

and overall mass (mole) conservation becomes

$$\chi_{CO} + \chi_{CO_2} + \chi_{O_2} + \chi_O = 1.$$

We now have a new set of four equations with four unknowns to solve. Since two of the four equations are nonlinear, it is likely that some method of simultaneously solving nonlinear equations would be applied. Appendix E presents the **Generalized Newton's Method**, which is easily applied to such systems.

An example of the above approach being applied to the C, H, N, O system is the computer code developed by Olikara and Borman [8]. This code solves for 12 species, invoking seven equilibrium reactions and four atom-conservation relations, one each for C, O, H, and N. This code was developed specifically for internal combustion engine simulations and is readily imbedded as a subroutine in simulation codes. This code is used in the software provided with this book, as explained in Appendix F.

One of the most frequently used general equilibrium codes is the powerful NASA Chemical Equilibrium Code [5], designated CEC86. The code is frequently updated so the "86" represents the update year. This code is capable of handling over 400 different species, and many special problem features are built into it. For example, rocket nozzle performance and shock calculations can be performed. The theoretical approach to the equilibrium calculation does not employ equilibrium constants, but rather techniques are applied to minimize either the Gibbs or Helmholz energies, subject to atom-balance constraints.

A more recent arrival on the equilibrium-calculation scene is the PC- or Macintosh-based STANJAN code [7]. This is an efficient, user-friendly code available as freeware through Stanford University. This robust and flexible code uses the element potential method to calculate equilibrium compositions.

EQUILIBRIUM PRODUCTS OF COMBUSTION

Full Equilibrium

When we combine the first law with complex chemical equilibrium principles, the adiabatic flame temperature and the detailed composition of the products of combustion can be obtained by solving Eqns. 2.40 (or 2.41) and 2.66 simultaneously, with appropriate atom-conservation constants. An example of such a calculation for constant-pressure (1 atm) combustion of propane with air is shown in Figs. 2.13 and 2.14, where it has been assumed that the only products occurring are CO_2, CO, H_2O, H_2, H, OH, O_2, O, NO, N_2, and N.

In Fig. 2.13, we see the adiabatic flame temperature and the **major species** as functions of equivalence ratio. Major products of lean combustion are H_2O, CO_2, O_2, and N_2; while for rich combustion, they are H_2O, CO_2, CO, H_2, and N_2. It is interesting to note that the maximum flame temperature 2278.4 K occurs not at stoichiometric, but, rather, at a slightly rich equivalence ratio ($\Phi \approx 1.05$), as does the water mole fraction ($\Phi \approx 1.15$). That the maximum temperature is at a slightly rich equivalence ratio is a consequence of both the heat of combustion and heat capacity of the products ($N_{\mathrm{prod}} \cdot \bar{c}_{p,\mathrm{prod}}$) declining beyond $\Phi = 1$. For equivalence ratios between $\Phi = 1$ and $\Phi(T_{\max})$, the heat capacity decreases more rapidly with Φ than ΔH_c; while beyond $\Phi(T_{\max})$, ΔH_c falls more rapidly than does the heat capacity. The decrease in heat capacity is dominated by the decrease in number of product moles formed per mole of fuel burned, with the decrease in the mean specific heat being less significant. Also in Fig. 2.13, we see, as a result of dissociation, the simultaneous presence of O_2, CO, and H_2 at stoichiometric conditions ($\Phi = 1$). Under conditions of "complete combustion," i.e., no dissociation, all three of these species would be zero; thus, we expose the approximate nature of the "complete-combustion" assumption. Later, we will quantify this effect.

Some of the **minor species** of equilibrium combustion of hydrocarbons in air are shown in Fig. 2.14. Here we see the atoms O and H and the diatomic species OH and NO, all below the 4000 ppm level, and that CO is a minor species in lean

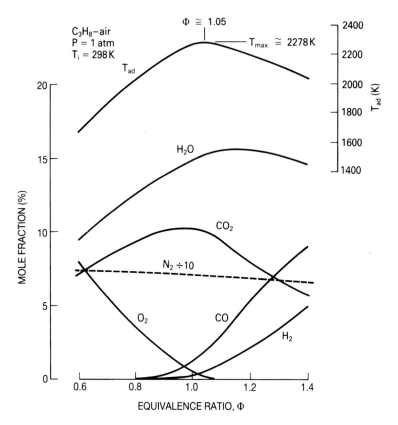

FIGURE 2.13
Equilibrium adiabatic flame temperatures and major product species for propane–air combustion at 1 atm.

products, and conversely, O_2 is a minor product of rich combustion. The CO and O_2 concentrations, however, head through the top of the graph on their way to becoming major species in rich and lean products, respectively. It is interesting to note that the level of the hydroxyl radical OH is more than an order of magnitude greater than the O atom, and that both peak slightly lean of stoichiometric conditions. Furthermore, although not shown, N-atom concentrations are several orders of magnitude less than those of the O atom. The lack of dissociation of the N_2 molecule is a result of the strong triple covalent bond. The O and OH maxima in the lean region have implications for the kinetics of NO formation. Equilibrium NO concentrations are rather flat and peak in the lean region, falling rapidly in the rich region. In most combustion systems, NO levels are well below the equilibrium concentrations shown, because of the relatively slow formation reactions, as we will see in Chapters 4 and 5.

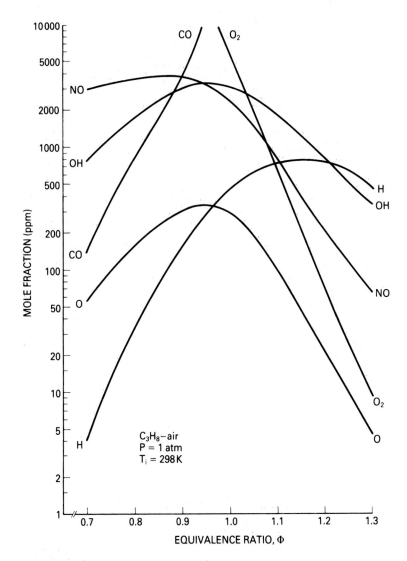

FIGURE 2.14
Minor species distributions for propane–air combustion at 1 atm.

Water-Gas Equilibrium

In this section, we will develop simple relations that allow the calculation of the ideal products of combustion (no dissociation producing minor species) for both lean and rich conditions. For lean combustion, nothing new is involved as we need employ only atom balances; for rich combustion, however, we employ a single equilibrium reaction, $CO + H_2O \Leftrightarrow CO_2 + H_2$, the so-called **water-gas**

shift reaction, to account for the simultaneous presence of the incomplete products of combustion, CO and H_2. This water-gas equilibrium is central to steam reforming of CO in the petroleum industry.

Assuming no dissociation, the combustion of an arbitrary hydrocarbon with our simplified air can be represented as

$$C_xH_y + a(O_2 + 3.76 N_2) \rightarrow b CO_2 + c CO + d H_2O + e H_2 + f O_2 + 3.76 a N_2,$$
$$(2.67a)$$

which for *lean or stoichiometric conditions* ($\Phi \leq 1$) becomes

$$C_xH_y + a(O_2 + 3.76 N_2) \rightarrow bCO_2 + d H_2O + f O_2 + 3.76 a N_2, \qquad (2.67b)$$

or for *rich conditions* ($\Phi > 1$),

$$C_xH_y + a(O_2 + 3.76 N_2) \rightarrow b CO_2 + c CO + d H_2O + e H_2 + 3.76 a N_2. \quad (2.67c)$$

Since the coefficient a represents the ratio of the number of moles of O_2 in the reactants to the number of moles of fuel, we can relate a to the equivalence ratio by using Eqn. 2.31, i.e.,

$$a = \frac{x + y/4}{\Phi}; \qquad (2.68)$$

thus, given the fuel type and Φ, a is a known quantity.

Our objective is to find the mole fractions of all of the product species. For lean or stoichiometric combustion, the coefficients c and e are zero because there is sufficient O_2 to have all the fuel C and H react to form CO_2 and H_2O, respectively. The coefficients b, d, and f can be found by C, H, and O-atom balances, respectively; thus,

$$b = x, \qquad (2.69a)$$
$$c = 0, \qquad (2.69b)$$
$$d = y/2, \qquad (2.69c)$$
$$e = 0, \qquad (2.69d)$$
$$f = \left(\frac{1 - \Phi}{\Phi}\right)(x + y/4) \qquad (2.69e)$$

The total number of moles of products (per mole of fuel burned) can be found by summing the above coefficients together with the 3.76a moles of N_2,

$$N_{TOT} = x + y/2 + \left(\frac{x + y/4}{\Phi}\right)(1 - \Phi + 3.76). \qquad (2.70)$$

The mole fractions are then determined by dividing each of the coefficients above by N_{TOT}:

Lean or stoichiometric $(\Phi \leq 1)$

$$\chi_{CO_2} = x/N_{TOT}, \tag{2.71a}$$

$$\chi_{CO} = 0, \tag{2.71b}$$

$$\chi_{H_2O} = (y/2)/N_{TOT}, \tag{2.71c}$$

$$\chi_{H_2} = 0, \tag{2.71d}$$

$$\chi_{O_2} = \left(\frac{1-\Phi}{\Phi}\right)(x + y/4)/N_{TOT}, \tag{2.71e}$$

$$\chi_{N_2} = 3.76(x + y/4)/(\Phi N_{TOT}). \tag{2.71f}$$

For rich combustion $(\Phi > 1)$, no oxygen appears, so the coefficient f is zero. That leaves us with four unknowns (b, c, d and e). To solve for these, we employ the three element balances (C, H, and O) and the water-gas shift equilibrium,

$$K_p = \frac{(P_{CO_2}/P^o) \cdot (P_{H_2}/P^o)}{(P_{CO}/P^o) \cdot (P_{H_2O}/P^o)} = \frac{b \cdot e}{c \cdot d}. \tag{2.72}$$

The use of Eqn. 2.72 causes the system of equations for b, c, d, and e to be nonlinear (quadratic). Solving the element balances in terms of the unknown coefficient b results in

$$c = x - b \tag{2.73a}$$

$$d = 2a - b - x \tag{2.73b}$$

$$e = -2a + b + x + y/2. \tag{2.73c}$$

Substituting Eqn. 2.73a–c into Eqn. 2.72 yields a quadratic equation in b, the solution of which is

$$b = \frac{2a(K_p - 1) + x + y/2}{2(K_p - 1)}$$
$$- \frac{1}{2(K_p - 1)}\left[(2a(K_p - 1) + x + y/2)^2 - 4K_p(K_p - 1)(2ax - x^2)\right]^{1/2}, \tag{2.74}$$

where the negative root is selected to yield physically realistic (positive) values of b. Again,

$$N_{TOT} = b + c + d + e + 3.76a = x + y/2 + 3.76a, \tag{2.75}$$

and the various mole fractions are expressed in terms of b (Eqn. 2.74):

Rich $(\Phi > 1)$

$$\chi_{CO_2} = b/N_{TOT}, \tag{2.76a}$$
$$\chi_{CO} = c/N_{TOT} = (x - b)/N_{TOT}, \tag{2.76b}$$
$$\chi_{H_2O} = d/N_{TOT} = (2a - b - x)/N_{TOT}, \tag{2.76c}$$
$$\chi_{H_2} = e/N_{TOT} = (-2a + b + x + y/2)/N_{TOT}, \tag{2.76d}$$
$$\chi_{O_2} = 0, \tag{2.76e}$$
$$\chi_{N_2} = 3.76a/N_{TOT}, \tag{2.76f}$$

where a is evaluated from Eqn. 2.68. Spreadsheet software can be used conveniently to solve Eqns. 2.76a–f and their ancillary relations for the mole fractions for various fuels (values of x and y) and equivalence ratios. Since K_p is a function of temperature, an appropriate temperature must be selected; however, at typical combustion temperatures, say 2000–2400 K, the mole fractions are not strongly dependent on the choice of temperature.

Table 2.3 shows comparisons between the full-equilibrium calculations and the approximate method above for CO and H_2 mole fractions for propane–air combustion products. The equilibrium constant for the water-gas shift was evaluated at 2200 K for all equivalence ratios. Here we see that for $\Phi \gtrsim 1.2$, the full-equilibrium and approximate methods yield concentrations that differ by only a few percent. As Φ approaches unity, the simple method becomes increasingly inaccurate, because dissociation was neglected.

To quantify the degree of dissociation at $\Phi = 1$, Table 2.4 shows CO_2 and H_2O mole fractions calculated using both full equilibrium and the assumption of

TABLE 2.3
CO and H_2 mole fractions for rich combustion, C_3H_8–air, $P = 1$ atm

	χ_{CO}			χ_{H_2}		
Φ	Full equilibrium	Water-gas equilibrium[a]	% Difference	Full equilibrium	Water-gas equilibrium[a]	% Difference
1.1	0.0317	0.0287	−9.5	0.0095	0.0091	−4.2
1.2	0.0537	0.0533	−0.5	0.0202	0.0203	+0.5
1.3	0.0735	0.0741	+0.8	0.0339	0.0333	−1.8
1.4	0.0903	0.0920	+1.9	0.0494	0.0478	−3.4

[a]For $K_p = 0.193$ ($T = 2200$ K).

TABLE 2.4
Degree of dissociation for propane–air combustion products ($P = 1$ atm, $\Phi = 1$)

	Mole fraction		
Species	Full equilibrium	No dissociation	% Dissociated
CO_2	0.1027	0.1163	11.7
H_2O	0.1484	0.1550	4.3

TABLE 2.5
Effect of pressure on dissociation of propane–air combustion products ($\Phi = 1$)

Pressure (atm)	T_{ad} (K)	χ_{CO_2}	% Dissociation	χ_{H_2O}	% Dissociation
0.1	2198	0.0961	17.4	0.1444	6.8
1.0	2268	0.1027	11.7	0.1484	4.3
10	2319	0.1080	7.1	0.1512	2.5
100	2353	0.1116	4.0	0.1530	1.3

no dissociation. Here we see that at 1 atm, approximately 12% of the CO_2 dissociates, while just over 4% of the H_2O dissociates.

Pressure Effects

Pressure has a significant effect on dissociation. Table 2.5 shows the decreasing degree of CO_2 dissociation with pressure. Since the only other carbon-containing species allowed in the product mixture is CO, the effect shown in Table 2.5 results from the equilibrium reaction $CO_2 \Leftrightarrow CO + \frac{1}{2}O_2$. Since the dissociation of CO_2 results in an increase in the total number of moles present, the pressure effect shown is consistent with the Principle of Le Châtelier discussed previously. The H_2O dissociation is more complex in that, in addition to H_2O, elemental hydrogen is present as OH, H_2, and H; thus, we cannot isolate the pressure effect on H_2O in a single equilibrium expression, but need to simultaneously consider other reactions. The net effect of pressure results in a decrease in the H_2O dissociation, as expected. We note also that the temperature increases as the dissociation is suppressed by increased pressure in accord with Le Châtelier's principle.

SOME APPLICATIONS

In this section, we present two practical applications: the use of recuperation or regeneration to improve energy utilization and/or increase flame temperatures, and the use of flue (or exhaust) gas recirculation to lower flame temperatures. Our intent here is to apply to "real world" examples the concepts previously developed in this chapter and to illustrate the use of some of the software included with this book.

Recuperation and Regeneration

A **recuperator** is a heat exchanger in which energy from a steady flow of hot combustion products, i.e., flue gases, is transferred to the air supplied to the combustion process. A general flow diagram is shown in Fig. 2.15. A wide variety of recuperators is used in practice, many of which employ radiation heat transfer from the flue gases, as well as convection. An example of a recuperator for an indirect-fired application is illustrated in Fig. 2.16.

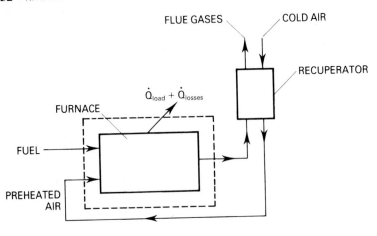

FIGURE 2.15
Schematic of furnace with air preheated by recuperation or regeneration. Dashed line indicates the control volume employed in Example 2.8.

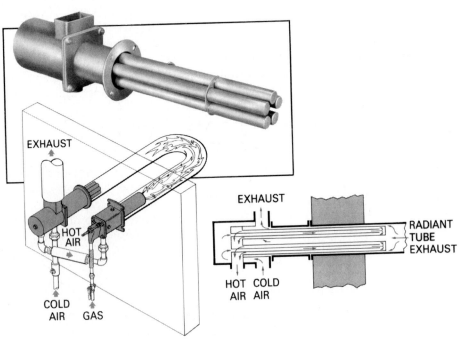

FIGURE 2.16
Radiant-tube burner with coupled recuperator for indirect firing. Note that all the flue gases pass through the recuperator. (Courtesy of Eclipse Combustion.)

A **regenerator** also transfers energy from the flue gases to the incoming combustion air, but, in this case, an energy storage medium, such as a corrugated steel or ceramic matrix, is alternately heated by the hot gases and cooled by the air. Figure 2.17 illustrates the application of a spinning-disk regenerator to an automotive gas-turbine engine, and Fig. 2.18 shows a similar concept applied to

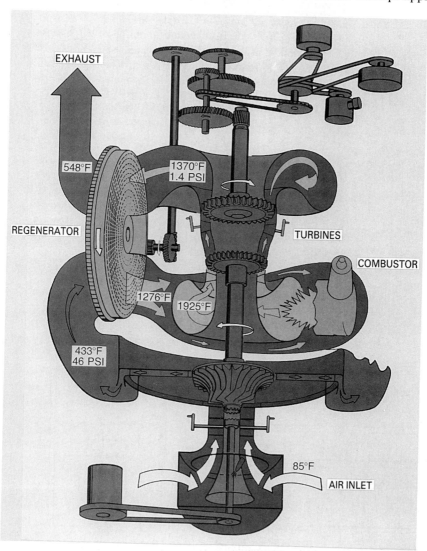

FIGURE 2.17

Flow schematic for automotive gas-turbine engine with spinning-disk regenerator. Ambient air is compressed to 46 psi and 433°F before passing through the regenerator. The thermal energy given up by the regenerator heats the air to 1276°F prior to combustion. After the products of combustion expand through the two turbines, they enter the opposite side of the regenerator at 1370°F, returning energy to the spinning disk, and exhaust at 548°F. (Courtesy of Chrysler Corporation.)

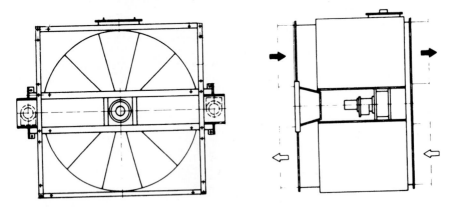

FIGURE 2.18
Steel rotary regenerator used in industrial furnace applications. Flow paths are indicated by the arrows in the sketch (lower right). (From Ref. [9]. Courtesy of Industrial Heating Equipment Association.)

an industrial furnace. In other regenerator concepts, the flow paths are switched alternately to heat and cool the thermal storage medium.

Example 2.8. A recuperator, such as shown in Fig. 2.16, is employed in a natural-gas-fired heat-treating furnace. The furnace operates at atmospheric pressure with an equivalence ratio of 0.9. The fuel gas enters the burner at 298 K, while the air is preheated.

A. Determine the effect of air preheat on the adiabatic temperature of the flame zone for a range of inlet air temperatures from 298 K to 1000 K.

B. What fuel savings result from preheating the air from 298 K to 600 K? Assume that the temperature of the flue gases at the furnace exit, prior to entering the recuperator, is 1700 K, both with and without air preheat.

Solution (Part A). We will employ the Fortran program HPFLAME, which incorporates the Olikara and Borman equilibrium routines [8], to solve the first-law problem, $H_{reac} = H_{prod}$. The input file for the program requires the definition of the fuel by providing the number of carbon, hydrogen, oxygen, and nitrogen atoms comprising the fuel molecule, the equivalence ratio, a guess for the adiabatic flame temperature, the pressure, and the reactants enthalpy. The input file for this example, treating natural gas as methane, is shown below:

Adiabatic Flame Calculation for Specified Fuel, Phi, P, & Reactant Enthalpy Using Olikara & Borman Equilibrium Routines
Problem Title: **EXAMPLE 2–8 Air Preheat at 1000 K**

```
01        /CARBON ATOMS IN FUEL
04        /HYDROGEN ATOMS IN FUEL
00        /OXYGEN ATOMS IN FUEL
00        /NITROGEN ATOMS IN FUEL
0.900     /EQUIVALENCE RATIO
2000.     /TEMPERATURE (K) (Initial Guess)
101325.0  /PRESSURE (Pa)
155037.0  /ENTHALPY OF REACTANTS PER KMOL FUEL (kJ/kmol-fuel)
```

The only quantity requiring calculation is the reactants enthalpy, expressed as kJ/kmol of fuel. To find the number of moles of O_2 and N_2 supplied per mole of fuel, we write our combustion equation as

$$CH_4 + a(O_2 + 3.76N_2) \rightarrow products$$

where (Eqn. 2.68)

$$a = \frac{x + y/4}{\Phi} = \frac{(1 + 4/4)}{0.9} = 2.22.$$

Thus,

$$CH_4 + 2.22O_2 + 8.35N_2 \rightarrow products.$$

The reactants' enthalpy (per mole of fuel) is then

$$H_{reac} = \bar{h}^o_{f,CH_4} + 2.22\Delta\bar{h}_{s,O_2} + 8.35\Delta\bar{h}_{s,N_2}.$$

Using Tables A.7, A.11, and B.1, the above expression can be evaluated for various air temperatures, as shown in the table below:

T (K)	$\Delta\bar{h}_{s,O_2}$ (kJ/kmol)	$\Delta\bar{h}_{s,N_2}$ (kJ/kmol)	H_{reac} (kJ/kmol-fuel)	T_{ad} (K)
298	0	0	−74,831	2134
400	3031	2973	−45,254	2183
600	9254	8905	+20,140	2283
800	15,838	15,046	+86,082	2373
1000	22,721	21,468	+155,037	2456

Using the H_{reac} values above, the constant-pressure adiabatic flame temperatures are calculated using HPFLAME. These results also are tabulated above and plotted in Figure 2.19.

Comment (Part A). We note from Fig. 2.19 that, for the range of preheat temperatures investigated, a 100 K increase in air temperature results in about a 50 K increase in flame temperature. This effect can be attributed to dissociation and to the larger specific heat of the product gases compared to the air.

Solution (Part B). To determine the amount of fuel saved as a result of preheating the air to 600 K, we will write an energy balance for the control volume indicated in Fig. 2.15, assuming both the heat transferred to the load and the heat losses are the same, with and without preheat. Assuming steady flow, we apply Eqn. 2.28, recognizing that heat is transferred out of the control volume:

$$-\dot{Q} = -\dot{Q}_{load} - \dot{Q}_{loss} = \dot{m}(h_{prod} - h_{reac})$$
$$= (\dot{m}_A + \dot{m}_F)h_{prod} - \dot{m}_F h_F - \dot{m}_A h_A.$$

For convenience, we define a fuel utilization efficiency as

$$\eta \equiv \frac{\dot{Q}}{\dot{m}_F \mathrm{LHV}} = \frac{-([(A/F) + 1]h_{prod} - (A/F)h_A - h_F)}{\mathrm{LHV}}.$$

To evaluate the above, we require:

$$(A/F) = \frac{(A/F)_{stoic}}{\Phi} = \frac{17.1}{0.9} = 19.0$$

$$h_F = \bar{h}^{\circ}_{f,F}/MW_F = \frac{-74,831}{16.043} = -4664.4 \, \mathrm{kJ/kg}$$

$h_{prod} = -923 \, \mathrm{kJ/kg}$ (Calculated by TPEQUIL code. See Appendix F.)

$$h_{A@298K} = 0$$

$$h_{A@600K} = (0.21\Delta\bar{h}_{s,O_2} + 0.79\Delta\bar{h}_{s,N_2})/MW_A$$
$$= \frac{0.21(9254) + 0.79(8905)}{28.85}$$
$$= 311.2 \, \mathrm{kJ/kg}.$$

Thus, with air entering at 298 K,

$$\eta_{298} = \frac{-[(19+1)(-923) - 19(0) - (-4664.4)]}{50,016}$$

$$= 0.276$$

and for air entering at 600 K,

$$\eta_{600} = \frac{-1[(19+1)(-923) - 19(311.2) - (-4664.4)]}{50,016}$$

$$= 0.394.$$

We now calculate the fuel savings, defined as,

$$\text{Savings} \equiv \frac{\dot{m}_{F,600} - \dot{m}_{F,298}}{\dot{m}_{F,298}} = 1 - \frac{\eta_{298}}{\eta_{600}}$$

$$= 1 - \frac{0.276}{0.394} = 0.30$$

or expressed as a percentage

$$\boxed{\text{Savings} = 30\%}$$

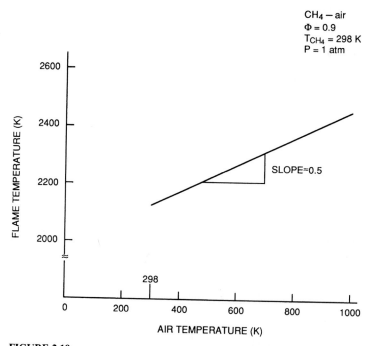

FIGURE 2.19
Effect of combustion air preheat on adiabatic flame temperature for methane combustion ($\Phi = 0.9$, $P = 1$ atm).

Comment (Part B). We see that substantial fuel savings can be realized by using recuperators to return some of the energy that would normally go up the stack. Note that the nitric oxide emissions may be affected, since peak temperatures will increase as a result of preheat. With air entering at 600 K, the adiabatic flame temperature increases 150 K (7.1%) above the 298 K air case.

Flue- (or Exhaust-) Gas Recirculation

In one strategy to decrease the amount of oxides of nitrogen (NO_x) formed and emitted from certain combustion devices, a portion of the burned product gases are recirculated and introduced with the air and fuel. This emission control strategy, and others, is discussed in Chapter 15. The effect of the recirculated gases is to decrease the maximum temperatures in the flame zone. Decreased flame temperatures result in less NO_x being formed. Figure 2.20a schematically illustrates the application of flue-gas recirculation (FGR) in a boiler or furnace, while Fig. 2.20b shows the exhaust-gas recirculation (EGR) system used in automotive engines. The following example shows how the principle of conservation of energy can be applied to determine the effect of product gas recirculation on flame temperatures.

Example 2.9. Consider a spark-ignition engine whose compression and combustion processes have been idealized as a polytropic compression from bottom-dead-center (state 1) to top-dead-center (state 2) and constant-volume combustion (state 2 to state 3), respectively, as shown in the sketch below. Determine the effect of EGR (0–20%, expressed as a volume percentage of the air and fuel) on the adiabatic flame temperature and pressure at state 3. The engine compression ratio ($CR \equiv V_1/V_2$) is 8.0, the polytropic exponent is 1.3, and the initial pressure and temperature (state 1) are fixed at 0.5 atm and 298 K, respectively, regardless of the quantity of recirculated gas. The fuel is isooctane and the equivalence ratio is unity.

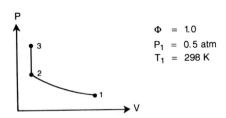

$$\Phi = 1.0$$
$$P_1 = 0.5 \text{ atm}$$
$$T_1 = 298 \text{ K}$$

Solution. To determine the initial temperature and pressure for the start of combustion (state 2), we apply the polytropic relations:

$$T_2 = T_1(V_1/V_2)^{n-1} = 298(8)^{0.3} = 556 \text{ K}$$

$$P_2 = P_1(V_1/V_2)^{n} = 0.5(8)^{1.3} = 7.46 \text{ atm } (755{,}885 \text{ Pa})$$

To analyze the combustion process, we will employ the code UVFLAME. Inputs required for the code that need to be calculated are H_{reac} (kJ/kmol—**fuel**), N_{reac}/N_{fuel}, and MW_{reac}. Each of these quantities will vary as %EGR is changed, although the temperature and pressure remain fixed. To determine these inputs, we first determine the composition of the recycled gases, assuming that they consist of undissociated products of the reaction

$$C_8H_{18} + 12.5(O_2 + 3.76N_2) \rightarrow 8CO_2 + 9H_2O + 47\,N_2.$$

Thus,

$$\chi_{CO_2} = \frac{8}{8+9+47} = \frac{8}{64} = 0.1250$$

$$\chi_{H_2O} = \frac{9}{64} = 0.1406$$

$$\chi_{N_2} = \frac{47}{64} = 0.7344.$$

Using Tables A.2, A.6, and A.7, we evaluate the molar specific enthalpy of the recycled gases at T_2 ($= 556\,K$):

$$\bar{h}_{EGR} = 0.1250(-382,707) + 0.1406(-232,906) + 0.7344(7588)$$
$$= -75,012.3 \text{ kJ/kmol-EGR}.$$

The molar specific enthalpy of the air at $T_2(= 556\,K)$ is:

$$\bar{h}_A = 0.21(7853) + 0.79(7588) = 7643.7 \text{ kJ/kmol-air}.$$

The fuel enthalpy at T_2 is calculated from the curvefit coefficients given in Table B.2. Note that the enthalpy generated from these coefficients is the sum of both the enthalpy of formation and sensible enthalpy:

$$\bar{h}_F = -161,221 \text{ kJ/kmol-fuel}.$$

The enthalpy of the reactants at state 2 can now be calculated:

$$H = N_F\bar{h}_F + N_A\bar{h}_A + N_{EGR}\bar{h}_{EGR}$$

where, by definition,

$$N_{EGR} \equiv (N_A + N_F)\%EGR.$$

From the stoichiometry given, $N_A = 12.5(4.76) = 59.5$ kmol, thus

$$H_{reac} = (1)\bar{h}_F + (59.5)\bar{h}_A + 60.5\,(\%EGR)\bar{h}_{EGR}.$$

Values of H_{reac} for various %EGR are shown in the table below.
    The reactant mixture molecular weight is

$$MW_{reac} = \frac{N_F MW_F + N_A MW_A + N_{EGR} MW_{EGR}}{N_F + N_A + N_{EGR}}$$

where

$$MW_{EGR} = \sum_{EGR} \chi_i MW_i$$
$$= 0.1250\,(44.011) + 0.1406\,(18.016) + 0.7344\,(28.013)$$
$$= 28.607 \text{ kg/kmol-EGR}.$$

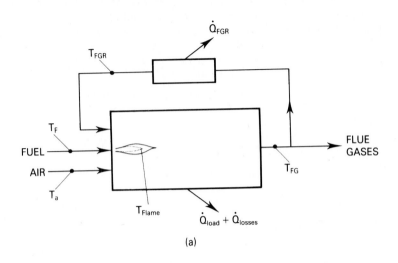

(a)

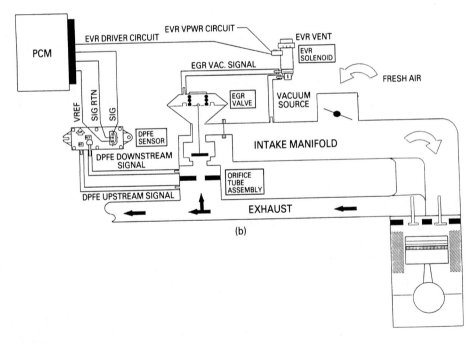

(b)

FIGURE 2.20
(a) Schematic of flue-gas recirculation applied to boiler or furnace. (b) Exhaust-gas recirculation system for spark-ignition engine. (Courtesy of Ford Motor Company.)

Values for MW_{reac} and $N_{tot} (= N_F + N_A + N_{EGR})$ are also shown in the table below.

%EGR	N_{EGR}	N_{tot}	MW_{reac}	H_{reac}(kJ/kmol-fuel)
0	0	60.50	30.261	$+293,579$
5	3.025	63.525	30.182	$+66,667$
10	6.050	66.55	30.111	$-160,245$
15	9.075	69.575	30.045	$-387,158$
20	12.100	72.60	29.98	$-614,070$

Using the above information, we exercise the code UVFLAME and calculate the following adiabatic temperatures and the corresponding pressures at state 3.

%EGR	$T_{ad} (= T_3)$ (K)	P_3 (atm)
0	2804	40.51
5	2740	39.36
10	2672	38.20
15	2600	37.01
20	2525	35.79

These results are plotted in Fig. 2.21.

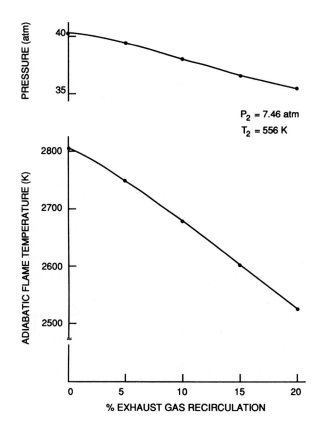

$P_2 = 7.46$ atm

$T_2 = 556$ K

FIGURE 2.21
Calculated adiabatic flame temperatures and peak pressures for constant-volume combustion, with combustion products recycled with the fresh air and fuel (Example 2.9).

Comments. From the table and the graph, we see that EGR can have a pronounced effect on peak temperatures, with 20% EGR resulting in a drop of about 275 K from the zero recycle condition. As we shall see in Chapters 4, 5, and 15, such temperature decreases can have a dramatic effect on NO_x formation.

We should note that in real applications, the temperature of the recycled gases is likely to vary with the amount recycled, which in turn affects the final peak temperature. Furthermore, we did not check to see if the initial (state 1) temperature was below the dew point of the recycled gases, as condensed water would be undesirable in a real EGR system.

SUMMARY

All of the concepts presented in this chapter are of fundamental importance to a study of combustion. We began this chapter with a brief review of basic thermodynamic properties of simple substances and ideal-gas mixtures. We also reviewed the conservation of energy principle, the first law of thermodynamics. The first law in its various forms should be an old friend by now. You should be familiar with the equivalence ratio and how it is used to define rich, lean, and stoichiometric mixtures. Other important thermodynamic properties defined include absolute (or standardized) enthalpies, which are used with the first law to define enthalpies of reaction, heating values, and constant-pressure and constant-volume adiabatic flame temperatures. You should be able to illustrate all of these properties graphically on appropriate thermodynamic coordinates (h–T or u–T). In our discussion of chemical equilibrium, we introduced the Gibbs function and demonstrated its utility in calculating the equilibrium composition of ideal-gas mixtures. You should be able to calculate equilibrium compositions for simple mixtures using equilibrium-constants (K_p), together with element conservation. You should also be able to formulate the more complex problems; however, a familiarity with one or more equilibrium computer codes is useful for their solution. The final topics in this chapter dealt with the variation of combustion product mixture composition with equivalence ratio and the importance of dissociation. You should understand which species may be considered major and which minor, and have an appreciation for the order of magnitude of the mole fractions of the 11 important species we considered. Also shown was the usefulness of water-gas equilibrium for dealing with rich product mixtures in a simplified way. You should be able to calculate the composition of combustion product mixtures assuming no dissociation. Although many seemingly diverse topics were discussed, you should appreciate how the principles of the first and second laws of thermodynamics underpin these topics.

NOMENCLATURE

a	Molar oxygen–fuel ratio (kmol/kmol)
A/F	Mass air–fuel ratio (kg/kg)
$c_p, \bar{c}_p,$	Constant-pressure specific heat (J/kg-K or J/kmol-K)

$c_v, \bar{c}_v$	Constant-volume specific heat (J/kg-K or J/kmol-K)
E, e	Total energy (J or J/kg)
F/A	Mass fuel-air ratio (kg/kg)
g	Gravitational acceleration (m/s^2)
$\bar{g}^o$	Pure-species Gibbs function (J/kmol)
$\bar{g}_f^o$	Gibbs function of formation (J/kmol)
$G, \bar{g}$	Gibbs function or free energy (J or J/kmol)
ΔG^o	Standard-state Gibbs function change, Eqn. 2.64 (J/kmol)
$h_f^0, \bar{h}_f^0$	Enthalpy of formation (J/kg or J/kmol)
$H, h, \bar{h}$	Enthalpy (J or J/kg or J/kmol)
$\Delta H_c, \Delta h_c, \Delta \bar{h}_c$	Heat of combustion (heating value) (J or J/kg or J/kmol)
$\Delta H_R, \Delta h_R, \Delta \bar{h}_R$	Enthalpy of reaction (J or J/kg or J/kmol)
HHV	Higher heating value
K_p	Equilibrium constant, Eqn. 2.65 (dimensionless)
LHV	Lower heating value
m	Mass (kg)
$\dot{m}$	Mass flowrate (kg/s)
MW	Molecular weight (kg/kmol)
N	Number of moles (kmol)
P	Pressure (Pa)
Q, q	Heat (J or J/kg)
$\dot{Q}, \dot{q}$	Heat-transfer rate (J/s = W or W/kg)
R	Specific gas constant (J/kg-K)
R_u	Universal gas constant (J/kmol-K)
$S, s, \bar{s}$	Entropy (J/K or J/kg-K or J/kmol-K)
t	Time (s)
T	Temperature (K)
$U, u, \bar{u}$	Internal energy (J or J/kg or J/kmol)
v	Velocity (m/s)
V, v	Volume (m^3 or m^3/kg)
W, w	Work (J or J/kg)
$\dot{W}, \dot{w}$	Rate of work or power (J/s = W or W/kg)
x	Number of carbon atoms in fuel
y	Number of hydrogen atoms in fuel
Y	Mass fraction (kg/kg)
z	Elevation (m)
Z	Element ratio

Greek Symbols

α	Fraction dissociated
κ	Proportionality constant, Eqn. 2.61
ρ	Density (kg/m^3)
Φ	Equivalence ratio
χ	Mole fraction

Subscripts

A	Air
ad	Adiabatic
cv	Control volume
F	Fuel
f	Final or formation
g	Gas
i	ith species or inlet
init	Initial
l	Liquid
mix	Mixture
o	Outlet
prod	Product
reac	Reactant
ref	Reference
sat	Saturation state
stoic	Stoichiometric
s	Sensible
T	At temperature T

Superscripts

o	Denotes standard-state pressure ($P^o = 1$ atm)

REFERENCES

1. Kee, R. J., Rupley, F. M., and Miller, J. A., "The Chemkin Thermodynamic Data Base," Sandia National Laboratories Report SAND87-8215 B, March 1991.
2. Moran, M. J., and Shapiro, H. N., *Fundamentals of Engineering Thermodynamics*, Wiley, New York, 1988.
3. Wark, K. Jr., *Thermodynamics*, 5th Ed., McGraw-Hill, New York, 1988.
4. Çengel, Y. A., and Boles, M. A., *Thermodynamics: An Engineering Approach*, McGraw-Hill, New York, 1989.
5. Gordon, S., and McBride, B. J., "Computer Program for Calculation of Complex Chemical Equilibrium Compositions, Rocket Performance, Incident and Reflected Shocks, and Chapman-Jouguet Detonations," NASA SP-273, 1976.
6. Stull, D. R., and Prophet, H., "JANAF Thermochemical Tables," 2nd Ed., NSRDS-NBS 37, National Bureau of Standards, June 1971. (The 3rd Edn. is available from NIST.)
7. Reynolds, W. C., "The Element Potential Method for Chemical Equilibrium Analysis: Implementation in the Interactive Program STANJAN," Department of Mechanical Engineering, Stanford University, January 1986.
8. Olikara, C., and Borman, G. L., "A Computer Program for Calculating Properties of Equilibrium Combustion Products with Some Applications to I. C. Engines," SAE Paper 750468, 1975.
9. Industrial Heating Equipment Association, *Combustion Technology Manual*, 4th Ed., IHEA, Arlington, VA, 1988.

REVIEW QUESTIONS

1. Make a list of all of the bold-faced words in Chapter 2. Make sure you understand the meaning of each.

2. Describe the temperature dependence of the specific heats of monatomic and polyatomic gases. What is the underlying cause of this dependence? What implications does the temperature dependence have for combustion?

3. Why is the equivalence ratio frequently more meaningful than the air–fuel (or fuel–air) ratio when comparing different fuels?

4. What three conditions define the standard reference state?

5. Sketch a graph showing H_{reac} and H_{prod} as functions of temperature, taking into account nonconstant specific heats.

6. Using your sketch from question 5, illustrate the effect of preheating the reactants on the constant-pressure adiabatic flame temperature.

7. Describe the effect of pressure on the equilibrium mole fractions for the following reactions:

$$O_2 \Leftrightarrow 2O$$
$$N_2 + O_2 \Leftrightarrow 2NO$$
$$CO + \tfrac{1}{2}O_2 \Leftrightarrow CO_2.$$

What is the effect of temperature?

8. Make a list of the major and minor species associated with combustion products at high temperature, ranking them from the highest to the lowest concentrations (mole fraction) and giving an approximate numerical value for each at $\Phi = 0.7$. Repeat for $\Phi = 1.3$. Compare your lists.

9. What is the significance of the water-gas shift reaction?

10. Describe the effect of increasing temperature on the equilibrium composition of combustion products.

11. Describe the effect of increasing pressure on the equilibrium composition of combustion products.

12. Why does flue-gas recirculation decrease flame temperatures? What happens if the flue gas recirculated is at the flame temperature?

PROBLEMS

2.1. Determine the mass fraction of O_2 and N_2 in air, assuming the molar composition is 21% O_2 and 79% N_2.

2.2. A mixture is composed of the following number of moles of various species:

Species	No. of moles
CO	0.095
CO_2	6
H_2O	7
N_2	34
NO	0.005

A. Determine the mole fraction of nitric oxide (NO) in the mixture. Also express your result as mole percent, and as parts-per-million.

B. Determine the molecular weight of the mixture.

C. Determine the mass fraction of each constituent.

2.3. Determine the molecular weight of a stoichiometric ($\Phi = 1.0$) methane–air mixture.

2.4. Determine the stoichiometric air–fuel ratio (mass) for propane (C_3H_8).

2.5. Propane burns in a premixed flame at an air–fuel ratio (mass) of 18:1. Determine the equivalence ratio Φ.

2.6. For an equivalence ratio of $\Phi = 0.6$, determine the associated air–fuel ratios (mass) for methane, propane, and decane ($C_{10}H_{22}$).

2.7. In a propane-fueled truck, 3% (by volume) oxygen is measured in the exhaust stream of the running engine. Assuming "complete" combustion without dissociation, determine the air–fuel ratio (mass) supplied to the engine.

2.8. Assuming "complete" combustion, write out a stoichiometric balance equation, like Eqn. 2.30, for 1 mole of an arbitrary alcohol $C_xH_yO_z$. Determine the number of moles of air required to burn 1 mole of fuel.

2.9. Using the results of problem 2.8, determine the stoichiometric air–fuel ratio (mass) for methanol (CH_3OH). Compare your result with the stoichiometric ratio for methane (CH_4). What implications does this comparison have?

2.10. Determine the enthalpy of formation in kJ/kmol for methane, given the lower heating value of 50,016 kJ/kg at 298 K.

2.11. Determine the absolute enthalpy of the mixture given in problem 2.2 for a temperature of 1000 K. Express your result in kJ/kmol of mixture.

2.12. The lower heating value of methane is 50,016 kJ/kg (of methane). Determine the heating value:

A. per mass of mixture.
B. per mole of air–fuel mixture.
C. per cubic meter of air–fuel mixture.

2.13. The higher heating value for liquid octane (C_8H_{18}) at 298 K is 47,893 kJ/kg and the heat of vaporization is 363 kJ/kg. Determine the enthalpy of formation at 298 K for octane vapor.

2.14. Verify the information in Table 2.1 under the headings Δh_R (kJ/kg of fuel), Δh_R (kJ/kg of mix), and $(O/F)_{stoic}$ for the following:

A. CH_4–air.
B. H_2–O_2.
C. $C(s)$–air.

Note that any H_2O in the product is assumed to be in the liquid state.

2.15. Generate the same information requested in problem 2.14 for a stoichiometric mixture of C_3H_8 (propane) and air.

2.16. Consider a liquid fuel. Draw a sketch on h–T coordinates illustrating the following quantities: $h_l(T)$; $h_v(T)$; heat of vaporization, h_{fg}; heat of formation for fuel vapor; enthalpy of formation for fuel liquid; lower heating value; higher heating value.

2.17. Determine the adiabatic flame temperature for constant-pressure combustion of a stoichiometric propane–air mixture assuming reactants at 298 K, no dissociation of the products, and constant specific heats evaluated at 298 K.

2.18. Repeat problem 2.17, but using constant specific heats evaluated at 2000 K. Compare your result with that of problem 2.17 and discuss.

2.19. Repeat problem 2.17, but now use property tables (Appendix A) to evaluate the sensible enthalpies.

2.20. Once more, repeat problem 2.17, but eliminate the unrealistic assumptions, i.e., allow for dissociation of the products and variable specific heats. Use HPFLAME

(Appendix F\,) or other appropriate software. Compare and contrast the results of problems 2.17–2.20. Explain why they differ.

2.21. Verify that the results given in Table 2.2 satisfy Eqns. 2.64 and 2.65 for the following conditions:

    A. $T = 2000$ K, $P = 0.1$ atm.
    B. $T = 2500$ K, $P = 100$ atm.
    C. $T = 3000$ K, $P = 1$ atm.

2.22. Consider the equilibrium reaction $O_2 \Leftrightarrow 2O$ in a closed vessel. Assume the vessel contains 1 mole of O_2 when there is no dissociation. Calculate the mole fractions of O_2 and O for the following conditions:

    A. $T = 2500$ K, $P = 1$ atm.
    B. $T = 2500$ K, $P = 3$ atm.

2.23. Repeat problem 2.22A, but add 1 mole of an inert diluent to the mixture, e.g., argon. What is the influence of the diluent? Discuss.

2.24. Calculate the equilibrium composition for the reaction $H_2 + \frac{1}{2}O_2 \Leftrightarrow H_2O$ when the ratio of the number of moles of elemental hydrogen to elemental oxygen is unity. The temperature is 2000 K, and the pressure is 1 atmosphere.

2.25. Reformulate problem 2.24 to include the species OH, O, and H. Identify the number of equations and the number of unknowns. They should, of course, be equal. Do not solve your system.

2.26. Use STANJAN or other appropriate software to calculate the complete equilibrium for the H–O system using the conditions and atom constraints given in problem 2.24.

2.27. Derive the equivalent system (fixed mass) form of the first law corresponding to Eqn. 2.35, which is used to define the heat of reaction. Treat the system as constant pressure with initial and final temperatures equal.

2.28. For the conditions given below, list from highest to lowest the mole fractions of CO_2, CO, H_2O, H_2, OH, O_2, O, N_2, NO, and N. Also give approximate values.

    A. Propane–air constant-pressure combustion products at their adiabatic flame temperature for $\Phi = 0.8$.
    B. As in part A above, but for $\Phi = 1.2$.
    C. Indicate which species may be considered major and which minor in parts A and B above.

2.29. Consider the combustion products of decane ($C_{10}H_{22}$) with air at an equivalence ratio of 1.25. Estimate the mixture composition assuming no dissociation except for the water-gas shift equilibrium.

2.30. A natural gas-fired industrial boiler operates with excess air such that the O_2 concentration in the flue gases is 2% (vol.), measured after removal of the moisture in the combustion products. The flue gas temperature is 700 K without air preheat.

    A. Determine the equivalence ratio for the system assuming that the properties of natural gas are the same as methane.
    B. Determine the thermal efficiency of the boiler, assuming both the air and fuel enter at 298 K.

C. With air preheat, the flue gases are at 433 K (320°F\,) after passing through the air preheater. Again, determine the thermal efficiency of the boiler for both air and fuel entering at the preheater and burner, respectively, at 298 K.

D. Assuming premixed operation of the burners, estimate the maximum temperature in the combustion space ($P = 1$ atm) with air preheat.

2.31. A furnace uses preheated air to improve its fuel efficiency. Determine the adiabatic flame temperature when the furnace is operating at a mass air–fuel ratio of 16 for air preheated to 600 K. The fuel enters at 300 K. Assume the following simplified thermodynamic properties:

$$T_{\text{ref}} = 300\,\text{K}$$
$$MW_{\text{fuel}} = MW_{\text{air}} = MW_{\text{prod}} = 29\,\text{kg/kmol}$$
$$c_{p,\text{fuel}} = c_{p,\text{air}} = c_{p,\text{prod}} = 1200\,\text{J/kg-K}$$
$$\bar{h}^{o}_{f,\text{air}} = h^{o}_{f,\text{prod}} = 0$$
$$h^{o}_{f,\text{fuel}} = 4 \cdot 10^{7}\,\text{J/kg}$$

CHAPTER
3

INTRODUCTION TO MASS TRANSFER

OVERVIEW

As indicated in Chapter 1, understanding combustion requires a combined knowledge of thermodynamics (Chapter 2), heat and mass transfer, and chemical reaction rate theory, or chemical kinetics (Chapter 4). Since most readers of this book are unlikely to have had much, if any, exposure to the subject of mass transfer, we present in this chapter a brief introduction to this topic. Mass transfer, a fundamental topic in chemical engineering, is quite complex, much more so than is suggested by the following discussion. We provide here only a rudimentary treatment of the fundamental rate laws and conservation principles governing mass transfer, leaving a more comprehensive treatment of mass transfer and its relation to combustion theory to other textbooks [1–4]. To develop some physical insight into mass transfer, we briefly examine the process from a molecular point of view. This has the added advantage of showing the fundamental similarity of mass transfer and heat conduction in gases. Lastly, we illustrate the application of mass transfer concepts to the mathematical descriptions of the evaporation of a liquid layer and a droplet.

RUDIMENTS OF MASS TRANSFER

Imagine opening a bottle of perfume and placing the opened bottle in the center of a room. Using your nose as a sensor, the presence of perfume molecules in the immediate vicinity of the bottle can be detected shortly after the bottle is opened. At a later time, you will find the perfume odor everywhere in the room. The processes whereby the perfume molecules are transported from a region of high concentration, near the bottle, to a region of low concentration, far from the bottle, are the subject of **mass transfer**. Like heat transfer and momentum transfer, mass may be transported by molecular processes (e.g., collisions in an ideal gas) and/or turbulent processes. The molecular processes are relatively slow and operate on small spatial scales, while turbulent transport depends upon the velocity and size of an eddy carrying the transported material. Our focus here is on molecular transport, while Chapters 11, 12, and 13 deal with the turbulent processes.

Mass Transfer Rate Laws

FICK'S LAW OF DIFFUSION. Let us consider a nonreacting gas mixture comprised of just two molecular species, species A and B. **Fick's Law** describes the rate at which one species diffuses through the other. For the case of **one-dimensional binary diffusion**, Fick's Law on a mass basis is

$$\dot{m}_A'' \quad = \quad Y_A\left(\dot{m}_A'' + \dot{m}_B''\right) \quad - \quad \rho \mathcal{D}_{AB}\frac{dY_A}{dx} \tag{3.1}$$

| Mass flow of species A per unit area | Mass flow of species A associated with bulk flow per unit area | Mass flow of species A associated with molecular diffusion per unit area |

where $\dot{m}_A''$ is the mass flux of species A and Y_A is the mass fraction. In this book, the **mass flux** is defined as the mass flowrate of species A per unit area perpendicular to the flow:

$$\dot{m}_A'' = \dot{m}_A/A. \tag{3.2}$$

The units of $\dot{m}_A''$ are kg/s-m^2. The idea of a "flux" should be familiar to you since the "heat flux" is the rate at which energy is transported per unit area, i.e., $\dot{Q}'' = \dot{Q}/A$ with units of J/s-m^2 or W/m^2. The **binary diffusivity**, $\mathcal{D}_{AB}$, is a property of the mixture and has units of m^2/s. Values for some binary diffusion coefficients, i.e., diffusivities, at 1 atmosphere are provided in Appendix D.

Equation 3.1 states that species A is transported by two means: the first term on the right-hand-side representing the transport of A resulting from the bulk motion of the fluid, and the second term representing the diffusion of A superimposed on the bulk flow. In the absence of diffusion, we obtain the obvious result that

$$\dot{m}_A'' = Y_A(\dot{m}_A'' + \dot{m}_B'') = Y_A\dot{m}'' \equiv \text{Bulk flux of species A} \qquad (3.3a)$$

where $\dot{m}''$ is the mixture mass flux. The diffusional flux adds an additional component to the flux of A:

$$-\rho \mathcal{D}_{AB} \frac{dY_A}{dx} \equiv \text{Diffusional flux of species A, } \dot{m}_{A,\text{diff}}'' \qquad (3.3b)$$

This expression says that the **diffusional flux of A**, $\dot{m}_{A,\text{diff}}''$, is proportional to the gradient of the mass fraction, where the constant of proportionality is $-\rho \mathcal{D}_{AB}$. Thus, we see that species A preferentially moves from a region of high concentration to a region of low concentration, analogous to energy traveling in the direction from high temperature to low. Note that the negative sign causes the flux to be positive in the x-direction when the concentration gradient is negative. An analogy between the diffusion of mass and the diffusion of heat (conduction) can be drawn by comparing **Fourier's law of conduction,**

$$\dot{Q}_x'' = -k\frac{dT}{dx}, \qquad (3.4)$$

with Fick's law of diffusion in the absence of bulk flow, Eqn. 3.3b. Both expressions indicate a flux ($\dot{m}_{A,\text{diff}}''$ or $\dot{Q}_x''$) being proportional to the gradient of a scalar quantity ((dY_A/dx) or (dT/dx)). We will explore this analogy further when we discuss the physical significance of the **transport properties**, $\rho \mathcal{D}$ and k, the proportionality constants in Eqns. 3.3b and 3.4, respectively.

Equation 3.1 is the one-dimensional component of the more general expression:

$$\dot{\mathbf{m}}_A'' = Y_A(\dot{\mathbf{m}}_A'' + \dot{\mathbf{m}}_B'') - \rho \mathcal{D}_{AB}\nabla Y_A \qquad (3.5)$$

where the bold symbols represent vector quantities. In many instances, the molar form of Eqn. 3.5 is useful:

$$\dot{\mathbf{N}}_A'' = \chi_A(\dot{\mathbf{N}}_A'' + \dot{\mathbf{N}}_B'') - c\mathcal{D}_{AB}\nabla\chi_A \qquad (3.6)$$

where $\dot{N}_A''$ is the molar flux (kmol/s-m²) of species A, χ_A is the mole fraction, and c is the mixture molar concentration (kmol$_{\text{mix}}$/m³).

The meanings of bulk flow and diffusional flux become clearer if we express the total mass flux for a binary mixture as the sum of the mass flux of species A and the mass flux of species B:

$$\dot{m}'' \quad = \quad \dot{m}_A'' \quad + \quad \dot{m}_B''. \qquad (3.7)$$

Mixture mass flux	Species A mass flux	Species B mass flux

The mixture mass flux on the left-hand-side of Eqn. 3.7 is the total mixture flowrate $\dot{m}$ per unit of area perpendicular to the flow. This is the $\dot{m}$ that you are familiar with from previous studies in thermodynamics, etc. Assuming one-dimensional flow for convenience, we now substitute the appropriate expressions for the individual species mass fluxes (Eqn. 3.1) into Eqn. 3.7 and obtain

$$\dot{m}'' = Y_A \dot{m}'' - \rho \mathcal{D}_{AB} \frac{dY_A}{dx} + Y_B \dot{m}'' - \rho \mathcal{D}_{BA} \frac{dY_B}{dx} \qquad (3.8a)$$

or

$$\dot{m}'' = (Y_A + Y_B)\dot{m}'' - \rho \mathcal{D}_{AB} \frac{dY_A}{dx} - \rho \mathcal{D}_{BA} \frac{dY_B}{dx}. \qquad (3.8b)$$

For a binary mixture, $Y_A + Y_B = 1$ (Eqn. 2.10), thus

$$-\rho \mathcal{D}_{AB} \frac{dY_A}{dx} - \rho \mathcal{D}_{BA} \frac{dY_B}{dx} = 0, \qquad (3.9)$$

$$\underbrace{\qquad\qquad}_{\substack{\text{Diffusional flux} \\ \text{of species A}}} \quad \underbrace{\qquad\qquad}_{\substack{\text{Diffusional flux} \\ \text{of species B}}}$$

i.e., the sum of the diffusional fluxes of the species is zero. In general, overall mass conservation requires that $\sum \dot{m}''_{i,\text{diff}} = 0$.

It is important at this point to emphasize that we are assuming a binary gas and that species diffusion is only a result of concentration gradients, which is termed **ordinary diffusion**. Real mixtures of interest in combustion contain many components, not just two. Our binary gas assumption, however, allows us to understand the essential physics of many situations without the complications inherent in an analysis of multi-component diffusion. Also, gradients of temperature and pressure can produce species diffusion, i.e., the **thermal diffusion (Soret)** and **pressure diffusion** effects, respectively. In many systems of interest, these effects are usually small, and, again, their neglect allows us to understand more clearly the essential physics of a problem.

MOLECULAR BASIS OF DIFFUSION. To obtain insight into the molecular processes that result in the macroscopic laws of mass diffusion (Fick's Law) and heat diffusion or conduction (Fourier's Law), we apply some concepts from the kinetic theory of gases, e.g., Refs. [5,6]. Consider a stationary (no bulk flow) plane layer of a binary gas mixture consisting of rigid, non-attracting molecules in which the molecular mass of each species A and B is essentially equal. A concentration (mass fraction) gradient exists in the gas layer in the x-direction and is sufficiently small that the temperature distribution can be considered linear over a distance of a few molecular mean free paths, λ, as illustrated in Fig. 3.1. With these assumptions, we can define the following average molecular properties derived from kinetic theory [1,5,6]:

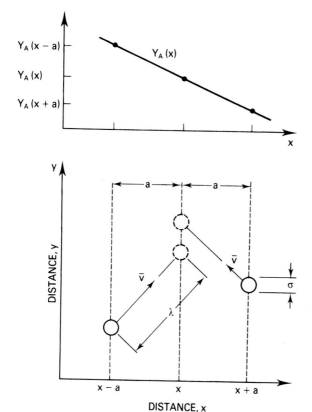

FIGURE 3.1
Schematic diagram illustrating mass diffusion of species A molecules from a region of high concentration to low concentration. Mass fraction distribution is shown at the top.

$$\bar{v} \equiv \begin{array}{c} \text{Mean speed of} \\ \text{species A molecules} \end{array} = \left(\frac{8k_B T}{\pi m_A}\right)^{1/2}, \tag{3.10a}$$

$$Z''_A \equiv \begin{array}{c} \text{Wall collision frequency} \\ \text{of A molecules per unit area} \end{array} = \frac{1}{4}\left(\frac{n_A}{V}\right)\bar{v}, \tag{3.10b}$$

$$\lambda \equiv \text{Mean free path} = \frac{1}{\sqrt{2}\pi\left(\frac{n_{tot}}{V}\right)\sigma^2}, \tag{3.10c}$$

$$a \equiv \begin{array}{c} \text{Average perpendicular distance} \\ \text{from plane of last collision to plane} \\ \text{where next collision occurs} \end{array} = \frac{2}{3}\lambda, \tag{3.10d}$$

where k_B is Boltzmann's constant, m_A the mass of a single A molecule, n_A/V the number of A molecules per unit volume, n_{tot}/V the total number of molecules per unit volume, and σ is the diameter of both A and B molecules.

Assuming no bulk flow for simplicity, the net flux of A molecules at the x-plane is the difference between the flux of A molecules in the positive x-direction and the flux of A molecules in the negative x-direction:

$$\dot{m}_A'' = \dot{m}_{A,(+)x\text{-dir}}'' - \dot{m}_{A,(-)x\text{-dir}}'' \tag{3.11}$$

which, when expressed in terms of the collision frequency, becomes

$$\dot{m}_A'' = (Z_A'')_{x-a} m_A - (Z_A'')_{x+a} m_A. \tag{3.12}$$

$$\begin{pmatrix} \text{Net mass} \\ \text{flux of} \\ \text{species A} \end{pmatrix} \begin{pmatrix} \text{Number of A} \\ \text{molecules crossing} \\ \text{plane at } x \text{ originating} \\ \text{from plane at } x-a \\ \text{per unit time and area} \end{pmatrix} \begin{pmatrix} \text{Mass of} \\ \text{single} \\ \text{molecule} \end{pmatrix} \begin{pmatrix} \text{Number of A} \\ \text{molecules crossing} \\ \text{plane at } x \text{ originating} \\ \text{from plane at } x+a \\ \text{per unit time and area} \end{pmatrix} \begin{pmatrix} \text{Mass of} \\ \text{single} \\ \text{molecule} \end{pmatrix}$$

We can use the definition of density $(\rho \equiv m_{\text{tot}}/V_{\text{tot}})$ to relate Z_A'' (Eqn. 3.10b) to the mass fraction of A molecules:

$$Z_A'' m_A = \frac{1}{4} \frac{n_A m_A}{m_{\text{tot}}} \rho \bar{v} = \frac{1}{4} Y_A \rho \bar{v}. \tag{3.13}$$

Substituting Eqn. 3.13 into Eqn. 3.12 and treating the mixture density and mean molecular speeds as constants yields

$$\dot{m}_A'' = \frac{1}{4} \rho \bar{v} (Y_{A,x-a} - Y_{A,x+a}). \tag{3.14}$$

With our assumption of a linear concentration distribution,

$$\frac{dY_A}{dx} = \frac{Y_{A,x+a} - Y_{A,x-a}}{2a} = \frac{Y_{A,x+a} - Y_{a,x-a}}{4\lambda/3}. \tag{3.15}$$

Solving Eqn. 3.15 for the concentration difference and substituting into Eqn. 3.14, we obtain our final result:

$$\dot{m}_A'' = -\rho \frac{\bar{v}\lambda}{3} \frac{dY_A}{dx}. \tag{3.16}$$

Comparing Eqn. 3.16 with Eqn. 3.3b, we identify the binary diffusivity $\mathcal{D}_{AB}$ as

$$\mathcal{D}_{AB} = \frac{\bar{v}\lambda}{3}. \tag{3.17}$$

Using the definitions of the mean molecular speed (Eqn. 3.10a) and mean free path (Eqn. 3.10c), together with the ideal-gas equation of state $PV = nk_BT$, the temperature and pressure dependence of $\mathcal{D}_{AB}$ can easily be determined, i.e.,

$$\mathcal{D}_{AB} = \frac{2}{3} \left(\frac{k_B^3 T}{\pi^3 m_A} \right)^{1/2} \frac{T}{\sigma^2 P} \tag{3.18a}$$

or

$$\mathcal{D}_{AB} \propto T^{3/2} P^{-1}. \tag{3.18b}$$

Thus, we see that the diffusivity depends strongly on temperature (to the $\frac{3}{2}$ power) and inversely with pressure. The mass flux of species A, however, depends on the product $\rho \mathcal{D}_{AB}$, which has a square-root temperature dependence and is independent of pressure:

$$\rho \mathcal{D}_{AB} \propto T^{1/2} P^0 = T^{1/2}. \tag{3.18c}$$

In many simplified analyses of combustion processes, the weak temperature dependence is neglected and $\rho \mathcal{D}$ is treated as a constant.

COMPARISON WITH HEAT CONDUCTION. To clearly see the relationship between mass and heat transfer, we now apply kinetic theory to the transport of energy. We assume a homogeneous gas consisting of rigid non-attracting molecules in which a temperature gradient exists. Again, the gradient is sufficiently small that the temperature distribution is essentially linear over several mean free paths, as illustrated in Fig. 3.2. The mean molecular speed and mean free path have the same definitions as given in Eqns. 3.10a and 3.10c, respectively; however, the molecular collision frequency of interest is now based on the total number density of molecules, n_{tot}/V, i.e.

$$Z'' \equiv \frac{\text{Average wall collision}}{\text{frequency per unit area}} = \frac{1}{4}\left(\frac{n_{tot}}{V}\right)\bar{v}. \tag{3.19}$$

In our no-interaction-at-a-distance hard-sphere model of the gas, the only energy storage mode is molecular translational, i.e., kinetic, energy. We write an energy balance at the x-plane (see Fig. 3.2) where the net energy flow (per unit area) in the x-direction is the difference between the kinetic energy flux associated with molecules traveling from $x - a$ to x and those traveling from $x + a$ to x:

$$\dot{Q}_x'' = Z''(ke)_{x-a} - Z''(ke)_{x+a}. \tag{3.20}$$

Since the mean kinetic energy of a molecule is given by [5]

$$ke = \frac{1}{2}m\bar{v}^2 = \frac{3}{2}k_B T, \tag{3.21}$$

the heat flux can be related to the temperature as

$$\dot{Q}_x'' = \frac{3}{2}k_B Z''(T_{x-a} - T_{x+a}). \tag{3.22}$$

The temperature difference in Eqn. 3.22 relates to the temperature gradient following the same form as Eqn. 3.15, i.e.,

$$\frac{dT}{dx} = \frac{T_{x+a} - T_{x-a}}{2a}. \tag{3.23}$$

Substituting Eqn. 3.23 into Eqn. 3.22, employing the definitions of Z'' and a, we obtain our final result for the heat flux:

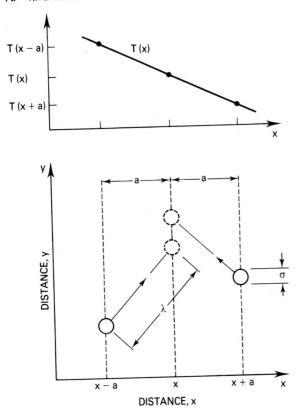

FIGURE 3.2
Schematic diagram illustrating energy transfer (heat conduction) associated with molecular motion in a gas. The temperature distribution is shown at the top.

$$\dot{Q}_x'' = -\frac{1}{2} k_B \left(\frac{n}{V}\right) \bar{v} \lambda \frac{dT}{dx}. \tag{3.24}$$

Comparing the above with Fourier's law of heat conduction (Eqn. 3.4), we can identify the thermal conductivity k as

$$k = \frac{1}{2} k_B \left(\frac{n}{V}\right) \bar{v} \lambda. \tag{3.25}$$

Expressed in terms of T and molecular mass and size, the thermal conductivity is

$$k = \left(\frac{k_B^3}{\pi^3 m \sigma^4}\right)^{1/2} T^{1/2}. \tag{3.26}$$

The thermal conductivity is thus proportional to the square-root of temperature

$$k \propto T^{1/2}, \tag{3.27}$$

as is the ρD_{AB} product. For real gases, the true temperature dependence is greater.

Species Conservation

In this section, we employ the rate law of species transport (Fick's Law) to develop a basic species mass conservation expression. Consider the one-dimensional control volume of Fig. 3.3, a plane layer Δx thick. Species A flows into and out of the control volume as a result of the combined action of bulk flow and diffusion. Within the control volume, species A may be created or destroyed as a result of chemical reaction.

The net rate of increase in the mass of A within the control volume relates to the mass fluxes and reaction rate as follows:

$$\underset{\substack{\text{Rate of increase} \\ \text{of mass of A} \\ \text{within control volume}}}{\frac{dm_{A,cv}}{dt}} = \underset{\substack{\text{Mass flow of A} \\ \text{into the} \\ \text{control volume}}}{[\dot{m}_A'' A]_x} - \underset{\substack{\text{Mass flow of A} \\ \text{out of the} \\ \text{control volume}}}{[\dot{m}_A'' A]_{x+\Delta x}} + \underset{\substack{\text{Mass production} \\ \text{rate of species A} \\ \text{by chemical reaction}}}{\dot{m}_A''' V}, \qquad (3.28)$$

where the species mass flux $\dot{m}_A''$ is given by Eqn. 3.1, and $\dot{m}_A'''$ is the mass production rate of species A per unit volume (kg_A/m^3-s). In Chapter 5, we specifically deal with how to determine $\dot{m}_A'''$. Recognizing that the mass of A within the control volume is $m_{A,cv} = Y_A m_{cv} = Y_A \rho V_{cv}$ and that the volume $V_{cv} = A\Delta x$, Eqn. 3.28 can be rewritten:

$$A\Delta x \frac{\partial(\rho Y_A)}{\partial t} = A\left[Y_A \dot{m}'' - \rho D_{AB} \frac{\partial Y_A}{\partial x} \right]_x - A\left[Y_A \dot{m}'' - \rho D_{AB} \frac{\partial Y_A}{\partial x} \right]_{x+\Delta x} + \dot{m}_A'' A\Delta x.$$
$$(3.29)$$

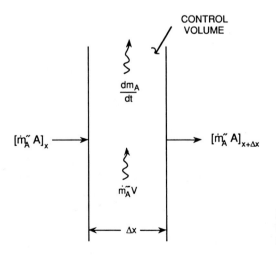

CONTROL
VOLUME

$\dfrac{dm_A}{dt}$

$[\dot{m}_A'' A]_x$ → → $[\dot{m}_A'' A]_{x+\Delta x}$

$\dot{m}_A'' V$

Δx

FIGURE 3.3
Control volume for one-dimensional analysis of conservation of species A.

Dividing through by $A\Delta x$ and taking the limit as $\Delta x \to 0$, Eqn. 3.29 becomes

$$\frac{\partial(\rho Y_A)}{\partial t} = -\frac{\partial}{\partial x}\left[Y_A \dot{m}'' - \rho D_{AB}\frac{\partial Y_A}{\partial x}\right] + \dot{m}_A''' \tag{3.30}$$

or, for the case of steady flow where $\partial(\rho Y_A)/\partial t = 0$,

$$\dot{m}_A''' - \frac{d}{dx}\left[Y_A \dot{m}'' - \rho D_{AB}\frac{d Y_A}{dx}\right] = 0. \tag{3.31}$$

Equation 3.31 is the steady-flow, one-dimensional form of species conservation for a binary gas mixture, assuming species diffusion occurs only as a result of concentration gradients, i.e., only ordinary diffusion is considered. For the multi-dimensional case, Eqn. 3.31 can be generalized as

$$\underset{\substack{\text{Net rate of production} \\ \text{of species A by} \\ \text{chemical reaction,} \\ \text{per unit volume}}}{\dot{m}_A'''} \quad - \quad \underset{\substack{\text{Net flow of species A} \\ \text{out of control volume,} \\ \text{per unit volume}}}{\nabla \cdot \dot{m}_A''} \quad = \quad 0. \tag{3.32}$$

In Chapter 7, we will employ Eqns. 3.31 and 3.32 to develop the conservation of energy principle for a reacting system.

SOME APPLICATIONS OF MASS TRANSFER

The Stefan Problem

Consider liquid A, maintained at a fixed height in a glass cylinder as illustrated in Fig. 3.4. A mixture of gas A and gas B flow across the top of the cylinder. If the concentration of A in the flowing gas is less than the concentration of A at the liquid–vapor interface, a driving force for mass transfer exists and species A will diffuse from the liquid–gas interface to the open end of the cylinder. If we assume a steady state exists (i.e., the liquid is replenished at a rate to keep the liquid level constant, or the interface regresses so slowly that its movement can be neglected) and, furthermore, assume that B is insoluble in liquid A, then there will be no net transport of B in the tube, producing a stagnant layer of B in the column.

Mathematically, the overall conservation of mass for this system can be expressed as

$$\dot{m}''(x) = \text{constant} = \dot{m}_A'' + \dot{m}_B''. \tag{3.33}$$

Since $\dot{m}_B'' = 0$, then

$$\dot{m}_A'' = \dot{m}(x) = \text{constant}. \tag{3.34}$$

Equation 3.1 now becomes

$$\dot{m}_A'' = Y_A \dot{m}_A'' - \rho D_{AB}\frac{d Y_A}{dx}. \tag{3.35}$$

Gas flow of A and B

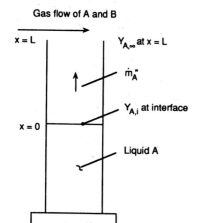

x = L

$Y_{A,\infty}$ at x = L

$\dot{m}_A''$

$Y_{A,i}$ at interface

x = 0

Liquid A

FIGURE 3.4
Diffusion of vapor A through a stagnant column of gas B, i.e., the Stefan problem.

Rearranging and separating variables, we obtain

$$-\frac{\dot{m}_A''}{\rho \mathcal{D}_{AB}} dx = \frac{dY_A}{1 - Y_A}. \tag{3.36}$$

Assuming the product $\rho \mathcal{D}_{AB}$ to be constant, Eqn. 3.36 can be integrated to yield

$$-\frac{\dot{m}_A''}{\rho \mathcal{D}_{AB}} x = -\ln[1 - Y_A] + C \tag{3.37}$$

where C is the constant of integration. With the boundary condition,

$$Y_A(x = 0) = Y_{A,i}, \tag{3.38}$$

we eliminate C and obtain the following mass fraction distribution after removing the logarithm by exponentiation:

$$Y_A(x) = 1 - (1 - Y_{A,i}) \exp\left[\frac{\dot{m}_A'' x}{\rho \mathcal{D}_{AB}}\right]. \tag{3.39}$$

The mass flux of A, $\dot{m}_A''$, can be found by letting $Y_A(x = L) = Y_{A,\infty}$ in Eqn. 3.39. Thus,

$$\dot{m}_A'' = \frac{\rho \mathcal{D}_{AB}}{L} \ln\left[\frac{1 - Y_{A,\infty}}{1 - Y_{A,i}}\right]. \tag{3.40}$$

From Eqn. 3.40, we see that the mass flux is directly proportional to the product of the density, ρ, and the mass diffusivity, $\mathcal{D}_{AB}$; and inversely proportional to the length, L. Larger diffusivities thus produce larger mass fluxes.

To see the effects of the concentrations at the interface and at the top of the tube, let the mass fraction of A in the freestream flow be zero, while arbitrarily varying $Y_{A,i}$ the interface mass fraction, from zero to unity. Physically, this could correspond to an experiment in which dry nitrogen is blown across the tube outlet and the interface mass fraction is controlled by the partial pressure of the liquid,

TABLE 3.1
Effect of interface mass fraction on mass flux

$Y_{A,i}$	$\dot{m}_A''/(\rho D_{AB}/L)$
0	0
0.05	0.0513
0.10	0.1054
0.20	0.2231
0.50	0.6931
0.90	2.303
0.999	6.908

which in turn is varied by changing the temperature. Table 3.1 shows that at small values of $Y_{A,i}$, the dimensionless mass flux is essentially proportional to $Y_{A,i}$. For $Y_{A,i}$ greater than about 0.5, the mass flux increases very rapidly.

Liquid–Vapor Interface Boundary Conditions

In the example above, we treated the gas-phase mass fraction of the diffusing species at the liquid–vapor interface, $Y_{A,i}$, as a known quantity. Unless this mass fraction is measured, which is unlikely, some means must be found to calculate or estimate its value. This can be done by assuming equilibrium exists between the liquid and vapor phases of species A. With this equilibrium assumption, and the assumption of ideal gases, the partial pressure of species A on the gas side of the interface must equal the saturation pressure associated with the temperature of the liquid, i.e.,

$$P_{A,i} = P_{\text{sat}}(T_{\text{liq},i}) \tag{3.41}$$

The partial pressure, $P_{A,i}$, can be related to the mole fraction of species A, $\chi_{A,i} = P_{\text{sat}}/P$, and to the mass fraction:

$$Y_{A,i} = \frac{P_{\text{sat}}(T_{\text{liq},i})}{P} \frac{MW_A}{MW_{\text{mix},i}} \tag{3.42}$$

where the molecular weight of the mixture also depends on $\chi_{A,i}$, and hence, P_{sat}.

The above analysis has transformed the problem of finding the vapor mass fraction at the interface to the problem of finding the temperature at the interface. In some cases, the interface temperature may be given or known, but, in general, the interface temperature must be found by writing energy balances for the liquid and gas phases and solving them with appropriate boundary conditions, including that at the interface. In the following, we will establish this interface boundary condition, but leave the gas-phase and liquid-phase energy balances for later.

Gas Phase

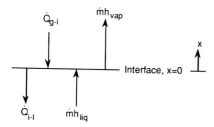

Interface, x=0

FIGURE 3.5
Energy balance at the surface of evaporating fluid.

In crossing the liquid–vapor boundary, we maintain continuity of temperature, i.e.,

$$T_{\text{liq},i}(x = 0^-) = T_{\text{vap},i}(x = 0^+) = T(0), \tag{3.43}$$

and energy is conserved at the interface as illustrated in Fig. 3.5. Heat is transferred from the gas to the liquid surface, $\dot{Q}_{g-i}$. Some of this energy goes into heating the liquid, $\dot{Q}_{i-l}$, while the remainder causes the phase change. This energy balance is expressed as

$$\dot{Q}_{g-i} - \dot{Q}_{g-l} = \dot{m}(h_{\text{vap}} - h_{\text{liq}}) = \dot{m}h_{fg} \tag{3.44}$$

or

$$\dot{Q}_{\text{net}} = \dot{m}h_{fg}. \tag{3.45}$$

Equation 3.45 can be used to calculate the net heat transferred to the interface if the evaporation rate, $\dot{m}$, is known. Conversely, if $\dot{Q}_{\text{net}}$ is known, the evaporation rate can be determined.

Example 3.1. Liquid benzene (C_6H_6) at 298 K, is contained in a 1-cm-diameter glass tube and maintained at a level 10 cm below the top of the tube, which is open to the atmosphere. The following properties of benzene are given:

$$T_{\text{boil}} = 353\,\text{K} @ 1\,\text{atm}$$
$$h_{fg} = 393\,\text{kJ/kg} @ T_{\text{boil}}$$
$$MW = 78.108\,\text{kg/kmol}$$
$$\rho_l = 879\,\text{kg/m}^3$$
$$\mathcal{D}_{C_6H_6-\text{air}} = 0.88 \cdot 10^{-5}\,\text{m}^2/\text{s} @ 298\,\text{K}$$

A. Determine the mass evaporation rate (kg/s) of the benzene.
B. How long does it take to evaporate 1 cm³ of benzene?
C. Compare the evaporation rate of benzene to that of water. Assume $\mathcal{D}_{H_2O-\text{air}} = 2.6 \cdot 10^{-5}\,\text{m}^2/\text{s}$.

Solution

A. Find $\dot{m}_{C_6H_6}$.

Since the configuration given represents the Stefan problem, we can apply Eqn. 3.40,

$$\dot{m}''_{C_6H_6} = \frac{\bar{\rho}D_{C_6H_6-\text{air}}}{L} \ln\left[\frac{1 - Y_{C_6H_6,\infty}}{1 - Y_{C_6H_6,i}}\right].$$

In the above, D, L, and $Y_{C_6H_6,\infty}(= 0)$ are all known; however, we need to evaluate the benzene mass fraction at the interface, $Y_{C_6H_6,i}$, and an appropriate mean density, $\bar{\rho}$, before proceeding.

From Eqn. 3.42, we know that

$$Y_{C_6H_6,i} = \chi_{C_6H_6,i}\frac{MW_{C_6H_6}}{MW_{\text{mix},i}},$$

where

$$\chi_{C_6H_6,i} = \frac{P_{\text{sat}}(T_{\text{liq},i})}{P}.$$

To evaluate P_{sat}/P, we integrate the Clausius–Clapeyron equation, Eqn. 2.19,

$$\frac{dP}{P} = \frac{h_{fg}}{R_u/MW_{C_6H_6}}\frac{dT}{T^2},$$

from the reference state ($P = 1$ atm, $T = T_{\text{boil}} = 353$ K) to the state at 298 K, i.e.,

$$\frac{P_{\text{sat}}}{P(= 1\,\text{atm})} = \exp\left[-\frac{h_{fg}}{(R_u/MW_{C_6H_6})}\left(\frac{1}{T} - \frac{1}{T_{\text{boil}}}\right)\right].$$

Evaluating the above,

$$\frac{P_{\text{sat}}}{P(= 1\,\text{atm})} = \exp\left[\frac{-393,000}{(8315/78.108)}\left(\frac{1}{298} - \frac{1}{353}\right)\right]$$
$$= \exp(-1.93) = 0.145.$$

So, $P_{\text{sat}} = 0.145$ atm and $\chi_{C_6H_6} = 0.145$. The interface mixture molecular weight is then

$$MW_{\text{mix},i} = 0.145(78.108) + (1 - 0.145)28.85$$
$$= 35.99\,\text{kg/kmol}$$

where the simplified composition of air is assumed. The interface benzene mass fraction is then

$$Y_{C_6H_6,i} = 0.145\frac{78.108}{35.99} = 0.3147.$$

For isothermal, isobaric conditions, we can estimate the mean gas density in the tube by using the ideal-gas law and the mean mixture molecular weight as follows:

$$\bar{\rho} = \frac{P}{(R_u/\overline{MW})T}$$

where

$$\overline{MW} = \frac{1}{2}(MW_{\text{mix},i} + MW_{\text{mix},\infty})$$

$$= \frac{1}{2}(35.99 + 28.85) = 32.42.$$

Thus,

$$\bar{\rho} = \frac{101,325}{\left(\dfrac{8315}{32.42}\right)298} = 1.326\,\text{kg/m}^3.$$

We can now evaluate the benzene mass flux (Eqn. 3.40):

$$\dot{m}''_{C_6H_6} = \frac{1.326(0.88 \cdot 10^{-5})}{0.1}\ln\left[\frac{1-0}{1-0.3147}\right]$$

$$= 1.167 \cdot 10^{-4}\ln(1.459)$$

$$= 1.167 \cdot 10^{-4}(0.378) = 4.409 \cdot 10^{-5}\ \text{kg/s-m}^2$$

and

$$\boxed{\dot{m}_{C_6H_6}} = \dot{m}''_{C_6H_6}\frac{\pi D^2}{4} = 4.409 \cdot 10^{-5}\frac{\pi(0.01)^2}{4} = \boxed{3.46 \cdot 10^{-9}\,\text{kg/s}}.$$

B. Find the time needed to evaporate 1 cm^3.
   Since the liquid level is maintained, the mass flux is constant during the time to evaporate the 1 cm^3, thus,

$$t = \frac{M_{\text{evap}}}{\dot{m}_{C_6H_6}} = \frac{\rho_{\text{liq}}V}{\dot{m}_{C_6H_6}},$$

$$\boxed{t} = \frac{879(\text{kg/m}^3)1 \cdot 10^{-6}(\text{m}^3)}{3.46 \cdot 10^{-9}\,(\text{kg/s})} = \boxed{2.54 \cdot 10^5 \text{ s or } 70.6 \text{ hr}}.$$

C. Find $\dot{m}_{C_6H_6}/\dot{m}_{H_2O}$.
   Finding $\dot{m}_{H_2O}$ follows the above; however, the problem is simplified since we can use the steam tables, e.g., Ref. [7], to find P_{sat} at 298 K rather than invoking the Clausius–Clapeyron approximation.
   From the steam tables

$$P_{\text{sat}}\,(298\ \text{K}) = 3.169\,\text{kPa}$$

so

$$\chi_{H_2O,i} = \frac{3169}{101,325} = 0.03128$$

and

$$MW_{\text{mix},i} = 0.03128(18.016) + (1 - 0.03128)28.85 = 28.51.$$

Thus,

$$Y_{H_2O,i} = \chi_{H_2O,i} \frac{MW_{H_2O}}{MW_{mix,i}} = 0.03128 = \frac{18.016}{28.51} = 0.01977.$$

The mean molecular weight and mean density in the tube are

$$\overline{MW} = \frac{1}{2}(28.51 + 28.85) = 28.68,$$

$$\bar{\rho} = \frac{101,325}{\left(\frac{8315}{28.68}\right)298} = 1.173\,\text{kg/m}^3,$$

where we assume the air outside of the tube is dry.
The evaporation flux is then

$$\dot{m}''_{H_2O} = \frac{1.173(2.6 \cdot 10^{-5})}{0.1} \ln\left[\frac{1-0}{1-0.01977}\right]$$

$$= 3.050 \cdot 10^{-4} \ln(1.020)$$

$$= 3.050 \cdot 10^{-4}(0.01997) = 6.09 \cdot 10^{-6}\,\text{kg/s-m}^2$$

so,

$$\boxed{\frac{\dot{m}_{C_6H_6}}{\dot{m}_{H_2O}}} = \frac{4.409 \cdot 10^{-5}}{6.09 \cdot 10^{-6}} = \boxed{7.2}.$$

Comment. Comparing the details of the calculations in parts A and C, we see that the higher vapor pressure of the benzene dominates over the higher diffusivity of the water, thus causing the benzene to evaporate more than seven times faster than the water.

Droplet Evaporation

The problem of the evaporation of a single liquid droplet in a quiescent environment is just the Stefan problem for a spherically symmetric coordinate system. Our treatment of droplet evaporation illustrates the application of mass transfer concepts to a problem of practical interest. In Chapter 10, we will deal with the droplet evaporation/combustion problem in greater detail; however, we fore-shadow the Chapter 10 development by introducing the concept of an evaporation constant and droplet lifetimes.

Figure 3.6 defines the spherically symmetric coordinate system. The radius r is the only coordinate variable. It has its origin at the center of the droplet, and the droplet radius at the liquid–vapor interface is denoted r_s. Very far from the droplet surface $(r \to \infty)$, the mass fraction of droplet vapor is $Y_{F,\infty}$.

Physically, heat from the ambient environment supplies the energy necessary to vaporize the liquid, and the vapor then diffuses from the droplet surface into the ambient gas. The mass loss causes the droplet radius to shrink with time until the droplet is completely evaporated $(r_s = 0)$. The problem that we wish to solve is the determination of the mass flowrate of the vapor from the surface at any

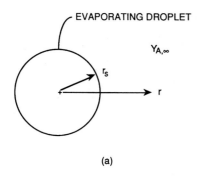

(a)

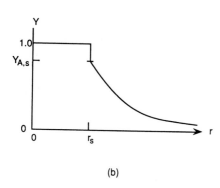

(b)

FIGURE 3.6
Evaporation of a liquid droplet in a quiescent environment.

instant in time. Knowledge of this will then enable us to calculate the droplet radius as a function of time and the droplet lifetime.

To mathematically describe this process completely, the following conservation laws are required:

Droplet: mass conservation, energy conservation.
Droplet vapor-ambient gas mixture $(r_s < r < \infty)$: overall mass conservation, droplet vapor (species) conservation, and energy conservation.

Thus, we see that for this complete description we need at least five equations. These equations, in general, take the form of either ordinary or partial differential equations, depending on the simplifying assumptions applied.

ASSUMPTIONS. For our brief treatment here, we can greatly reduce the number of unknowns and, hence, equations, by invoking the same assumptions that we employed in the one-dimensional cartesian problem.

1. The evaporation process is quasi-steady. This means that at any instant in time the process can be described as if it were in steady state. This assumption eliminates the need to deal with partial differential equations.

2. The droplet temperature is uniform and, furthermore, the temperature is assumed to be some fixed value below the boiling point of the liquid. In many problems, the transient heating of the liquid does not greatly affect the droplet lifetime. Determination of the temperature at the droplet surface depends on the heat transfer rate to the droplet. Thus, our assumption of a specified temperature eliminates the need to apply conservation of energy to the gas phase surrounding the liquid droplet and to the droplet itself. As will be shown in Chapter 10, heat-transfer considerations frequently dominate the droplet evaporation problem.

3. The mass fraction of vapor at the droplet surface is determined by liquid–vapor equilibrium at the droplet temperature.

4. We also assume that all thermophysical properties, specifically, the ρD product, are constant. Although properties may vary greatly as we move through the gas phase from the droplet surface to the faraway surroundings, constant properties allow a simple closed-form solution.

EVAPORATION RATE. With the above assumptions, we can find the mass evaporation rate, $\dot{m}$, and the droplet radius history, $r_s(t)$, by writing a droplet vapor species conservation equation, and a droplet liquid mass conservation equation. From species conservation, we determine the evaporation rate $\dot{m}$, and thus, knowing $\dot{m}(t)$, we can easily find the drop size as a function of time.

As in the cartesian-coordinate Stefan problem, the species originally in the liquid phase is the species transported, while the ambient fluid is stagnant. Thus, our previous analysis (Eqns. 3.33–3.35) only needs to be modified to take into account the change in coordinate system. Overall mass conservation is expressed

$$\dot{m}(r) = \text{constant} = 4\pi r^2 \dot{m}'', \tag{3.46}$$

where $\dot{m}'' = \dot{m}''_A + \dot{m}''_B = \dot{m}''_A$, since $\dot{m}''_B = 0$. Note that it is the mass flowrate, not the mass flux, that is constant. Species conservation for the droplet vapor (Eqn. 3.5) becomes

$$\dot{m}''_A = Y_A \dot{m}''_A - \rho D_{AB} \frac{dY_A}{dr}. \tag{3.47}$$

Substituting Eqn. 3.46 into Eqn. 3.47 and rearranging to solve for the evaporation rate $\dot{m}(= \dot{m}_A)$, yields

$$\dot{m} = -4\pi r^2 \frac{\rho D_{AB}}{1 - Y_A} \frac{dY_A}{dr}. \tag{3.48}$$

Integrating Eqn. 3.48 and applying the boundary condition that at the droplet surface the vapor mass fraction is $Y_{A,s}$, i.e.,

$$Y_A(r = r_s) = Y_{A,s}, \tag{3.49}$$

yields

$$Y_A(r) = 1 - \frac{(1 - Y_{A,s})\exp\left(\dfrac{-\dot{m}}{4\pi\rho D_{AB}r}\right)}{\exp\left(\dfrac{-\dot{m}}{4\pi\rho D_{AB}r_s}\right)} \tag{3.50}$$

The evaporation rate can be determined from Eqn. 3.50 by letting $Y_A = Y_{A,\infty}$ for $r \to \infty$ and solving for $\dot{m}$:

$$\dot{m} = 4\pi r_s \rho D_{AB} \ln\left[\frac{(1 - Y_{A,\infty})}{(1 - Y_{A,s})}\right]. \tag{3.51}$$

This result (Eqn. 3.51) is analogous to Eqn. 3.40 for the cartesian problem.

To more conveniently see how the vapor mass fractions at the droplet surface, $Y_{A,s}$, and far from the surface, $Y_{A,\infty}$, affect the evaporation rate, the argument of the logarithm in Eqn. 3.51 is used to define the dimensionless **transfer number, B_Y**:

$$1 + B_Y \equiv \frac{1 - Y_{A,\infty}}{1 - Y_{A,s}} \tag{3.52a}$$

or

$$B_Y = \frac{Y_{A,s} - Y_{A,\infty}}{1 - Y_{A,s}}. \tag{3.52b}$$

Using the transfer number, B_Y, the evaporation rate is expressed as

$$\dot{m} = 4\pi r_s \rho D_{AB} \ln(1 + B_Y). \tag{3.53}$$

From this result, we see that when the transfer number is zero, the evaporation rate is zero; and, correspondingly, as the transfer number increases, so does the evaporation rate. This makes physical sense in that, from the appearance of the mass fraction difference $Y_{A,s} - Y_{A,\infty}$ in its definition, B_Y can be interpreted as a "driving potential" for mass transfer.

DROPLET MASS CONSERVATION. We obtain the droplet radius (or diameter) history by writing a mass balance that states that the rate at which the mass of the droplet decreases is equal to the rate at which the liquid is vaporized, i.e.,

$$\frac{dm_d}{dt} = -\dot{m}, \tag{3.54}$$

where the droplet mass, m_d, is given by

$$m_d = \rho_l V = \rho_l \pi D^3/6, \tag{3.55}$$

and V and $D(= 2r_s)$ are the droplet volume and diameter, respectively.

Substituting Eqns. 3.55 and 3.53 into Eqn. 3.54 and performing the differentiation yields:

$$\frac{dD}{dt} = -\frac{4D_{AB}}{\rho_l D}\ln(1 + B_Y). \tag{3.56}$$

In the combustion literature, however, Eqn. 3.56 is more commonly expressed in terms of D^2 rather than D. This form is

$$\frac{dD^2}{dt} = -\frac{8\rho D_{AB}}{\rho_l}\ln(1 + B_Y). \tag{3.57}$$

Equation 3.57 tells us that the time derivative of the square of the droplet diameter is constant; hence, D^2 varies linearly with t with the slope $-(8\rho D_{AB}/\rho_l)\ln(1 + B_Y)$, as illustrated in Fig. 3.7a. This slope is defined to be the **evaporation constant** K,

$$K = \frac{8\rho D_{AB}}{\rho_l}\ln(1 + B_Y). \tag{3.58}$$

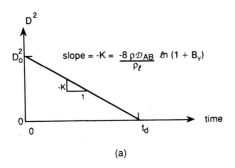

(a)

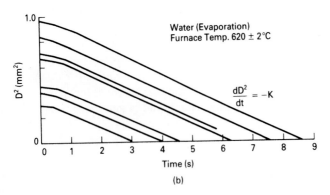

(b)

FIGURE 3.7
D^2 law for droplet evaporation. (a) Simplified analysis. (b) Experimental data from Ref. [8] for water droplets with $T_\infty = 620°C$. (Reprinted by permission of The Combustion Institute.)

We can use Eqn. 3.57 (or 3.56) to find the time it takes a droplet of given initial size to completely evaporate, i.e., the droplet lifetime, t_d. Thus,

$$\int_{D_0^2}^{0} dD^2 = -\int_{0}^{t_d} K dt, \qquad (3.59)$$

which yields

$$t_d = D_0^2/K. \qquad (3.60)$$

We can change the upper limits in Eqn. 3.59 to provide a general relationship expressing the variation of D with time (t):

$$D^2(t) = D_0^2 - Kt. \qquad (3.61)$$

Equation 3.61 is referred to as the **D^2 law** for droplet evaporation. Experimental data show that the D^2 law holds after an initial transient period as shown in Fig. 3.7b. The D^2 law is also used to describe burning of fuel droplets, which is discussed in Chapter 10.

Example 3.2. In mass-diffusion-controlled evaporation of a fuel droplet, the droplet surface temperature is an important parameter. Estimate the droplet lifetime of a 100-μm-diameter n-dodecane droplet evaporating in dry nitrogen at 1 atm if the droplet temperature is 10 K below the dodecane boiling point. Repeat the calculation for a temperature 20 K below the boiling point, and compare the results. For simplicity, assume that, in both cases, the mean gas density is that of nitrogen at a mean temperature of 800 K. Use this same temperature to estimate the fuel vapor diffusivity. The density of liquid dodecane is 749 kg/m^3.

Given: n-dodecane droplet

$$D = 100\ \mu m$$
$$P = 1\ atm$$
$$\rho_l = 749\ kg/m^3$$
$$T_s = T_{boil} - 10\ (or\ 20)$$
$$\rho = \rho_{N_2}\ @\ \bar{T} = 800\ K$$

Find: droplet lifetime, t_d.

Solution. We can estimate the droplet lifetimes by employing Eqn. 3.60, after calculating the evaporation rate constants, K, from Eqn. 3.58. Evaluation of properties will be important in our solution.

Properties required:

$$T_{boil} = 216.3°C + 273.15 = 489.5\ K\ (Table\ B.1)$$
$$h_{fg} = 256\ kJ/kg\ (Table\ B.1)$$
$$MW_A = 170.337$$
$$\mathcal{D}_{AB} = 8.1 \cdot 10^{-6}\ m^2/s\ @\ 399\ K\ (Table\ D.1).$$

We start by calculating B_Y which requires knowledge of the fuel mass fraction at the surface. As in Example 3.1, we integrate the Clausius–Clapeyron equation to find the saturation pressure at the given droplet surface temperature. For $T = T_{boil} - 10 \, (= 479.5 \, K)$,

$$\frac{P_{sat}}{P(= 1 \, atm)} = \exp\left[\frac{-256,000}{(8315/170.337)}\left(\frac{1}{479.5} - \frac{1}{489.5}\right)\right] = 0.7998$$

so $P_{sat} = 0.7998$ and $\chi_A \, (= \chi_{dodecane}) = 0.7998$. We employ Eqn. 2.11 to calculate the fuel mass fraction at the surface:

$$Y_{A,s} = 0.7998 \frac{170.337}{0.7998(170.337) + (1 - 0.7998)28.014} = 0.9605.$$

We now evaluate the transfer number B_Y (Eqn. 3.52b):

$$B_Y = \frac{Y_{A,s} - Y_{A,\infty}}{1 - Y_{A,s}} = \frac{0.9605 - 0}{1 - 0.9605} = 24.32.$$

To evaluate the evaporation constant, we need to estimate ρD_{AB}, which we treat as $\bar{\rho}_{N_2} D_{AB}(\bar{T} = 800 \, K)$. Extrapolating the tabulated value to 800 K using Eqn. 3.18b,

$$D_{AB}(\bar{T}) = 8.1 \cdot 10^{-6}\left(\frac{800}{399}\right)^{3/2} = 23.0 \cdot 10^{-6} \, m^2/s,$$

and using the ideal-gas law to evaluate $\bar{\rho}_{N_2}$,

$$\bar{\rho}_{N_2} = \frac{101,325}{(8315/28.014)800} = 0.4267 \, kg/m^3.$$

Thus,

$$K = \frac{8\bar{\rho}D_{AB}}{\rho_\ell} \ln(1 + B_Y)$$

$$= \frac{8(0.4267)23.0 \cdot 10^{-6}}{749} \ln(1 + 24.32),$$

$$= 3.39 \cdot 10^{-7} \, m^2/s$$

and the droplet lifetime is

$$t_d = D^2/K = \frac{(100 \cdot 10^{-6})^2}{3.39 \cdot 10^{-7}}$$

$$\boxed{t_d = 0.030 \, s}.$$

Repeating the calculations for $T = T_{boil} - 20 = 469.5 \, K$, we can compare the various parameters:

ΔT (K)	T (K)	P_{sat} (atm)	Y_s	B_Y	K (m²/s)	t_d (s)
10	479.5	0.7998	0.9605	24.32	$3.39 \cdot 10^{-7}$	0.030
20	469.5	0.6336	0.9132	10.52	$2.56 \cdot 10^{-7}$	0.039

From the above table, we see that about a 2% change in the droplet surface temperature results in a 34.3% increase in the droplet lifetime. This large effect of temperature manifests itself in the B_Y term, where the denominator, $1 - Y_{A,s}$, is clearly sensitive to temperature when $Y_{A,s}$ is large.

Comments. Evaporation of fuel droplets at elevated temperatures is important for many practical devices, particularly gas-turbine engines, and diesel engines. In these devices, evaporation occurs when droplets are injected into hot compressed air or into zones where combustion is already in progress. In spark-ignition engines employing fuel injection, temperatures in the intake system are typically much closer to ambient levels and pressures are subatmospheric. In most cases, forced-convection effects are important in the evaporation process. These effects will be discussed in Chapter 10, which focuses on droplet combustion.

SUMMARY

In this chapter, you were introduced to the concept of mass diffusion or mass transfer, and Fick's Law governing the rate of species mass transfer in a binary mixture was presented. A new transport property, the mass diffusivity, provides the proportionality between the species diffusional flux and the species concentration gradient, analogous to the kinematic viscosity and thermal diffusivity in momentum and heat transfer, respectively. You should be familiar with the physical interpretation of Fick's Law and how to apply it to simple binary systems. As an example of simple binary diffusion, the Stefan problem was developed. From this example, you saw how overall mass and species mass conservation equations apply to a single species diffusing through a stagnant layer of a second species. With application of appropriate boundary conditions, we were able to solve for the liquid evaporation rate. A similar analysis was performed for the spherically symmetric problem of droplet evaporation. You should have some physical appreciation for this problem, as well as being familiar with how to calculate droplet evaporation rates and droplet lifetimes.

NOMENCLATURE

a	Defined in Eqn. 3.10d
A	Area (m^2)
B_Y	Dimensionless transfer number or Spalding number, Eqn. 3.52
c	Molar concentration ($kmol/m^3$)
D	Diameter (m)
$\mathcal{D}_{AB}$	Binary diffusivity or diffusion coefficient (m^2/s)
h	Enthalpy (J/kg)
h_{fg}	Heat of vaporization (J/kg)
k	Thermal conductivity (W/m-K)
k_B	Boltzmann constant
ke	Kinetic energy (J)
K	Evaporation constant, Eqn. 3.58 (m^2/s)
L	Tube height (m)

m	Mass (kg)
$\dot{m}$	Mass flowrate (kg/s)
$\dot{m}''$	Mass flux (kg/s-m^2)
MW	Molecular weight (kg/kmol)
n	Number of molecules
N	Number of moles
$\dot{N}$	Molar flowrate (kmol/s)
$\dot{N}''$	Molar flux (kmol/s-m^2)
P	Pressure (Pa)
$\dot{Q}$	Heat-transfer rate (W)
$\dot{Q}''$	Heat flux (W/m^2)
r	Radius (m)
R_u	Universal gas constant
t	Time (s)
T	Temperature (K)
$\bar{v}$	Average molecular speed (m/s)
V	Volume (m^3)
x	Cartesian coordinate (m)
y	Cartesian coordinate (m)
Y	Mass fraction (kg/kg)
Z''	Molecular collision frequency per unit area (No./m^2-s)

Greek symbols

λ	Molecular mean free path (m)
ρ	Density (kg/m^3)
σ	Molecular diameter (m)
χ	Mole fraction (kmol/kmol)

Subscripts

A	Species A
B	Species B
boil	Boiling point
cv	Control volume
d	Droplet
diff	Diffusion
g	Gas
i	Interface
l, liq	Liquid
mix	Mixture
s	Surface
sat	Saturation
vap	Vapor
∞	Freestream or far removed from surface

REFERENCES

1. Bird, R. B., Stewart, W. E., and Lightfoot, E. N., *Transport Phenomena*, John Wiley & Sons, New York, 1960.
2. Thomas, L. C., *Heat Transfer–Mass Transfer Supplement*, Prentice-Hall, Englewood Cliffs, NJ, 1991.
3. Williams, F. A., *Combustion Theory*, 2nd Ed., Addison-Wesley, Redwood City, CA, 1985.
4. Kuo, K. K., *Principles of Combustion*, John Wiley & Sons, New York, 1986.
5. Pierce, F. J., *Microscopic Thermodynamics*, International, Scranton, PA, 1968.
6. Daniels, F., and Alberty, R. A., *Physical Chemistry*, 4th Ed., John Wiley & Sons, New York, 1975.
7. Irvine, T. F., Jr., and Hartnett, J. P. (eds.), *Steam and Air Tables in SI Units*, Hemisphere, Washington, 1976.
8. Nishiwaki, N., "Kinetics of Liquid Combustion Processes: Evaporation and Ignition Lag of Fuel Droplets," *Fifth Symposium (International) on Combustion*, Reinhold, New York, pp. 148–158, 1955.

REVIEW QUESTIONS

1. Make a list of all of the bold-faced words in Chapter 3. Make sure you understand the meaning of each.
2. Assuming constant properties, recast Eqn. 3.4 into a form where the constant of proportionality in Fourier's Law is the thermal diffusivity, $\alpha = k/\rho c_p$, rather than k. The gradient (or spatial derivative) of what property now appears?
3. Starting with the sketch in Fig. 3.3, derive the species conservation equation (Eqn. 3.30) without reference to the text derivation.
4. Using words only, explain what is happening in the Stefan problem.
5. How is the evaporating droplet problem similar to the Stefan problem?
6. If no heat is supplied to the liquid A (Fig. 3.4), what happens to the temperature of the liquid? Can you write a simple energy conservation equation to justify your answer?
7. Define a transfer number, B_Y, that can be used with Eqn. 3.40. Furthermore, assume the flow area is A, and write an expression for in $\dot{m}$ terms of fluid properties, geometrical parameters, and B_Y. Compare your result with Eqn. 3.53 and discuss.
8. Why, and in what way, does the presence of species A in the free stream (Fig. 3.4) affect the evaporation rate?
9. How does the mass average velocity vary with distance from the surface of an evaporating droplet at any instant in time?
10. Explain what is meant by "quasi-steady" flow.
11. Starting with Eqns. 3.53 and 3.54, derive the "D^2 law" for droplet evaporation.

PROBLEMS

3.1. Consider an equimolar mixture of oxygen (O_2) and nitrogen (N_2) at 400 K and 1 atm. Calculate the mixture density ρ and the mixture molar concentration c.

3.2. Calculate the mass fractions of O_2 and N_2 in the mixture given in problem 3.1.

3.3. Estimate the value of the binary diffusivity of *n*-octane in air at a temperature of 400 K and pressure of 3.5 atm utilizing the value given in Appendix D. Also, compare the ratio $\mathcal{D}_{ref}/\mathcal{D}(T = 400\,K,\ P = 3.5\,atm)$ to the ratio of the $\rho\mathcal{D}$ products, i.e., $(\rho\mathcal{D})_{ref}/(\rho\mathcal{D})(T = 400\,K,\ P = 3.5\,atm)$.

3.4. Equation 3.18a was derived assuming molecules A and B are essentially the same mass and size. Reference [1] indicates that Eqn. 3.18a can be generalized for the case where $m_A \neq m_B$ and $\sigma_A \neq \sigma_B$ by using

$$m = \frac{m_A m_B}{(m_A + m_B)/2}, \quad \text{and} \quad \sigma = \frac{1}{2}(\sigma_A + \sigma_B).$$

With this information, estimate the binary diffusivity for O_2 in N_2 at 273 K for $\sigma_{O_2} = 3.467$ and $\sigma_{N_2} = 3.798$ Å. Compare your simple estimate with the handbook value of $1.8 \cdot 10^{-5}$ m^2/s. Should you expect good agreement? Why not? Note: You will need to use Avogadro's number $6.022 \cdot 10^{26}$ molecules/kmol to calculate the mass of a molecule.

3.5. Consider water in a 25-mm-diameter test tube evaporating into dry air at 1 atm. The distance from the water–air interface to the top of the tube is $L = 15$ cm. The mass fraction of the water vapor at the water–air interface is 0.0235, and the binary diffusivity for water vapor in air is $2.6 \cdot 10^{-5}$ m^2/s.

A. Determine the mass evaporation rate of the water.
B. Determine the water vapor mass fraction at $x = L/2$.
C. Determine the fraction of the water mass flow that is contributed by bulk flow and the fraction contributed by diffusion at $x = L/2$.
D. Repeat part C for $x = 0$ and $x = L$. Plot your results. Discuss.

3.6. Consider the same physical situation described above in problem 3.5, except that the interface vapor mass fraction is unknown. Find the mass evaporation rate of the water when the liquid water is at 21°C. Assume equilibrium at the interface, i.e., $P_{H_2O}(x = 0) = P_{sat}(T)$. The air outside the tube is dry.

3.7. Repeat problem 3.6 when the air outside the tube is at 21°C and has a relative humidity of 50%. Also determine the rate of heat transfer required to maintain the liquid water at 21°C.

3.8. Consider liquid n-hexane in a 50-mm-diameter graduated cylinder. Air blows across the top of the cylinder. The distance from the liquid–air interface to the open end of the cylinder is 20 cm. Assume the diffusivity of n-hexane is $8.8 \cdot 10^{-6}$ m^2/s. The liquid n-hexane is at 25°C. Estimate the evaporation rate of the n-hexane. (Hint: Review the Clausius–Clapeyron relation as applied in Example 3.1.)

3.9. Calculate the evaporation rate constant for a 1-mm-diameter water droplet at 75°C evaporating into dry, hot air at 500 K and 1 atm.

3.10. Determine the influence of the ambient water vapor mole fraction on the lifetimes of 50-μm-diameter water droplets. The droplets are evaporating in air at 1 atm. Assume the droplet temperature is 75°C and the mean air temperature is 200°C. Use values of $\chi_{H_2O,\infty} = 0.1, 0.2,$ and 0.3.

CHAPTER
4

CHEMICAL
KINETICS

OVERVIEW

Understanding the underlying chemical processes is an essential element in our study of combustion. In many combustion processes, chemical reaction rates control the rate of combustion, and, in essentially all combustion processes, chemical rates determine pollutant formation and destruction. Also, ignition and flame extinction are intimately related to chemical processes. The study of the elementary reactions and their rates, **chemical kinetics**, is a specialized field of physical chemistry. In the past few decades, much progress has been made in combustion because chemists have been able to define the detailed chemical pathways leading from reactants to products, and to measure or calculate their associated rates. With this knowledge, combustion scientists and engineers are able to construct computer models that simulate reacting systems. Although a tremendous amount of progress has been made, the problem of predicting the details of combustion in a complex flow field, where both fluid mechanics and chemistry are treated from first principles, is still under attack. In general, the fluid mechanical problem alone still taxes the largest computers (Chapter 11), and the addition of detailed chemistry makes the solution impossible.

In this chapter, we will look at basic chemical kinetics concepts. The subsequent chapter outlines the most important, or at least most well known, chemical mechanisms of importance to combustion; and, in Chapter 6, we will also see how models of chemical processes can be coupled to simple thermodynamic models of some reacting systems of interest to combustion engineers.

GLOBAL VERSUS ELEMENTARY REACTIONS

The overall reaction of a mole of fuel with a moles of an oxidizer to form b moles of combustion products can be expressed by the **global reaction mechanism**

$$F + aOx \rightarrow bPr. \qquad (4.1)$$

From experimental measurements, the rate at which the fuel is consumed can be expressed as

$$\frac{d[X_F]}{dt} = -k_G(T)[X_F]^n[X_{Ox}]^m, \qquad (4.2)$$

where the notation $[X_i]$ is used to denote the molar concentration (kmol/m^3 in SI units or gmol/cm^3 in CGS units) of the ith species in the mixture. Equation 4.2 states that the rate of disappearance of the fuel is proportional to each of the reactants raised to a power. The constant of proportionality, k_G, is called the **global rate coefficient**, and in general is not constant, but rather a strong function of temperature. The minus sign indicates that the fuel concentration decreases with time. The exponents n and m relate to the **reaction order**. Equation 4.2 says that the reaction is nth order with respect to the fuel, mth order with respect to the oxidizer, and $(n + m)$th order overall. For global reactions, n and m are not necessarily integers and arise from curvefitting experimental data. Later we will see that for elementary reactions, reaction orders will always be integers. In general, a particular global expression in the form of Eqn. 4.2 holds only over a limited range of temperatures and pressures, and may depend on the details of the apparatus used to define the rate parameters. For example, different expressions for $k_G(T)$ and different values for n and m must be applied to cover a wide range of temperatures.

The use of global reactions to express the chemistry in a specific problem is frequently a "black box" approach. Although this approach may be useful in solving some problems, it does not provide a basis for understanding what is actually happening chemically in a system. For example, it is totally unrealistic to believe that a oxidizer molecules simultaneously collide with a single fuel molecule to form b product molecules, since this would require breaking several bonds and subsequently forming many new bonds. In reality, many sequential processes can occur involving many **intermediate species**. For example, consider the global reaction

$$2H_2 + O_2 \rightarrow 2H_2O. \qquad (4.3)$$

To effect this global conversion of hydrogen and oxygen to water, the following **elementary reactions** are important:

$$H_2 + O_2 \rightarrow HO_2 + H, \qquad (4.4)$$

$$H + O_2 \rightarrow OH + O, \qquad (4.5)$$

$$OH + H_2 \rightarrow H_2O + H, \tag{4.6}$$

$$H + O_2 + M \rightarrow HO_2 + M, \tag{4.7}$$

among others.

In this partial mechanism for hydrogen combustion, we see from reaction 4.4 that when oxygen and hydrogen molecules collide and react, they do not yield water, but instead, form the intermediate species HO_2, the hydroperoxy radical, and a hydrogen atom, H, another radical. **Radicals** or **free radicals** are reactive molecules, or atoms, that have unpaired electrons. To form HO_2 from H_2 and O_2, only one bond is broken and one bond formed. Alternatively, one might consider that H_2 and O_2 would react to form two hydroxyl radicals (OH); however, such a reaction is unlikely since it requires the breaking of two bonds and the creation of two new bonds. The hydrogen atom created in reaction 4.4 then reacts with O_2 forming two additional radicals, OH and O (reaction 4.5). It is the subsequent reaction (4.6) of the hydroxyl radical (OH) with molecular hydrogen that forms water. To have a complete picture of the combustion of H_2 and O_2, more than 20 elementary reactions can be considered [1,2]. These we consider in Chapter 5. The collection of elementary reactions necessary to describe an overall reaction is called a reaction **mechanism**. Reaction mechanisms may involve only a few steps (i.e., elementary reactions) or as many as several hundred. A field of active research involves selecting the minimum number of elementary steps necessary to describe a particular global reaction.

ELEMENTARY REACTION RATES

Bimolecular Reactions and Collision Theory

Most elementary reactions of interest in combustion are **bimolecular**, that is, two molecules collide and react to form two different molecules. For an arbitrary bimolecular reaction, this is expressed as

$$A + B \rightarrow C + D. \tag{4.8}$$

Reactions 4.4–4.6 are examples of bimolecular elementary reactions.

The rate at which the reaction proceeds is directly proportional to the concentrations ($kmol/m^3$) of the two reactant species, i.e.,

$$\frac{d[A]}{dt} = -k_{bimolec}[A][B]. \tag{4.9}$$

All elementary bimolecular reactions are overall second order, being first order with respect to each of the reacting species. The rate coefficient, $k_{bimolec}$, again is a function of temperature, but unlike the global rate coefficient, this rate coefficient has a theoretical basis. The SI units for $k_{bimolec}$ are $m^3/kmol$-s; however, much of the chemistry and combustion literature still use CGS units.

Molecular collision theory can be used to provide insight into the form of Eqn. 4.9 and to suggest the temperature dependence of the bimolecular rate coefficient. As we will see, the collision theory for bimolecular reactions has many shortcomings; nevertheless, the approach is important for historical reasons and provides a way to visualize bimolecular reactions. In our discussion of molecular transport in Chapter 3, we introduced the concepts of wall collision frequency, mean molecular speed, and mean free path (Eqn. 3.10). These same concepts are important in our discussion of molecular collision rates. To determine the collision frequency of a pair of molecules, we start with the simpler case of a single molecule of diameter σ traveling with constant speed v and experiencing collisions with identical, but stationary, molecules. The random path of the molecule is illustrated in Fig. 4.1. If the distance traveled between collisions, i.e., the mean free path, is large, then the moving molecule sweeps out a cylindrical volume in which collisions are possible, equal to $v\pi\sigma^2\Delta t$, in the time interval Δt. If the stationary molecules are distributed randomly and have a number density n/V, the number of collisions experienced by the traveling molecule per unit time can be expressed

$$Z \equiv \frac{\text{collisions}}{\text{per unit time}} = (n/V)v\pi\sigma^2. \tag{4.10}$$

In an actual gas, all of the molecules are moving. If we assume Maxwellian velocity distributions for all the molecules, the collisions frequency for identical molecules is given by [2,3]

$$Z_c = \sqrt{2}(n/V)\pi\sigma^2\bar{v} \tag{4.11}$$

where $\bar{v}$ is the mean speed whose value depends on temperature (Eqn. 3.10a).

Equation 4.11 applies to identical molecules. We can extend our analysis to collisions between unlike molecules having hard-sphere diameters of σ_A and σ_B. The diameter of the collision volume (Fig. 4.1) is then $\sigma_A + \sigma_B \equiv 2\sigma_{AB}$. Thus, Eqn. 4.11 becomes

$$Z_c = \sqrt{2}(n_B/V)\pi\sigma_{AB}^2\bar{v}_A, \tag{4.12}$$

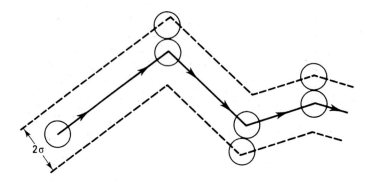

FIGURE 4.1
Collision volume swept out by a molecule, with diameter σ, striking like molecules.

which expresses the frequency of collision of a single A molecule with all B molecules. We are interested, however, in the collision frequency associated with all A and B molecules. Thus, the total number of collisions per unit volume and per unit time is obtained by multiplying the collision frequency of a single A molecule (Eqn. 4.12) by the number of A molecules per unit volume, and using the appropriate mean molecular speeds, i.e.,

$$Z_{AB}/V = \frac{\text{No. of collisions between all A and all B}}{\text{Unit volume} \cdot \text{unit time}}$$

$$= (n_A/V)(n_B/V)\pi\sigma_{AB}^2(\bar{v}_A^2 + \bar{v}_B^2)^{1/2},$$

(4.13)

which can be expressed in terms of temperature as [2,3]

$$Z_{AB}/V = (n_A/V)(n_B/V)\pi\sigma_{AB}^2\left(\frac{8k_BT}{\pi\mu}\right)^{1/2},$$

(4.14)

where

$k_B = $ Boltzmann constant $= 1.381 \cdot 10^{-23}$ J/K;

$\mu = \dfrac{m_A m_B}{m_A + m_B} = $ reduced mass where m_A and m_B are the masses of species A and B, respectively, in kilograms;

$T = $ absolute temperature (K).

Note that the average speed is obtained by replacing the mass of the single molecule in Eqn. 3.10a with the reduced mass μ.

To relate the above to the problem of reaction rates, we write

$$-\frac{d[A]}{dt} = \left[\begin{array}{c}\text{No. of collisions}\\ \text{A and B molecules}\\ \overline{\text{Unit volume} \cdot \text{unit time}}\end{array}\right] \cdot \left[\begin{array}{c}\text{Probability that a}\\ \text{collision leads to}\\ \text{reaction}\end{array}\right] \cdot \left[\dfrac{\text{kmol of A}}{\text{No. of molecules of A}}\right],$$

(4.15a)

or

$$-\frac{d[A]}{dt} = (Z_{AB}/V)PN_{AV}^{-1},$$

(4.15b)

where N_{AV} is the Avogadro number ($6.022 \cdot 10^{26}$ molecules/kmol). The probability that a collision leads to reaction can be expressed as a product of two factors: an energy factor, $\exp[-E_A/R_uT]$, which expresses the fraction of collisions that occur with an energy above the threshold level necessary for reaction, E_A, or **activation energy**; and a geometrical or **steric factor, p,** that takes into account the geometry of collisions between A and B. For example, in the reaction of OH and H to form H_2O, intuitively one expects a reaction to be more likely if the H atom strikes the O side of the hydroxyl rather than the H side, since the product has bonds of the form H–O–H. In general, steric factors are much less than unity; however, there are exceptions. Thus, Eqn. 4.15b becomes

$$-\frac{d[A]}{dt} = pN_{AV}\sigma_{AB}^2\left[\frac{8\pi k_BT}{\mu}\right]^{1/2}\exp[-E_A/R_uT][A][B],$$

(4.16)

where the substitutions $n_A/V = [A]N_{AV}$ and $n_B/V = [B]N_{AV}$ have been employed. Comparing Eqn. 4.9 with Eqn. 4.16, we see that the bimolecular rate coefficient, based on collision theory, is

$$k(T) = pN_{AV}\sigma_{AB}^2 \left[\frac{8\pi k_B T}{\mu}\right]^{1/2} \exp[-E_A/R_u T]. \tag{4.17}$$

Unfortunately, collision theory provides no means to determine the activation energy or the steric factor. More-advanced theories, which postulate the structure of the molecule in the process of breaking and forming bonds, i.e., an **activated complex**, do allow calculation of $k_{bimolec}$ from first principles. A discussion of such theories is beyond the scope of this book and the interested reader is referred to Refs. [2] and [3].

If the temperature range of interest is not too great, the bimolecular rate coefficient can be expressed by the empirical **Arrhenius form**,

$$k(T) = A \exp(-E_A/R_u T), \tag{4.18}$$

where A is a constant termed the **pre-exponential factor** or the **frequency factor**. Comparing Eqns. 4.17 and 4.18, we see that A is not strictly constant but depends, based on collision theory, on $T^{1/2}$. **Arrhenius plots** of log k versus $1/T$ for experimental data are used to extract values for the activation energy, since the slope of such plots is $-E_A/R_u$.

Although tabulation of experimental values for rate coefficients in Arrhenius form is common, current practice frequently utilizes the three-parameter functional form:

$$k(T) = AT^b \exp(-E_A/R_u T), \tag{4.19}$$

where A, b, and E_A, are the three empirical parameters. Table 4.1 illustrates the three-parameter form showing the recommendations of Warnatz [4] for the H_2–O_2 system.

Example 4.1. Determine the collision-theory steric factor for the reaction

$$O + H_2 \rightarrow OH + H$$

at 2000 K given the hard-sphere diameters $\sigma_O = 3.050$ and $\sigma_{H_2} = 2.827$ Å and the experimental parameters of Table 4.1.

Solution. Equating the collision-theory rate coefficient (Eqn. 4.17) with the three-parameter experimental rate coefficient (Eqn. 4.19) yields

$$k(T) = pN_{AV}\sigma_{AB}^2 \left[\frac{8\pi k_B T}{\mu}\right]^{1/2} \exp[-E_A/R_u T] = AT^b \exp[-E_A/R_u T],$$

where we assume the activation energy E_A is the same for both expressions. Solving for the steric factor, p, is straightforward, although care must be exercised in treating the units:

TABLE 4.1
Recommended rate coefficients for H_2/O_2 reactions from Ref. [4]

Reaction	A $((cm^3/gmol)^{n-1}/s)^a$	b	E_A (kJ/gmol)	Temperature range (K)
$H + O_2 \rightarrow OH + O$	$1.2 \cdot 10^{17}$	-0.91	69.1	300–2500
$OH + O \rightarrow O_2 + H$	$1.8 \cdot 10^{13}$	0	0	300–2500
$O + H_2 \rightarrow OH + H$	$1.5 \cdot 10^{7}$	2.0	31.6	300–2500
$OH + H_2 \rightarrow H_2O + H$	$1.0 \cdot 10^{8}$	1.6	13.8	300–2500
$H + H_2O \rightarrow OH + H_2$	$4.6 \cdot 10^{8}$	1.6	77.7	300–2500
$O + H_2O \rightarrow OH + OH$	$1.5 \cdot 10^{10}$	1.14	72.2	300–2500
$H + H + M \rightarrow H_2 + M$				
M = Ar (low P)	$6.4 \cdot 10^{17}$	-1.0	0	300–5000
M = H_2 (low P)	$9.7 \cdot 10^{16}$	-0.6	0	100–5000
$H_2 + M \rightarrow H + H + M$				
M = Ar (low P)	$2.2 \cdot 10^{14}$	0	402	2500–8000
M = H_2 (low P)	$8.8 \cdot 10^{14}$	0	402	2500–8000
$H + OH + M \rightarrow H_2O + M$				
M = H_2O (low P)	$1.4 \cdot 10^{23}$	-2.0	0	1000–3000
$H_2O + M \rightarrow H + OH + M$				
M = H_2O (low P)	$1.6 \cdot 10^{17}$	0	478	2000–5000
$O + O + M \rightarrow O_2 + M$				
M = Ar (low P)	$1.0 \cdot 10^{17}$	-1.0	0	300–5000
$O_2 + M \rightarrow O + O + M$				
M = Ar (low P)	$1.2 \cdot 10^{14}$	0	451	2000–10,000
	$1.5 \cdot 10^{9}$	1.14	0	300–2500

[a] n is the reaction order.

$$p = \frac{AT^b}{N_{AV}\left(\dfrac{8\pi k_B T}{\mu}\right)^{1/2} \sigma_{AB}^2}.$$

To evaluate the above, we employ

$$A = 1.5 \cdot 10^7 \ cm^3/gmol\text{-}s \qquad \text{(Table 4.1)}$$

$$b = 2.0 \qquad \text{(Table 4.1)}$$

$$\sigma_{AB} = (\sigma_O + \sigma_{H_2})/2$$

$$= (3.050 + 2.827)/2 = 2.939 \ \text{A}$$

$$= 2.939 \cdot 10^{-8} \ cm$$

$$m_O = \frac{16\,\text{g/gmol}}{6.022 \cdot 10^{23} \text{ molecules/gmol}} = 2.66 \cdot 10^{-23}\,\text{g}$$

$$m_{H_2} = \frac{2.008}{6.022 \cdot 10^{23}} = 0.332 \cdot 10^{-23}\,\text{g}$$

$$\mu = \frac{m_O m_{H_2}}{m_O + m_{H_2}} = \frac{2.66(0.332)}{2.66 + 0.332} \cdot 10^{-23} = 2.95 \cdot 10^{-24}\,\text{g}$$

$$k_B = 1.381 \cdot 10^{-23}\,\text{J/K} = 1.381 \cdot 10^{-16}\,\text{g-cm}^2/\text{s}^2\text{-K}.$$

Thus,

$$p = \frac{1.5 \cdot 10^7 (2000)^2}{6.022 \cdot 10^{23} \left(\dfrac{8\pi(1.381 \cdot 10^{-16})2000}{2.95 \cdot 10^{-24}}\right)^{1/2} (2.939 \cdot 10^{-8})^2}$$

$$= 0.075$$

Units check:

$$p [=] \frac{\text{cm}^3}{\text{gmol-s}} \frac{1}{\dfrac{1}{\text{gmol}} \left(\dfrac{\text{g-cm}^2}{\text{s}^2\text{-K}} \dfrac{K}{g}\right)^{1/2} \text{cm}^2} = 1$$

$$\boxed{p = 0.075 \text{ (dimensionless)}}.$$

Comment. The value of $p = 0.075$ is less than unity, as expected, and its small value points out the shortcomings of the simple theory. Note that CGS units were employed and the use of the Avogadro number to calculate the species mass in grams. Note also that all of the units for $k(T)$ are in the pre-exponential factor A; thus, the factor T^b is dimensionless by definition.

Other Elementary Reactions

As the name suggests, **unimolecular** reactions involve a single species undergoing a rearrangement (isomerization or decomposition) to form one or two product species, i.e.,

$$A \rightarrow B \tag{4.20}$$

or

$$A \rightarrow B + C. \tag{4.21}$$

Examples of unimolecular reactions include the typical dissociation reactions important to combustion, e.g., $O_2 \rightarrow O + O$, $H_2 \rightarrow H + H$, etc.

Unimolecular reactions are first order at high pressures,

$$\frac{d[A]}{dt} = -k_{\text{uni}}[A], \tag{4.22}$$

while at low pressures, the reaction rate also depends on the concentration of any molecules, M, with which the reacting species may collide. In this case,

$$\frac{d[A]}{dt} = -k[A][M].$$
(4.23)

To explain this interesting behavior requires postulating a three-step mechanism. Since we have yet to explore some of the concepts required to deal with this, we conclude our treatment of unimolecular reactions for the time being.

    Termolecular reactions involve three reactant species and correspond to the reverse of the unimolecular reaction at low pressures. The general form of a termolecular reaction is

$$A + B + M \rightarrow C + M.$$
(4.24)

Recombination reactions such as $H + H + M \rightarrow H_2 + M$ and $H + OH + M \rightarrow H_2O + M$ are important examples of termolecular reactions in combustion. Termolecular reactions are third order, and their rates can be expressed

$$\frac{d[A]}{dt} = -k_{ter}[A][B][M],$$
(4.25)

where again M may be any molecule and is frequently referred to as a **third body**. When A and B are the same species, as in $H + H + M$, a factor of two must multiply the right-hand-side of Eqn. 4.25 since two A molecules disappear to form C. In radical–radical reactions, the third body is required to carry away the energy liberated in forming the stable species. During the collision, the internal energy of the newly formed molecule is transferred to the third body, M, and is manifest as kinetic energy of M. Without this energy transfer, the newly formed molecule would dissociate back to its constituent atoms.

RATES OF REACTION FOR MULTI-STEP MECHANISMS

Net Production Rates

In the previous sections, we introduced the idea of a sequence of elementary reactions that leads from reactants to products, which we termed the reaction mechanism. Knowing how to express the rates of elementary reactions, we can now mathematically express the net rates of production or destruction for any species participating in a series of elementary steps. For example, let's return to the H_2–O_2 reaction mechanism, which is incompletely given by Eqns. 4.4–4.7, and include both forward and reverse reactions as indicated by the ⇔ symbol:

$$H_2 + O_2 \overset{k_{f1}}{\underset{k_{r1}}{\Leftrightarrow}} HO_2 + H, \tag{R.1}$$

$$H + O_2 \overset{k_{f2}}{\underset{k_{r2}}{\Leftrightarrow}} OH + O, \tag{R.2}$$

$$OH + H_2 \overset{k_{f3}}{\underset{k_{r3}}{\Leftrightarrow}} H_2O + H, \tag{R.3}$$

$$H + O_2 + M \overset{k_{f4}}{\underset{k_{r4}}{\Leftrightarrow}} HO_2 + M, \tag{R.4}$$

$$\vdots$$

where k_{fi} and k_{ri} are the elementary forward and reverse rate coefficients, respectively, for the ith reaction. The net rate of production of O_2, for example, is the sum of all of the individual elementary rates producing O_2 minus the sum of all of the rates destroying O_2, i.e.,

$$
\begin{aligned}
\frac{d[O_2]}{dt} &= k_{r1}[HO_2][H] + k_{r2}[OH][O] \\
&+ k_{r4}[HO_2][M] + \ldots \\
&- k_{f1}[H_2][O_2] - k_{f2}[H][O_2] \\
&- k_{f4}[H][O_2][M] - \ldots
\end{aligned}
\tag{4.26}
$$

and for H atoms,

$$
\begin{aligned}
\frac{d[H]}{dt} &= k_{f1}[H_2][O_2] + k_{r2}[OH][O] \\
&+ k_{f3}[OH][H_2] + k_{r4}[HO_2][M] + \ldots \\
&- k_{r1}[HO_2][H] - k_{f2}[H][O_2] \\
&- k_{r3}[H_2O][H] - k_{f4}[H][O_2][M] - \ldots.
\end{aligned}
\tag{4.27}
$$

We can write similar expressions for each species participating in the mechanism, which yields a system of first-order ordinary differential equations that describes the evolution of the chemical system starting from given initial conditions, i.e.,

$$\frac{d[X_i](t)}{dt} = f_i([X_1](t), [X_2](t), \ldots [X_n](t)) \tag{4.28a}$$

with

$$[X_i](0) = [X_i]_0. \tag{4.28b}$$

For a particular system, this set of equations (4.28a), together with any necessary statements of conservation of mass, momentum, or energy, and state equations, can be integrated numerically using a computer. Packaged routines, such as IMSL's DGEAR [5], efficiently integrate the **stiff** system of equations that arise in chemical systems. A set of equations is considered stiff when one or more variables change very rapidly, while others change very slowly. This disparity in time scales is common in chemical systems where radical reactions are very fast compared to reactions involving stable species. Several numerical integration routines have been used or developed specifically for reacting chemical systems [1,6-8].

Compact Notation

Since mechanisms may involve many elementary steps and many species, a compact notation has been developed to represent both the mechanism, e.g., R1–R4 . . . , and the individual species production rates, e.g., Eqns. 4.26 and 4.27. For the mechanism, one can write

$$\sum_{j=1}^{N} \nu'_{ji} X_j \Leftrightarrow \sum_{j=1}^{N} \nu''_{ji} X_j \text{ for } i = 1, 2 \ldots L \quad (4.29)$$

where ν'_{ji} and ν''_{ji} are the **stoichiometric coefficients** on the reactants and products side of the equation, respectively, for the jth species in the ith reaction. For example, consider the four reactions, R.1–R.4, involving the eight species, O_2, H_2, H_2O, HO_2, O, H, OH, and M. Defining j and i as follows:

j	Species	i	Reaction
1	O_2	1	R.1
2	H_2	2	R.2
3	H_2O	3	R.3
4	HO_2	4	R.4
5	O		
6	H		
7	OH		
8	M		

Using j as the column index and i as the row index, we can write the stoichiometric coefficient matrices as

$$\nu'_{ji} = \begin{bmatrix} 1 & 1 & 0 & 0 & 0 & 0 & 0 & 0 \\ 1 & 0 & 0 & 0 & 0 & 1 & 0 & 0 \\ 0 & 1 & 0 & 0 & 0 & 0 & 1 & 0 \\ 1 & 0 & 0 & 0 & 0 & 1 & 0 & 1 \end{bmatrix} \quad (4.30a)$$

and

$$\nu''_{ji} = \begin{bmatrix} 0 & 0 & 0 & 1 & 0 & 1 & 0 & 0 \\ 0 & 0 & 0 & 0 & 1 & 0 & 1 & 0 \\ 0 & 0 & 1 & 0 & 0 & 1 & 0 & 0 \\ 0 & 0 & 0 & 1 & 0 & 0 & 0 & 1 \end{bmatrix}. \quad (4.30b)$$

Since elementary reactions involve, at most, three species, the coefficient matrices will always be sparse (many more zero than non-zero elements) when the number of species involved is large.

The following three relations compactly express the net production rate of each species in a multi-step mechanism:

$$\dot{\omega}_j = \sum_{i=1}^{L} \nu_{ji}\, q_i \quad \text{for} \quad j = 1, 2 \ldots N \tag{4.31}$$

where

$$\nu_{ji} = \left(\nu_{ji}'' - \nu_{ji}'\right) \tag{4.32}$$

and

$$q_i = k_{fi} \prod_{j=1}^{N} [X_j]^{\nu_{ji}'} - k_{ri} \prod_{j=1}^{N} [X_j]^{\nu_{ji}''}. \tag{4.33}$$

The **production rates**, $\dot{\omega}_j$, correspond to the left-hand-sides of Eqns. 4.26 and 4.27, for example. In other words, $\dot{\omega}_j \equiv d[X_j]/dt$ for the complete mechanism. Equation 4.33 defines the **rate-of-progress variable**, q_i, for the ith elementary reaction. The symbol $\prod$ is used to denote a product of terms in the same sense that $\sum$ is used to represent a summation of terms. For example, q_i for reaction R.1 is expressed

$$
\begin{aligned}
q_i &= k_{f1}[O_2]^1[H_2]^1[H_2O]^0[HO_2]^0[O]^0[H]^0[OH]^0[M]^0 \\
&\quad - k_{r1}[O_2]^0[H_2]^0[H_2O]^0[HO_2]^1[O]^0[H]^1[OH]^0[M]^0 \\
&= k_{f1}[O_2][H_2] - k_{r1}[HO_2][H].
\end{aligned}
\tag{4.34}
$$

Writing similar expressions for $i = 2$, 3 and 4 and summing (Eqn. 4.31), taking into account whether the jth species is created, destroyed, or does not participate in the ith step (Eqn. 4.32), completes the total rate expression for $\dot{\omega}_j$.

The compact notation embodied in Eqns. 4.29 and 4.31–4.34 is particularly useful in solving chemical kinetics problems using a computer. The software CHEMKIN [1] is a widely used general-purpose package for solving chemical kinetics problems and is available through Sandia (Livermore) National Laboratories.

Relation between Rate Coefficients and Equilibrium Constants

Measuring rate coefficients of elementary reactions is a difficult task that frequently leads to results that possess a rather large degree of uncertainty. The more reliable rate coefficients often are known no better than within a factor of two, while others may be uncertain by an order of magnitude, or more. On the other hand, equilibrium constants, which are based on thermodynamic measurements or calculations, are very accurate and precise in most cases. We can take advantage of accurate thermodynamic data in solving chemical kinetics problems by recognizing that at equilibrium the forward and reverse reaction rates must be equal. For example, consider both the forward and reverse rates for the arbitrary bimolecular reaction

$$A + B \overset{k_f}{\underset{k_r}{\rightleftharpoons}} C + D. \qquad (4.35)$$

For species A, we can write

$$\frac{d[A]}{dt} = -k_f [A][B] + k_r [C][D]. \qquad (4.36)$$

For the equilibrium condition, $A + B = C + D$, the time rate of change of [A] must be zero, as must also be the time rates of change of species B, C, and D. Thus, we can express equilibrium as

$$0 = -k_f [A][B] + k_r [C][D], \qquad (4.37)$$

which upon rearranging becomes

$$\frac{[C][D]}{[A][B]} = \frac{k_f(T)}{k_r(T)}. \qquad (4.38)$$

In Chapter 2, we defined the equilibrium constant based on partial pressures for an arbitrary equilibrium reaction to be

$$K_p = \frac{(P_C/P^o)^c (P_D/P^o)^d \cdots}{(P_A/P^o)^a (P_B/P^o)^b \cdots} \qquad (4.39)$$

where the superscripts are the stoichiometric coefficients, i.e., $\nu_i' = a, b, \ldots$ and $\nu_i'' = c, d, \ldots$. Since the molar concentrations relate to the mole fractions and partial pressures as follows,

$$[X_i] = \chi_i P/R_u T = P_i/R_u T, \qquad (4.40)$$

we can define an equilibrium constant based on molar concentrations, K_c. The relationship between K_c and K_p is

$$K_p = K_c (R_u T/P^o)^{c+d+\cdots-a-b-\cdots} \qquad (4.41a)$$

or

$$K_p = K_c (R_u T/P^o)^{\Sigma\nu'' - \Sigma\nu'}, \qquad (4.41b)$$

where

$$K_c = \frac{[C]^c [D]^d \cdots}{[A]^a [B]^b \cdots} = \frac{\prod_{\text{prod}} [X_i]^{\nu_i''}}{\prod_{\text{react}} [X_i]^{\nu_i'}}. \qquad (4.42)$$

From the above, we see that the ratio of the forward and reverse rate coefficients equals the equilibrium constant K_c,

$$\frac{k_f(T)}{k_r(T)} = K_c(T), \qquad (4.43)$$

and that for a bimolecular reaction $K_c = K_p$. Using Eqn. 4.43, one can compute a reverse reaction rate from a knowledge of the forward rate and the equilibrium coefficient for the reaction; or conversely, one can calculate the forward rate knowing the reverse rate. In performing kinetic calculations, the most accurate experimental rate coefficient over the temperature range of interest should be used, and the rate in the opposite direction calculated from the equilibrium constant. Over a wide range of temperatures, different choices may have to be made. The National Institute of Standards and Technology (formerly the U.S. Bureau of Standards) maintains a chemical kinetics database providing rate information on well over 6000 reactions [9].

Example 4.2. In their survey of experimental determinations of rate coefficients for the N–H–O system, Hanson and Salimian [10] recommend the following rate coefficient for the reaction $NO + O \rightarrow N + O_2$:

$$k_f = 3.80 \cdot 10^9 \ T^{1.0} \exp(-20,820/T) \ [=] \ cm^3/gmol\text{-}s$$

Determine the rate coefficient k_r for the reverse reaction, i.e., $N + O_2 \rightarrow NO + O$, at 2300 K.

Solution. The forward and reverse rate coefficients are related to the equilibrium constant, K_p, via Eqn. 4.43,

$$\frac{k_f(T)}{k_r(T)} = K_c(T) = K_p(T).$$

Thus, to find k_r, we need to evaluate k_f and K_p at 2300 K. From Eqns. 2.66 and 2.64, we can evaluate K_p:

$$K_p = \exp\left(\frac{-\Delta G_T^o}{R_u T}\right)$$

where

$$\Delta G_{2300K}^o = \left[\bar{g}_{f,N}^o + \bar{g}_{f,O_2}^o - \bar{g}_{f,NO}^o - \bar{g}_{f,O}^o\right]_{2300\ K}$$
$$= 326,331 + 0 - 61,243 - 101,627 \quad \text{(Tables A.8, A.9, A.11, A.12)}$$
$$= 163,461 \ \text{kJ/kmol}$$
$$K_p = \exp\left(\frac{-163,461}{8.315\,(2300)}\right) = 1.94 \cdot 10^{-4} \quad \text{(dimensionless)}.$$

The forward rate coefficient at 2300 K is

$$k_f = 3.8 \cdot 10^9 \,(2300) \exp\left(\frac{-20,820}{2300}\right).$$
$$= 1.024 \cdot 10^9 \ cm^3/gmol\text{-}s$$

So,

$$\boxed{k_r} = k_f/K_p = \frac{1.024 \cdot 10^9}{1.94 \cdot 10^{-4}} = \boxed{5.28 \cdot 10^{12}\,\text{cm}^3/\text{gmol-s}}.$$

Comment. The reactions used in this example are part of the important Zeldovich or thermal NO mechanism: $O + N_2 \Leftrightarrow NO + O$ and $N + O_2 \Leftrightarrow NO + O$. We will explore this mechanism further in a subsequent example, as well as in Chapters 5 and 15.

Steady-State Approximation

In many chemical systems of interest to combustion, highly reactive intermediate species, e.g., radicals, are formed. Analyses of such systems can sometimes be simplified by applying the **steady-state approximation** to these reactive intermediates or radicals. Physically, what occurs is that, after a rapid initial build-up in concentration, the radical is destroyed as rapidly as it is formed, so that its rate of formation and its rate of destruction are equal [11]. This situation typically occurs when the reaction forming the intermediate species is slow, while the reaction destroying the intermediate is very fast. As a result, the concentrations of the radical are quite small in comparison to those of the reactants and products. A good example of this is the Zeldovich mechanism for the formation of nitric oxide, where the reactive intermediate of interest is the N atom:

$$O + N_2 \xrightarrow{k_1} NO + N$$

$$N + O_2 \xrightarrow{k_2} NO + O.$$

The first reaction in this pair is slow and, hence, rate limiting; while the second is extremely fast. We can write the net production rate of N atoms as

$$\frac{d[N]}{dt} = k_1[O][N_2] - k_2[N][O_2]. \tag{4.44}$$

After a rapid transient allowing the build-up of N atoms to some low concentration, the two terms on the right-hand-side of Eqn. 4.44 become equal, and $d[N]/dt$ approaches zero. With $d[N]/dt \to 0$, we are able to determine the steady concentration of N atoms:

$$0 = k_1[O][N_2] - k_2[N]_{ss}[O_2] \tag{4.45}$$

or

$$[N]_{ss} = \frac{k_1[O][N_2]}{k_2[O_2]}. \tag{4.46}$$

Although involving the steady-state approximation suggests that $[N]_{ss}$ does not change with time, $[N]_{ss}$ may change as it rapidly readjusts according to Eqn. 4.46. To determine the time rate-of-change, requires differentiating Eqn. 4.46, rather than applying Eqn. 4.44:

$$\frac{d[N]_{ss}}{dt} = \frac{d}{dt}\left[\frac{k_1[O][N_2]}{k_2[O_2]}\right]. \tag{4.47}$$

In the next section, we apply the steady-state approximation to the mechanism for unimolecular reactions.

The Mechanism for Unimolecular Reactions

In a previous section we deferred discussing the pressure dependence of unimolecular reactions until we had a grasp of the multi-step mechanism concept. To explain the pressure dependence requires a three-step mechanism:

$$A + M \xrightarrow{k_e} A^* + M \tag{4.48a}$$

$$A^* + M \xrightarrow{k_{de}} A + M \tag{4.48b}$$

$$A^* \xrightarrow{k_{uni}} \text{products}. \tag{4.48c}$$

In the first step, Eqn. 4.48a, molecule A collides with the "third body," M. As a result of the collision, some of the translational kinetic energy from M is transferred to molecule A, resulting in an increase in A's internal vibrational and rotational energies. The high-internal-energy A molecule is referred to as the *energized* A molecule, A^*. After the energizing of A, two things may happen: A* may collide with another molecule resulting in A^*'s internal energy being converted back to translational energy in the reverse of the energizing process (Eqn. 4.48b), or the energized A^* may fly apart in a true unimolecular process (Eqn. 4.48c). To observe the pressure dependence, we can write an expression that describes the rate at which products are formed:

$$\frac{d[\text{products}]}{dt} = k_{uni}[A^*]. \tag{4.49}$$

To evaluate $[A^*]$, we will employ the steady-state approximation discussed above. The net production of A^* can be expressed

$$\frac{d[A^*]}{dt} = k_e[A][M] - k_{de}[A^*][M] - k_{uni}[A^*]. \tag{4.50}$$

If we assume that $d[A^*]dt = 0$, following some initial rapid transient during which $[A^*]$ reaches a steady state, then we can solve for $[A^*]$:

$$[A^*] = \frac{k_e[A][M]}{k_{de}[M] + k_{uni}}. \tag{4.51}$$

Substituting Eqn. 4.51 into Eqn. 4.49 yields

$$\frac{d[\text{products}]}{dt} = \frac{k_{uni}k_e[A][M]}{k_{de}[M] + k_{uni}} = \frac{k_e[A][M]}{\dfrac{k_{de}}{k_{uni}}[M] + 1}. \tag{4.52}$$

For the overall reaction,

$$A \xrightarrow{k_{app}} \text{products},$$

(4.53)

we write

$$-\frac{d[A]}{dt} = \frac{d[\text{products}]}{dt} = k_{app}[A]$$

(4.54)

where k_{app} is defined as the apparent unimolecular rate coefficient. Equating Eqns. 4.52 and 4.54, we find that the apparent rate coefficient is of the form

$$k_{app} = \frac{k_e[M]}{\dfrac{k_{de}}{k_{uni}}[M] + 1}$$

(4.55)

Analyzing Eqn. 4.55, we can explain the interesting pressure dependence of unimolecular reactions. When the pressure is increased, [M] (kmol/m^3) increases. At high enough pressures, the term $k_{de}[M]/k_{uni}$ becomes much larger than unity, and the [M]s in the numerator and denominator of Eqn. 4.55 cancel. Thus,

$$k_{app}(P \rightarrow \infty) = k_{uni}k_e/k_{de}.$$

(4.56)

At sufficiently low pressures, $k_{de}[M]/k_{uni}$ is much less than unity and can be neglected in comparison; hence,

$$k_{app}(P \rightarrow 0) = k_e[M],$$

(4.57)

and the dependence of the reaction rate on [M] becomes apparent. Thus, we see that the three-step mechanism indeed provides a logical explanation for the high- and low-pressure limits of unimolecular reactions. Procedures for obtaining rate coefficients for pressures between the two limits are discussed by Gardiner and Troe [12].

Chain and Chain-Branching Reactions

Chain reactions involve the production of a radical species that subsequently reacts to produce another radical. This radical in turn reacts to produce yet another radical. This sequence of events, or chain reaction, continues until a reaction involving the formation of a stable species from two radicals breaks the chain. Chain reactions can occur in many chemical processes of importance to combustion, as you will see in Chapter 5.

In the following, we illustrate some of the features of chain reactions by exploring a hypothetical chain mechanism, which is globally represented as

$$A_2 + B_2 \rightarrow 2AB$$

(C.1)

The **chain-initiation reaction** is

$$A_2 + M \xrightarrow{k_1} A + A + M$$

(C.2)

and the **chain-propagating reactions** involving the free radicals A and B are

$$A + B_2 \xrightarrow{k_2} AB + B \tag{C.2}$$

$$B + A_2 \xrightarrow{k_3} AB + A. \tag{C.3}$$

The **chain-terminating reaction** is

$$A + B + M \xrightarrow{k_4} AB + M. \tag{C.4}$$

In the early stages of reaction, the concentration of the product AB is small, as are the concentrations of A and B throughout the course of the reaction; thus we can neglect the reverse reactions to determine the reaction rates for the stable species at this reaction stage:

$$\frac{d[A_2]}{dt} = -k_1[A_2][M] - k_3[A_2][B] \tag{4.58}$$

$$\frac{d[B_2]}{dt} = -k_2[B_2][A] \tag{4.59}$$

$$\frac{d[AB]}{dt} = k_2[A][B_2] + k_3[B][A_2] + k_4[A][B][M]. \tag{4.60}$$

For the radicals A and B, the steady-state approximation is invoked. Thus,

$$2k_1[A_2][M] - k_2[A][B_2] + k_3[B][A_2] - k_4[A][B][M] = 0 \tag{4.61}$$

and

$$k_2[A][B_2] - k_3[B][A_2] - k_4[A][B][M] = 0. \tag{4.62}$$

Solving Eqns. 4.61 and 4.62 simultaneously for [A] yields

$$[A] = \frac{k_1}{2k_2} \frac{[M][A_2]}{[B_2]} + \frac{k_3}{k_4} \frac{[A_2]}{[M]} \left\{ \left[1 + \left(\frac{k_1 k_4}{2k_2 k_3} \frac{[M]^2}{[B_2]} \right)^2 \right]^{1/2} - 1 \right\}. \tag{4.63}$$

A similarly complicated expression results for [B]. Knowing the steady-state values for [A] and [B], the initial reaction rates $d[A_2]/dt$ and $d[B_2]/dt$, and $d[AB]/dt$, can be determined for some initial concentrations of $[A_2]$ and $[B_2]$. Of the three reaction rates, $d[B_2]/dt$ is the simplest and is expressed

$$\frac{d[B_2]}{dt} = -\frac{k_1}{2}[A_2][M] - \frac{k_2 k_3}{k_4} \frac{[A_2][B_2]}{[M]} \left\{ \left[1 + \left(\frac{k_1 k_4}{2k_2 k_3} \frac{[M]^2}{[B_2]} \right)^2 \right]^{1/2} - 1 \right\}. \tag{4.64}$$

Equations 4.63 and 4.64 can be simplified further by recognizing that, in the second term, $k_1 k_4[M]^2/(2k_2 k_3[B]) \ll 1$. This inequality holds since the rate coefficients for the radical reactions, k_2 and k_3, must be much larger than k_1 and k_4 for the steady-state approximation to apply. Using a truncated Taylor series, we can now write expressions for [A] and $d[B_2]/dt$ that can be easily analyzed:

$$[A] \approx \frac{k_1}{2k_2} \frac{[A_2][M]}{[B_2]} + \frac{k_1^2 k_4}{8k_2^2 k_3} \frac{[A_2][M]^3}{[B_2]^2} \tag{4.65}$$

and

$$\frac{d[B_2]}{dt} \approx -\frac{k_1}{2}[A_2][M] - \frac{k_1^2 k_4}{4k_1 k_3} \frac{[A_2][M]^3}{[B_2]}. \tag{4.66}$$

A simple order-of-magnitude analysis shows that the first term in both Eqns. 4.65 and 4.66 dominates at low pressures; thus, the concentration of A depends directly on the ratio of the initiation-step (C.1) rate coefficient to the first propagation-step (C.2) rate coefficient, and the rate at which B_2 disappears is governed solely by the initiation step. The effect of k_1 on [A] and $d[B_2]/dt$ is illustrated in Table 4.2, which shows spreadsheet calculations for assumed initial reactant concentrations, $[A_2] = [B_2] = 1$ and $[M] = [A_2] + [B_2] = 2$, and rate coefficients, all in arbitrary units.

Table 4.3 shows the influence of the chain-propagating steps rate coefficients. Here we see that the radical concentrations decrease as k_2 and k_3 increase, and that k_2 and k_3 have virtually no effect on the products production rate. In Table 4.4, we see that the radical concentrations are directly proportional to pressure and that the reaction rates of the major species scale with the pressure squared. These relationships hold as long as the second terms on the right-hand-sides of Eqns. 4.65 and 4.66 remain small in comparison to the first terms.

The influence of the termolecular chain-terminating-step (C.4) rate coefficient k_4 is shown in Tables 4.5 and 4.6. At low pressures (Table 4.5), k_4 has virtually no effect on either the radical concentrations or the overall reaction rate; however, at high pressures k_4 does have an influence. This is a direct result of the second terms in Eqns. 4.65 and 4.66 becoming important at high pressures, since they increase with pressure faster than the first terms. Recall that the molar concentration ($kmol/m^3$) scales directly with pressure if the mole fractions and temperature are fixed.

Chain-branching reactions involve the formation of two radical species from a reaction that consumes only one radical. The reaction, $O + H_2O \rightarrow OH + OH$, is an example of a chain-branching reaction. The existence of a chain-branching step in a chain mechanism can have an explosive effect, literally, and the interesting explosion behavior of mixtures of H_2 and O_2 (Chapter 5) is a result of chain-branching steps.

In a system with chain branching, it is possible for the concentration of a radical species to build up geometrically, causing the rapid formation of products. Unlike in the previous example (cf. Table 4.2), the rate of the chain-initiation step does not control the overall reaction rate. With chain branching, the rates of radical reactions dominate. Chain-branching reactions are responsible for a flame being self-propagating and are an essential ingredient in combustion chemistry.

TABLE 4.2
Effect of initiation-step rate coefficient k_1

Pressure	1	1	1	1	1
Rate coefficient k_1	**0.001**	**0.01**	**0.1**	**1**	**10**
Rate coefficient k_2	1000	1000	1000	1000	1000
Rate coefficient k_3	1000	1000	1000	1000	1000
Rate coefficient k_4	10	10	10	10	10
$[A_2]$ Concentration	1	1	1	1	1
$[B_2]$ Concentration	1	1	1	1	1
$[M]$ Concentration	2	2	2	2	2
$[A]$ Concentration	1.00000E-6	1.00000E-5	1.00000E-4	0.00100000	0.01000099
$[B]$ Concentration	9.9999999E-7	9.9999990E-6	9.9999900E-5	9.9999000E-4	0.0009990000
$d[A_2]/dt$	-0.002999999	-0.029999999	-0.299999899	-2.999990000	-29.99900000
$d[B_2]/dt$	-0.0010000	-0.0100000	-0.1000001	-1.0000100	-10.001000
$d[AB]/dt$	0.0020000000	0.020000002	0.2000002	2.0000200000	20.002000000

TABLE 4.3
Effect of chain-propagating-steps rate coefficients k_2 and k_3

Pressure	1	1	1	1	1	1	1
Rate coefficient k_1	1	1	1	1	1	1	1
Rate coefficient k_2	**100**	**500**	**1000**	**5000**	**10,000**	**50,000**	**100,000**
Rate coefficient k_3	**100**	**500**	**1000**	**5000**	**10,000**	**50,000**	**100,000**
Rate coefficient k_4	10	10	10	10	10	10	10
$[A_2]$ Concentration	1	1	1	1	1	1	1
$[B_2]$ Concentration	1	1	1	1	1	1	1
$[M]$ Concentration	2	2	2	2	2	2	2
$[A]$ Concentration	0.01000999	0.0020007	0.00100000	2.00000E-4	1.00000E-4	2.00000E-5	1.00000E-5
$[B]$ Concentration	0.0099990000	0.0019999200	9.9999000E-4	1.9999992E-4	9.9999990E-5	2.0000000E-5	1.0000000E-5
$d[A_2]/dt$	-2.999000001	-2.999960000	-2.999990000	-2.999999600	-2.999999900	-2.999999996	-2.999999999
$d[B_2]/dt$	-1.0010000	-1.0000400	-1.0000100	-1.0000004	-1.0000001	-1.0000000	-1.0000000
$d[AB]/dt$	2.0019999980	2.0000800000	2.0000200000	2.0000008	2.0000002	2.000000008	2.000000002

TABLE 4.4
Effect of pressure

Pressure	0.1	0.5	1	5	10	50
Rate coefficient k_1	1	1	1	1	1	1
Rate coefficient k_2	1000	1000	1000	1000	1000	1000
Rate coefficient k_3	1000	1000	1000	1000	1000	1000
Rate coefficient k_4	10	10	10	10	10	10
$[A_2]$ Concentration	0.1	0.5	1	5	10	50
$[B_2]$ Concentration	0.1	0.5	1	5	10	50
$[M]$ Concentration	0.2	1	2	10	20	100
$[A]$ Concentration	1.00000E-4	5.00002E-4	0.00100000	0.00500024	0.01000099	0.05002499
$[B]$ Concentration	9.9999900E-5	4.9999750E-4	9.9999000E-4	0.0049997500	0.0099999000	0.0499750000
$d[A_2]/dt$	−0.029999989	−0.749998750	−2.999990000	−74.99875000	−299.9900000	−7,498.75000
$d[B_2]/dt$	−0.0100000	−0.2500012	−1.0000100	−25.001250	−100.01000	−2,501.250
$d[AB]/dt$	0.02000002	0.5000024999	2.0000200000	50.002500000	200.0200000	5,002.499999

TABLE 4.5
Effect of chain-termination-step rate coefficient k_4 at low pressure

Pressure	1	1	1	1	1	1	1
Rate coefficient k_1	1	1	1	1	1	1	1
Rate coefficient k_2	1000	1000	1000	1000	1000	1000	1000
Rate coefficient k_3	1000	1000	1000	1000	1000	1000	1000
Rate coefficient k_4	**0.001**	**0.01**	**0.1**	**1**	**10**	**100**	**1000**
[A$_2$] Concentration	1	1	1	1	1	1	1
[B$_2$] Concentration	1	1	1	1	1	1	1
[M] Concentration	2	2	2	2	2	2	2
[A] Concentration	0.00100000	0.00100000	0.00100000	0.00100000	0.00100000	0.00100009	0.00100099
[B] Concentration	1.0000000E-3	9.9999999E-4	9.9999990E-4	9.9999900E-4	9.9990000E-4	9.9990000E-4	9.9900000E-4
d[A$_2$]/dt	-2.999999999	-2.99999990	-2.999999900	-2.999999000	-2.999990000	-2.999900000	-2.999000001
d[B$_2$]/dt	-1.0000000	-1.0000000	-1.0000001	-1.0000010	-1.0000100	-1.0001000	-1.0010000
d[AB]/dt	2.000000002	2.00000002	2.0000002	2.0000200	2.0002000000	2.0002000000	2.0019999980

TABLE 4.6
Effect of chain-termination-step rate coefficient k_4 at high pressure

Pressure	100,000	100,000	100,000	100,000	100,000	100,000	100,000
Rate coefficient k_1	1	1	1	1	1	1	1
Rate coefficient k_2	1000	1000	1000	1000	1000	1000	1000
Rate coefficient k_3	1000	1000	1000	1000	1000	1000	1000
Rate coefficient k_4	**0.001**	**0.01**	**0.1**	**1**	**10**	**100**	**1000**
[A$_2$] Concentration	100,000	100,000	100,000	100,000	100,000	100,000	100,000
[B$_2$] Concentration	100,000	100,000	100,000	100,000	100,000	100,000	100,000
[M] Concentration	200,000	200,000	200,000	200,000	200,000	200,000	200,000
[A] Concentration	100.010000000	100.100000000	100.999900	109.901951	161.803399	195.124922	199.501250
[B] Concentration	99.990000000	99.900000100	99.000099980	90.09804641	38.196601125	4.8750780275	0.4987500078
$d[A_2]/dt$	-2.99990E + 10	-2.99900E + 10	-2.99000E + 10	-2.90098E + 10	-2.38197E + 10	-2.04875E + 10	-2.00499E + 10
$d[B_2]/dt$	-1.000E + 10	-1.001E + 10	-1.010E + 10	-1.099E + 10	-1.618E + 10	-1.951E + 10	-1.995E + 10
$d[AB]/dt$	2.000200E + 10	2.002000E + 10	2.019998E + 10	2.198039E + 10	3.236068E + 10	3.902498E + 10	3.990025E + 10

Example 4.3. As mentioned previously, a famous chain mechanism is the Zeldovich, or thermal, mechanism for the formation of nitric oxide from atmospheric nitrogen:

$$N_2 + O \xrightarrow{k_{1f}} NO + N,$$
$$N + O_2 \xrightarrow{k_{2f}} NO + O.$$

Because the second reaction is much faster than the first, the steady-state approximation can be used to evaluate the N-atom concentration. Furthermore, in high-temperature systems, the NO formation reaction is typically much slower than other reactions involving O_2 and O. Thus, O_2 and O can be assumed to be in equilibrium

$$O_2 \overset{K_p}{\Longleftrightarrow} 2O.$$

Construct a global mechanism

$$N_2 + O_2 \xrightarrow{k_G} 2NO$$

represented as

$$\frac{d[NO]}{dt} = k_G [N_2]^m [O_2]^n,$$

i.e., determine k_G, m, and n using the elementary rate coefficients, etc., from the detailed mechanism.

Solution. From the elementary reactions, we can write

$$\frac{d[NO]}{dt} = k_{1f} [N_2][O] + k_{2f} [N][O_2],$$

$$\frac{d[N]}{dt} = k_{1f} [N_2][O] - k_{2f} [N][O_2],$$

where we assume reverse reaction rates are negligible.

With the steady-state approximation, $d[N]/dt = 0$, thus

$$[N]_{ss} = \frac{k_{1f} [N_2][O]}{k_{2f} [O_2]}.$$

Substituting $[N]_{ss}$ into the above expression for $d[NO]/dt$, yields

$$\frac{d[NO]}{dt} = k_{1f} [N_2][O] + k_{2f} [O_2] \left(\frac{k_{1f} [N_2][O]}{k_{2f} [O_2]} \right)$$

$$= 2 k_{1f} [N_2][O].$$

We now eliminate [O] through our equilibrium approximation

$$K_p = \frac{P_O^2}{P_{O_2} P^o} = \frac{[O]^2 (R_u T)^2}{[O_2] (R_u T) P^o} = \frac{[O]^2}{[O_2]} \frac{R_u T}{P^o}$$

or

$$[O] = \left[[O_2] \frac{K_p P^o}{R_u T} \right]^{1/2}.$$

Thus,

$$\frac{d[NO]}{dt} = 2k_{1f}\left(\frac{K_p P^o}{R_u T}\right)^{1/2} [N_2][O_2]^{1/2}.$$

From the above, we can identify the global parameters:

$$\boxed{k_G \equiv 2k_{1f}\left(\frac{K_p P^o}{R_u T}\right)^{1/2}}$$

$$\boxed{\begin{aligned} m &= 1 \\ n &= 1/2 \end{aligned}}.$$

Comment. In many cases where global reactions are invoked, the detailed kinetics are not known. This example shows that global parameters can be interpreted or inferred from a knowledge of detailed chemistry. This allows the testing or verification of elementary mechanisms in terms of global measurements. Note, also, that the global mechanism developed above only applies to the initial formation rate of NO. This is because we have ignored the reverse reactions, which would become important as NO concentrations rise.

Example 4.4. Consider the shock-heating of air to 2500 K and 3 atm. Use the results of Example 4.3 to determine:

A. The initial nitric oxide formation rate in ppm/s.
B. The amount of nitric oxide formed (in ppm) in 0.25 ms.

The rate constant, k_{1f}, is given by [10]:

$$k_{1f} = 1.82 \cdot 10^{14} \exp[-38,370/T(K)]$$

$$[=] cm^3/gmol\text{-}s.$$

Solution

A. Find $d\chi_{NO}/dt$. We can evaluate $d[NO]/dt$ from

$$\frac{d[NO]}{dt} = 2k_{1f}\left(\frac{K_p P^o}{R_u T}\right)^{1/2} [N_2][O_2]^{1/2}$$

where we assume that

$$\chi_{N_2} \cong \chi_{N_2,i} = 0.79,$$

$$\chi_{O_2,e} \cong \chi_{O_2,i} = 0.21,$$

since χ_{NO} and χ_O are both likely to be quite small and, hence, can be neglected in estimating the values of χ_{N_2} and $\chi_{O_2,e}$.

We can convert the mole fractions to molar concentrations (Eqn. 4.40)

$$[\text{N}_2] = \chi_{\text{N}_2} \frac{P}{R_u T} = 0.79 \frac{3(101,325)}{8315(2500)},$$

$$= 1.155 \cdot 10^{-2} \, \text{kmol/m}^3,$$

$$[\text{O}_2] = \chi_{\text{O}_2} \frac{P}{R_u T} = 0.21 \frac{3(101,325)}{8315(2500)},$$

$$= 3.071 \cdot 10^{-3} \, \text{kmol/m}^3,$$

and evaluate the rate coefficient,

$$k_{1f} = 1.82 \cdot 10^{14} \exp[-38,370/2500]$$

$$= 3.93 \cdot 10^7 \, \text{cm}^3/\text{gmol-s}$$

$$= 3.93 \cdot 10^4 \, \text{m}^3 \text{kmol-s}.$$

To find the equilibrium constant, we employ Eqns. 2.64 and 2.66:

$$\Delta G_T^o = \left[(2)\bar{g}_{f,\text{O}}^o - (1)\bar{g}_{f,\text{O}_2}^o \right]_{2500\,\text{K}}$$

$$= 2(88,203) - (1)0 = 176,406 \, \text{kJ/kmol} \quad \text{(Tables A.11 and A.12)}$$

$$K_p = \frac{P_{\text{O}}^2}{P_{\text{O}_2} P^o} = \exp\left(\frac{-\Delta G_T^o}{R_u T} \right)$$

$$K_p P^o = \exp\left(\frac{-176,406}{8.315(2500)} \right) 1 \, \text{atm} = 2.063 \cdot 10^{-4} \, \text{atm} = 20.90 \, \text{Pa}.$$

We can now numerically evaluate d[NO]/dt:

$$\frac{d[\text{NO}]}{dt} = 2(3.93 \cdot 10^4) \left(\frac{20.90}{8315(2500)} \right)^{1/2} 1.155 \cdot 10^{-2} (3.071 \cdot 10^{-3})^{1/2}$$

$$= 0.0505 \, \text{kmol/m}^3\text{-s}$$

or, in terms of parts-per-million

$$\frac{d\chi_{\text{NO}}}{dt} = \frac{R_u T}{P} \frac{d[\text{NO}]}{dt}$$

$$= \frac{8315(2500)}{3(101,325)} 0.0505 = 3.45 \, (\text{kmol/kmol})/\text{s}$$

$$\boxed{\frac{d\chi_{\text{NO}}}{dt} = 3.45 \cdot 10^6 \, \text{ppm/s}}.$$

The reader should verify that the units are correct in the above calculations of d[NO]/dt and dχ_{NO}/dt.

B. Find $\chi_{\text{NO}}(t = 0.25\,\text{ms})$. If we assume that the N_2 and O_2 concentrations do not change with time and that reverse reactions are unimportant over the 0.25-ms interval, we can quite simply integrate d[NO]/dt or χ_{NO}/dt, i.e.,

$$\int_0^{[\text{NO}](t)} d[\text{NO}] = \int_0^t k_G[\text{N}_2][\text{O}_2]^{1/2} dt$$

so

$$[NO](t) = k_G[N_2][O_2]^{1/2} t$$
$$= 0.0505\,(0.25 \cdot 10^{-3}) = 1.263 \cdot 10^{-5}\,\text{kmol/m}^3$$

or

$$\chi_{NO} = [NO]\frac{R_u T}{P}$$
$$= 1.263 \cdot 10^{-5}\left(\frac{8315\,(2500)}{3\,(101,325)}\right) = 8.64 \cdot 10^{-4}\,\text{kmol/kmol}$$

$$\boxed{\chi_{NO} = 864\,\text{ppm}}\,.$$

Comment. We could use the above value of NO together with the appropriate reverse reaction rate coefficients to see the relative importance of the reverse reactions in the Zeldovich mechanism (Example 4.3) to determine if our approach to Part B was valid.

The next chapter outlines several chemical mechanisms that have importance to combustion and shows the usefulness of the theoretical concepts presented in this chapter.

SUMMARY

In this chapter, we explored many concepts essential to the understanding of combustion chemistry. You should be able to distinguish between global and elementary reactions and mechanisms and have an appreciation for the types of elementary reactions, i.e., bimolecular, termolecular, and unimolecular. You should also have an understanding of the relation between molecular collision theory and reaction rates. In particular, you should understand the physical meaning of the steric factor, pre-exponential factor, and activation energy—components of the rate coefficient that have their origins in collision theory. We also developed the concept of net species production rates and procedures to formulate appropriate equations from complex mechanisms. A compact notation was introduced to facilitate numerical calculations using a computer. The final topic of discussion was chain mechanisms and the concepts of chain initiation, chain propagation, and chain termination. The idea of a steady state for highly reactive species, such as atoms and other radicals, was introduced and used to simplify chain mechanisms. The Zeldovich nitric oxide formation mechanism, introduced in the examples, was used to illustrate many of the concepts in concrete ways.

NOMENCLATURE

A	Pre-exponential factor (various units)
b	Temperature exponent
E_A	Activation energy (J/kmol)

k	Rate constant (various units)
k_B	Boltzmann constant, $1.381 \cdot 10^{-23}$ (J/K)
K_c	Equilibrium constant based on concentrations
K_p	Equilibrium constant based on partial pressures
m	Mass (kg) or reaction order
M	Third-body collision partner
n	Reaction order
n/V	Number density (molecules/m^3 or 1/m^3)
N_{AV}	Avogadro number, $6.022 \cdot 10^{26}$ (molecules/kmol)
p	Steric factor
P	Pressure
$\mathcal{P}$	Probability
q	Rate-of-progress variable, Eqn. 4.33
R_u	Universal gas constant (J/kmol-K)
t	Time (s)
T	Temperature (K)
v	Velocity (m/s)
$\bar{v}$	Maxwellian mean velocity (m/s)
V	Volume (m^3)
X_j	Chemical formula of species j, Eqn. 4.29
Z_c	Collision frequency (1/s)

Greek symbols

Δt	Time interval(s)
μ	Reduced mass (kg)
ν'	Reactant stoichiometric coefficient
ν''	Product stoichiometric coefficient
ν_{ji}	$\nu_{ji}'' - \nu_{ji}'$, Eqn. 4.32
χ	Mole fraction
$\dot{\omega}$	Net species volumetric production rate (kmol/m^3-s)

Subscripts

app	Apparent
bimolec	Bimolecular
de	De-energized
e	Energized
f	Forward
F	Fuel
G	Global or overall
i	ith species
Ox	Oxidizer
Pr	Products
r	Reverse

ss	Steady state
ter	Termolecular
uni	Unimolecular

Other notation

$[X]$	Molar concentration of species X (kmol/m^3)
$\prod$	Multiplication

REFERENCES

1. Kee, R. J., Rupley, F. M., and Miller, J. A., "Chemkin-II: A Fortran Chemical Kinetics Package for the Analysis of Gas-Phase Chemical Kinetics," Sandia National Laboratories Report SAND89-8009, March 1991.
2. Gardiner, W. C., Jr., *Rates and Mechanisms of Chemical Reactions*, Benjamin, Menlo Park, CA, 1972.
3. Benson, S. W., *The Foundations of Chemical Kinetics*, McGraw-Hill, New York, 1960.
4. Warnatz, J., "Rate Coefficients in the C/H/O System," Chapter 5 in *Combustion Chemistry* (W. C. Gardiner, Jr., ed.), Springer-Verlag, New York, pp. 197–360, 1984.
5. IMSL, Inc., "DGEAR," IMSL Library, Houston, TX.
6. Hindmarsh, A. C., "ODEPACK, A Systematic Collection of ODE Solvers," *Scientific Computing—Applications of Mathematics and Computing to the Physical Sciences* (R. S. Stapleman, ed.), North-Holland, Amsterdam, p. 55, 1983.
7. Bittker, D. A., and Soullin, V. J., "GCKP-84-General Chemical Kinetics Code for Gas Flow and Batch Processing Including Heat Transfer," NASA TP-2320, 1984.
8. Pratt, D. T., and Radhakrishnan, K., "CREK-ID: A Computer Code for Transient, Gas-Phase Combustion Kinetics," NASA Technical Memorandum TM-83806, 1984.
9. National Institute of Standards and Technology, NIST Chemical Kinetics Database, NIST, Gaithersburg, MD, published annually.
10. Hanson, R. K., and Salimian, S., "Survey of Rate Constants in the N/H/O System," Chapter 6 in *Combustion Chemistry* (W. C. Gardiner, Jr., ed.), Springer-Verlag, New York, pp. 361–421, 1984.
11. Williams, F. A., *Combustion Theory*, 2nd Ed., Addison-Wesley, Redwood City, CA, p. 565, 1985.
12. Gardiner, W. C., Jr., and Troe, J., "Rate Coefficients of Thermal Dissociation, Isomerization, and Recombination Reactions," Chapter 4 in *Combustion Chemistry* (W. C. Gardiner, Jr., ed.), Springer-Verlag, New York, pp. 173–196, 1984.
13. Svehla, R. A., "Estimated Viscosities and Thermal Conductivities of Gases at High Temperature," NASA Technical Report R-132, 1962.

QUESTIONS AND PROBLEMS

4.1. Make a list of all of the bold-faced words in Chapter 4 and discuss their meanings.

4.2. Several species and their structural forms are given below. Using sketches of colliding molecules, show that the reaction $2H_2 + O_2 \rightarrow 2H_2O$ is highly improbable based on simple collisions and the given structures.

$$H_2 \quad : \quad H - H$$
$$O_2 \quad : \quad O = O$$
$$H_2O \quad : \quad H \overset{\frown}{} O \overset{\frown}{} H$$

4.3. Consider the reaction $H_2 + O_2 \rightarrow HO_2 + H$. Show that this is likely to be an elementary reaction. Use a sketch, as in problem 4.2. The structure of the hydroperoxy radical is $H - O - O$.

4.4. Consider the overall oxidation reaction of propane:

$$C_3H_8 + 5O_2 \rightarrow 3CO_2 + 4H_2O.$$

The following global mechanism has been proposed for this reaction:

$$\text{Reaction rate} = 8.6 \cdot 10^{11} \exp(-30/R_u T)[C_3H_8]^{0.1}[O_2]^{1.65}$$

where CGS units (cm, s, gmol, kcal, K) are employed.

A. Identify the order of the reaction with respect to propane.
B. Identify the order of the reaction with respect to O_2.
C. What is the overall order of the global reaction?
D. Identify the activation energy for the reaction.

4.5. Classify the following reactions as being either global or elementary. For those identified as elementary, further classify them as unimolecular, bimolecular or termolecular. Give reasons for your classification.

A. $CO + OH \rightarrow CO_2 + H$
B. $2CO + O_2 \rightarrow 2CO_2$
C. $H_2 + O_2 \rightarrow H + H + O_2$
D. $HOCO \rightarrow H + CO_2$
E. $CH_4 + 2O_2 \rightarrow CO_2 + 2H_2O$
F. $OH + H + M \rightarrow H_2O + M.$

4.6. The following hard-sphere collision diameters, σ, are take from Svehla [13]:

Molecule	σ (Å)
H	2.708
H_2	2.827
OH	3.147
H_2O	2.641
O	3.050
O_2	3.467

Using the above data with Eqn. 4.17 and Table 4.1, determine a temperature-dependent expression for the steric factors for the rate constants of the following reactions. Evaluate the steric factor at a temperature of 2500 K. Be careful with units and remember that the reduced mass should be in grams or kilograms.

$$H + O_2 \rightarrow OH + O$$

$$OH + O \rightarrow O_2 + H$$

4.7. Plot the forward rate constant for the reaction $O + N_2 \rightarrow NO + N$ versus temperature for the temperature range $1500\,K < T < 2500\,K$. The rate constant is given as [10] $k(T) = 1.82 \cdot 10^{14} \exp[-38,370/T(K)]$ in units of $cm^3/gmol$-s. What conclusions can you draw?

4.8. Consider the following mechanism for the production of ozone from the heating of oxygen:

$$O_3 \underset{k_{1r}}{\overset{k_{1f}}{\rightleftharpoons}} O_2 + O \tag{R.1}$$

$$O + O_3 \underset{k_{2r}}{\overset{k_{2f}}{\rightleftharpoons}} 2O_2 \tag{R.2}$$

A. Write out the coefficient matrices for ν'_{ji} and ν''_{ji}. Use the convention that species 1 is O_3, species 2 is O_2, and species 3 is O.
B. Starting with the compact notation defined by Eqns. 4.31–4.33, express the rate of progress variables, $\dot{\omega}_j$, for the three species involved in the above mechanism. Retain all terms without simplifying, i.e., retain terms raised to the zero power.

4.9. Generate the coefficient matrices ν'_{ji} and ν''_{ji} for the H_2–O_2 reaction mechanism (H.1–H.20) given in Chapter 5. Consider both forward and reverse reactions. Do not attempt to include the radical destruction at the walls (Eqn. H.21).

4.10. Consider the following chain-reaction mechanism for the high-temperature formation of nitric oxide, i.e., the Zeldovich mechanism:

$$O + N_2 \overset{k_{1f}}{\rightarrow} NO + N \qquad \text{Reaction 1}$$

$$N + O_2 \overset{k_{2f}}{\rightarrow} NO + O \qquad \text{Reaction 2.}$$

A. Write out expressions for $d[NO]/dt$ and $d[N]/dt$.
B. Assuming N atoms exist in steady state and that the concentrations of O, O_2, and N_2 are at their equilibrium values for a specified temperature and composition, simplify your expression obtained above for $d[NO]/dt$ for the case of negligible reverse reactions. (Answer: $d[NO]/dt = 2k_{1f}[O]_{eq}[N_2]_{eq}$.)
C. Write out the expression for the steady-state N-atom concentration used in part B above.
D. For the conditions given below and using the assumptions of part B above, how long does it take to form 50 ppm (mole fraction $\cdot 10^6$) of NO?

$$T = 2100\,\text{K}$$
$$p = 0.167\,\text{kg/m}^3$$
$$MW = 28.778$$
$$\chi_{O,eq} = 7.6 \cdot 10^{-5} \qquad \text{(mole fraction)}$$
$$\chi_{O_2,eq} = 3.025 \cdot 10^{-3} \qquad \text{(mole fraction)}$$
$$\chi_{N_2,eq} = 0.726 \qquad \text{(mole fraction)}$$
$$k_{1f} = 1.82 \cdot 10^{14} \exp[-38,370/T(\text{K})] \text{ with units of cm}^3/\text{gmol-s}.$$

E. Calculate the value of the reverse reaction rate constant for the first reaction, i.e., $O + N_2 \leftarrow NO + N$, for a temperature of 2100 K.
F. For your computations in part D above, how good is the assumption that reverse reactions are negligible? Be quantitative.
G. For the conditions of part D above, determine numerical values for [N] and χ_N. (Note: $k_{2f} = 1.8 \cdot 10^{10}\, T \exp(-4680/T)$ with units of cm^3/gmol-s.)

4.11. When the following reaction is added to the two reactions in problem 4.10 above, the NO formation mechanism is called the extended Zeldovich mechanism:

$$N + OH \xrightarrow{k_{3f}} NO + H.$$

With the assumption of equilibrium concentrations of O, O_2, N_2, H, and OH applied to this three-step mechanism, find expressions for:

A. The steady-state N-atom concentration, neglecting reverse reactions.
B. The NO formation rate $d[NO]/dt$, again neglecting reverse reactions.

CHAPTER

5

SOME
IMPORTANT
CHEMICAL
MECHANISMS

OVERVIEW

Our approach in this chapter will be to present, or outline, the elementary steps involved in a number of chemical mechanisms of major importance to combustion and combustion-generated air pollution. For detailed discussions of these mechanisms, the reader is referred to the original literature, reviews, and more advanced textbooks that emphasize kinetics [1,2]. Our purpose is simply to illustrate real systems, which are generally complex, and to show that the fundamentals discussed in the previous chapter are indeed important to understanding such systems.

It is important to point out that complex mechanisms are evolutionary products of chemists' thoughts and experiments, and, as such, they may change with time as new insights are developed. Thus when we discuss a particular mechanism, we are not referring to *the* mechanism in the same sense that we refer to *the* first law of thermodynamics, or other well-known conservation principles.

THE H_2–O_2 SYSTEM

The hydrogen–oxygen system is important in its own right as, for example, in rocket propulsion. This system is also important as a subsystem in the oxidation of hydrocarbons and moist carbon monoxide. Detailed reviews of H_2–O_2 kinetics can be found in Refs. [3]–[5]. Relying heavily on Glassman [1], we outline the oxidation of hydrogen as follows.

The initiation reactions are:

$$H_2 + M \rightarrow H + H + M \quad \text{(very high temperatures)} \tag{H.1}$$

$$H_2 + O_2 \rightarrow HO_2 + H \quad \text{(other temperatures).} \tag{H.2}$$

Chain-reaction steps involving O, H, and OH radicals are:

$$H + O_2 \rightarrow O + OH \tag{H.3}$$

$$O + H_2 \rightarrow H + OH \tag{H.4}$$

$$H_2 + OH \rightarrow H_2O + H \tag{H.5}$$

$$O + H_2O \rightarrow OH + OH. \tag{H.6}$$

Chain-terminating steps involving O, H, and OH radicals are the three-body recombination reactions,

$$H + H + M \rightarrow H_2 + M \tag{H.7}$$

$$O + O + M \rightarrow O_2 + M \tag{H.8}$$

$$H + O + M \rightarrow OH + M \tag{H.9}$$

$$H + OH + M \rightarrow H_2O + M. \tag{H.10}$$

To complete the mechanism, we need to include reactions involving HO_2, the hydroperoxy radical, and H_2O_2, hydrogen peroxide. When

$$H + O_2 + M \rightarrow HO_2 + M \tag{H.11}$$

becomes active, then the following reactions, and the reverse of H.2 come into play:

$$HO_2 + H \rightarrow OH + OH \tag{H.12}$$

$$HO_2 + H \rightarrow H_2O + O \tag{H.13}$$

$$HO_2 + O \rightarrow O_2 + OH \tag{H.14}$$

and

$$HO_2 + HO_2 \rightarrow H_2O_2 + O_2 \tag{H.15}$$

$$HO_2 + H_2 \rightarrow H_2O_2 + H \tag{H.16}$$

with

$$H_2O_2 + OH \rightarrow H_2O + HO_2 \tag{H.17}$$

$$H_2O_2 + H \rightarrow H_2O + OH \tag{H.18}$$

$$H_2O_2 + H \rightarrow HO_2 + H_2 \tag{H.19}$$

$$H_2O_2 + M \rightarrow OH + OH + M. \tag{H.20}$$

Depending upon the temperature, pressure, and extent of reaction, the reverse reactions of all of the above can be important; therefore, in modeling the H_2–O_2 system as many as 40 reactions can be taken into account involving the eight species: H_2, O_2, H_2O, OH, O, H, HO_2, and H_2O_2.

The H_2–O_2 system has interesting explosion characteristics (Fig. 5.1) that can be explained using the above mechanism. Figure 5.1 shows that there are distinct regions in temperature–pressure coordinates where a stoichiometric mixture of H_2 and O_2 will and will not explode. The temperatures and pressures correspond to the initial charging conditions of the spherical vessel containing the reactants. To explore the explosion behavior, let us follow a vertical line, say at 500°C, from the lowest pressure shown (1 mm Hg) upwards to pressures of several atmospheres. Up until about 1.5 mm Hg, there is no explosion. This lack of explosion is the result of the free radicals produced in the initiation step (H.2) and chain sequence (H.3–H.6) being destroyed by reactions on the walls of the vessel. These wall reactions break the chain, preventing the rapid build-up of radicals that leads to explosion. The wall reactions are not explicitly included in the mechanism since they are not strictly gas-phase reactions. We can symbolically write a first-order reaction for wall destruction of radicals as

$$\text{Radical} \xrightarrow{k_{wall}} \text{absorbed products} \tag{H.21}$$

Where k_{wall} is a function of both diffusion (transport) and chemical processes, as well as the nature of the wall surface. Reactions of gaseous species at solid surfaces are called **heterogeneous** reactions and are quite important in solids combustion (Chapter 14) and catalysis.

When the initial pressure is set above approximately 1.5 mm Hg, the mixture explodes. This is a direct result of the gas-phase chain sequence H.3–H.6 prevailing over the radical destruction at the wall. Recall from our examination of a generic chain mechanism that increasing pressure increased the radical concentration linearly, while increasing the reaction rate geometrically (cf. Table 4.4).

Continuing our journey up the 500°C isotherm, we remain in an explosive regime until about 50 mm Hg; at this point, the mixture ceases to be explosive. The cessation of explosive behavior can be explained by the competition for H atoms between the chain-branching reaction, H.3, and what is effectively a chain-terminating step at low temperatures, reaction H.11 [1,2]. Reaction H.11 is chain-terminating because the hydroperoxy radical, HO_2, is relatively unreactive at these conditions, and because of this, it can diffuse to the wall where it is destroyed (H.21).

At the third limit, we cross over again into an explosive regime at about 3000 mm Hg. At these conditions, reaction H.16 adds a chain-branching step which opens up the H_2O_2 chain sequence [1,2].

From this brief discussion of the explosion limits of the H_2–O_2 system, it is clear how useful an understanding of the *detailed* chemistry of a system is in

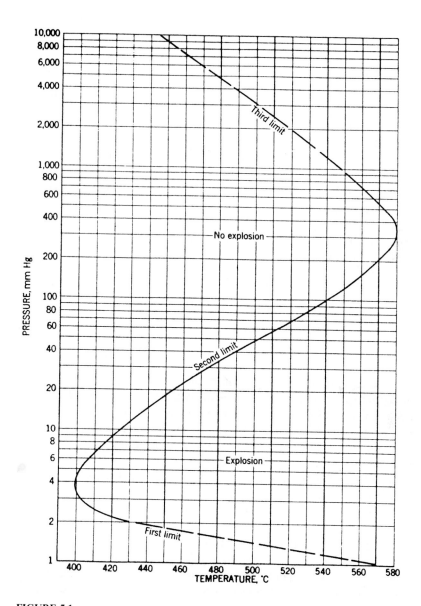

FIGURE 5.1
Explosion limits for a stoichiometric hydrogen–oxygen mixture in a spherical vessel. (From Ref. [2].
Reprinted by permission of Academic Press.)

explaining experimental observations. It is also clear that such understanding is essential to the development of predictive models of combustion phenomena when chemical effects are important.

CARBON MONOXIDE OXIDATION

Although the oxidation of carbon monoxide has importance in its own right, it is extremely important to the oxidation of hydrocarbons. Hydrocarbon combustion simplistically can be characterized as a two-step process: the first step involves the breakdown of the fuel to carbon monoxide, with the second step being the final oxidation of carbon monoxide to carbon dioxide.

It is well known that CO is slow to oxidize unless there are some hydrogen-containing species present; small quantities of H_2O or H_2 can have a tremendous effect on the oxidation rate. This is because the CO oxidation step involving the hydroxyl radical is much faster than the steps involving O_2 and O.

Assuming water is the primary hydrogen-containing species, the following four steps describe the oxidation of CO [1]:

$$CO + O_2 \rightarrow CO_2 + O \tag{CO.1}$$

$$O + H_2O \rightarrow OH + OH \tag{CO.2}$$

$$CO + OH \rightarrow CO_2 + H \tag{CO.3}$$

$$H + O_2 \rightarrow OH + O. \tag{CO.4}$$

The reaction CO.1 is slow and does not contribute significantly to the formation of CO_2, but rather serves as the initiator of the chain sequence. The actual CO oxidation step, CO.3, is also a chain-propagating step, producing H atoms that react with O_2 to form OH and O (Reaction CO.4). These radicals in turn feed back into the oxidation step (CO.3) and the first chain-branching step (CO.2). The $CO + OH \rightarrow CO_2 + H$ (CO.3) is a key reaction in the overall scheme.

If hydrogen is the catalyst instead of water, the following steps are involved [1]:

$$O + H_2 \rightarrow OH + H \tag{CO.5}$$

$$OH + H_2 \rightarrow H_2O + H. \tag{CO.6}$$

With hydrogen present, the entire H_2–O_2 reaction system (H.1–H.21) needs to be included to describe the CO oxidation. Glassman [1] indicates that with HO_2 present, another route for CO oxidation opens up:

$$CO + HO_2 \rightarrow CO_2 + OH, \tag{CO.7}$$

although this reaction is not nearly as important as the OH attack on CO, i.e., reaction CO.3. A comprehensive CO oxidation mechanism is presented in Ref. [5].

OXIDATION OF HIGHER PARAFFINS

General Scheme

Paraffins, or **alkanes**, are saturated, straight-chain or branched-chain, single-bonded hydrocarbons with the general molecular formula, C_nH_{2n+2}. In this section, we briefly discuss the generic oxidation of the higher paraffins, i.e., $n > 2$. The oxidation of methane (and ethane) exhibits unique characteristics and will be discussed in the next section.

Our discussion of higher paraffins is different from the preceding sections in that no attempt is made to explore or list the many elementary reactions involved; rather we will present an overview of the oxidation process, indicating key reaction steps, and then briefly discuss multi-step global approaches that have been applied with some success.

The oxidation of paraffins can be characterized by three sequential processes [1], given below, and illustrated by the species and temperature distributions shown in Fig. 5.2:

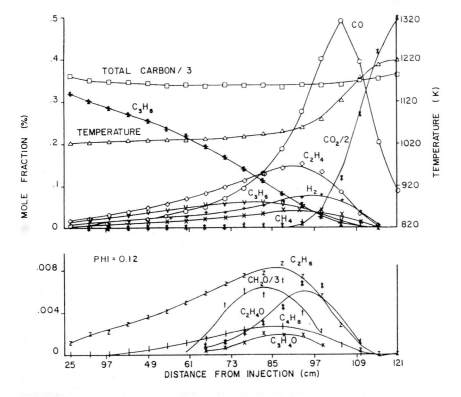

FIGURE 5.2
Species mole fractions and temperature as functions of distance (time) for the oxidation of propane in a steady-flow reactor. (From Ref. [7]. Reprinted by permission of Gordon & Breach Science Publishers.)

I. The fuel molecule is attacked by O and H atoms, breaks down, primarily forming olefins and hydrogen. The hydrogen oxidizes to water, subject to available oxygen.

II. The unsaturated olefins further oxidize to CO and H_2. Essentially, all of the H_2 is converted to water.

III. The CO burns out via reaction (CO.3), $CO + OH \rightarrow CO_2 + H$. Nearly all of the heat release associated with the overall combustion process occurs in this step.

We will now flesh out these three processes in steps 1–8, following Glassman [1], and illustrate them with the example of propane (C_3H_8) oxidation.

Step 1. A carbon–carbon (C–C) bond is broken in the original fuel molecule. The C–C bonds are preferentially broken over hydrogen–carbon bonds because the C–C bonds are weaker.

$$\text{Example}: \quad C_3H_8 + M \rightarrow C_2H_5 + CH_3 + M. \tag{P.1}$$

Step 2. The two resulting hydrocarbon radicals break down further, creating olefins (hydrocarbons with double carbon bonds) and hydrogen atoms. The removal of an H atom from the hydrocarbon is termed **H-atom abstraction**. In the example for this step, ethylene and methylene are produced.

$$\text{Example}: \quad C_2H_5 + M \rightarrow C_2H_4 + H + M \tag{P.2a}$$

$$CH_3 + M \rightarrow CH_2 + H + M. \tag{P.2b}$$

Step 3. The creation of H atoms from Step 2 starts the development of a pool of radicals.

$$\text{Example}: \quad H + O_2 \rightarrow O + OH. \tag{P.3}$$

Step 4. With the establishment of the radicals, new fuel-molecule attack pathways open up.

$$\text{Example}: \quad C_3H_8 + OH \rightarrow C_3H_7 + H_2O \tag{P.4a}$$

$$C_3H_8 + H \rightarrow C_3H_7 + H_2 \tag{P.4b}$$

$$C_3H_8 + O \rightarrow C_3H_7 + OH. \tag{P.4c}$$

Step 5. As in Step 2, the hydrocarbon radicals again decay into olefins and H atoms via H-atom abstraction,

$$\text{Example}: \quad C_3H_7 + M \rightarrow C_3H_6 + H + M, \tag{P.5}$$

and following the β-**scission rule** [1]. This rule states that the C–C or C–H bond broken will be the one that is one place removed from the radical site, i.e., the site of the unpaired electron. The unpaired electron at the radical site strengthens the adjacent bonds at the expense of those one place removed from the site. For the C_3H_7 radical created in Step 4, we have two possible paths:

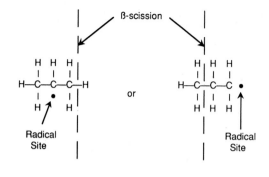

FIGURE 5.3

β-scission rule applied to bond breaking in C_3H_7 where the radical site occurs at different locations. Note the intervening C—C bond between the radical site and the broken bond.

$$\textit{Example}: C_3H_7 + M \nearrow \begin{array}{l} C_3H_6 + H + M \\[1em] C_2H_4 + CH_3 + M \end{array} \quad (P.6)$$

The application of the β-scission rule to the C_3H_7 radical breakdown (P.6) is illustrated in Fig. 5.3.

Step 6. The oxidation of the olefins created in Steps 2 and 5 is initiated by O-atom attack, which produces formyl radicals (HCO) and formaldehyde (H_2CO).

$$\textit{Example}: \quad C_3H_6 + O \rightarrow C_2H_5 + HCO \quad (P.7a)$$
$$C_3H_6 + O \rightarrow C_2H_4 + H_2CO. \quad (P.7b)$$

Step 7a. Methyl radicals (CH_3) oxidize.

Step 7b. Formaldehyde (H_2CO) oxidizes.

Step 7c. Methylene (CH_2) oxidizes.

The details of Steps 7a–7c can be found in Ref. [1]; however, each of these steps produce carbon monoxide, the oxidation of which is the final step (Step 8).

Step 8. The carbon monoxide oxidizes following the moist CO mechanism defined by CO.1–CO.7.

As can be seen from the above, the mechanism of higher-paraffin oxidation is quite complex indeed. The details of such mechanisms are still the subject of research.

Global and Quasi-Global Mechanisms

The sequential nature of the processes I–III above has led to empirical global models that capture the overall behavior in a sequence of global or quasi-global steps. Westbrook and Dryer [6] present and evaluate one-step, two-step, and multi-step global kinetics for a wide variety of hydrocarbons. Gobal models, by definition, do not capture the details of hydrocarbon oxidation; they may, however, be useful for engineering approximations, if their limitations are recognized. The following single-step expression [6] is suggested for engineering approximations for the global reaction,

$$C_xH_y + (x + y/4)O_2 \xrightarrow{k_G} xCO_2 + (y/2)H_2O \qquad (5.1)$$

$$\frac{d[C_xH_y]}{dt} = -A \exp(-E_a/R_uT)[C_xH_y]^m[O_2]^n \qquad (5.2)$$

$$[=] \text{ gmol/cm}^3\text{-s}$$

where the parameters A, E_a/R_u, m, and n, shown in Table 5.1 have been chosen to provide best agreement between experimental and predicted flame speeds and flammability limits (see Chapter 8).

An example of a multi-step, quasi-global mechanism is that of Hautman *et al.* [7], modeling propane oxidation using a four-step scheme:

$$C_nH_{2n+2} \rightarrow (n/2)C_2H_4 + H_2 \qquad (HC.1)$$

$$C_2H_4 + O_2 \rightarrow 2CO + 2H_2 \qquad (HC.2)$$

$$CO + \tfrac{1}{2}O_2 \rightarrow CO_2 \qquad (HC.3)$$

$$H_2 + \tfrac{1}{2}O_2 \rightarrow H_2O \qquad (HC.4)$$

where the reaction rates (in gmol/cm³-s) are expressed

$$\frac{d[C_nH_{2n+2}]}{dt} = -10^x \exp(-E_A/R_uT)[C_nH_{2n+2}]^a[O_2]^b[C_2H_4]^c \qquad (5.3)$$

$$\frac{d[C_2H_4]}{dt} = -10^x \exp(-E_A/R_uT)[C_2H_4]^a[O_2]^b[C_nH_{2n+2}]^c \qquad (5.4)$$

$$\frac{d[CO]}{dt} = -10^x \exp(-E_A/R_uT)[CO]^a[O_2]^b[H_2O]^c 7.93 \exp(-2.48\Phi) \qquad (5.5)$$

$$\frac{d[H_2]}{dt} = -10^x \exp(-E_A/R_uT)[H_2]^a[O_2]^b[C_2H_4]^c \qquad (5.6)$$

where Φ is the equivalence ratio. The exponents x, a, b, and c for each reaction are given in Table 5.2.

Notice that in the mechanism it is assumed that ethylene (C_2H_4) is the intermediate hydrocarbon; and that in the rate equations, C_3H_8 and C_2H_4 inhibit the oxidation of C_2H_4 and H_2, respectively, since the C_3H_8 and C_2H_4 exponents are negative. Note also that the rate equations do not directly follow from the global steps, since Eqns. 5.3–5.6 involve the product of three species, not just two, as suggested by the individual global steps HC.1–HC.4. More recent approaches to simplified hydrocarbon oxidation are discussed in Ref. [8].

TABLE 5.1
Single-step reaction rate parameters for use with Eqn. 5.2. (Adapted from Ref. [6])

Fuel	Pre-exponential factor, A^a	Activation temperature, E_a/R_u (K)	m	n
CH_4	$1.3 \cdot 10^8$	$24{,}358^b$	-0.3	1.3
CH_4	$8.3 \cdot 10^5$	$15{,}098^c$	-0.3	1.3
C_2H_6	$1.1 \cdot 10^{12}$	$15{,}098$	0.1	1.65
C_3H_8	$8.6 \cdot 10^{11}$	$15{,}098$	0.1	1.65
C_4H_{10}	$7.4 \cdot 10^{11}$	$15{,}098$	0.15	1.6
C_5H_{12}	$6.4 \cdot 10^{11}$	$15{,}098$	0.25	1.5
C_6H_{14}	$5.7 \cdot 10^{11}$	$15{,}098$	0.25	1.5
C_7H_{16}	$5.1 \cdot 10^{11}$	$15{,}098$	0.25	1.5
C_8H_{18}	$4.6 \cdot 10^{11}$	$15{,}098$	0.25	1.5
C_8H_{18}	$7.2 \cdot 10^{12}$	$20{,}131^d$	0.25	1.5
C_9H_{20}	$4.2 \cdot 10^{11}$	$15{,}098$	0.25	1.5
$C_{10}H_{22}$	$3.8 \cdot 10^{11}$	$15{,}098$	0.25	1.5
CH_3OH	$3.2 \cdot 10^{12}$	$15{,}098$	0.25	1.5
C_2H_5OH	$1.5 \cdot 10^{12}$	$15{,}098$	0.15	1.6
C_6H_6	$2.0 \cdot 10^{11}$	$15{,}098$	-0.1	1.85
C_7H_8	$1.6 \cdot 10^{11}$	$15{,}098$	-0.1	1.85
C_2H_4	$2.0 \cdot 10^{12}$	$15{,}098$	0.1	1.65
C_3H_6	$4.2 \cdot 10^{11}$	$15{,}098$	-0.1	1.85
C_2H_2	$6.5 \cdot 10^{12}$	$15{,}098$	0.5	1.25

^{a}Units of A are consistent with concentrations in Eqn. 5.1 expressed in units of gmol/cm^3, i.e., $A[=]$ (gmol/cm$^3)^{1-m-n}$/s.

$^b E_a = 48.4$ kcal/gmol.

$^c E_a = 30$ kcal/gmol.

$^d E_a = 40$ kcal/gmol.

TABLE 5.2
Constants^a for multi-step global mechanism for C_nH_{2n+2} oxidation [7]

	Propane ($n = 3$)			
Rate eqn.	5.3	5.4	5.5	5.6
x	17.32	14.7	14.6	13.52
$[E_A/R_u]$ (K)	$24{,}962$	$25{,}164$	$20{,}131$	$20{,}634$
a	0.50	0.90	1.0	0.85
b	1.07	1.18	0.25	1.42
c	0.40	-0.37	0.50	-0.56

^{a}Initial conditions: T(K): 960–1145; $[C_3H_8]_i$ (gmol/cm^3): $1 \cdot 10^{-8}$–$1 \cdot 10^{-7}$; $[O_2]_i$ (gmol/cm^3): $1 \cdot 10^{-7}$–$5 \cdot 10^{-6}$; Φ : 0.03–2.0.

METHANE COMBUSTION

Complex Mechanism

Because of its unique tetrahedral molecular structure with large C–H bond energies, methane exhibits some unique combustion characteristics. For example, it has a high ignition temperature, low flame speed, and is essentially unreactive in photochemical smog chemistry.

Methane chemical kinetics are perhaps the most widely researched, and, hence, most well understood. Kaufman [9], in a review of combustion kinetics, indicated that the methane combustion mechanism evolved in the period 1970–1982, from less than 15 elementary steps with 12 species to 75 elementary steps, plus the 75 reverse reactions, with 25 species. The mechanism has evolved further to date (1992): Frenklach *et al.* [10] discuss the optimization of a methane kinetic mechanism that considers 149 elementary steps, with 144 reverse reactions, involving 33 species. This mechanism is shown in Table 5.3. Many of these steps we have seen before as part of the H_2 and CO oxidation mechanisms.

To make some sense of this complex system, we present Glassman's [1] overview of the low-temperature and high-temperature regimes of CH_4 oxidation.

Low-Temperature Simplified Mechanism

The following steps provide a description of the methane oxidation at temperatures below approximately 800 K:

$CH_4 + O_2 \rightarrow CH_3 + HO_2$	chain initiation	(M.1)
$CH_3 + O_2 \rightarrow CH_2O + OH$	chain propagating	(M.2)
$OH + CH_4 \rightarrow H_2O + CH_3$	chain propagating	(M.3)
$OH + CH_2O \rightarrow H_2O + HCO$	chain propagating	(M.4)
$CH_2O + O_2 \rightarrow HO_2 + HCO$	chain branching	(M.5)
$HCO + O_2 \rightarrow CO + HO_2$	chain propagating	(M.6)
$HO_2 + CH_4 \rightarrow H_2O_2 + CH_3$	chain propagating	(M.7)
$HO_2 + CH_2O \rightarrow H_2O_2 + HCO$	chain propagating	(M.8)
$OH \rightarrow wall$	chain termination	(M.9)
$HCO \rightarrow wall$	chain termination	(M.10)
$HO_2 \rightarrow wall$	chain termination	(M.11)

In the above, we see that CH_4 is first transformed to the methyl radical, CH_3, via the initiation step M.1. The methyl radical is oxidized in step M.2. The products of combustion formed in the low-temperature regime include: H_2O from steps M.3 and M.4, CO via reaction M.6; and H_2O_2 from steps M.7 and M.8. Thus, we see that complete combustion of CH_4 to CO_2 and H_2O is not possible at low temperatures in the absence of a catalyst.

TABLE 5.3
Complex methane mechanism from Frenklach *et al.* [10]

No.	Reaction[a]	ΔH^o_{298} (kJ/mol)	Forward rate coefficient[b]		
			A	n	E
	H_2/O_2 reactions				
1	$H + O_2 \Leftrightarrow OH + O$	70.5	1.59 (+17)	−0.927	70.6
2	$O + H_2 \Leftrightarrow OH + H$	8.2	3.87 (+04)	2.70	26.2
3	$OH + H_2 \Leftrightarrow H_2O + H$	−63.2	2.16 (+08)	1.51	14.4
4	$OH + OH \Leftrightarrow O + H_2O$	−71.3	2.10 (+08)	1.40	−1.6
5	$O + O + M \Leftrightarrow O_2 + M$	−498.3	1.00 (+17)	−1.00	
6	$H + H + M \Leftrightarrow H_2 + M$	−436.0	6.40 (+17)	−1.00	
7	$H + OH + M \Leftrightarrow H_2O + M$	−499.2	8.40 (+21)	−2.00	
	HO_2 reactions				
8	$H + O_2 + M \Leftrightarrow HO_2 + M$	−205.4	7.00 (+17)	−0.80	
9	$HO_2 + H \Leftrightarrow OH + OH$	−151.9	1.50 (+14)		4.2
10	$HO_2 + H \Leftrightarrow H_2 + O_2$	−230.5	2.50 (+13)		2.9
11	$HO_2 + H \Leftrightarrow H_2O + O$	−223.2	5.00 (+12)		5.9
12	$HO_2 + O \Leftrightarrow O_2 + OH$	−222.4	2.00 (+13)		
13	$HO_2 + OH \Leftrightarrow H_2O + O_2$	−293.7	6.02 (+13)		
14	$HO_2 + HO_2 \Leftrightarrow H_2O_2 + O_2$	−161.2	1.06 (+11)		−7.1
	H_2O_2 reactions				
15	$H_2O_2 + M \Leftrightarrow OH + OH + M$	214.8	1.00 (+17)		190.0
16	$H_2O_2 + H \Leftrightarrow HO_2 + H_2$	−69.3	1.70 (+12)		15.7
17	$H_2O_2 + H \Leftrightarrow H_2O + OH$	−284.4	1.00 (+13)		15.0
18	$H_2O_2 + O \Leftrightarrow HO_2 + OH$	−61.2	2.80 (+13)		26.8
19	$H_2O_2 + OH \Leftrightarrow H_2O + HO_2$	−132.5	7.00 (+12)		6.0
	CO/CO_2 reactions				
20	$HOCO (+M) \Leftrightarrow H + CO_2 (+M)$	38.9	2.29 (+26)	−3.02	146.7
			1.74 (+12)	0.31	137.8
21	$HOCO (+M) \Leftrightarrow CO + OH (+M)$	143.3	2.19 (+23)	−1.89	147.6
			5.89 (+12)	0.53	142.2
22	$CO + OH \Leftrightarrow CO_2 + H$	−104.3	1.17 (+07)	1.35	−3.0
			2.45 (−03)	3.68	−5.2
23	$CO + HO_2 \Leftrightarrow CO_2 + OH$	−256.2	1.50 (+14)		98.7
24	$CO + O + M \Leftrightarrow CO_2 + M$	−532.1	3.01 (+14)		12.6
25	$CO + O_2 \Leftrightarrow CO_2 + O$	−33.8	2.50 (+12)		200.0
	Reactions of CH_1 species				
26	$CH (X^2\Pi) + O \Leftrightarrow CO + H$	−739.1	1.00 (+14)		
27	$CH (X^2\Pi) + OH \Leftrightarrow HCO + H$	−376.7	3.00 (+13)		
28	$CH (X^2\Pi) + O_2 \Leftrightarrow CO + OH$	−668.5	2.00 (+13)		
29	$CH (A^2\Delta) \rightarrow CH (X^2\Pi)$	−274.0	1.90 (+06)		
30	$CH (A^2\Delta) + M \rightarrow CH (X^2\Pi) + M$	−274.0	4.00 (+10)	0.50	
31	$CH (A^2\Delta) + O_2 \rightarrow CH (X^2\Pi) + O_2$	−274.0	2.40 (+12)	0.50	
32	$HCO + H \Leftrightarrow H_2 + CO$	−370.5	7.23 (+13)		
33	$HCO + O \Leftrightarrow OH + CO$	−362.4	3.00 (+13)		
34	$HCO + O \Leftrightarrow H + CO_2$	−466.7	3.00 (+13)		
35	$HCO + OH \Leftrightarrow H_2O + CO$	−433.7	1.00 (+14)		
36	$HCO + O_2 \Leftrightarrow HO_2 + CO$	−140.0	4.20 (+12)		
37	$HCO + HCO \Leftrightarrow CH_2O + CO$	−303.1	2.00 (+13)		
38	$HCO + M \Leftrightarrow H + CO + M$	65.5	1.86 (+17)	−1.00	71.1

TABLE 5.3
(Continued)

No.	Reaction[a]	ΔH^o_{298} (kJ/mol)	Forward rate coefficient[b]		
			A	n	E
	Reactions of CH₂ species				
39	$^1CH_2 + H \Leftrightarrow CH\,(X^2\Pi) + H_2$	−45.4	3.00 (+13)		
40	$^1CH_2 + H_2 \Leftrightarrow CH_3 + H$	−59.9	7.23 (+13)		
41	$^1CH_2 + O \Leftrightarrow CO + H + H$	−348.4	1.50 (+13)		
42	$^1CH_2 + O \Leftrightarrow CO + H_2$	−784.4	1.50 (+13)		
43	$^1CH_2 + OH \Leftrightarrow CH_2O + H$	−354.7	3.00 (+13)		
44	$^1CH_2 + O_2 \Leftrightarrow CO + OH + H$	−277.9	3.10 (+13)		
45	$^1CH_2 + CH_3 \Leftrightarrow C_2H_4 + H$	−301.3	1.80 (+13)		
46	$^1CH_2 + M \Leftrightarrow {}^3CH_2 + M$	−34.3	6.00 (+12)		
47	$^3CH_2 + H \Leftrightarrow CH\,(X^2\Pi) + H_2$	−11.1	4.00 (+13)		
48	$^3CH_2 + O \Leftrightarrow CO + H + H$	−314.1	5.00 (+13)		
49	$^3CH_2 + OH \Leftrightarrow CH\,(X^2\Pi) + H_2O$	−74.2	1.13 (+07)	2.00	12.6
50	$^3CH_2 + OH \Leftrightarrow CH_2O + H$	−320.3	2.50 (+13)		
51	$^3CH_2 + O_2 \Leftrightarrow CO_2 + H + H$	−347.9	1.60 (+12)		4.2
52	$^3CH_2 + O_2 \Leftrightarrow CH_2O + O$	−249.8	5.00 (+13)		37.7
53	$^3CH_2 + O_2 \Leftrightarrow CO_2 + H_2$	−783.9	6.90 (+11)		2.1
54	$^3CH_2 + O_2 \Leftrightarrow CO + OH + H$	−243.6	8.60 (+10)		−2.1
55	$^3CH_2 + O_2 \Leftrightarrow HCO + OH$	−309.1	4.30 (+10)		−2.1
56	$^3CH_2 + {}^3CH_2 \Leftrightarrow C_2H_2 + H + H$	−117.4	1.00 (+14)		
57	$CH_2O + H \Leftrightarrow HCO + H_2$	−67.4	1.26 (+08)	1.62	9.1
58	$CH_2O + O \Leftrightarrow HCO + OH$	−59.2	3.50 (+13)		14.7
59	$CH_2O + OH \Leftrightarrow HCO + H_2O$	−130.6	7.23 (+05)	2.46	−4.1
60	$CH_2O + O_2 \Leftrightarrow HCO + HO_2$	163.1	1.00 (+14)		167.4
61	$CH_2O + HO_2 \Leftrightarrow HCO + H_2O_2$	1.9	1.00 (+12)		33.5
62	$CH_2O + CH_3 \Leftrightarrow HCO + CH_4$	−71.2	8.91 (−13)	7.40	−4.0
63	$CH_2O + M \Leftrightarrow HCO + H + M$	368.6	5.00 (+16)		320.0
64	$CH_2O + M \Leftrightarrow CO + H_2 + M$	−2.0	8.20 (+15)		291.0
	CH₃ reactions				
65	$CH_3 + H \Leftrightarrow {}^3CH_2 + H_2$	25.6	1.80 (+14)		63.2
66	$CH_3 + O \Leftrightarrow CH_2O + H$	−286.6	8.43 (+13)		
67	$CH_3 + OH \Leftrightarrow CH_2O + H_2$	−294.8	8.00 (+12)		
68	$CH_3 + OH \Leftrightarrow {}^3CH_2 + H_2O$	−37.6	1.13 (+06)	2.13	10.2
69	$CH_3 + O_2 \Leftrightarrow CH_3O + O$	118.6	1.00 (+14)		128.9
70	$CH_3 + O_2 \Leftrightarrow CH_2O + OH$	−216.1	5.20 (+13)		146.0
71	$CH_3 + HO_2 \Leftrightarrow CH_3O + OH$	−103.7	2.00 (+13)		
72	$CH_3 + HCO \Leftrightarrow CH_4 + CO$	−374.3	3.20 (+11)	0.50	
73	$CH_3 + M \Leftrightarrow {}^3CH_2 + H + M$	461.6	1.00 (+16)		379.0
74	$CH_3 + CH_3 \Leftrightarrow C_2H_5 + H$	31.3	5.00 (+12)	0.10	44.4
			3.80 (−07)	4.84	32.2
75	$CH_3 + CH_3 \Leftrightarrow CH_4 + {}^3CH_2$	21.8	1.70 (+09)	0.56	52.6
76	$CH_3 + {}^3CH_2 \Leftrightarrow C_2H_4 + H$	−267.0	5.00 (+13)		
	CH₄ reactions				
77	$CH_4\,(+M) \Leftrightarrow CH_3 + H\,(+M)$	439.7	1.29 (+33)	−3.73	445.6
			3.71 (+17)	−0.56	438.8
78	$CH_4 + H \Leftrightarrow CH_3 + H_2$	3.7	3.90 (+06)	2.11	32.4
79	$CH_4 + O \Leftrightarrow CH_3 + OH$	11.9	1.90 (+09)	1.44	36.3

TABLE 5.3
(Continued)

No.	Reaction[a]	ΔH^o_{298} (kJ/mol)	Forward rate coefficient[b]		
			A	n	E
	CH_4 reactions				
80	$CH_4 + O_2 \Leftrightarrow CH_3 + HO_2$	234.3	8.00 (+13)		234.3
81	$CH_4 + OH \Leftrightarrow CH_3 + H_2O$	−59.4	1.50 (+06)	2.13	10.2
82	$CH_4 + HO_2 \Leftrightarrow CH_3 + H_2O_2$	73.1	2.00 (+13)		75.3
	CH_3O reactions				
83	$CH_3O + H \Leftrightarrow CH_2O + H_2$	−342.9	2.00 (+13)		
84	$CH_3O + O \Leftrightarrow CH_2O + OH$	−334.7	5.00 (+12)		
85	$CH_3O + OH \Leftrightarrow CH_2O + H_2O$	−406.1	5.00 (+12)		
86	$CH_3O + O_2 \Leftrightarrow CH_2O + HO_2$	−112.3	4.28 (−13)	7.60	−14.8
87	$CH_3O + CO \Leftrightarrow CO_2 + CH_3$	−152.4	4.68 (+02)	3.16	22.5
88	$CH_3O + M \Leftrightarrow CH_2O + H + M$	93.1	1.00 (+14)		105.0
	CH_2OH reactions				
89	$CH_3 + OH \Leftrightarrow CH_2OH + H$	14.6	5.00 (+13)		20.0
90	$CH_2OH + H \Leftrightarrow CH_2O + H_2$	−309.4	2.00 (+13)		
91	$CH_2OH + O \Leftrightarrow CH_2O + OH$	−301.2	5.00 (+12)		
92	$CH_2OH + OH \Leftrightarrow CH_2O + H_2O$	−372.6	5.00 (+12)		
93	$CH_2OH + O_2 \Leftrightarrow CH_2O + HO_2$	−78.9	1.80 (+13)		3.3
94	$CH_2OH + M \Leftrightarrow CH_2O + H + M$	126.6	1.54 (+13)		138.3
	Reactions of C_2H_1 species				
95	$C_2H + H_2 \Leftrightarrow C_2H_2 + H$	−89.1	1.10 (+13)		12.0
96	$C_2H + O \Leftrightarrow CO + CH\,(X^2\Pi)$	−296.9	1.00 (+13)		
97	$C_2H + OH \Leftrightarrow CHCO + H$	−194.8	2.00 (+13)		
98	$C_2H + O_2 \Leftrightarrow CHCO + O$	−124.3	6.02 (+11)		
99	$C_2H + O_2 \to CH\,(A^2\Delta) + CO_2$	−56.6	4.50 (+15)		105.0
100	$C_2H + O_2 \Leftrightarrow HCO + CO$	−603.0	2.41 (+12)		
101	$C_2H + C_2H_2 \Leftrightarrow C_4H_2 + H$	−103.4	3.50 (+13)		
102	$CHCO + H \Leftrightarrow {}^1CH_2 + CO$	−64.9	1.50 (+14)		
103	$CHCO + O \Leftrightarrow HCO + CO$	−413.3	1.00 (+14)		
104	$CHCO + M \Leftrightarrow CH\,(X^2\Pi) + CO + M$	325.7	6.00 (+15)		246.1
	Reactions of C_2H_2 species				
105	$C_2H_2 + O \Leftrightarrow {}^3CH_2 + CO$	−196.7	7.81 (+03)	2.80	2.1
106	$C_2H_2 + O \Leftrightarrow CHCO + H$	−97.5	1.39 (+04)	2.80	2.1
107	$C_2H_2 + OH \Leftrightarrow C_2H + H_2O$	25.9	2.71 (+13)		43.9
108	$C_2H_2 + OH \Leftrightarrow HCCOH + H$	36.7	5.06 (+05)	2.30	56.5
109	$C_2H_2 + OH \Leftrightarrow CH_2CO + H$	−100.6	2.19 (−04)	4.50	−4.2
110	$C_2H_2 + OH \Leftrightarrow CH_3 + CO$	−230.4	4.85 (−04)	4.00	−8.4
111	$C_2H_2 + M \Leftrightarrow C_2H + H + M$	525.1	4.17 (+16)		448.0
112	$HCCOH + H \Leftrightarrow CH_2CO + H$	−137.4	1.00 (+13)		
113	$CH_2CO + H \Leftrightarrow CHCO + H_2$	−5.0	3.00 (+13)		36.0
114	$CH_2CO + O \Leftrightarrow HCO + HCO$	−113.3	1.00 (+13)		25.0
115	$CH_2CO + OH \Leftrightarrow CHCO + H_2O$	−68.2	1.00 (+13)		11.0
116	$CH_2CO\,(+M) \Leftrightarrow {}^3CH_2 + CO\,(+M)$	331.8	3.60 (+15)		248.0
			3.00 (+14)		297.0
	Reactions of C_2H_3 species				
117	$C_2H_3 + H \Leftrightarrow C_2H_2 + H_2$	−270.1	3.00 (+13)		
118	$C_2H_3 + OH \Leftrightarrow C_2H_2 + H_2O$	−333.3	4.00 (+12)		

TABLE 5.3
(Continued)

No.	Reaction[a]	ΔH^o_{298} (kJ/mol)	Forward rate coefficient[b]		
			A	n	E
	Reactions of C$_2$H$_3$ species				
119	C$_2$H$_3$ + O ⇔ CH$_2$CO + H	−362.5	3.00 (+13)		
120	C$_2$H$_3$ + O$_2$ ⇔ CH$_2$O + HCO	−346.1	4.00 (+12)		−1.0
121	C$_2$H$_3$ + M ⇔ C$_2$H$_2$ + H + M	165.9	2.00 (+38)	−7.17	211.7
122	CH$_3$CO + H ⇔ CH$_2$CO + H$_2$	−247.3	2.00 (+13)		
123	CH$_3$CO + O ⇔ CH$_3$ + CO$_2$	−473.2	2.00 (+13)		
124	CH$_3$CO (+M) ⇔ CH$_3$ + CO (+M)	58.9	1.20 (+15)		52.4
			3.00 (+12)		70.0
	Reactions of C$_2$H$_4$ species				
125	C$_2$H$_4$ + H ⇔ C$_2$H$_3$ + H$_2$	9.2	3.16 (+11)	0.70	33.5
126	C$_2$H$_4$ + O ⇔ CH$_3$ + HCO	−112.6	1.60 (+08)	1.44	2.2
127	C$_2$H$_4$ + O ⇔ CH$_3$CO + H	−106.1	1.60 (+08)	1.44	2.2
128	C$_2$H$_4$ + O ⇔ CH$_2$O + ^{3}CH$_2$	17.4	7.11 (+08)	1.55	31.3
129	C$_2$H$_4$ + OH ⇔ C$_2$H$_3$ + H$_2$O	−54.0	3.00 (+13)		12.5
130	C$_2$H$_4$ + CH$_3$ ⇔ C$_2$H$_3$ + CH$_4$	5.4	3.92 (+12)		54.5
131	C$_2$H$_4$ + M ⇔ C$_2$H$_2$ + H$_2$ + M	175.1	2.60 (+17)		331.7
132	C$_2$H$_4$ + M ⇔ C$_2$H$_3$ + H + M	445.2	3.80 (+17)		410.7
133	CH$_3$CHO + H ⇔ CH$_3$CO + H$_2$	−74.4	4.00 (+13)		17.6
134	CH$_3$CHO + O ⇔ CH$_3$CO + OH	−66.2	5.00 (+12)		7.5
135	CH$_3$CHO + OH ⇔ CH$_3$CO + H$_2$O	−137.6	1.00 (+13)		
136	CH$_3$CHO + CH$_3$ ⇔ CH$_3$CO + CH$_4$	−78.2	8.50 (+10)		25.1
137	CH$_3$CHO ⇔ CH$_3$ + HCO	355.0	2.00 (+15)		331.0
	C$_2$H$_5$ reactions				
138	C$_2$H$_5$ + H ⇔ C$_2$H$_4$ + H$_2$	−272.7	3.00 (+13)		
139	C$_2$H$_5$ + O$_2$ ⇔ C$_2$H$_4$ + HO$_2$	−42.2	2.00 (+12)		20.9
140	C$_2$H$_5$ + O ⇔ CH$_2$O + CH$_3$	−317.9	4.24 (+13)		
141	C$_2$H$_5$ + O ⇔ CH$_3$CHO + H	−304.4	5.32 (+13)		
142	C$_2$H$_5$ + O ⇔ C$_2$H$_4$ + OH	−264.5	3.06 (+13)		
143	C$_2$H$_5$ (+M) ⇔ C$_2$H$_4$ + H (+M)	163.3	2.44 (+36)	−5.36	175.3
			4.97 (+10)	0.73	154.2
	C$_2$H$_6$ reactions				
144	C$_2$H$_6$ (+M) ⇔ CH$_3$ + CH$_3$ (+M)	377.6	1.81 (+58)	−10.61	412.4
			1.06 (+26)	−2.79	389.6
145	C$_2$H$_6$ (+M) ⇔ C$_2$H$_5$ + H (+M)	408.9	4.90 (+42)	−6.43	448.4
			8.85 (+20)	−1.23	427.7
146	C$_2$H$_6$ + H ⇔ C$_2$H$_5$ + H$_2$	−27.1	5.40 (+02)	3.50	21.8
147	C$_2$H$_6$ + O ⇔ C$_2$H$_5$ + OH	−19.0	1.40 (+00)	4.30	11.6
148	C$_2$H$_6$ + OH ⇔ C$_2$H$_5$ + H$_2$O	−90.3	2.20 (+07)	1.90	4.7
149	C$_2$H$_6$ + CH$_3$ ⇔ C$_2$H$_5$ + CH$_4$	−30.9	5.50 (−01)	4.00	34.7

[a]Reactions with the sign "⇔" were treated as reversible; those with "→" were treated as irreversible.

[b]The forward rate constant $k = AT^n \exp(-E/RT)$. R is the universal gas constant, T is the temperature in K. The units of A involve gmol/cm^3 and s, and those of E, kJ/gmol.

Source: From Ref. [10], reprinted with kind permission from Elsevier Science Ltd., The Boulevard, Langford Lane, Kidlington OX5 1GB, U.K.

High-Temperature Simplified Mechanism

At higher temperatures, say greater than 1500 K, the following reactions capture the several important features of methane oxidation [1]. In the following, X represents any radical species:

$CH_4 + M \rightarrow CH_3 + H + M$	chain initiation	(M.12)
$CH_4 + X \rightarrow CH_3 + XH$	chain branching/propagating	(M.13)
$CH_3 + O_2 \rightarrow CH_3O + O$	chain branching	(M.14)
$CH_3O + M \rightarrow H_2CO + H + M$	chain propagating	(M.15)
$H_2CO + X \rightarrow HCO + XH$	chain branching/propagating	(M.16)
$HCO + M \rightarrow H + CO + M$	chain propagating	(M.17)
$CH_3 + CH_3 \rightarrow C_2H_6$	ethane-intermediate formation	(M.18)
$CO + OH \rightarrow CO_2 + H$	final oxidation	(M.19)

$$+$$
$$H_2\text{--}O_2 \text{ system (H.1--H.20)}$$
$$+$$
$$\text{CO oxidation system (CO.1, CO.3, CO.7)}$$
$$+$$
$$C_2H_6 \text{ oxidation steps.}$$

Two interesting features of the above mechanism are, first, the multiple chain-branching steps (M.13, M.14, M.16), which cause CO formation to be relatively fast; and, second, the formation of ethane, C_2H_6, which must subsequently oxidize. The ethane oxidation clearly complicates the mechanism. Note the C_2H_6 reactions in Table 5.3. Also of interest is the formation of formaldehyde, H_2CO, as an intermediate species (M.15). Because of the importance of methane oxidation, there has been much effort directed to formulating reduced (simplified) mechanisms. References [11] and [12] illustrate promising approaches.

OXIDES OF NITROGEN FORMATION

Nitric oxide, introduced in Chapter 1 and more fully discussed in Chapter 4, is an important minor species in combustion because of its contribution to air pollution. In the combustion of fuels that contain no nitrogen, nitric oxide is formed by three chemical mechanisms or routes that involve nitrogen from the air: the **thermal** or **Zeldovich mechanism**, the **Fenimore** or **prompt mechanism**, and the **N_2O-intermediate mechanism**. The thermal mechanism dominates in high-temperature combustion over a fairly wide range of equivalence ratios, while the Fenimore mechanism is particularly important in rich combustion. It appears that the N_2O-intermediate mechanism plays an important role in the production of NO in very lean, low-temperature combustion processes. Recent studies show the relative contributions of the three mechanisms in premixed [13] and diffusion flames [14,15]. For more information than is provided in this section, the reader is referred to Miller and Bowman [16], which provides a comprehensive, state-of-the-art (c. 1989) review of the chemistry involved in forming and controlling oxides of nitrogen in combustion processes. Additional information and references also are provided in Chapter 15.

The **thermal** or **Zeldovich mechanism** consists of the two chain reactions:

$$O + N_2 \Leftrightarrow NO + N \tag{N.1}$$

$$N + O_2 \Leftrightarrow NO + O \tag{N.2}$$

which can be extended by adding the reaction:

$$N + OH \Leftrightarrow NO + H. \tag{N.3}$$

The rate coefficients for N.1–N.3 are [17]

$$k_{N1,f} = 1.8 \cdot 10^{11} \exp[-38,370/T(K)] \qquad [=]m^3/kmol\text{-}s$$
$$k_{N1,r} = 3.8 \cdot 10^{10} \exp[-425/T(K)] \qquad [=]m^3/kmol\text{-}s$$
$$k_{N2,f} = 1.8 \cdot 10^{7} T \exp[-4680/T(K)] \qquad [=]m^3/kmol\text{-}s$$
$$k_{N2,r} = 3.8 \cdot 10^{6} T \exp[-20,820/T(K)] \qquad [=]m^3/kmol\text{-}s$$
$$k_{N3,f} = 7.1 \cdot 10^{10} \exp[-450/T(K)] \qquad [=]m^3/kmol\text{-}s$$
$$k_{N3,r} = 1.7 \cdot 10^{11} \exp[-24,560/T(K)] \qquad [=]m^3/kmol\text{-}s$$

This three-reaction set is referred to as the **extended Zeldovich mechanism**. In general, this mechanism is coupled to the fuel combustion chemistry through the O_2, O, and OH species; however, in processes where the fuel combustion is complete before NO formation becomes significant, the two processes can be uncoupled. In this case, if the relevant time scales are sufficiently long, one can assume that the N_2, O_2, O, and OH concentrations are at their equilibrium values and N atoms are in steady state. These assumptions greatly simplify the problem of calculating the NO formation. If we make the additional assumption that the NO concentrations are much less than their equilibrium values, the reverse reactions can be neglected. This yields the following rather simple rate expression:

$$\frac{d[NO]}{dt} = 2k_{N1,f}[O]_{eq}[N_2]_{eq}. \tag{5.7}$$

In Chapter 4 (Example 4.3), we showed that Eqn. 5.7 obtains for the above assumptions. Within flame zones proper and in short-timescale, post-flame processes, the equilibrium assumption is not valid. Superequilibrium concentrations of O atoms, up to several orders of magnitude greater than equilibrium, greatly increase NO formation rates. This **superequilibrium O** (and OH) atom contribution to NO production rates is sometimes classified as part of the so-called prompt-NO mechanism; however, for historical reasons, we refer to prompt-NO only in conjunction with the Fenimore mechanism.

The activation energy for (N.1) is relatively large (319,050 kJ/kmol); thus, this reaction has a very strong temperature dependence (cf. problem 4.7). As a rule-of-thumb, the thermal mechanism is usually unimportant at temperatures below 1800 K. Compared to the time scales of fuel oxidation processes, NO is formed rather slowly by the thermal mechanism; thus, thermal NO is generally considered to be formed in the post-flame gases.

The **N_2O-intermediate mechanism** is important in fuel-lean ($\Phi < 0.8$), low-temperature conditions. The three steps of this mechanism are

$$O + N_2 + M \Leftrightarrow N_2O + M \tag{N.4}$$

$$H + N_2O \Leftrightarrow NO + NH \tag{N.5}$$

$$O + N_2O \Leftrightarrow NO + NO \tag{N.6}$$

This mechanism becomes important in NO control strategies that involve lean premixed combustion, which are currently being explored by gas-turbine manufacturers [18].

The **Fenimore mechanism** is intimately linked to the combustion chemistry of hydrocarbons. Fenimore [19] discovered that some NO was rapidly produced in the flame zone of laminar premixed flames long before there would be time to form NO by the thermal mechanism, and he gave this rapidly formed NO the appellation **prompt NO**. The general scheme of the Fenimore mechanism is that hydrocarbon radicals react with molecular nitrogen to form amines or cyano compounds. The amines and cyano compounds are then converted to intermediate compounds that ultimately form NO. Ignoring the processes that form CH radicals to initiate the mechanism, the Fenimore mechanism can be written

$$CH + N_2 \Leftrightarrow HCN + N \tag{N.7}$$

$$C + N_2 \Leftrightarrow CN + N \tag{N.8}$$

where (N.7) is the primary path and is the rate-limiting step in the sequence. For equivalence ratios less than about 1.2, the conversion of hydrogen cyanide, HCN, to form NO follows the following chain sequence:

$$HCN + O \Leftrightarrow NCO + H \tag{N.9}$$

$$NCO + H \Leftrightarrow NH + CO \tag{N.10}$$

$$NH + H \Leftrightarrow N + H_2 \tag{N.11}$$

$$N + OH \Leftrightarrow NO + H \tag{N.3}$$

For equivalence ratios richer than 1.2, other routes open up and the chemistry becomes much more complex. Miller and Bowman [16] point out that the above scheme is no longer rapid and that NO is recycled to HCN, inhibiting NO production. Furthermore, the Zeldovich reaction that couples with the prompt mechanism actually destroys rather than forms NO, i.e., $N + NO \rightarrow N_2 + O$. Figure 5.4 schematically illustrates the processes involved, and the reader is referred to Refs. [16] and [20] for further details.

Certain fuels contain nitrogen in their molecular structure. Coal, in particular, may contain bound nitrogen up to about 2% by mass. In the combustion of fuels with bound nitrogen, the nitrogen in the parent fuel is rapidly converted to hydrogen cyanide, HCN, or ammonia, NH_3. The remaining steps follow the prompt-NO mechanism discussed above and outlined in Fig. 5.4.

In the atmosphere, nitric oxide ultimately oxidizes to form **nitrogen dioxide**, which is important to the production of acid rain and photochemical smog. Many

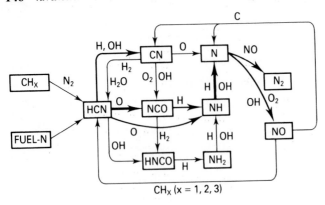

FIGURE 5.4
NO production associated with the Fenimore prompt mechanism. (Reprinted from Ref. [20] by permission of The Combustion Institute.)

combustion processes, however, emit significant fractions of their total oxides of nitrogen ($NO_x = NO + NO_2$) as NO_2. The elementary reactions responsible for forming NO_2 prior to the exhausting of the combustion products into the atmosphere are the following:

$$NO + HO_2 \Leftrightarrow NO_2 + OH \quad \text{(formation)} \tag{N.12}$$

$$NO_2 + H \Leftrightarrow NO + OH \quad \text{(destruction)} \tag{N.13}$$

$$NO_2 + O \Leftrightarrow NO + O_2 \quad \text{(destruction)} \tag{N.14}$$

where the HO_2 radical is formed by the three-body reaction

$$H + O_2 + M \Leftrightarrow HO_2 + M. \tag{N.15}$$

The HO_2 radicals are formed in relatively low-temperature regions; hence, NO_2 formation occurs when NO molecules from high-temperature regions diffuse or are transported by fluid mixing into the HO_2-rich regions. The NO_2 destruction reactions (N.13) and (N.14) are active at high temperatures, thus preventing the formation of NO_2 in high-temperature zones.

SUMMARY

In this chapter, we outlined the kinetic mechanisms for five chemical systems of importance to combustion: H_2 oxidation, CO oxidation, higher paraffin oxidation, CH_4 oxidation, and oxides of nitrogen (NO and NO_2) formation. In the H_2–O_2 system, we discovered how the changes in reaction pathways with temperature and pressure result in various regimes of explosive and nonexplosive behavior. The idea of heterogeneous, or wall, reactions was introduced to explain the destruction of radicals at low pressures where mean free paths are long. We also saw the importance of moisture, or other H_2-containing species, in the oxidation of CO. Without a trace of these species, CO oxidation is very slow. The $CO + OH \rightarrow CO_2 + H$ reaction was found to be a key step in CO oxidation. The oxidation of higher paraffins (C_nH_{2n+2} with $n > 2$) can be characterized as a three-step process: first, the fuel molecule is attracted by radicals producing intermediates (olefins and H_2); second, the intermediates oxidize to CO and H_2O; and, third, the CO and any remaining H_2 are oxidized to CO_2 and H_2O, respectively. Global and quasi-global mechanisms were presented for use in engineering approximations. Methane was shown to be unique among hydrocarbons in that it is significantly less reactive. The mechanism for CH_4 oxidation is perhaps the best elaborated of all hydrocarbons, and an example was presented that consists of 149 elementary steps involving 33 species. Simplified, yet still relatively complex, mechanisms for low- and high-temperature CH_4 oxidation were outlined. The chapter concludes with a discussion of the various NO formation pathways: the extended Zeldovich, or thermal route, together with the superequilibrium O (and OH) contributions; the Fenimore prompt mechanism; the N_2O-intermediate path; and, lastly, the fuel-N mechanism. Although an overwhelming number of reactions were discussed in this chapter, the reader should still be able to grasp certain key features of each system, without getting bogged down in a myriad of elementary reactions. Moreover, this chapter should provide a heightened awareness of the importance of chemistry in combustion.

REFERENCES

1. Glassman, I., *Combustion*, 2nd Ed., Academic Press, Orlando, 1987.
2. Lewis, B., and VonElbe, G., *Combustion, Flames and Explosions of Gases*, 3rd Ed., Academic Press, Orlando, 1987.
3. Gardiner, W. C., Jr., and Olson, D. B., "Chemical Kinetics of High Temperature Combustion," *Annual Review of Physical Chemistry*, 31: 377–399 (1980).
4. Westbrook, C. K., and Dryer, F. L., "Chemical Kinetic Modeling of Hydrocarbon Combustion," *Progress in Energy and Combustion Science*; 10: 1–57 (1984).
5. Yetter, Y. A., Dryer, F. L., and Rabitz, H., "A Comprehensive Reaction Mechanism for Carbon Monoxide/Hydrogen/Oxygen Kinetics," *Combustion Science and Technology* 79: 97–128 (1991).
6. Westbrook, C. K., and Dryer, F. L., "Simplified Reaction Mechanisms for the Oxidation of Hydrocarbon Fuels in Flames," *Combustion Science and Technology*, 27: 31–43 (1981).
7. Hautman, D. J., Dryer, F. L., Schug, K. P., and Glassman, I., "A Multiple-Step Overall Kinetic Mechanism for the Oxidation of Hydrocarbons," *Combustion Science and Technology*, 25: 219–235 (1981).
8. Card, J. M., and Williams, F. A., "Asymptotic Analysis with Reduced Chemistry for the Burning of n-Heptane Droplets, *Combustion and Flame*, 91: 187–199 (1992).
9. Kaufman, F., "Chemical Kinetics and Combustion: Intricate Paths and Simple Steps," *Nineteenth Symposium (International) on Combustion*, The Combustion Institute, Pittsburgh, pp. 1–10, 1982.
10. Frenklach, M., Wang, H., and Rabinowitz, M. J., "Optimization and Analysis of Large Chemical Kinetic Mechanisms Using the Solution Mapping Method—Combustion of Methane," *Progress in Energy and Combustion Science*, 18: 47–73 (1992).
11. Peters, N., and Kee, R. J., "The Computation of Stretched Laminar Methane–Air Diffusion Flames Using a Reduced Four-Step Mechanism," *Combustion and Flame*, 68: 17–29 (1987).
12. Smooke, M. D. (ed.), *Reduced Kinetic Mechanisms and Asymptotic Approximations for Methane–Air Flames*, Lecture Notes in Physics, 384, Springer-Verlag, New York, 1991.

13. Drake, M. C., and Blint, R. J., "Calculations of NO_x Formation Pathways in Propagating Laminar, High Pressure Premixed CH_4/Air Flames," *Combustion Science and Technology*, 75: 261–285 (1991).
14. Drake, M. C., and Blint, R. J., "Relative Importance of Nitric Oxide Formation Mechanisms in Laminar Opposed-Flow Diffusion Flames," *Combustion and Flame*, 83: 185–203 (1991).
15. Nishioka, M., Nakagawa, S., Ishikawa, Y., and Takeno, T., "NO Emission Characteristics of Methane–Air Double Flame," *Combustion and Flame*, 98: 127–138 (1994).
16. Miller, J. A., and Bowman, C. T., "Mechanism and Modeling of Nitrogen Chemistry in Combustion," *Progress in Energy and Combustion Science*, 15: 287–338 (1989).
17. Hanson, R. K., and Salimian, S., "Survey of Rate Constants in the N/H/O System," Chapter 6 in *Combustion Chemistry* (W. C. Gardiner, Jr., ed.), Springer-Verlag, New York, pp. 361–421, 1984.
18. Correa, S. M., "A Review of NO_x Formation under Gas-Turbine Combustion Conditions," *Combustion Science and Technology*, 87: 329–362 (1992).
19. Fenimore, C. P., "Formation of Nitric Oxide in Premixed Hydrocarbon Flames," *Thirteenth Symposium (International) on Combustion*, The Combustion Institute, Pittsburgh, pp. 373–380, 1970.
20. Bowman, C. T., "Control of Combustion-Generated Nitrogen Oxide Emissions: Technology Driven by Regulations," *Twenty-Fourth Symposium (International) on Combustion*, The Combustion Institute, Pittsburgh, pp. 859–878, 1992.
21. Weast, R. C. (ed.), *Handbook of Chemistry and Physics*, 56th Ed., CRC Press, Cleveland, 1976.

QUESTIONS AND PROBLEMS

5.1. Identify and discuss the processes involved in the H_2–O_2 system that result in:

    A. The first explosion limit (cf. Fig. 5.1).
    B. The second explosion limit.
    C. The third explosion limit.

5.2. What is the difference between a homogeneous reaction and a heterogeneous reaction? Give examples of each.

5.3. Why is moisture, or other H_2-containing species, important for the rapid oxidation of CO?

5.4. Identify the primary elementary reaction step in which CO is converted to CO_2.

5.5. The oxidation of higher paraffins can be treated as three major sequential steps. What are the key features of each step?

5.6. Show how the β-scission rule would apply to the breaking of C–C bonds in the following hydrocarbon radicals. The line indicates a C–H bond and the dot the radical site.

    A. *n*-butyl radical—C_4H_9

$$\bullet \ \overset{|}{\underset{|}{C}} - \overset{|}{\underset{|}{C}} - \overset{|}{\underset{|}{C}} - \overset{|}{\underset{|}{C}} -$$

B. *sec*-butyl radical—C_4H_9

$$-\,C - C - C - C -$$

with vertical bonds above each carbon and a radical dot (•) below the second carbon.

5.7. The oxidation of C_3H_8 has been broken down into eight semi-detailed steps (P.1 through P.7 plus other steps). Following the example of C_3H_8, show the first five steps in the oxidation of butane, C_4H_{10}.

5.8. Using the single-step global mechanism given by Eqns. 5.1 and 5.2 for combustion of a hydrocarbon with air, compare the rates of fuel carbon conversion to CO_2 for $\Phi = 1$, $P = 1$ atm, and $T = 1600$ K for the following fuels:

i. CH_4—methane
ii. C_3H_8—propane
iii. C_8H_{18}—octane.

Hint: Make sure that you include the nitrogen from the air in determining your reactants' concentrations.

5.9. What features of the methane molecule contribute to its low reactivity? Use data from the *CRC Handbook of Chemistry and Physics* [21] (or other reference book) to support your statements.

5.10. The production of nitric oxide from the combustion of nitrogen-free fuels with air occurs by several mechanisms. List and discuss these mechanisms.

5.11. Many experiments have shown that nitric oxide is formed very rapidly within flame zones, and more slowly in post-flame gases. What factors contribute to this rapid formation of NO in flame zones?

5.12. Identify the key radical in the conversion of NO to NO_2 in combustion systems. Why does NO_2 not appear in high-temperature flame regions?

5.13. Consider the production of nitric oxide (NO) in the following combustion systems using the Zeldovich mechanism given in Eqn. 5.7. (See also Chapter 4, Examples 4.3 and 4.4.) In each case, assume that the environment is well mixed; O, O_2, and N_2 are at their equilibrium values (given); N atoms are in steady state; the temperature is fixed (given); and reverse reactions are negligible. Calculate the NO concentration in parts-per-million and the ratio of the kinetically formed NO to the given equilibrium NO concentration. Comment on the validity of neglecting reverse reactions. Do your results make sense?

A. Consider the operation of a stationary power-generation, gas-turbine engine operating without any emission controls. The primary zone of this gas-turbine combustor has an equivalence ratio of 1.0. The mean residence time of the combustion products at the conditions below is 7 ms.

n-Decane/air	$\chi_{O,eq} = 7.93 \cdot 10^{-5}$
$T = 2300$ K	$\chi_{O_2,eq} = 3.62 \cdot 10^{-3}$
$P = 14$ atm	$\chi_{N_2,eq} = 0.7295$
$MW = 28.47$	$\chi_{NO,eq} = 2.09 \cdot 10^{-3}$

B. The residence time in the primary combustion zone of a gas-fired (methane/air) furnace is 200 ms for conditions given below.

$$\Phi = 1.0 \qquad\qquad \chi_{O,eq} = 1.99 \cdot 10^{-4}$$
$$T = 2216\,K \qquad\qquad \chi_{O_2,eq} = 4.46 \cdot 10^{-3}$$
$$P = 1\,atm \qquad\qquad \chi_{N_2,eq} = 0.7088$$
$$MW = 27.44 \qquad\qquad \chi_{NO,eq} = 1.91 \cdot 10^{-3}$$

C. Additional air is added after the primary zone combustion of part A above to form a secondary combustion zone. How much additional NO is formed in the secondary zone of the combustor, assuming a step change to the conditions given below? The mean residence time of the gases in the secondary zone is 10 ms. Use the NO formed in part A as the initial condition for your calculation.

$$\Phi = 0.55 \qquad\qquad \chi_{O_2,eq} = 0.0890$$
$$P = 14\,atm \qquad\qquad \chi_{O,eq} = 2.77 \cdot 10^{-5}$$
$$T = 1848\,K \qquad\qquad \chi_{N_2,eq} = 0.7570$$
$$MW = 28.73 \qquad\qquad \chi_{NO,eq} = 3.32 \cdot 10^{-3}$$

D. How much additional NO is formed in the secondary combustion zone of the furnace of part B above? The residence time in the secondary zone is 0.5 s. Again, assume instantaneous mixing.

$$\Phi = 0.8958 \qquad\qquad \chi_{O,eq} = 9.149 \cdot 10^{-5}$$
$$T = 2000\,K \qquad\qquad \chi_{O_2,eq} = 0.0190$$
$$P = 1\,atm \qquad\qquad \chi_{N_2,eq} = 0.720$$
$$MW = 27.72 \qquad\qquad \chi_{NO,eq} = 2.34 \cdot 10^{-3}$$

5.14. Determine the units conversion factor required to express the pre-exponential factors in Table 5.1 in SI units, i.e., kmol, m, and s. Perform the conversion for the first and last entries in the table.

CHAPTER 6

COUPLING CHEMICAL AND THERMAL ANALYSES OF REACTING SYSTEMS

OVERVIEW

In Chapter 2, we reviewed the thermodynamics of reacting systems, considering only the initial and final states. For example, the concept of an adiabatic flame temperature was derived based on the knowledge of the initial state of the reactants and the final composition of the products, as determined by equilibrium. Performing an adiabatic flame temperature calculation required no knowledge of chemical rate processes. In the present chapter, we couple the knowledge gained of chemical kinetics in Chapter 4 with fundamental conservation principles (e.g., mass and energy conservation) for various archetypal thermodynamic systems. This coupling allows us to describe the detailed evolution of the system from its initial reactant state to its final product state, which may or may not be in chemical equilibrium. In other words, we will be able to calculate the system temperature and the various species concentrations as functions of time as the system proceeds from reactants to products.

Our analyses in this chapter will be simple, without the complication of mass diffusion. The systems that are chosen for study in this chapter, shown in Fig. 6.1,

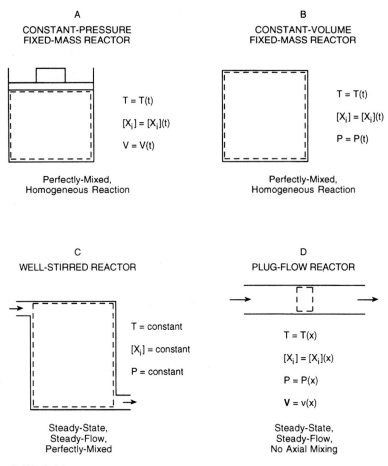

FIGURE 6.1
Simple chemically reacting systems: (A) constant-pressure, fixed mass; (B) constant-volume, fixed mass; (C) well-stirred reactor; (D) plug-flow reactor.

make bold assumptions about the mixedness of the system. Three of the four systems assume that the systems are perfectly mixed and homogeneous in composition; the fourth system, the plug-flow reactor, totally ignores mixing and diffusion in the flow (axial) direction, while assuming perfect mixedness in the radial direction perpendicular to the flow. Although the concepts developed here can be used as building blocks for modeling more complex flows, perhaps more importantly, they are pedagogically useful for developing a very basic understanding of the interrelationships among thermodynamics, chemical kinetics, and fluid mechanics. In the next chapter, we will extend our simple analysis to include the effects of mass diffusion.

CONSTANT-PRESSURE, FIXED-MASS REACTOR

Application of Conservation Laws

Consider reactants contained in a piston-cylinder arrangement (Fig. 6.1a) that react at each and every location within the gas volume at the same rate. Thus, there are no temperature or composition gradients within the mixture, and a single temperature and set of species concentrations suffice to describe the evolution of this system. For exothermic combustion reactions, the temperature and volume will both increase with time, and there may be heat transfer through the reaction vessel walls.

In the following, we will develop a system of first-order ordinary differential equations whose solution describes the desired temperature and species evolution. These equations and their initial conditions define an **initial-value problem**. Starting with the rate form of the conservation of energy for a fixed-mass system, we write

$$\dot{Q} - \dot{W} = m\frac{du}{dt}.\tag{6.1}$$

Applying the definition of enthalpy, $h \equiv u + Pv$, and differentiating,

$$\frac{du}{dt} = \frac{dh}{dt} - P\frac{dv}{dt}.\tag{6.2}$$

Assuming the only work is the P–dv work at the piston,

$$\frac{\dot{W}}{m} = P\frac{dv}{dt}.\tag{6.3}$$

Substituting Eqns. 6.2 and 6.3 into Eqn. 6.1, the $P\,dv/dt$ terms cancel leaving

$$\frac{\dot{Q}}{m} = \frac{dh}{dt}.\tag{6.4}$$

We can express the system enthalpy in terms of the system chemical composition as

$$h = \frac{H}{m} = \frac{\sum\limits_{i=1}^{N} N_i \bar{h}_i}{m},\tag{6.5}$$

where N_i and $\bar{h}_i$ are the number of moles and molar enthalpy of species i, respectively. Differentiation of Eqn. 6.5 yields

$$\frac{dh}{dt} = \frac{1}{m}\left[\sum_i \left(\bar{h}_i \frac{dN_i}{dt}\right) + \sum_i \left(N_i \frac{d\bar{h}_i}{dt}\right)\right].\tag{6.6}$$

Assuming ideal-gas behavior, i.e., $\bar{h}_i = \bar{h}_i(T$ only$)$,

$$\frac{d\bar{h}_i}{dt} = \frac{\partial \bar{h}_i}{\partial T}\frac{dT}{dt} = \bar{c}_{p,i}\frac{dT}{dt} \qquad (6.7)$$

where $\bar{c}_{p,i}$ is the molar constant-pressure specific heat of species i. Equation 6.7 provides the desired link to the system temperature, while the definition of the molar concentration $[X_i]$ and the mass-action expressions, $\dot{\omega}_i =$ etc., provide the necessary link to the system composition, N_i, and chemical dynamics, dN_i/dt. These expressions are

$$N_i = V[X_i], \qquad (6.8)$$

$$\frac{dN_i}{dt} \equiv V\dot{\omega}_i, \qquad (6.9)$$

where the $\dot{\omega}_i$ values are calculated from the detailed chemical mechanism as discussed in Chapter 4 (cf. Eqns. 4.31–4.33).

Substituting Eqns. 6.7 and 6.9 into Eqn. 6.6, our statement of energy conservation (Eqn. 6.4) becomes, after rearrangement,

$$\frac{dT}{dt} = \frac{(\dot{Q}/V) - \sum_i \left(\bar{h}_i\dot{\omega}_i\right)}{\sum_i \left([X_i]\bar{c}_{p,i}\right)}, \qquad (6.10)$$

where we use the following calorific equation of state to evaluate the enthalpies:

$$\bar{h}_i = \bar{h}^o_{f,i} + \int_{T_{\text{ref}}}^{T} \bar{c}_{p,i}dT. \qquad (6.11)$$

To obtain the volume, we apply mass conservation and the definition of $[X_i]$ in Eqn. 6.8:

$$V = \frac{m}{\sum_i \left([X_i]MW_i\right)}. \qquad (6.12)$$

The species molar concentrations, $[X_i]$, change with time as a result of both chemical reactions and changing volume, i.e.,

$$\frac{d[X_i]}{dt} = \frac{d(N_i/V)}{dt} = \frac{1}{V}\frac{dN_i}{dt} - N_i\frac{1}{V^2}\frac{dV}{dt} \qquad (6.13a)$$

or

$$\frac{d[X_i]}{dt} = \dot{\omega}_i - [X_i]\frac{1}{V}\frac{dV}{dt}, \qquad (6.13b)$$

where the first term on the right-hand-side is the chemical production term and the second term accounts for the changing volume.

The ideal-gas law can be used to eliminate the dV/dt term. Differentiating

$$PV = \sum_i N_i R_u T \tag{6.14a}$$

for the case of constant pressure, and rearranging, yields

$$\frac{1}{V}\frac{dV}{dt} = \frac{1}{\sum_i N_i}\sum_i \frac{dN_i}{dt} + \frac{1}{T}\frac{dT}{dt}. \tag{6.14b}$$

First substituting Eqn. 6.9 into Eqn. 6.14b and then substituting the result into Eqn. 6.13b, provides, after rearrangement, our final expression for the rate of change of the species molar concentrations:

$$\frac{d[X_i]}{dt} = \dot{\omega}_i - [X_i]\left[\frac{\sum_j \dot{\omega}_i}{\sum_j [X_j]} + \frac{1}{T}\frac{dT}{dt}\right]. \tag{6.15}$$

Reactor Model Summary

Succinctly stated, our problem is to find the solution to

$$\frac{dT}{dt} = f([X_i], T) \tag{6.16a}$$

$$\frac{d[X_i]}{dt} = f([X_i], T) \quad i = 1, 2, \ldots N \tag{6.16b}$$

with initial conditions

$$T(t = 0) = T_0 \tag{6.17a}$$

and

$$[X_i](t = 0) = [X_i]_0. \tag{6.17b}$$

The functional expressions for Eqns. 6.16a and 6.16b are obtained from Eqn. 6.10 and Eqn. 6.15, respectively. Enthalpies are calculated using Eqn. 6.11, and the volume is obtained from Eqn. 6.12.

To carry out the solution of the above system, an integration routine capable of handling stiff equations should be employed, as discussed in Chapter 4.

CONSTANT-VOLUME, FIXED-MASS REACTOR

Application of Conservation Laws

The application of energy conservation to the constant-volume reactor follows closely that of the constant-pressure reactor, with the major difference being the absence of work in the former. Starting with Eqn. 6.1, with $\dot{W} = 0$, the first law takes the following form:

$$\frac{du}{dt} = \frac{\dot{Q}}{m}.$$
(6.18)

Recognizing that the specific internal energy, u, now plays the same mathematical role as the specific enthalpy, h, in our previous analysis, expressions equivalent to Eqns. 6.5–6.7 are developed and substituted into Eqn. 6.18. This yields, after rearrangement,

$$\frac{dT}{dt} = \frac{(\dot{Q}/V) - \sum_i (\bar{u}_i \dot{\omega}_i)}{\sum_i ([X_i]\bar{c}_{v,i})}.$$
(6.19)

Recognizing that, for ideal gases, $\bar{u}_i = \bar{h}_i - R_u T$ and $\bar{c}_{v,i} = \bar{c}_{p,i} - R_u$, we can express Eqn. 6.19 using enthalpies and constant-pressure specific heats:

$$\frac{dT}{dt} = \frac{(\dot{Q}/V) + R_u T \sum_i \dot{\omega}_i - \sum_i (\bar{h}_i \dot{\omega}_i)}{\sum_i [[X_i](\bar{c}_{p,i} - R_u)]}.$$
(6.20)

In constant-volume explosion problems, the time-rate-of-change of the pressure is of interest. To calculate dP/dt, we differentiate the ideal-gas law, subject to the constant volume constraint, i.e.,

$$PV = \sum_i N_i R_u T$$
(6.21)

and

$$V\frac{dP}{dt} = R_u T \frac{d\sum_i N_i}{dt} + R_u \sum_i N_i \frac{dT}{dt}.$$
(6.22)

Applying the definitions of $[X_i]$ and $\dot{\omega}_i$ (cf. Eqns. 6.8 and 6.9), Eqns. 6.21 and 6.22 become

$$P = \sum_i [X_i] R_u T$$
(6.23)

and

$$\frac{dP}{dt} = R_u T \sum_i \dot{\omega}_i + R_u \sum_i [X_i]\frac{dT}{dt},$$
(6.24)

which completes our simple analysis of homogeneous constant-volume combustion.

Reactor Model Summary

Equation 6.20 can be integrated simultaneously with the chemical rate expressions to determine $T(t)$ and $[X_i](t)$, i.e.,

$$\frac{dT}{dt} = f([X_i], T) \tag{6.25a}$$

$$\frac{d[X_i]}{dt} = \dot{\omega}_i = f([X_i], T) \quad i = 1, 2, \ldots N \tag{6.25b}$$

with initial conditions

$$T(t = 0) = T_0 \tag{6.26a}$$

and

$$[X_i](t = 0) = [X_i]_0. \tag{6.26b}$$

The required enthalpies are evaluated using Eqn. 6.11, and the pressure from Eqn. 6.23. Again, a stiff equation solver should be used to carry out the integration.

Example 6.1. In spark-ignition engines, knock occurs when the unburned fuel–air mixture ahead of the flame reacts homogeneously, i.e., it autoignites. The rate-of-pressure rise is a key parameter in determining knock intensity and propensity for mechanical damage to the piston-crank assembly. Pressure-versus-time traces for normal and knocking combustion in a spark-ignition engine are illustrated in Fig. 6.2. Note the very rapid pressure rise in the case of heavy knock. Figure 6.3 shows schlieren (index-of-refraction gradient) photographs of flame propagation for normal and knocking combustion.

Create a simple constant-volume model of the autoignition process and determine the temperature and fuel and product concentration histories. Also determine dP/dt as a function of time. Assume initial conditions corresponding to compression of a fuel–air mixture from 300 K and 1 atm to top-dead-center for a compression ratio of 10:1. The initial volume before compression is $3.68 \cdot 10^{-4}\,\mathrm{m}^3$, which corresponds to an engine with both a bore and stroke of 75 mm. Use ethane as fuel.

Solution. We will make some bold and sweeping assumptions about the thermodynamics and the chemical kinetics to keep the computational complexity to a minimum. Our solution, however, will still retain the strong coupling between the thermochemistry and chemical kinetics. Our assumptions are:

i. One-step global kinetics using the rate parameters for ethane C_2H_6 (cf. Table 5.1).

ii. The fuel, air, and products all have equal molecular weights; $MW_F = MW_{Ox} = MW_{Pr} = 29$.

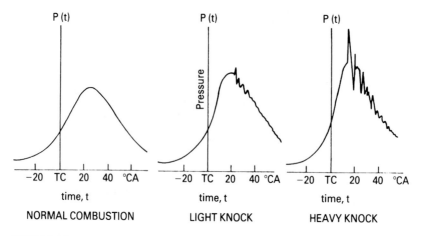

FIGURE 6.2
Cylinder pressure-versus-time measurements in a spark-ignition engine for normal combustion, light knock, and heavy knock cycles. The crank angle interval of 40° corresponds to 1.67 ms. (Adapted from Refs. [1] and [17] by permission of McGraw-Hill, Inc.)

iii. The specific heats of the fuel air, and products are constants and equal; $c_{p,F} = c_{p,Ox} = c_{p,Pr} = 1200\,\text{J/kg-K}$.

iv. The enthalpy of formation of the air and products are zero; the enthalpy of formation of the fuel is $4 \cdot 10^7\,\text{J/kg}$.

v. We assume that the stoichiometric air–fuel ratio is 16.0 and restrict combustion to stoichiometric or lean conditions.

The use of global kinetics is hard to justify for a problem like engine knock where detailed chemistry is important [3]. Our only justification is that we are trying to illustrate principles, recognizing that our answers may be inaccurate in detail. Assumptions ii–iv provide values that give reasonable estimates of flame temperatures, yet trivialize the problem of obtaining thermodynamic properties [4].

With these assumptions, we can now formulate our model. From Eqn. 5.2 and Table 5.1, the fuel (ethane) reaction rate is

$$\frac{d[F]}{dt} = -6.19 \cdot 10^9 \exp\left(\frac{-15,098}{T}\right) [F]^{0.1} [O_2]^{1.65},$$

$$[=]\ \text{kmol/m}^3\text{-s},\tag{I}$$

where, assuming 21% O_2 in the air,

$$[O_2] = 0.21[Ox].$$

Note the conversion of units for the pre-exponential factor $(1.1 \cdot 10^{12} \cdot [1000]^{1-0.1-1.65} = 6.19 \cdot 10^9)$ from a gmol-cm³ to a kmol-m³ basis.

We can simply relate the oxidizer and product reaction rates to the fuel rate through the stoichiometry (assmptions ii and v):

$$\frac{d[Ox]}{dt} = (A/F)_s \frac{MW_F}{MW_{Ox}} \frac{d[F]}{dt} = 16 \frac{d[F]}{dt}\tag{II}$$

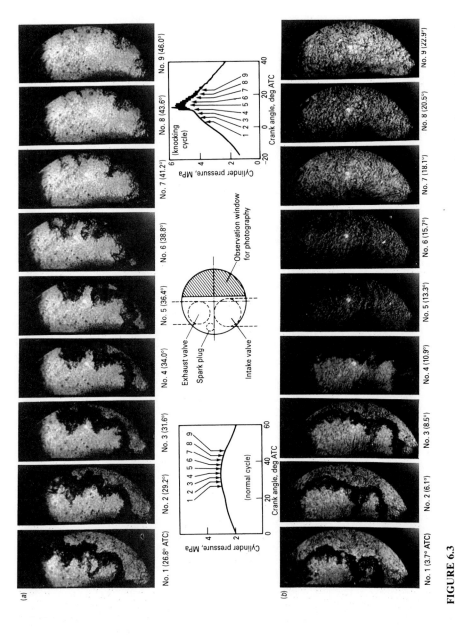

FIGURE 6.3
Schlieren photographs from high-speed movies of normal combustion (top) and knocking combustion (bottom). Pressure–time traces corresponding to the photographs are also shown. (From Refs. [2] and [17]. Reprinted by permission of McGraw-Hill, Inc.)

and

$$\frac{d[Pr]}{dt} = -[(A/F)_s + 1]\frac{MW_F}{MW_{Pr}}\frac{d[F]}{dt} = -17\frac{d[F]}{dt}. \tag{III}$$

We complete our model by applying Eqn. 6.20:

$$\frac{dT}{dt} = \frac{(\dot{Q}/V) + R_u T \sum \dot{\omega}_i - \sum (\bar{h}_i \dot{\omega}_i)}{\sum [[X_i](\bar{c}_{p,i} - R_u)]}.$$

This simplifies, by noting that

$$\dot{Q}/V = 0 \quad \text{(adiabatic)},$$

$$\sum \dot{\omega}_i = 0 \quad \text{(assumptions ii and v)},$$

$$\sum \bar{h}_i \dot{\omega}_i = \dot{\omega}_F \bar{h}_{f,F}^o \quad \text{(assumptions ii–v)},$$

and

$$\sum [X_i](\bar{c}_{p,i} - R_u) = (\bar{c}_p - R_u) \sum [X_i] = (\bar{c}_p - R_u) \sum \chi_i \frac{P}{R_u T} = (\bar{c}_p - R_u)\frac{P}{R_u T},$$

to be

$$\frac{dT}{dt} = \frac{-\dot{\omega}_F \bar{h}_{f,F}^o}{(\bar{c}_p - R_u)P/(R_u T)}. \tag{IV}$$

Although our basic model is complete, we can add ancillary relations for the pressure and pressure-derivative. From Eqn. 6.23 and 6.24,

$$P = R_u T([F] + [Ox] + [Pr]),$$

or

$$P = P_0 \frac{T}{T_0},$$

and

$$\frac{dP}{dt} = \frac{P}{T}\frac{dT}{dt} = \frac{P_0}{T_0}\frac{dT}{dt}.$$

Before we can integrate our system of first-order ODEs (Eqns. I–IV\,), we need to determine initial conditions for each of the variables: $[F]$, $[Ox]$, $[Pr]$, and T. Assuming isentropic compression from bottom-dead-center to top-dead-center and a specific heat ratio of 1.4, the initial temperature and pressure can be found:

$$T_0 = T_{\text{TDC}} = T_{\text{BDC}}\left(\frac{V_{\text{BDC}}}{V_{\text{TDC}}}\right)^{\gamma-1} = 300\left(\frac{10}{1}\right)^{1.4-1} = 753 \, \text{K},$$

$$P_0 = P_{\text{TDC}} = P_{\text{BDC}}\left(\frac{V_{\text{BDC}}}{V_{\text{TDC}}}\right)^{\gamma} = (1)\left(\frac{10}{1}\right)^{1.4} = 25.12 \, \text{atm}.$$

The initial concentrations can be found by employing the given stoichiometry. The oxidizer and fuel mole fractions are

$$\chi_{Ox,0} = \frac{(A/F)_s/\Phi}{[(A/F)_s/\Phi]+1},$$

$$\chi_{Pr} = 0,$$

$$\chi_F = 1 - \chi_{Ox,0}.$$

The molar concentrations, $[X_i] = \chi_i P/(R_u T)$, are

$$[Ox]_0 = \left[\frac{(A/F)_s/\Phi}{((A/F)_s/\Phi)+1}\right]\frac{P}{R_u T_0},$$

$$[F]_0 = \left[1 - \frac{(A/F)_s/\Phi}{((A/F)_s/\Phi)+1}\right]\frac{P}{R_u T_0},$$

$$[Pr]_0 = 0.$$

Equations I–IV were integrated numerically, and the results are shown in Fig. 6.4. From this figure, we see that the temperature increases only about 200 K in the first 3 ms, while, thereafter, it rises to the adiabatic flame temperature (c. 3300 K) in less than 0.1 ms. This rapid temperature rise and concomitant rapid consumption of the fuel is characteristic of a **thermal explosion**, where the energy released and temperature rise from reaction feeds back to produce ever-increasing reaction rates because of the $[-E_a/R_u T]$ temperature dependence of the reaction rate. From Fig. 6.4, we also see the huge pressure derivative in the explosive stage, with a peak value of about $1.9 \cdot 10^{13}$ Pa/s.

Comments. Although this model predicted the explosive combustion of the mixture after an initial period of slow combustion, as is observed in real knocking combustion, the single-step kinetics mechanism does not model the true behavior of auto-igniting mixtures. In reality, the **induction period**, or **ignition delay**, is controlled by the formation of intermediate species, which subsequently react. Recall the three basic stages of hydrocarbon oxidation presented in Chapter 5. To accurately model knock, a more detailed mechanism would be required. Ongoing research efforts aim at elucidating the details of the "low-temperature" kinetics of the induction period [3].

Control of engine knock has always been important to performance improvements, and, more recently, has received attention because of legislated requirements to remove lead-based antiknock compounds from gasoline.

WELL-STIRRED REACTOR

The well-stirred, or perfectly stirred, reactor is an ideal reactor in which perfect mixing is achieved inside the control volume, as shown in Fig. 6.5. Experimental reactors employing high-velocity inlet jets approach this ideal and have been used to study many aspects of combustion, such as flame stabilization [5] and NO_x formation [6–8] (Fig. 6.6). Well-stirred reactors also have been used to obtain values for global reaction parameters [9]. The well-stirred reactor is sometimes called a Longwell reactor in recognition of the early work of Longwell and Weiss [5]. Chomiak [10] cites that Zeldovich [11] described the operation of the well-stirred reactor nearly a decade earlier.

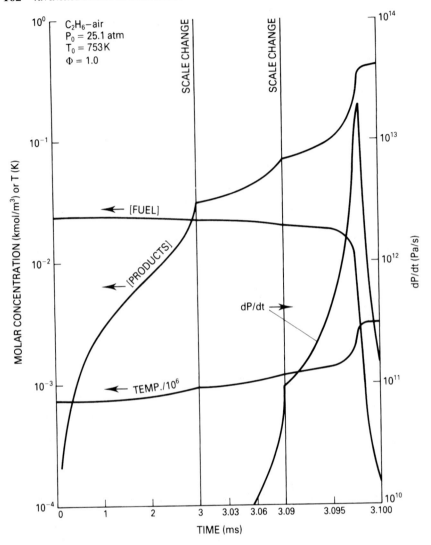

FIGURE 6.4
Results for the constant-volume reactor model of Example 6.1. Temperature, fuel and products concentrations, and rate-of-pressure rise (dP/dt) are shown. Note the expansion of the time scale at 3 ms and again at 3.09 ms allows the explosion to be resolved.

Application of Conservation Laws

To develop the theory of well-stirred reactors, we review the concept of mass conservation of individual species. In Chapter 3, we developed a species conservation equation for a differential control volume. We now write mass conservation for an arbitrary species i, for an integral control volume (cf. Fig. 6.5), as:

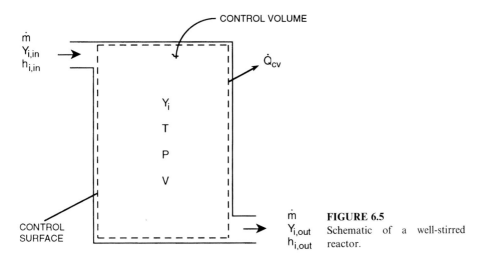

FIGURE 6.5
Schematic of a well-stirred reactor.

FIGURE 6.6
Longwell reactor with one hemisphere removed. Fuel–air mixture enters through small holes in central hollow steel sphere, and products exit through larger holes in firebrick lining. Scale shown is in inches. (From Ref. [5]. Reprinted by permission, © The American Chemical Society.)

$$\underbrace{\frac{dm_{i,cv}}{dt}}_{\substack{\text{Rate at which mass} \\ \text{of } i \text{ accumulates} \\ \text{within } CV}} = \underbrace{\dot{m}_i''' V}_{\substack{\text{Rate at which} \\ \text{mass of } i \\ \text{is generated} \\ \text{within } CV}} + \underbrace{\dot{m}_{i,in}}_{\substack{\text{Mass flow} \\ \text{of } i \\ \text{into } CV}} - \underbrace{\dot{m}_{i,out}}_{\substack{\text{Mass flow} \\ \text{of } i \\ \text{out of } CV}}. \qquad (6.27)$$

What distinguishes Eqn. 6.27 from the overall continuity equation is the presence of the generation term $\dot{m}_i''' V$. This term arises because chemical reactions transform one species into another; hence, a positive generation rate indicates the formation of a species, while a negative generation rate signifies that the species is being destroyed during the reaction. In the combustion literature, this generation term is frequently referred to as a **source** or **sink**. When the appropriate form of Eqn. 6.27 is written for each of the species in the reactor $(i = 1, 2, \ldots N)$, the sum of these equations yields the familiar form of the continuity equation,

$$\frac{dm_{cv}}{dt} = \dot{m}_{in} - \dot{m}_{out} \qquad (6.28)$$

The mass generation rate of a species, $\dot{m}_i'''$, is easily related to the net production rate, $\dot{\omega}_i$, developed in Chapter 4:

$$\dot{m}_i''' = \dot{\omega}_i MW_i. \qquad (6.29)$$

Ignoring any diffusional flux, the individual species mass flowrate is simply the product of the total mass flowrate and that species mass fraction, i.e.,

$$\dot{m}_i = \dot{m} Y_i. \qquad (6.30)$$

When we apply Eqn. 6.27 to the well-stirred reactor, assuming steady-state operation, the time derivative of the left-hand-side disappears. With this assumption, and substituting Eqns. 6.29 and 6.30, Eqn. 6.27 becomes

$$\dot{\omega}_i MW_i V + \dot{m}(Y_{i,in} - Y_{i,out}) = 0 \quad \text{for} \quad i = 1, 2, \ldots N \text{ species.} \qquad (6.31)$$

Furthermore, we can identify the outlet mass fractions, $Y_{i,out}$ as being equal to the mass fractions within the reactor. Since the composition within the reactor is everywhere the same, the composition at the outlet of the control volume must be the same as in the interior. With this knowledge, the species product rates are of the form

$$\dot{\omega}_i = f([X_i]_{cv}, T) = f([X_i]_{out}, T), \qquad (6.32)$$

where the mass fractions and molar concentrations are related by

$$Y_i = \frac{[X_i]MW_i}{\sum\limits_{j=1}^{N}[X_j]MW_j}. \qquad (6.33)$$

Equation 6.31, when written for each species, provides N equations with $N + 1$ unknowns, with the assumed known parameters $\dot{m}$ and V. An energy balance provides the additional equation needed for closure.

The steady-state, steady-flow conservation of energy equation (Eqn. 2.28) applied to the well-stirred reactor is

$$\dot{Q} = \dot{m}(h_{\text{out}} - h_{\text{in}}), \tag{6.34}$$

where we neglect changes in kinetic and potential energies. Rewriting Eqn. 6.34 in terms of the individual species, we obtain

$$\dot{Q} = \dot{m}\left(\sum_{i=1}^{N} Y_{i,\text{out}} h_i(T) - \sum_{i=1}^{N} Y_{i,\text{in}} h_i(T)\right), \tag{6.35}$$

where

$$h_i(T) = h_{f,i}^o + \int_{T_{\text{ref}}}^{T} c_{p,i} dT. \tag{6.36}$$

Solving for the temperature, T, and species mass fractions, $Y_{i,\text{out}}$, is quite similar to our computation of equilibrium flame temperatures in Chapter 2; however, now the product composition is constrained by chemical kinetics, rather than by chemical equilibrium.

It is common in the discussion of well-stirred reactors to define a mean **residence time** for the gases in the reactor:

$$t_R = \rho V / \dot{m} \tag{6.37}$$

where the mixture density is calculated from the ideal-gas law

$$\rho = P M W_{\text{mix}} / R_u T. \tag{6.38}$$

The mixture molecular weight is readily calculated from a knowledge of the mixture composition. Appendix 6A provides relationships between MW_{mix} and Y_i, χ_i, and $[X_i]$.

Reactor Model Summary

Because the well-stirred reactor is assumed to be operating at steady state, there is no time dependence in the mathematical model. The equations describing the reactor are a set of coupled nonlinear algebraic equations, rather than a system of ordinary differential equations, which was the result for the previous two examples. Thus, the $\dot{\omega}_i$ appearing in Eqn. 6.31 depends only on the Y_i (or $[X_i]$) and temperature, not time. To solve this system of $N+1$ equations, Eqns. 6.31 and 6.35, the generalized Newton's method (Appendix E) can be employed. Depending on the chemical system under study, it may be difficult to achieve convergence with Newton's method and more sophisticated numerical techniques may be necessary [12].

> **Example 6.2.** Develop a simplified model of a well-stirred reactor using the same simplified chemistry and thermodynamics used in Example 6.1 (equal and constant

c_ps and MWs, and one-step global kinetics). Use the model to determine the blowout characteristics of a spherical (80-mm-diameter) reactor with premixed reactants (C_2H_6–air) entering at 298 K. Plot the equivalence ratio at blowout as a function of mass flowrate for $\Phi \leq 1.0$. Assume the reactor is adiabatic.

Solution. Noting that the molar concentrations relate to mass fractions as

$$[X_i] = \frac{PMW_{\text{mix}}}{R_u T} \frac{Y_i}{MW_i},$$

our global reaction rate, $\dot{\omega}_F$, can be expressed as

$$\dot{\omega}_F = \frac{d[F]}{dt} = -k_G \left(\frac{PMW_{\text{mix}}}{R_u T}\right)^{m+n} \left(\frac{Y_F}{MW_F}\right)^m \left(\frac{0.233 Y_{Ox}}{MW_{Ox}}\right)^n,$$

where $m = 0.1$ and $n = 1.65$, the factor 0.233 is the mass fraction of O_2 in the oxidizer (air), and the mixture molecular weight is given by

$$MW_{\text{mix}} = \left[\frac{Y_F}{MW_F} + \frac{Y_{Ox}}{MW_{Ox}} + \frac{Y_{Pr}}{MW_{Pr}}\right]^{-1}.$$

The global rate coefficient is, as in Example 6.1,

$$k_G = 6.19 \cdot 10^9 \exp\left(\frac{-15,098}{T}\right).$$

We can now write species conservation equations for the fuel by applying Eqn. 6.31:

$$f_1 \equiv \dot{m}(Y_{F,\text{in}} - Y_F) - k_G MW_F V \left(\frac{P}{R_u T}\right)^{1.75} \frac{\left(\frac{Y_F}{MW_F}\right)^{0.1} \left(\frac{0.233 Y_{Ox}}{MW_{Ox}}\right)^{1.65}}{\left[\frac{Y_F}{MW_F} + \frac{Y_{Ox}}{MW_{Ox}} + \frac{Y_{Pr}}{MW_{Pr}}\right]^{1.75}} = 0,$$

which further simplifies by applying our assumption of equal molecular weights and noting that $\sum Y_i = 1$:

$$f_1 \equiv \dot{m}(Y_{F,\text{in}} - Y_F) - k_G MW V \left(\frac{P}{R_u T}\right)^{1.75} \frac{Y_F^{0.1}(0.233 \, Y_{Ox})^{1.65}}{1} = 0. \qquad \text{(I)}$$

For the oxidizer (air):

$$f_2 \equiv \dot{m}(Y_{Ox,\text{in}} - Y_{Ox}) - (A/F)_s k_G MW V \left(\frac{P}{R_u T}\right)^{1.75} \frac{Y_F^{0.1}(0.233 \, Y_{Ox})^{1.65}}{1} = 0. \qquad \text{(II)}$$

For the product mass fraction, we write

$$f_3 \equiv 1 - Y_F - Y_{Ox} - Y_{Pr} = 0. \qquad \text{(III)}$$

Our final equation in the model results from the application of Eqn. 6.35:

$$f_4 \equiv Y_F \left[h_{f,F}^o + c_{p,F}(T - T_{ref}) \right]$$
$$+ Y_{Ox} \left[h_{f,Ox}^o + c_{p,Ox})(T - T_{ref}) \right]$$
$$+ Y_{Pr} \left[h_{f,Pr}^o + c_{p,Pr}(T - T_{ref}) \right]$$
$$- Y_{F,in} \left[h_{f,F}^o + c_{p,F}(T_{in} - T_{ref}) \right]$$
$$- Y_{Ox,in} \left[h_{f,Ox}^o + c_{p,Ox}(T_{in} - T_{ref}) \right] = 0,$$

which also further simplifies by the assumptions of equal specific heats and $h_{f,Ox}^o = h_{f,Pr}^o = 0$:

$$f_4 \equiv (Y_F - Y_{F,in})h_{f,F}^o + c_p(T - T_{in}) = 0. \tag{IV}$$

Equations I–IV constitute our reactor model and involve the four unknowns: Y_F, Y_{Ox}, Y_{Pr}, and T, and the parameter $\dot{m}$. To determine the reactor blowout characteristic, we solve the nonlinear algebraic equation set (I–IV\,) for a sufficiently small value of $\dot{m}$ that allows combustion for a given equivalence ratio. We then increase $\dot{m}$ until we fail to achieve a solution, or the solution yields the input values. Figure 6.7 illustrates the results of such a procedure for $\Phi = 1$. The generalized Newton's method (Appendix E) was used to solve the equation set.

In Fig. 6.7, we see the decreasing conversion of fuel to products and decreased temperature as the flowrate increases to the blowout condition ($\dot{m} > 0.193$ kg/s). The ratio of the temperature at blowout to the adiabatic flame temperature is (1738 K/ 2381 K = 0.73), which is in agreement with the results in Ref. [5]. Repeating the calculations at various equivalence ratios generates the blowout characteristics shown in Fig. 6.8. Note that the reactor is more easily blown out as the fuel–air mixture becomes leaner. The shape of the blowout curve in Fig. 6.8 is similar to those determined for experimental reactors and turbine combustors.

Comment. Well-stirred-reactor theory and experiments were used in the 1950s as a guide to the development of high-intensity combustors for gas turbines and ramjets. This example provides a good illustration of how reactor theory can be applied to the problem of blowout. The blowout condition, plus some margin of safety, determines the maximum-load condition for continuous-flow combustors. Although well-stirred-reactor theory captures some of the characteristics of blowout, other theories also have been proposed to explain flameholding. We explore this topic further in Chapter 12.

PLUG-FLOW REACTOR

Assumptions

A plug-flow reactor represents an ideal reactor that has the following attributes:

1. Steady-state, steady flow.
2. No mixing in the axial direction. This implies that molecular and/or turbulent mass diffusion is negligible in the flow direction.

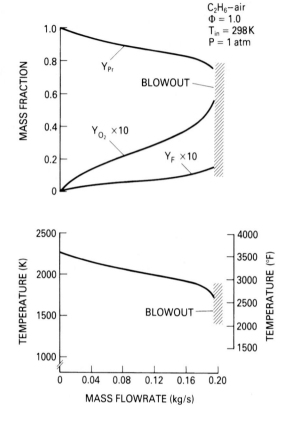

FIGURE 6.7
Effect of flowrate on conditions inside a model well-stirred reactor. For flowrates greater than 0.193 kg/s, combustion cannot be sustained within the reactor (blowout).

3. Uniform properties in the direction perpendicular to the flow, i.e., one-dimensional flow. This means that at any cross-section, a single velocity, temperature, composition, etc., completely characterizes the flow.

4. Ideal frictionless flow. This assumption allows the use of the simple Euler equation to relate pressure and velocity.

5. Ideal-gas behavior. This assumption allows simple state relations to be employed to relate T, P, ρ, Y_i, and h.

Application of Conservation Laws

Our goal here is to develop a system of first-order ODEs whose solution describes the reactor flow properties, including composition, as functions of distance, x. The geometry and coordinate definition are schematically illustrated at the top of Fig. 6.9. Table 6.1 provides an overview of the analysis listing the physical and chemical principles that generate $6 + 2N$ equations and a like number of unknown variables and functions. The number of unknowns could be easily reduced by N, by recognizing that the species production rates, $\dot{\omega}_i$, can be immediately expressed

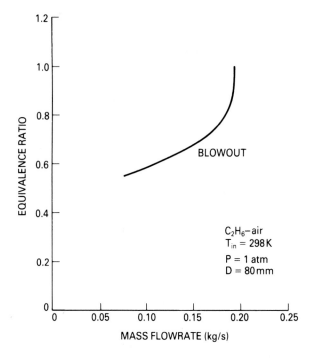

FIGURE 6.8
Blowout characteristics of a model well-stirred reactor.

in terms of the mass fractions (see Appendix 6A) without the need to explicitly involve the $\dot{\omega}_1$. Explicitly retaining them, however, clearly reminds us of the importance of chemical reactions in our analysis. Although not shown in Table 6.1, the following parameters are treated as known quantities, or functions, and are necessary to obtain a solution: $\dot{m}$, $k_i(T)$, $A(x)$, and $\dot{Q}''(x)$. The area function $A(x)$ defines the cross-sectional area of the reactor as a function of x; thus, our model reactor could represent a nozzle, or a diffuser, or any particular one-dimensional geometry, and not just a constant cross-sectional device as suggested by the top sketch in Fig. 6.9. The heat flux function $\dot{Q}(x)$, although explicitly indicating that the wall heat flux is known, is also intended to indicate that the heat flux may be calculated from a given wall-temperature distribution.

With reference to the fluxes and control volumes illustrated in Fig. 6.9, we can easily derive the following conservation relationships:

MASS CONSERVATION

$$\frac{\mathrm{d}(\rho v_x A)}{\mathrm{d}x} = 0. \tag{6.39}$$

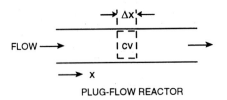

PLUG-FLOW REACTOR

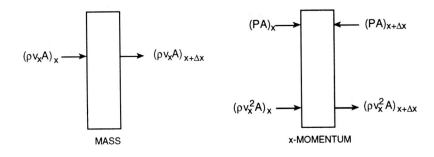

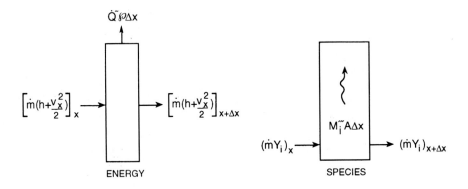

FIGURE 6.9
Control volumes showing fluxes of mass, x-momentum, energy, and species for a plug-flow reactor.

TABLE 6.1
Overview of relationships and variables for plug-flow reactor with N species

Source of equations	Number of equations	Variables or derivatives involved
Fundamental conservation principles: mass, x-momentum energy, species	$3 + N$	$\dfrac{d\rho}{dx}, \dfrac{dv_x}{dx}, \dfrac{dP}{dx}, \dfrac{dh}{dx}, \dfrac{dY_i}{dx}(i = 1, 2, \ldots, N), \dot{\omega}_i(i = 1, 2, \ldots, N)$
Mass action laws	N	$\dot{\omega}_i(i = 1, 2, \ldots, N)$
Equation of state	1	$\dfrac{d\rho}{dx}, \dfrac{dP}{dx}, \dfrac{dT}{dx}, \dfrac{dMW_{\text{mix}}}{dx}$
Calorific equation of state	1	$\dfrac{dh}{dx}, \dfrac{dT}{dx}, \dfrac{dY_i}{dx}(i = 1, 2, \ldots, N)$
Definition of mixture molecular weight	1	$\dfrac{dMW_{\text{mix}}}{dx}, \dfrac{dY_i}{dx}(i = 1, 2, \ldots, N)$

X-MOMENTUM CONSERVATION

$$\frac{dP}{dx} + \rho v_x \frac{dv_x}{dx} = 0. \tag{6.40}$$

ENERGY CONSERVATION

$$\frac{d(h + v_x^2/2)}{dx} + \frac{\dot{Q}''\mathcal{P}}{\dot{m}} = 0. \tag{6.41}$$

SPECIES CONSERVATION

$$\frac{dY_i}{dx} - \frac{\dot{\omega}_i MW_i}{\rho v_x} = 0. \tag{6.42}$$

The symbols v_x and $\mathcal{P}$ represent the axial velocity and local perimeter of the reactor, respectively. All of the other quantities have been defined previously. The derivation of these equations is left as a homework exercise (cf. problem 6.1).

To obtain a useful form of the equations where the individual variable derivatives can be isolated, Eqns. 6.39 and 6.41 can be expanded and rearranged to yield the following:

$$\frac{1}{\rho}\frac{d\rho}{dx} + \frac{1}{v_x}\frac{dv_x}{dx} + \frac{1}{A}\frac{dA}{dx} = 0, \tag{6.43}$$

$$\frac{dh}{dx} + v_x\frac{dv_x}{dx} + \frac{\dot{Q}''\mathcal{P}}{\dot{m}} = 0. \tag{6.44}$$

The $\dot{\omega}_i$s appearing in Eqn. 6.42 can be expressed using Eqn. 4.31, with the $[X_i]$s transformed to Y_is.

The functional relationship of the ideal-gas calorific equation of state,

$$h = h(T, Y_i), \quad i = 1, 2, \ldots, N, \tag{6.45}$$

can be exploited using the chain rule to relate dh/dx and dT/dx, yielding

$$\frac{dh}{dx} = c_p \frac{dT}{dx} + \sum_{i=1}^{N} h_i \frac{dY_i}{dx}. \tag{6.46}$$

To complete our mathematical description of the plug-flow reactor, we differentiate the ideal-gas equation of state,

$$P = \rho R_u T / MW_{\text{mix}}, \tag{6.47}$$

to yield

$$\frac{1}{P}\frac{dP}{dx} = \frac{1}{\rho}\frac{d\rho}{dx} + \frac{1}{T}\frac{dT}{dx} - \frac{1}{MW_{\text{mix}}}\frac{dMW_{\text{mix}}}{dx} \tag{6.48}$$

where the mixture molecular weight derivative follows simply from its definition expressed in terms of species mass fractions, i.e.,

$$MW_{\text{mix}} = \left[\sum_{i=1}^{N} Y_i / MW_i \right]^{-1} \tag{6.49}$$

and

$$\frac{dMW_{\text{mix}}}{dx} = -MW_{\text{mix}}^2 \sum_{i=1}^{N} \frac{1}{MW_i}\frac{dY_i}{dx}. \tag{6.50}$$

Equations 6.40, 6.42, 6.43, 6.44, 6.46, 6.48, and 6.49 contain in a linear fashion the derivatives $d\rho/dx$, dv_x/dx, dP/dx, dh/dx, dY_i/dx $(i = 1, 2, \ldots, N)$, dT/dx, and dMW_{mix}/dx. The number of equations can be reduced by eliminating some of the derivatives by substitution. One logical choice is to retain the derivatives dT/dx, $d\rho/dx$, and dY_i/dx $(i = 1, 2 \ldots, N)$. With this choice, the following equations comprise the system of ODEs that must be integrated starting from an appropriate set of initial conditions:

$$\frac{d\rho}{dx} = \frac{\left(1 - \dfrac{R_u}{c_p MW_{\text{mix}}}\right)\rho^2 v_x^2 \left(\dfrac{1}{A}\dfrac{dA}{dx}\right) + \dfrac{\rho R_u}{v_x c_p MW_{\text{mix}}} \sum_{i=1}^{N} MW_i \dot{\omega}_i \left(h_i - \dfrac{MW_{\text{mix}}}{MW_i} c_p T\right)}{P\left(1 + \dfrac{v_x^2}{c_p T}\right) - \rho v_x^2}, \tag{6.51}$$

$$\frac{dT}{dx} = \frac{v_x^2}{\rho c_p}\frac{d\rho}{dx} + \frac{v_x^2}{c_p}\left(\frac{1}{A}\frac{dA}{dx}\right) - \frac{1}{v_x \rho c_p}\sum_{i=1}^{N} h_i \dot{\omega}_i MW_i, \tag{6.52}$$

$$\frac{dY_i}{dx} = \frac{\dot{\omega}_i MW_i}{\rho v_x}. \tag{6.53}$$

Note that in Eqns. 6.41 and 6.52, $\dot{Q}''$ has been set to zero for simplicity.

A residence time, t_R, can also be defined, and one more equation added to the set:

$$\frac{dt_R}{dx} = \frac{1}{v_x}. \tag{6.54}$$

Initial conditions necessary to solve Eqns. 6.51–6.54 are

$$T(0) = T_0, \tag{6.55a}$$

$$\rho(0) = \rho_0, \tag{6.55b}$$

$$Y_i(0) = Y_{i0} \quad i = 1, 2, \dots N, \tag{6.55c}$$

$$t_R(0) = 0. \tag{6.55d}$$

In summary, we see that the mathematical description of the plug-flow reactor is similar to the constant-pressure and constant-volume reactor models in that all three result in a coupled set of ordinary differential equations; the plug-flow reactor, however, is expressed as a function of a spatial coordinate rather than time.

APPLICATIONS TO COMBUSTION SYSTEM MODELING

Various combinations of well-stirred reactors and plug-flow reactors are frequently used to approximate more complex combustion systems. A simple illustration of this approach is shown in Fig. 6.10. Here we see a gas-turbine combustor modeled as two well-stirred reactors and a plug-flow reactor, all in series, with provisions for some recycle (recirculation) of combustion products in the first reactor, which represents the primary zone (see Fig. 10.4a in Chapter 10). The secondary zone and dilution zones are modeled by the second well-stirred reactor and the plug-flow reactor, respectively. To accurately model a real combustion device, many reactors may be required, with judicious selection of the proportioning of the various flows into each reactor. This approach relies much

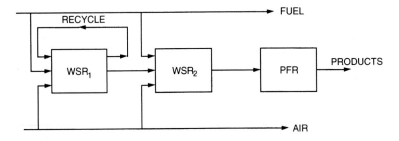

FIGURE 6.10
Conceptual model of gas-turbine combustor using combinations of well-stirred and plug-flow reactors. (After Ref. [13].)

on the art and craft of an experienced designer to achieve useful results. Reactor modeling approaches are often used to complement more sophisticated finite-difference or finite-element numerical models of turbine combustors, furnaces, and boilers, etc.

SUMMARY

In this chapter, four model reactors were explored: a constant-pressure reactor, a constant-volume reactor, a well-stirred reactor, and a plug-flow reactor. A description of each of these systems was developed from fundamental conservation principles and linked to chemical kinetics. You should be familiar with these principles and be able to apply them to the model reactors. A numerical example of a constant-volume reactor was developed employing three species (fuel, oxidizer, and products) with one-step global kinetics and simplified thermochemistry. With the model, some characteristics of thermal explosions were elucidated and related to autoignition (knock) in reciprocating engines. As a second example, an equally simple numerical model of a well-stirred reactor was developed. This model was exercised to demonstrate the concept of blowout and the dependence of the blowout mass flowrate on equivalence ratio. With a firm grasp of these simple models, you should be in a good position to understand more complex and more rigorous analyses of combustion systems. Nevertheless, these simple models frequently are useful as a first step in analyzing many real devices.

NOMENCLATURE

A	Area (m^2)
A/F	Mass air–fuel ratio (kg/kg)
$c_p, \bar{c}_p$	Constant-pressure specific heat (J/kg-K or J/kmol-K)
$c_v, \bar{c}_v$	Constant-volume specific heat (J/kg-K or J/kmol-K)
$h_f^o, \bar{h}_f^o$	Enthalpy of formation (J/kg or J/kmol)
$H, h, \bar{h}$	Enthalpy (J or J/kg or J/kmol)
k	Chemical kinetic rate coefficient (various units)
m	Mass (kg) or reaction order with respect to fuel
$\dot{m}$	Mass flowrate (kg/s)
$\dot{m}'''$	Volumetric mass production rate (kg/s-m^3)
MW	Molecular weight (kg/kmol)
n	Reaction order with respect to oxygen
N	Number of moles
P	Pressure (Pa)
$\mathcal{P}$	Perimeter (m)
$\dot{Q}$	Heat transfer rate (W)
$\dot{Q}''$	Heat flux (W/m^2)
R_u	Universal gas constant (J/kmol-K)
t	Time (s)
T	Temperature (K)

$U, u, \bar{u}$	Internal energy (J or J/kg or J/kmol)
v	Velocity (m/s)
v	Specific volume (m³/kg)
V	Volume (m³)
V	Velocity vector (m/s)
$\dot{W}$	Power (W)
x	Distance (m)
Y	Mass fraction (kg/kg)

Greek symbols

γ	Specific heat ratio, c_p/c_v
ρ	Density (kg/m³)
Φ	Equivalence ratio
χ	Mole fraction (kmol/kmol)
$\dot{\omega}$	Species production rate (kmol/s-m³)

Subscripts

BDC	Bottom-dead-center
cv	Control volume
F	Fuel
G	Global
i	ith species
in	Inlet condition
mix	Mixture
out	Outlet condition
Ox	Oxidizer
Pr	Product
R	Residence
ref	Reference state
s	Stoichiometric
TDC	Top-dead-center
x	x-Direction
0	Initial

Other

$[X]$	Molar concentration of species X (kmol/m³)

REFERENCES

1. Douaud, A., and Eyzat, P., "DIGITAP—An On-Line Acquisition and Processing System for Instantaneous Engine Data—Applications," SAE Paper 770218, 1977.
2. Nakajima, Y., et al., "Analysis of Combustion Patterns Effective in Improving Anti-Knock Performance of a Spark-Ignition Engine," *Japan Society of Automotive Engineers Review*, 13: 9–17 (1984).
3. Litzinger, T. A., "A Review of Experimental Studies of Knock Chemistry in Engines," *Progress in Energy and Combustion Science*, 16: 155–167 (1990).

4. Spalding, D. B., *Combustion and Mass Transfer*, Pergamon, New York, 1979.
5. Longwell, J. P., and Weiss, M. A., "High Temperature Reaction Rates in Hydrocarbon Combustion," *Industrial & Engineering Chem.*, 47: 1634–1643 (1955).
6. Glarborg, P., Miller, J. A., and Kee, R. J., "Kinetic Modeling and Sensitivity Analysis of Nitrogen Oxide Formation in Well-Stirred Reactors," *Combustion and Flame*, 65: 177–202 (1986).
7. Duterque, J., Avezard, N., and Borghi, R., "Further Results on Nitrogen Oxides Production in Combustion Zones," *Combustion Science and Technology*, 25: 85–95 (1981).
8. Malte, P. C., Schmidt, S. C., and Pratt, D. T., "Hydroxyl Radical and Atomic Oxygen Concentrations in High-Intensity Turbulent Combustion," *Sixteenth Symposium (International) on Combustion*, The Combustion Institute, Pittsburgh, p. 145, 1977.
9. Bradley, D., Chin, S. B., and Hankinson, G., "Aerodynamic and Flame Structure Within a Jet-Stirred Reactor," *Sixteenth Symposium (International) on Combustion*, The Combustion Institute, Pittsburgh, p. 1571, 1977.
10. Chomiak, J., *Combustion: A Study in Theory, Fact and Application*, Gordon & Breach, New York, p. 334, 1990.
11. Zeldovich, Y. B., and Voyevodzkii, V. V., *Thermal Explosion and Flame Propagation in Gases*, Izd. MMI, Moscow, 1947.
12. Glarborg, P., Kee, R. J., Grcar, J. F., and Miller, J. A., "PSR: A Fortran Program for Modeling Well-Stirred Reactors", Sandia National Laboratories Report SAND86-8209, 1986.
13. Swithenbank, J., Poll, I., Vincent, M. W., and Wright, D. D., "Combustion Design Fundamentals," *Fourteenth Symposium (International) on Combustion*, The Combustion Institute, Pittsburgh, p. 627, 1973.
14. Dryer, F. L., and Glassman, I., "High-Temperature Oxidation of CO and H_2," *Fourteenth Symposium (International) on Combustion*, The Combustion Institute, Pittsburgh, pp. 987–1003, 1972.
15. Westbrook, C. K., and Dryer, F. L., "Simplified Reaction Mechanisms for the Oxidation of Hydrocarbon Fuels in Flames," *Combustion Science and Technology*, 27: 31–43 (1981).
16. Kee, R. J., Rupley, F. M., and Miller, J. A., "Chemkin-II: A Fortran Chemical Kinetics Package for the Analysis of Gas-Phase Chemical Kinetics," Sandia National Laboratories Report SAND89-8009, March 1991.
17. Heywood, J. B., *Internal Combustion Engine Fundamentals*, McGraw-Hill, New York, 1988.

PROBLEMS AND PROJECTS

6.1. Derive the basic differential conservation equations for the plug-flow reactor (Eqns. 6.39–6.42) using Fig. 6.9 as a guide. Hint: This is relatively straightforward and does not involve much manipulation.

6.2. Show that:

$$\frac{d(\rho v_x A)}{dx} = 0 = \frac{1}{\rho}\frac{d\rho}{dx} + \dots, \text{etc.} \qquad (\text{cf. Eqn. 6.43})$$

6.3. Show that:

$$\frac{d}{dx}\left(P = \rho\frac{R_u T}{MW_{mix}}\right) \Rightarrow \frac{1}{P}\frac{dP}{dx} = \frac{1}{\rho}\frac{d\rho}{dx} + \dots, \text{etc.} \qquad (\text{cf. Eqn. 6.48})$$

6.4. Show that:

$$\frac{dMW_{mix}}{dx} = -MW_{mix}^2 \sum_i (dY_i/dx)MW_i^{-1}.$$

6.5. A. Use Mathematica or other symbolic manipulation software to verify Eqns. 6.51–6.53.

B. Add the heat flux distribution, $\dot{Q}''(x)$ to the problem defined by Eqns. 6.51–6.53.

6.6. In the well-stirred-reactor literature, a "reactor loading parameter" is frequently encountered. This single parameter lumps together the effect of pressure, mass flow-rate, and reactor volume. Can you identify (create) such a parameter for the well-stirred-reactor model developed in Example 6.2? Hint: The parameter is expressed as $P^a \dot{m}^b V^c$. Find the exponents a, b, and c.

6.7. Create a computer code embodying the simple constant-volume reactor developed in Example 6.1. Verify that it reproduces the results shown in Fig. 6.4 and then use the model to explore the effects of P_0, T_0, and Φ on combustion times and maximum rates-of-pressure rise. Discuss your results. Hint: You will need to decrease the time interval between output printings when combustion rates are rapid.

6.8. Develop a constant-pressure-reactor model using the same chemistry and thermo-dynamics as in Example 6.1. Using an initial volume of $0.008 \, \text{m}^3$, explore the effects of P and T_0 on combustion durations. Use $\Phi = 1$ and assume the reactor is adiabatic.

6.9. Develop a plug-flow-reactor model using the same chemistry and thermodynamics as in Example 6.1. Assume the reactor is adiabatic. Use the model to:

A. Determine the mass flowrate such that the reaction is 99% complete in a flow length of 10 cm for $T_{in} = 1000 \, \text{K}$, $P_{in} = 0.2 \, \text{atm}$, and $\Phi = 0.2$. The circular duct has a diameter of 3 cm.

B. Explore the effects of P_{in}, T_{in}, and Φ on the flow length required for 99% complete combustion using the flowrate determined in part A above.

6.10. Develop a model of the combustion of carbon monoxide with moist air in a constant-volume adiabatic reactor. Assume the following global mechanism of Dryer and Glassman [14] applies:

$$CO + \tfrac{1}{2}O_2 \underset{k_r}{\overset{k_f}{\rightleftharpoons}} CO_2$$

where the forward and reverse reaction rates are expressed as:

$$\frac{d[CO]}{dt} = -k_f[CO][H_2O]^{0.5}[O_2]^{0.25},$$

$$\frac{d[CO_2]}{dt} = -k_r[CO_2],$$

where

$$k_f = 2.24 \cdot 10^{12} \left[\left(\frac{\text{kmol}}{\text{m}^3} \right)^{-0.75} \frac{1}{\text{s}} \right] \exp \left[\frac{-1.674 \cdot 10^8 \, (\text{J/kmol})}{R_u T(\text{K})} \right],$$

$$k_r = 5.0 \cdot 10^8 \left(\frac{1}{\text{s}} \right) \exp \left[\frac{-1.674 \cdot 10^8 \, (\text{J/kmol})}{R_u T(\text{K})} \right].$$

In your model, assume constant (but not equal) specific heats evaluated at 2000 K.

A. Write out all of the necessary equations to describe your model, explicitly expressing them in terms of the molar concentrations of CO, CO_2, H_2O, and N_2; individual $\bar{c}_p$ values, $\bar{c}_{p,CO}$, $\bar{c}_{p,CO_2}$, etc.; and individual enthalpies of forma-tion. Note that the H_2O is a catalyst so its mass fraction is preserved.

B. Exercise your model to determine the influence of the initial H_2O mole fraction (0.1–3.0%) on the combustion process. Use maximum rates-of-pressure rise and combustion durations to characterize the process. Use the following initial conditions: $T_0 = 1000\,K$, $P = 1\,atm$, and $\Phi = 0.25$.

6.11. Incorporate the global CO oxidation kinetics given in problem 6.10 above in a model of a well-stirred reactor. Assume constant (but not equal) specific heats evaluated at 2000 K.

A. Write out all of the necessary equations to describe your model, explicitly expressing them in terms of the molar concentrations of CO, CO_2, H_2O, and N_2; individual $\bar{c}_p$ values, $\bar{c}_{p,CO}$, $\bar{c}_{p,CO_2}$, etc.; and individual enthalpies of formation.
B. Exercise your model to determine the influence of the initial H_2O mole fraction (0.1–3.0%) on the blowout-limit mass flowrate. The incoming gases are a stoichiometric mixture of CO and air (plus moisture) at 298 K. The reactor operates at atmospheric pressure.

6.12. Incorporate Zeldovich NO formation kinetics in the well-stirred-reactor model presented in Example 6.2. Assume that the NO formation kinetics are *uncoupled* from the combustion process, i.e., the heat lost or evolved from the NO reactions can be neglected, as can the small amount of mass. Assume equilibrium O-atom concentrations.

A. Write out explicitly all of the equations required by your model.
B. Determine the NO mass fraction as a function of Φ (0.8–1.2) for $\dot{m} = 0.2\,kg/s$, $T_{in} = 298\,K$, and $P = 1\,atm$. The equilibrium constant for

$$\tfrac{1}{2}O_2 \overset{K_p}{\Leftrightarrow} O,$$

is given by

$$K_p = 3030\exp(-30,790/T).$$

6.13. Develop a model of a gas-turbine combustor as two well-stirred reactors in series, where the first reactor represents the primary zone, and the second reactor the secondary zone. Assume the fuel is decane. Use the following two-step hydrocarbon oxidation mechanism [15]:

$$C_xH_y + \left(\frac{x}{2}+\frac{y}{4}\right)O_2 \overset{k_F}{\rightarrow} xCO + \frac{y}{2}H_2O,$$

$$CO + \tfrac{1}{2}O_2 \underset{k_{CO,r}}{\overset{k_{CO,f}}{\Leftrightarrow}} CO_2.$$

The rate expressions for the CO oxidation step are given in problem 6.10 above, while the rate expression for decane conversion to CO is given by:

$$\frac{d[C_{10}H_{22}]}{dt} = -k_F[C_{10}H_{22}]^{0.25}[O_2]^{1.5},$$

where

$$k_F = 2.64 \cdot 10^9 \exp\left[\frac{-15,098}{T}\right]. \qquad \text{(SI units)}$$

A. Write out all of the governing equations treating the equivalence ratios, Φ_1 and Φ_2, of the two zones as known parameters. Assume constant (but not equal) specific heats.

B. Write a computer code embodying your model from part A above. Perform a design exercise with objectives and constraints provided by your instructor.

6.14. Use CHEMKIN [16] subroutines to model H_2–air combustion and thermal NO formation, including superequilibrium O-atom contributions, for the following systems:

A. A constant-volume reactor.

B. A plug-flow reactor.

C. Exercise your models using initial and/or flow conditions provided by your instructor.

APPENDIX 6A
SOME USEFUL RELATIONSHIPS AMONG MASS FRACTIONS, MOLE FRACTIONS, MOLAR CONCENTRATIONS, AND MIXTURE MOLECULAR WEIGHTS

Mole fraction/mass fractions

$$\chi_i = Y_i M W_{\text{mix}} / M W_i \tag{6A.1}$$

$$Y_i = \chi_i M W_i / M W_{\text{mix}} \tag{6A.2}$$

Mass fraction/molar concentration

$$[X_i] = P M W_{\text{mix}} Y_i / (R_u T M W_i) = Y_i \rho / M W_i \tag{6A.3}$$

$$Y_i = \frac{[X_i] M W_i}{\sum_j [X_j] M W_j} \tag{6A.4}$$

Mole fraction/molar concentration

$$[X_i] = \chi_i P / R_u T = \chi_i \rho / M W_{\text{mix}} \tag{6A.5}$$

$$\chi_i = [X_i] / \sum_j [X_j] \tag{6A.6}$$

$M W_{\text{mix}}$ defined in terms of mass fractions

$$M W_{\text{mix}} = \frac{1}{\sum_i Y_i / M W_i} \tag{6A.7}$$

MW_{mix} defined in terms of mole fractions

$$MW_{mix} = \sum_i \chi_i MW_i \tag{6A.8}$$

MW_{mix} defined in terms of molar concentrations

$$MW_{mix} = \frac{\sum_i [X_i] MW_i}{\sum_i [X_i]} \tag{6A.9}$$

CHAPTER
7

SIMPLIFIED CONSERVATION EQUATIONS FOR REACTING FLOWS[1]

OVERVIEW

One of the objectives of this book is to present in as simple as possible a manner the essential physics and chemistry of combustion. When one considers the details of multi-component reacting mixtures, a somewhat complex situation arises, both physically and mathematically, which can be somewhat intimidating to a newcomer to the field. The primary objective of this chapter is to present the simplified governing equations expressing the conservation of mass, species, momentum, and energy for reacting flows. In particular, we wish to treat the following three situations:

1. Steady flow for a one-dimensional *planar* (*x*-coordinate only) geometry.
2. Steady flow for a one-dimensional *spherical* (*r*-coordinate only) geometry.
3. Steady flow for a two-dimensional *axisymmetric* (*r*- and *x*-coordinates) geometry.

[1]This chapter may be skipped in its entirety without any loss of continuity. It is recommended that the chapter be treated as a reference when dealing with the simplified fundamental conservation relations employed in various subsequent chapters.

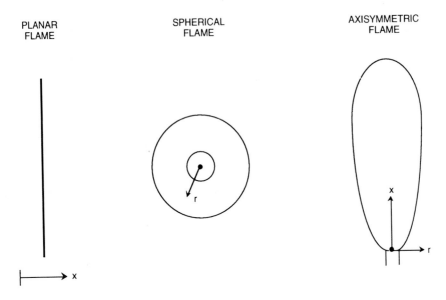

FIGURE 7.1
Coordinate systems for planar flames, spherically symmetric flames (droplet burning), and axisymmetric flames (jet flames).

From the first of these, we will develop an analysis of premixed laminar flames in Chapter 8; from the second, analyses of evaporation and combustion of fuel droplets in Chapter 10; and from the third, analyses of laminar (Chapter 9) and turbulent (Chapter 13) axisymmetric jet flames. These systems and the coordinate geometries are illustrated in Fig. 7.1.

Our approach is first to develop quite simple forms of the conservation equations, usually focusing on one-dimensional cartesian systems, to illustrate the essential physics of each conservation principle. We then present more general relationships from which the basic conservation equations are obtained for the radial and axisymmetric geometries of interest. Although much of the physics can be captured in such simple analyses, it is important to caution that certain interesting and important phenomena will be excluded with this approach. For example, recent research [1] shows that the unequal rates of temperature-gradient-induced diffusion among species (thermal diffusion) in premixed flames have a profound effect on turbulent flame propagation. In our analysis, we neglect thermal diffusion and assume all species diffuse at the same rate, thereby making it impossible to capture this effect. More detailed treatments can be found in Refs. [2–4].

The use of "conserved scalars" to simplify and analyze certain combustion problems is quite common in the literature. To introduce this concept, we discuss and develop equations for the conserved scalars of mixture fraction and mixture enthalpy.

OVERALL MASS CONSERVATION (CONTINUITY)

Consider the one-dimensional control volume of Fig. 7.2, a plane layer Δx thick. Mass enters at x and exits at $x + \Delta x$, with the difference between the flow in and out being the rate at which mass accumulates within the control volume, i.e.,

$$\frac{dm_{cv}}{dt} = [\dot{m}]_x - [\dot{m}]_{x+\Delta x}. \qquad (7.1)$$

| Rate of increase of mass within control volume | Mass flow into the control volume | Mass flow out of the control volume |

Recognizing that the mass within the control volume is $m = \rho V_{cv}$, where the volume $V_{cv} = A\Delta x$, and that the mass flowrate is $\dot{m} = \rho v_x A$, we rewrite Eqn. 7.1 as:

$$\frac{d(\rho A \Delta x)}{dt} = [\rho v_x A]_x - [\rho v_x A]_{x+\Delta x}. \qquad (7.2)$$

Dividing through by $A\Delta x$ and taking the limit as $\Delta x \to 0$, Eqn. 7.2 becomes

$$\frac{\partial \rho}{\partial t} = \frac{\partial(\rho v_x)}{\partial x}. \qquad (7.3)$$

In the case of steady flow, where $\partial \rho / \partial t = 0$,

$$\boxed{\frac{d(\rho v_x)}{dx} = 0} \qquad (7.4a)$$

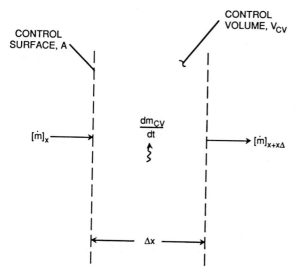

CONTROL VOLUME, V_{CV}

CONTROL SURFACE, A

$[\dot{m}]_x$

$\dfrac{dm_{CV}}{dt}$

$[\dot{m}]_{x+x\Delta}$

Δx

FIGURE 7.2
Control volume for one-dimensional analysis of mass conservation.

or

$$\boxed{\rho v_x = \text{constant}}.$$ (7.4b)

In combustion systems, the density will vary greatly with position in the flow; thus, we see from Eqn. 7.4 that the velocity must also vary with position such that the product ρv_x, the mass flux $\dot{m}''$, remains constant. In its most general form, conservation of mass associated with a fixed point in a flow can be expressed:

$$\frac{\partial \rho}{\partial t} \quad + \quad \nabla \cdot (\rho \mathbf{V}) = 0.$$ (7.5)

| Rate of gain of mass per unit volume | Net rate of mass flow out per unit volume |

Assuming steady flow and applying the vector operations appropriate for the coordinate system of interest (for example, see Ref. [2] for a complete compilation), we obtain, first for the spherical system,

$$\frac{1}{r^2}\frac{\partial}{\partial r}(r^2 \rho v_r) + \frac{1}{r\sin\theta}\frac{\partial}{\partial\theta}(\rho v_\theta \sin\theta) + \frac{1}{r\sin\theta}\frac{\partial(\rho v_\phi)}{\partial\phi} = 0,$$

which simplifies for our 1-D spherically symmetric system, where $v_\theta = v_\phi = 0$, and $\partial(\ )/\partial\theta = \partial(\ )/\partial\phi = 0$, to be

$$\boxed{\frac{1}{r^2}\frac{d}{dr}(r^2 \rho v_r) = 0}$$ (7.6a)

or

$$\boxed{r^2 \rho v_r = \text{constant}}.$$ (7.6b)

Equation 7.6b is equivalent to writing $\dot{m} = \text{constant} = \rho v_r A(r)$ where $A(r) = 4\pi r^2$.
For our axisymmetric system with steady flow, the general continuity equation (Eqn. 7.5) yields

$$\boxed{\frac{1}{r}\frac{\partial}{\partial r}(r\rho v_r) + \frac{\partial}{\partial x}(\rho v_x) = 0}$$ (7.7)

which results from setting $v_\theta = 0$ in the complete cylindrical formulation. Note that now, for the first time, two velocity components, v_r and v_x, appear, rather than just a single component as in previous analyses.

SPECIES MASS CONSERVATION (SPECIES CONTINUITY)

In Chapter 3, we derived the one-dimensional species conservation equation with the assumptions that species diffused only as a result of concentration gradients and that the mixture was comprised of only two species, i.e., a binary mixture. We will not repeat that development here, but, rather restate our final result (Eqn. 3.31) which for steady flow is written as

$$\frac{d}{dx}\left[\dot{m}'' Y_A \quad - \quad \rho D_{AB} \frac{dY_A}{dx}\right] \quad = \quad \dot{m}_A'''$$

or

$$\frac{d}{dx}(\dot{m}'' Y_A) \quad - \quad \frac{d}{dx}\left(\rho D_{AB} \frac{dY_A}{dx}\right) \quad = \quad \dot{m}_A'''$$

Mass flow of species A due to convection (advection by bulk flow) per unit volume (kg/s-m³)	Mass flow of species A due to molecular diffusion per unit volume (kg/s-m³)	Net mass production rate of species A by chemical reaction per unit volume (kg/s-m³)

(7.8)

where $\dot{m}''$ is the mass flux ρv_x, and $\dot{m}_A'''$ is the net production rate of species A per unit volume associated with chemical reaction. A more general one-dimensional form of species continuity can be expressed as

$$\frac{d\dot{m}_i''}{dx} = \dot{m}_i''' \qquad i = 1, 2, \dots N \tag{7.9}$$

where the subscript i represents the ith species. In this relation, no restrictions, such as binary diffusion governed by Fick's Law, have been imposed to describe the species flux $\dot{m}_i''$.

The general vector form for mass conservation of the ith species is expressed:

$$\frac{\partial(\rho Y_i)}{\partial t} \quad + \quad \nabla \cdot \dot{\mathbf{m}}_i'' \quad = \quad \dot{m}_i''' \quad \text{for } i = 1, 2, \dots N. \tag{7.10}$$

Rate of gain of mass of species i per unit volume	Net rate of mass flow of species i out by diffusion and bulk flow per unit volume	Net rate of mass production of species i per unit volume

At this juncture, it is worthwhile to digress somewhat to discuss the species mass flux in a bit more detail. The mass flux of i, $\dot{m}_i''$, is defined by the species i mass average velocity v_i, as follows:

$$\dot{m}_i'' \equiv \rho Y_i \mathbf{v}_i, \tag{7.11}$$

where the **species velocity** $\mathbf{v}_i$ is, in general, a quite complicated expression that takes into account mass diffusion associated with concentration gradients **(ordinary diffusion)**, temperature gradients **(thermal diffusion)**, and pressure gradients **(pressure diffusion)**. The sum of all the individual species mass fluxes is the mixture mass flux, i.e.,

$$\sum \dot{m}_i'' = \sum \rho Y_i \mathbf{v}_i = \dot{m}''. \tag{7.12}$$

Thus, we see that, since $\dot{m}'' \equiv \rho \mathbf{V}$, the mixture mass average velocity $\mathbf{V}$ is given as

$$\mathbf{V} = \sum Y_i \mathbf{v}_i. \tag{7.13}$$

This is the fluid velocity with which you are familiar and is referred to as the mass average **bulk velocity**. The difference between the species velocity and the bulk velocity is defined as the **diffusional velocity**, $\mathbf{v}_i - \mathbf{V}$, i.e., the velocity of an individual species relative to the bulk velocity. The diffusional mass flux can be expressed in terms of the diffusional velocity.

$$\dot{m}_{i,\mathbf{diff}}'' \equiv \rho Y_i(\mathbf{v}_i - \mathbf{V}). \tag{7.14}$$

As discussed in Chapter 3, the total species mass flux is the sum of the bulk flow and diffusion contributions, i.e.,

$$\dot{m}_i'' = \dot{m}'' Y_i + \dot{m}_{i,\mathbf{diff}}'' \tag{7.15a}$$

or, in terms of velocities,

$$\rho Y_i \mathbf{v}_i = \rho Y_i \mathbf{V} + \rho Y_i(\mathbf{v}_i - \mathbf{V}). \tag{7.15b}$$

Depending on the direction of the species concentration gradients, the diffusional flux, or velocity, can be directed either against or with the bulk flow. For example, a high concentration of a species downstream creates a diffusional flux upstream against the bulk flow. We end our digression here and return to the development of the simplified species conservation equations for the spherical and axisymmetrical geometries.

For the case of ordinary diffusion only (no thermal or pressure diffusion) in a binary mixture, the general form of Fick's Law given below can be used to evaluate the species mass flux, $\dot{m}_i''$, which appears in our general species conservation relation (Eqn. 7.10):

$$\dot{m}_A'' = \dot{m}'' Y_A - \rho \mathcal{D}_{AB} \nabla Y_A. \tag{7.16}$$

For the spherically symmetric system with steady flow, Eqn. 7.10 becomes

$$\frac{1}{r^2} \frac{d}{dr} \left(r^2 \dot{m}_i'' \right) = \dot{m}_i''' \qquad i = 1, 2, \ldots N \tag{7.17}$$

or, with the assumption of binary diffusion, Eqn. 7.16,

$$\boxed{\frac{1}{r^2}\frac{d}{dr}\left[r^2\left(\rho v_r Y_A - \rho D_{AB}\frac{dY_A}{dr}\right)\right] = \dot{m}_A'''}.$$

(7.18)

The physical interpretation of the above relation is the same as previously shown (Eqn. 7.8) except that the mass flow of species A is directed in the radial direction, rather than in the x-direction.

For the axisymmetric geometry (r, x-coordinates), the corresponding species conservation equation for a binary mixture is

$$\frac{1}{r}\frac{\partial}{\partial r}(r\rho v_r Y_A) \qquad + \qquad \frac{1}{r}\frac{\partial}{\partial x}(r\rho v_x Y_A)$$

Mass flow of species A
due to radial convection
(radial advection by bulk flow)
per unit volume ($kg_A/s\text{-}m^3$)

Mass flow of species A
due to axial convection
(axial advection by bulk flow)
per unit volume ($kg_A/s\text{-}m^3$)

$$-\frac{1}{r}\frac{\partial}{\partial r}\left[r\rho D_{AB}\frac{\partial Y_A}{\partial r}\right] \qquad = \qquad \dot{m}_A'''$$

(7.19)

Mass flow of species A
due to molecular diffusion
in radial direction per unit volume
($kg_A/s\text{-}m^3$)

Net mass production rate
of species A by chemical
reaction per unit volume
($kg_A/s\text{-}m^3$)

In the above equation, we have assumed that axial diffusion is negligible in comparison to radial diffusion and both axial and radial convection (advection).

MOMENTUM CONSERVATION

One-Dimensional Forms

Momentum conservation for our 1-D planar and spherical systems is exceedingly simple because we neglect both viscous forces and the gravitational body force. Figure 7.3 illustrates that the only forces acting on our planar control volume are those due to pressure. Also, there is only a single momentum flow in and a single momentum flow out of the control volume because of the simple geometry. For steady state, the general statement of momentum conservation is that the sum of all forces acting in a given direction on a control volume equals the net flow of momentum out of the control volume in the same direction, i.e.,

$$\sum \mathbf{F} = \dot{m}\mathbf{v_{out}} - \dot{m}\mathbf{v_{in}}.$$

(7.20)

For the 1-D system shown in Fig. 7.3, Eqn. 7.20 is written

$$[PA]_x - [PA]_{x+\Delta x} = \dot{m}([v_x]_{x+\Delta x} - [v_x]_x).$$

(7.21)

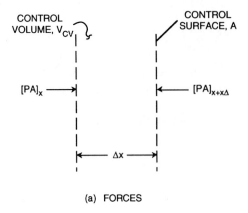

(a) FORCES

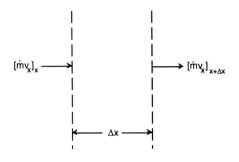

FIGURE 7.3
Control volume for one-dimensional analysis of momentum conservation, neglecting all effects of viscosity.

Dividing the left- and right-hand-sides of the above equation by Δx, recognizing that both A and $\dot{m}$ are constant, and taking the limit $\Delta x \to 0$, we recover the following ordinary differential equation:

$$-\frac{dP}{dx} = \dot{m}'' \frac{dv_x}{dx}.$$

(7.22)

Expressing the mass flux in terms of the velocity ($\dot{m}'' = \rho v_x$), Eqn. 7.22 becomes

$$-\frac{dP}{dx} = \rho v_x \frac{dv_x}{dx}.$$

(7.23)

This is the 1-D Euler equation with which you are probably familiar. For the spherically symmetric flow, a similar result is found where r and v_r replace x and v_x, respectively.

For the 1-D laminar premixed flame (Chapter 8), and droplet combustion (Chapter 10), we will assume that kinetic energy change across the flame is small, i.e.,

$$\frac{d\left(v_x^2/2\right)}{dx} = v_x \frac{dv_x}{dx} \approx 0.$$

Hence, the momentum equation simplifies to the trivial result that

$$\frac{dP}{dx} = 0, \qquad (7.24)$$

which implies that the pressure is constant throughout the flowfield. The same result obtains for the spherical system.

Two-Dimensional Forms

Rather than proceeding directly with the axisymmetric problem, we first illustrate the essential elements of momentum conservation for a two-dimensional viscous flow in cartesian (x, y) coordinates. Working in the cartesian system allows us to visualize and assemble the various terms in the momentum equation in a more straightforward manner than is possible in cylindrical coordinates. Following this development, we present the analogous axisymmetric formulation and simplify this for the boundary-layer-like jet flow.

Figure 7.4 illustrates the various forces acting in the x-direction on a control volume having a width Δx, height Δy, and unit depth in a steady two-dimensional flow. Acting normal to the x-faces are the normal viscous stresses τ_{xx}, and the pressure P, each multiplied by the area over which they act, $\Delta y\,(1)$. Acting on the y-faces, but generating a force in the x-direction, are the viscous shear stresses τ_{yx}, also multiplied by the area over which they act, $\Delta x\,(1)$. Acting at the center of

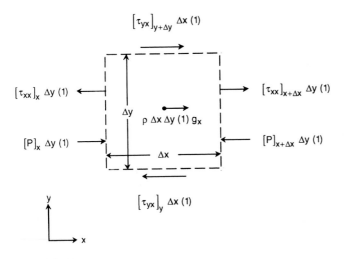

FIGURE 7.4
Forces in the x-direction acting on x- and y-faces of a two-dimensional control volume of unit depth (perpendicular to page).

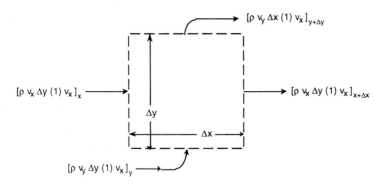

FIGURE 7.5
Momentum flows through x- and y-faces of a two-dimensional control volume of unit depth (perpendicular to page).

mass of the control volume is the body force associated with gravity, $m_{cv}g_x(=\rho\Delta x\Delta y(1)g_x)$. The various x-direction momentum flows associated with the same control volume are shown in Fig. 7.5. Each of these corresponds to the product of the mass flowrate through the control-volume face of interest and the x-component of the velocity at that face. Applying the principle of momentum conservation, which states that the sum of the forces in the x-direction must equal the net momentum flow out of the control volume, we write

$$
\begin{aligned}
&([\tau_{xx}]_{x+\Delta x} - [\tau_{xx}]_x)\Delta y(1) + \left([\tau_{yx}]_{y+\Delta y}-[\tau_{yx}]_y\right)\Delta x(1) \\
&+ ([P]_x - [P]_{x+\Delta x})\Delta y(1) + \rho\Delta x\Delta y(1)g_x \\
&= ([\rho v_x v_x]_{x+\Delta x} - [\rho v_x v_x]_x)\Delta y(1) \\
&+ ([\rho v_y v_x]_{y+\Delta y} - [\rho v_y v_x]_y)\Delta x(1).
\end{aligned}
\tag{7.25}
$$

Dividing each term above by $\Delta x\,\Delta y$, taking the limits $\Delta x\to 0$ and $\Delta y\to 0$, and recognizing the definitions of the various partial derivatives, Eqn. 7.25 becomes

$$
\frac{\partial(\rho v_x v_x)}{\partial x} + \frac{\partial(\rho v_y v_x)}{\partial y} = \frac{\partial\tau_{xx}}{\partial x} + \frac{\partial\tau_{yx}}{\partial y} - \frac{\partial P}{\partial x} + \rho g_x,
\tag{7.26}
$$

where the momentum flows have been placed on the left-hand-side, and the forces on the right.

A similar procedure yields the steady-flow y-component of the momentum equation:

$$
\frac{\partial(\rho v_x v_y)}{\partial x} + \frac{\partial(\rho v_y v_y)}{\partial y} = \frac{\partial\tau_{xy}}{\partial x} + \frac{\partial\tau_{yy}}{\partial y} - \frac{\partial P}{\partial y} + \rho g_y.
\tag{7.27}
$$

The corresponding equations for the axial and radial components of the momentum equation for the axisymmetric flow expressed in cylindrical coordinates are:

axial (x) component

$$\frac{\partial}{\partial x}(r\rho v_x v_x) + \frac{\partial}{\partial r}(r\rho v_x v_r) = \frac{\partial}{\partial r}(r\tau_{rx}) + r\frac{\partial \tau_{xx}}{\partial x} - r\frac{\partial P}{\partial x} + \rho g_x r \qquad (7.28)$$

radial (r) component

$$\frac{\partial}{\partial x}(r\rho v_r v_x) + \frac{\partial}{\partial r}(r\rho v_r v_r) = \frac{\partial}{\partial r}(r\tau_{rr}) + r\frac{\partial \tau_{rx}}{\partial x} - r\frac{\partial P}{\partial r}. \qquad (7.29)$$

To preserve axisymmetry in the presence of a gravitational field, we assume that the gravitational acceleration is aligned with the x-direction.

For a Newtonian fluid, the viscous stresses appearing in the above equations are given by

$$\tau_{xx} = \mu\left[2\frac{\partial v_x}{\partial x} - \frac{2}{3}(\nabla \cdot \mathbf{V})\right], \qquad (7.30a)$$

$$\tau_{rr} = \mu\left[2\frac{\partial v_r}{\partial r} - \frac{2}{3}(\nabla \cdot \mathbf{V})\right], \qquad (7.30b)$$

$$\tau_{rx} = \mu\left[2\frac{\partial v_x}{\partial r} + \frac{\partial v_r}{\partial x}\right], \qquad (7.30c)$$

where μ is the fluid viscosity and

$$(\nabla \cdot \mathbf{V}) = \frac{1}{r}\frac{\partial}{\partial r}(rv_r) + \frac{\partial v_x}{\partial x}.$$

Our purpose in developing the axisymmetric flow momentum equations is to apply them to jet flames in subsequent chapters. Jets have characteristics very similar to boundary layers which develop in flows adjoining a solid surface. First, the jet width is typically small in comparison to its length in the same sense that a boundary layer is thin in comparison to its length. Second, velocities change much more rapidly in the direction transverse to the flow than they do in the axial direction, i.e., $\partial(\ )/\partial r \gg \partial(\ )/\partial x$. And lastly, axial velocities are much larger than the transverse velocities, i.e., $v_x \gg v_r$. Using these properties of a jet (boundary layer) flow, the axial component of the momentum equation (Eqn. 7.28) can be simplified using dimensional (order-of-magnitude) analysis. Specifically, for the axial component, $r(\partial \tau_{xx}/\partial x)$ is neglected, since

$$\frac{\partial}{\partial r}(r\tau_{rx}) \gg r\frac{\partial \tau_{xx}}{\partial x},$$

and τ_{rx} simplifies to

$$\tau_{rx} = \mu\frac{\partial v_x}{\partial r},$$

since

$$\frac{\partial v_x}{\partial r} \gg \frac{\partial v_r}{\partial x}.$$

With these simplifications, the axial momentum equation becomes

$$\frac{\partial}{\partial x}(r\rho v_x v_x) + \frac{\partial}{\partial r}(r\rho v_x v_r) = \frac{\partial}{\partial r}\left(r\mu \frac{\partial v_x}{\partial r}\right) - r\frac{\partial P}{\partial x} + \rho g_x r. \tag{7.31}$$

From a similar order-of-magnitude analysis of the radial momentum equation, one comes to the conclusion that $\partial P/\partial r$ is very small (see, for example, Schlichting [5]). This implies that the pressure inside the jet at any axial station is essentially the same as the pressure in the ambient fluid, outside of the jet, at the same axial position. With this knowledge, we can equate $\partial P/\partial x$ appearing in the axial momentum equation to the hydrostatic pressure gradient in the ambient fluid; and, furthermore, the velocity components v_x and v_r can be determined by simultaneously solving the overall continuity (Eqn. 7.7) and axial momentum (Eqn. 7.31) equations, with no need to include the radial momentum equation explicitly.

   In our future developments (Chapters 9 and 13), we will assume that the jet is oriented vertically upwards with gravity acting downwards, thus providing a positive buoyancy effect, or, in some cases, neglect gravity altogether. For the first case, then, we recognize, as mentioned above, that

$$\frac{\partial P}{\partial x} \approx \frac{\partial P_\infty}{\partial x} = -\rho_\infty g \tag{7.32}$$

where $g(=-g_x)$ is the scalar gravitational acceleration ($9.81\,\text{m/s}^2$), and P_∞ and ρ_∞ are the ambient fluid pressure and density, respectively. Combining Eqn. 7.32 with Eqn. 7.31 yields our final form of the axial momentum equation:

$$
\begin{array}{ccc}
\dfrac{1}{r}\dfrac{\partial}{\partial x}(r\rho v_x v_x) & + & \dfrac{1}{r}\dfrac{\partial}{\partial r}(r\rho v_x v_r) \\[2mm]
\begin{array}{c}\text{x-momentum flow}\\\text{by axial convection}\\\text{per unit volume}\end{array} & & \begin{array}{c}\text{x-momentum flow}\\\text{by radial convection}\\\text{per unit volume}\end{array} \\[6mm]
= \quad \dfrac{1}{r}\dfrac{\partial}{\partial r}\left(r\mu \dfrac{\partial v_x}{\partial r}\right) & + & (\rho_\infty - \rho)g \\[2mm]
\begin{array}{c}\text{Viscous force}\\\text{per unit volume}\end{array} & & \begin{array}{c}\text{Buoyant force}\\\text{per unit volume}\end{array}
\end{array}
\tag{7.33}
$$

Note that the above relation allows for variable density, an inherent characteristic of combusting flows, and variable (temperature-dependent) viscosity.

ENERGY CONSERVATION

General One-Dimensional Form

Starting with a one-dimensional cartesian system, we consider the control volume in Fig. 7.6, where the various energy flows into and out of a plane layer, Δx in length, are shown. Following Eqn. 2.28, the first law of thermodynamics can be expressed:

$$(\dot{Q}''_x - \dot{Q}''_{x+\Delta x})A - \dot{W}_{cv} = \dot{m}''A\left[\left(h + \frac{v_x^2}{2} + gz\right)_{x+\Delta x} - \left(h + \frac{v_x^2}{2} + gz\right)_x\right]. \quad (7.34)$$

From the outset, we assume steady state; thus, no energy accumulation within the control volume is indicated. We also assume that no work is done by the control volume and that there is no change in potential energies of the inlet and outlet streams. With these assumptions, dividing through by the area A, and rearranging, Eqn. 7.34 becomes

$$-(\dot{Q}''_{x+\Delta x} - \dot{Q}''_x) = \dot{m}''\left[\left(h + \frac{v_x^2}{2}\right)_{x+\Delta x} - \left(h + \frac{v_x^2}{2}\right)_x\right]. \quad (7.35)$$

Dividing both sides of Eqn. 7.35 by Δx, taking the limit $\Delta x \to 0$, and recognizing the definition of a derivative, we obtain the following differential equation:

$$-\frac{d\dot{Q}''_x}{dx} = \dot{m}''\left(\frac{dh}{dx} + v_x\frac{dv_x}{dx}\right). \quad (7.36)$$

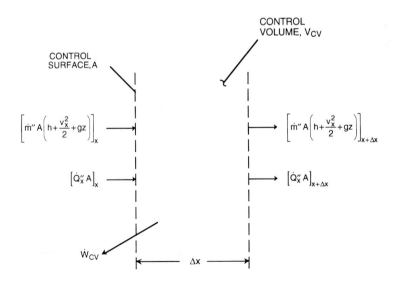

FIGURE 7.6
Control volume analysis for one-dimensional, steady-state analysis of energy conservation.

If we were dealing with a system where there was no species diffusion, we would simply replace the heat flux $\dot{Q}''_x$ with Fourier's Law for conduction; however, in our system, which assumes species are diffusing, the heat flux consists of both conduction and an additional enthalpy flux resulting from the diffusing species. Assuming there is no radiation, the general vector form of the heat flux is given by

$$\dot{\mathbf{Q}}'' \quad = \quad -k\nabla T \quad + \quad \sum \dot{m}''_{i,\text{diff}} h_i \qquad (7.37a)$$

Heat flux vector	Conduction contribution	Species diffusion contribution

where $\dot{m}''_{i,\text{diff}}$ is the diffusional flux of the ith species, which was introduced in our discussion of species conservation. For our 1-D plane layer, the heat flux is

$$\dot{Q}''_x = -k\frac{dT}{dx} + \sum \rho Y_i (v_{ix} - v_x) h_i, \qquad (7.37b)$$

where we have related the diffusional flux to the diffusion velocity (Eqn. 7.14). At this juncture, we have all the physics we wish to consider defined by Eqn. 7.36 with Eqn. 7.37b. The following development is primarily mathematical manipulation and coupling with concepts and definitions from our discussion of species conservation.

Before substituting $\dot{Q}''_x$ back into our expression for overall energy conservation, we rewrite Eqn. 7.37b in terms of the bulk and species mass fluxes, i.e.,

$$\dot{Q}''_x = -k\frac{dT}{dx} + \sum \rho v_{ix} Y_i h_i - \rho v_x \sum Y_i h_i = -k\frac{dT}{dx} + \sum \dot{m}''_i h_i - \dot{m}'' h, \quad (7.38)$$

where we recognize that $\dot{m}''_i = \rho v_{ix} Y_i$, $\rho v_x = \dot{m}''$, and $\sum Y_i h_i = h$. Now substituting Eqn. 7.38 into Eqn. 7.36, canceling the $\dot{m}'' dh/dx$ terms which appear on each side, and rearranging, results in

$$\frac{d}{dx}\left(\sum h_i \dot{m}''_i\right) + \frac{d}{dx}\left(-k\frac{dT}{dx}\right) + \dot{m}'' v_x \frac{dv_x}{dx} = 0. \qquad (7.39)$$

We now expand the first term in Eqn. 7.39, i.e.,

$$\frac{d}{dx}\left(\sum h_i \dot{m}''_i\right) = \sum \dot{m}''_i \frac{dh_i}{dx} + \sum h_i \frac{d\dot{m}''_i}{dx}.$$

The term $d\dot{m}''/dx$, that now appears, is key in that from species conservation (Eqn. 7.9),

$$\frac{d\dot{m}''_i}{dx} = \dot{m}'''_i.$$

With the substitution of the above, energy conservation (Eqn. 7.39) is explicitly linked to the species production rates associated with chemical reactions. Our final 1-D energy conservation equation is

$$\sum \dot{m}_i'' \frac{dh_i}{dx} + \frac{d}{dx}\left(-k\frac{dT}{dx}\right) + \dot{m}'' v_x \frac{dv_x}{dx} = -\sum h_i \dot{m}_i''' . \qquad (7.40)$$

Equation 7.40 is often the starting point for further simplification and, as such, applies equally well to multi-component (nonbinary) and binary systems. It is also important to note that, so far, no assumptions have been made with regard to the thermophysical properties $(k, \rho, c_p, \mathcal{D})$; we have, however, assumed that there is no radiation, no viscous dissipation, and no potential energy changes. Table 7.1 summarizes the assumptions inherent in the various energy conservation expressions developed in this chapter.

Shvab–Zeldovich Forms

The **Shvab–Zeldovich energy equation**, so named in recognition of the researchers who first developed it, is particularly useful in that the species mass fluxes and

TABLE 7.1
Energy equation assumptions

Equation	Basic assumptions/neglected effects	Properties	Mass transfer laws	Geometry
Eqn. 7.40	i. Steady state ii. No effect of gravity iii. No shaft work or viscous dissipation iv. No radiation heat transfer	Variable, temperature-dependent properties	Ordinary (concentration gradient) diffusion only	Constant-area plane layer (1-D cartesian)
Eqn. 7.46	i–iv above + thermal diffusivity (α) equals mass diffusivity $(\mathcal{D})$, i.e., the Lewis number (Le) is unity	As above	As above + binary (or effective binary) diffusion governed by Fick's Law	As above
Eqn. 7.47	As above + kinetic energy changes are negligible, which implies that the pressure is constant	As above	As above	As above
Eqn. 7.49	As above	As above	As above	One-dimensional, spherically symmetric
Eqn. 7.50	As above + negligible diffusion in the axial (x) direction	As above	As above	Two-dimensional, axisymmetric

enthalpies are eliminated from the left-hand-side of Eqn. 7.40 and replaced with terms having temperature as the only dependent variable. A key assumption in the development of the Shvab–Zeldovich equation is that the **Lewis number** $(Le = k/\rho c_p D)$ is unity. The **unity Le assumption** is frequently invoked in the analysis of combustion problems, and the great simplification that it affords will be emphasized here. Another key assumption in our development is that Fick's Law can be used to describe the species mass fluxes.

We begin by examining the heat flux for a reacting flow defined in Eqn. 7.37a:

$$\dot{Q}''_x = -k\frac{dT}{dx} + \sum \dot{m}''_{i,\mathrm{diff}} h_i.$$

(7.41)

Using the definition of the species flux (Eqn. 7.15a) and Fick's Law (Eqn. 3.1 or 7.16), Eqn. 7.41 becomes

$$\dot{Q}''_x = -k\frac{dT}{dx} - \sum \rho D \frac{dY_i}{dx} h_i$$

(7.42a)

or, assuming a single diffusivity characterizes the mixture,

$$\dot{Q}''_x = -k\frac{dT}{dx} - \rho D \sum h_i \frac{dY_i}{dx}.$$

(7.42b)

By applying the definition of the derivative of the product,

$$\frac{d\sum h_i Y_i}{dx} = \sum h_i \frac{dY_i}{dx} + \sum Y_i \frac{dh_i}{dx},$$

the heat flux is now expressed

$$\dot{Q}''_x = -k\frac{dT}{dx} - \rho D \frac{d\sum h_i Y_i}{dx} + \rho D \sum Y_i \frac{dh_i}{dx}.$$

(7.42c)

We use the definition of $h \equiv \sum h_i Y_i$ to simplify the second term on the right-hand-side; while the third term can be expressed in terms of c_p and T by recognizing that

$$\sum Y_i \frac{dh_i}{dx} = \sum Y_i c_{p,i} \frac{dT}{dx} = c_p \frac{dT}{dx}.$$

The three terms comprising the heat flux are now

$$\dot{Q}''_x = -k\frac{dT}{dx} - \rho D \frac{dh}{dx} + \rho D c_p \frac{dT}{dx}.$$

(7.42d)

Using the definition of the thermal diffusivity, $\alpha \equiv k/\rho c_p$, to express the thermal conductivity appearing in the above, results in

$$\dot{Q}_x'' = \underbrace{-\rho\alpha c_p\frac{dT}{dx}}_{\substack{\text{Flux of sensible} \\ \text{enthalpy due to} \\ \text{conduction}}} - \underbrace{\rho D\frac{dh}{dx}}_{\substack{\text{Flux of absolute} \\ \text{enthalpy due to} \\ \text{species diffusion}}} + \underbrace{\rho D c_p\frac{dT}{dx}}_{\substack{\text{Flux of sensible} \\ \text{enthalpy due to} \\ \text{species diffusion}}} \qquad (7.42e)$$

where a physical interpretation of each of the terms is shown. In general, all three terms contribute to the total heat flux; however, for the special case where $\alpha = D$, we see that the sensible enthalpy flux due to conduction cancels with the sensible enthalpy flux arising from species diffusion. Since the Lewis number is defined as the ratio of α to D,

$$Le \equiv \frac{\alpha}{D} = 1 \qquad (7.43)$$

for this special case. For many species of interest in combustion, Lewis numbers are of the order of unity, thus providing some physical justification for equating α and D. With this assumption, the heat flux is simply

$$\dot{Q}_x'' = -\rho D\frac{dh}{dx}. \qquad (7.44)$$

We now employ the above in our basic energy conservation equation (Eqn. 7.36); thus,

$$\frac{d}{dx}\left(\rho D\frac{dh}{dx}\right) = \dot{m}''\frac{dh}{dx} + \dot{m}''v_x\frac{dv_x}{dx}. \qquad (7.45)$$

Employing the definition of the absolute (or standardized) enthalpy,

$$h = \sum Y_i h_{f,i}^o + \int_{T_{\text{ref}}}^{T} c_p dT,$$

Eqn. 7.45 becomes

$$\frac{d}{dx}\left[\rho D\sum h_{f,i}^o\frac{dY_i}{dx} + \rho D\frac{d\int c_p dT}{dx}\right] = \dot{m}''\sum h_{f,i}^o\frac{dY_i}{dx} + \dot{m}''\frac{d\int c_p dT}{dx} + \dot{m}''v_x\frac{dv_x}{dx}.$$

Rearranging the above yields

$$\dot{m}''\frac{d\int c_p dT}{dx} - \frac{d}{dx}\left[\rho D\frac{d\int c_p dT}{dx}\right] + \dot{m}''v_x\frac{dv_x}{dx} = -\frac{d}{dx}\left[\sum h_{f,i}^o\left(\dot{m}''Y_i - \rho D\frac{dY_i}{dx}\right)\right].$$

The right-hand-side of the above is simplified by employing both Fick's Law and species conservation (Eqn. 7.9):

$$-\frac{d}{dx}\left[\sum h_{f,i}^o\left(\dot{m}''Y_i - \rho D\frac{dY_i}{dx}\right)\right] = -\frac{d}{dx}\left[\sum h_{f,i}^o\dot{m}_i''\right] = -\sum h_{f,i}^o\dot{m}_i'''.$$

We now reassemble our final result,

$$\dot{m}''\frac{d\int c_p dT}{dx} - \frac{d}{dx}\left[\rho D\frac{d\int c_p dT}{dx}\right] + \dot{m}''v_x\frac{dv_x}{dx} = -\sum h_{f,i}^o \dot{m}_i'''. \qquad (7.46)$$

Thus far, we have retained the kinetic energy change term for completeness; however, this term is usually small and generally neglected in most developments of the Shvab–Zeldovich energy equation. Dropping this term, we have the following result, which has the simple physical interpretation that the combined rates of convection (advection) and diffusion of sensible enthalpy (thermal energy) equal the rate at which chemical energy is converted to thermal energy by chemical reaction:

$$\underbrace{\dot{m}''\frac{d\int c_p dT}{dx}}_{\substack{\text{Rate of sensible}\\\text{enthalpy transport by}\\\text{convection (advection)}\\\text{per unit volume (W/m}^3)}} + \underbrace{\frac{d}{dx}\left[-\rho D\frac{d\int c_p dT}{dx}\right]}_{\substack{\text{Rate of sensible}\\\text{enthalpy transport}\\\text{by diffusion per unit}\\\text{volume (W/m}^3)}} = \underbrace{-\sum h_{f,i}^o \dot{m}_i'''}_{\substack{\text{Rate of sensible}\\\text{enthalpy production}\\\text{by chemical reaction}\\\text{per unit volume (W/m}^3)}}$$

$$(7.47)$$

The general form of the Shvab–Zeldovich energy equation is

$$\nabla \cdot \left[\dot{m}'' \int c_p dT - \rho D \nabla \left(\int c_p dT\right)\right] = -\sum h_{f,i}^o \dot{m}_i'''. \qquad (7.48)$$

We can apply the definitions of the vector operators to obtain the Shvab–Zeldovich energy equation for our spherical and axisymmetric geometries. The 1-D spherical form is

$$\boxed{\frac{1}{r^2}\frac{d}{dr}\left[r^2\left(\rho v_r \int c_p dT - \rho D\frac{d\int c_p dT}{dr}\right)\right] = -\sum h_{f,i}^o \dot{m}_i'''} \qquad (7.49)$$

and the axisymmetrix form is

$$\underbrace{\frac{1}{r}\frac{\partial}{\partial x}\left(r\rho v_x \int c_p dT\right)}_{\substack{\text{Rate of sensible}\\\text{enthalpy transport}\\\text{by axial convection}\\\text{(advection) per unit}\\\text{volume (W/m}^3)}} + \underbrace{\frac{1}{r}\frac{\partial}{\partial r}\left(r\rho v_r \int c_p dT\right)}_{\substack{\text{Rate of sensible}\\\text{enthalpy transport}\\\text{by radial convection}\\\text{(advection) per unit}\\\text{volume (W/m}^3)}} - \underbrace{\frac{1}{r}\frac{\partial}{\partial r}\left(r\rho D\frac{\partial\int c_p dT}{\partial r}\right)}_{\substack{\text{Rate of sensible}\\\text{enthalpy transport}\\\text{by radial diffusion}\\\text{per unit volume}\\\text{(W/m}^3)}} = \underbrace{-\sum h_{f,i}^o \dot{m}'''}_{\substack{\text{Rate of sensible}\\\text{enthalpy production}\\\text{by chemical reaction}\\\text{per unit volume}\\\text{(W/m}^3)}}$$

$$(7.50)$$

Note that, in all of the forms of the energy equation given above, we have made no assumptions that the properties are constant; however, in many simplified analyses of combustion systems, as we will employ in subsequent chapters, it is useful to treat c_p and the product $\rho\mathcal{D}$ as constants. Table 7.1 summarizes the assumptions we have employed in developing our various energy conservation equations.

THE CONCEPT OF A CONSERVED SCALAR

The **conserved scalar** concept greatly simplifies the solution of reacting flow problems (i.e., the determination of the fields of velocity, species, and temperature), particularly those involving nonpremixed flames. A somewhat tautological definition of a conserved scalar is any scalar property that is conserved throughout the flowfield. For example, with certain restrictions, the absolute enthalpy is conserved at every point in a flow when there are no sources (or sinks) of thermal energy, such as radiation into or out of the flow or viscous dissipation. In this case, then, the absolute enthalpy would qualify as being a conserved scalar. Element mass fractions are also conserved scalars, since elements are neither created nor destroyed by chemical reaction. There are many conserved scalars that can be defined [6]; however, in the development here we choose to deal with only two: the mixture fraction, defined below, and the previous mentioned mixture absolute enthalpy.

Definition of Mixture Fraction

If we restrict our flow system to consist of a single inlet stream of pure fuel together with a single stream of pure oxidizer, which react to form a single product, we can define the **mixture fraction**, f, a conserved scalar, as

$$f \equiv \frac{\text{mass of material having its origin in the fuel stream}}{\text{mass of mixture}} \qquad (7.51)$$

Since Eqn. 7.51 applies to an infinitesimally small volume, f is just a special kind of mass fraction, formed as a combination of fuel, oxidizer, and product mass fractions, as shown below. For example, f is unity in the fuel stream and zero in the oxidizer stream; and within the flowfield, f takes on values between unity and zero.

For our three-"species" system, we can define f in terms of the fuel, oxidizer, and product mass fractions at any point in the flow, when

$$1 \text{ kg fuel} + \nu \text{ kg oxidizer} \rightarrow (\nu + 1) \text{ kg products.} \qquad (7.52)$$

That is

$$f \qquad = (1) \qquad Y_F \quad +$$

Mass fraction of
material having $\qquad \left(\dfrac{\text{kg fuel stuff}}{\text{kg fuel}}\right) \quad \left(\dfrac{\text{kg fuel}}{\text{kg mixture}}\right)$
its origin in the
fuel stream

$$\left(\dfrac{1}{\nu + 1}\right) \qquad Y_{Pr} \qquad + \qquad (0) \qquad Y_{Ox},$$

$$\left(\dfrac{\text{kg fuel stuff}}{\text{kg products}}\right) \left(\dfrac{\text{kg products}}{\text{kg mixture}}\right) \qquad \left(\dfrac{\text{kg fuel stuff}}{\text{kg oxidizer}}\right) \left(\dfrac{\text{kg oxidizer}}{\text{kg mixture}}\right)$$

$$(7.53)$$

where "fuel stuff" is that material originating in the fuel stream. For a hydrocarbon fuel, fuel stuff is carbon and hydrogen. Equation 7.53 is more simply
written

$$\boxed{f = Y_F + \left(\dfrac{1}{\nu + 1}\right) Y_{Pr}} \; . \qquad\qquad (7.54)$$

This conserved scalar is particularly useful in dealing with diffusion flames where
the fuel and oxidizer streams are initially segregated. For premixed combustion,
the mixture fraction is everywhere uniform, assuming all species diffuse at the
same rate; hence, a conservation equation for f provides no new information.

Conservation of Mixture Fraction

The utility of the conserved scalar, f, is that it can be used to generate a species
conservation equation that has no reaction rate terms appearing, i.e., the equation
is "sourceless." We can develop this idea simply using the 1-D cartesian species
equations as an example. Writing out Eqn. 7.8 for the fuel and product species, we
have

$$\dot{m}'' \frac{\mathrm{d}Y_F}{\mathrm{d}x} - \frac{\mathrm{d}}{\mathrm{d}x}\left(\rho D \frac{\mathrm{d}Y_F}{\mathrm{d}x}\right) = \dot{m}_F''', \qquad\qquad (7.55)$$

$$\dot{m}'' \frac{\mathrm{d}Y_{Pr}}{\mathrm{d}x} - \frac{\mathrm{d}}{\mathrm{d}x}\left(\rho D \frac{\mathrm{d}Y_{Pr}}{\mathrm{d}x}\right) = \dot{m}_{Pr}''', \qquad\qquad (7.56)$$

Dividing Eqn. 7.56 by $(\nu + 1)$ results in

$$\dot{m}'' \frac{\mathrm{d}(Y_{Pr}/(\nu + 1))}{\mathrm{d}x} - \frac{\mathrm{d}}{\mathrm{d}x}[\rho D \mathrm{d}(Y_{Pr}/(\nu + 1))] = \frac{1}{\nu + 1}\dot{m}_{Pr}'''. \qquad (7.57)$$

Mass conservation (Eqn. 7.52) also implies that

$$\dot{m}_{Pr}'''/(\nu + 1) = -\dot{m}_F''', \qquad\qquad (7.58)$$

where the minus sign reflects that fuel is being consumed and products are being generated. Substituting Eqn. 7.58 into Eqn. 7.57 and adding the resultant equation to Eqn. 7.55 yields

$$\dot{m}'' \frac{d(Y_F + Y_{Pr}/(\nu + 1))}{dx} - \frac{d}{dx}\left(\rho D \frac{d}{dx}(Y_F + Y_{Pr}/(\nu + 1))\right) = 0. \qquad (7.59)$$

We note that Eqn. 7.59 is "sourceless," i.e., the right-hand-side is zero, and that the quantity in the derivatives is our conserved scalar, the mixture fraction, f. Recognizing this, Eqn. 7.59 is rewritten

$$\boxed{\dot{m}'' \frac{df}{dx} - \frac{d}{dx}\left(\rho D \frac{df}{dx}\right) = 0}. \qquad (7.60)$$

Similar manipulations can be performed on the 1-D spherical and the 2-D axisymmetric system equations. For the spherical system, we obtain:

$$\boxed{\frac{d}{dr}\left[r^2\left(\rho v_r f - \rho D \frac{df}{dr}\right)\right] = 0}, \qquad (7.61)$$

and for the axisymmetric geometry:

$$\boxed{\frac{\partial}{\partial x}(r\rho v_x f) + \frac{\partial}{\partial r}(r\rho v_r f) - \frac{\partial}{\partial r}\left(r\rho D \frac{\partial f}{\partial r}\right) = 0}. \qquad (7.62)$$

Example 7.1. Consider a nonpremixed, ethane (C_2H_6)–air flame in which the mole fractions of the following species are measured using various techniques: C_2H_6, CO, CO_2, H_2, H_2O, N_2, O_2, and OH. The mole fractions of all other species are assumed to be negligible. Define a mixture fraction f expressed in terms of the mole fractions of the measured species.

Solution. Our approach will be to first express f in terms of the known species mass fractions by exploiting the definition of f (Eqn. 7.51), and then express the mass fractions in terms of the mole fractions (Eqn. 2.11). Thus,

$$f \equiv \frac{\text{Mass of material originating in fuel stream}}{\text{Mass of mixture}}$$

$$= \frac{[m_C + m_H]_{mix}}{m_{mix}},$$

since the fuel stream consists only of carbon and hydrogen, and assuming that no carbon or hydrogen are present in the oxidizer stream, i.e., the air consists solely of N_2 and O_2.

In the flame gases, carbon is present in any unburned fuel and in the CO and CO_2; while hydrogen is present in unburned fuel, H_2, H_2O, and OH. Summing the mass fractions of carbon and hydrogen associated with each species yields,

$$f = Y_{C_2H_6} \frac{2MW_C}{MW_{C_2H_6}} + Y_{CO} \frac{MW_C}{MW_{CO}} + Y_{CO_2} \frac{MW_C}{MW_{CO_2}}$$
$$+ Y_{C_2H_6} \frac{3MW_{H_2}}{MW_{C_2H_6}} + Y_{H_2} + Y_{H_2O} \frac{MW_{H_2}}{MW_{H_2O}} + Y_{OH} \frac{0.5MW_{H_2}}{MW_{OH}},$$

where the weighted ratios of molecular weights are the fractions of the element (C or H_2) in each of the species. Substituting for the mass fractions, $Y_i = \chi_i MW_i / MW_{mix}$, yields

$$f = \chi_{C_2H_6} \frac{MW_{C_2H_6}}{MW_{mix}} \frac{2MW_C}{MW_{C_2H_6}} + \chi_{CO} \frac{MW_{CO}}{MW_{mix}} \frac{MW_C}{MW_{CO}} + \cdots$$
$$= \frac{(2\chi_{C_2H_6} + \chi_{CO} + \chi_{CO_2})MW_C + (3\chi_{C_2H_6} + \chi_{H_2} + \chi_{H_2O} + \frac{1}{2}\chi_{OH})MW_{H_2}}{MW_{mix}}$$

where

$$MW_{mix} = \sum \chi_i MW_i$$
$$= \chi_{C_2H_6} MW_{C_2H_6} + \chi_{CO} MW_{CO} + \chi_{CO_2} MW_{CO_2}$$
$$+ \chi_{H_2} MW_{H_2} + \chi_{H_2O} MW_{H_2O} + \chi_{N_2} MW_{N_2}$$
$$+ \chi_{O_2} MW_{O_2} + \chi_{OH} MW_{OH}.$$

Comment. Here we see that although the mixture fraction is simple in concept, experimental determinations of f may require the measurement of many species. Approximate values, of course, can be obtained by neglecting the minor species that are difficult to measure.

Example 7.2. For the experiment discussed in Example 7.1, determine a numerical value for the mixture fraction, where the mole fractions measured at a point in the flame are the following:

χ_{CO} = 949 ppm	χ_{H_2O} = 0.1488
χ_{CO_2} = 0.0989	χ_{O_2} = 0.0185
χ_{H_2} = 315 ppm	χ_{OH} = 1350 ppm.

Assume the balance of the mixture is N_2. Also, determine the equivalence ratio for the mixture using the calculated mixture fraction.

Solution. Calculation of the mixture fraction is a straightforward application of the result obtained in Example 7.1. We start by calculating the N_2 mole fraction,

$$\chi_{N_2} = 1 - \sum \chi_i$$
$$= 1 - 0.0989 - 0.1488 - 0.0185 - (949 + 315 + 1350)1 \cdot 10^{-6}$$
$$\chi_{N_2} = 0.7312.$$

The mixture molecular weight can now be determined:

$$MW_{mix} = \sum \chi_i MW_i$$
$$= 28.16 \text{ kg}_{mix}/\text{kmol}_{mix}.$$

Substituting numerical values into the expression for f from Example 7.1, yields

$$f = \frac{(949 \cdot 10^{-6} + 0.0989)12.011 + (315 \cdot 10^{-6} + 0.1488 + (0.5)1350 \cdot 10^{-6})2.016}{28.16}$$

$$\boxed{f = 0.0533} \; .$$

To calculate the equivalence ratio, we first recognize that, through its definition, the mixture fraction is related to the fuel–air ratio, (F/A), by

$$(F/A) = f/(1-f),$$

and that

$$\Phi = (F/A)/(F/A)_{\text{stoic}}.$$

For an arbitrary hydrocarbon C_xH_y, the stoichiometric fuel–air ratio is calculated from Eqn. 2.32,

$$(F/A)_{\text{stoic}} = \left[4.76(x + y/4) \frac{MW_{\text{air}}}{MW_{C_xH_y}} \right]^{-1}$$

$$= \left[4.76(2 + 6/4) \frac{28.85}{30.07} \right]^{-1}$$

$$= 0.0626.$$

Thus,

$$\Phi = \frac{f/(1-f)}{(F/A)_{\text{stoic}}} = \frac{0.0533/(1 - 0.0533)}{0.0626}$$

$$\boxed{\Phi = 0.90} \; .$$

Comment. Here we see how the mixture fraction relates to previously defined measures of stoichiometry. You should be able to develop relationships among these various measures, f, (A/F), (F/A), and Φ, through a knowledge of their fundamental definitions.

Conserved Scalar Energy Equation

Subject to all of the assumptions underlying the Shvab–Zeldovich energy equation (Eqns. 7.47–7.50), the mixture enthalpy, h, is also a conserved scalar:

$$h \equiv \sum Y_i h_{f,i}^o + \int_{T_{\text{ref}}}^{T} c_p dT. \tag{7.63}$$

This can be seen directly from energy conservation expressed by Eqn. 7.45 when the kinetic energy term $\dot{m}'' v_x dv_x/dx$ is assumed to be negligible. For our three geometries of interest, the 1-D planar, 1-D spherical, and 2-D axisymmetric, the conserved scalar forms of energy conservation are expressed, respectively, as

$$\dot{m}'' \frac{dh}{dx} - \frac{d}{dx}\left(\rho D \frac{dh}{dx}\right) = 0 \qquad (7.64)$$

$$\frac{d}{dr}\left[r^2\left(\rho v_r h - \rho D \frac{dh}{dr}\right)\right] = 0 \qquad (7.65)$$

and

$$\frac{\partial}{\partial x}(r\rho v_x h) + \frac{\partial}{\partial r}(r\rho v_r h) - \frac{\partial}{\partial r}\left(r\rho D \frac{\partial h}{\partial r}\right) = 0. \qquad (7.66)$$

The derivations of Eqns. 7.65 and 7.66 are left as exercises for the reader.

SUMMARY

In this chapter, the general forms of the conservation equations for mass, species, momentum, and energy have been presented along with their brief description. You should be able to recognize these equations and have some appreciation of the physical meaning of each term. Simplified equations were developed for three different geometries and are summarized in Table 7.2 for easy reference. These equations will be the starting point for subsequent developments throughout the text. The concept of a conserved scalar was also introduced in this chapter. Conservation equations for mixture fraction and mixture enthalpy, two conserved scalars, were developed and are also cited in Table 7.2.

TABLE 7.2
Summary of conservation equations for reacting flows

Conserved quantity	General forms	1-D planar	1-D spherical	2-D axisymmetric
Mass	Eqn. 7.5	Eqn. 7.4	Eqn. 7.6	Eqn. 7.7
Species	Eqn. 7.10	Eqns. 7.8 and 7.9	Eqn. 7.18	Eqn. 7.19
Momentum	N/A	Eqn. 7.23 and 7.24	See discussion of Eqn. 7.24	Eqn. 7.33
Energy	Eqn. 7.48 (Shvab–Zeldovich form)	Eqn. 7.40 and Eqn. 7.47 (Shvab–Zeldovich form)	Eqn. 7.49 (Shvab–Zeldovich form)	Eqn. 7.50 (Shvab–Zeldovich form)
Mixture fraction[a]	—	Eqn. 7.60	Eqn. 7.61	Eqn. 7.62
Enthalpy[a]	—	Eqn. 7.64	Eqn. 7.65	Eqn. 7.66

[a]These are just alternate conserved scalar forms of species and energy conservation, respectively, and are not separate conservation principles.

NOMENCLATURE

A	Area
c_p	Constant-pressure specific heat (J/kg-K)
$\mathcal{D}$	Mass diffusivity (m^2/s)
$\mathcal{D}_{AB}$	Binary mass diffusivity (m^2/s)
f	Mixture fraction, Eqn. 7.53
F	Force (N)
g	Gravitational acceleration (m/s^2)
h	Enthalpy (J/kg)
h_f^o	Enthalpy of formation (J/kg)
k	Thermal conductivity (W/m-K)
Le	Lewis number, $\alpha/\mathcal{D}$
m	Mass (kg)
$\dot{m}$	Mass flowrate (kg/s)
$\mathbf{\dot{m}}'', \dot{m}''$	Mass flux (kg/s-m^2)
$\dot{m}'''$	Mass production rate per unit volume (kg/s-m^3)
P	Pressure (Pa)
$\mathbf{\dot{Q}}''$	Heat flux vector, Eqn. 7.37 (W/m^2)
r	Radial coordinate (m)
t	Time (s)
T	Temperature (K)
$\mathbf{v}_i$	Mass average velocity of species i (m/s)
v_x, v_y, v_z	Cartesian coordinate velocity components (m/s)
v_r, v_θ, v_x	Cylindrical coordinate velocity components (m/s)
v_r, v_θ, v_ϕ	Spherical coordinate velocity components (m/s)
V	Volume (m^3)
$\mathbf{V}$	Velocity vector (m/s)
x	Cartesian or cylindrical axial coordinate (m)
y	Cartesian coordinate (m)
Y	Mass fraction (kg/kg)
z	Cartesian coordinate (m)

Greek symbols

α	Thermal diffusivity (m^2/s)
θ	Spherical coordinate circumferential angle (rad)
μ	Absolute or dynamic viscosity (N-s/m^2)
ν	Kinematic viscosity, μ/ρ (m^2/s), or stoichiometric oxidizer-to-fuel ratio (kg/kg)
ρ	Density (kg/m^3)
τ	Viscous stress (N/m^2)
ϕ	Spherical coordinate azimuthal angle (rad)

Subscripts

A	Species A

cv	Control volume
diff	Diffusion
F	Fuel
i	*i*th species
Ox	Oxidizer
Pr	Products
ref	Reference state
∞	Ambient condition

REFERENCES

1. Tseng, L.-K., Ismail, M. A., and Faeth, G. M., "Premixed Flame Surface Statistics at Various Preferential Diffusion Conditions in Isotropic Turbulence," Central and Eastern States Sections, The Combustion Institute, Joint Technical Meeting, New Orleans, 15–17 March 1993.
2. Bird, R. B., Stewart, W. E., and Lightfoot, E. N., *Transport Phenomena*, John Wiley & Sons, New York, 1960.
3. Williams, F. A., *Combustion Theory*, 2nd Ed., Addison-Wesley, Redwood City, CA, 1985.
4. Kuo, K. K., *Principles of Combustion*, John Wiley & Sons, New York, 1986.
5. Schlichting, H., *Boundary-Layer Theory*, 6th Ed., McGraw-Hill, New York, 1968.
6. Bilger, R. W., "Turbulent Flows with Nonpremixed Reactants," in *Turbulent Reacting Flows* (P. A. Libby, and F. A. Williams, eds.), Springer-Verlag, New York, 1980.

REVIEW QUESTIONS

1. What are the three types of mass diffusion? Which one(s) do we neglect?
2. Discuss how the heat flux vector, $\dot{Q}''$, in a multi-component mixture with diffusion differs from that used in a single-component gaseous system.
3. Define the Lewis number, Le, and discuss its physical significance. What role does the assumption that the Lewis number is unity play in simplifying the conservation of energy equation?
4. We considered three mass-average velocities in our discussion of species conservation: the bulk flow velocity, the individual species velocities, and the individual species diffusion velocities. Define each and discuss their physical significance. How do the various velocities relate to each other?
5. What does it mean for a conservation equation to be "sourceless." Give examples of both governing equations that contain sources and those that are sourceless.
6. Discuss what is meant by a conserved scalar.
7. Define the mixture fraction.

PROBLEMS

7.1. With the aid of overall continuity (Eqn. 7.7), transform the left-hand-side of the axial momentum equation, Eqn. 7.33, to a form involving the substantial (or material) derivative, where the cylindrical-coordinate substantial derivative operator is given by

$$\frac{D(\ )}{Dt} \equiv \frac{\partial(\ )}{\partial t} + v_r \frac{\partial(\ )}{\partial r} + \frac{v_\theta}{r}\frac{\partial(\ )}{\partial \theta} + v_x \frac{\partial(\ )}{\partial x}.$$

7.2. Equation 7.40 expresses conservation of energy for a 1-D (cartesian) reacting flow where no assumptions are made regarding the form of the species transport law (i.e., Fick's Law has not been invoked) or the relationship among properties (i.e., $Le = 1$ has not been assumed). Starting with this equation, derive the Shvab–Zeldovich energy equation (Eqn. 7.47) by applying Fick's Law with effective binary diffusion and assuming $Le = 1$.

7.3. Derive the conserved scalar equation for enthalpy for a 1-D spherical flow (Eqn. 7.65) starting with Eqn. 7.49.

7.4. Derive the conserved scalar equation for enthalpy for an axisymmetric flow (Eqn. 7.66) starting with Eqn. 7.50.

7.5. Consider the combustion of propane with air with products consisting of CO, CO_2, H_2O, H_2, O_2, and N_2. Define the mixture fraction in terms of the various product species mole fractions, χ_i.

7.6. So-called "state relations" are frequently employed in the analysis of diffusion flames. These state relations relate various mixture properties to the mixture fraction, or other appropriate conserved scalars. Construct state relations for the adiabatic flame temperature T_{ad} and mixture density ρ for ideal combustion (no dissociation) of propane with air. Plot T_{ad} and ρ as functions of the mixture fraction f for the range $0 \le f \le 0.12$.

7.7. Laser-based techniques are used to measure the major species, N_2, O_2, H_2, and H_2O (spontaneous Raman scattering), and the minor species OH and NO (laser-induced fluorescence), in turbulent hydrogen jet flames burning in air. The hydrogen fuel is diluted, in some cases, with helium. A mixture fraction is defined as follows:

$$f = \frac{(MW_{H_2} + \alpha MW_{He})([H_2O] + [H_2]) + (MW_H + \frac{\alpha}{2} MW_{He})[OH]}{\underset{A}{} + \underset{B}{}}$$

where $A = MW_{N_2}[N_2] + MW_{O_2}[O_2] + (MW_{H_2O} + \alpha MW_{He})[H_2O]$

and $B = (MW_{H_2} + \alpha MW_{He})[H_2] + (MW_{OH} + \frac{\alpha}{2} MW_{He})[OH]$

and where the concentrations $[X_i]$ are expressed as $kmol/m^3$ and α is the mole ratio of helium to hydrogen in the fuel stream. Here, it is assumed that there are no effects of differential diffusion and that the NO concentration is negligible.

Show that the mixture fraction defined above is the same as mass of fuel stuff per mass of mixture defined by Eqn. 7.51.

CHAPTER
8

LAMINAR PREMIXED FLAMES

OVERVIEW

In previous chapters, we introduced the concepts of mass transfer (Chapter 3) and chemical kinetics (Chapters 4 and 5) and linked them with familiar thermodynamic and heat transfer concepts in Chapters 6 and 7. Understanding premixed laminar flames requires us to utilize all of these concepts. Our development in Chapter 7 of the one-dimensional conservation equations for a reacting flow will be the starting point for analyzing laminar flames.

Laminar premixed flames, frequently in conjunction with diffusion flames, have application in many residential, commercial, and industrial devices and processes. Examples include gas ranges and ovens, heating appliances, and bunsen burners. An advanced cooktop burner for a gas range is illustrated in Fig. 8.1. Laminar, premixed, natural-gas flames also are frequently employed in the manufacturing of glass products. As suggested by the examples given above, laminar premixed flames are by themselves important; but, perhaps more importantly, understanding laminar flames is a necessary prerequisite to the study of turbulent flames. In both laminar and turbulent flows, the same physical processes are active, and many turbulent flame theories are based on an underlying laminar flame structure. In the following, we will qualitatively describe the essential characteristics of laminar premixed flames and develop a simplified analysis of these flames that allows us to see what factors influence the laminar flame speed and the

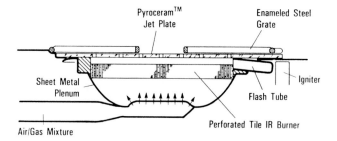

Pyroceram™
Jet Plate

Enameled Steel
Grate

Sheet Metal
Plenum

Igniter

Flash Tube

Air/Gas Mixture

Perforated Tile IR Burner

FIGURE 8.1
Advanced residential cook-
top burner for gas ranges.
(Courtesy of the Gas
Research Institute.)

flame thickness. We also will examine experimental data that illustrate how equivalence ratio, temperature, pressure, and fuel type affect flame speed and flame thickness. Flame speed is emphasized because it is this property that dictates flame shape and important flame stability characteristics, such as blowoff and flashback. The chapter concludes with discussion of flammability limits and ignition and extinction phenomena.

PHYSICAL DESCRIPTION

Definition

Before proceeding, it is useful to define what we mean by a flame. A **flame** is a self-sustaining propagation of a localized combustion zone at subsonic velocities. There are several key words in this definition. First, we require a flame to be localized, i.e., the flame occupies only a small portion of the combustible mixture at any one time. This is in contrast to the various homogeneous reactors we studied in Chapter 6, where reaction was assumed to occur uniformly throughout the reaction vessel. The second key word is subsonic. A discrete combustion wave that travels subsonically is termed a **deflagration**. It is also possibe for combustion waves to propagate at supersonic velocities. Such a wave is called a **detonation**. The fundamental propagation mechanisms are different in deflagrations and detonations, and because of this, these are distinct phenomena. Detonations will not be discussed in this book; however, the interested reader can find abundant information in the many advanced combustion textbooks [1–6] and their literature citations.

Principal Characteristics

The temperature profile through a flame is perhaps its most important characteristic. Figure 8.2 illustrates a typical flame temperature profile, together with other essential flame features.

To understand this figure, we need to establish a reference frame for our coordinate system. A flame may be freely propagating, as occurs when a flame is initiated in a tube containing a combustible gas mixture. The appropriate coordinate system would be fixed to the propagating combustion wave. An observer

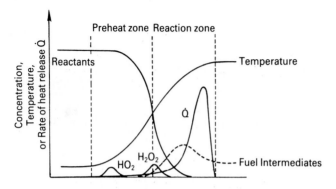

FIGURE 8.2
Laminar flame structure. (From Ref. [3]. Reprinted by permission of the author and Academic Press.)

riding with the flame would experience the unburned mixture approaching at the **flame speed, S_L.** This is equivalent to a flat flame stabilized on a burner. Here, the flame is stationary relative to the laboratory reference frame and, once again, the reactants enter the flame with a velocity equal to the flame propagation velocity, S_L. In both examples, we assume that the flame is one dimensional and that the unburned gas enters the flame in a direction normal to the flame sheet. Since a flame heats the products, the product density is less than the reactant density. Continuity thus requires that the burned gas velocity be greater than the velocity of the unburned gas:

$$\rho_u S_L A \equiv \rho_u v_u A = \rho_b v_b A, \tag{8.1}$$

where the subscripts u and b refer to the unburned and burned gases, respectively. For a typical hydrocarbon–air flame at atmospheric pressure, the density ratio is approximately seven. Thus, there is considerable acceleration of the gas flow across the flame.

It is convenient to divide a flame into two zones: the **preheat zone**, where little heat is released; and the **reaction zone**, where the bulk of the chemical energy is released. At atmospheric pressure, the flame thickness is quite thin, of the order of a millimeter. Because the flame is thin, temperature gradients and species concentration gradients are very large. These gradients provide the driving forces that cause the flame to be self-sustaining: the diffusion of heat and radical species from the reaction zone to the preheat zone.

Hydrocarbon flames are also characterized by their visible radiation. With an excess of air, the reaction zone appears blue. This blue radiation results from excited CH radicals in the high-temperature zone. When the air is decreased to less than stoichiometric proportions, the flame zone appears blue-green, now as a result of radiation from excited C_2. In both flames, OH radicals also contribute to the visible radiation, and to a lesser degree, chemiluminescence from the reaction $CO + O \rightarrow CO_2 + h\nu$ [1]. If the flame is made richer still, soot will form, with its consequent blackbody continuum radiation. Although the soot radiation has its maximum intensity in the infrared (recall Wien's Law?), the spectral sensitivity of the human eye causes us to see a bright yellow (nearly white) to dull orange emission, depending on the flame temperature. References [7] and [8] provide a wealth of information on radiation from flames.

Typical Laboratory Flames

The Bunsen-burner flame provides an interesting example of laminar premixed flames with which most students have some familiarity and that can be easily used in classroom demonstrations. Figure 8.3a schematically illustrates a bunsen burner and the flame it produces. A jet of fuel at the base induces a flow of air through the variable area port, and the air and fuel mix as they flow up through the tube. The typical Bunsen-burner flame is a dual flame: a fuel-rich premixed inner flame surrounded by a diffusion flame. The secondary diffusion flame results when the carbon monoxide product from the rich inner flame encounters the ambient air. The shape of the flame is determined by the combined effects of the velocity profile and heat losses to the tube wall. For the flame to remain stationary, the flame speed must equal the speed of the normal component of unburned gas at each location, as illustrated in the vector diagram in Fig. 8.3b. Thus,

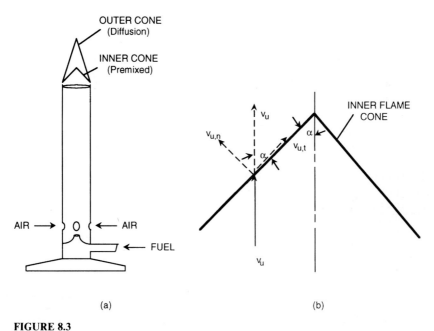

(a)   (b)

FIGURE 8.3
(a) Bunsen-burner schematic. (b) Laminar flame speed equals normal component of unburned gas velocity, $v_{u,n}$.

$$S_L = v_u \sin \alpha, \tag{8.2}$$

where S_L is the laminar burning velocity. This principle causes the essential conical character of the flame.

One-dimensional flat flames are frequently studied in the laboratory and are also used in some radiant heating burners (Fig. 8.4). Figure 8.5 illustrates the laboratory genre. In the adiabatic burner, a flame is stabilized over a bundle of small tubes through which the fuel–air mixture passes laminarly [9]. Over a narrow range of conditions, a stable flat flame is produced. The non-adiabatic burner utilizes a water-cooled face that allows heat to be extracted from the flame, which, in turn, decreases the flame speed, allowing flames to be stabilized over a relatively wide range of flow conditions [10].

Example 8.1. A premixed laminar flame is stabilized in a one-dimensional gas flow where the vertical velocity of the unburned mixture, v_u, varies linearly with the horizontal coordinate, x, as shown in the lower half of Fig. 8.5. Determine the flame shape and the distribution of the local angle of the flame surface from vertical. Assume the flame speed is independent of position and equal to 0.4 m/s, a nominal value for a stoichiometric methane–air flame.

Solution. From Fig. 8.5, we see that the local angle, α, which the flame sheet makes with a vertical plane is (Eqn. 8.2)

$$\alpha = \sin^{-1}(S_L/v_u)$$

where, from Fig. 8.6,

$$v_u \,(\text{mm/s}) = 800 + \frac{1200 - 800}{20} x \,(\text{mm}).$$

So,

$$\alpha = \sin^{-1}\left(\frac{400}{800 + 20x(\text{mm})}\right),$$

and has values ranging from 30° at $x = 0$ to 19.5° at $x = 20$ mm as shown in the top part of Fig. 8.6.

To calculate the flame position, we first obtain an expression for the local slope of the flame sheet (dz/dx) in the x–z plane, and then integrate this expression with respect to x to find $z(x)$. From Fig. 8.7, we see that

$$\frac{dz}{dx} = \tan \beta = \left(\frac{v_u^2(x) - S_L^2}{S_L^2}\right)^{1/2},$$

which, for $v_u \equiv A + Bx$, becomes

$$\frac{dz}{dx} = \left[\left(\frac{A}{S_L} + \frac{B_x}{S_L}\right)^2 - 1\right]^{1/2}.$$

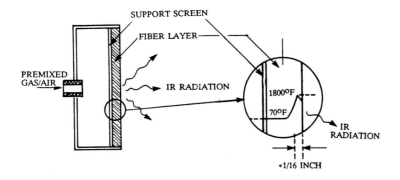

Fiber Matrix Burner (Ceramic or Metal)

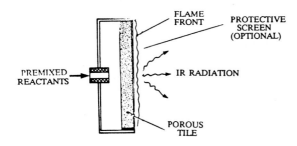

Porous Ceramic Foam Burner

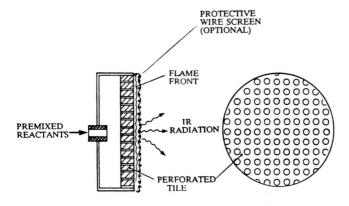

Ported Ceramic Tile Burner

FIGURE 8.4
Direct-fired radiant burners provide uniform heat flux and high efficiency. (Reprinted with permission
from the Center for Advanced Materials, *Newsletter*, (1), 1990, Penn State University.)

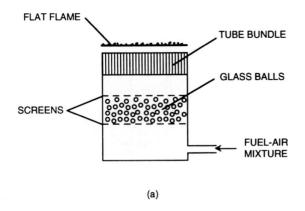

(a)

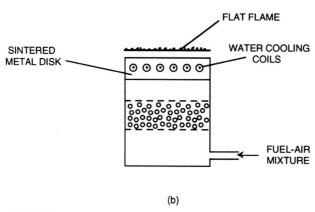

(b)

FIGURE 8.5
(a) Adiabatic flat-flame burner. (b) Nonadiabatic flat-flame burner.

Integrating the above with $A/S_L = 2$ and $B/S_L = 0.05$ yields

$$z(x) = \int_0^x \left(\frac{dz}{dx}\right) dx$$

$$= (x^2 + 80x + 1200)^{1/2}\left(\frac{x}{40} + 1\right)$$
$$- 10 \ln[(x^2 + 80x + 1200)^{1/2} + (x + 40)]$$
$$- 20\sqrt{3} + 10 \ln(20\sqrt{3} + 40).$$

The flame position $z(x)$ is plotted in the upper half of Fig. 8.6. Here we see that the flame sheet is quite steeply inclined. (Note that the horizontal scale is twice the vertical.)

Comment. From this example, we see how the flame shape is intimately linked to the velocity distribution of the oncoming unburned gas.

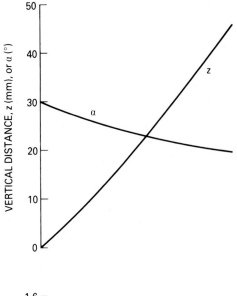

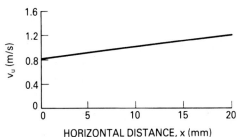

HORIZONTAL DISTANCE, x (mm)

FIGURE 8.6
Flow velocity, flame position, and angle from vertical of line tangent to flame, for Example 8.1.

In the next section, we turn our attention to establishing some theoretical basis for how various parameters, such as pressure, temperature, and fuel type, affect laminar flame speeds.

SIMPLIFIED ANALYSIS

Theories of laminar flames abound and have occupied many researchers for many decades. For example, Kuo [5] cites more than a dozen major papers dealing with laminar flame theory published between 1940 and 1980. Various approaches have assumed that either heat diffusion or mass diffusion effects dominate, while other detailed theories include both effects, assuming both phenomena are important. The earliest description of a laminar flame is that of Mallard and Le Chatelier [11] in 1883. Our simplified approach here follows that of Spalding [12], which lays bare the essential physics of the problem without a great deal of mathematics. The analysis couples principles of heat transfer, mass transfer, chemical kinetics, and thermodynamics to understanding the factors governing flame speed and thick-

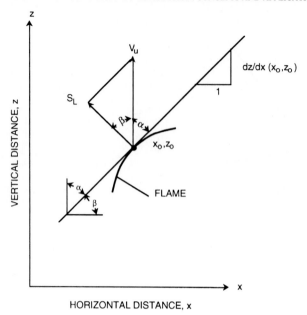

FIGURE 8.7
Definition of flame geometry for Example 8.1.

ness. The simplified analysis presented below relies on the one-dimensional conservation relations developed in the previous chapter, with additional simplifying assumptions for thermodynamic and transport properties applied. Our objective is to find a simple analytical expression for the laminar flame speed.

Assumptions

1. One-dimensional, constant-area, steady flow.
2. Kinetic and potential energies, viscous shear work, and thermal radiation are all neglected.
3. The small pressure difference across the flame is neglected; thus, the pressure is constant.
4. The diffusion of heat and mass are governed by Fourier's and Fick's Laws, respectively. Binary diffusion is assumed.
5. The **Lewis number**, **Le**, which expresses the ratio of thermal diffusivity to mass diffusivity, i.e.,

$$Le \equiv \frac{\alpha}{D} = \frac{k}{\rho c_p D}, \tag{8.3}$$

is unity. This has the result that $k/c_p = \rho D$, which greatly simplifies the energy equation.

6. The mixture specific heat depends neither on temperature nor on the mixture composition. This is equivalent to assuming that the individual species specific heats are all equal and constant.

7. Fuel and oxidizer form products in a single-step exothermic reaction.

8. The oxidizer is present in stoichiometric or excess proportions; thus, the fuel is completely consumed at the flame.

Conservation Laws

To understand flame propagation, we apply conservation of mass, species, and energy to the differential control volume illustrated in Fig. 8.8. Using the relationships from Chapter 7, these conservation principles are expressed:

MASS CONSERVATION

$$\frac{d(\rho v_x)}{dx} = 0, \tag{7.4a}$$

or

$$\dot{m}'' = \rho v_x = \text{constant.} \tag{7.4b}$$

SPECIES CONSERVATION

$$\frac{d\dot{m}_i''}{dx} = \dot{m}_i''', \tag{7.9}$$

or, with the application of Fick's Law,

$$\frac{d\left[\dot{m}'' Y_i - \rho D \dfrac{dY_i}{dx}\right]}{dx} = \dot{m}_i'''. \tag{7.8}$$

where $\dot{m}_i'''$ is the mass production rate of species i per unit volume (kg/s-m^3).

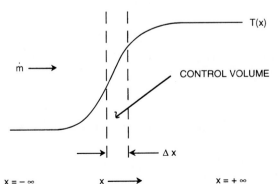

$x = -\infty$ $x \longrightarrow$ $x = +\infty$

FIGURE 8.8
Control volume for flame analysis.

Equation 7.8 can be written for each of the three species, where the mass production rates of the oxidizer and products are related to the fuel production rate. Obviously, the production rates of the fuel, $\dot{m}_F'''$, and oxidizer, $\dot{m}_{Ox}'''$, are negative since these species are being consumed, not produced. For our simple reaction, the overall stoichiometry is

$$1 \text{ kg fuel} + \nu \text{ kg oxidizer} \rightarrow (\nu + 1) \text{ kg products.} \qquad (8.4)$$

Thus,

$$\dot{m}_F''' = \frac{1}{\nu}\dot{m}_{Ox}''' = -\frac{1}{\nu + 1}\dot{m}_{Pr}'''. \qquad (8.5)$$

Equation 7.8 becomes for each species:

Fuel

$$\dot{m}''\frac{dY_F}{dx} - \frac{d\left(\rho D \frac{dY_f}{dx}\right)}{dx} = \dot{m}_F''' \qquad (8.6a)$$

Oxidizer

$$\dot{m}''\frac{dY_{Ox}}{dx} - \frac{d\left(\rho D \frac{dY_{Ox}}{dx}\right)}{dx} = \nu\dot{m}_F''' \qquad (8.6b)$$

Products

$$\dot{m}''\frac{dY_{Pr}}{dx} - \frac{d\left(\rho D \frac{dY_{Pr}}{dx}\right)}{dx} = -(\nu + 1)\dot{m}_F'''. \qquad (8.6c)$$

In this analysis, the species conservation relations are used only to simplify the energy equation. Because of the assumptions of binary diffusion governed by Fick's Law and unity Lewis number, there will be no need to solve the species equations.

ENERGY CONSERVATION. The assumptions we have adopted for our analysis are consistent with those embodied in the Shvab–Zeldovich form of energy conservation (Eqn. 7.47), which, for a constant mixture specific heat, is written as

$$\dot{m}''c_p\frac{dT}{dx} - \frac{d}{dx}\left[(\rho D c_p)\frac{dT}{dx}\right] = -\sum h_{f,i}^o \dot{m}_i'''. \qquad (8.7a)$$

With the overall stoichiometry expressed by Eqns. 8.4 and 8.5, the right-hand-side of the above becomes

$$-\sum h_{f,i}^o \dot{m}_i''' = -\left[h_{f,F}^o \dot{m}_F''' + h_{f,Ox}^o \nu\dot{m}_F''' - h_{f,Pr}^o (\nu + 1)\dot{m}_F'''\right]$$

or

$$-\sum h_{f,i}^o \dot{m}_i''' = -\dot{m}_F'''\Delta h_c$$

where Δh_c is the heat of combustion of the fuel, $\Delta h_c \equiv h^o_{f,F} + \nu h^o_{f,Ox} - (\nu + 1)h^o_{f,Pr}$, based on the given stoichiometry. Because of the unity Lewis number approximation, we also can replace $\rho D c_p$ by k. With these two substitutions, Eqn. 8.7a becomes

$$\dot{m}'' \frac{dT}{dx} - \frac{1}{c_p} \frac{d\left(k \frac{dT}{dx}\right)}{dx} = -\frac{\dot{m}'''_F \Delta h_c}{c_p}. \qquad (8.7b)$$

Recall that our objective is to find a useful expression for the laminar flame speed, which is related simply to the mass flux, $\dot{m}''$, appearing in Eqn. 8.7b, by

$$\dot{m}'' = \rho_u S_L. \qquad (8.8)$$

To achieve this objective, we again follow Spalding's [12] approach.

Solution

To find the mass burning rate, we will assume a temperature profile that satisfies the boundary conditions given below and then integrate Eqn. 8.7b using the assumed temperature distribution. The boundary conditions far upstream of the flame are

$$T(x \rightarrow -\infty) = T_u, \qquad (8.9a)$$

$$\frac{dT}{dx}(x \rightarrow -\infty) = 0, \qquad (8.9b)$$

and far downstream of the flame,

$$T(x \rightarrow +\infty) = T_b, \qquad (8.9c)$$

$$\frac{dT}{dx}(x \rightarrow +\infty) = 0. \qquad (8.9d)$$

For simplicity, we assume a simple linear temperature profile that goes from T_u to T_b over the small distance, δ, as shown in Fig. 8.9. We define δ to be the flame thickness. Mathematically, we have a second-order ordinary differential equation (Eqn. 8.7b) with two unknown parameters, which are referred to in the combustion literature as the **eigenvalues**, $\dot{m}''$ and δ. The specification of *four* boundary conditions, rather than just *two*, allows us to determine the eigenvalues. (It is interesting to note the similarity of the present analysis to von Karman's integral analysis of the flat plate boundary layer that you may have studied in fluid mechanics. In the fluid mechanics problem, reasonable estimates of boundary layer thickness and shear stresses were obtained using an assumed velocity profile.)

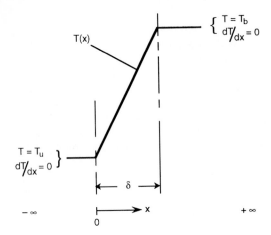

FIGURE 8.9
Assumed temperature profile for laminar premixed flame analysis.

Integrating Eqn. 8.7b over x and applying the conditions at $-\infty$ and $+\infty$, yields:

$$[T]_{T=T_u}^{T=T_b} - \left[\frac{dT}{dx}\right]_{dT/dx=0}^{dT/dx=0} = \frac{-\Delta h_c}{c_p} \int_{-\infty}^{\infty} \dot{m}_F''' \, dx \qquad (8.10)$$

which, by evaluating the limits, simplifies to

$$\dot{m}''(T_b - T_u) = -\frac{\Delta h_c}{c_p} \int_{-\infty}^{\infty} \dot{m}_F''' \, dx. \qquad (8.11)$$

We can change the limits on the reaction rate integral appearing on the right-hand-side of Eqn. 8.11 from space to temperature, since $\dot{m}_F'''$ is only non-zero between T_u and T_b over the region δ, i.e.,

$$\frac{dT}{dx} = \frac{T_b - T_u}{\delta} \quad \text{or} \quad dx = \frac{\delta}{T_b - T_u} dT. \qquad (8.12)$$

With the change of variables,

$$\dot{m}''(T_b - T_u) = -\frac{\Delta h_c}{c_p} \frac{\delta}{(T_b - T_u)} \int_{T_u}^{T_b} \dot{m}_F''' \, dT, \qquad (8.13)$$

and recognizing the definition of the average reaction rate,

$$\bar{\dot{m}}_F''' \equiv \frac{1}{(T_b - T_u)} \int_{T_u}^{T_b} \dot{m}_F''' \, dT, \qquad (8.14)$$

we obtain the simple result, that

$$\dot{m}''(T_b - T_u) = -\frac{\Delta h_c}{c_p} \delta \bar{\dot{m}}_F'''. \tag{8.15}$$

This result, Eqn. 8.15, is a simple algebraic equation involving the two unknowns $\dot{m}''$ and δ; thus, we need to find another equation to complete the solution. This can be done by following the same procedure as before, but now integrating from $x = -\infty$ to $x = \delta/2$. Since the reaction zone of a flame lies in the high-temperature region, it is reasonable to assume that $\dot{m}_F'''$ is zero in the interval $-\infty < x \leq \delta/2$. Noting that at $x = \delta/2$,

$$T = \frac{T_b + T_u}{2} \tag{8.16}$$

and

$$\frac{dT}{dx} = \frac{T_b - T_u}{\delta}, \tag{8.12}$$

we obtain from Eqn. 8.10, with the modified limits,

$$\dot{m}''\delta/2 - k/c_p = 0. \tag{8.17}$$

Solving Eqns. 8.15 and 8.17 simultaneously, yields

$$\dot{m}'' = \left[2\frac{k}{c_p^2} \frac{(-\Delta h_c)}{(T_b - T_u)} \bar{\dot{m}}_F''' \right]^{1/2} \tag{8.18}$$

and

$$\delta = 2k/(c_p \dot{m}''). \tag{8.19}$$

Applying the definitions of flame speed, $S_L \equiv \dot{m}''/\rho_u$, and thermal diffusivity, $\alpha \equiv k/\rho_u c_p$, and recognizing that $\Delta h_c = (\nu + 1)c_p(T_b - T_u)$, we obtain the final results:

$$S_L = \left[-2\alpha(\nu + 1)\frac{\bar{\dot{m}}_F'''}{\rho_u} \right]^{1/2} \tag{8.20}$$

$$\delta = \left[\frac{-2\rho_u \alpha}{(\nu + 1)\bar{\dot{m}}_F'''} \right]^{1/2} \tag{8.21a}$$

or in terms of S_L,

$$\delta = 2\alpha/S_L. \tag{8.21b}$$

We can now use Eqns. 8.20 and 8.21 to analyze how S_L and δ theoretically are affected by the fuel–air mixture properties. This is done in the next section, where, also, comparisons are made with experimental observations.

Example 8.2. Estimate the laminar flame speed of a stoichiometric propane–air mixture using the simplified-theory result (Eqn. 8.20). Use the global one-step reaction mechanism (Eqn. 5.2, Table 5.1) to estimate the mean reaction rate.

Solution. To find the laminar flame speed, we evaluate Eqn. 8.20,

$$S_L = \left[-2\alpha(\nu + 1)\frac{\bar{\dot{m}}_F'''}{\rho_u} \right]^{1/2}.$$

The essence of this problem is how to evaluate $\bar{\dot{m}}_F'''$ and α. Since the simple theory assumed that the reaction was confined to the second half of the flame thickness ($\delta/2 < x < \delta$), we will choose a mean temperature to evaluate the reaction rate as

$$\bar{T} = \frac{1}{2}\left(\tfrac{1}{2}(T_b + T_u) + T_b \right)$$

$$= 1770\,\text{K}$$

where we assume $T_b = T_{ad} = 2260\,\text{K}$ (Chapter 2) and $T_u = 300\,\text{K}$. Assuming there is neither fuel nor oxygen in the burned gas, the mean concentrations used in the rate equation are

$$\bar{Y}_F = \frac{1}{2}(Y_{F,u} + 0)$$

$$= 0.06015/2 = 0.0301,$$

and

$$\bar{Y}_{O_2} = \frac{1}{2}\left[0.233(1 - Y_{F,u}) + 0 \right]$$

$$= 0.1095,$$

where the A/F of a stoichiometric propane–air mixture is 15.625 ($= \nu$) and the mass fraction of O_2 in the air is 0.233.

The reaction rate, given by

$$\dot{\omega}_F \equiv \frac{d[C_3H_8]}{dt} = -k_G[C_3H_8]^{0.1}[O_2]^{1.65},$$

with

$$k_G = 4.836 \cdot 10^9 \exp\left(\frac{-15,098}{T} \right) [=] \left(\frac{\text{kmol}}{\text{m}^3} \right)^{-0.75} \frac{1}{s},$$

can be transformed to

$$\bar{\dot{\omega}}_F = -k_G(\bar{T})\bar{\rho}^{1.75}\left(\frac{\bar{Y}_F}{MW_F} \right)^{0.1}\left(\frac{\bar{Y}_{O_2}}{MW_{O_2}} \right)^{1.65}$$

where we now use our judiciously selected mean values. Evaluating, using the appropriate units conversion for Table 5.1,

$$k_G = 4.836 \cdot 10^9 \exp\left(\frac{-15,098}{1770}\right) = 9.55 \cdot 10^5 \left(\frac{\text{kmol}}{\text{m}^3}\right)^{-0.75} \frac{1}{\text{s}}$$

$$\bar{\rho} = \frac{P}{\frac{R_u}{MW}\bar{T}} = \frac{101,325}{\left(\frac{8315}{29}\right)1770} = 0.1997 \,\text{kg/m}^3$$

$$\bar{\omega}_F = -9.55 \cdot 10^5 (0.1997)^{1.75}\left(\frac{0.0301}{44}\right)^{0.1}\left(\frac{0.1095}{32}\right)^{1.65}$$

$$= -2.439 \,\text{kmol/s-m}^3.$$

Then, from Eqn. 6.29,

$$\dot{m}_F''' = \bar{\omega}_F MW_F = -2.439\,(44)$$

$$= -107.3 \,\text{kg/s-m}^3.$$

The thermal diffusivity employed in Eqn. 8.20 is defined as

$$\alpha = \frac{k(\bar{T})}{\rho_u c_p(\bar{T})}.$$

The appropriate mean temperature, however, is now the average over the entire flame thickness $(0 \le x \le \delta)$ since conduction occurs over this interval, not just the half-interval as assumed for the reaction. Thus,

$$\bar{T} = \frac{1}{2}(T_b + T_u)$$

$$= 1280 \,\text{K}$$

and

$$\alpha = \frac{0.0809}{1.16\,(1186)} = 5.89 \cdot 10^{-5}\,\text{m}^2/\text{s}$$

where air properties were used to evaluate k, c_p, and ρ.

We can now substitute numerical values into Eqn. 8.20:

$$S_L = \left[\frac{-2(5.89 \cdot 10^{-5})(15.625 + 1)(-107.3)}{1.16}\right]^{1/2}$$

$$\boxed{S_L = 0.425 \,\text{m/s or } 42.5 \,\text{cm/s}}.$$

Comment. From correlations yet to be discussed [13], the experimental value of S_L for this mixture is 33.3 cm/s. Considering the crude nature of our theoretical analysis, this is excellent agreement with the calculated value of 42.5 cm/s. Of course, rigorous theory with detailed kinetics can be used to obtain much more accurate predictions. We also note that, with the assumptions embodied in our analysis, the fuel and oxidizer concentrations can be related linearly to the temperature and $\dot{m}_F'''$ can be evaluated exactly by integrating the single-step, irreversible global reaction rate, rather than using estimated mean concentrations and temperature as was done in the example.

FACTORS INFLUENCING FLAME VELOCITY AND THICKNESS

Temperature

The temperature dependencies of S_L and δ can be inferred from Eqns. 8.20 and 8.21, recognizing the following approximate temperature scalings. For simplicity, we use T_b to estimate $\bar{m}_F'''$. The pressure dependencies also are indicated.

$$\alpha \propto \bar{T}^{1.75} P^{-1}, \tag{8.22}$$

$$\bar{m}_F'''/\rho_u \propto T_u T_b^{-n} P^{n-1} \exp(-E_A/R_u T_b), \tag{8.23}$$

where the exponent n is the overall reaction order, and $\bar{T} \equiv 0.5(T_b + T_u)$. Combining the above scalings yields

$$S_L \propto \bar{T}^{0.875} T_u^{0.5} T_b^{-n/2} \exp(-E_A/2R_u T_b) P^{(n-2)/2} \tag{8.24}$$

and

$$\delta \propto \bar{T}^{0.875} T_u^{-0.5} T_b^{n/2} \exp(+E_A/2R_u T_b) P^{-n/2}. \tag{8.25}$$

We see that the laminar flame speed has a strong temperature dependence, since global reaction orders for hydrocarbons are about two, and apparent activation energies approximately $1.67 \cdot 10^8$ J/kmol (40 kcal/gmol) (cf. Table 5.1). For example, Eqn. 8.24 predicts the flame speed to increase by a factor of 2.89 when the unburned gas temperature is increased from 300 K to 600 K. Increasing the unburned gas temperature also will increase the burned gas temperature by about the same amount, if we neglect dissociation and temperature-dependent specific heats. Table 8.1 shows comparisons of flame speeds and flame thicknesses for the case just mentioned (Case B), and for the use of fixed unburned gas temperature but a decreased burned gas temperature (Case C). Case A is the reference condition. Case C captures the effect of heat transfer or changing the equivalence ratio, either rich or lean, from the maximum-temperature condition. In this case, we see flame speeds decrease, while flame thicknesses increase significantly.

TABLE 8.1
Estimate of effects of unburned and burned gas temperature on laminar flame speeds and thickness using Eqns. 8.24 and 8.25

Case	A	B	C
T_u (K)	300	600	300
T_b (K)	2000	2300	1700
$S_L/S_{L,A}$	1	2.89	0.43
δ/δ_A	1	0.52	1.82

We can compare our simple estimates of the influence of temperature on flame speeds using the empirical correlation of Andrews and Bradley [14] for stoichiometric methane–air flames,

$$S_L(\text{cm/s}) = 10 + 3.71 \cdot 10^{-4}[T_u(\text{K})]^2, \tag{8.26}$$

which is shown in Fig. 8.10, along with data from several experimenters. Using Eqn. 8.26, an increase in T_u from 300 K to 600 K results in S_L increasing by a factor of 3.3, which compares quite favorably with our estimate of 2.89 (Table 8.1).

Useful correlations of flame speed with unburned gas temperature have been developed by Metghalchi and Keck [13] and are presented in the next section.

Pressure

Equation 8.25 shows that $S_L \propto P^{(n-2)/2}$. If, again, we assume a global reaction order of two, flame speed should be independent of pressure. Experimental measurements generally show a negative dependence on pressure. Andrews and Bradley [14] found that

$$S_L(\text{cm/s}) = 43[P(\text{atm})]^{-0.5} \tag{8.27}$$

fits their data for $P > 5$ atmospheres for methane–air flames (Fig. 8.11). Law [15] provides a summary of flame speed data for a range of pressure (up to 5 atm or less) for the following fuels: H_2, CH_4, C_2H_2, C_2H_4, C_2H_6, and C_3H_8. The previously cited work by Metghalchi and Keck [13] also provides flame speed–pressure correlations for selected fuels.

Equivalence Ratio

Except for very rich mixtures, the primary effect of equivalence ratio on flame speed for similar fuels is a result of how this parameter affects flame temperatures; thus, we would expect flame speeds to be a maximum at a slightly rich mixture and falling off on either side (cf. Fig. 2.13). Figure 8.12 indeed shows this behavior for methane. Flame thickness shows the inverse trend, having a minimum near stoichiometric (Fig. 8.13). Note that many definitions of δ are applied in experimental measurements, so caution should be exercised when comparing numerical values from different investigations.

Fuel Type

An extensive, but somewhat dated, summary of flame speed measurements for a wide variety of fuels is contained in Ref. [16]. Data from this report are shown in Fig. 8.14 for C_2–C_6 paraffins (single bonds), olefins (double bonds), and acetylenes (triple bonds). Also shown are CH_4 and H_2. The flame velocity of propane is

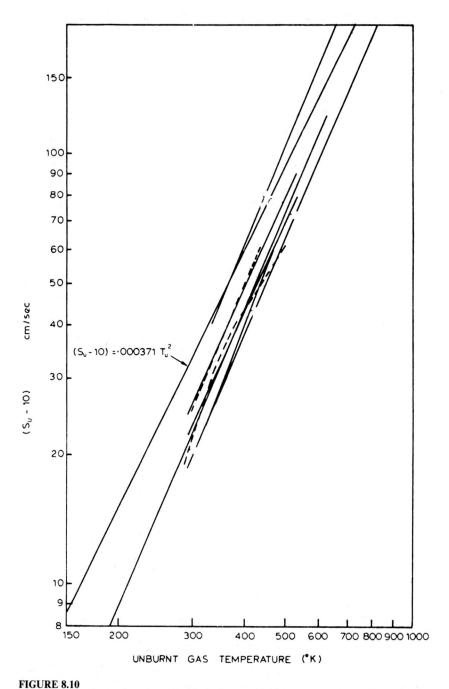

FIGURE 8.10
Effect of unburned gas temperature on laminar flame speeds of stoichiometric methane–air mixtures at 1 atm. Various lines are data from various investigators. (Reprinted with permission, Elsevier Science, Inc., from Ref. [14], © 1972, The Combustion Institute.)

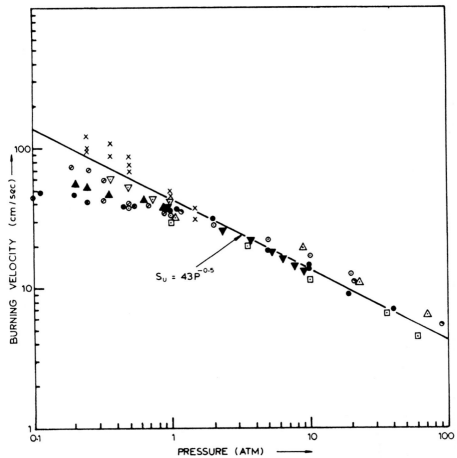

FIGURE 8.11
Effect of pressure on laminar flame speeds of stoichiometric methane–air mixtures for $T_u = 16$–$27°C$. (Reprinted with permission, Elsevier Science, Inc., from Ref. [14], © 1972, The Combustion Institute.)

used as a reference. Roughly speaking, the C_3–C_6 hydrocarbons all follow the same trend as a function of flame temperature. Ethylene (C_2H_4) and acetylene (C_2H_2) have velocities greater than the C_3–C_6 group, while methane lies somewhat below. Hydrogen's maximum flame speed is many times greater than propane. Several factors combine to give H_2 its high flame speed: First, the thermal diffusivity of pure H_2 is many times greater than the hydrocarbon fuels; second, the mass diffusivity of hydrogen likewise is much greater than for the hydrocarbons; and third, the reaction kinetics for H_2 are very rapid since the relatively slow $CO \rightarrow CO_2$ step that is a major factor in hydrocarbon combustion is absent. Law [15] presents a compilation of laminar flame-speed data for various pure fuels and mixtures which are considered to be some of the more reliable data obtained to date. Table 8.2 shows a subset of these data.

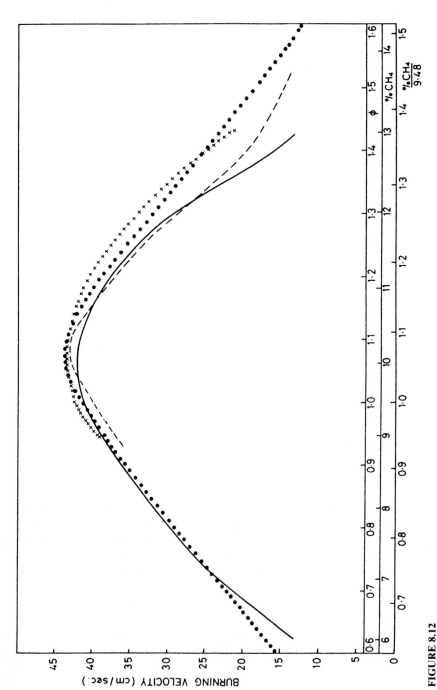

FIGURE 8.12

Effect of equivalence ratio on the laminar flame speed of methane–air mixtures at atmospheric pressure. (Reprinted with permission, Elsevier Science, Inc., from Ref. [14], © 1972, The Combustion Institute.)

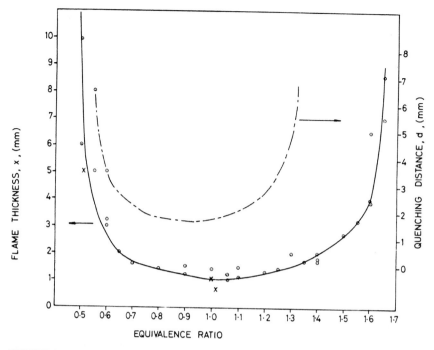

FIGURE 8.13
Flame thickness for laminar methane–air flames at atmospheric pressure. Also shown is the quenching distance. (Reprinted with permission, Elsevier Science, Inc., from Ref. [14], © 1972, The Combustion Institute.)

FLAME SPEED CORRELATIONS FOR SELECTED FUELS

Meghalchi and Keck [13] experimentally determined laminar flame speeds for various fuel–air mixtures over a range of temperatures and pressures typical of conditions associated with reciprocating internal combustion engines and gas-turbine combustors. Several forms for correlations were tried [13], including one similar to Eqn. 8.24, with the most useful being

$$S_L = S_{L,\text{ref}}\left(\frac{T_u}{T_{u,\text{ref}}}\right)^{\gamma}\left(\frac{P}{P_{\text{ref}}}\right)^{\beta}(1 - 2.1\,Y_{\text{dil}}). \qquad (8.28)$$

The subscript ref refers to reference conditions defined by

$$T_{u,\text{ref}} = 298\,\text{K},$$

$$P_{\text{ref}} = 1\,\text{atm},$$

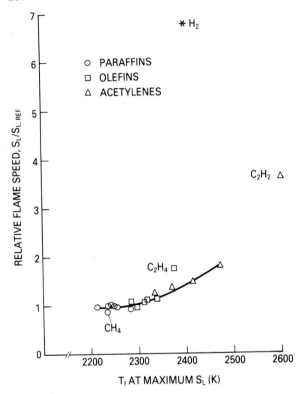

FIGURE 8.14
Relative flame speeds for C_1–C_6 hydrocarbon fuels. The reference flame speed is based on propane using the tube method [16].

TABLE 8.2
Laminar flame speeds for various pure fuels burning in air at 1 atm (T_u = room temperature) from Ref. [15]

Fuel	Formula	Laminar flame speeds, S_L (cm/s)
Methane	CH_4	40
Acetylene	C_2H_2	136
Ethylene	C_2H_4	67
Ethane	C_2H_6	43
Propane	C_3H_8	44
Hydrogen	H_2	210

and

$$S_{L,\text{ref}} = B_M + B_2(\Phi - \Phi_M)^2,$$

where the constants B_M, B_2, and Φ_M depend on fuel type and are given in Table 8.3. The temperature and pressure exponents, γ and β, are functions of the equivalence ratio, expressed as

$$\gamma = 2.18 - 0.8(\Phi - 1),$$

TABLE 8.3
Values for B_M, B_2, and Φ_M used with Eqn. 8.28 [13]

Fuel	Φ_M	B_M(cm/s)	B_2(cm/s)
Methanol	1.11	36.92	−140.51
Propane	1.08	34.22	−138.65
Isooctane	1.13	26.32	−84.72
RMFD-303	1.13	27.58	−78.34

$$\beta = -0.16 + 0.22(\Phi - 1).$$

Y_{dil} is the mass fraction of diluent present in the air–fuel mixture, specifically included in Eqn. 8.28 to account for any recirculated combustion products. Recirculation of exhaust or flue gases is a common technique used to control oxides of nitrogen in many combustion systems (Chapter 15); and in internal combustion engines, residual combustion products mix with the incoming charge under most operating conditions.

Example 8.3. Compare the laminar flame speeds of gasoline–air mixtures with $\Phi = 0.8$ for the following three cases:

i. At reference conditions of $T = 298\,\text{K}$ and $P = 1\,\text{atm}$.
ii. At conditions typical of a spark-ignition engine operating at wide-open throttle: $T = 685\,\text{K}$ and $P = 18.38\,\text{atm}$.
iii. Same as condition ii above, but with 15% (by mass) exhaust-gas recirculation.

Solution. We will employ the correlation of Metghalchi and Keck, Eqn. 8.28, for RMFD-303. This research fuel (also called indolene) has a controlled composition simulating typical gasolines. The flame speed at 298 K and 1 atm is given by

$$S_{L,\text{ref}} = B_M + B_2(\Phi - \Phi_M)^2$$

where, from Table 8.3,

$$B_M = 27.58\,\text{cm/s},$$
$$B_2 = -78.34\,\text{cm/s},$$
$$\phi_M = 1.13.$$

Thus,

$$S_{L,\text{ref}} = 27.58 - 78.34(0.8 - 1.13)^2,$$

$$\boxed{S_{L,\text{ref}} = 19.05\,\text{cm/s}}.$$

To find the flame speed at temperatures and pressures other than the reference state, we employ (Eqn. 8.28)

$$S_L(T_u, P) = S_{L,\text{ref}}\left(\frac{T_u}{T_{u,\text{ref}}}\right)^{\gamma}\left(\frac{P}{P_{\text{ref}}}\right)^{\beta}$$

where

$$\gamma = 2.18 - 0.8(\Phi - 1)$$
$$= 2.34$$
$$\beta = -0.16 + 0.22(\Phi - 1)$$
$$= -0.204.$$

Thus,

$$S_L(685\,\text{K},\ 18.38\,\text{atm}) = 19.05 \left(\frac{685}{298}\right)^{2.34} \left(\frac{18.38}{1}\right)^{-0.204}$$
$$= 19.05\ (7.012)\ (0.552)$$

$$\boxed{S_L = 73.8\,\text{cm/s}}.$$

With dilution by exhaust-gas recirculation, the flame speed above is reduced by the factor $(1 - 2.1\,Y_{\text{dil}})$:

$$S_L(685\,\text{K},\ 18.38\,\text{atm},\ 15\%\,\text{EGR}) = 73.8[1 - 2.1(0.15)]$$

$$\boxed{S_L = 50.6\,\text{cm/s}}.$$

Comments. We see that the laminar flame velocity is much greater at engine conditions than at the reference state, with the dominant influence being the temperature. In Chapter 12, we will learn that the laminar flame speed is an important factor in determining the turbulent flame speed, which controls the burning rate in spark-ignition engines. Results of this example also show that dilution decreases the flame speed, which can have a detrimental effect on engine performance if too much gas is recirculated.

QUENCHING, FLAMMABILITY, AND IGNITION

So far in this chapter we have considered only the steady propagation of premixed laminar flames. We now turn our attention to what are essentially transient processes: flame quenching and ignition. Although the processes are transient, we will confine our attention to examining limit behavior, i.e., conditions under which a flame will either extinguish or not, or ignite or not, and ignore the time-dependent details of the extinction and ignition processes.

There are many ways in which a flame can be extinguished. For example, flames will extinguish while passing through narrow passageways. This phenomenon is the basis for many practical flame-arresting devices in use today, and was first put into practice by Sir Humphrey Davey in his invention of the miner's safety lamp in 1815. Other techniques for extinguishing premixed flames are the addition of diluents, such as water, which have primarily a thermal effect, or chemical suppressants, such as halogens, which alter the chemical kinetics. Blowing the flame away from the reactants is also effective in extinguishing flames, as is easily demonstrated with a weakly burning Bunsen-burner flame. A more practical application is the blowout of oil-well fires with explosive charges; although in this case, the flames may have a strongly nonpremixed character, rather than being premixed.

In the following, we discuss three concepts: quenching distances, flammability limits, and minimum ignition energies. In all of these, heat losses are assumed to control the phenomena. For more detailed analyses and discussions, the reader is referred to the literature [2–6, 17–22].

Quenching by a Cold Wall

As mentioned above, flames extinguish upon entering a sufficiently small passageway. If the passageway is not too small, the flame will propagate through it. The critical diameter of a circular tube where a flame extinguishes, rather than propagates, is referred to as the **quenching distance**. Experimentally, quenching distances are determined by observing whether a flame stabilized above a tube does or does not **flashback** for a particular tube diameter when the reactant flow is rapidly shut off. Quenching distances are also determined using high-aspect-ratio rectangular-slot burners. In this case, the quenching distance is the distance between the long sides, i.e., the slit width. Tube-based quenching distances are somewhat larger (~ 20–50%) than slit-based ones [16].

IGNITION AND QUENCHING CRITERIA. Williams [2] provides the following two rules-of-thumb governing ignition and its converse, flame extinction. The second criterion is the one applicable to the problem of flame quenching by a cold wall.

> Criterion I—Ignition will only occur if enough energy is added to the gas to heat a slab about as thick as a steadily propagating laminar flame to the adiabatic flame temperature.

> Criterion II—The rate of liberation of heat by chemical reactions inside the slab must approximately balance the rate of heat loss from the slab by thermal conduction.

In the following section, we employ these criteria to develop a greatly simplified analysis of flame quenching.

SIMPLIFIED QUENCHING ANALYSIS. Consider a flame that has just entered a slot formed by two plane-parallel plates as shown in Fig. 8.15. Applying Williams' second criterion and following the approach of Friedman [19], we write an energy balance equating the heat produced by reaction to the heat lost by conduction to the walls, i.e.,

$$\dot{Q}''' V = \dot{Q}_{\text{cond,tot}} \tag{8.29}$$

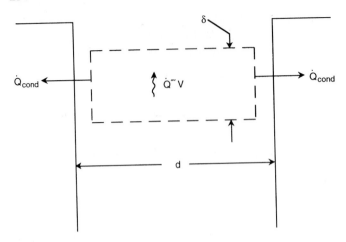

FIGURE 8.15
Schematic of flame quenching between two parallel walls.

where the volumetric heat release rate $\dot{Q}'''$ is related to the previously defined $\bar{\dot{m}}_F'''$ as

$$\dot{Q}''' = -\bar{\dot{m}}_F''' \Delta h_c. \tag{8.30}$$

Before proceeding, it is important to note that the thickness of the slab of gas analyzed (Fig. 8.15) has been taken to be δ, the adiabatic laminar flame thickness as expressed in Eqn. 8.21. Our objective now is to determine the distance d, the quenching distance, that satisfies the quenching criterion expressed by Eqn. 8.29.

The heat loss from the flame slab to the wall can be expressed using Fourier's Law as

$$\dot{Q}_{cond} = -kA\frac{dT}{dx}\bigg|_{\substack{\text{In gas} \\ \text{at wall}}}, \tag{8.31}$$

where both the conductivity, k, and temperature gradient are evaluated in the gas at the wall. The area A is easily expressed as $2\delta L$, where L is the slot width (perpendicular to the page) and the factor 2 accounts for the flame being in contact with walls on each side. The temperature gradient dT/dx, however, is much more difficult to approximate. A reasonable lower bound for the magnitude of dT/dx is $(T_b - T_w)/(d/2)$, where we assume a linear distribution from the centerline plane at T_b to the wall at T_w. Since dT/dx is likely to be much greater than this, we introduce an arbitrary constant b, defined by

$$\left|\frac{dT}{dx}\right| \equiv \frac{T_b - T_w}{d/b}, \tag{8.32}$$

where b is a number generally much greater than 2. Utilizing Eqns. 8.30–8.32, the quenching criterion (Eqn. 8.29) becomes

$$\left(-\bar{\dot{m}}_F''' \Delta h_c\right)(\delta dL) = k(2\delta L)\frac{T_b - T_w}{d/b},\tag{8.33a}$$

or

$$d^2 = \frac{2kb(T_b - T_w)}{-\bar{\dot{m}}_F''' \Delta h_c}.\tag{8.33b}$$

Assuming $T_w = T_u$, using the previously developed relationship between $\bar{\dot{m}}_F'''$ and S_L (Eqn. 8.21), and relating $\Delta h_c = (\nu + 1)c_p(T_b - T_u)$, Eqn. 8.33b becomes

$$d = 2\sqrt{b}\alpha/S_L,\tag{8.34a}$$

or in terms of δ,

$$d = \sqrt{b}\delta.\tag{8.34b}$$

Equation 8.34b is in agreement with the experimental results shown in Fig. 8.13 for methane, which show quenching distances to be greater than the flame thickness δ. Quenching distances for a wide variety of fuels are shown in Table 8.4. It should be pointed out that the temperature and pressure dependencies of the quenching distance can be estimated using Eqn. 8.25.

Example 8.4. Consider the design of a laminar-flow, adiabatic, flat-flame burner consisting of a square arrangement of thin-walled tubes as illustrated in the sketch below. Fuel–air mixture flows through both the tubes and the interstices between the tubes. It is desired to operate the burner with a stoichiometric methane–air mixture exiting the burner tubes at 300 K and 5 atm.

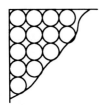

Burner Tube Layout

A. Determine mixture mass flowrate per unit cross-sectional area at the design condition.

B. Estimate the maximum tube diameter allowed so that flashback will be prevented.

Solution

A. To establish a flat flame, the mean flow velocity must equal the laminar flame speed at the design temperature and pressure. From Fig. 8.11,

TABLE 8.4
Flammability limits, quenching distances, and minimum ignition energies for various fuels[a]

Fuel	Flammability limits		Stoichiometric mass air–fuel ratio	Quenching distance		Minimum ignition energy	
	Φ_{min} (Lean or lower limit)	Φ_{max} (Rich or upper limit)		For $\Phi = 1$ (mm)	Absolute minimum (mm)	For $\Phi = 1$ (10^{-5} J)	Absolute minimum (10^{-5} J)
Acetylene, C_2H_2	0.19[b]	∞[b]	13.3	2.3	—	3	—
Carbon monoxide, CO	0.34	6.76	2.46	—	—	—	—
n-Decane, $C_{10}H_{22}$	0.36	3.92	15.0	2.1[c]	—	—	—
Ethane, C_2H_6	0.50	2.72	16.0	2.3	1.8	42	24
Ethylene, C_2H_4	0.41	>6.1	14.8	1.3	—	9.6	—
Hydrogen, H_2	0.14[b]	2.54[b]	34.5	0.64	0.61	2.0	1.8
Methane, CH_4	0.46	1.64	17.2	2.5	2.0	33	29
Methanol, CH_3OH	0.48	4.08	6.46	1.8	1.5	21.5	14
n-Octane, C_8H_{18}	0.51	4.25	15.1	—	—	—	—
Propane, C_3H_8	0.51	2.83	15.6	2.0	1.8	30.5	26

[a]Data from Ref. [16] unless otherwise noted.
[b]Zabetakis (U.S. Bureau of Mines, Bulletin 627, 1965).
[c]Chomiak [6].

$$S_L(300\,\text{K},\,5\,\text{atm}) = 43/\sqrt{P\,(\text{atm})}$$
$$= 43/\sqrt{5} = 19.2\,\text{cm/s}.$$

The mass flux, $\dot{m}''$, is

$$\dot{m}'' = \dot{m}/A = \rho_u S_L.$$

We can approximate the density by assuming an ideal-gas mixture, where

$$MW_{\text{mix}} = \chi_{CH_4} MW_{CH_4} + (1 - \chi_{CH_4}) MW_{\text{air}}$$

$$= 0.095\,(16.04) + 0.905\,(28.85)$$

$$= 27.6\,\text{kg/kmol}$$

and

$$\rho_u = \frac{P}{\dfrac{R_u}{MW_{\text{mix}}} T_u} = \frac{5\,(101,325)}{\dfrac{8315}{27.6}\,(300)}$$

$$= 5.61\,\text{kg/m}^3.$$

Thus, the mass flux is

$$\dot{m}'' = \rho_u S_L = 5.61\,(0.192)$$

$$\boxed{\dot{m}'' = 1.08\,\text{kg/s-m}^2}.$$

B. We assume that if the tube diameter is less than the quenching distance, with some factor-of-safety applied, the burner will operate without danger of flashback. Thus, we need to find the quench distance at the design conditions. From Fig. 8.13, we see that the 1-atm quench distance for a slit is approximately 1.7 mm. Since slit quenching distances are 20–50% smaller than for tubes, we will use this value outright, with the difference being our factor-of-safety. We now need to correct this value to the 5-atm condition. From Eqn. 8.34a, we see that

$$d \propto \alpha/S_L,$$

and from Eqn. 8.22,

$$\alpha \propto T^{1.75}/P.$$

Combining the pressure effects on α and S_L, we have

$$d_2 = d_1 \frac{\alpha_2}{\alpha_1} \frac{S_{L,1}}{S_{L,2}} = d_1 \frac{P_1}{P_2} \frac{S_{L,1}}{S_{L,2}}$$

$$d(5\,\text{atm}) = 1.7\,\text{mm} \frac{1\,\text{atm}}{5\,\text{atm}} \frac{43\,\text{cm/s}}{19.2\,\text{cm/s}}$$

so,

$$\boxed{d_{\text{design}} \le 0.76\,\text{mm}}.$$

We need to verify that, when using this diameter, laminar flow is maintained in the tube, i.e., $Re_d < 2300$. Using air properties for the viscosity,

$$Re_d = \frac{\rho_u d_{\text{design}} S_L}{\mu}$$

$$= \frac{5.61 \, (0.00076) \, (0.192)}{15.89 \cdot 10^{-6}}$$

$$Re_d = 51.5.$$

This value is well below the transitional value; hence, the quenching criteria rols the design.

Comment. The final design should be based on the worst-case scenario where the quenching distance is a minimum. From Fig. 8.13, we see that the minimum quenching distance is close to the value used above for $\Phi = 0.8$.

Flammability Limits

Experiments show that a flame will propagate only within a range of mixture strengths between the so-called lower and upper limits of flammability. The **lower limit** is the leanest mixture ($\Phi < 1$) that will allow steady flame propagation, while the **upper limit** represents the richest mixture ($\Phi > 1$). Flammability limits are frequently quoted as percent fuel by volume in the mixture, or as a percentage of the stoichiometric fuel requirement, i.e., $\Phi \times 100\%$.

Table 8.4 shows flammability limits for a number of fuel–air mixtures at atmospheric pressure obtained from experiments employing the "tube method." In this method, it is ascertained whether or not a flame initiated at the bottom of a vertical tube (approximately 50-mm diameter by 1.2-m long) propagates the length of the tube. A mixture that sustains the flame is said to be flammable. By adjusting the mixture strength, the flammability limit can be ascertained.

Although flammability limits can be defined that are physiochemical properties of the fuel–air mixture, experimental flammability limits are related to heat losses from the system, in addition to the mixture properties, and, hence, are generally apparatus dependent [22].

Even if conduction losses are minimal, radiation losses can account for the existence of flammability limits. Figure 8.16 illustrates an intantaneous axial temperature profile along the centerline of a tube in which a flame is propagating. Because the high-temperature product gases radiate to a lower-temperature environment, they cool. Their cooling creates a negative temperature gradient at the rear of the flame zone; hence, heat is lost by conduction from the flame proper. When sufficient heat is removed, such that Williams' criteria are not met, the flame ceases to propagate. Williams [2] provides a theoretical analysis for the situation described in Fig. 8.16, a discussion of which is beyond the scope of this book.

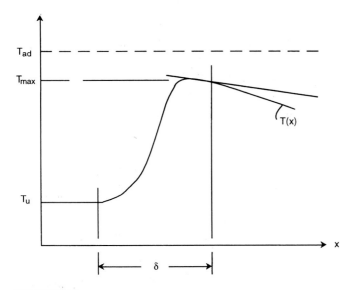

FIGURE 8.16
Temperature profile through flame with heat losses.

Example 8.5. A full propane cylinder from a camp stove leaks its contents of 1.02 lb (0.464 kg) into a 12′ × 14′ × 8′ (3.66 m × 4.27 m × 2.44 m) room at 20°C and 1 atm. After a long time, the fuel gas and room air are well mixed. Is the mixture in the room flammable?

Solution. From Table 8.4, we see that propane–air mixtures are flammable for $0.51 < \Phi < 2.83$. Our problem, thus, is to determine the equivalence ratio of the mixture filling the room. We can determine the partial pressure of the propane by assuming ideal-gas behavior,

$$P_F = \frac{m_F(R_u/MW_F)T}{V_{\text{room}}}$$

$$= \frac{0.464\,(8315/44.094)\,(20+273)}{3.66\,(4.27)\,(2.44)}$$

$$= 672.3 \text{ Pa}.$$

The propane mole fraction is

$$\chi_F = \frac{P_F}{P} = \frac{672.3}{101,325} = 0.00664$$

and

$$\chi_{\text{air}} = 1 - \chi_F = 0.99336.$$

The air–fuel ratio of the mixture in the room is

$$(A/F) = \frac{\chi_{air} MW_{air}}{\chi_F MW_F} = \frac{0.99336\,(28.85)}{0.00664\,(44.094)}$$
$$= 97.88.$$

From the definition of Φ and the value of $(A/F)_{stoic}$ from Table 8.4, we have

$$\Phi = \frac{15.6}{97.88} = 0.159.$$

Since $\Phi = 0.159$ is less than the lower limit of flammability ($\Phi_{min} = 0.51$), the mixture in the room is not capable of supporting a flame.

Comment. Although our calculations show that in the fully mixed state the mixture is not flammable, it is quite possible that during the transient leaking process, a flammable mixture can exist somewhere within the room. Propane is heavier than air and would tend to accumulate near the floor until it is mixed by bulk motion and molecular diffusion. In environments employing flammable gases, monitors should be located both at low and high positions to detect leakage of heavy and light fuels, respectively.

Ignition

In this section, we limit our discussion to ignition by electrical sparks and, in particular, focus on the concept of **minimum ignition energy**. Spark ignition is perhaps the most frequently employed means of ignition in practical devices, for example, spark-ignition and gas-turbine engines, and various industrial, commercial, and residential burners. Spark ignition is highly reliable and does not require a pre-existing flame, as required by pilot ignition. In the following, a simple analysis is presented from which the pressure and temperature dependencies of the minimum ignition energy are determined. Experimental data are also presented and compared with the predictions of the simple theory.

SIMPLIFIED IGNITION ANALYSIS. Consider Williams' second criterion, applied now to a spherical volume of gas, which represents the incipient propagating flame created by a point spark. Using this criterion, we can define a critical gas-volume radius such that a flame will not propagate if the actual radius is smaller than the critical value. The second step of the analysis is to assume that the minimum ignition energy to be supplied by the spark is the energy required to heat the critical gas volume from its initial state to the flame temperature.

To determine the critical radius, R_{crit}, we equate the rate of heat liberated by reaction to the rate of heat lost to the cold gas by conduction, as illustrated in Fig. 8.17, i.e.,

$$\dot{Q}''' V = \dot{Q}_{cond}, \tag{8.35}$$

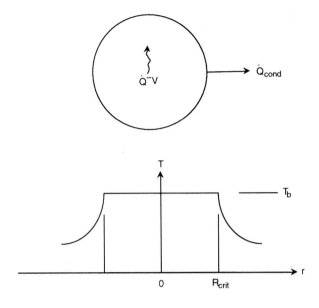

FIGURE 8.17
Critical volume of gas for spark ignition.

or

$$-\bar{\dot{m}}_F''' \Delta h_c 4\pi R_{crit}^3/3 = -k4\pi R_{crit}^2 \frac{\mathrm{d}T}{\mathrm{d}r}\bigg|_{R_{crit}}, \qquad (8.36)$$

where Eqn. 8.30 has been substituted for $\dot{Q}'''$, Fourier's Law employed, and the volume and surface area of the sphere expressed in terms of the critical radius, R_{crit}.

The temperature gradient in the cold gas at the sphere boundary, $(\mathrm{d}T/\mathrm{d}r)_{crit}$, can be evaluated by determining the temperature distribution in the gas beyond the sphere ($R_{crit} \leq r \leq \infty$) with the boundary conditions $T(R_{crit}) = T_b$ and $T(\infty) = T_u$. (The well-known result that $Nu = 2$ follows from this analysis, where Nu is the Nusselt number.) This results in

$$\frac{\mathrm{d}T}{\mathrm{d}r}\bigg|_{R_{crit}} = -\frac{(T_b - T_u)}{R_{crit}}. \qquad (8.37)$$

Substituting Eqn. 8.37 into Eqn. 8.36 yields

$$R_{crit}^2 = \frac{3k(T_b - T_u)}{-\bar{\dot{m}}_F''' \Delta h_c}. \qquad (8.38)$$

The critical radius can be related to the laminar flame speed, S_L, and flame thickness, δ, by solving Eqn. 8.20 for $\bar{\dot{m}}_F'''$ and substituting the result into Eqn. 8.38. This substitution, together with the recognition that $\Delta h_c = (\nu + 1)c_p(T_b - T_u)$, yields

$$R_{\text{crit}} = \sqrt{6}\frac{\alpha}{S_L}, \tag{8.39a}$$

where $\alpha = k/\rho_u c_p$ with k and c_p evaluated at some appropriate mean temperature. The critical radius can also be expressed in terms of δ (Eqn. 8.21b):

$$R_{\text{crit}} = \sqrt{6}\delta/2. \tag{8.39b}$$

Considering the crudeness of our analysis, the constant $\sqrt{6}/2$ should not be construed to be in any way precise but, rather, expresses an order of magnitude. Thus, from Eqn. 8.39b, we see that the critical radius is roughly equal to, or at most, a few times larger than the laminar flame thickness. In contrast, the quenching distance, d, as expressed by Eqn. 8.34b, can be many times larger than the flame thickness.

Knowing the critical radius, we now turn our attention to determining the minimum ignition energy, E_{ign}. This is done simply by assuming the energy added by the spark heats the critical volume to the burned-gas temperature, i.e.,

$$E_{\text{ign}} = m_{\text{crit}} c_p(T_b - T_u), \tag{8.40}$$

where the mass of the critical sphere, m_{crit}, is $\rho_b 4\pi R_{\text{crit}}^3/3$, or

$$E_{\text{ign}} = 61.6\rho_b c_p(T_b - T_u)(\alpha/S_L)^3. \tag{8.41}$$

Eliminating ρ_b using the ideal-gas law yields our final result

$$E_{\text{ign}} = 61.6P\left(\frac{c_p}{R_b}\right)\left(\frac{T_b - T_u}{T_b}\right)\left(\frac{\alpha}{S_L}\right)^3, \tag{8.42}$$

where $R_b = R_u/MW_b$.

PRESSURE AND TEMPERATURE DEPENDENCIES. The effect of pressure on minimum ignition energy is the result of the obvious direct influence seen in Eqn. 8.42, and the indirect influences buried in the thermal diffusivity, α, and the flame speed, S_L. Using Eqns. 8.22 and 8.24 ($n \approx 2$), with Eqn. 8.42, shows the combined pressure effects to be

$$E_{\text{ign}} \propto P^{-2}, \tag{8.43}$$

which agrees remarkably well with experimental results. Figure 8.18 shows experimental ignition energies as a function of pressure [20], together with the power law of Eqn. 8.43 fitted to match the central data point.

In general, increasing the initial mixture temperature results in decreased ignition energies, as shown in Table 8.5. Determining the theoretical influence from the simplified analyses presented in this chapter is left as an exercise for the reader.

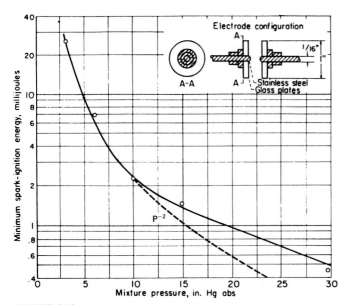

FIGURE 8.18
Effect of pressure on minimum spark-ignition energy. (From Ref. [20]. Reprinted by permission of the American Institute of Physics.)

TABLE 8.5
Temperature influence on spark-ignition energy [21]

Fuel	Initial temperature (K)	E_{ign} (mJ)[a]
n-Heptane	298	14.5
	373	6.7
	444	3.2
Isooctane	298	27.0
	373	11.0
	444	4.8
n-Pentane	243	45.0
	253	14.5
	298	7.8
	373	4.2
	444	2.3
Propane	233	11.7
	243	9.7
	253	8.4
	298	5.5
	331	4.2
	356	3.6
	373	3.5
	477	1.4

[a] $P = 1$ atm.

FLAME STABILIZATION

Important design criteria for gas burners are the avoidance of **flashback** and **liftoff**. Flashback occurs when the flame enters and propagates through the burner tube or port without quenching; while liftoff is the condition where the flame is not attached to the burner tube or port but, rather, is stabilized at some distance from the port. Flashback is not only a nuisance, but is a safety hazard as well. In a gas appliance, propagation of a flame through a port can ignite the relatively large volume of gas in the mixer leading to the port, which might result in an explosion. Conversely, flame propagation through a "flash tube" from the pilot flame to the burner proper is used for ignition. In practical burners, flame lifting is generally undesirable for several reasons [23]. First, it can contribute to some escape of unburned gas or incomplete combustion. Also, ignition is difficult to achieve above the lifting limit. Accurate control of the position of a lifted flame is hard to achieve so that poor heat-transfer characteristics can result. Lifted flames can also be noisy.

The phenomena of flashback and liftoff are both related to matching the local laminar flame speed to the local flow velocity. These matching conditions are schematically illustrated by the velocity vector diagrams of Fig. 8.19. Flashback is generally a transient event, occurring as the fuel flow is decreased or turned off. When the local flame speed exceeds the local flow velocity, the flame propagates upstream through the tube or port (Fig. 8.19a). When the fuel flow is stopped, flames will flashback through any tubes or ports that are larger than the quenching distance. Thus, we expect the controlling parameters for flashback to be the same as those affecting quenching, e.g., fuel type, equivalence ratio, flow velocity, and burner geometry.

Figure 8.20 illustrates flashback stability for a fixed burner geometry (a straight row of 2.7-mm-diameter ports with 6.35-mm spacing) for two different fuels, natural gas (top), and a manufactured gas that contains hydrogen (bottom). For a fixed gas and port size, the abscissa is proportional to the port exit velocity. Operation in the region to the left of the flashback zone line results in flashback, while flashback-free operation occurs to the right, where velocities are higher. We see that for both fuels, slightly rich stoichiometries provide the least tolerance to flashback, as expected, since maximum laminar flame speeds generally occur with slightly rich mixtures (cf. Fig. 8.12). We also observe from Fig. 8.20 that the flashback stability of natural gas, which is primarily methane, is much greater than for the manufactured gas. This is primarily a result of the high flame speed associated with the hydrogen in the manufactured gas. (Referring to Table 8.2, we see that the flame speed of H_2 is more than five times that of CH_4.)

Flame lifting depends on local flame and flow properties near the edges of the burner port. Consider a flame stabilized on a circular tube. At low flow velocities, the edge of the flame lies quite close to the burner lip and is said to be **attached**. When the velocity is increased, the cone angle of the flame decreases in accordance with the condition $\alpha = \sin^{-1}(S_L/v_u)$, Eqn. 8.2, and the edge of the flame is displaced a small distance downstream. With further increases in flow

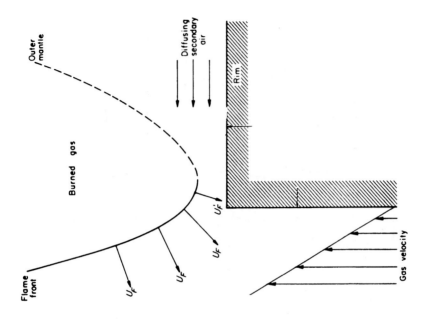

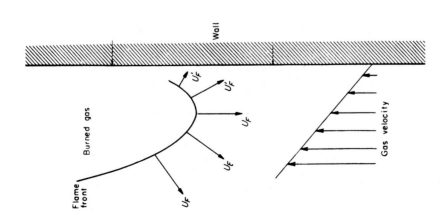

FIGURE 8.19
Velocity vectors showing flow velocities and local flame velocity for flashback (left) and liftoff (right). (Reprinted with permission from Ref. [24]. © 1955, American Chemical Society.)

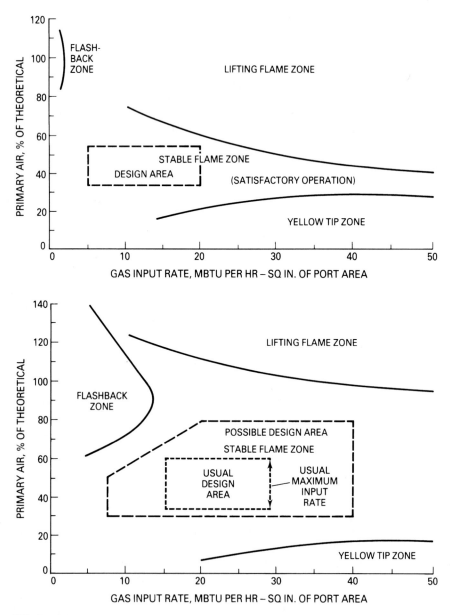

FIGURE 8.20
Stability diagrams for flashback, liftoff, and yellow-tipping for natural gas (top) and manufactured gas (bottom) for a burner with a single row of 2.7-mm-diameter ports with 6.35-mm spacing. Yellow-tipping indicates soot formation within the flame. (From Ref. [23]. Reprinted with permission of Industrial Press.)

velocity, a critical velocity is reached where the flame edge jumps to a downstream position far from the burner lip. When the flame jumps to this position, it is said to be lifted. Increasing the velocity beyond the liftoff value results in increasing the liftoff distance until the flame abruptly blows off the tube altogether, an obviously undesirable condition.

Liftoff and blowoff can be explained by the countervailing effects of decreased heat and radical loss to the burner tube and increased dilution with ambient fluid, which occur as the flow velocity is increased. Consider a flame that is stabilized quite close to the burner rim. The local flow velocity at the stabilization location is small as a result of the boundary layer that develops in the tube. Inside the tube, the velocity at the wall is zero. Because of the close proximity of the flame to the cold wall, both heat and reactive species diffuse to the wall causing the local laminar flame speed at the stabilization point also to be small. With the flame speed and flow velocities equal and of relatively small magnitude, the flame edge lies close to the burner tube. When the flow velocity is increased, the flame anchor point moves downstream; however, S_L increases since the heat/radical losses are less because the flame is now not as close to the cold wall. This increase in the burning velocity results in only a small downstream adjustment; and, hence, the flame remains attached. With yet further increases in flow velocity, another effect becomes important—dilution of the mixture with ambient fluid as a result of diffusion. Since dilution tends to offset the effects of less heat loss, the flame lifts, as shown in Fig. 8.19b. With further increases in flow velocity, a point is reached at which there is no location across the flow at which the local flame speed matches the flow velocity and the flame blows off the tube.

Figure 8.20 shows how the region of lift-free operation varies as function of stoichiometry (% primary air) and flow velocity (gas input rate per unit port area). Here we see that natural gas flames are more prone to lifting than the manufactured gas flame. Again, the high flame speed of the hydrogen in the manufactured gas explains the greater stability of this fuel. For more detailed information on laminar flame stability, the reader is referred to Refs. [1] and [16].

SUMMARY

In this chapter, we considered the properties of laminar flames: their propagation velocity and thickness, quenching distances, flammability limits, and minimum ignition energies. Simplified theories were presented to illuminate the underlying physics and chemistry of these flame properties. We used the results of one such analysis to explore the pressure and temperature dependencies of flame speed and flame thickness, drawing from our conclusion that $S_L \propto \left(\alpha \bar{\dot{m}}_F''' / \rho_u\right)^{1/2}$, and finding that S_L increases rapidly with temperature and has a weak inverse dependence on pressure. We saw that maximum laminar flame speeds for hydrocarbons typically occur in slightly rich mixtures, as do peak adiabatic flame temperatures. Correlations of laminar flame speeds for several fuels were presented. These correlations are useful for estimating flame properties in practical devices, such as engines, and you should be familiar with their use. Simple criteria for flame quenching and ignition were presented and used to develop simplistic models of these phenomena. Our analyses showed that the quenching distance is directly proportional to the thermal diffusivity and inversely proportional to the flame speed. We defined the upper and lower flammability limits and presented data for several fuels. In an analysis of the ignition process, the ideas of a critical radius and minimum energy input required to produce a self-propagating flame were developed. We saw that the minimum ignition energy exhibits a strong inverse pressure dependence, which has strong implications for engine applications where reliable ignition must be assured over a wide range of pressures. The chapter concluded with a discussion of the stabilization of laminar flames, i.e., their flashback and liftoff behavior, topics of great practical importance.

NOMENCLATURE

A	Area (m^2)
b	Dimensionless parameter defined in Eqn. 8.32
B_M, B_2	Parameters defined in Table B.3
c_p	Specific heat (J/kg-K)
d	Quenching distance (m)
$\mathcal{D}$	Mass diffusivity (m^2/s)
E_A	Activation energy (J/kmol)
E_{ign}	Minimum ignition energy (J)
h	Enthalpy (J/kg)
k	Thermal conductivity (W/m-K)
L	Slot width (m)
Le	Lewis number, $\alpha/\mathcal{D}$
m	Mass (kg)
$\dot{m}$	Mass flowrate (kg/s)
$\dot{m}''$	Mass flux (kg/s-m^2)
$\dot{m}'''$	Volumetric mass production rate (kg/s-m^3)
MW	Molecular weight (kg/kmol)
Nu	Nusselt number
P	Pressure (Pa)
$\dot{Q}$	Heat-transfer rate (W)
$\dot{Q}'''$	Volumetric energy generation rate (W/m^3)
r	Radial coordinate (m)
R	Radius (m) or specific gas constant (J/kg-K)
R_u	Universal gas constant (J/kmol-K)
Re_d	Reynolds number
S_L	Laminar flame speed (m/s)
T	Temperature (K)
v	Velocity (m/s)
x	Distance (m)
Y	Mass fraction (kg/kg)

Greek symbols

α	Angle (rad) or thermal diffusivity (m^2/s)
β	Pressure exponent, Eqn. 8.28
γ	Temperature exponent, Eqn. 8.28
δ	Laminar flame thickness (m)
Δh_c	Heat of combustion (J/kg)
ν	Mass oxidizer to fuel ratio (kg/kg)
ρ	Density (kg/m^3)
Φ	Equivalence ratio
Φ_M	Parameter defined in Table B.3
$\dot{\omega}$	Species production rate (kmol/s)

Subscripts

ad	Adiabatic
b	Burned gas
cond	Conduction
crit	Critical
dil	Diluent
F	Fuel
i	ith species
max	Maximum
mix	Mixture
Ox	Oxidizer
Pr	Product
ref	Reference state
u	Unburned gas

Other

$\overline{(\ )}$	Average over reaction zone

REFERENCES

1. Lewis, B., and Von Elbe, G., *Combustion, Flames and Explosions of Gases*, 3rd Ed., Academic Press, Orlando, 1987.
2. Williams, F. A., *Combustion Theory*, 2nd Ed., Addison-Wesley, Redwood City, CA, 1985.
3. Glassman, I., *Combustion*, 2nd Ed., Academic Press, Orlando, 1987.
4. Strehlow, R. A., *Fundamentals of Combustion*, Krieger, Huntington, NY, 1979.
5. Kuo, K. K., *Principles of Combustion*, John Wiley & Sons, New York, 1986.
6. Chomiak, J., *Combustion: A Study in Theory, Fact and Application*, Gordon & Breach, New York, 1990.
7. Gordon, A. G., *The Spectroscopy of Flames*, 2nd Ed., Halsted Press, New York, 1974.
8. Gordon, A. G., and Wolfhard, H. G., *Flames: Their Structure, Radiation and Temperature*, 4th Edn., Halsted Press, New York, 1979.
9. Powling, J., "A New Burner Method for the Determination of Low Burning Velocities and Limits of Inflammability," *Fuel*, 28: 25–28 (1949).

10. Botha, J. P., and Spalding, D. B., "The Laminar Flame Speed of Propane–Air Mixtures with Heat Extraction from the Flame," *Proceedings of the Royal Society of London Series A*, 225: 71–96 (1954).
11. Mallard, E., and Le Chatelier, H. L., *Ann. Mines*, 4: 379–568 (1883).
12. Spalding, D. B., *Combustion and Mass Transfer*, Pergamon, New York, 1979.
13. Metghalchi, M., and Keck, J. C., "Burning Velocities of Mixtures of Air with Methanol, Isooctane, and Indolene at High Pressures and Temperatures," *Combustion and Flame*, 48: 191–210 (1982).
14. Andrews, G. E., and Bradley, D., "The Burning Velocity of Methane–Air Mixtures," *Combustion and Flame*, 19: 275–288 (1972).
15. Law, C. K., "A Compilation of Experimental Data on Laminar Burning Velocities," in *Reduced Kinetic Mechanisms for Applications in Combustion Systems* (N. Peters, and B. Rogg, eds.), Springer-Verlag, New York, pp. 15–26, 1993.
16. Barnett, H. C., and Hibbard, R. R. (eds.), "Basic Considerations in the Combustion of Hydrocarbon Fuels with Air," NACA Report 1300, 1959.
17. Frendi, A., and Sibulkin, M., "Dependence of Minimum Ignition Energy on Ignition Parameters," *Combustion Science and Technology*, 73: 395–413 (1990).
18. Lovachev, L. A., *et al.*, "Flammability Limits: An Invited Review," *Combustion and Flame*, 20: 259–289 (1973).
19. Friedman, R., "The Quenching of Laminar Oxyhydrogen Flames by Solid Surfaces," *Third Symposium on Combustion and Flame and Explosion Phenomena*, Williams & Wilkins, Baltimore, p. 110, 1949.
20. Blanc, M. V., Guest, P. G., von Elbe, G., and Lewis, B., "Ignition of Explosive Gas Mixture by Electric Sparks. I. Minimum Ignition Energies and Quenching Distances of Mixtures of Methane, Oxygen, and Inert Gases," *Journal of Chemical Physics*, 15(11): 798–802 (1947).
21. Fenn, J. B., "Lean Flammability Limit and Minimum Spark Ignition Energy," *Industrial & Engineering Chemistry*, 43(12): 2865–2868 (1951).
22. Law, C. L., and Egolfopoulos, F. N., "A Unified Chain-Thermal Theory of Fundamental Flammability Limits," *Twenty-Fourth Symposium (International) on Combustion*, The Combustion Institute, Pittsburgh, p. 137, 1992.
23. Weber, E. J., and Vandaveer, F. E., "Gas Burner Design," *Gas Engineers Handbook*, Industrial Press, New York, pp. 12/193–12/210, 1965.
24. Dugger, G. L., "Flame Stability of Preheated Propane–Air Mixtures," *Industrial & Engineering Chemistry*, 47(1): 109–114, 1955.

REVIEW QUESTIONS

1. Make a list of all the bold-faced words in Chapter 8 and discuss each.
2. Distinguish between deflagration and detonation.
3. Discuss the structure/appearance of a Bunsen-burner flame where the air–fuel mixture in the tube is rich.
4. What is the physical significance of the Lewis number? What role does the $Le = 1$ assumption play in the analysis of laminar flame propagation?
5. In the context of laminar flame theory, what is an eigenvalue? Discuss.
6. Discuss the origins of the pressure- and temperature-dependencies of the laminar flame speed. Hint: Refer to the global hydrocarbon oxidation mechanism in Chapter 5.
7. What are the basic criteria for ignition and quenching?

PROBLEMS

8.1. Consider the outward propagation of a spherical laminar flame into an infinite medium of unburned gas. Assuming that S_L, T_u, and T_b are all constants, determine an expression for the radial velocity of the flame front for a fixed coordinate system with its origin at the center of the sphere.

8.2. Prove that, for the simplified thermodynamics employed in Chapter 8, flame speed theory, $\Delta h_c = (\nu + 1)c_p(T_b - T_u)$.

8.3. Using the simplified theory, estimate the laminar flame speed of CH_4 for $\Phi = 1$ and $T_u = 300$ K. Use the global, single-step kinetics given in Chapter 5. Compare your estimate with experimental results. Also compare your results for CH_4 with those for C_3H_8 from Example 8.2.

8.4. Consider a one-dimensional, adiabatic, laminar, flat flame stabilized on a burner such as in Fig. 8.5a. The fuel is propane and the mixture ratio is stoichiometric. Determine the velocity of the burned gases for operation at atmospheric pressure and an unburned gas temperature of 300 K.

8.5. Consider a premixed flame stabilized above a circular tube. For the flame to be conical (constant angle α), what is the shape of the velocity profile at the tube exit? Explain.

8.6. Derive the theoretical flame shape for a premixed laminar flame stabilized over a circular tube, assuming the unburned mixture velocity profile is parabolic: $v(r) = v_o(1 - r^2/R^2)$, where v_o is the centerline velocity and R is the burner-tube radius. Ignore the region close to the tube wall where S_L is greater than $v(r)$. Discuss your results.

8.7. Derive the pressure and temperature dependencies of the laminar flame speed, as shown in Eqn. 8.24, starting with Eqn. 8.20 and utilizing Eqn. 8.22 as given.

8.8. Using the correlations of Metghalchi and Keck [13], calculate laminar flame speeds for the stoichiometric mixtures of the following fuels for $P = 1$ atm and $T_u = 400$ K: propane; isooctane; and indolene (RMFD-303), a gasoline reference fuel.

8.9. Use Eqn. 8.28 to estimate the laminar flame speed of a laminar flamelet in a spark-ignition internal combustion engine for conditions shortly after the spark is fired and a flame is established. The conditions are as follows:

$$\text{Fuel: indolene (gasoline)} \qquad \Phi = 1.0$$
$$P = 13.4 \text{ atm} \qquad T = 560 \text{ K.}$$

8.10. Repeat problem 8.9 for an equivalence ratio of $\Phi = 0.80$ with all other conditions the same. Compare your results with those of problem 8.9 and discuss the practical implications of your comparison.

8.11. Use Eqn. 8.28 to calculate the laminar flame speed of propane for the following sets of conditions:

	Set 1	Set 2	Set 3	Set 4
P (atm)	1	1	1	10
T_u (K)	350	700	350	350
Φ	0.9	0.9	1.2	0.9

Using your results, discuss the effects of T_u, P, and Φ on S_L.

8.12. Using a combination of correlations and simplified theory, estimate propane–air flame thicknesses for $P = 1$, 10, and 100 atm for $\Phi = 1$ and $T_u = 300$ K. What are the implications of your calculations for the design of explosion-proof housings for electrical devices?

8.13. Estimate values of the parameter b employed in quenching theory for methane–air mixtures over the range of $0.6 \leq \Phi \leq 1.2$. Plot your results and discuss.

8.14. Determine the critical radius for ignition of a stoichiometric propane–air mixture at 1 atm.

8.15. How many tmes more ignition energy is required to achieve ignition of a fuel–air mixture at sea level with $T = 298$ K than at an altitude of 6000 m (19,685 ft) where $P = 47,166$ Pa and $T = 248$ K? Discuss the implications of your calculations for high-altitude relight in aircraft gas-turbine engines.

CHAPTER 9

LAMINAR DIFFUSION FLAMES— BURNING JETS

OVERVIEW

In this chapter, we begin our study of laminar diffusion flames by focusing on burning jets of fuel. Laminar jet flames have been the subject of much fundamental research, and, more recently, have been used to develop an understanding of how soot is formed in diffusion burning, e.g., Refs. [1–3]. A familiar example of a nonpremixed jet flame is the Bunsen-burner outer-cone flame, which was briefly mentioned in Chapter 8. Many residential gas appliances, e.g., cooking ranges and ovens, employ laminar jet flames. In these applications, the fuel stream is usually partially premixed with air, which is essential to provide nonsooting operation. Although many analytical [4–8] and numerical [9–13] analyses of laminar jet flames have been performed, much of current design practices rely on the art and craft of experienced burner designers [14, 15]; however, recent concerns with indoor air quality and pollutant emissions have resulted in the use of more sophisticated design methods. Of particular concern are the emissions of nitrogen dioxide (NO_2) and carbon monoxide (CO), both of which are toxic gases.

A primary concern in the design of any system utilizing laminar jet flames is flame geometry, with short flames frequently being desired. Also of interest is the effect of fuel type. For example, some appliances may be designed to operate on natural gas (primarily methane) or propane. In the following sections, we will develop analyses that allow us to see what parameters control flame size and shape. We will also examine the factors controlling soot from laminar jet flames.

NONREACTING CONSTANT-DENSITY LAMINAR JET

Physical Description

Before discussing jet flames proper, let us consider the simpler case of a nonreacting laminar jet of fluid (fuel) flowing into an infinite reservoir of quiescent fluid (oxidizer). This simpler case allows us to develop an understanding of the basic flow and diffusional processes that occur in laminar jets uncomplicated by the effects of chemical reaction.

Figure 9.1 illustrates the essential features of a fuel jet issuing from a nozzle of radius R into still air. For simplicity, we assume that the velocity profile is uniform at the tube exit. Close to the nozzle, there exists a region called the **potential core** of the jet. In the potential core, the effects of viscous shear and diffusion have yet to be felt; hence, both the velocity and nozzle-fluid mass fraction remain unchanged from their nozzle-exit values and are uniform in this region. This situation is quite similar to the developing flow in a pipe, except that, in the pipe, conservation of mass requires the uniform core flow to accelerate.

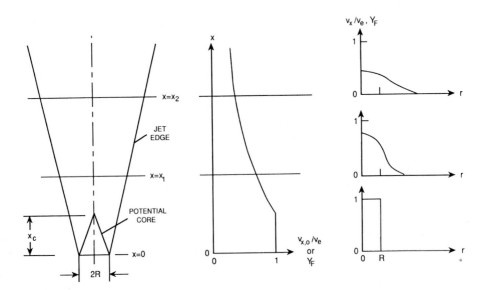

FIGURE 9.1
Nonreacting, laminar fuel jet issuing into an infinite into reservoir of quiescent air.

In the region between the potential core and the jet edge, both the velocity and fuel concentration (mass fraction) decrease monotonically to zero at the edge of the jet. Beyond the potential core $(x > x_c)$, the effects of viscous shear and mass diffusion are active across the whole width of the jet.

Throughout the entire flowfield, the initial jet momentum is conserved. As the jet issues into the surrounding air, some of its momentum is transferred to the air. Thus, the velocity of the jet decreases, while greater and greater quantities of air are **entrained** into the jet as it proceeds downstream. This idea can be expressed mathematically using an integral form of momentum conservation:

$$\begin{array}{ccc} \text{Momentum flow of the} & = & \text{Momentum flow} \\ \text{jet at any } x, J & & \text{issuing from the nozzle, } J_e \end{array}$$

or

$$2\pi \int_0^\infty \rho(r, x) v_x^2(r, x) r \, dr \quad = \quad \rho_e v_e^2 \pi R^2. \tag{9.1}$$

where ρ_e and v_e are the density and velocity of the fuel at the nozzle exit, respectively. The central graph of Fig. 9.1 illustrates the decay of the centerline velocity with distance beyond the potential core, while the right-hand graphs of Fig. 9.1 show the radial velocity decay from the maximum, which occurs at the centerline, to zero at the edge of the jet.

The processes that control the velocity field, i.e., the convection and diffusion of momentum, are similar to the processes that control the fuel concentration field, i.e., the convection and diffusion of mass. Thus, we expect that the distribution of the fuel mass fraction, $Y_F(r, x)$, should be similar to the dimensionless velocity distribution, $v_x(r, x)/v_e$, as indicated in Fig. 9.1. Because of the high concentration of fuel in the center of the jet, fuel molecules diffuse radially outward in accordance with Fick's Law. The effect of moving downstream is to increase the time available for diffusion to take place; hence, the width of the region containing fuel molecules grows with axial distance, x, and the centerline fuel concentration decays. Similar to the initial jet momentum, the mass of the fluid issuing from the nozzle is conserved, i.e.,

$$2\pi \int_0^\infty \rho(r, x) v_x(r, x) Y_F(r, x) r \, dr = \rho_e v_e \pi R^2 Y_{F,e} \tag{9.2}$$

where $Y_{F,e} = 1$. The problem now before us is the determination of the detailed velocity and fuel mass fraction fields.

Assumptions

In order to provide a very simple analysis of a nonreacting laminar jet, we employ the following assumptions:

1. The molecular weights of the jet and reservoir fluids are equal. This assumption, combined with ideal-gas behavior and the further assumptions of con-

stant pressure and temperature, provide a uniform fluid density throughout the flowfield.

2. Species molecular transport is by simple binary diffusion governed by Fick's Law.

3. Momentum and species diffusivities are constant and equal; thus, the **Schmidt number**, $Sc \equiv \nu/\mathcal{D}$, which expresses the ratio of these two quantities, is unity.

4. Only radial diffusion of momentum and species is important; axial diffusion is neglected. This implies that our solution only applies some distance downstream of the nozzle exit, since near the exit, axial diffusion is quite important.

Conservation Laws

The basic governing equations expressing conservation of mass, momentum, and species appropriate for our purposes are the so-called **boundary-layer equations**, which are obtained by simplifying the more general equations of motion and species conservation, as discussed in Chapter 7. The pertinent equations (Eqns. 7.7, 7.33, and 7.19) are simplified for our assumptions of constant density, viscosity, and mass diffusivity to yield:

MASS CONSERVATION

$$\frac{\partial v_x}{\partial x} + \frac{1}{r}\frac{\partial (v_r r)}{\partial r} = 0. \tag{9.3}$$

AXIAL MOMENTUM CONSERVATION

$$v_x \frac{\partial v_x}{\partial x} + v_r \frac{\partial v_x}{\partial r} = \nu \frac{1}{r}\frac{\partial}{\partial r}\left(r \frac{\partial v_x}{\partial r} \right). \tag{9.4}$$

SPECIES CONSERVATION. For the jet fluid, i.e., the fuel,

$$v_x \frac{\partial Y_F}{\partial x} + v_r \frac{\partial Y_F}{\partial r} = \mathcal{D}\frac{1}{r}\frac{\partial}{\partial r}\left(r \frac{\partial Y_F}{\partial r} \right), \tag{9.5}$$

and since there are only two species, fuel and oxidizer, the mass fractions of the two must sum to unity, i.e.,

$$Y_{Ox} = 1 - Y_F. \tag{9.6}$$

Boundary Conditions

In order to solve the above equations for the unknown functions, $v_x(r, x)$, $v_r(r, x)$, and $Y_F(r, x)$, requires three boundary conditions each for v_x and Y_F (two as functions of x and specified r, and one as a function of r at specified x) and one boundary condition for v_r (as a function of x at specified r). These are:

Along the jet centerline $(r = 0)$,

$$v_r(0, x) = 0, \tag{9.7a}$$

$$\frac{\partial v_x}{\partial r}(0, x) = 0, \tag{9.7b}$$

$$\frac{\partial Y_F}{\partial r}(0, x) = 0. \tag{9.7c}$$

where the first condition (9.7a) implies that there is no source or sink of fluid along the jet axis, while the second two, (9.7b and c), result from symmetry. At large radii $(r \to \infty)$, the fluid is stagnant and no fuel is present, i.e.,

$$v_x(\infty, x) = 0, \tag{9.7d}$$

$$Y_F(\infty, x) = 0. \tag{9.7e}$$

At the jet exit $(x = 0)$, we assume the axial velocity and fuel mass fraction are uniform at the mouth of the nozzle $(r \le R)$ and zero elsewhere:

$$\begin{aligned} v_x(r \le R, 0) &= v_e \\ v_x(r > R, 0) &= 0 \end{aligned} \tag{9.7f}$$

$$\begin{aligned} Y_F(r \le R, 0) &= Y_{F,e} = 1 \\ Y_F(r > R, 0) &= 0 \end{aligned} \tag{9.7g}$$

Solution

The velocity field can be obtained by assuming the profiles to be **similar**. The idea of similarity is that the intrinsic shape of the velocity profiles is the same everywhere in the flowfield. For the present problem, this implies that the radial distribution of $v_x(r, x)$, when normalized by the local centerline velocity $v_x(0, x)$, is a universal function that depends only on the **similarity variable**, r/x. The solution for the axial and radial velocities is [16]

$$v_x = \frac{3}{8\pi} \frac{J_e}{\mu x} \left[1 + \frac{\xi^2}{4} \right]^{-2}, \tag{9.8}$$

$$v_r = \left(\frac{3J_e}{16\pi \rho_e} \right)^{1/2} \frac{1}{x} \frac{\xi - \frac{\xi^3}{4}}{\left(1 + \frac{\xi^2}{4} \right)^2}, \tag{9.9}$$

where J_e is the jet initial momentum flow,

$$J_e = \rho_e v_e^2 \pi R^2, \tag{9.10}$$

and ξ contains the similarity variable r/x,

$$\xi = \left(\frac{3\rho_e J_e}{16\pi}\right)^{1/2}\frac{1}{\mu}\frac{r}{x}. \tag{9.11}$$

The axial velocity distribution in dimensionless form can be obtained by substituting Eqn. 9.10 into Eqn. 9.8 and rearranging:

$$v_x/v_e = 0.375(\rho_e v_e R/\mu)(x/R)^{-1}[1+\xi^2/4]^{-2}, \tag{9.12}$$

and the dimensionless centerline velocity decay is obtained by setting $r = 0(\xi = 0)$:

$$v_{x,0}/v_e = 0.375(\rho_e v_e R/\mu)(x/R)^{-1}. \tag{9.13}$$

Equation 9.12 shows that the velocity decays inversely with axial distance and is directly proportional to the jet Reynolds number $(Re_j \equiv \rho_e v_e R/\mu)$. Furthermore, Eqn. 9.13 reminds us that the solution is not valid near the nozzle, since $v_{x,0}/v_e$ should not exceed unity. The centerline velocity decay pattern predicted by Eqn. 9.13 is shown in Fig. 9.2. Here we see that the decay is more rapid with the lower-Re_j jets. This behavior occurs because as the Reynolds number is decreased, the relative importance of the initial jet momentum becomes smaller in comparison to the viscous shearing action that slows the jet.

Other parameters frequently used to characterize jets are the **spreading rate** and **spreading angle**, α. To define these parameters, we need to introduce the idea

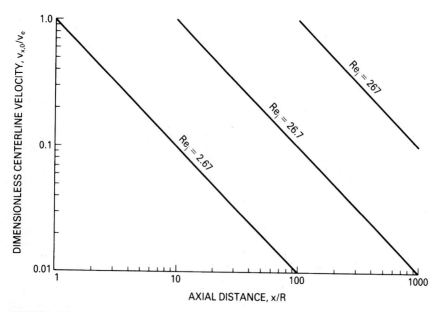

FIGURE 9.2
Centerline velocity decay for laminar jets.

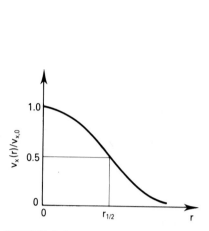
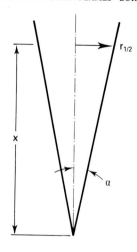

FIGURE 9.3
Definitions of jet half-width, $r_{1/2}$, and jet spreading angle, α.

of the **jet half-width**, $r_{1/2}$. The jet half-width is simply the radial location where the jet velocity has decayed to one half of its centerline value (Fig. 9.3). An expression for $r_{1/2}$ can be derived by setting $v_x/v_{x,0}$, obtained by taking the ratio of Eqns. 9.12 and 9.13, to be one half and solving for $r(= r_{1/2})$. The ratio of the jet half-width to the axial distance x is termed the jet spreading rate, and the spreading angle is the angle whose tangent is the spreading rate. Thus,

$$r_{1/2}/x = 2.97\left(\frac{\mu}{\rho v_e R}\right) = 2.97 Re_j^{-1}, \tag{9.14}$$

and

$$\alpha \equiv \tan^{-1}(r_{1/2}/x). \tag{9.15}$$

Equations 9.14 and 9.15 reveal that high-Re_j jets are narrow, while low-Re_j jets are wide. This result is consistent with the Reynolds number dependence of the velocity decay discussed above.

Let us now examine the solution for the concentration field. Referring to the governing equations for momentum conservation (Eqn. 9.4) and species conservation (Eqn. 9.5), we see that the fuel mass fraction, Y_F plays the same mathematical role as the dimensionless axial velocity, v_x/v_e, if ν and $\mathcal{D}$ are equal. Since the equality of ν and $\mathcal{D}$ was one of our original assumptions, $Sc = \nu/\mathcal{D} = 1$, the functional form of the solution for Y_F is identical to that for v_x/v_e, i.e.,

$$Y_F = \frac{3}{8\pi}\frac{Q_F}{\mathcal{D}x}\left[1 + \xi^2/4\right]^{-2} \tag{9.16}$$

where Q_F is the volumetric flowrate of fuel from the nozzle ($Q_F = v_e\pi R^2$).

By applying $Sc = 1 (\nu = \mathcal{D})$ to Eqn. 9.16, we can identify again the jet Reynolds number as a controlling parameter, i.e.,

$$Y_F = 0.375 Re_j (x/R)^{-1} [1 + \xi^2/4]^{-2}, \qquad (9.17)$$

and for the centerline values of the mass fraction,

$$Y_{F,0} = 0.375 Re_j (x/R)^{-1}. \qquad (9.18)$$

Again, we see that the solutions above can only be applied far from the nozzle, that is, the dimensionless distance downstream where the solution is valid must exceed the jet Reynolds number, i.e.,

$$(x/R) \tilde{>} 0.375 Re_j. \qquad (9.19)$$

Note that Fig. 9.2 also represents the decay of the centerline mass fractions, since Eqns. 9.18 and 9.13 are identical.

Example 9.1. A jet of ethylene (C_2H_4) exits a 10-mm-diameter nozzle into still air at 300 K and 1 atm. Compare the spreading angles and axial locations where the jet centerline mass fraction drops to the stoichiometric value for initial jet velocities of 10 cm/s and 1.0 cm/s. The viscosity of ethylene at 300 K is $102.3 \cdot 10^{-7}$ N-s/m^2.

Solution. Since the molecular weight of C_2H_4 and air are nearly the same ($MW = 28.05$ and 28.85, respectively), we assume that the constant-density jet solutions (Eqns. 9.8–9.15) can be applied to this problem. Designating the 10 cm/s case as Case I and the 1 cm/s as Case II, we determine the jet Reynolds numbers to be

$$Re_{j,I} = \frac{\rho v_{e,I} R}{\mu} = \frac{1.14 (0.10) 0.005}{102.3 \cdot 10^{-7}} = 55.7$$

and

$$Re_{j,II} = \frac{\rho v_{e,II} R}{\mu} = \frac{1.14 (0.01) 0.005}{102.3 \cdot 10^{-7}} = 5.57$$

where the density has been estimated from the ideal-gas law, i.e.,

$$\rho = \frac{P}{\left(\dfrac{R_u}{MW}\right) T} = \frac{101,325}{\left(\dfrac{8315}{28.05}\right) 300} = 1.14 \, \text{kg/m}^3.$$

A. The spreading angle is determined by combining Eqns. 9.14 and 9.15 to yield

$$\alpha = \tan^{-1} [2.97 / Re_j]$$

where

$$\alpha_I = \tan^{-1} [2.97 / 55.7]$$

$$\boxed{\alpha_I = 3.05°}$$

and

$$\alpha_{II} = \tan^{-1}[2.97/5.57]$$

$$\boxed{\alpha_{II} = 28.1°} \ .$$

Comment. From these calculations, we see that the low-velocity jet is much wider, with a spreading angle about nine times larger than the high-velocity jet.

B. The stoichiometric fuel mass fraction can be calculated as

$$Y_{F,stoic} = \frac{m_F}{m_A + m_F} = \frac{1}{(A/F)_{stoic} + 1}$$

where

$$(A/F)_{stoic} = (x + (y/4))4.76 \frac{MW_A}{MW_F}$$

$$= (2 + (4/4))4.76 \frac{28.85}{28.05} = 14.7.$$

Thus,

$$Y_{F,stoic} = \frac{1}{14.7 + 1} = 0.0637.$$

To find the axial location where the centerline fuel mass fraction takes on the stoichiometric value, we set $Y_{F,0} = Y_{F,stoic}$ in Eqn. 9.18 and solve for x:

$$x = \left(\frac{0.375 Re_j}{Y_{F,stoic}} \right) R,$$

which, when evaluated for the two cases, becomes

$$\boxed{x_I} = \left(\frac{0.375\,(55.7)\,0.005}{0.0637} \right) = \boxed{1.64\,m}$$

and

$$\boxed{x_{II}} = \left(\frac{0.375\,(5.57)\,0.005}{0.0637} \right) = \boxed{0.164\,m} \ .$$

Comment. We see that the fuel concentration of the low-velocity jet decays to the same value as the high-velocity jet in 1/10 the distance.

Example 9.2. Using the Case II ($v_e = 1.0\,cm/s$, $R = 5\,mm$) jet from Example 9.1 as the base case, determine what nozzle exit radius is required to maintain the same flowrate if the exit velocity is increased by a factor of ten to $10\,cm/s$. Also determine the axial location for $Y_{F,0} = Y_{F,stoic}$ for this condition and compare it to the base case.

Solution

A. We can relate the velocities and exit radii to the flowrate as

$$Q = v_{e,1} A_1 = v_{e,2} A_2$$

$$Q = v_{e,1} \pi R_1^2 = v_{e,2} \pi R_2^2.$$

Thus,

$$R_2 = \left(\frac{v_{e,1}}{v_{e,2}}\right)^{1/2} R_1 = \left(\frac{1}{10}\right)^{1/2} 5 \text{ mm}$$

$$\boxed{R_2 = 1.58 \text{ mm}}.$$

B. For the high-velocity, small-diameter jet, the Reynolds number is

$$Re_j = \frac{\rho v_{e,2} R}{\mu} = \frac{1.14 \, (0.1) \, 0.00158}{102.3 \cdot 10^{-7}} = 17.6,$$

and from Eqn. 9.18

$$x = \left(\frac{0.375 \, Re_j}{Y_{F,\text{stoic}}}\right) R = \frac{0.375 \, (17.6) \, 0.00158}{0.0637}$$

$$\boxed{x = 0.164 \text{ m}}.$$

Comment. The distance calculated in part B is identical to the Case II value from Example 9.1. Thus, we see that the spatial fuel mass fraction distribution depends only on the initial volumetric flow rate for a given fuel (μ/ρ constant).

JET FLAME PHYSICAL DESCRIPTION

The burning laminar fuel jet has much in common with our previous discussion of the isothermal jet. Some essential features of the jet flame are illustrated in Fig. 9.4. As the fuel flows along the flame axis, it diffuses radially outward, while the oxidizer (e.g., air) diffuses radially inward. The flame surface is nominally defined to exist where the fuel and oxidizer meet in stoichimetric proportions, i.e.,

$$\text{Flame surface} \quad \equiv \quad \begin{array}{l} \text{Locus of points where the} \\ \text{equivalence ratio, } \Phi, \text{ equals unity.} \end{array} \quad (9.20)$$

Note that, although the fuel and oxidizer are consumed at the flame, the equivalence ratio still has meaning since the products composition relates to a unique value of Φ. The products formed at the flame surface diffuse both radially inward and outward. For an **overventilated** flame, where there is more than enough oxidizer in the surroundings to continuously burn the fuel, the flame length, L_f, is simply determined by the axial location where

$$\Phi(r = 0, x = L_f) = 1. \quad (9.21)$$

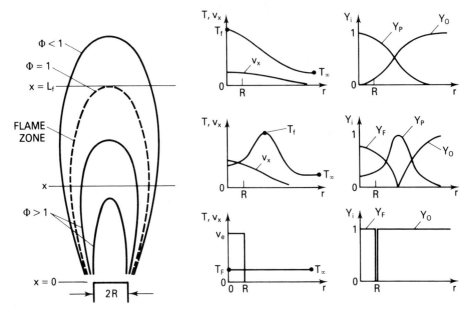

FIGURE 9.4
Laminar diffusion flame structure.

The region where chemical reactions occur is generally quite narrow. As seen in Fig. 9.4, the high-temperature reaction zone occurs in an annular region until the flame tip is reached. That the flame zone is an annulus can be demonstrated in a simple experiment where a metal screen is placed perpendicular to the axis of an unaerated bunsen-burner flame. In the flame zone, the screen becomes hot and glows, showing the annular structure.

In the upper regions of a vertical flame, there is a sufficient quantity of hot gases that buoyant forces become important. Buoyancy accelerates the flow and causes a narrowing of the flame, since conservation of mass requires streamlines to come closer together as the velocity increases. The narrowing of the flow increases the fuel concentration gradients, dY_F/dr, thus enhancing diffusion. The effects of these two phenomena on the length of flames issuing from circular nozzles tend to cancel [6,7]; thus, simple theories that neglect buoyancy fortuitously are able to predict flame lengths reasonably well for the circular- (and square-) port geometry.

For hydrocarbon flames, soot is frequently present, giving the flame its typical orange or yellow appearance. Given sufficient time, soot is formed on the fuel side of the reaction zone and is consumed when it flows into an oxidizing region, for example, the flame tip. Figure 9.5 illustrates soot formation and destruction zones in a simple jet flame. Depending on the fuel type and flame residence times, all of the soot that is formed may not be oxidized on its journey through high-temperature oxidizing regions. In this case, soot "wings" may

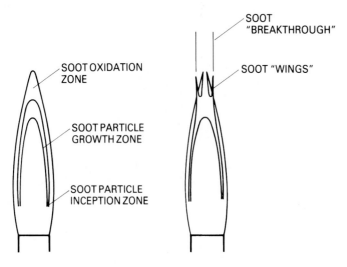

FIGURE 9.5
Soot formation and destruction zones in laminar jet flames.

appear, with the soot breaking through the flame. This soot that breaks through is generally referred to as **smoke**. Figure 9.6 shows a photograph of an ethylene flame where a soot wing is apparent on the right-hand-side of the flame tip. We will discuss the formation and destruction of soot in greater detail in a later section of this chapter.

The last feature of laminar jet diffusion flames we wish to highlight is the relationship between flame length and initial conditions. For circular-port flames, the flame length does not depend on initial velocity or diameter but, rather, on the initial volumetric flowrate, Q_F. Since $Q_F = v_e \pi R^2$, various combinations of v_e and R can yield the same flame length. We can show that this is reasonable by appealing to our previous analysis of the nonreacting laminar jet (cf. Example 9.2). By ignoring the effects of heat released by reaction, Eqn. 9.16 provides a crude description of the flame boundaries when Y_F is set equal to $Y_{F,\text{stoic}}$. The flame length is then obtained when r equals zero, i.e.,

$$L_f \approx \frac{3}{8\pi} \frac{Q_F}{\mathcal{D} Y_{F,\text{stoic}}}. \tag{9.22}$$

Thus we see that the flame length is indeed proportional to the volumetric flow-rate; furthermore, we see that the flame length is inversely proportional to the stoichiometric fuel mass fraction. This implies that fuels that require less air for complete combustion produce shorter flames, as one might expect. In a subsequent section, we present better approximations that can be used in engineering calculations of flame lengths.

FIGURE 9.6
Laminar ethylene jet diffusion flame. Note soot "wings" at sides of flame near the tip. (Photograph courtesy of R.J. Santoro.)

SIMPLIFIED THEORETICAL DESCRIPTIONS

The earliest theoretical description of the laminar jet diffusion flame is that of Burke and Schumann [4] published in 1928. Although many simplifying assumptions were employed, e.g., the velocity field was everywhere constant and parallel to the flame axis, their theory predicted flame lengths reasonably well for axisymmetric (circular-port) flames. This good agreement led other investigators to refine the original theory, yet retaining the constant-velocity assumption. In 1977, Roper [6–8] published a new theory that retained the essential simplicity of the Burke–Schumann analysis, but relaxed the requirement of a single constant velocity. Roper's approach provides reasonable estimates of flame lengths for both circular and noncircular nozzles. Subsequently, we will present his results, which are useful for engineering calculations. Before doing so, however, let us describe the problem mathematically so that we can see the inherent difficulty of the problem and thus appreciate the elegance of the simplified theories. We begin by first presenting a somewhat general formulation using the more familiar variables: velocities, mass fractions, and temperature; then, with a few additional assumptions, we develop the conserved scalar approach that requires the solution of only *two* partial differential equations. More complete mathematical descriptions can be found in advanced texts [17] and original references [12].

Primary Assumptions

In the same spirit as Chapter 8, we can greatly simplify the basic conservation equations, yet retain the essential physics, by invoking the following assumptions:

1. The flow is laminar, steady, and axisymmetric, produced by a jet of fuel emerging from a circular nozzle of radius R, which burns in a quiescent, infinite reservoir of oxidizer.
2. Only three "species" are considered: fuel, oxidizer, and products. Inside the flame zone, only fuel and products exist; while beyond the flame, only oxidizer and products exist.
3. Fuel and oxidizer react in stoichiometric proportions at the flame. Chemical kinetics are assumed to be infinitely fast, resulting in the flame being represented as an infinitesimally thin sheet. This is commonly referred to as the **flame-sheet approximation**.
4. Species molecular transport is by simple binary diffusion governed by Fick's Law.
5. Thermal energy and species diffusivities are equal; thus, the Lewis number $(Le = \alpha/\mathcal{D})$ is unity.
6. Radiation heat transfer is negligible.
7. Only radial diffusion of momentum, thermal energy, and species is important; axial diffusion is neglected.
8. The flame axis is oriented vertically upward.

Basic Conservation Equations

With these assumptions, the differential equations that govern the velocity, temperature, and species distributions throughout the flowfield are developed as follows:

MASS CONSERVATION. The appropriate mass conservation equation is identical to the axisymmetric continuity equation (Eqn. 7.7) developed in Chapter 7, since none of the flame assumptions above result in any further simplification:

$$\frac{1}{r}\frac{\partial(r\rho v_r)}{\partial r} + \frac{\partial(\rho v_x)}{\partial x} = 0. \tag{9.23}$$

AXIAL MOMENTUM CONSERVATION. Similarly, the axial momentum equation (Eqn. 7.33) also stands as previously developed:

$$\frac{1}{r}\frac{\partial}{\partial x}(r\rho v_x v_x) + \frac{1}{r}\frac{\partial}{\partial r}(r\rho v_x v_r) - \frac{1}{r}\frac{\partial}{\partial r}\left(r\mu\frac{\partial v_x}{\partial r}\right) = (\rho_\infty - \rho)g. \tag{9.24}$$

This equation applies throughout the entire domain, i.e., both inside and outside of the flame boundary, with no discontinuities at the flame sheet.

SPECIES CONSERVATION. With the flame-sheet assumption, the chemical production rates $(\dot{m}_i''')$ become zero in the species conservation equation (Eqn. 7.19), with all chemical reaction phenomena embodied in the boundary conditions. Thus,

$$\frac{1}{r}\frac{\partial}{\partial x}(r\rho v_x Y_i) + \frac{1}{r}\frac{\partial}{\partial r}(r\rho v_r Y_i) - \frac{1}{r}\frac{\partial}{\partial r}\left(r\rho D\frac{Y_i}{\partial r}\right) = 0, \tag{9.25}$$

where i represents fuel, and Eqn. 9.25 applies inside the flame boundary, or oxidizer, and Eqn. 9.25 applies outside of the flame boundary. Since there are only three species, the product mass fraction can be found from

$$Y_{Pr} = 1 - Y_F - Y_{Ox}. \tag{9.26}$$

ENERGY CONSERVATION. The Shvab–Zeldovich form of energy conservation (Eqn. 7.50) is consistent with all of our assumptions and simplifies further in the same manner as the species equation, in that the production term $(\sum h_{f,i}^o \dot{m}_i''')$ becomes zero everywhere except at the flame boundary. Thus, Eqn. 7.50 becomes

$$\frac{\partial}{\partial x}(r\rho v_x \int c_p dT) + \frac{\partial}{\partial r}(r\rho v_r \int c_p dT) - \frac{\partial}{\partial r}\left(r\rho D\frac{\partial \int c_p dT}{\partial r}\right) = 0, \tag{9.27}$$

and applies both inside and outside of the flame, but with discontinuities at the flame itself. Thus, the heat release from reaction must enter the problem formulation as a boundary condition, where the boundary is the flame surface.

Additional Relations

To completely define our problem, an equation of state is needed to relate density and temperature:

$$\rho = \frac{PMW_{\text{mix}}}{R_u T} \tag{9.28}$$

where the mixture molecular weight is determined from the species mass fractions (Eqn. 2.12b) as

$$MW_{\text{mix}} = (\Sigma Y_i / WM_i)^{-1}. \tag{9.29}$$

Before proceeding, it is worthwhile to summarize our jet flame model equations and point out the intrinsic difficulties associated with obtaining their solutions, for it is these difficulties that motivate reformulating the problem in terms of conserved scalars. We have a total of five conservation equations, mass, axial momentum, energy, fuel species, and oxidizer species; involving five unknown functions, $v_r(r, x)$, $v_x(r, x)$, $T(r, x)$, $Y_F(r, x)$, and $Y_{Ox}(r, x)$. Determining the five functions that simultaneously satisfy all five equations, subject to appropriate boundary conditions, defines our problem. Simultaneously solving five partial differential equations is itself a formidable task. The problem becomes even more complicated when we realize that some of the boundary conditions necessary to solve the fuel and oxidizer species and energy equations must be specified at the flame, the location of which is not known a priori. To eliminate this problem of the unknown location of the flame sheet, we seek to recast the governing equations, i.e., employ conserved scalars, which require boundary conditions only along the flame axis $(r = 0, x)$, far from the flame $(r \to \infty, x)$, and at the nozzle exit plane $(r, x = 0)$.

Conserved Scalar Approach

MIXTURE FRACTION. We can eliminate our boundary-condition dilemma, without reducing the complexity of the problem much, by replacing the two species conservation equations with the single mixture fraction equation (Eqn. 7.62) developed in Chapter 7:

$$\frac{\partial}{\partial x}(r\rho v_x f) + \frac{\partial}{\partial r}(r\rho v_r f) - \frac{\partial}{\partial r}\left(r\rho D \frac{\partial f}{\partial r}\right) = 0. \tag{9.30}$$

This equation involves no discontinuities at the flame and requires no additional assumptions beyond those previously listed. Recall that the definition of the mixture fraction, f, is the mass fraction of material having its origin in the fuel system (cf. Eqns. 7.51 and 7.53), and, as such, has a maximum value of unity at the nozzle exit and a value of zero far from the flame. The appropriate boundary conditions for f can be given by

$$\frac{\partial f}{\partial r}(0, x) = 0 \text{ (symmetry)} \tag{9.31a}$$

$$f(\infty, x) = 0 \text{ (no fuel in oxidizer)} \tag{9.31b}$$

$$f(r \le R, 0) = 1$$
$$f(r > R, 0) = 0$$ (top-hat exit profile). (9.31c)

Once the function $f(r, x)$ is known, the location of the flame is easily found, since $f = f_{\text{stoic}}$ at this location.

ABSOLUTE ENTHALPY. We continue our development by turning our attention now to the energy equation. Here, again with no additional simplifying assumptions, we can replace the Shvab–Zeldovich energy equation, which explicitly involves $T(r, x)$, with the conserved scalar form, Eqn. 7.66, which involves the absolute (or standardized) enthalpy function, $h(r, x)$, with temperature no longer appearing explicitly:

$$\frac{\partial}{\partial x}(r\rho v_x h) + \frac{\partial}{\partial r}(r\rho v_r h) - \frac{\partial}{\partial r}\left(r\rho D \frac{\partial h}{\partial r}\right) = 0. \tag{9.32}$$

As with the mixture fraction, no discontinuities in h occur at the flame, and the boundary conditions are given by

$$\frac{\partial h}{\partial r}(0, x) = 0 \tag{9.33a}$$

$$h(\infty, x) = h_{Ox} \tag{9.33b}$$

$$h(r \le R, 0) = h_F$$
$$h(r > R, 0) = h_{Ox} \tag{9.33c}$$

The continuity and axial momentum equations remain as given above, i.e., Eqns. 9.23 and 9.24, respectively, unaffected by our desire to use the conserved scalars to replace the species and energy equations. The boundary conditions for the velocities are the same as given previously for the nonreacting jet, i.e.,

$$v_r(0, x) = 0 \tag{9.34a}$$

$$\frac{\partial v_x}{\partial r}(0, x) = 0 \tag{9.34b}$$

$$v_x(\infty, x) = 0 \tag{9.34c}$$

$$v_x(r \le R, 0) = v_e$$
$$v_x(r > R, 0) = 0 \tag{9.34d}$$

Before our system of equations (Eqns. 9.23, 9.24, 9.30, and 9.32) can be solved, we need to be able to determine the density, $\rho(r, x)$, which appears in each conservation equation, using some appropriate state relationship. Before we do so, however, we can effect further simplification of our problem by recasting the governing equations to a nondimensional form.

NONDIMENSIONAL EQUATIONS. Frequently, valuable insights can be obtained by defining dimensionless variables and substituting these into the governing equations. Such procedures result in the identification of important dimensionless parameters, such as the Reynolds number, with which you are well acquainted. We start by using the nozzle radius R as the characteristic length scale, and the nozzle exit velocity v_e as the characteristic velocity, to define the following dimensionless spatial coordinates and velocities:

$$x^* \equiv \begin{array}{c}\text{dimensionless axial}\\ \text{distance}\end{array} = x/R \qquad (9.35a)$$

$$r^* \equiv \begin{array}{c}\text{dimensionless radial}\\ \text{distance}\end{array} = r/R \qquad (9.35b)$$

$$v_x^* \equiv \begin{array}{c}\text{dimensionless axial}\\ \text{velocity}\end{array} = v_x/v_e \qquad (9.35c)$$

$$v_r^* \equiv \begin{array}{c}\text{dimensionless radial}\\ \text{velocity}\end{array} = v_r/v_e \qquad (9.35d)$$

Since the mixture fraction f is already a dimensionless variable with the desired property that $0 \leq f \leq 1$, we will use it directly. The mixture absolute enthalpy h, however, is not dimensionless; thus, we define

$$h^* \equiv \begin{array}{c}\text{dimensionless}\\ \text{absolute enthalpy}\end{array} = \frac{h - h_{Ox,\infty}}{h_{F,e} - h_{Ox,\infty}} \qquad (9.35e)$$

Note that at the nozzle exit, $h = h_{F,e}$ and thus, $h^* = 1$; and in the ambient $(r \rightarrow \infty)$, $h = h_{Ox,\infty}$, and $h^* = 0$.

To make our governing equations completely dimensionless, we also define the density ratio

$$\rho^* \equiv \begin{array}{c}\text{dimensionless}\\ \text{density}\end{array} = \frac{\rho}{\rho_e} \qquad (9.35f)$$

where ρ_e is the fuel density at the nozzle exit.

Relating each of the dimensional variables or parameters to its dimensionless counterpart, and substituting these back into the basic conservation equations, results in the following dimensionless governing equations:

Continuity

$$\frac{\partial}{\partial x^*}\left(\rho^* v_x^*\right) + \frac{1}{r^*}\frac{\partial}{\partial r^*}\left(r^* \rho^* v_r^*\right) = 0. \qquad (9.36)$$

Axial momentum

$$\frac{\partial}{\partial x^*}\left(r^* \rho^* v_x^* v_x^*\right) + \frac{\partial}{\partial r^*}\left(r^* \rho^* v_r^* v_x^*\right) - \frac{\partial}{\partial r^*}\left[\left(\frac{\mu}{\rho_e v_e R}\right) r^* \frac{\partial v_x^*}{\partial r^*}\right] = \frac{gR}{v_e^2}\left(\frac{\rho_\infty}{\rho_e} - 1\right) r^*.$$
$$(9.37)$$

Mixture fraction

$$\frac{\partial}{\partial x^*}\left(r^*\rho^* v_x^* f\right) + \frac{\partial}{\partial r^*}\left(r^*\rho^* v_r^* f\right) - \frac{\partial}{\partial r^*}\left[\left(\frac{\rho D}{\rho_e v_e R}\right) r^* \frac{\partial f}{\partial r^*}\right] = 0. \tag{9.38}$$

Dimensionless enthalpy

$$\frac{\partial}{\partial x^*}\left(r^*\rho^* v_x^* h^*\right) + \frac{\partial}{\partial r^*}\left(r^*\rho^* v_r^* h\right) - \frac{\partial}{\partial r^*}\left[\left(\frac{\rho D}{\rho_e v_e R}\right) r^* \frac{\partial h^*}{\partial r^*}\right] = 0. \tag{9.39}$$

The dimensionless boundary conditions for the above are

$$v_r^*(0, x^*) = 0 \tag{9.40a}$$

$$\frac{\partial v_x^*}{\partial r^*}(0, x^*) = \frac{\partial f}{\partial r^*}(0, x^*) = \frac{\partial h^*}{\partial r^*}(0, x^*) = 0 \tag{9.40b}$$

$$v_x^*(r^* \leq 1, 0) = f(r^* \leq 1, 0) = h^*(r^* \leq 1, 0) = 1$$
$$v_x^*(r^* > 1, 0) = f(r^* > 1, 0) = h^*(r^* > 1, 0) = 0. \tag{9.40c}$$

Inspection of the dimensionless governing equation and boundary conditions shows some very interesting features. First, we see that the mixture fraction and dimensionless enthalpy equations, and their boundary conditions, are of identical form, that is, f and h^* play the same role in their respective governing equations. Therefore, we do not need to solve both Eqn. 9.38 and Eqn. 9.39, but, rather, one or the other. For example, if we were to solve for $f(r^*, x^*)$, then simply, $h^*(r^*, x^*) = f(r^*, x^*)$.

ADDITIONAL ASSUMPTIONS. We also note that, if buoyancy were neglected, the right-hand-side of the axial momentum equation (Eqn. 9.37) becomes zero and the general form of this equation is the same as the mixture fraction and dimensionless enthalpy equations except that μ appears in the former where ρD appears in the latter. Our problem can be simplified even further if we assume that viscosity μ equals the ρD product. Since the **Schmidt number, Sc,** is defined

$$Sc \equiv \frac{\text{momentum diffusivity}}{\text{mass diffusivity}} = \frac{\nu}{D} = \frac{\mu}{\rho D}, \tag{9.41}$$

we see that with $\mu = \rho D$, the Schmidt number is unity ($Sc = 1$). Assuming that the momentum diffusivity and mass diffusivity are equal ($Sc = 1$) is analogous to our previous assumption of equal thermal and mass diffusivities ($Le = 1$).

With the assumptions of negligible buoyancy and $Sc = 1$, the following single conservation equation replaces the individual momentum, mixture fraction (species mass), and enthalpy (energy) equations (Eqns. 9.37–9.39):

$$\frac{\partial}{\partial x^*}\left(r^*\rho^* v_x^* \zeta\right) + \frac{\partial}{\partial r^*}\left(r^*\rho^* v_r^* \zeta\right) - \frac{\partial}{\partial r^*}\left(\frac{1}{Re} r^* \frac{\partial \zeta}{\partial r^*}\right) = 0, \tag{9.42}$$

where our generic conserved scalar variable $\zeta = v_x^* = f = h^*$ and $Re = \rho_e v_e R/\mu$. Since $\zeta = v_x^*$, our problem is now completely defined by only two conservation equations, Eqn. 9.42 above, and continuity Eqn. 9.36, together with the boundary conditions of Eqn. 9.40.

STATE RELATIONSHIPS. To be able to solve the jet flame problem as developed above requires that the density $\rho^* (= \rho/\rho_e)$ be related to the mixture fraction, f, or any of the other conserved scalars. To do this, we employ the ideal-gas equation of state (Eqn. 9.28); however, this requires a knowledge of the species mass fractions and temperature. Our immediate problem then is to relate the Y_is and T as functions of the mixture fraction. Knowing these primary relationships, they can be combined to obtain the needed relationship $\rho = \rho(f)$. For our simple system, which consists only of products and fuel inside the flame sheet, and only products and oxidizer outside the flame sheet (see assumption 2), our task is to find the following **state relationships**:

$$Y_F = Y_F(f) \tag{9.43a}$$

$$Y_{Pr} = Y_{Pr}(f) \tag{9.43b}$$

$$Y_{Ox} = Y_{Ox}(f) \tag{9.43c}$$

$$T = T(f) \tag{9.43d}$$

$$\rho = \rho(f). \tag{9.43e}$$

With our flame-sheet approximation (assumption 3), the definition of the mixture fraction (Eqn. 7.52) can be used to relate the species mass fractions, Y_F, Y_{Ox}, and Y_{Pr} to f in the region inside the flame sheet, at the flame, and beyond the flame sheet, as illustrated in Fig. 9.7, as follows:

Inside the flame ($f_{stoic} < f \leq 1$)

$$Y_F = \frac{f - f_{stoic}}{1 - f_{stoic}} \tag{9.44a}$$

$$Y_{Ox} = 0 \tag{9.44b}$$

$$Y_{Pr} = \frac{1 - f}{1 - f_{stoic}}. \tag{9.44c}$$

At the flame ($f = f_{stoic}$)

$$Y_F = 0 \tag{9.45a}$$

$$Y_{Ox} = 0 \tag{9.45b}$$

$$Y_{Pr} = 1. \tag{9.45c}$$

Outside the flame ($0 \leq f < f_{stoic}$)

$$Y_F = 0 \tag{9.46a}$$

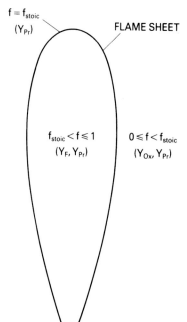

$f = f_{\text{stoic}}$
(Y_{Pr})

FLAME SHEET

$f_{\text{stoic}} < f \leqslant 1$
(Y_F, Y_{Pr})

$0 \leqslant f < f_{\text{stoic}}$
(Y_{Ox}, Y_{Pr})

FIGURE 9.7
Simplified model of jet diffusion flame employing the flame-sheet approximation where inside the flame sheet only fuel and products exist, and outside the sheet are only oxidizer and products.

$$Y_{Ox} = 1 - f/f_{\text{stoic}} \qquad (9.46b)$$

$$Y_{Pr} = f/f_{\text{stoic}} \qquad (9.46c)$$

where the stoichiometric mixture fraction relates to the stoichiometric (mass) coefficient ν as

$$f_{\text{stoic}} = \frac{1}{\nu + 1}. \qquad (9.47)$$

Note that all of the mass fractions are related linearly to the mixture fraction (Fig. 9.8a).

To determine the mixture temperature as a function of mixture fraction requires a calorific equation of state (cf. Eqn. 2.4). As we have done in previous chapters, we follow Spalding [18] and make the following assumptions:

1. The specific heats of each species (fuel, oxidizer and products) are constant and equal: $c_{p,F} = c_{p,Ox} = c_{p,Pr} \equiv c_p$.
2. The enthalpies of formation of the oxidizer and the products are zero: $h_{f,Ox}^o = h_{f,Pr}^o = 0$. This results in the enthalpy of formation of the fuel equaling its heat of combustion.

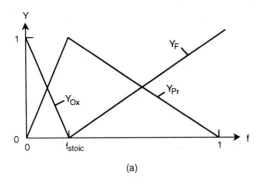

(a)

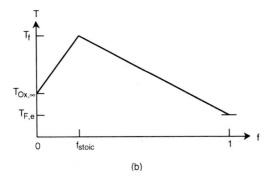

(b)

FIGURE 9.8
(a) Simplified-state relationships for species mass fractions $Y_F(f)$, $Y_{Ox}(f)$, and $Y_{Pr}(f)$. (b) Simplified-state relationships for mixture temperature $T(f)$.

These assumptions are invoked only to provide a simple illustration of how to construct state relationships and are not essential to the basic concept. With these assumptions, our calorific equation of state is simply

$$h = \sum Y_i h_i = Y_F \Delta h_c + c_p(T - T_{\text{ref}}). \tag{9.48}$$

Substituting Eqn. 9.48 into the definition of the dimensionless enthalpy h^* (Eqn. 9.35e) and recalling that, because of the similarity of the governing equations, $h^* = f$, we obtain

$$h^* = \frac{Y_F \Delta h_c + c_p(T - T_{Ox,\infty})}{\Delta h_c + c_p(T_{F,e} - T_{Ox,\infty})} \equiv f \tag{9.49}$$

where the definitions $h_{Ox,\infty} \equiv c_p(T_{Ox,\infty} - T_{\text{ref}})$ and $h_{F,e} \equiv c_p(T_{F,e} - T_{\text{ref}})$ also have been substituted. Solving Eqn. 9.49 for T provides the following general state relationship, $T = T(f)$, recognizing that Y_F is also a function of the mixture fraction f:

$$T = (f - Y_F)\frac{\Delta h_c}{c_p} + f(T_{F,e} - T_{Ox,\infty}) + T_{Ox,\infty}. \tag{9.50}$$

Using Eqn. 9.50 with the appropriate expressions for Y_F inside (Eqn. 9.44a), at (Eqn. 9.45a), and outside (Eqn. 9.46a) the flame sheet, yields:

Inside the flame $(f_{stoic} < f \le 1)$

$$T = T(f) = f\left[(T_{F,e} - T_{Ox,\infty}) - \frac{f_{stoic}}{1 - f_{stoic}}\frac{\Delta h_c}{c_p}\right] + T_{Ox,\infty} + \frac{f_{stoic}}{(1 - f_{stoic})c_p}\Delta h_c.$$

$$(9.51a)$$

At the flame $(f = f_{stoic})$

$$T \equiv T(f) = f_{stoic}\left(\frac{\Delta h_c}{c_p} + T_{F,e} - T_{Ox,\infty}\right) + T_{Ox,\infty}. \qquad (9.51b)$$

Outside the flame $(0 \le f < f_{stoic})$

$$T = T(f) = f\left(\frac{\Delta h_c}{c_p} + T_{F,e} - T_{Ox,\infty}\right) + T_{Ox,\infty}. \qquad (9.51c)$$

Note that with our simplified thermodynamics, the temperature depends linearly on f in the regions inside and outside the flame with a maximum at the flame, as illustrated in Fig. 9.8b. It is also interesting to note that the flame temperature given by Eqn. 9.51b is identical to the constant-pressure adiabatic flame temperature calculated from the first law (Eqn. 2.40) for fuel and oxidizer with initial temperatures of $T_{F,e}$ and $T_{Ox,\infty}$, respectively. Our task is now complete in that, with the state relationships $Y_F(f)$, $Y_{Ox}(f)$, $Y_{Pr}(f)$, and $T(f)$, the mixture density can be determined solely as a function of mixture fraction f using the ideal-gas equation of state (Eqn. 9.28). It is important to point out that our use of only three species (fuel, oxidizer, and products) and greatly simplified thermodynamics allows us to formulate simple, closed-form state relationships and illustrate the basic concepts and procedures involved in creating a conserved scalar model of diffusion flames. More sophisticated state relationships are frequently employed using equilibrium, partial equilibrium, or experimental state relationships for complex mixtures. Nevertheless, the basic concepts are essentially as presented here.

Table 9.1 summarizes our developments of conserved scalar models of laminar jet diffusion flames, while the following sections discuss various solutions to the problem.

Various Solutions

BURKE–SCHUMANN. As mentioned previously, the earliest approximate solution to the laminar jet flame problem is that of Burke and Schumann [4], who analyzed circular and two-dimensional fuel jets emerging into coflowing annular oxidizer streams. For both the axisymmetric and two-dimensional problems, they used the flame-sheet approximation and assumed that a single velocity characterized the flow $(v_x = v, v_r = 0)$. This latter assumption eliminates the need to solve the axial-momentum equation (Eqn. 9.24) and, by default, neglects buoyancy.

TABLE 9.1
Summary of conserved scalar models of laminar jet diffusion flame

Assumptions	Solution variables required	Conservation equations required	State relationships required[a]
Primary assumptions only for conservation equations	$v_r^*(r^*, x^*)$, $v_x^*(r^*, x^*)$, $f(r^*, x^*)$ or $h^*(r^*, x^*)$	Eqns. 9.36, 9.37, 9.38, or 9.39	Eqn. 9.28 and Eqns. 9.44, 9.45, 9.46, and 9.51 (or equivalent)
+ Simplified thermodynamics for state relationships			
Primary assumptions + No buoyancy and $Sc = 1$ + Simplified thermodynamics for state relationships	$v_r^*(r^*, x^*)$, $\zeta(r^*, x^*)$, i.e., v_x^* or f for h^*	Eqns. 9.36 and 9.42	As above

[a]Additional relations required for temperature-dependent transport properties μ and/or $\rho\mathcal{D}$.

Although the concept of a conserved scalar had not been formally developed at the time of Burke and Schumann's study (1928), their treatment of species conservation cast the problem in a form equivalent to that of a conserved scalar. With the assumption that $v_r = 0$, mass conservation (Eqn. 9.23) requires that ρv_x be a constant; thus, the variable-density species conservation equation (Eqn. 9.25) becomes

$$\rho v_x \frac{\partial Y_i}{\partial x} - \frac{1}{r}\frac{\partial}{\partial r}\left(r\rho\mathcal{D}\frac{\partial Y_i}{\partial r}\right) = 0. \quad (9.52)$$

Since the above equation has no species production term, its solution requires a priori knowledge of the flame boundary. Burke and Schumann circumvented this problem by defining the flowfield in terms of a single fuel species whose mass fraction takes on a value of unity in the fuel stream, zero at the flame, and $-1/\nu$, or $-f_{\text{stoic}}/(1 - f_{\text{stoic}})$, in the pure oxidizer. Thus, with this convention, "negative" fuel concentrations occur outside of the flame. In a modern context, their fuel mass fraction Y_F is defined by the mixture fraction as

$$Y_F = \frac{f - f_{\text{stoic}}}{1 - f_{\text{stoic}}}. \quad (9.53)$$

Substitution of this definition into Eqn. 9.52 recovers the familiar conserved scalar equation (Eqn. 9.30). Although Burke and Schumann assumed constant properties and constant v_x, we can recover their governing equation by making the less restrictive assumption that the product of the density and diffusivity is constant, i.e., $\rho\mathcal{D} = $ constant $\equiv \rho_{ref}\mathcal{D}_{ref}$. In Chapter 3, we saw that the $\rho\mathcal{D}$ product varies approximately as $T^{1/2}$; thus, this assumption is clearly an approximation. Substituting $\rho_{ref}\mathcal{D}_{ref}$ for $\rho\mathcal{D}$ into Eqn. 9.52, removing this product from inside the radial derivative, and noting that $\rho v_x = $ constant $\equiv \rho_{ref}v_{x,ref}$, we see that the density ρ_{ref} cancels, yielding the following final result:

$$v_{x,ref}\frac{\partial Y_F}{\partial x} = \mathcal{D}_{ref}\frac{1}{r}\frac{\partial}{\partial r}\left(r\frac{\partial Y_F}{\partial r}\right) \tag{9.54}$$

where $v_{x,ref}$ and $\mathcal{D}_{ref}$ are reference values of velocity and diffusivity, respectively, both evaluated at the same temperature.

The solution to the above partial differential equation, $Y_F(x, r)$, is a rather complicated expression involving **Bessel functions**. The flame length is not given explicitly but can be found by solving the following transcendental equation for the flame length, L_f:

$$\sum_{m=1}^{\infty}\frac{J_1(\lambda_m R)}{\lambda_m[J_0(\lambda_m R_o)]^2}\exp\left(-\frac{\lambda_m^2 \mathcal{D}}{v}L_f\right) - \frac{R_o^2}{2R}\left(1+\frac{1}{S}\right) + \frac{R}{2} = 0. \tag{9.55}$$

In the above, J_0 and J_1 are the zeroth- and first-order Bessel functions, which are described in mathematical reference books, e.g. Ref. [19]; the λ_m are defined by all the positive roots of the equation $J_1(\lambda_m R) = 0$ [19]; R and R_o are the fuel tube and outer flow radii, respectively; and S is the molar stoichiometric ratio of oxidizer (outer flow fluid) to fuel (nozzle fluid). Flame lengths predicted by the Burke–Schumann theory are in reasonable agreement with theory for circular-port burners, primarily as a result of offsetting assumptions; the effect of buoyancy is to cause a narrowing of the flame, which, in turn, increases diffusion rates. Burke and Schumann recognized this possibility, foreshadowing the work of Roper [6] that showed this to be true. The numerical study of Kee and Miller [10] also explicitly showed this effect by running comparison cases with and without buoyancy.

ROPER. Roper [6] proceeded in the spirit of the Burke–Schumann approach, but allowed the characteristic velocity to vary with axial distance as modified by buoyancy and in accordance with continuity. In addition to circular-port burners, Roper analyzed rectangular-slot and curved-slot [6,8] burners. Roper's analytical solutions, and as modified slightly by experiment, are presented in a separate section below.

CONSTANT-DENSITY SOLUTION. If the density is assumed to be constant, the solutions to Eqns. 9.23, 9.24, and 9.30 are identical to those of the nonreacting jet. In this case, the flame length is given by Eqn. 9.22:

$$L_f \approx \frac{3}{8\pi}\frac{1}{D}\frac{Q_F}{Y_{F,stoic}}. \tag{9.56}$$

TABLE 9.2
Momentum integral estimates[a] for variable-density laminar jet flames

ρ_∞/ρ_f	ρ_∞/ρ_{ref}	$I(\rho_\infty/\rho_f)$
1	1	1
3	2	2.4
5	3	3.7
7	4	5.2
9	5	7.2

[a]Estimated from Fig. 3 of Ref. [5].

VARIABLE-DENSITY APPROXIMATE SOLUTION. Fay [5] solved the variable-density, laminar, jet-flame problem. In his solution, buoyancy is neglected, thereby simplifying the axial momentum equation. With regard to properties, the Schmidt and Lewis numbers are assumed to be unity, consistent with our formation of the governing equations, and furthermore, that the absolute viscosity, μ, is directly proportional to temperature, i.e.,

$$\mu = \mu_{ref} T / T_{ref}.$$

Fay's solution for the flame length is

$$L_f \approx \frac{3}{8\pi} \frac{1}{Y_{F,\text{stoic}}} \frac{\dot{m}_F}{\mu_{ref}} \frac{\rho_\infty}{\rho_{ref}} \frac{1}{I(\rho_\infty/\rho_f)}, \qquad (9.57)$$

where $\dot{m}_F$ is the mass flow issuing from the nozzle, ρ_∞ is the ambient fluid density far from the flame, and $I(\rho_\infty/\rho_f)$ is a function obtained by numerical integration as a part of Fay's solution. Tabulated values of $I(\rho_\infty/\rho_f)$ and ρ_∞/ρ_{ref} are given in Table 9.2 for various ratios of ambient to flame densities, ρ_∞/ρ_f.

Equation 9.57 can be recast in a form similar to the constant-density solution, Eqn. 9.56, by noting that $\dot{m}_F = \rho_F Q_F$ and $\mu_{ref} = \rho_{ref} \mathcal{D}_{ref}$ $(Sc = 1)$:

$$L_f \approx \frac{3}{8\pi} \frac{1}{\mathcal{D}_{ref}} \frac{Q_F}{Y_{F,\text{stoic}}} \left(\frac{\rho_F \rho_\infty}{\rho_{ref}^2} \right) \frac{1}{I(\rho_\infty/\rho_f)}. \qquad (9.58)$$

Thus, we see that the flame lengths predicted by the variable-density theory are longer than those of the constant-density theory by the factor

$$\frac{\rho_F \rho_\infty}{\rho_{ref}^2} \frac{1}{I(\rho_\infty/\rho_f)}.$$

For $\rho_\infty/\rho_f = 5$ and $\rho_F = \rho_\infty$ (reasonable values for hydrocarbon/air flames) the predicted flame length for the variable-density theory is about 2.4 times that of the constant-density theory. Regardless of the ability of either theory to predict actual flame lengths, they both show that flame length is directly proportional to the nozzle-fluid volumetric flowrate and inversely proportional to the stoichiometric nozzle-fluid mass fraction, independent of the nozzle diameter.

NUMERICAL SOLUTIONS. The use of digital computers and finite-difference techniques allows laminar jet flames to be modeled in much greater detail than the analytical approaches discussed above. For example, the flame-sheet approximation with **frozen flow** assumed inside and outside of the flame can be replaced by a reacting mixture governed by chemical kinetics (cf. Chapter 4). Kee and Miller [9,10] modeled an H_2–air flame using 16 reversible reactions involving 10 species. Smooke et al. [13], more recently, modeled a CH_4–air flame taking into account 79 reactions with 26 species. With chemical transformation effects no longer relegated to boundary conditions, the species conservation equations, Eqn. 9.25, would now have to include species production (source) and destruction (sink) terms (cf. Chapter 7). Numerical models also allow the relaxation of the assumption of simple binary diffusion. Detailed multi-component diffusion is included in the computer models of Heys et al. [12] and Smooke et al. [13]. Similarly, temperature-dependent properties can be incorporated easily into numerical models [9–13]. In the Mitchell et al. [11] and Smooke et al. [13] models, both radial and axial diffusion terms are retained in the conservation equation, thereby avoiding the boundary-layer approximations. Lastly, Heys et al. [12] incorporate thermal radiation in their model of a CH_4–air flame and show that its inclusion results in peak temperature predictions of about 150 K lower than when no radiation losses are considered. Temperature difference of this order can greatly affect temperature-sensitive chemical reaction rates, such as those involved in nitric oxide formation (cf. Chapter 5).

FLAME LENGTHS FOR CIRCULAR-PORT AND SLOT BURNERS

Roper's Correlations

Roper developed [6,8], and verified by experiment [7,8], expressions to predict laminar jet flame lengths for various burner geometries (circular, square, slot, and curved slot) and flow regimes (momentum-controlled, buoyancy-controlled, and transitional). Roper's results [6,7] are summarized in Table 9.3 and detailed below.

For circular and square burner ports, the following expressions can be used to estimate flame lengths. These results apply regardless of whether or not buoyancy is important, and are applicable for fuel jets emerging into either a quiescent oxidizer or a coflowing stream, as long as the oxidizer is in excess, i.e., the flames are overventilated.

CIRCULAR PORT

$$L_{f,\text{thy}} = \frac{Q_F(T_\infty/T_F)}{4\pi \mathcal{D}_\infty \ln(1 + 1/S)} \left(\frac{T_\infty}{T_f}\right)^{0.67}, \tag{9.59}$$

TABLE 9.3
Empirical and theoretical correlations for estimating lengths of vertical laminar jet flames

Port Geometry	Conditions	Applicable equation[a]
Circular	Momentum- or Buoyancy-controlled	Circular—Eqns. 9.59 and 9.60
Square	Momentum- or Buoyancy-controlled	Square—Eqn. 9.61 and 9.62
Slot	Momentum-controlled	Eqns. 9.63 and 9.64
	Buoyancy-controlled	Eqns. 9.65 and 9.66
	Mixed momentum–Buoyancy-controlled	Eqn. 9.70

[a]For the circular and square geometries, the indicated equations apply for either a stagnant or coflowing oxidizer stream. For the slot geometry, the equations apply only to the stagnant oxidizer case.

$$L_{f,\text{expt}} = 1330 \frac{Q_F(T_\infty/T_F)}{\ln(1 + 1/S)}, \tag{9.60}$$

where S is the molar stoichiometric oxidizer–fuel ratio, $\mathcal{D}_\infty$ is a mean diffusion coefficient evaluated for the oxidizer at the oxidizer stream temperature, T_∞, and T_F and T_f are the fuel stream and mean flame temperatures, respectively. In Eqn. 9.60, all quantities are evaluated in SI units (m, m^3/s, etc.). Note that the burner diameter does not explicitly appear in either of these expressions.

SQUARE PORT

$$L_{f,\text{thy}} = \frac{Q_F(T_\infty/T_F)}{16\mathcal{D}_\infty \left[\text{inverf}\left((1+S)^{-0.5}\right) \right]^2} \left(\frac{T_\infty}{T_f} \right)^{0.67}, \tag{9.61}$$

$$L_{f,\text{expt}} = 1045 \frac{Q_F(T_\infty/T_F)}{\left[\text{inverf}\left((1+S)^{-0.5}\right) \right]^2}, \tag{9.62}$$

where **inverf** is the **inverse error function**. Values of the **error function erf** are tabulated in Table 9.4. Values for the inverse error function are generated from the error function tables in the same way that you would deal with inverse trigonometric functions, i.e., $\omega = \text{inverf}(\text{erf}\,\omega)$. Again, all quantities are evaluated in SI units.

TABLE 9.4
Gaussian error function[a]

ω	erf ω	ω	erf ω	ω	erf ω
0.00	0.00000	0.36	0.38933	1.04	0.85865
0.02	0.02256	0.38	0.40901	1.08	0.87333
0.04	0.04511	0.40	0.42839	1.12	0.88679
0.06	0.06762	0.44	0.46622	1.16	0.89910
0.08	0.09008	0.48	0.50275	1.20	0.91031
0.10	0.11246	0.52	0.53790	1.30	0.93401
0.12	0.13476	0.56	0.57162	1.40	0.95228
0.14	0.15695	0.60	0.60386	1.50	0.96611
0.16	0.17901	0.64	0.63459	1.60	0.97635
0.18	0.20094	0.68	0.66378	1.70	0.98379
0.20	0.22270	0.72	0.69143	1.80	0.98909
0.22	0.24430	0.76	0.71754	1.90	0.99279
0.24	0.26570	0.80	0.74210	2.00	0.99532
0.26	0.28690	0.84	0.76514	2.20	0.99814
0.28	0.30788	0.88	0.78669	2.40	0.99931
0.30	0.32863	0.92	0.80677	2.60	0.99976
0.32	0.34913	0.96	0.82542	2.80	0.99992
0.34	0.36936	1.00	0.84270	3.00	0.99998

[a]The Gaussian error function is defined as

$$\text{erf}\,\omega \equiv \frac{2}{\sqrt{\pi}} \int_0^\omega e^{-v^2}\, dv.$$

The complementary error function is defined as
$$\text{erfc}\,\omega \equiv 1 - \text{erf}\,\omega.$$

SLOT BURNER—MOMENTUM-CONTROLLED

$$L_{f,\text{thy}} = \frac{b\beta^2 Q_F}{hID_\infty Y_{F,\text{stoic}}} \left(\frac{T_\infty}{T_F}\right)^2 \left(\frac{T_f}{T_\infty}\right)^{0.33}, \tag{9.63}$$

$$L_{f,\text{expt}} = 8.6 \cdot 10^4 \frac{b\beta^2 Q_F}{hIY_{F,\text{stoic}}} \left(\frac{T_\infty}{T_F}\right)^2, \tag{9.64}$$

where b is the slot width, h is the slot length (cf. Table 9.3), and the function β is given by

$$\beta = \frac{1}{4\,\text{inverf}\,[1/(1+S)]},$$

and I is the ratio of the actual initial momentum flow from the slot to that of uniform flow, i.e.,

$$I = \frac{J_{e,\text{act}}}{\dot{m}_F v_e}.$$

If the flow is uniform, $I = 1$, and for a fully developed, parabolic exit velocity profile (assuming $h \gg b$), $I = 1.5$. Equations 9.63 and 9.64 apply only if the oxidizer is stagnant. For a coflowing oxidizer stream, the reader is referred to Refs. [6] and [7].

SLOT BURNER–BUOYANCY-CONTROLLED

$$L_{f,\text{thy}} \left[\frac{9\beta^4 Q_F^4 T_\infty^4}{8D_\infty^2 ah^4 T_F^4}\right]^{1/3} \left[\frac{T_f}{T_\infty}\right]^{2/9}, \tag{9.65}$$

$$L_{\text{expt}} = 2 \cdot 10^3 \left[\frac{\beta^4 Q_F^4 T_\infty^4}{ah^4 T_F^4}\right]^{1/3}, \tag{9.66}$$

where a is the mean buoyant acceleration evaluated from

$$a \cong 0.6g\left(\frac{T_f}{T_\infty} - 1\right) \tag{9.67}$$

where g is the gravitational acceleration. Roper *et al.* [7] used a mean flame temperature, $T_f = 1500\,\text{K}$, to evaluate the acceleration. As can be seen in Eqns. 9.65 and 9.66, the predicted flame length depends only weakly ($-1/3$ power) on a.

SLOT BURNER—TRANSITION REGIME. To determine whether a flame is momentum-or buoyancy-controlled, the flame **Froude number, Fr_f,** must be evaluated. The Froude number physically represents the ratio of the initial jet momentum flow to the buoyant force experienced by the flame. For the laminar jet flame issuing into a stagnant medium,

$$Fr_f \equiv \frac{(v_e I Y_{F,\text{stoic}})^2}{aL_f},$$ (9.68)

and the flow regime can be established by the following criteria:

$Fr_f \gg 1$	Momentum-controlled	(9.69a)
$Fr_f \approx 1$	Mixed (transition)	(9.69b)
$Fr_f \ll 1$	Buoyancy-controlled.	(9.69c)

Note that in order to establish the appropriate flow regime, a value for L_f is required; thus, an a posteriori check is required to see if the correct flow regime has been selected.

For the transitional region where both jet momentum and buoyancy are important, Roper [6,7] recommends the following treatment:

$$L_{f,T} = \frac{4}{9} L_{f,M} \left(\frac{L_{f,B}}{L_{f,M}}\right)^3 \left\{ \left[1 + 3.38 \left(\frac{L_{f,M}}{L_{f,B}}\right)^3\right]^{2/3} - 1\right\},$$ (9.70)

where the subscripts M, B, and T refer to momentum-controlled, buoyancy-controlled, and transition (mixed), respectively.

Example 9.3. It is desired to operate a square-port diffusion flame burner with a 50-mm-high flame in a laboratory. Determine the volumetric flowrate required if the fuel is propane. Also, determine the heat release ($\dot{m}\Delta h_c$) of the flame. What flowrate is required if methane is substituted for propane?

Solution. We will apply Roper's correlation for square-port burners (Eqn. 9.62) to determine the volumetric flowrate:

$$L_f = \frac{1045 Q_F (T_\infty / T_F)}{\left[\text{inverf}\left((1 + S)^{-0.5}\right)\right]^2}.$$

If we assume that $T_\infty = T_F = 300\,\text{K}$, the only parameter we need to calculate before we can find Q_F is the molar stoichiometric air–fuel ratio, S. From Chapter 2, $S = (x + y/4)\,4.76$; so, for propane (C_3H_8),

$$S = (3 + 8/4)4.76 = 23.8 \,\frac{\text{kmol}}{\text{kmol}}.$$

Thus,

$$\text{inverf}[(1 + 23.8)^{-0.5}] = \text{inverf}\,(0.2008) = 0.18$$

where Table 9.4 was used to evaluate inverf (0.2008). Solving Eqn. 9.62 for Q_F, and evaluating, yields

$$Q_F = \frac{0.050(0.18)^2}{1045\,(300/300)} = 1.55 \cdot 10^{-6}\,\text{m}^3/\text{s}$$

or

$$Q_F = 1.55\,\text{cm}^3/\text{s}.$$

Using the ideal-gas law to estimate the propane density ($P = 1\,\text{atm}$, $T = 300\,\text{K}$), and taking the heat of combustion from Appendix B, the heat release rate is

$$\dot{m}\Delta h_c = \rho_F Q_F \Delta h_c$$
$$= 1.787\,(1.55 \cdot 10^{-6})\,46{,}357{,}000$$

$$\dot{m}\Delta h_c = 128\,\text{W}.$$

Repeating the problem for methane, we find $S = 9.52$, $\rho_F = 0.65$, and $\Delta h_c = 50{,}016{,}000\,\text{J/kg}$; thus,

$$Q = 3.75\,\text{cm}^3/\text{s}$$

and

$$\dot{m}\Delta h_c = 122\,\text{W}.$$

Comment. Here we see that, although the volumetric flowrate required for CH_4 is about 2.4 times greater than the C_3H_8 requirement, both flames release approximately the same energy.

In the next two sections, we will explore the correlations above to see how various important engineering parameters affect flame lengths.

Flowrate and Geometry Effects

Figure 9.9 compares flame lengths for a circular-port burner with slot burners having various exit aspect ratios, h/b, with all burners having the same port area. With the port area fixed, the mean exit velocity is the same for each configuration. From the figure, we see the linear dependence of flame length on flowrate for the circular port and the somewhat greater-than-linear dependence for the slot burners. For the conditions selected, flame Froude numbers are quite small, and, hence, the flames are dominated by buoyancy. As the slot-burner ports become more narrow (h/d increasing), the flames become significantly shorter for the same flowrate.

Factors Affecting Stoichiometry

The molar stoichiometric ratio, S, employed in the above expressions is defined in terms of the nozzle fluid and the surrounding reservoir fluid, i.e.,

$$S = \left(\frac{\text{moles ambient fluid}}{\text{moles nozzle fluid}}\right)_{\text{stoic}}. \tag{9.71}$$

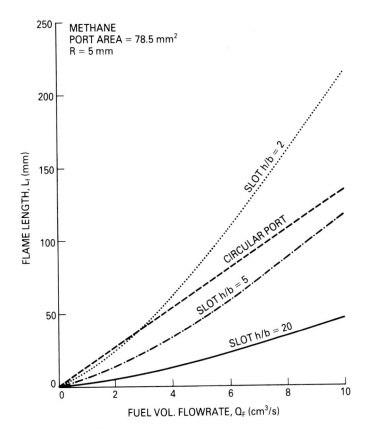

FIGURE 9.9
Predicted flame lengths for circular and slot burners having equal port areas.

Thus, S depends on the chemical compositions of both the nozzle fluid stream and surrounding fluid. For example, the values of S would be different for a pure fuel burning in air and a nitrogen-diluted fuel burning in air. Similarly, the mole fraction of oxygen in the ambient also affects S. In many applications, the following parameters, all of which affect S, are of interest.

FUEL TYPE. The molar stoichiometric air–fuel ratio for a pure fuel can be calculated by applying simple atom balances (cf. Chapter 2). For a generic hydrocarbon, C_xH_y, the stoichiometric ratio can be expressed

$$S = \frac{x + y/4}{\chi_{O_2}}, \tag{9.72}$$

where χ_{O_2} is the mole fraction of oxygen in the air.

Figure 9.10 shows flame lengths, relative to methane, for hydrogen, carbon monoxide, and the C_1–C_4 paraffins, calculated using the circular-port expression,

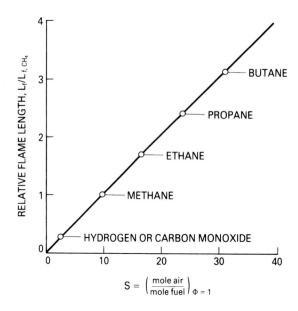

FIGURE 9.10
Dependence of flame length on fuel stoichiometry. Flame lengths for various fuels are shown relative to methane.

Eqn. 9.60, assuming equal flowrates for all fuels. Note that in using this expression, it is assumed that the same mean diffusivity applies to all of the mixtures, which is only approximately true. For hydrogen, this assumption may not be very good at all.

From Fig. 9.10, we see that flame lengths increase as the H/C ratio of the fuel decreases. For example, the propane flame is nearly two and one-half times as long as the methane flame. The flame lengths of the higher hydrocarbons, within a hydrocarbon family, do not differ greatly since the H/C ratios change much less with the addition of each C atom in comparison to the light hydrocarbons. We also see from Fig. 9.10 that carbon monoxide and hydrogen flames are much smaller than the hydrocarbon flames.

PRIMARY AERATION. Gas-burning appliances premix some air with the fuel gas before it burns as a laminar jet diffusion flame. This **primary aeration**, which is typically 40–60% of the stoichiometric air requirement, makes the flames short and prevents soot from forming, resulting in the familiar blue flame. The maximum amount of air that can be added is limited by safety considerations. If too much air is added, the rich flammability limit may be exceeded, which implies that the mixture will support a premixed flame. Depending on flow conditions and burner geometry, this flame may propagate upstream, a condition referred to as **flashback**. If the flow velocity is too great for flashback to occur, an inner premixed flame will form inside the diffusion flame envelope, as in the Bunsen burner. Flashback limits are illustrated in Fig. 8.20.

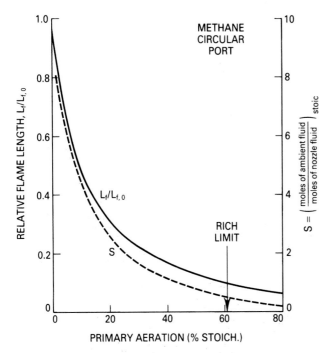

FIGURE 9.11

Effect of primary aeration on laminar jet flame lengths. For primary aerations greater than the rich limit, premixed burning (and flashback) is possible.

Figure 9.11 shows the effect of primary aeration on the length of methane flames on circular-port burners. Note that in the range of 40–60% primary aeration, flame lengths are reduced approximately 85–90% from their original no-air-added lengths. The stoichiometric ratio S, defined by Eqn. 9.71, can be evaluated for the case of primary air addition by treating the "fuel", i.e., the nozzle fluid, as a mixture of the true fuel and primary air:

$$S = \frac{1 - \psi_{pri}}{\psi_{pri} + \dfrac{1}{S_{\text{pure}}}}, \tag{9.73}$$

where ψ_{pri} is the fraction of the stoichiometric requirement met by the primary air, i.e., the primary aeration, and S_{pure} is the molar stoichiometric ratio associated with the pure fuel.

OXYGEN CONTENT OF OXIDIZER. The amount of oxygen in the oxidizer has a strong influence on flame lengths, as can be seen in Fig. 9.12. Small reductions in O_2 content from the nominal 21% value for air result in greatly lengthened flames. With a pure-O_2 oxidizer, flame lengths for methane are about one-fourth

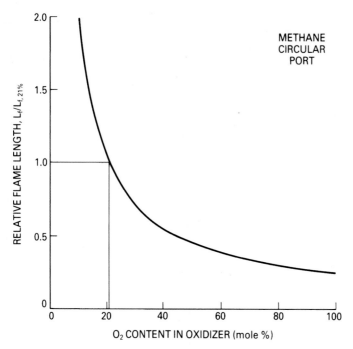

FIGURE 9.12
Effect of oxygen content in the oxidizing stream on flame length.

their value in air. To calculate the effect of O_2 content, Eqn. 9.72 can be used to evaluate the stoichiometric ratio for hydrocarbon fuels.

FUEL DILUTION WITH INERT GAS. Diluting the fuel with an inert gas also has the effect of reducing flame length via its influence on the stoichiometric ratio. For hydrocarbon fuels,

$$S = \frac{x + y/4}{\left(\dfrac{1}{1 - \chi_{\text{dil}}}\right)\chi_{O_2}}, \tag{9.74}$$

where χ_{dil} is the diluent mole fraction in the fuel stream.

> **Example 9.4.** Design a natural-gas burner for a commercial cooking range that has a number of circular ports arranged in a circle. The circle diameter is constrained to be 160 mm (6.3 in.). The burner must deliver 2.2 kW at full load and operate with 40% primary aeration. For stable operation, the loading of an individual port should not exceed 10 W per mm^2 of port area. (See Fig. 8.20 for typical design constraints for natural-gas burners.) Also, the full-load flame height should not exceed 20 mm. Determine the number and the diameter of the ports.

Solution. We will assume that the fuel gas is methane, although for an accurate design, actual natural-gas properties should be used. Our overall strategy will be to relate the number of ports, N, and their diameter, D, to the port loading constraint; choose an N and D that satisfy this constraint; and then check to see if the flame-length constraint is violated. Having a design that meets these two constraints, we will check to see that the overall design makes physical sense.

Step 1. Apply port loading constraint. The total port area is

$$A_{tot} = N\pi D^2/4,$$

and the constraint is

$$\frac{\dot{m}_F \Delta h_c}{A_{tot}} = \frac{2200\,\text{W}}{A_{tot}(\text{mm}^2)} = 10\,\text{W/mm}^2;$$

thus,

$$ND = \frac{4\,(2200)}{10\pi} = 280\,\text{mm}^2.$$

At this point, we can choose (more or less arbitrarily) a value for N (or D) and calculate D (or N) as a first trial for the design. Choosing $N = 36$ yields $D = 2.79\,\text{mm}$.

Step 2. Determine flowrates. The design heat-release rate determines the fuel flowrate:

$$\dot{Q} = 2200\,\text{W} = \dot{m}_F \Delta h_c$$

$$\dot{m}_F = \frac{2200\,\text{W}}{1{,}010{,}100\,\text{J/kg}} = 4.4 \cdot 10^{-5}\,\text{kg/s}.$$

The primary aeration determines the flowrate of air premixed with the fuel:

$$\dot{m}_{A,pri} = 0.40\,(A/F)_{stoic}\dot{m}_F$$

$$= 0.40\,(17.1)\,4.4 \cdot 10^{-5} = 3.01 \cdot 10^{-4}\,\text{kg/s}.$$

The total volumetric flowrate is

$$Q_{tot} = (\dot{m}_{A,pri} + \dot{m}_F)/\bar{\rho}.$$

To determine $\bar{\rho}$, we apply the ideal-gas law where the mean molecular weight is calculated from the composition of the air–fuel mixture:

$$\chi_{A,pri} = \frac{N_A}{N_A + N_F} = \frac{Z}{Z+1}$$

where Z is the primary molar air–fuel ratio:

$$Z = (x + y/4)\,4.76\,(\%\ \text{aeration}/100)$$
$$= (1 + 4/4)\,(4.76)\,(40/100)$$
$$= 3.81.$$

Thus,

$$\chi_{A,\,pri} = \frac{3.81}{3.81 + 1} = 0.792,$$

$$\chi_{F,\,pri} = 1 - \chi_A = 0.208,$$

$$MW_{\mathrm{mix}} = 0.792\,(28.85) + 0.208\,(16.04) = 26.19,$$

$$\bar{\rho} = \frac{P}{\left(\dfrac{R_u}{MW_{\mathrm{mix}}}\right)T} = \frac{101,325}{\left(\dfrac{8315}{26.19}\right)300} = 1.064\,\mathrm{kg/m^3}$$

and

$$Q_{\mathrm{TOT}} = \frac{3.01 \cdot 10^{-4} + 4.4 \cdot 10^{-5}}{1.064} = 3.24 \cdot 10^{-4}\,\mathrm{m^3/s}.$$

Step 3. Check flame length constraint. The flowrate per port is

$$Q_{\mathrm{PORT}} = Q_{\mathrm{TOT}}/N = 3.24 \cdot 10^{-4}/36$$
$$= 9 \cdot 10^{-6}\,\mathrm{m^3/s}.$$

The molar ambient-air to nozzle fluid stoichiometric ratio, S, is given by Eqn. 9.73 and evaluated as

$$S = \frac{1 - \psi_{pri}}{\psi_{pri} + \dfrac{1}{S_{\mathrm{pure}}}} = \frac{1 - 0.40}{0.40 + \dfrac{1}{9.52}} = 1.19.$$

We can calculate the flame length using Eqn. 9.60:

$$L_f = 1330\,\frac{Q_F(T_\infty/T_F)}{\ln(1 + 1/S)}$$

$$= \frac{1330\,(9 \cdot 10^{-6})(300/300)}{\ln(1 + 1/1.19)} = 0.0196\,\mathrm{m}$$

$$L_f = 19.6\,\mathrm{mm}.$$

A flame length of 19.6 mm meets our requirement of $L_f \leq 20\,\mathrm{mm}$.

Step 4. Check practicability of design. If we arrange 36 ports equally spaced on a 160-mm-diameter circle, the spacing between ports is

$$\ell = r\theta = \frac{160}{2}\,(\mathrm{mm})\frac{2\pi}{36}\,(\mathrm{rad})$$

$$\ell = 14\,\mathrm{mm}.$$

Comment. This spacing seems reasonable, although it is not clear whether or not the flames will form independently or merge. If the flames merge, our method of estimating flame height would not be valid. Since all of the constraints are satisfied with the 36-port design, iteration is not required.

SOOT FORMATION AND DESTRUCTION

As mentioned in our overview of laminar flame structure at the beginning of this chapter, the formation and destruction of soot is an important feature of non-premixed hydrocarbon/air flames. The incandescent soot within the flame is the primary source of the diffusion flames' luminosity, and the oil lamp is a prime example of a practical application dating back to ancient times. Soot also contributes to radiant heat losses from flames, with peak emission at wavelengths in the infrared region of the spectrum. Although soot formation in practical applications of laminar diffusion flames, e.g., in gas ranges, is to be avoided, the laminar diffusion flame is frequently used as a research tool in fundamental studies of soot formation in combustion systems and, hence, has a large literature associated with it. References [20–25] provide general reviews of soot formation in combustion.

It is generally agreed that soot is formed in diffusion flames over a limited range of temperatures, say, $1300\,K < T < 1600\,K$. Figure 9.13 illustrates this

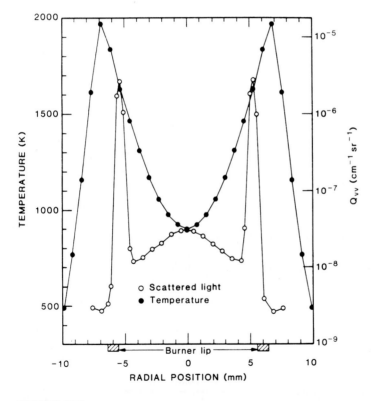

FIGURE 9.13
Radial profiles of temperature and scattered light for a laminar ethylene jet diffusion flame. Soot is contained in the region where the scattered light intensity is high. (Reprinted from Ref. [1] by permission of Gordon & Breach Science Publishers, © 1987.)

point for an ethylene jet flame. Here we see radial temperature profiles measured at an axial location between the burner and the flame tip. Also shown are measurements of light scattered by soot particles, where the two peaks correspond to regions containing significant amounts of soot. Note that the soot peaks are at radial locations interior to the temperature peaks and correspond to temperatures of about 1600 K. The soot region is very narrow and confined to a restricted range of temperatures. Although the chemistry and physics of soot formation in diffusion flames is exceedingly complex, the view has emerged that soot formation proceeds in a four-step sequence:

1. Formation of precursor species.
2. Particle inception.
3. Surface growth and particle agglomeration.
4. Particle oxidation.

In the first step, the formation of soot precursor species, polycyclic aromatic hydrocarbons (PAH) are thought to be important intermediates between the original fuel molecule and what can be considered a primary soot particle [20]. Chemical kinetics plays an important role in this first step. Although the detailed chemical mechanisms involved and the identity of the specific precursors are still subjects of research, the formation of ring structures and their growth via reactions with acetylene have been identified as important processes. The particle inception step involves the formation of small particles of a critical size (3000—10,000 atomic mass units) from growth by both chemical means and coagulation. It is in this step that large molecules are transformed to, or become identified as, particles. When the small primary soot particles continue to be exposed to the bath of species from the pyrolyzing fuel as they travel through the flame, they experience surface growth and agglomeration, the third step. At some point in their history, the soot particles must pass through an oxidizing region of the flame. For a jet flame, this region is invariably the flame tip, since the soot is always formed interior to the reaction zone lower in the flame, and the flow streamlines, which the particles largely follow, do not cross the reaction zone until near the flame tip [1]. If all of the soot particles are oxidized, the flame is termed nonsooting, while, conversely, incomplete oxidation yields a sooting flame. Figure 9.14 illustrates sooting and non-sooting conditions for nonpremixed laminar propylene and butane fuels. The non-zero value of the soot volume fraction beyond the flame tip ($x/x_{\text{stoic}} \overset{\sim}{>} 1.1$) indicates a sooting flame.

As suggested by Fig. 9.14, the amount of soot formed in a diffusion flame is strongly dependent on fuel type. An experimentally determined measure of a fuel's tendency to soot is the so-called **smoke point**. The smoke-point test was originally devised for liquid fuels and has also been used to characterize gaseous fuels. The basic concept is to increase the fuel flowrate until smoke is observed to escape from the flame tip. The greater the fuel flowrate at the incipient sooting condition, the lower the sooting propensity of the fuel. Sometimes smoke points

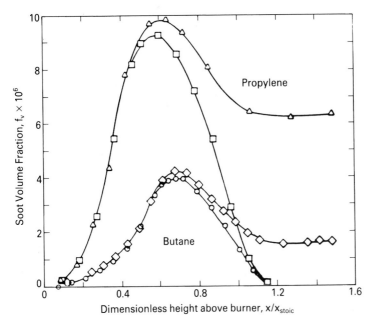

FIGURE 9.14

Measured soot volume fractions as functions of height above burner for propylene and butane at both sooting and nonsooting conditions. (Reprinted by permission of Elsevier Science, Inc., from Ref. [26]. ©1986, The Combustion Institute.)

are expressed as the height of the flame at the incipient sooting condition. As with flowrates, the larger the flame height, the lower the sooting propensity. Table 9.5, from Kent [26], lists smoke points for a large number of fuels. It is interesting to note that methane does not appear on the list since it is not possible to produce a stable sooting laminar methane flame.

If we group the fuels listed in Table 9.5 by families, we note that the fuel sooting propensities, from least to greatest, are in the order of alkanes, alkenes, alkynes, and aromatics. Table 9.6 shows these groupings. Quite obviously, the parent-fuel molecular structure is very important in determining the fuel's sooting propensity, and the groupings given above are consistent with the ideas that ring compounds and their growth via acetylene are important features of soot-formation chemistry. In the design of practical burners, soot formation is generally avoided altogether. The effects of port loading and primary aeration on the "yellow-tip" zone conditions, where soot is formed within the flame, are shown for natural gas and for manufactured gas flames in Fig. 8.20.

SUMMARY

This chapter opened with a discussion of laminar constant-density jets, whose behavior has much in common with laminar jet flames, but is easier to describe

TABLE 9.5
Smoke points, $\dot{m}_{sp}$; maximum soot volume fractions, $f_{v,m}$; and maximum soot yields, Y_s; for selected fuels[a]

Fuel		$\dot{m}_{sp}$ (mg/s)	$f_{v,m} \times 10^6$	$Y_s(\%)$
Acetylene	C_2H_2	0.51	15.3	23
Ethylene	C_2H_4	3.84	5.9	12
Propylene	C_3H_6	1.12	10.0	16
Propane	C_3H_8	7.87	3.7	9
Butane	C_4H_{10}	7.00	4.2	10
Cyclohexane	C_6H_{12}	2.23	7.8	19
n-Heptane	C_7H_{16}	5.13	4.6	12
Cyclooctane	C_8H_{16}	2.07	10.1	20
Isooctane	C_8H_{18}	1.57	9.9	27
Decalin	$C_{10}H_{18}$	0.77	15.4	31
4-Methylcyclohexene	C_7H_{12}	1.00	13.3	22
1-Octene	C_8H_{16}	1.73	9.2	25
1-Decene	$C_{10}H_{20}$	1.77	9.9	27
1-Hexadecene	$C_{16}H_{32}$	1.93	9.2	22
1-Heptyne	C_7H_{12}	0.65	14.7	30
1-Decyne	$C_{10}H_{18}$	0.80	14.7	30
Toluene	C_7H_8	0.27	19.1	38
Styrene	C_8H_8	0.22	17.9	40
o-Xylene	C_8H_{10}	0.28	20.0	37
1-Phenyl-1-propyne	C_9H_8	0.15	24.8	42
Indene	C_9H_8	0.18	20.5	33
n-Butylbenzene	$C_{10}H_{14}$	0.27	14.5	29
1-Methylnaphthalene	$C_{11}H_{10}$	0.17	22.1	41

[a]From Ref. [26].

TABLE 9.6
Smoke points by hydrocarbon family[a]

Alkanes		Alkenes		Alkynes		Aliphatic-aromatics	
Fuel	$\dot{m}_{sp}$[b]	Fuel	$\dot{m}_{sp}$[b]	Fuel	$\dot{m}_{sp}$[b]	Fuel	$\dot{m}_{sp}$[b]
Propane	7.87	Ethylene	3.84	Acetylene	0.51	Toluene	0.27
Butane	7.00	Propylene	1.12	1-Heptyne	0.65	Styrene	0.22
n-Heptane	5.13	1-Octene	1.73	1-Decyne	0.80	o-Xylene	0.28
Isooctane	1.57	1-Decene	1.77			n-Butylbenzene	0.27
		1-Hexadecene	1.93				

[a]Data from Ref. [26].
[b]Smoke point flowrate in mg/s.

mathematically. You should be able to describe the general characteristics of the velocity and nozzle-fluid concentration fields of laminar jets and understand the Reynolds-number dependence of the spreading characteristics. We also saw that the nozzle-fluid concentration distribution is identical for equal flowrates, which translates to flame lengths depending only on flowrate for a given fuel–oxidizer combination. You should be able to describe the general characteristics of the temperature, fuel and oxidizer mass fractions, and velocity fields of laminar jet flames, and have a firm grasp of how stoichiometry determines the flame contour. The conserved scalar formulation of the laminar jet diffusion flame problem was developed and emphasized. This approach results in a considerable mathematical simplification. For historical perspective, we reviewed the theoretical Burke–Schumann and Fay solutions of the laminar jet flame problem and then focused on Roper's simplified analyses, presenting flame length correlations for circular-, square-, and slot-port burners. You should be familiar with the use of these relationships. The Roper theory clearly showed the importance of the ambient oxidizer to nozzle-fluid stoichiometric ratio, which is determined by fuel type, O_2 content in the oxidizer, primary aeration, and fuel dilution by an inert gas. We also saw in this chapter how soot formation is an essential characteristic of diffusion flames, although soot formation can be avoided if residence times (flame lengths) are short enough. You should be familiar with the four-step sequence of soot formation and destruction occurring in flames and have an appreciation of the importance of fuel type (structure) in determining sooting propensities.

NOMENCLATURE

a	Buoyant acceleration, Eqn. 9.67 (m/s^2)
A/F	Mass air–fuel ratio
b	Port width, Table 9.3 (m)
c_p	Specific heat (J/kg-K)
$\mathcal{D}$	Mass diffusivity (m^2/s)
f	Mixture fraction (kg/kg)
f_v	Soot volume fraction
Fr	Froude number, Eqn. 9.68
g	Gravitational acceleration (m/s^2)
h	Enthalpy (J/kg) or port length, Table 9.3 (m)
h_f^o	Enthalpy of formation (J/kg)
I	Momentum flow ratio or momentum integral, Table 9.2
J	Momentum flow, Eqn. 9.1 (kg-m/s^2)
J_0, J_1	Bessel functions
k	Thermal conductivity (W/m-K)
L_f	Flame length (m)
Le	Lewis number
m	Mass (kg)
$\dot{m}$	Mass flowrate (kg/s)
MW	Molecular weight (kg/kmol)
N	Number of moles (kmol)
Q	Volumetric flowrate (m^3/s)
r	Radial coordinate (m)
$r_{1/2}$	Radius at half-height (m)

R	Radius (m)
R_o	Outer flow radius, Eqn. 9.55 (m)
R_u	Universal gas constant (J/kmol-K)
Re	Reynolds number
S	Molar stoichiometric oxidizer to nozzle fluid ratio (kmol/kmol)
Sc	Schmidt number
T	Temperature (K)
v	Velocity (m/s)
v_r, v_x	Radial and axial velocity components, respectively (m/s)
x	Axial coordinate (m) or number of carbon atoms in fuel molecule
y	Number of hydrogen atoms in fuel molecule
Y	Mass fraction (kg/kg)

Greek symbols

α	Spreading angle (rad) or thermal diffusivity (m^2/s)
β	Defined following Eqn. 9.64
ζ	General conserved scalar variable, Eqn. 9.42
μ	Absolute viscosity (N-s/m^2)
ν	Kinematic viscosity (m^2/s) or stoichiometric air–fuel ratio (kg/kg)
ξ	Defined by Eqn. 9.11
ρ	Density (kg/m^3)
Φ	Equivalence ratio
χ	Mole fraction (kmol/kmol)
ψ	Primary aeration

Subscripts

A	Air
act	Actual
B	Buoyancy-controlled
c	Core
dil	Diluent
expt	Experiment
e	Exit
f	Flame
F	Fuel
i	ith species
j	Jet
m	Maximum
mix	Mixture
M	Momentum-controlled
O, Ox	Oxidizer
P, Pr	Products
pri	Primary
pure	Pure fuel
ref	Reference

sp	Smoke point
stoic	Stoichiometric
thy	Theory
T	Transition
0	Centerline
∞	Ambient

Superscripts

*	Nondimensional quantity

REFERENCES

1. Santoro, R. J., Yeh, T. T., Horvath, J. J., and Semerjian, H. G., "The Transport and Growth of Soot Particles in Laminar Diffusion Flames," *Combustion Science and Technology*, 53: 89–115 (1987).

2. Santoro, R. J., and Semerjian, H. G., "Soot Formation in Diffusion Flames: Flow Rate, Fuel Species and Temperature Effects," *Twentieth Symposium (International) on Combustion*, The Combustion Institute, Pittsburgh, p. 997, 1984.

3. Santoro, R. J., Semerjian, H. G., and Dobbins, R. A., "Soot Particle Measurements in Diffusion Flames," *Combustion and Flame*, 51: 203–218 (1983).

4. Burke, S. P., and Schumann, T. E. W., "Diffusion Flames," *Industrial & Engineering Chemistry*, 20(10): 998–1004 (1928).

5. Fay, J. A., "The Distributions of Concentration and Temperature in a Laminar Jet Diffusion Flame," *Journal of Aeronautical Sciences*, 21: 681–689 (1954).

6. Roper, F. G., "The Prediction of Laminar Jet Diffusion Flame Sizes: Part I. Theoretical Model," *Combustion and Flame*, 29: 219–226 (1977).

7. Roper, F. G., Smith, C., and Cunningham, A. C., "The Prediction of Laminar Jet Diffusion Flame Sizes: Part II. Experimental Verification," *Combustion and Flame*, 29: 227–234 (1977).

8. Roper, F. G., "Laminar Diffusion Flame Sizes for Curved Slot Burners Giving Fan-Shaped Flames," *Combustion and Flame*, 31: 251–259 (1978).

9. Miller, J. A., and Kee, R. J., "Chemical Nonequilibrium Effects in Hydrogen–Air Laminar Jet Diffusion Flames," *Journal of Physical Chemistry*, 81(25): 2534–2542 (1977).

10. Kee, R. J., and Miller, J. A., "A Spit-Operator, Finite-Difference Solution for Axisymmetric Laminar-Jet Diffusion Flames," *AIAA Journal*, 16(2): 169–176 (1978).

11. Mitchell, R. E., Sarofin, A. F., and Clomburg, L. A., "Experimental and Numerical Investigation of Confined Laminar Diffusion Flames," *Combustion and Flame*, 37: 227–244 (1980).

12. Heys, N. W., Roper, F. G., and Kayes, P. J., "A Mathematical Model of Laminar Axisymmetrical Natural Gas Flames," *Computers and Fluids*, 9: 85–103 (1981).

13. Smooke, M. D., Lin, P., Lam, J. K., and Long, M. B., "Computational and Experimental Study of a Laminar Axisymmetric Methane–Air Diffusion Flame," *Twenty-Third Symposium (International) on Combustion*, The Combustion Institute, Pittsburgh, p. 575, 1990.

14. Anon., *Fundamentals of Design of Atmospheric Gas Burner Ports*, Research Bulletin No. 13, American Gas Association Testing Laboratories, Cleveland, August 1942.

15. Weber, E. J., and Vandaveer, F. E., "Gas Burner Design," Chapter 12 in *Gas Engineers Handbook*, The Industrial Press, New York, pp. 12/193–12/210, 1965.

16. Schlichting, H., *Boundary-Layer Theory*, 6th Ed., McGraw-Hill, New York, 1968.

17. Kuo, K. K., *Principles of Combustion*, John Wiley & Sons, New York, 1986.

18. Spalding, D. B., *Combustion and Mass Transfer*, Pergamon, New York, 1979.

19. Beyer, W. H. (ed.), *Standard Mathematical Tables*, 28th Ed., The Chemical Rubber Co., Cleveland, 1987.

20. Glassman, I., "Soot Formation in Combustion Processes," *Twenty-Second Symposium (International) on Combustion*, The Combustion Institute, Pittsburgh, p. 295, 1988.

21. Wagner, H. G., "Soot Formation—An Overview," in *Particulate Carbon Formation During Combustion* (D. C. Siegla, and G. W. Smith, eds.), Plenum Press, New York, p. 1, 1981.

22. Calcote, H. F., "Mechanisms of Soot Nucleation in Flames—A Critical Review," *Combustion and Flame*, 42: 215–242 (1981).

23. Haynes, B. S., and Wagner, H. G., "Soot Formation," *Progress in Energy and Combustion Science*, 7: 229–273 (1981).

24. Wagner, H. G., "Soot Formation in Combustion," *Seventeenth Symposium (International) on Combustion*, The Combustion Institute, Pittsburgh, p. 3, 1979.

25. Palmer, H. B., and Cullis, C. F., "The Formation of Carbon in Gases," *The Chemistry and Physics of Carbon* (P. L. Walker, Jr., ed.), Marcel Dekker, New York, p. 265, 1965.

26. Kent, J. H., "A Quantitative Relationship Between Soot Yield and Smoke Point Measurements," *Combustion and Flame*, 63: 349–358 (1986).

REVIEW QUESTIONS

1. Make a list of all the bold-faced words in Chapter 9 and define each.

2. Describe the velocity and nozzle-fluid concentration fields of a constant-density laminar jet.

3. Describe the fields of velocity; temperature; and the fuel, oxidizer, and product mass fractions of a laminar jet flame.

4. Explain why the flame boundary is at the $\Phi = 1$ contour. Hint: Consider what would happen if the flame boundary were slightly inside of the $\Phi = 1$ contour ($Y_{Ox} = 0$, $Y_F > 0$) or outside of the $\Phi = 1$ contour ($Y_F = 0$, $Y_{Ox} > 0$).

5. How do the combined assumptions of unity Lewis number and unity Schmidt number simplify the governing conservation equations for a laminar flame?

6. Explain what it means for a jet flame to be buoyancy- or momentum-controlled. What dimensionless parameter determines the flow regime? What is the physical meaning of this parameter?

7. Light a flame on a butane lighter. Hold the lighter at an angle from the vertical, being careful not to burn your fingers. What happens to the flame shape? Explain.

8. List and discuss the four steps involved in soot formation and destruction in diffusion flames.

9. Explain how the use of conserved scalars simplifies the mathematical description of laminar jet flames. What assumptions are required to effect these simplifications?

PROBLEMS

9.1. Starting with the more general axial momentum equation for a reacting axisymmetric flow (Eqn. 7.33), derive the constant-property, constant-density form given by Eqn. 9.4. Hint: you will need to apply continuity.

9.2. Repeat problem 9.1 for species conservation, starting with Eqn. 7.19 to obtain Eqn. 9.5.

9.3. Using the definition of the volumetric flowrate ($Q = v_e \pi R^2$), show that the centerline mass fraction $Y_{F,0}$ for a laminar jet (Eqn. 9.18) depends only on Q and v.

9.4. Calculate the velocity decay for a jet with an initial top-hat velocity profile (Eqn. 9.13) and for a jet where the profile is parabolic, i.e., $v(r) = 2v_e[1 - (r/R)^2]$, where v_e is the mean velocity. Both jets have same flowrates. Plot your results versus axial distance and discuss.

9.5. Two isothermal (300 K, 1 atm) air-in-air laminar jets with different diameters have the same volumetric flowrates.

    A. Expressed in terms of R, what is the ratio of their Reynolds numbers?

    B. For $Q = 5\,cm^3/s$, and $R_1 = 3\,mm$ and $R_2 = 5\,mm$ for the two jets, respectively, calculate and compare $r_{1/2}/x$ and α for the two jets.

    C. Determine the axial location where the centerline fuel velocity has decayed to $1/10$ of the nozzle-exit velocity for each jet.

9.6. Using isothermal jet theory, estimate the length of an ethane–air diffusion flame for an initial velocity of 5 cm/s. The velocity profile issuing from the 10-mm-diameter port is uniform. Both the air and ethane are at 300 K and 1 atm. The viscosity of ethane is approximately $9.5 \cdot 10^{-6}\,N\text{-}s/m^2$. Compare your estimate using an average viscosity, $(\mu_{air} + \mu_{ethane})/2$, with the predicted value from Roper's experimental correlations.

9.7. A circular-port and a square-port burner operate with the same mean velocities and produce the same flame lengths. What is the ratio of the circular-port diameter, D, to the length of a side b, of the square port? The fuel is methane.

9.8. Consider a slot burner with an aspect ratio $h/b = 10$ and slot width $b = 2\,mm$. The slot has a contoured entrance that produces a uniform exit flow. Operating with methane, the burner has a heat release of 500 W. Determine the flame length.

9.9. Two circular-port burners have the same mean velocity $\bar{v}_e$, but the velocity profile of one burner is uniform, while the other has a parabolic distribution, $v(r) = 2\bar{v}_e[1 - (r/R)^2]$. Determine the ratio of the momentum flow of the two burners.

9.10. In a study of nitric oxide formation in laminar jet flames, the propane fuel is diluted with N_2 to suppress soot formation. The nozzle fluid is 60% N_2 by mass. The burner has a circular port. The fuel, nitrogen, and the air are all at 300 K and 1 atm. Compare the flame lengths for the following two cases with the undiluted base case ($\dot{m}_F = 5 \cdot 10^{-6}\,kg/s$). What is the physical significance of your results? Discuss.

    A. The total flowrate of the diluted flow $(C_3H_8 + N_2)$ is $5 \cdot 10^{-6}\,kg/s$.

    B. The flowrate of the C_3H_8 in the diluted flow is $5 \cdot 10^{-6}\,kg/s$.

9.11. In determining the constant associated with the experimental flame-length correlation (Eqn. 9.60), Roper used a flame temperature of 1500 K. What value of the mean diffusion coefficient $\mathcal{D}_\infty$ appearing in Eqn. 9.59 is consistent with the constant in Eqn. 9.60? How does this value compare with the value of the binary diffusivity for oxygen in air at 298 K ($\mathcal{D}_{O_2-air} = 2.1 \cdot 10^{-5}\,m^2/s$)?

9.12. Estimate both the Lewis and Schmidt numbers for a dilute mixture of O_2 in air at 298 K and 1 atm. Assume $\mathcal{D}_{O_2-air} = 2.1 \cdot 10^{-5}\,m^2/s$ at these conditions. Discuss the implications of your results.

9.13. The following fuels are burned in laminar jet flames, each with a mass flowrate of 3 mg/s: acetylene, ethylene, butane, and isooctane. Which flames emit soot from their tips? Discuss your answer.

CHAPTER 10

DROPLET EVAPORATION AND BURNING

OVERVIEW

In this chapter, we consider our second nonpremixed combustion system, the evaporation and burning of spherical liquid droplets. With appropriate assumptions, this system is relatively simple to analyze and, thus, provides a good opportunity to see clearly how various physical phenomena interrelate. For both droplet evaporation and burning, closed-form analytic solutions to the simplified governing conservation equations are possible. These solutions allow us to explore the influence of droplet size and ambient conditions on droplet evaporation or burning times. Knowledge of droplet gasification rates and droplet lifetimes are important in the design and operation of practical devices. In addition to developing simple droplet gasification models, we show how the simple evaporation model can be incorporated into a one-dimensional analysis of a combustor. Before we begin our various analyses, however, it is worthwhile to review some of the practical applications that are related to or impacted by droplet evaporation and/or burning.

SOME APPLICATIONS

Droplet burning has relevance to many practical combustion devices, including diesel, rocket and gas-turbine engines, as well as oil-fired boilers, furnaces, and process heaters. To maintain perspective, it is important to point out that in these devices, spray combustion, rather than individual droplet burning, is the dominant feature; however, understanding isolated droplet burning is an essential prerequisite to dealing with more complex flames, as well as being important in its own right in some situations.

Diesel Engines

There are two primary types of diesel engines, the indirect-injection type and the direct-injection type, shown in Figs. 10.1 and 10.2, respectively. In the **indirect-injection** engine, fuel is injected under high pressure into a precombustion cham-

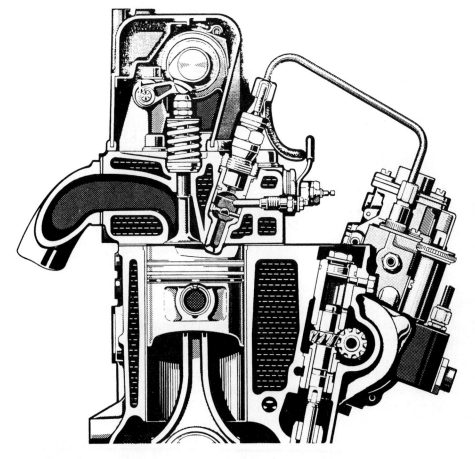

FIGURE 10.1
Light-duty indirect-injection diesel engine. Cutaway shows prechamber with glow plug, used for starting, and fuel injector. (Reprinted from Ref. [1] with permission, ©1971, Society of Automotive Engineers, Inc.)

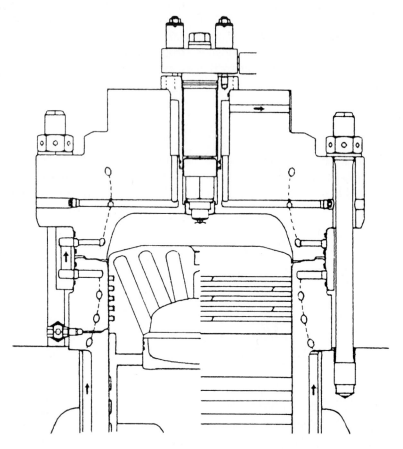

FIGURE 10.2
Combustion chamber and piston cutaway view of large direct-injection diesel engine. (Reprinted from Ref. [2] by permission of the American Society of Mechanical Engineers.)

ber. The fuel droplets begin to evaporate and the fuel vapor mixes with the air in the chamber. Portions of this fuel–air mixture autoignite (Example 6.1) and initiate nonpremixed combustion. Because of the heat release, the pressure rises inside the prechamber forcing its contents through a throat or orifice into the main chamber. The partially reacted fuel–air mixture and any remaining fuel droplets mix with additional air in the main chamber and burn to completion. In the **direct-injection** engine, the fuel is introduced by a multi-holed fuel injector. Fuel–air mixing is governed by both the injection process and the air motion within the combustion space. As suggested above, diesel-engine combustion takes place in both premixed and diffusion-controlled modes. Diesel fuels are much less volatile than spark-ignition fuels, but are more readily autoigniting. The rate at which the fuel vaporizes and mixes with the air is in competition with the rate of reaction leading to autoignition. Thus, the first fuel injected into the chamber may become premixed before it is subjected to an ignition source (a pocket of gas that has autoignited) and burns in a premixed flame; the fuel injected subsequently, however, burns in a diffusion mode, since an ignition source (the pre-existing flame) is present as the fuel is injected. Clearly, droplet evaporation and burning are important in both indirect- and direct-injection engines.

Gas-Turbine Engines

Liquid-fueled, gas-turbine engines are the primary powerplant used in aircraft. Figure 10.3 shows a cutaway view of an aircraft turbine engine. In spite of the critical importance of the combustor to the engine system, it occupies a suprisingly small amount of space. Fuel is injected into and atomized within the annular combustor where the flame is typically stabilized by swirling air that creates a recirculation zone. Aircraft gas-turbine combustor design is influenced by several factors: combustion efficiency, combustion stability, relight-at-altitude capability, and emissions, among others. Typically, aircraft engines employ nonpremixed combustion systems, with a near-stoichiometric primary flame zone integrated with secondary air streams to complete combustion and dilute the products to the proper temperature before entry into the turbine (Fig. 10.4a). Some designs and experimental systems utilize various degrees of premixing to avoid

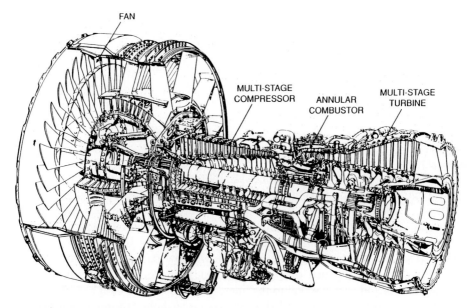

FIGURE 10.3
Aircraft gas-turbine engine. Note, the combustor is a small part of the total volume of the engine. (Reprinted from Ref. [3] by permission of Gordon & Breach Science Publishers, SA.)

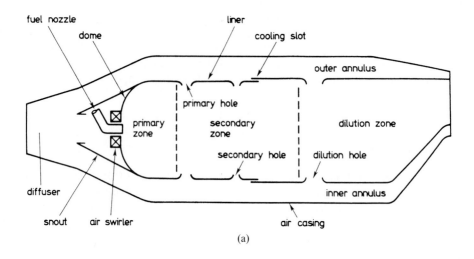

(a)

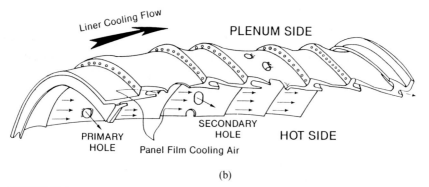

(b)

FIGURE 10.4
(a) Schematic of annular turbine combustor showing primary, secondary, and dilution zones. (Reprinted from Ref. [6] by permission of Taylor & Francis.) (b) Schematic of panel film cooling of combustor liner walls. (Reprinted from Ref. [3] by permission of Gordon & Breach Science Publishers, SA.)

high-temperature, NO_x-forming zones [4,5]. Premixed combustion is achieved by vaporizing the fuel and mixing with air before the mixture enters the hot combustion zone where it then ignites and burns. Figure 10.4a illustrates the **primary, secondary**, and **dilution zones** of an aircraft gas-turbine combustor.

Figure 10.4b shows the metal liner that separates the inner combustion space from the surrounding outer annular air flow passage. A portion of the air is used to cool the liner on the hot-gas side. This air flows through the ring of small holes and runs parallel to the liner, thus providing a cool boundary-layer flow. Combustion air is directed through the larger holes, forming high-velocity jets that penetrate into the core of the combustion space and rapidly mix with the hot gases. A critical concern in the design of turbine combustors is the gas temperature distribution in the radial direction when it enters the turbine section. Air injection in the dilution zone is used to control this distribution. Hot spots that can damage turbine blades are avoided, and the gas temperature profile is tailored to increase from the blade root through a maximum and then decrease at the tip. At the root, the blade stresses are greatest; hence, the cooler gas at the root allows the blade to be cooler in this region. This is important since the blade material strength decreases with temperature. Optimizing the temperature profile allows the maximum average turbine inlet temperature and high efficiencies as a result. The temperature distribution at the combustor outlet is frequently referred to as the **pattern factor**.

Liquid-Rocket Engines

Of all the combustion devices considered here, the modern rocket engine produces the most intense combustion, i.e., the greatest energy release per volume of combustion space. There are two types of liquid rockets: **pressure-fed**, in which the fuel and oxidizer are pushed into the combustion chamber by a high-pressure gas; and **pump-fed**, where turbopumps deliver the propellants. These two arrangements are illustrated in Fig. 10.5. The pump-fed system delivers the higher performance of the two systems; however, it is much more complex. Figure 10.6 shows the liquid-hydrogen, liquid-oxygen pump-fed J-2 rocket engine used in both the second and third stages of the Saturn vehicle used in the Apollo program.

The thrust of the engine is produced by creating a hot, high-pressure gas from the combustion of the fuel and oxidizer in the combustion chamber, that is subsequently accelerated through a supersonic, converging–diverging nozzle. Unlike any of the other combustion devices discussed previously, the oxidizer for the rocket engine is supplied as a liquid. To establish combustion thus requires the vaporization of both the fuel and the oxidizer. It is likely that both modes of combustion, premixed and diffusion burning, play a role in rocket engine combustion. Because of the extreme difficulty of instrumenting the interior of the combustion chamber, relatively little is known about the details of the combustion process. Work is in progress [8,9] to learn more about the processes going on in a rocket combustion chamber using laser probes and other techniques.

SIMPLE MODEL OF DROPLET EVAPORATION

To illustrate principles of mass transfer in Chapter 3, we developed a droplet evaporation model by transforming the Stefan problem to spherical coordinates. That model involved only mass transfer, since it was assumed that the droplet surface temperature was a known parameter. In the present analysis, we assume that the droplet surface temperature is near the droplet boiling point and, hence, the evaporation rate is controlled by the heat transfer rate from the ambient to the droplet surface. This can be a good approximation in combustion environments where ambient temperatures are high, and the mathematical description of the

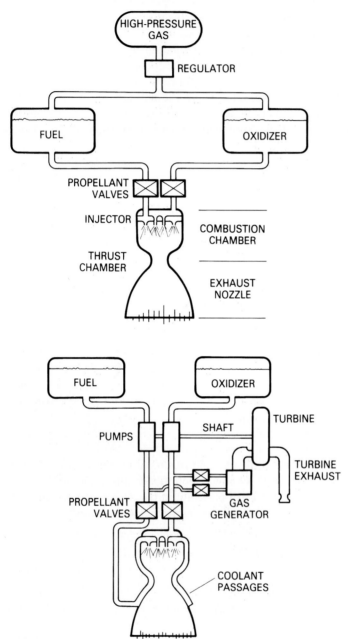

FIGURE 10.5
Schematic illustration of the two types of liquid-rocket systems: (top) pressure-fed system, (lower) pump-fed system. (From Ref. [7]. Reprinted with permission of the Jet Propulsion Laboratory.)

FIGURE 10.6
J-2 engine test firing (top) and Saturn V second stage with cluster of five J-2 engines. (Courtesy of Rockwell Aerospace, Rocketdyne Division.)

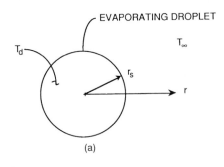

(a)

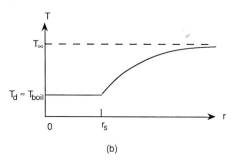

(b)

FIGURE 10.7
Evaporation of a liquid fuel droplet in a quiescent
environment, where it is assumed that the droplet
surface temperature is nearly at the liquid boiling
point.

evaporation process is, perhaps, the simplest possible and, yet, is useful for engineering calculations. Later in this chapter, we develop a more general droplet
burning model, which can also be used to deal with pure evaporation, that couples
both heat and mass transfer.

Figure 10.7 defines the spherically symmetric coordinate system. The radius
r is the only coordinate variable. It has its origin at the center of the droplet, and
the droplet radius at the liquid–vapor interface is denoted r_s. Very far from the
droplet surface ($r \to \infty$), the temperature is T_∞.

Physically, heat from the ambient environment supplies the energy necessary
to vaporize the liquid fuel, and the fuel vapor then diffuses from the droplet
surface into the ambient gas. The mass loss causes the droplet radius to shrink
with time until the droplet is completely evaporated ($r_s = 0$). The problem that we
wish to solve is the determination of the mass flowrate of the fuel vapor from the
surface at any instant in time. Knowledge of this will then enable us to calculate
the droplet radius as a function of time and the droplet lifetime.

Assumptions

The following assumptions for a droplet evaporating in a hot gas are commonly
invoked because they lead to great simplification, principally by eliminating the
need to deal with the mass-transfer aspects of the problem, yet still agree reasonably well with experimental results:

1. The droplet evaporates in a quiescent, infinite medium.
2. The evaporation process is quasi-steady. This means that at any instant in time the process can be described as if it were in steady state. This assumption eliminates the need to deal with partial differential equations.
3. The fuel is a single-component liquid with zero solubility for gases.
4. The droplet temperature is uniform, and, furthermore, the temperature is assumed to be the boiling point of the fuel, $T_d = T_{boil}$. In many problems, the transient heating of the liquid does not greatly affect the droplet lifetime, and more rigorous calculations show that the droplet surface temperature is only slightly less than the liquid boiling point in combustion environments. This assumption eliminates the need to solve a liquid-phase (droplet) energy equation, and, more importantly, eliminates the need to solve the fuel vapor transport (species) equation in the gas phase! Implicit in this assumption is that $T_\infty > T_{boil}$. In our subsequent analysis, when we eliminate the assumption that the droplet is at the boiling point, you will see how much more complicated the analysis becomes.
5. We assume binary diffusion with a unity Lewis number ($\alpha = \mathcal{D}$). This permits us to use the simple Shvab–Zeldovich energy equation developed previously, in Chapter 7.
6. We also assume that all thermophysical properties, such as thermal conductivity, density, and specific heat, are constant. Although these properties may vary greatly as we move through the gas phase from the droplet surface to the faraway surroundings, constant properties allow a simple closed-form solution. In the final analysis, a judicious choice of mean values allows reasonably accurate predictions to be made.

Gas-Phase Analysis

With the above assumptions, we can find the mass evaporation rate, $\dot{m}$, and the droplet radius history, $r_s(t)$, by writing a gas-phase mass conservation equation, a gas-phase energy equation, a droplet gas-phase interface energy balance, and a droplet liquid mass conservation equation. The gas-phase energy equation gives us the temperature distribution in the gas-phase, which in turn allows us to evaluate the conduction heat transfer into the droplet at the surface. This is necessary to evaluate the surface energy balance that yields the evaporation rate $\dot{m}$. Knowing $\dot{m}(t)$, we can easily find the drop size as a function of time.

MASS CONSERVATION. With the assumption of quasi-steady burning, the mass flowrate, $\dot{m}(r)$, is a constant, independent of radius; thus,

$$\dot{m} = \dot{m}_F = \rho v_r 4\pi r^2 = \text{constant} \tag{10.1}$$

and

$$\frac{d(\rho v_r r^2)}{dr} = 0,\qquad(10.2)$$

where v_r is the bulk flow velocity.

ENERGY CONSERVATION. As previously derived in Chapter 7, conservation of energy for the situation depicted in Fig. 10.8a is expressed by Eqn. 7.49. With the assumption of constant properties and unity Lewis number, this can be re-arranged and written as:

$$\frac{d\left(r^2\dfrac{dT}{dr}\right)}{dr} = \frac{\dot{m}c_{pg}}{4\pi k}\frac{dT}{dr},\qquad(10.3)$$

where the reaction rate term is zero, since no reactions occur for pure evaporation.

For convenience in the following development, we define $Z \equiv c_{pg}/4\pi k$; thus,

$$\frac{d\left(r^2\dfrac{dT}{dr}\right)}{dr} = Z\dot{m}\frac{dT}{dr}.\qquad(10.4)$$

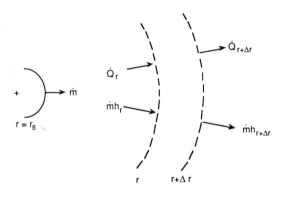

(a)

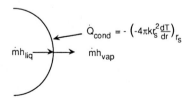

(b)

FIGURE 10.8
Evaporating-droplet energy balance for (a) gas phase and (b) droplet surface.

Solving Eqn. 10.4 gives us the temperature distribution, $T(r)$, in the gas phase. To effect this solution requires two boundary conditions:

Boundary condition 1: $\qquad T(r \rightarrow \infty) = T_\infty$ $\hfill$ (10.5a)

Boundary condition 2: $\qquad T(r = r_s) = T_{\text{boil}}.$ $\hfill$ (10.5b)

Equation 10.4 can be easily solved by twice separating variables and integrating. After the first integration, we obtain

$$r^2 \frac{dT}{dr} = Z\dot{m}T + C_1$$

where C_1 is the integration constant. Separating and integrating again, yields the general solution,

$$\frac{1}{Z\dot{m}} \ln(Z\dot{m}T + C_1) = -\frac{1}{r} + C_2, \tag{10.6}$$

where C_2 is the second integration constant. Applying Eqn. 10.5a to Eqn. 10.6 gives C_2 in terms of C_1:

$$C_2 = \frac{1}{Z\dot{m}} \ln(Z\dot{m}T_\infty + C_1).$$

Substituting C_2 back into Eqn. 10.6, applying the second boundary condition (Eqn. 10.5b), and using exponentiation to remove the logarithm, we can find C_1, i.e.,

$$C_1 = \frac{Z\dot{m}[T_\infty(-Z\dot{m}/r_s) - T_{\text{boil}}]}{1 - \exp(-Z\dot{m}/r_s)}.$$

The second constant is now readily found by substituting C_1 into the expression for C_2 above. Thus,

$$C_2 = \frac{1}{Z\dot{m}} \ln \left[\frac{Z\dot{m}(T_\infty - T_{\text{boil}})}{1 - \exp(-Z\dot{m}/r_s)} \right].$$

Finally, the temperature distribution can be found by substituting these expressions for C_1 and C_2 back into the general solution given by Eqn. 10.6. The final, and somewhat complicated, result is

$$T(r) = \frac{(T_\infty - T_{\text{boil}}) \exp(-Z\dot{m}/r) - T_\infty \exp(-Z\dot{m}/r_s) + T_{\text{boil}}}{1 - \exp(-Z\dot{m}/r_s)}. \tag{10.7}$$

DROPLET-GAS-PHASE INTERFACE ENERGY BALANCE. By itself, Eqn. 10.7 does not allow us to solve for the evaporation rate $\dot{m}$; however, it does allow us to evaluate the heat transferred to the droplet surface, which appears in the interface (surface) energy balance illustrated in Fig. 10.8b. Heat is conducted to the interface from the hot gas, and since we assume that the droplet temperature is uniform at T_{boil}, all of this heat must be used to vaporize the fuel, with no heat flowing into the droplet interior. It is relatively easy to allow transient droplet heating, as will be shown in our burning droplet analysis. The surface energy balance can be written:

$$\dot{Q}_{\text{cond}} = \dot{m}(h_{\text{vap}} - h_{\text{liq}}) = \dot{m}h_{fg}. \tag{10.8}$$

Substituting Fourier's Law for $\dot{Q}_{\text{cond}}$, paying careful attention to sign conventions, we have

$$4\pi k_g r_s^2 \frac{dT}{dr}\bigg|_{r_s} = \dot{m}h_{fg}. \tag{10.9}$$

Differentiating Eqn. 10.7, the temperature gradient in the gas phase at the droplet surface is

$$\frac{dT}{dr}\bigg|_{r_s} = \frac{Z\dot{m}}{r_s^2} \left[\frac{(T_\infty - T_{\text{boil}})\exp(-Z\dot{m}/r_s)}{1 - \exp(-Z\dot{m}/r_s)} \right]. \tag{10.10}$$

Substituting this result into Eqn. 10.9 and solving for $\dot{m}$, we obtain

$$\dot{m} = \frac{4\pi k_g r_s}{c_{pg}} \ln\left[\frac{c_{pg}(T_\infty - T_{\text{boil}})}{h_{fg}} + 1 \right]. \tag{10.11}$$

In the combustion literature, the first term in the brackets is defined

$$B_q = \frac{c_{pg}(T_\infty - T_{\text{boil}})}{h_{fg}}, \tag{10.12}$$

so

$$\dot{m} = \frac{4\pi k_g r_s}{c_{pg}} \ln(B_q + 1). \tag{10.13}$$

The parameter B is one of those dimensionless parameters, such as the Reynolds number, that has special significance in combustion and is commonly referred to by those knowledgeable in the field. It is sometimes referred to as the **Spalding number**, or simply as the **transfer number, B**. Recall that, in Chapter 3, we developed a similar expression for droplet evaporization controlled by mass transfer. The definition of B given by Eqn. 10.12 applies only to the set of assumptions listed previously, with the subscript q indicating that it is based on heat transfer considerations alone. Other definitions exist and their functional form depends on the assumptions made. For example, B has a different definition if a spherically symmetric flame is assumed to surround the droplet. This will be elaborated on later.

 This completes our analysis of the gas phase. Knowing the instantaneous (quasi-steady) evaporation rate allows us now to calculate the droplet lifetime.

Droplet Lifetimes

Following the same analysis as in Chapter 3 for mass-transfer controlled evaporation, we obtain the droplet radius (or diameter) history by writing a mass balance that states that the rate at which the mass of the droplet decreases is equal to the rate at which the liquid is vaporized, i.e.,

$$\frac{dm_d}{dt} = -\dot{m},$$ (10.14)

where the droplet mass, m_d, is given by

$$m_d = \rho_\ell V = \rho_\ell \pi D^3/6$$ (10.15)

and V and D are the droplet volume and diameter, respectively.

Substituting Eqns. 10.15 and 10.13 into Eqn. 10.14, and performing the differentiation, yields:

$$\frac{dD}{dt} = -\frac{4k_g}{\rho_\ell c_{pg} D} \ln(B_q + 1).$$ (10.16)

As discussed previously (cf. Chapter 3), Eqn. 10.16 is more commonly expressed in terms of D^2 rather than D, i.e.,

$$\frac{dD^2}{dt} = -\frac{8k_g}{\rho_\ell c_{pg}} \ln(B_q + 1).$$ (10.17)

Equation 10.17 shows that the time derivative of the square of the droplet diameter is constant; hence, D^2 varies linearly with t with the slope $-(8k/\rho_\ell c_{pg}) \ln(B_q + 1)$ as illustrated in Fig. 10.9a. This slope is defined to be the **evaporation constant K**,

$$K = \frac{8k_g}{\rho_\ell c_{pg}} \ln(B_q + 1).$$ (10.18)

Note the similarity of this relation to Eqn. 3.58: the form of each equation is the same, and the equations become identical if the Lewis number is unity $(k_g/c_{pg} = \rho D)$, although different definitions apply to B. We can integrate Eqn. 10.17 to provide a general relationship expressing the variation of D (or D^2) with time:

$$\int_{D_0^2}^{D^2} d\hat{D}^2 = -\int_0^t K d\hat{t},$$

which yields

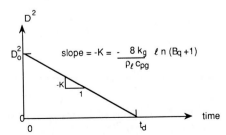

slope = $-K = -\dfrac{8 k_g}{\rho_\ell c_{pg}} \ell n (B_q + 1)$

FIGURE 10.9

D^2 law for droplet evaporation resulting from simplified analysis.

$$D^2(t) = D_0^2 - Kt. \tag{10.19}$$

Equation 10.19 is the same D^2 **law** for droplet evaporation that we introduced in Chapter 3. Experiments, e.g. Ref. [10], show that the D^2 law holds after an initial transient period associated with the heating of the droplet to near the boiling point (cf. Fig. 3.7b).

We can find the time it takes a droplet of given initial size to completely evaporate, i.e., the droplet lifetime, t_d, by letting $D^2(t_d) = 0$:

$$t_d = D_0^2/K. \tag{10.20}$$

To use Eqns. 10.19 and 10.20 to predict droplet evaporation is straightforward; however, we have the problem of choosing appropriate mean values for c_{pg} and k_g, the gas-phase specific heat and thermal conductivity, respectively, which appear in the evaporation rate constant. In our analysis, we assumed that c_{pg} and k_g were constant, while, in reality, they vary considerably in going from the droplet surface to the freestream conditions. Following the approach of Law and Williams [11] for burning droplets, the following approximations for c_{pg} and k_g are suggested:

$$c_{pg} = c_{pF}(\bar{T}), \tag{10.21}$$

$$k_g = 0.4 k_F(\bar{T}) + 0.6 k_\infty(\bar{T}), \tag{10.22}$$

where the subscript F represents the fuel vapor and $\bar{T}$ is the average of the fuel boiling point temperature and that of the free stream,

$$\bar{T} = (T_{\text{boil}} + T_\infty)/2. \tag{10.23}$$

Other approximations for property evaluations exist that are more accurate [12]; however, the above technique is the easiest to apply.

Example 10.1. Consider a 500-μm-diameter liquid n-hexane (C_6H_{14}) droplet evaporating in hot, stagnant nitrogen at 1 atm. The N_2 temperature is 850 K. Determine the lifetime of the n-hexane droplet, assuming the droplet temperature is at its boiling point.

Solution. Find t_d. The droplet lifetime is evaluated from,

$$t_d = D_0^2/K, \tag{Eqn. 10.20}$$

where

$$K = \frac{8 k_g}{\rho_\ell c_{pg}} \ln(B_q + 1) \tag{Eqn. 10.18}$$

and

$$B_q = \frac{c_{pg}(t_\infty - T_{\text{boil}})}{h_{fg}}. \tag{Eqn. 10.12}$$

The solution is straightforward, with, perhaps, the greatest complication being the property evaluations. The n-hexane properties are evaluated at

$$\bar{T} = \frac{1}{2}(T_{\text{boil}} + T_\infty) = \frac{1}{2}(342 + 850) = 596\,\text{K},$$

where the boiling point ($T_{\text{boil}} = 342\,\text{K}$) is found in Appendix B, Table B.1, as are the liquid density and heat of vaporization. The n-hexane specific heat and thermal conductivity are evaluated from the curvefit coefficients provided in Tables B.2 and B.3.

$$c_{pg} = c_{pC_6H_{14}}(\bar{T}) = 2872\,\text{J/kg-K} \qquad \text{(Table B.2)}$$

$$k_F = k_{C_6H_{14}}(\bar{T}) = 0.0495\,\text{W/m-K} \qquad \text{(Table B.3)}$$

$$k_\infty = k_{N_2}(\bar{T}) = 0.0444\,\text{W/m-K}. \qquad \text{(Table C.2)}$$

The appropriate mean thermal conductivity is (Eqn. 10.22)

$$k_g = 0.4(0.0495) + 0.6(0.0444) = 0.0464\,\text{W/m-K}$$

and the n-hexane heat of vaporization and liquid density are, respectively,

$$h_{fg} = 335,000\,\text{J/kg}, \qquad \text{(Table B.1)}$$

$$\rho_\ell \approx 659\,\text{kg/m}^3. \qquad \text{(Table B.1)}$$

The dimensionless transfer number B can now be evaluated using the properties estimated above:

$$B_q = \frac{2872(850 - 342)}{335,000} = 4.36$$

and the evaporation constant K is

$$K = \frac{8(0.0464)}{659(2872)}\ln(1 + 4.36)$$
$$= 1.961 \cdot 10^{-7}(1.679) = 3.29 \cdot 10^{-7}\,\text{m}^2/\text{s}.$$

Thus, the droplet lifetime is

$$\boxed{t_d} = D_0^2/K = \frac{(500 \cdot 10^{-6})^2}{3.29 \cdot 10^{-7}} = \boxed{0.76\,\text{s}}.$$

Comments. The example results can give us a physical feel for the time scales involved in droplet evaporation. Using the evaporation constant calculated above, but with $d \approx 50\,\mu\text{m}$, t_d is of the order of 10 ms. In many spray combustion systems, mean drop sizes are of the order of $50\,\mu\text{m}$ and smaller.

SIMPLE MODEL OF DROPLET BURNING

Our approach here extends the development above to include a spherically symmetric diffusion flame that surrounds the droplet. We will retain the assumption of a quiescent environment and spherical symmetry in the initial development, but subsequently show how the spherically symmetric results can be adjusted to take into account the enhancement of burning caused by convection, either natural convection produced by the flame or a forced flow. We will also remove the restriction that the droplet is at the boiling point, which requires using species conservation in the gas phase.

Assumptions

The following assumptions lead to a greatly simplified model of droplet combustion that preserves the essential physics and agrees reasonably well with experimental results:

1. The burning droplet, surrounded by a spherically symmetric flame, exists in a quiescent, infinite medium. There are no interactions with any other droplets, and the effects of convection are ignored.
2. As in our previous analysis, the burning process is quasi-steady.
3. The fuel is a single-component liquid with zero solubility for gases. Phase equilibrium prevails at the liquid–vapor interface.
4. The pressure is uniform and constant.
5. The gas phase consists of only three "species:" fuel vapor, oxidizer,[1] and combustion products. The gas-phase region is divided into two zones. The inner zone between the droplet surface and the flame contains only fuel vapor and products, while the outer zone consists of oxidizer and products. Thus, binary diffusion prevails in each region.
6. Fuel and oxidizer react in stoichiometric proportions at the flame. Chemical kinetics are assumed to be infinitely fast, resulting in the flame being represented as an infinitesimally thin sheet.
7. The Lewis number, $Le = \alpha/\mathcal{D} = k_g/\rho c_{pg}\mathcal{D}$, is unity.
8. Radiation heat transfer is negligible.
9. The gas-phase thermal conductivity, k_g, specific heat, c_{pg}, and the product of the density and mass diffusivity, $\rho\mathcal{D}$, are all constants.
10. The liquid fuel droplet is the only condensed phase; no soot or liquid water is present.

The basic model embodied by the above assumptions is illustrated in Fig. 10.10, which shows temperature and species profiles through the inner region between the droplet surface and the flame, $r_s \leq r \leq r_f$, and the outer region beyond the flame, $r_f \leq r < \infty$. We see that there are three important temperatures: the

---

[1]The oxidizer may be a mixture of gases, some of which may be inert. For example, we here consider air to be an oxidizer, even though only approximately 21% of the air chemically reacts. At the flame, the nitrogen conceptually is transformed from oxidizer to products even though it does not actually react.

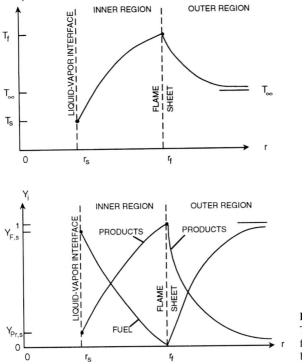

FIGURE 10.10
Temperature (top) and species profiles (bottom) for simple droplet burning model.

droplet surface temperature, T_s; the flame temperature, T_f; and the temperature of the medium at infinity, T_∞. The fuel vapor mass fraction, Y_F, is a maximum at the droplet surface and monotonically decreases to zero at the flame, where the fuel is totally consumed. The oxidizer mass fraction, Y_{Ox}, mirrors this, being a maximum (unity) far from the flame and decreasing to zero at the flame sheet. The combustion products have their maximum concentration at the flame sheet (unity) diffusing both inward toward the droplet and outward away from the flame. Since assumption 3 prevents the products from dissolving in the liquid, there can be no net flow of products inward from the flame to the droplet surface. Thus, the products in the inner region form a stagnant film through which fuel vapor moves. The species fluxes in this inner region behave in a manner reminiscent of the Stefan problem discussed in Chapter 3.

Problem Statement

In the following analysis, our number one objective is to determine the droplet mass burning rate, $\dot{m}_F$, given the initial droplet size and the conditions far from the droplet, i.e., the temperature, T_∞, and the oxidizer mass fraction, $Y_{Ox,\infty}(=1)$. On the way to achieving this objective, we will also obtain expressions describing the temperature and species profiles in each region, together with relationships that allow us to calculate the flame radius, r_f; flame temperature, T_f; droplet surface temperature, T_s; and the fuel vapor mass fraction at the droplet surface, $Y_{F,s}$. In summary, we seek expressions that allow us to evaluate a total of five parameters: $\dot{m}_F$, $Y_{F,s}$, T_s, T_f, and r_f.

As an overview, the five relationships needed to solve for the five unknowns have their origins in the following: (1) an energy balance at the droplet surface, (2) an energy balance at the flame sheet, (3) the oxidizer distribution in the outer region, (4) the fuel vapor distribution in the inner region, and (5) phase equilibrium at the liquid–vapor interface expressed, for example, by the Clausius–Clapeyron relationship. Finally, knowing the instantaneous mass burning rate, droplet lifetimes will be calculated in the same manner as employed in our evaporation analysis. In the analysis, we will recover a D^2 law for burning droplets.

The problem of droplet combustion has been widely studied and has a very large literature associated with it, as evidenced by the reviews of the past few decades [13–17]. The physical model we describe here has its origins in the 1950s [18,19]. The solution approach taken here is not elegant. Our treatment, however, seeks to maintain a view of the physical processes at all times by retaining the important physical variables, temperature and species mass fractions. A more elegant approach, which is described in more-advanced textbooks, e.g., Ref. [20], combines the species and energy equations to create a conserved-scalar variable.

Mass Conservation

Overall mass conservation in the gas phase is described as in our previous development (Eqns. 10.1 and 10.2), i.e.,

$$\dot{m}(r) = \dot{m}_F = \text{constant.} \tag{10.1}$$

Note that the total flowrate is everywhere identical to the fuel flowrate, that is, the burning rate. This will be important in applying species conservation.

Species Conservation

INNER REGION. In the *inner region*, the important diffusing species is the *fuel vapor*. We can apply Fick's Law (Eqn. 3.5) to the inner region:

$$\dot{m}_A'' = Y_A\left(\dot{m}_A'' + \dot{m}_B''\right) - \rho D_{AB} \nabla Y_A \tag{3.5}$$

where the subscripts A and B here denote fuel and products, respectively:

$$\dot{m}_A'' \equiv \dot{m}_F'' = \dot{m}_F/4\pi r^2, \tag{10.24}$$

$$\dot{m}_B'' \equiv \dot{m}_{Pr}'' = 0, \tag{10.25}$$

and the ∇-operator in spherical coordinates, where the only variations are in the r-direction, is $\nabla(\ ) = d(\ )/dr$. Thus, Fick's Law is

$$\dot{m}_F = -4\pi r^2 \frac{\rho D}{1 - Y_F} \frac{dY_F}{dr}. \tag{10.26}$$

This first-order ordinary differential equation must satisfy two boundary conditions: at the droplet surface, liquid–vapor equilibrium prevails; thus,

$$Y_F(r_s) = Y_{F,s}(T_s), \tag{10.27a}$$

and at the flame, the fuel disappears, so

$$Y_F(r_f) = 0. \tag{10.27b}$$

The existence of two boundary conditions allows us to treat the burning rate, $\dot{m}_F$, as an eigenvalue, i.e., a parameter that can be calculated from the solution of Eqn. 10.26 subject to Eqns. 10.27a and b. Defining $Z_F \equiv 1/4\pi\rho D$, the general solution to Eqn. 10.26 is

$$Y_F(r) = 1 + C_1 \exp(-Z_F \dot{m}_F/r). \tag{10.28}$$

Applying the droplet surface condition (Eqn. 10.27a) to evaluate C_1, we obtain

$$Y_F(r) = 1 - \frac{(1 - Y_{F,s})\exp(-Z_F \dot{m}_F/r)}{\exp(-Z_F \dot{m}_F/r_s)}. \tag{10.29}$$

Applying the flame boundary condition (Eqn. 10.27b), we obtain a relationship involving the three unknowns $Y_{F,s}$, $\dot{m}_F$, and r_f:

$$Y_{F,s} = 1 - \frac{\exp(-Z_F \dot{m}_F/r_s)}{\exp(-Z_F \dot{m}_F/r_f)}. \tag{10.30}$$

Completing the species conservation solution in the inner region—although not necessary to accomplish our objective—the combustion product mass fraction can be expressed

$$Y_{Pr}(r) = 1 - Y_F(r). \tag{10.31}$$

OUTER REGION. In the *outer region*, the important diffusing species is the *oxidizer*, which is transported radially inward to the flame. At the flame, the oxidizer and fuel combine in stoichiometric proportions according to

$$1 \text{ kg fuel} + \nu \text{ kg oxidizer} = (\nu + 1) \text{ kg products}, \tag{10.32}$$

where ν is the stoichiometric (mass) ratio and includes any nonreacting gases that may be a part of the oxidizer stream. This relationship is illustrated in Fig. 10.11. The vector mass fluxes in Fick's Law are thus:

$$\dot{m}_A'' \equiv \dot{m}_{Ox}'' = -\nu \dot{m}_F'', \tag{10.33a}$$

$$\dot{m}_B'' \equiv \dot{m}_{Pr}'' = +(\nu + 1)\dot{m}_F''. \tag{10.33b}$$

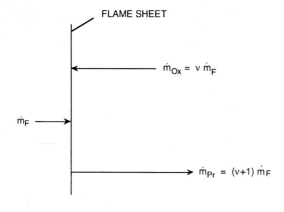

FLAME SHEET

$\dot{m}_{Ox} = \nu \, \dot{m}_F$

$\dot{m}_F$

$\dot{m}_{Pr} = (\nu+1) \, \dot{m}_F$

FIGURE 10.11
Mass flow relationships at flame sheet. Note that the net mass flow in both the inner and outer regions is equal to the fuel flowrate, $\dot{m}_F$.

Fick's Law in the outer region is thus,

$$\dot{m}_F = +4\pi r^2 \frac{\rho \mathcal{D}}{\nu + Y_{Ox}} \frac{d Y_{Ox}}{dr}, \tag{10.34}$$

with boundary conditions

$$Y_{Ox}(r_f) = 0. \tag{10.35a}$$

$$Y_{Ox}(r \to \infty) = Y_{Ox,\infty} \equiv 1. \tag{10.35b}$$

Integrating Eqn. 10.34 yields

$$Y_{Ox}(r) = -\nu + C_1 \exp(-Z_F \dot{m}_F/r). \tag{10.36}$$

Applying the flame condition (Eqn. 10.35a) to eliminate C_1 yields

$$Y_{Ox}(r) = \nu \left[\frac{\exp(-Z_F \dot{m}_F/r)}{\exp(-Z_F \dot{m}_F/r_f)} - 1 \right]. \tag{10.37}$$

Applying the condition at $r \to \infty$ (Eqn. 10.35b), we obtain an algebraic relation between the burning rate, $\dot{m}_F$, and the flame radius, r_f, i.e.,

$$\exp(+Z_F \dot{m}_F/r_f) = (\nu + 1)/\nu. \tag{10.38}$$

Complementing the oxidizer distribution (Eqn. 10.37), the product mass fraction distribution is

$$Y_{Pr}(r) = 1 - Y_{Ox}(r). \tag{10.39}$$

Energy Conservation

Again, we use the Shvab–Zeldovich form of the energy equation. Since we confine chemical reactions to occur at the boundary, i.e., the flame sheet, the reaction rate term is zero both inside the flame and outside the flame. Thus, the same energy equation that we developed for pure evaporation (Eqn. 10.4) also applies to the burning droplet:

$$\frac{d\left(r^2 \dfrac{dT}{dr}\right)}{dr} = \frac{\dot{m}_F c_{pg}}{4\pi k_g} \frac{dT}{dr}. \tag{10.4}$$

Again, for convenience, we define $Z_T = c_{pg}/4\pi k_g$; thus, our governing equation is

$$\frac{d\left(r^2 \dfrac{dT}{dr}\right)}{dr} = Z_T \dot{m}_F \frac{dT}{dr}. \tag{10.40}$$

As an aside, note that the parameter Z_F, defined in the species conservation analysis, equals Z_T when the Lewis number is unity, since, then, $c_{pg}/k_g = \rho D$. Since the form of Eqn. 10.4 is predicated on equal diffusivities for heat and mass, i.e., unity Lewis number (refer to the derivation of the Shvab–Zeldovich energy equation in Chapter 7), we require $Z_F = Z_T$.

The boundary conditions applied to Eqn. 10.40 are

$$\text{Inner region} \begin{cases} T(r_s) & = & T_s \tag{10.41a} \\ T(r_f) & = & T_f \tag{10.41b} \end{cases}$$

$$\text{Outer region} \begin{cases} T(r_f) & = & T_f \tag{10.41c} \\ T(r \to \infty) & = & T_\infty. \tag{10.41d} \end{cases}$$

Of the three temperatures, only T_∞ is considered to be known; T_s and T_f are two of the five unknowns in our problem.

TEMPERATURE DISTRIBUTIONS. The general solution to Eqn. 10.40 is

$$T(r) = \frac{C_1 \exp(-Z_T \dot{m}_F/r)}{Z_T \dot{m}_F} + C_2, \tag{10.42}$$

and in the *inner zone*, the temperature distribution resulting from application of Eqns. 10.41a and b is

$$T(r) = \frac{(T_s - T_f)\exp(-Z_T \dot{m}_F/r) + T_f\exp(-Z_T \dot{m}_F/r_s) - T_s \exp(-Z_T \dot{m}_F/r_f)}{\exp(-Z_T \dot{m}_F/r_s) - \exp(-Z_T \dot{m}_F/r_f)} \tag{10.43}$$

for $r_s \leq r \leq r_f$.

In the *outer region*, application of Eqns. 10.41c and d to Eqn. 10.42 yields

$$T(r) = \frac{(T_f - T_\infty)\exp(-Z_T \dot{m}_F/r) + \exp(-Z_T \dot{m}_F/r_f)T_\infty - T_f}{\exp(-Z_T \dot{m}_F/r_f) - 1}, \tag{10.44}$$

for $r_f < r < \infty$.

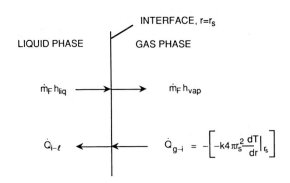

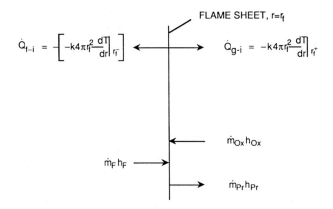

FIGURE 10.12
Surface energy balance at droplet liquid–vapor interface (top) and surface energy balance at flame sheet (bottom).

ENERGY BALANCE AT DROPLET SURFACE. Figure 10.12 shows the conduction heat transfer rates and the enthalpy fluxes at the surface of the evaporating droplet. Heat is conducted from the flame through the gas phase to the droplet surface. Some of this energy is used to vaporize fuel, with the remainder con- ducted into the droplet interior. Mathematically, this is expressed as

$$\dot{Q}_{g-i} = \dot{m}_F(h_{vap} - h_{liq}) + \dot{Q}_{i-\ell} \qquad (10.45a)$$

or

$$\dot{Q}_{g-i} = \dot{m}_F h_{fg} + \dot{Q}_{i-\ell}. \qquad (10.45b)$$

The heat conducted into the droplet interior, $\dot{Q}_{i-\ell}$, can be handled in several ways. One common approach is to model the droplet as consisting of two zones: an interior region existing uniformly at its initial temperature, T_0; and a thin surface layer at the surface temperature, T_s. For this so-called "onion-skin" model,

$$\dot{Q}_{i-\ell} = \dot{m}_F c_{p\ell}(T_s - T_0) \qquad (10.46)$$

is the energy required to heat up from T_0 to T_s the fuel that is vaporized. For convenience, we define

$$q_{i-\ell} \equiv \dot{Q}_{i-\ell}/\dot{m}_F, \qquad (10.47)$$

so for the *onion-skin model*,

$$q_{i-\ell} = c_{p\ell}(T_s - T_0) \qquad (10.48)$$

Another common treatment of $\dot{Q}_{i-\ell}$ is to assume that the droplet behaves as a lumped parameter, i.e., it has a uniform temperature, with a transient heat-up period. For the *lumped parameter*,

$$\dot{Q}_{i-\ell} = m_d c_{p\ell} \frac{dT_s}{dt}, \qquad (10.49)$$

and

$$q_{i-\ell} = \frac{m_d c_{p\ell}}{\dot{m}_F} \frac{dT_s}{dt} \qquad (10.50)$$

where m_d is the droplet mass. Implementation of the lumped-parameter model requires solving energy and mass conservation equations for the droplet as a whole in order to obtain dT_s/dt.

A third approach, and the simplest, is to assume the droplet rapidly heats up to a steady temperature, T_s. This, in effect, says the thermal inertia of the droplet is negligible. With this assumption of *negligible thermal inertia*,

$$q_{i-\ell} = 0. \qquad (10.51)$$

Returning to the surface energy balance expressed by Eqn. 10.45b, the conduction heat transfer from the gas phase, $\dot{Q}_{g-i}$, can be evaluated by applying Fourier's Law and using the temperature distribution in the inner region (Eqn. 10.43) to obtain the temperature gradient, i.e.,

$$-\left[-k_g 4\pi r^2 \frac{dT}{dr}\right]_{r_s} = \dot{m}_F(h_{fg} + q_{i-\ell}) \qquad (10.52)$$

where

$$\frac{dT}{dr} = \frac{(T_s - T_f)Z_T \dot{m}_F \exp(-Z_T \dot{m}_F/r)}{r^2[\exp(-Z_T \dot{m}_F/r_s) - \exp(-Z_T \dot{m}_F/r_f)]} \qquad (10.53)$$

for $r_s \leq r \leq r_f$.

Evaluating the heat-transfer rate at $r = r_s$, Eqn. 10.52 becomes, after rearranging and substituting the definition of Z_T,

$$\frac{c_{pg}(T_f - T_s)}{(q_{i-\ell} + h_{fg})} \frac{\exp(-Z_T \dot{m}_F/r_s)}{[\exp(-Z_T \dot{m}_F/r_s) - \exp(-Z_T \dot{m}_F/r_f)]} + 1 = 0. \qquad (10.54)$$

Equation 10.54 contains four unknowns: $\dot{m}_F, T_f, T_s$, and r_f.

ENERGY BALANCE AT FLAME SHEET. Referring to Fig. 10.12, we see how the various energy fluxes at the flame sheet relate. Since the flame temperature is the highest temperature in the system, heat is conducted both toward the droplet, $\dot{Q}_{f-i}$, and away to infinity, $\dot{Q}_{f-\infty}$. The chemical energy released at the flame is taken into account by using absolute enthalpy fluxes for the fuel, oxidizer, and products. A surface energy balance at the flame sheet can be written

$$\dot{m}_F h_F + \dot{m}_{Ox} h_{Ox} - \dot{m}_{Pr} h_{Pr} = \dot{Q}_{f-i} + \dot{Q}_{f-\infty}. \tag{10.55}$$

The enthalpies are defined as

$$h_F \equiv h_{f,F}^o + c_{pg}(T - T_{\text{ref}}), \tag{10.56a}$$

$$h_{Ox} \equiv h_{f,Ox}^o + c_{pg}(T - T_{\text{ref}}), \tag{10.56b}$$

$$h_{Pr} \equiv h_{f,Pr}^o + c_{pg}(T - T_{\text{ref}}), \tag{10.56c}$$

and the heat of combustion, Δh_c, per unit mass of fuel is given by

$$\Delta h_c(T_{\text{ref}}) = (1)h_{f,F}^o + (\nu)h_{f,Ox}^o - (1 + \nu)h_{f,Pr}^o. \tag{10.57}$$

The mass flowrates of fuel, oxidizer, and products are related by stoichiometry (cf. Eqns. 10.32 and 10.33a and b). Note that although products exist in the inner region, there is no net flow of products between the droplet surface and the flame; thus, all of the products flow radially outward away from the flame. Knowing this, Eqn. 10.55 becomes

$$\dot{m}_F[h_F + \nu h_{Ox} - (\nu + 1)h_{Pr}] = \dot{Q}_{f-i} + \dot{Q}_{f-\infty}. \tag{10.58}$$

Substituting Eqns. 10.56 and 10.57 into the above, yields

$$\dot{m}_F \Delta h_c + \dot{m}_F c_{pg}[(T_f - T_{\text{ref}}) + \nu(T_f - T_{\text{ref}}) - (\nu + 1)(T_f - T_{\text{ref}})] = \dot{Q}_{f-i} + \dot{Q}_{f-\infty}. \tag{10.59}$$

Since we assume that c_{pg} is constant, then Δh_c is independent of temperature; thus, we can choose the flame temperature as a reference state to simplify Eqn. 10.59:

$$\underset{\substack{\text{Rate at which chemical} \\ \text{energy is converted to} \\ \text{thermal energy at the flame}}}{\dot{m}_F \Delta h_c} \quad = \quad \underset{\substack{\text{Rate at which heat} \\ \text{is conducted away} \\ \text{from the flame}}}{\dot{Q}_{f-i} + \dot{Q}_{f-\infty}.} \tag{10.60}$$

Once again, we rely on Fourier's Law and the previously derived temperature distributions to evaluate the conduction heat-transfer terms, $\dot{Q}_{f-i}$ and $\dot{Q}_{f-\infty}$, i.e.,

$$\dot{m}_F \Delta h_c = k_g 4\pi r_f^2 \frac{dT}{dr}\bigg|_{r_f^-} - k_g 4\pi r_f^2 \frac{dT}{dr}\bigg|_{r_f^+}. \tag{10.61}$$

To evaluate the temperature gradient at $r = r_f^-$, we can employ Eqn. 10.53; for the gradient at $r = r_f^+$, the temperature distribution in the outer region is differentiated to yield

$$\frac{dT}{dr} = \frac{Z_T \dot{m}_F (T_\infty - T_f) \exp(-Z_T \dot{m}_F / r)}{r^2 [1 - \exp(-Z_T \dot{m}_F / r_f)]} \tag{10.62}$$

and evaluated at r_f^+. Performing these substitutions and rearranging, the flame sheet energy balance is finally expressed as

$$\frac{c_{pg}}{\Delta h_c} \left[\frac{(T_s - T_f) \exp(-Z_T \dot{m}_F / r_f)}{\exp(-Z_T \dot{m}_F / r_s) - \exp(-Z_T \dot{m}_F / r_f)} - \frac{(T_\infty - T_f) \exp(-Z_T \dot{m}_F / r_f)}{[1 - \exp(-Z_T \dot{m}_F / r_f)]} \right] - 1 = 0. \tag{10.63}$$

Equation 10.63 is a nonlinear algebraic relation involving the same four unknowns ($\dot{m}_F, T_f, T_s$, and r_f) that appear in Eqn. 10.54.

LIQUID–VAPOR EQUILIBRIUM. Thus far in our development, we have four equations and five unknowns. Assuming equilibrium between the liquid and vapor phases of the fuel at the surface, and applying the Calusius–Clapeyron equation, we obtain a fifth equation to provide closure to the problem. Of course, other, more accurate expressions could be used to express this equilibrium; however, the Clausius–Clapeyron approach is quite simple to apply. At the liquid–vapor interface, the partial pressure of the fuel vapor is given by

$$P_{F,s} = A \exp(-B / T_s) \tag{10.64}$$

where A and B are constants obtained from the Clausius–Clapeyron equation and take on different values for different fuels. The fuel partial pressure can be related to the fuel mole fraction and mass fraction as follows:

$$\chi_{F,s} = P_{F,s} / P \tag{10.65}$$

and

$$Y_{F,s} = \chi_{F,s} \frac{MW_F}{\chi_{F,s} MW_F + (1 - \chi_{F,s}) MW_{Pr}}. \tag{10.66}$$

Substituting Eqns. 10.64 and 10.65 into Eqn. 10.66 yields an explicit relation between $Y_{F,s}$ and T_s:

$$Y_{F,s} = \frac{A \exp(-B / T_s) MW_F}{A \exp(-B / T_s) MW_F + [P - A \exp(-B / T_s)] MW_{Pr}}. \tag{10.67}$$

This completes the mathematical description of our simplified droplet burning model. It is important to note that if we allow $T_f \to T_\infty$ and $r_f \to \infty$, we recover a pure evaporation model, but with coupled heat and mass-transfer effects, unlike the previous simple models that assume either heat or mass-transfer effects dominate.

Example 10.2. Determine the Clausius–Clapeyron constants, A and B, which appear in Eqn. 10.64, for n-hexane. The 1-atm boiling point for n-hexane is 342 K, its enthalpy of vaporization is 334,922 J/kg, and its molecular weight is 86.178.

Solution. For an ideal gas, the Clausius–Clapeyron relationship between vapor pressure and temperature is

$$\frac{dP_v}{dT} = \frac{P_v h_{fg}}{RT^2},$$

which can be separated and then integrated as follows:

$$\frac{dP_v}{P_v} = \frac{h_{fg}}{R} \frac{dT}{T^2}$$

and

$$\ln P_v = -\frac{h_{fg}}{R} \frac{1}{T} + C$$

or

$$P_v = \exp(C) \exp\left[\frac{-h_{fg}}{RT}\right].$$

Letting $P_v = 1$ atm and $T = T_{\text{boil}}$

$$\exp(C) = \exp\left[\frac{h_{fg}}{RT_{\text{boil}}}\right],$$

which we identify as the constant A. By inspection

$$B = h_{fg}/R.$$

We can now numerically evaluate A and B:

$$A = \exp\left[\frac{334,922}{\left(\dfrac{8315}{86.178}\right)342}\right]$$

$$\boxed{A = 25,580\,\text{atm}}$$

and

$$B = \frac{334,922}{\left(\dfrac{8315}{86.178}\right)}$$

$$\boxed{B = 3471.2\,\text{K}}.$$

Comments. For conditions not too far from the normal boiling point, the vapor pressure equation above, with the calculated values of A and B, should be a useful approximation.

TABLE 10.1
Summary of droplet burning model

Equation no.	Unknowns involved	Underlying physical principles
I (10.30)	$\dot{m}_F, r_f, Y_{F,s}$	Fuel species conservation in the inner region
II (10.38)	$\dot{m}_F, r_f$	Oxidizer species conservation in the outer region
III (10.54)	$\dot{m}_F, r_f, T_f, T_s$	Energy balance at droplet liquid–vapor interface
IV (10.63)	$\dot{m}_F, r_f, T_f, T_s$	Energy balance at flame sheet
V (10.67)	$T_s, Y_{F,s}$	Liquid–vapor phase equilibrium at interface with Clausius–Clapeyron applied

Summary and Solution

Table 10.1 summarizes the five equations that must be solved for the five unknowns: $\dot{m}_F, r_f, T_f, T_s$, and $Y_{F,s}$. The system of nonlinear equations can be reduced to a useful level by simultaneously solving Eqns. II, III, IV for $\dot{m}_F, r_f$, and T_f, treating T_s as a known parameter for the time being. Following this procedure, the burning rate is

$$\dot{m}_F = \frac{4\pi k_g r_s}{c_{pg}} \ln\left[1 + \frac{\Delta h_c/\nu + c_{pg}(T_\infty - T_s)}{q_{i-\ell} + h_{fg}}\right], \tag{10.68a}$$

or in terms of the **transfer number, $B_{o,q}$**, defined as

$$B_{o,q} = \frac{\Delta h_c/\nu + c_{pg}(T_\infty - T_s)}{q_{i-\ell} + h_{fg}}, \tag{10.68b}$$

$$\dot{m}_F = \frac{4\pi k_g r_s}{c_{pg}} \ln(1 + B_{o,q}). \tag{10.68c}$$

The flame temperature is

$$T_f = \frac{q_{i-\ell} + h_{fg}}{c_{pg}(1 + \nu)} [\nu B_{o,q} - 1] + T_s, \tag{10.69}$$

and the flame radius is

$$r_f = r_s \frac{\ln[1 + B_{o,q}]}{\ln[(\nu + 1)/\nu]}. \tag{10.70}$$

The fuel mass fraction at the droplet surface is

$$Y_{F,s} = \frac{B_{o,q} - 1/\nu}{B_{o,q} + 1}. \tag{10.71}$$

Equations 10.68–10.71 can all be evaluated for an assumed value of T_s. Equation V (10.67) can be used to provide an improved value for T_s (shown below as Eqn. 10.72, where T_s has been isolated on the left-hand-side) and then Eqns. 10.68–10.71 can be re-evaluated and the process repeated until convergence is obtained.

$$T_s = \frac{-B}{\ln \left[\dfrac{-Y_{F,s}PMW_{Pr}}{A(Y_{F,s}MW_F - Y_{F,s}MW_{Pr} - MW_F)} \right]} . \qquad (10.72)$$

As in our pure evaporation analysis, if we assume the fuel is at the boiling point, the problem is greatly simplified. With this assumption, Eqns. 10.68–10.70 are used to find $\dot{m}_F$, T_f, and r_f without iteration, and Eqn. 10.71 is irrelevant since $Y_{F,s}$ is unity when $T_s = T_{boil}$. This is a reasonable assumption when the droplet is burning vigorously after its initial heat-up transient.

Burning Rate Constant and Droplet Lifetimes

The droplet mass burning rate in terms of the transfer number, $B_{o,q}$, expressed by Eqn. 10.68c, is of identical form to the expression derived for the evaporation rate (cf. Eqn. 10.13). Thus, without further development we can immediately define the **burning rate constant, K**, as

$$K = \frac{8k_g}{\rho_\ell c_{pg}} \ln(1 + B_{o,q}). \qquad (10.73)$$

The burning rate constant is truly a constant only after a steady-state surface temperature is reached, since, then, $B_{o,q}$ is a constant.

Assuming the transient heat-up period is small in comparison to the droplet lifetime, we recover once again a **D^2 law** for droplet burning:

$$D^2(t) = D_0^2 - Kt \qquad (10.74)$$

where the droplet lifetime is found by letting $D^2(t_d) = 0$, i.e.,

$$t_d = D_0^2/K. \qquad (10.75)$$

Figure 10.13 shows that the D^2 law is a good representation of experimental results [21] after the heat-up transient.

As with the pure evaporation problem, we need to define appropriate values of the properties c_{pg}, k_g, and ρ_ℓ that appear in Eqn. 10.73. Law and Williams [11] suggest the following empiricism:

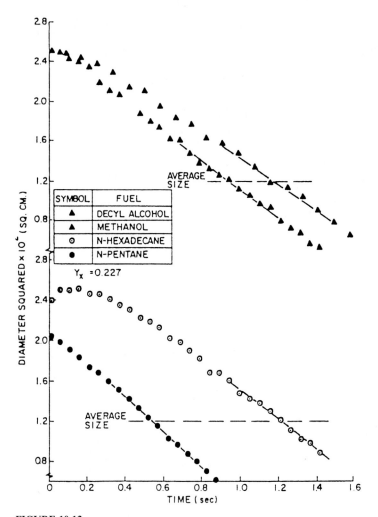

FIGURE 10.13
Experimental data for burning droplets illustrating D^2 law behavior after initial transient. (Reprinted from Ref. [21] with permission, ©1971, AIAA.)

$$c_{pg} = c_{pF}(\bar{T}),\qquad(10.76a)$$

$$k_g = 0.4k_F(\bar{T}) + 0.6k_{Ox}(\bar{T}),\qquad(10.76b)$$

$$\rho_\ell = \rho_\ell(T_s),\qquad(10.76c)$$

where

$$\bar{T} = 0.5(T_s + T_f).\qquad(10.76d)$$

Example 10.3. Consider the combustion of an n-heptane (C_7H_{16}) droplet when its diameter is $100 \, \mu m$. Determine (A) the mass burning rate, (B) the flame temperature, and (C) the ratio of the flame radius to the droplet radius for $P = 1$ atm and $T_\infty = 300$ K. Assume quiescent surroundings and that the droplet is at its boiling point.

Solution. We will employ Eqns. 10.68, 10.69, and 10.70 to find $\dot{m}_F$, T_f, and r_f/r_s, respectively. Our first task will be to determine values for the average properties required (Eqn. 10.76). From our knowledge of Chapter 2, we guess that the flame temperature will be about 2200 K; thus,

$$\bar{T} = 0.5(T_s + T_f) = 0.5\,(371.5 + 2200) \cong 1285 \text{ K}$$

where $T_{\text{boil}}(= T_s)$ was obtained from Table B.1.
From Appendices B and C, we obtain

$$k_{Ox}(\bar{T}) = 0.081 \text{ W/m-K} \qquad \text{(Table C.1)}$$

$$k_F(\bar{T}) = k_F(1000 \text{ K})\left(\frac{\bar{T}}{1000 \text{ K}}\right)^{1/2}$$

$$= 0.0971\left(\frac{1285}{1000}\right)^{1/2} = 0.110 \text{ W/m-K}, \qquad \text{(Table B.3)}$$

where we use the $T^{1/2}$-dependence (cf. Eqn. 3.27) to extrapolate from 1000 K to 1285 K. Thus,

$$k_g = 0.4\,(0.110) + 0.6\,(0.081) = 0.0926 \text{ W/m-K}$$

and

$$c_{p,F}(\bar{T}) = 4.22 \text{ kJ/kg-K} \qquad \text{(Table B.3)}$$

$$h_{fg}(T_{\text{boil}}) = 316 \text{ kJ/kg} \qquad \text{(Table B.1)}$$

$$\Delta h_c = 44{,}926 \text{ kJ/kg.} \qquad \text{(Table B.1)}$$

The stoichiometric air–fuel ratio, ν, is (Eqns. 2.31 and 2.32)

$$\nu = (x + y/4)4.76\frac{MW_{Ox}}{MW_F}$$

$$= (7 + 16/4)\,(4.76)\frac{28.85}{100.20} = 15.08.$$

We can now evaluate the transfer number, $B_{o,q}$,

$$B_{o,q} = \frac{\Delta h_c/\nu + c_{pg}(T_\infty - T_s)}{q_{i-\ell} + h_{fg}}$$

$$= \frac{\dfrac{44{,}926}{15.08} + 4.22\,(300 - 371.5)}{0 + 316} = 8.473,$$

where droplet heating is ignored ($q_{i-\ell} = 0$).

A. The mass burning rate is found from (Eqn. 10.68):

$$\dot{m}_F = \frac{4\pi k_g r_s}{c_{pg}} \ln(1 + B_{o,q})$$

$$= \frac{4\pi 0.0926 \left(\dfrac{100 \cdot 10^{-6}}{2} \right)}{4220} \ln(1 + 8.473)$$

$$\boxed{\dot{m}_F = 3.10 \cdot 10^{-8} \, \text{kg/s}} \, .$$

B. To find the flame temperature, we evaluate (Eqn. 10.69):

$$T_f = \frac{q_{i-\ell} + h_{fg}}{c_{pg}(1 + \nu)} (\nu B_{o,q} - 1) + T_s$$

$$= \frac{0 + 316}{4.22 \, (1 + 15.08)} [15.08 \, (8.473) - 1] + 371.5$$

$$= 590.4 + 371.5$$

$$\boxed{T_f = 961.8 \, \text{K}} \, .$$

This value is quite low. See comments below.

C. The dimensionless flame radius can be calculated from (Eqn. 10.70):

$$\frac{r_f}{r_s} = \frac{\ln[1 + B_{o,q}]}{\ln[(\nu + 1)/\nu]} = \frac{\ln[1 + 8.473]}{\ln(16.08/15.08)}$$

$$\boxed{\frac{r_f}{r_s} = 35} \, .$$

Comments. We note that the calculated temperature is much less than our guess of 2200 K! Unfortunately, the problem is not with our guess, but, rather, with the simplified theory. The choice of $c_{pg} = c_{pF}(\bar{T})$ does a good job at predicting $\dot{m}_F$; however, the large value $(c_{pF} = 4.22 \, \text{kJ/kg-K})$ is inappropriate for calculating T_f. A more reasonable choice would be to use a value that is typical of air (or products). For example, using $c_{pg}(\bar{T}) = c_{p,\text{air}} = 1.187 \, \text{kJ/kg-K}$, yields $T_f = 2470 \, \text{K}$, a much more reasonable temperature.

Experimental values of dimensionless flame radii (~ 10) are considerably smaller than that calculated above. Law [15] indicates that fuel-vapor accumulation effects account for the difference. In spite of the shortcomings of the theory, useful estimates of burning rates and droplet lifetimes are obtained.

Example 10.4. Determine the lifetime of the 100-μm-diameter n-heptane droplet from Example 10.3. How does the result compare with that for pure vaporization (no flame) with $T_\infty = 2200 \, \text{K}$?

Solution. We first evaluate the burning rate constant using a liquid density of 684 kg/m^3 (Table B.1):

$$K = \frac{8k_g}{\rho_\ell c_{pg}} \ln(1 + B_{o,q})$$

$$= \frac{8\,(0.0926)}{684\,(4220)} \ln(1 + 8.473) = 5.77 \cdot 10^{-7}\, \text{m}^2/\text{s}.$$

The lifetime of the burning droplet is then (Eqn. 10.75)

$$t_d = D_0^2/K = (100 \cdot 10^{-6})^2/5.77 \cdot 10^{-7}$$

$$\boxed{t_d = 0.0173\, \text{s}}\,.$$

For the pure evaporation problem, we use the same expression to evaluate K and t_d; however, the transfer number is now expressed (Eqn. 10.12):

$$B = \frac{c_{pg}(T_\infty - T_{\text{boil}})}{h_{fg}}$$

$$= \frac{4.220\,(2200 - 371.5)}{316} = 24.42.$$

The evaporation rate constant is then $K = 8.30 \cdot 10^{-7}\, \text{m}^2/\text{s}$ and the droplet lifetime is

$$\boxed{t_d = 0.0120\, \text{s}}\,.$$

Comments. We expect that the droplet lifetime should be longer for the pure evaporation case when $T_f = T_\infty$; however, the "theoretical" flame temperature of 961.8 K (Example 10.2) is much less than the 2200 K ambient. Using the pure evaporation model with $T_\infty = 961.8$ K, yields a predicted droplet lifetime of 0.0178 s, which is slightly longer than that for the burning droplet, as expected.

Extension to Convective Environments

To achieve the conditions of spherically symmetric burning in a stagnant medium, as assumed in our analysis above, requires no relative velocity between the droplet and the free stream, and no buoyancy. This latter condition can only be achieved in the absence of gravity or in a weightless freefall. Interest in buoyancy-free combustion has a long history, e.g. Refs [22–24], while a renewed interest has been shown with the advent of the space shuttle and the anticipation of a permanent space station in low-earth orbit [25–28].

There are several approaches to incorporating convection in the droplet-burning problem [13–17]. The approach taken here is that of chemical engineering "film theory". This approach is straightforward and in keeping with our desire for simplicity.

The essence of film theory is the replacement of the heat and mass transfer boundary conditions at infinity with the same conditions moved inward to the

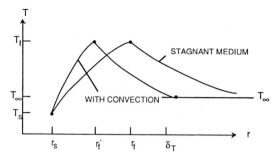

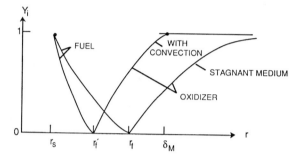

FIGURE 10.14

Comparison of temperature and species profiles with and without convection. Theoretical film thicknesses are indicated by δ_T (temperature) and δ_M (species).

so-called film radius, δ_M for species, and δ_T for energy. Figure 10.14 illustrates how the film radius steepens concentration and temperature gradients, and, hence, increases mass- and heat-transfer rates at the droplet surface. This, of course, means that convection enhances droplet burning rates and, as a result, burning times decrease.

The film radii are defined in terms of the **Nusselt number, Nu,** for heat transfer, and the **Sherwood number, Sh,** for mass transfer. Physically, the Nusselt number is the dimensionless temperature gradient at the droplet surface, and the Sherwood number is the dimensionless concentration (mass fraction) gradient at the surface. Formally, the film radii are given by

$$\frac{\delta_T}{r_s} = \frac{Nu}{Nu - 2}, \tag{10.77a}$$

$$\frac{\delta_M}{r_s} = \frac{Sh}{Sh - 2}. \tag{10.77b}$$

Note that for a stagnant medium, $Nu = 2$; thus, we recover $\delta_T \to \infty$ in the absence of convection. Consistent with the unity Lewis number assumption, we assume $Sh = Nu$. For droplet burning with forced convection, Faeth [13] recommends the following correlation to evaluate Nu:

$$Nu = 2 + \frac{0.555 \, Re^{1/2} \, Pr^{1/3}}{[1 + 1.232/(RePr^{4/3})]^{1/2}}, \tag{10.78}$$

where the Reynolds number, Re, is based on the droplet diameter and the relative velocity. For simplicity, thermophysical properties can be evaluated at the mean temperature (Eqn. 10.76d).

In terms of the basic conservation principles, convection affects the species conservation relations in the outer region (oxidizer distribution, Eqns. 10.37 and 10.38), and the energy conservation relations that involve the outer region (T-distribution in the outer region, Eqn. 10.44, and the energy balance at the flame sheet, Eqn. 10.63).

Application of the film-theory boundary condition for species conservation,

$$Y_{Ox}(\delta_M) = 1,\qquad(10.79)$$

to Eqn. 10.37, yields

$$\frac{\exp[-Z_M \dot{m}_F/[r_s Nu/(Nu-2)]]}{\exp(-Z_M \dot{m}_F/r_f)} - \frac{\nu+1}{\nu} = 0.\qquad(10.80)$$

Equation 10.80 (with convection) above is equivalent to Eqn. 10.38 (without convection).

Application of the film-theory boundary condition for energy conservation,

$$T(\delta_T) = T_\infty,\qquad(10.81)$$

to Eqn. 10.40 yields the outer-zone temperature distribution

$$T(r) = [(T_\infty - T_f)\exp(-Z_T \dot{m}_F/r) + T_\infty \exp(-Z_T \dot{m}_F/r_f)$$
$$-T_f \exp(-Z_T \dot{m}_F(Nu-2)/r_s Nu)]/[\exp(-Z_T \dot{m}_F/r_f) - \exp(-Z_T \dot{m}_F(Nu-2)/r_s Nu)].$$
$$(10.82)$$

Using Eqn. 10.82 to evaluate the energy balance at the flame (Eqn. 10.61), yields

$$\frac{c_{pg}}{\Delta h_c}\left[\frac{(T_f - T_s)\exp(-Z_T \dot{m}_F/r_f)}{\exp(-Z_T \dot{m}_F/r_f) - \exp(-Z_T \dot{m}_F/r_s)}\right.$$
$$\left. - \frac{(T_f - T_\infty)\exp(-Z_T \dot{m}_F/r_f)}{\exp(-Z_T \dot{m}_F/r_f) - \exp(-Z_T \dot{m}_F(Nu-2)/r_s Nu)}\right] - 1 = 0,\qquad(10.83)$$

which is the film-theory equivalent to Eqn. 10.54 for the stagnant case.

We now, once again, have a system of five nonlinear algebraic equations involving the five unknowns $\dot{m}_F$, T_f, r_f, $Y_{F,s}$, and T_s (cf. Table 10.1). Simultaneously solving for three of these, $\dot{m}_F$, T_f, and r_f, gives the burning rate

$$\dot{m}_F = \frac{2\pi k_g r_s Nu}{c_{pg}}\ln\left[1 + \frac{\Delta h_c/\nu + c_{pg}(T_\infty - T_s)}{q_{i-\ell} + h_{fg}}\right],\qquad(10.84a)$$

or

$$\dot{m}_F = \frac{2\pi k_g r_s Nu}{c_{pg}}\ln(1 + B_{o,q})\qquad(10.84b)$$

where the transfer number has been introduced (cf. Eqn. 10.68b). Note that this expression (Eqn. 10.84b) differs from that for the stagnant case (Eqn. 10.68c) only by the explicit appearance of the Nusselt number. In the stagnant flow case, $Nu = 2$, and the two expressions are identical, as expected.

MORE-ADVANCED APPROACHES

There are many complicating features of real burning droplets that are ignored in the simplified theory presented above. It is beyond the scope of this book to discuss any of the topics in detail; instead, we merely list some of them and cite a few references to provide starting points for further study.

In the simplified model, all properties are treated as constants, and a judicious selection of mean values is used to provide agreement with experiment. In reality, many of the properties possess strong temperature and/or composition dependencies. Various approaches have been taken to include **variable properties**, with, perhaps, the most comprehensive treatment found in Refs. [29] and [30]. Reference [12] compares various simplified approaches with comprehensive numerical results. Also related to the issue of variable properties is the correct formulation of the conservation equations when the ambient temperature and/or pressure exceeds the thermodynamic critical point of the evaporating liquid. This is an important issue for modeling burning droplets in both diesel and rocket engines. More information on **supercritical droplet combustion and evaporation** can be found in Refs. [31] and [32].

The unrealistically large flame stand-off distances predicted by the D^2 law (see Example 10.3) are shown by Law *et al.* [33] to be a result of neglecting the unsteady effect of **fuel vapor accumulation** between the droplet surface and the flame. Inclusion of this effect in a modified D^2-law model results in capturing the flame movement observed in experiments [15,33].

More sophisticated models of **droplet heating** have also been developed that take into account the time-varying temperature field within the droplet [34]. Proper treatment of the liquid phase is important in the evaporation and combustion of **multi-component fuel** droplets [35,36]. Related to this issue is the shear-driven fluid motion within droplets in a convective environment, i.e., **internal recirculation** [16,36].

More recent approaches to single droplet gasification include numerical models that treat the problem in its appropriate axisymmetric coordinate system. This approach incorporates the effects of convection directly, rather than as an ad-hoc modification to assumed spherical symmetry [36].

Finally, we come to the issue of **interactions among multiple droplets**, as would be present in a fuel spray. Spray evaporation and combustion is of great practical importance and has a huge literature associated with it. Useful starting points for further study of sprays are Refs. [14,20,37]. A primary issue in spray combustion is the coupling of the variable ambient conditions, to which a droplet is exposed during its lifetime, and the droplet evaporation rate.

ONE-DIMENSIONAL VAPORIZATION-CONTROLLED COMBUSTION

In this section, we will apply the concepts developed above to the analysis of a simple, one-dimensional, steady-flow, liquid-fuel combustor. This section stands alone in that it is a large-scale example of how droplet evaporation and equilibrium concepts (Chapter 2) can be combined to model spray combustors, such as are used in gas-turbine and rocket engines (cf. Figs. 10.4a and 10.5), and brings together the previously developed theory and applications, albeit in a simplified fashion. Since the primary objective of this section is to provide a framework from which various design problems or projects can be developed, no new fundamental combustion concepts are introduced here; therefore, depending on the reader's objectives, this section can be skipped without jeopardizing understanding of subsequent chapters.

Physical Model

Figure 10.15a schematically illustrates a simple combustor with a constant cross-sectional area. Fuel droplets, uniformly distributed across the combustor, evaporate as they move downstream in an oxidizer stream. The fuel vapor is assumed to mix with the gas phase and burn instantaneously. This causes the gas temperature to rise, speeding the vaporization of the droplets. The gas velocity increases because droplet vaporization, and, possibly, secondary oxidizer addition, add mass to the gas phase, and because combustion decreases the gas density.

Obviously, the model discussed above neglects many detailed phenomena occurring in a real combustor; however, for flows without recirculation and backmixing, or downstream of such regions, the model is a useful first approximation when mixing and burning rates are substantially faster than fuel vaporization rates. Priem and Heidmann [38] and Dipprey [7] have applied one-dimensional, vaporization-controlled models to liquid-rocket engine combustion, and Turns and Faeth [39] have used the approach to model slurry-fuel combustion in a gas-turbine combustor. In the following sections, we develop the analysis of a one-dimensional combustor that can be easily implemented in a computer code.

Assumptions

The following assumptions will be embodied in our simple analysis of a liquid-fueled combustor:

1. The system comprises only two phases: a gas phase, consisting of combustion products; and a liquid, single-component fuel phase.
2. The properties of the gas phase and liquid phase depend only on the coordinate in the flow direction, i.e., the flow is one-dimensional. This implies that the gas phase has uniform properties in the radial direction perpendicular to

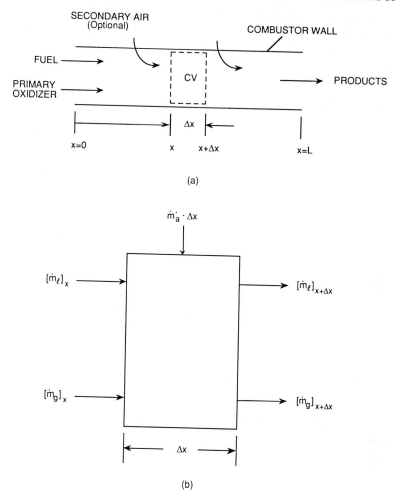

SECONDARY AIR
(Optional)

COMBUSTOR WALL

FUEL

PRIMARY
OXIDIZER

CV

PRODUCTS

Δx

$x=0$ x $x+\Delta x$ $x=L$

(a)

$\dot{m}_a' \cdot \Delta x$

$[\dot{m}_\ell]_x$ $[\dot{m}_\ell]_{x+\Delta x}$

$[\dot{m}_g]_x$ $[\dot{m}_g]_{x+\Delta x}$

Δx

(b)

FIGURE 10.15
(a) Overall schematic of one-dimensional combustor with (b) details of control-volume analysis for overall mass conservation.

the flow at any axial position, x. Furthermore, we neglect diffusion, even though axial concentration gradients exist.

3. The effects of friction and velocity changes on pressure are neglected. This implies the pressure is constant, i.e., $dP/dx = 0$, and simplifies the vaporization problem.

4. The fuel is introduced as a stream of monodisperse droplets, i.e., all droplets have the same diameter and velocity at any axial location.

5. The droplets in the stream all obey the droplet evaporation theory presented earlier in Chapter 10, with the droplet temperature assumed fixed at the boiling point.

6. The gas-phase properties are determined by equilibrium or, alternatively, by the even simpler no-dissociation model with water-gas equilibrium (cf. Chapter 2).

Mathematical Problem Statement

Given a set of initial conditions for the gas phase and the liquid phase, we wish to determine the following functions:

gas phase:
$T_g(x)$, temperature
$\dot{m}_g(x)$, mass flowrate
$\Phi_g(x)$, equivalence ratio
$v_g(x)$, velocity

liquid phase:
$D(x)$, droplet diameter
$\dot{m}_\ell(x)$, fuel evaporation rate
$v_d(x)$, droplet velocity

In the section below, we apply the basic conservation principles (mass, momentum, and energy conservation) to determine the desired functions listed above.

Analysis

For this problem, we choose a steady-state, steady-flow, control-volume analysis. The selected control volume extends across the combustor and is Δx in length (Fig. 10.15a).

MASS CONSERVATION. Figure 10.15b shows the mass flows of both the liquid and gas phases into and out of the control volume. Since there is no change in mass within the control volume, the total mass flows entering and exiting the control volume are equal:

$$[\dot{m}_\ell]_x + [\dot{m}_g]_x + \dot{m}'_a \cdot \Delta x = [\dot{m}_\ell]_{x+\Delta x} + [\dot{m}_g]_{x+\Delta x}$$

where $\dot{m}_\ell$ and $\dot{m}_g$ are the mass flowrates (kg/s) of the liquid and gas phases, respectively, and $\dot{m}'_a$ is the mass flow of secondary oxidizer per unit length (kg/s-m) entering the control volume. We assume that $\dot{m}'_a$ is a given function of x.

Rearranging the above, we obtain

$$\frac{[\dot{m}_\ell]_{x+\Delta x} - [\dot{m}_\ell]_x}{\Delta x} + \frac{[\dot{m}_g]_{x+\Delta x} - [\dot{m}_g]_x}{\Delta x} = \dot{m}'_a.$$

Taking the limit of $\Delta x \to 0$ and recognizing the definition of a derivative, we obtain the following governing equation for conservation of total mass:

$$\frac{d\dot{m}_\ell}{dx} + \frac{d\dot{m}_g}{dx} = \dot{m}'_a. \tag{10.85}$$

Equation 10.85 can be integrated to provide an expression for $\dot{m}_g(x)$,

$$\dot{m}_g(x) = \dot{m}_g(0) + \dot{m}_\ell(0) - \dot{m}_\ell(x) + \int_0^x \dot{m}_a' dx. \qquad (10.86)$$

We next focus solely on the liquid phase; thus, the control volume shown in Fig. 10.16a contains only liquid. The $\dot{m}_{\ell g}'$ term is the mass flowrate of fuel per unit length going from the liquid phase into the gas phase, i.e., the fuel vaporization rate. Thus, the rate at which liquid fuel exits the control volume at $x + \Delta x$ is less than that entering at x by the amount $\dot{m}_{\ell g}' \Delta x$, i.e.,

$$[\dot{m}_\ell]_x - [\dot{m}_\ell]_{x+\Delta x} = \dot{m}_{\ell g}' \cdot \Delta x.$$

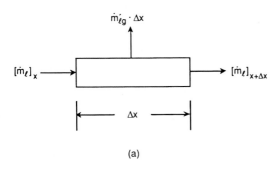

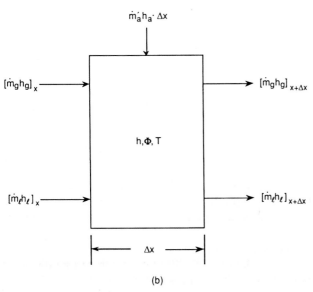

FIGURE 10.16
Control-volume analysis for (a) fuel mass conservation and (b) overall energy conservation.

Rearranging and taking the limit $\Delta x \rightarrow 0$, yields,

$$\frac{dm_\ell}{dx} = -\dot{m}'_{\ell g}.$$

The flowrate of liquid through the combustor can be related to the number of fuel droplets entering the chamber per unit time, $\dot{N}$, and the mass of an individual droplet, m_d. Thus,

$$\dot{m}_\ell = \dot{N}m_d, \tag{10.87}$$

or

$$\dot{m}_\ell = \dot{N}\rho_\ell \pi D^3 / 6, \tag{10.88}$$

where ρ_ℓ and D are the droplet density and diameter, respectively.

Differentiating Eqn. 10.88, we obtain

$$\frac{d\dot{m}_\ell}{dx} = (\pi/4)\dot{N}\rho_\ell D \frac{dD^2}{dx}. \tag{10.89}$$

The derivative of D^2 with respect to x can be related to the time derivative through the droplet velocity v_d, i.e., $dx = v_d dt$; thus,

$$\frac{dD^2}{dx} = \frac{1}{v_d}\frac{dD^2}{dt}. \tag{10.90}$$

In an earlier section, we derived an expression for dD^2/dt. Substituting Eqn. 10.17 into Eqn. 10.90 yields

$$\frac{dD^2}{dx} = -K/v_d, \tag{10.91}$$

where K is the evaporation coefficient (cf. Eqn. 10.18).

The number of droplets entering the combustor per unit time is easily related to the initial fuel flowrate and the assumed initial droplet size, D_0, i.e.,

$$\dot{m}_{\ell,0} = \dot{N}\rho_\ell \pi D_0^3 / 6, \tag{10.92a}$$

or

$$\dot{N} = 6\dot{m}_{\ell,0} / (\pi\rho_\ell D_0^3). \tag{10.92b}$$

The above mass conservation analysis provides a single ordinary differential equation, Eqn. 10.91, which, when solved, yields $D^2(x)$ or $D(x)$. Knowing the droplet diameter, $\dot{m}_g$ can be calculated using Eqn. 10.86 and appropriate ancillary relations.

To find the droplet velocity as a function of axial distance, $v_d(x)$, requires application of conservation of momentum to a droplet, which will be discussed subsequently. The velocity of the gas phase can be written as

$$v_g = \dot{m}_g / \rho_g A, \tag{10.93}$$

where ρ_g is the gas-phase density, and A is the cross-sectional area of the combustor. The density can be related to the gas temperature and pressure through the ideal-gas law:

$$\rho_g = P/R_g T_g, \tag{10.94}$$

where

$$R_g = R_u/MW_g. \tag{10.95}$$

Gas-phase energy conservation is required to find T_g, and since the composition of the gas phase is continually varying as we move downstream, the molecular weight, MW_g, is a variable as well. Substituting Eqns. 10.94 and 10.95 into Eqn. 10.93 yields

$$v_g = \dot{m}_g R_u T_g / (MW_g PA). \tag{10.96}$$

GAS-PHASE ENERGY CONSERVATION. With reference to Fig. 10.16b, and following the same procedures used to derive the mass conservation relationships, conservation of energy for the control volume is expressed

$$\frac{d(\dot{m}_g h_g)}{dx} + \frac{d(\dot{m}_\ell h_\ell)}{dx} = \dot{m}'_a h_a, \tag{10.97}$$

where we assume no heat of work interactions. Expanding the derivatives of the products and recognizing that the enthalpy of the liquid is a constant, Eqn. 10.97 becomes, after rearrangement,

$$\frac{dh_g}{dx} = \left[\dot{m}'_a h_a - h_g \frac{d\dot{m}_g}{dx} - h_\ell \frac{d\dot{m}_\ell}{dx} \right] / \dot{m}_g. \tag{10.98}$$

Since we are interested in finding the temperature distribution, $T(x)$, the enthalpy can be related to the temperature and the other thermodynamic variables:

$$h_g = f(T_g, P_g, \Phi_g), \tag{10.99}$$

where the relationships among these variables are determined by equilibrium. Applying the chain rule, recognizing that P_g is constant, dh_g/dx can be expressed

$$\frac{dh_g}{dx} = \frac{\partial h_g}{\partial T} \frac{dT}{dx} + \frac{\partial h_g}{\partial \Phi} \frac{d\Phi}{dx}, \tag{10.100}$$

where the subscript g has been dropped from T and Φ.

Equating the right-hand-sides of Eqns. 10.98 and 10.100, and solving for dT/dx, yields

$$\frac{dT}{dx} = \left[\left(\dot{m}'_a h_a - h_g \frac{d\dot{m}_g}{dx} - h_\ell \frac{d\dot{m}_\ell}{dx} \right) \Big/ \dot{m}_g - \frac{\partial h_g}{\partial \Phi} \frac{d\Phi}{dx} \right] \Big/ \frac{\partial h_g}{\partial T}. \tag{10.101}$$

The gas enthalpy, h_g and its partial derivatives, $\partial h_g/\partial T$ and $\partial h_g/\partial \Phi$, can all be calculated knowing the equilibrium state at T, P, and Φ. The Olikara and Borman [40] equilibrium code (see Appendix F) can be employed to perform these calculations. Equation 10.101 can be simplified further by using Eqn. 10.85 to eliminate $d\dot{m}_g/dx$, i.e.,

$$\frac{dT}{dx} = \left\{ \left[(h_a - h_s)\dot{m}_a' + (h_g - h_\ell)\frac{d\dot{m}_\ell}{dx} \right] \bigg/ \dot{m}_g - \frac{\partial h_g}{\partial \Phi}\frac{d\Phi}{dx} \right\} \bigg/ \frac{\partial h_g}{\partial T}. \qquad (10.102)$$

To maintain perspective on where we have been and where we are going, a brief summary is helpful at this point in our analysis. So far, we have derived first-order ordinary differential equations giving expressions for dD^2/dx and dT_g/dx. These equations can be integrated (numerically) to yield $D(x)$ and $T_g(x)$ for given initial conditions. It remains for us to determine expressions for Φ and $d\Phi/dx$, and to derive one more differential equation that can be integrated to find the droplet velocity, $v_d(x)$.

GAS-PHASE COMPOSITION. Our goal here is to determine the axial distribution of the equivalence ratio, $\Phi(x)$. This calculation is just a subset of mass conservation, since all that is required is a knowledge of the mass of the fuel and oxidizer at any axial location.

Assume that at $x = 0$, the chamber entrance, there is an initial gas-phase flow. This flow may be a burned or unburned mixture of oxidizer and fuel (or pure oxidizer or pure fuel), and can be expressed

$$\dot{m}_g(0) = \dot{m}_F(0) + \dot{m}_a(0). \qquad (10.103)$$

The fuel–oxidizer ratio at an arbitrary position, x, downstream, is just the ratio of the mass flow of the gas phase that had its origin as fuel, to the mass flow of the gas phase that had its origin as oxidizer:

$$(F/O)_x = \frac{\dot{m}_{F,x}}{\dot{m}_{a,x}} = \frac{\dot{m}_g(x) - \dot{m}_{a,0} - \int_0^x \dot{m}_a' dx}{\dot{m}_{a,0} + \int_0^x \dot{m}_a' dx}. \qquad (10.104a)$$

Equation 10.104a can be rearranged to yield,

$$(F/O)_x = \dot{m}_g \left[\dot{m}_{a,0} + \int_0^x \dot{m}_a' dx \right]^{-1} - 1, \qquad (10.104b)$$

which, when differentiated with respect to x, becomes

$$\frac{d(F/O)_x}{dx} = \frac{d\dot{m}_g}{dx} \left[\dot{m}_{a,0} + \int_0^x \dot{m}_a' dx \right]^{-1} - \dot{m}_g \dot{m}_a' \left[\dot{m}_{a,0} + \int_0^x \dot{m}_a' dx \right]^{-2}. \qquad (10.105)$$

The equivalence ratio and its derivative are then easily obtained by definition:

$$\Phi(x) \equiv (F/O)_x / (F/O)_{\Phi=1} \qquad (10.106)$$

and

$$\frac{d\Phi(x)}{dx} = \frac{1}{(F/O)_{\Phi=1}} \frac{d(F/O)_x}{dx},$$ (10.107)

where we assume that the fuel entering the chamber in the gas phase $(\dot{m}_F(0))$ has the same hydrogen-to-carbon ratio as the injected liquid fuel $(\dot{m}_\ell(0))$. If this is not true, then $(F/O)_{\Phi=1}$ varies through the chamber, and this variation would have to be taken into account.

DROPLET MOMENTUM CONSERVATION. Fuel droplets initially injected at high velocities into the lower-velocity gas stream will slow down because of drag. As the fuel evaporates and burns, the velocity of the gas increases. This may cause the droplets to decelerate at a lesser rate, or accelerate, depending on the relative velocity between the gas and the droplet. The relative velocity also affects the evaporation rate. We assume that drag is the only force acting on the particle. This force will act in the same direction as V_{rel}. Figure 10.17a defines the relative velocity, V_{rel}. Applying Newton's Second Law ($F = ma$) to the droplet, yields

$$F_d = m_d \frac{dv_d}{dt}.$$ (10.108)

Transforming from the time to space domain via $dx = v_d dt$, we obtain

$$F_d = m_d v_d \frac{dv_d}{dx}.$$ (10.109)

The drag force can be obtained by using an appropriate drag coefficient correlation [41], i.e.,

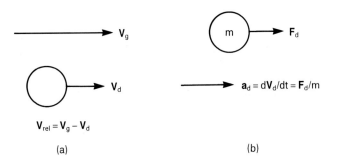

(a)

(b)

FIGURE 10.17
(a) Definition of relative velocity for droplet in a gas stream and (b) Newton's Second Law applied to droplet.

$$C_D = \mathrm{f}(Re_{D,\mathrm{rel}}) \approx \frac{24}{Re_{D,\mathrm{rel}}} + \frac{6}{1 + \sqrt{Re_{D,\mathrm{rel}}}} + 0.4 \tag{10.110}$$

for $0 \leq Re_{D,\mathrm{rel}} \leq 2 \cdot 10^5$, where

$$C_D = \frac{F_d/(\pi D^2/4)}{\rho_g v_{\mathrm{rel}}^2/2}. \tag{10.111}$$

Substituting Eqn. 10.111 into 10.109 and rearranging gives

$$\frac{dv_d}{dx} = \frac{3C_D \rho_g v_{\mathrm{rel}}^2}{4\rho_\ell D v_d}, \tag{10.112}$$

where the sign of dv_d/dx is the same as v_{rel}, or

$$\frac{dv_d}{dx} = \frac{3C_D \rho_g (v_g - v_d)|v_g - v_d|}{4\rho_\ell D v_d}. \tag{10.113}$$

Model Summary

In the preceding, we developed a system of ordinary differential equations and ancillary algebraic relations that describe the operation of a vaporization-controlled, one-dimensional combustor. Mathematically, the problem is an initial-value problem, with the temperatures and flowrates specified at the inlet $(x = 0)$. To make the solution procedure clear, the governing equations and their initial conditions are summarized below.

Liquid mass (droplet diameter)

$$\frac{dD^2}{dx} = f_1, \tag{10.91}$$

with

$$D(0) = D_0.$$

Gas-phase mass

$$\dot{m}_g(x) = \dot{m}_g(0) + \dot{m}_\ell(0) - \dot{m}_\ell(x) + \int_0^x \dot{m}_a dx \tag{10.86}$$

where

$$\dot{m}_g(0) = \dot{m}_{F,0} + \dot{m}_{a,0}.$$

Gas-phase energy

$$\frac{dT_g}{dx} = f_2 \tag{10.102}$$

with

$$T_g(0) = T_{g,0}.$$

Droplet momentum (velocity)

$$\frac{dv_d}{dx} = f_3, \qquad (10.113)$$

with

$$v_d(0) = v_{d,0}.$$

In addition to the above, there are several other purely algebraic relationships necessary to provide closure, together with the relationships expressing the complex equilibrium for the C–H–O–N system.

To solve the problem, the above governing equations can be integrated numerically using one of the many readily available packaged subroutines [42,43]. To calculate the equilibrium properties of the gas phase, the methods presented in Chapter 2 can be employed to solve the problem, or an existing program or subroutine, e.g. Ref. [40], can be adopted for this purpose. The Olikara and Borman code [40] is convenient to use since it routinely calculates the various useful partial derivatives $((\partial h/\partial T), (\partial h/\partial \Phi),$ etc.) in its determination of the equilibrium composition.

Example 10.5. Consider the liquid-fueled rocket engine illustrated in Fig. 10.18, where a cylindrical combustion chamber is attached to a converging–diverging supersonic nozzle. A portion of the fuel is used to cool the nozzle and, hence, is vaporized; thus, both gaseous and liquid fuel enter the combustion chamber along with the gaseous oxidizer. The liquid fuel is atomized into small droplets at the injector plate (head end of combustion chamber at $x = 0$). Using the parameters shown below, apply the one-dimensional analysis developed above to explore the effects of initial droplet diameter, D_0, on the temperature distribution, $T(x)$, and the gas-phase equivalence ratio distribution, $\Phi(x)$, along the axis of the combustion chamber. Also show the droplet diameter history and the droplet- and gas-phase velocities.

Combustor cross-sectional area	$0.157\,\mathrm{m^2}$
Combustor length	$0.725\,\mathrm{m}$
Total fuel injection area	$0.0157\,\mathrm{m^2}$
Fuel	n-heptane (C_7H_{16})
Overall equivalence ratio, Φ_{OA}	2.3
Premixed equivalence ratio, $\Phi(0)$	0.45
Initial temperature, $T(0)$	801 K
Combustion chamber pressure	$3.4474\,\mathrm{MPa}$
Initial droplet velocity, $v_d(0)$	10 m/s

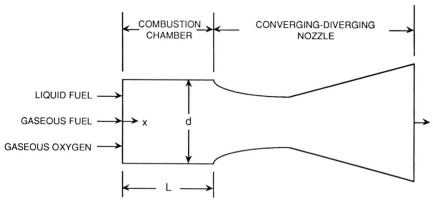

FIGURE 10.18
Schematic diagram of liquid-fueled rocket engine with cylindrical combustion chamber.

Solution. The mathematical one-dimensional combustor model, as summarized above (Eqns. 10.91, 10.86, 10.102, and 10.113), was coded in Fortran. A main program calculated the initial conditions from the given input parameters, and carried out the integration of the governing ordinary differential equations by calling the IMSL routine DGEAR [42]. The equilibrium properties and the thermodynamic partial derivatives were obtained using a version of the Olikara and Borman routine [40], modified to deal with a nitrogen-free oxidizer. Curvefit properties (k, μ, and c_p) for *n*-heptane vapor were taken from Appendix B, and the heptane heat of vaporization was estimated from vapor-pressure data [45] using the Clausius–Clapeyron relation. For simplicity, the gas-phase transport properties were assumed to be those of pure oxygen and obtained from curvefits [44]. Convective enhancement of evaporation was ignored.

Results from exercising this model for five different initial droplet diameters, ranging from 30 μm to 200 μm, are shown in Figs. 10.19 and 10.20. Here we see that, for the two smallest initial droplet sizes ($D_0 = 30$ and 50μm), combustion is complete within the length of the combustion chamber, i.e., D/D_0 becomes zero at a distance less than $L(= 725$ mm). The larger droplets, however, exit the chamber after being partially vaporized. To achieve complete combustion within the combustion chamber, we see from Fig. 10.19 that the initial drop size must be somewhat less than 80 μm. Since the combustor operates rich overall, the gas-phase equivalence ratio, Φ_g, monotonically increases from the initial value based on the entering fuel vapor. Peak temperatures of approximately 3400 K occur near $\Phi_g = 1$ (cf. Chapter 2). From Fig. 10.19, we see that for the smallest droplets (30 μm), temperatures are highest near the injector face, while for the largest droplets (200 μm), the peak temperature is not quite reached before the exit of the combustor. In practice, excessive heat transfer from the combustion gases can damage or destroy the injector assembly. We see then, that an optimum initial droplet size exists such that combustion can be completed within the combustion chamber, while maintaining the highest-temperature zone as far downstream from the injector face as possible. Figure 10.20 shows the tremendous increase in gas velocity associated with the vaporization and combustion of the fuel droplets. With the assumption that the initial droplet velocity is 10 m/s, we see that the droplet is always moving more slowly than the gas and, hence, is

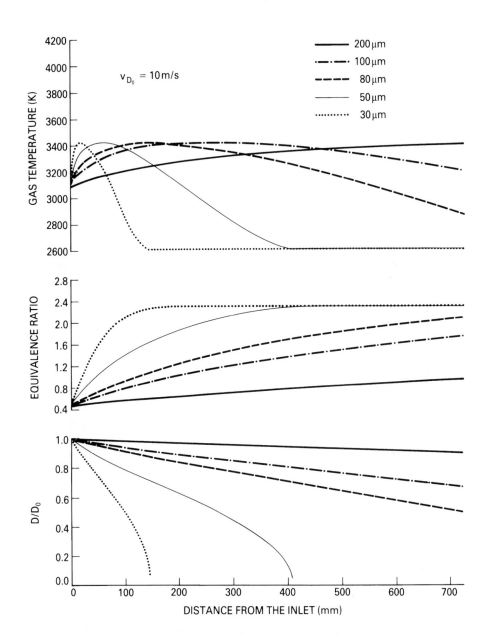

FIGURE 10.19
The effects of initial droplet size on gas temperature, equivalence ratio, and droplet size. The initial droplet velocity is 10 m/s.

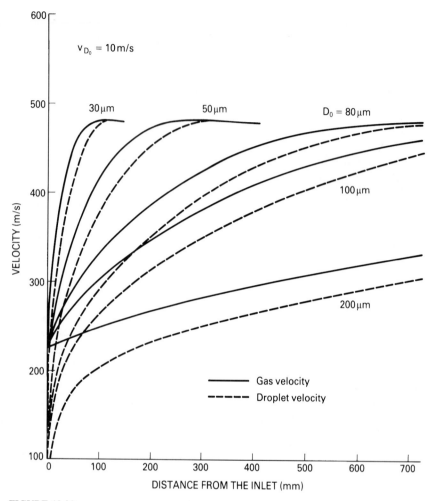

FIGURE 10.20
The effects of initial droplet size on gas and droplet velocities. The initial droplet velocity is 10 m/s.

continually being accelerated. We also see that with such relatively large slip velocities, neglecting convective enhancement of vaporization is not justified.

Comments. This example clearly shows how even a simple model can be used to gain insight into complex situations. Since parametric investigations are easily conducted, such models can be used to provide guidance in both engine design and development efforts. One must be cautious, however, in that a model is only as good as its incorporated physics, which is always incomplete. Nevertheless, computer codes, much more sophisticated than those employed here, are routinely used in the design and development of combustion systems.

SUMMARY

In this chapter, we first saw how the operation of many practical devices depends on the evaporation and/or combustion of fuel droplets. To illuminate these processes, several mathematical models were developed. The first of these was a simple heat-transfer-controlled model of droplet vaporization in a hot gas. This model is analogous to the mass-transfer-controlled evaporation model introduced in Chapter 3. With the assumption that the droplet surface is at the boiling point, the problem is uncoupled from mass-transfer considerations and very simple and easy-to-use expressions result for calculating evaporation rates and droplet lifetimes. The second, more general, analysis models droplet gasification with a spherically symmetric flame surrounding the droplet. The flame is assumed to be an infinitesimally thin sheet where the fuel vapor from the evaporating droplet reacts instantaneously with the inward-diffusing oxidizer. This simple model allows prediction of the droplet burning rate, flame radius, droplet surface and flame temperatures, and fuel vapor concentration at the droplet surface. You should be thoroughly familiar with the conservation principles involved and how they apply to this particular problem. In particular, you should have a physical understanding of the various mass flux relationships. In the burning droplet model, we have coupled the heat-transfer and mass-transfer problems, unlike the isolated mass-transfer analysis (Stefan problem) of Chapter 3 and the heat-transfer (evaporating droplet) analyses presented in this chapter. Of course, if one assumes that the droplet surface is at the boiling point, we return to the heat-transfer dominated problem. You should be able to apply the Clausius–Clapeyron relationship relating vapor pressure and temperature to determine the fuel vapor concentration at the droplet surface. Applying the results of the simple gas-phase theory to estimate droplet lifetimes, we recovered the D^2 law for droplet combustion. Lumped-parameter and onion-skin models treating transient droplet heat-up were also developed. Using film theory, we extended the analysis to a droplet burning in a convective environment and saw that convection enhances burning rates and, thus, shortens droplet lifetimes. The chapter also contains a brief discussion of the many complicating factors ignored in the simple model of which you should be aware.

The chapter concludes with the development of a simple, but general, one-dimensional model of a combustion chamber in which the combustion rate is governed by the vaporization rate of the fuel droplets injected into the chamber. Applications of this model include liquid-rocket engine and gas-turbine combustors. You saw how a steady-flow, control-volume approach could be coupled with droplet evaporation theory and chemical equilibrium (Chapter 2). The control-volume analyses (mass, energy, and droplet momentum) are sufficiently simple that you should be able to develop similar analyses on your own. The 1-D model was applied to the problem of a liquid-hydrocarbon-fueled rocket engine, and the effects of initial droplet size on important chamber design parameters were explored. With appropriate computer codes, you should be able to conduct similar design analyses.

NOMENCLATURE

A	Clausius–Clapeyron constant, Eqn. 10.64 (Pa or atm), or combustor flow area (m^2)
B	Clausius–Clapeyron constant, Eqn. 10.64 (K)
$B_q, B_{o,q}$	Transfer, or Spalding, number
c_p	Specific heat (J/kg-K)
C_D	Drag coefficient
C_1, C_2	Integration constants
D	Diameter (m)
$\mathcal{D}$	Mass diffusivity (m^2/s)
F	Force (N)
F/O	Mass fuel–oxidizer ratio (kg/kg)
h	Enthalpy (J/kg)
h_f^o	Enthalpy of formation (J/kg)
h_{fg}	Latent heat of vaporization (J/kg)
k	Thermal conductivity (W/m-K)
K	Evaporation rate constant (m^2/s)
L	Combustor length (m)
Le	Lewis number, $\alpha/\mathcal{D}$
m	Mass (kg)
$\dot{m}$	Mass flowrate (kg/s)
$\dot{m}'$	Mass flowrate per unit length of combustor (kg/s-m)
$\dot{m}''$	Mass flux (kg/s-m^2)
MW	Molecular weight (kg/kmol)
$\dot{N}$	Number of droplets per unit time (1/s)
Nu	Nusselt number
P	Pressure (Pa or atm)
Pr	Prandtl number
q	Heat per unit mass (J/kg)
$\dot{Q}$	Heat-transfer rate (W)
r	Radial coordinate or radius (m)
R	Specific gas constant (J/kg-K)
R_u	Universal gas constant (J/mol-K)
Re	Reynolds number
Sh	Sherwood number
t	Time (s)
T	Temperature (K)
v	Velocity (m/s)
v_r	Radial velocity (m/s)
$\mathbf{V}$	Velocity vector (m/s)
V	Volume (m^3)
x	Number of carbon atoms in fuel molecule or axial coordinate (m)
y	Number of hydrogen atoms in fuel molecule
Y	Mass fraction (kg/kg)

Z, Z_T $c_{pg}/(4\pi k_g)$ (m-s/kg)

Z_F $1/(4\pi\rho\mathcal{D})$ (m-s/kg)

Greek symbols

α	Thermal diffusivity (m^2/s)
δ_T, δ_M	Film thickness based on heat or mass transfer, respectively (m)
Δh_c	Enthalpy of combustion (J/kg)
ν	Oxidizer to fuel stoichiometric ratio (kg/kg)
ρ	Density (kg/m^3)
Φ	Equivalence ratio
χ	Mole fraction (kmol/kmol)

Subscripts

a	Oxidizer (or air)
boil	Boiling point
d	Droplet
f	Flame
F	Fuel
g	Gas
i	Interface
ℓ, liq	Liquid
ℓg	Liquid to gas
Ox	Oxidizer
Pr	Product
rel	Relative
s	Surface
sat	Saturation
vap	Vapor
∞	Freestream or far removed from surface
0	Initial condition

REFERENCES

1. Hoffman, H., "Development Work on the Mercedes-Benz Commercial Diesel Engine, Model Series 400," SAE Paper 710558, 1971.
2. Eberle, M. L., "The Marine Diesel Engine—The Answer to Low-Grade Fuels," ASME Paper 80-DGP-16, 1980.
3. Correa, S. M., "A Review of NO$_x$ Formation Under Gas-Turbine Combustion Conditions," *Combustion Science and Technology*, 87: 329–362 (1992).
4. Davis, L. B., and Washam, R. M., "Development of a Dry Low NO$_x$ Combustor," ASME 89-GT-255, Gas Turbine and Aeroengine Congress and Exposition, Toronto, ON, 4–8 June, 1988.
5. Shaw, R. J., "Engine Technology Challenges for a 21st Century High Speed Civil Transport," NASA Technical Memorandum 104363, 1991.
6. Lefebvre, A. H., *Gas Turbine Combustion*, Hemisphere, Washington, DC, 1983.
7. Dipprey, D. F., "Liquid Rocket Engines," in *Chemistry in Space Research* (R. F. Landel, and A. Rembaum, eds.), Elsevier, New York, pp. 464–597, 1972.

8. Moser, M. D., Merenich, J. J., Pal, S., and Santoro, R. J., "OH-Radical Imaging and Velocity Field Measurements in a Gaseous Hydrogen/Oxygen Rocket," AIAA Paper 93-2036, 1993.
9. Pal, S., Moser, M. D., Ryan, H. M., Foust, M. J., and Santoro, R. J., "Flowfield Characteristics in a Liquid Propellant Rocket," AIAA Paper 93-1882, 1993.
10. Nishiwaki, N., "Kinetics of Liquid Combustion Processes: Evaporation and Ignition Lag of Fuel Droplets," *Fifth Symposium (International) on Combustion*, Reinhold, New York, pp. 148–158, 1955.
11. Law, C. K., and Williams, F. A., "Kinetics and Convection in the Combustion of Alkane Droplets," *Combustion and Flame*, 19(3): 393–406 (1972).
12. Hubbard, G. L., Denny, V. E., and Mills, A. F., "Droplet Evaporation: Effects of Transients and Variable Properties," *International Journal of Heat and Mass Transfer*, 18: 1003–1008 (1975).
13. Faeth, G. M., "Current Status of Droplet and Liquid Combustion," *Progress in Energy and Combustion Science*, 3: 191–224 (1977).
14. Faeth, G. M., "Evaporation and Combustion of Sprays," *Progress in Energy and Combustion Science*, 9: 1–76 (1983).
15. Law, C. K., "Recent Advances in Droplet Vaporization and Combustion," *Progress in Energy and Combustion Science*, 8: 171–201 (1982).
16. Sirignano, W. A., "Fuel Droplet Vaporization and Spray Combustion Theory," *Progress in Energy and Combustion Science*, 9: 291–322 (1983).
17. Williams, A., "Combustion of Droplets of Liquid Fuels: A Review," *Combustion and Flame*, 21: 1–21 (1973).
18. Godsave, G. A. E., "Studies of the Combustion of Drops in a Fuel Spray: The Burning of Single Drops of Fuel," *Fourth Symposium (International) on Combustion*, Williams & Wilkins, Baltimore, pp. 818–830, 1953.
19. Spalding, D. B., "The Combustion of Liquid Fuels," *Fourth Symposium (International) on Combustion*, Williams & Wilkins, Baltimore, pp. 847–864, 1953.
20. Kuo, K. K., *Principles of Combustion*, John Wiley & Sons, New York, 1986.
21. Faeth, G. M., and Lazar, R. S., "Fuel Droplet Burning Rates in a Combustion Gas Environment," *AIAA Journal*, 9: 2165–2171 (1971).
22. Kumagai, S., and Isoda, H., "Combustion of Fuel Droplets in a Falling Chamber," *Sixth Symposium (International) on Combustion*, Reinhold, New York, pp. 726–731, 1957.
23. Faeth, G. M., "The Kinetics of Droplet Ignition in a Quiescent Air Environment," Ph.D. Thesis, The Pennsylvania State University, University Park, PA, 1964.
24. Kumagai, S., Sakai, T., and Okajima, S., "Combustion of Free Fuel Droplets in a Freely Falling Chamber," *Thirteenth Symposium (International) on Combustion*, The Combustion Institute, Pittsburgh, pp. 779–785, 1971.
25. Choi, M. Y., Dryer, F. L., and Haggard, J. B., Jr., "Observations on a Slow Burning Regime for Hydrocarbon Droplets: *n*-Heptane/Air Results," *Twenty-Third Symposium (International) on Combustion*, The Combustion Institute, Pittsburgh, pp. 1597–1604, 1990.
26. Hara, H., and Kumagai, S., "Experimental Investigation of Free Droplet Combustion Under Microgravity," *Twenty-Third Symposium (International) on Combustion*, The Combustion Institute, Pittsburgh, pp. 1605–1610, 1990.
27. Cho, S. Y., Choi, M. Y., and Dryer, F. L., "Extinction of a Free Methanol Droplet in Microgravity," *Twenty-Third Symposium (International) on Combustion*, The Combustion Institute, Pittsburgh, pp. 1611–1617, 1990.
28. Yang, J. C., Jackson, G. S., and Avedisian, C. T., "Combustion of Unsupported Methanol/Dodecanol Mixture Droplets at Low Gravity," *Twenty-Third Symposium (International) on Combustion*, The Combustion Institute, Pittsburgh, pp. 1619–1625, 1990.
29. Law, C. K., and Law, H. K., "Theory of Quasi-Steady One-Dimensional Diffusional Combustion with Variable Properties Including Distinct Binary Diffusion Coefficients," *Combustion and Flame*, 29: 269–275 (1977).
30. Law, C. K., and Law, H. K., "Quasi-Steady Diffusion Flame Theory with Variable Specific Heats and Transport Coefficients," *Combustion Science and Technology*, 12: 207–216 (1977).

31. Shuen, J. S., Yang, V., and Hsiao, C. C., "Combustion of Liquid-Fuel Droplets in Supercritical Conditions," *Combustion and Flame*, 89: 299–319 (1992).
32. Canada, G. S., and Faeth, G. M., "Combustion of Liquid Fuels in a Flowing Combustion Gas Environment at High Pressures," *Fifteenth Symposium (International) on Combustion*, The Combustion Institute, Pittsburgh, pp. 419–428, 1975.
33. Law, C. K., Chung, W. H. and Srinivasan, N., "Gas-Phase Quasi-Steadiness and Fuel Vapor Accumulation Effects in Droplet Burning," *Combustion and Flame*, 38: 173–198 (1980).
34. Law, C. K., and Sirignano, W. A., "Unsteady Droplet Combustion and Droplet Heating II: Conduction Limit," *Combustion and Flame*, 28: 175–186 (1977).
35. Law, C. K., "Multicomponent Droplet Combustion with Rapid Internal Mixing," *Combustion and Flame*, 26: 219–233 (1976).
36. Megaridis, C. M., and Sirignano, W. A., "Numerical Modeling of a Vaporizing Multicomponent Droplet," *Twenty-Third Symposium (International) on Combustion*, The Combustion Institute, Pittsburgh, pp. 1413–1421, 1990.
37. Sirignano, W. A., "Fluid Dynamics of Sprays—1992 Freeman Scholar Lecture," *Journal of Fluids Engineering*, 115: 345–378 (1993).
38. Priem, R. J., and Heidmann, M. F., "Propellant Vaporization as a Design Criterion for Rocket-Engine Combustion Chambers," NASA Technical Report R-67, 1960.
39. Turns, S. R., and Faeth, G. M., "A One-Dimensional Model of a Carbon-Black Slurry-Fueled Combustor," *Journal of Propulsion and Power*, 1(1): 5–10 (1985).
40. Olikara, C., and Borman, G. L., "A Computer Program for Calculating Properties of Equilibrium Combustion Products with Some Application to I. C. Engines," SAE Paper 750468, 1975.
41. White, F. M., *Viscous Fluid Flow*, McGraw-Hill, New York, p. 209, 1974.
42. IMSL, Inc., "DGEAR," IMSL Library, Houston, TX.
43. Press, W. H., Teukolsky, S. A., Vetterling, W. T., and Flannery, B. P., *Numerical Recipes in FORTRAN—The Art of Scientific Computing*, 2nd Ed., Cambridge University Press, New York, 1992.
44. Andrews, J. R., and Biblarz, O., "Temperature Dependence of Gas Properties in Polynomial Form," Naval Postgraduate School, NPS67-81-001, January 1981.
45. Weast, R. C. (ed.), *CRC Handbook of Chemistry and Physics*, 56th Ed., CRC Press, Cleveland, 1975.

PROBLEMS

10.1. Calculate the evaporation rate constant for a 1-mm-diameter water droplet evaporating into dry, hot air at 500 K and 1 atm.

10.2. Calculate the lifetimes for n-hexane droplets evaporating in a quiescent ambient environment of air at 800 K and 1 atm for initial diameters of 1000, 100, and 10 μm. Also calculate the mean evaporation rate defined as m_0/t_d, where m_0 is the initial droplet mass. Assume the liquid density is 664 kg/m^3.

10.3. Determine the influence of ambient temperature on droplet lifetimes. Use as a base case n-hexane with $D_0 = 100\,\mu$m and $T = 800$ K, as determined above in problem 10.2. Use temperatures of 600, 800, and 1000 K. Separate the effects of temperature proper and temperature-dependent properties by first calculating lifetimes assuming properties fixed at the same values as the base case, and then repeat your calculations with appropriate properties. Plot your results. Discuss.

10.4. Determine the influence of pressure on the lifetimes of 500-μm water droplets. The ambient environment is dry air at 1000 K. Use pressures of 0.1, 0.5, and 1.0 MPa. Plot your results. Discuss.

10.5. Estimate the mass burning rate of a 1-mm-diameter n-hexane droplet burning in air at atmospheric pressure. Assume no heat is conducted into the interior of the liquid droplet and that the droplet temperature is equal to the boiling point. The ambient air is at 298 K.

10.6. Calculate the ratio of the flame radius to droplet radius and flame temperature corresponding to the conditions given in problem 10.5.

10.7. For the conditions associated with problems 10.5 and 10.6, plot the temperature distribution for the region $r_s \leq r \leq 2r_f$. Based on your plot, determine which is greater: the heat conduction from the flame toward the droplet, or the heat conduction from the flame to the surroundings. Discuss the physical significance of your result.

10.8. Repeat problems 10.5 and 10.6 removing the assumption that the droplet temperature is at the boiling point. The Clausius–Clapeyron constants for n-hexane are $A = 25,591$ atm and $B = 3471.2$ K. Compare these results with those of problems 10.5 and 10.6 and discuss.

10.9. A rogue fuel droplet escapes from the primary zone of a gas-turbine combustor. If both the droplet and the combustion gases are traveling at 50 m/s through the combustor, estimate the combustor length required to burn out the rogue droplet. Discuss the implications of your results.

To simplify property evaluation, assume the combustion products have the same properties as air. For the fuel droplet, use n-hexane properties. Assume the liquid density is 664 kg/m³. Also assume $T_s = T_{boil}$, using the Clausius–Clapeyron constants to evaluate T_{boil} at the given pressure. Other pertinent data are $P = 10$ atm, $T_\infty = 1400$ K, and drop diameter $D = 200 \, \mu m$.

10.10. What is the influence of introducing a 10 m/s slip velocity between the droplet and gas stream in problem 10.9? Answer this by comparing the initial burning rates with and without slip.

10.11. Derive a "power-law" expression for droplet burning in a convective environment, i.e.,

$$D^n(t) = D_0^n(t) - K't$$

where the value for n results from your analysis. You will also have to define an appropriate burning rate constant K'. To keep your analysis simple, assume

$$Nu = CRe^{0.8} Pr^{1/3},$$

where C is a known constant, rather than trying to employ Eqn. 10.78.

10.12. Determine the influence of droplet heat-up on droplet lifetimes. Use the results from problem 10.5 as the base case (heat-up ignored) and compare to results obtained using the "onion-skin" model to account for droplet heat-up. For the heat-up model, assume the bulk droplet temperature is 300 K and the liquid specific heat is 2265 J/kg-K.

10.13. Starting with Eqn. 10.69, and assuming that the heat transfer into the interior of the droplet, g_{i-l}, is zero, show that

$$\Delta h_c = c_{pg}(T_f - T_s) + \nu c_{pg}(T_f - T_\infty) + h_{fg}.$$

Discuss the physical significance of each term in the above expression.

PROJECTS

Note: The detailed implementations of the suggested projects below depend upon available software. It is assumed that subroutines to calculate equilibrium properties and their partial derivatives (Appendix F) and a numerical integration routine are available.

1. Model the primary zone of a gas-turbine combustor can assuming one-dimensionality and the other Chapter 10 assumptions. The following conditions are known or given:

$$\Phi_{supplied} = 1.0$$

$$\dot{m}_{a,0} = 0.66 \text{ kg/s}$$

$$A = 0.0314 \text{ m}^2$$

$$L = 0.30 \text{ m}$$

$$P = 10 \text{ atm}$$

$$T_{inlet,air} = 600 \text{ K}.$$

A. Determine the maximum allowed drop size if 95% of the fuel is to be burned in the primary zone. Simplify the vaporization problem by using the following approximate properties and treating them as independent of temperature:

$$C_{12}H_{26} \text{ (n-dodecane)}$$

$$\rho_\ell = 749 \text{ kg/m}^3$$

$$h_{fg} \approx 263 \text{ kJ/kg}$$

$$k_g = 0.05 \text{ W/m-K}$$

$$c_{pg} = 1200 \text{ J/kg-K}$$

$$T_b = 447 \text{ K}.$$

Use properties of air at 1600 K to evaluate Re, Pr, and Nu.

B. Plot $D(x)$, $T_g(x)$, $v_g(x)$, and $\Phi_g(x)$ for the conditions determined in part A above. Discuss.

2. Consider a gas-turbine combustor can that has a diameter of 0.2 m. Assume the fuel can be approximated as *n*-dodecane with the properties as listed in Project 1 above. Gas-phase conditions at the exit of the primary zone are:

$$\Phi_g = 1.0$$

$$P = 10 \text{ atm}$$

$$T_g = 2500 \text{ K}$$

$$\dot{m}_g = 0.6997 \, \text{kg/s}.$$

Not all of the fuel injected into the combustor is burned in the primary zone, with 0.00441 kg/s of fuel entering the secondary zone as liquid drops of $25 \, \mu$m diameter.

Determine the length of the secondary zone required to completely burn the remaining fuel, assuming secondary air is added at a constant rate per unit length, $\dot{m}'_a$, and that the total amount of secondary air added is 1.32 kg/s.

How much time is required to burn out the droplets? (Hint: $dt = dx/v_d$.) Also determine the temperature and equivalence ratio at the end of the secondary zone.

Discuss your results and support your discussion with various graphs showing variation of key parameters with axial distance, x.

CHAPTER
11

INTRODUCTION TO TURBULENT FLOWS

OVERVIEW

In practical devices that involve flowing fluids, turbulent flows are more frequently encountered than are laminar flows. This rule-of-thumb is especially true for combustion devices such as reciprocating internal combustion engines, gas turbines, furnaces, boilers, rocket engines, etc. Unfortunately, the mathematical description of a turbulent flow and the solution of the resulting governing conservation equations is much more difficult than for laminar flows. Analytical and numerical solutions to turbulent flows are engineering approximations even for the most simple geometries and can be subject to large errors. In contrast, exact solutions can be found for many laminar flows, especially simple geometries, and very accurate solutions are obtainable for even complicated situations using numerical methods. The essential dilemma of solving a turbulent flow problem is that if all the information necessary for describing a flow is tracked, there is no computer in the world large enough to handle the job; on the other hand, if the problem is simplified to be tractable using available computers, large errors may result, especially for flow conditions that have not been studied experimentally. Considerable progress, however, is being made on this front. Because of the tremendous importance of turbulent flows in engineering and other applications, considerable effort has been expended over many decades to understand

357

turbulence and to develop descriptive and predictive methods that are useful in the design of practical devices.

Our objectives in this chapter are by necessity quite limited. First, we will review a few key concepts related to turbulent flow that you may have seen in an introductory fluid mechanics course. These include the general behavior of the velocity and scalars (e.g., temperature and species) in turbulent flows, some physical notions of turbulence, definitions of length scales, and the most simple mathematical description of a turbulent flow. Our second objective is to discuss the essential features of free (unconfined), turbulent jets. This archetypal flow occurs frequently in many practical combustion devices, and, hence, is a useful starting point to understand more complex flows. For example, during the intake stroke of a spark-ignition engine, a jet-like flow is created as the incoming charge passes into the cylinder through the relatively narrow passage created by the opening intake valve. Inside the cylinder, the intake jet, and other flows created by piston motion, then interact with the cylinder walls and head. In gas-turbine engines, the secondary and dilution zones comprise a combination of jet and wall flows (cf. Fig. 10.4). Industrial burners and furnaces also are examples of practical devices where both turbulent jet and wall flows are important. Of course, in all of these devices, the actual flows are much more complicated than the simple situation that we will study in this chapter; however, an understanding of simpler flows is an essential prerequisite to dealing with complex flows.

In this chapter, we treat only nonreacting, incompressible flows to illuminate the essential features of turbulent flows uncomplicated by combustion. Subsequent chapters explore premixed turbulent flames, with the specific application of spark-ignition engines in mind (Chapter 12), and nonpremixed turbulent jet flames (Chapter 13).

DEFINITION OF TURBULENCE

Turbulent flow results when instabilities in a flow are not sufficiently damped by viscous action and the fluid velocity at each point in the flow exhibits random fluctuations. All students of fluid mechanics should be familiar with the famous experiment of Osborne Reynolds [1] in which the transition from a laminar to a turbulent flow in a tube was visualized with a dye streak and related to the dimensionless parameter that now bears the name of this important early fluid mechanician, i.e., the **Reynolds number**. The random unsteadiness associated with various flow properties is the hallmark of a turbulent flow and is illustrated for the axial velocity component in Fig. 11.1. One particularly useful way to characterize a turbulent flowfield is to define **mean** and **fluctuating** quantities. Mean properties are defined by taking a time-average of the flow property over a sufficiently large time interval, $\Delta t = t_2 - t_1$, i.e.,

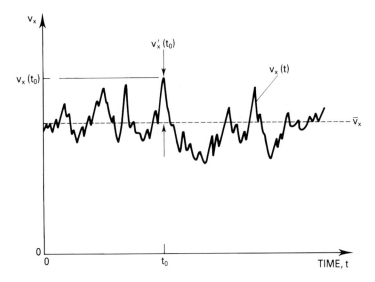

FIGURE 11.1
Velocity as a function of time at a fixed point in a turbulent flow.

$$\bar{p} \equiv \frac{1}{\Delta t} \int_{t_i}^{t_2} p(t) dt, \tag{11.1}$$

where p is any flow property, e.g., velocity, temperature, pressure, etc. The fluctuation, $p'(t)$, is the difference between the instantaneous value of the property, $p(t)$, and the mean value, $\bar{p}$, or

$$p(t) = \bar{p} + p'(t). \tag{11.2}$$

Figure 11.1 illustrates the fluctuating component of v_x at a specific time, t_0, i.e., $v_x(t_0) = \bar{v}_x + v'_x(t_0)$. In turbulent flows with combustion, there are also frequently large random fluctuations in temperature, density, and species, as defined by

$$T(t) = \bar{T} + T'(t),$$
$$\rho(t) = \bar{\rho} + \rho'(t),$$

and

$$Y_i(t) = \bar{Y}_i + Y'_i(t).$$

This manner of expressing variables as a mean and fluctuating component is referred to as the **Reynolds decomposition**.

It is common practice to define the **intensity** of the turbulent fluctuations in terms of root-mean-square quantities, that is,

$$p'_{rms} \equiv \sqrt{\overline{p'^2}}. \tag{11.3a}$$

The **relative intensity** is defined as

$$p'_{rms}/\bar{p}, \tag{11.3b}$$

and is usually expressed as a percentage.

What is the physical nature of a turbulent flow? Figures 11.2 and 11.3 give a partial answer to this question. In each of these figures, we see fluid blobs and filaments of fluid intertwining. A common notion in fluid mechanics is the idea of a fluid **eddy**. An eddy is considered to be a macroscopic fluid element in which the microscopic elements comprising the eddy behave in some ways as a unit. For example, a **vortex** imbedded in a flow would be considered an eddy. A turbulent flow is comprised of many eddies with a multitude of sizes and **vorticities**, a measure of angular velocities. A number of smaller eddies may be imbedded in a larger eddy. A characteristic of a fully turbulent flow is the existence of a wide range of length scales, i.e., eddy sizes. For a turbulent flow, the Reynolds number is a measure of the range of scales present; the greater the Reynolds number, the greater the range of sizes from the smallest eddy to the largest. It is this large range of length scales that makes calculating turbulent flows from first principles intractable. We will discuss length scales in more detail in the next section.

The rapid intertwining of fluid elements is a characteristic that distinguishes turbulent flow from laminar flow. The turbulent motion of fluid elements allows momentum, species, and energy to be transported in the cross-stream direction much more rapidly than is possible by the molecular diffusion processes controlling transport in laminar flows. Because of this, most practical combustion devices employ turbulent flows to enable rapid mixing and heat release in relatively small volumes.

LENGTH SCALES IN TURBULENT FLOWS

We can improve our qualitative understanding of the structure of turbulent flows by exploring some of the length scales that are used to characterize such flows. Furthermore, some understanding of the important length scales will be essential to our discussion of premixed turbulent combustion in Chapter 12, since the relationships among length scales determine the intrinsic character of turbulent combustion.

Four Length Scales

In the turbulence literature, many length scales have been defined; however, the following four scales are of general relevance to our discussion and, in general, are frequently cited. In decreasing order of size, these scales are:

L Characteristic width of flow or macroscale
ℓ_0 Integral scale or Taylor macroscale

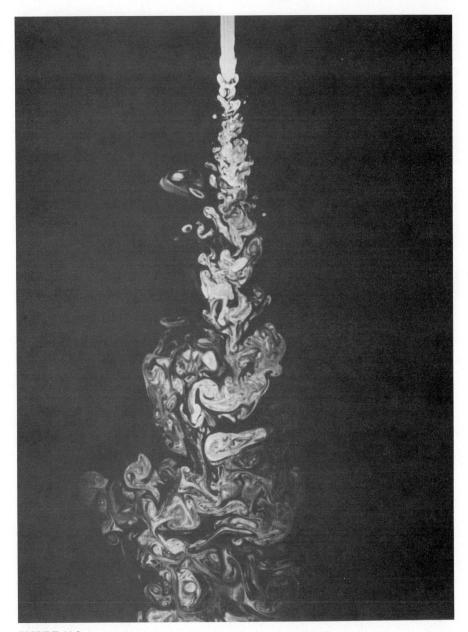

FIGURE 11.2
Turbulent jet issuing into a quiescent reservoir. The flow visualization technique makes visible the jet fluid in a plane containing the jet centerline. (From Ref. [2], reprinted by permission of PWN-Polish Scientific Publishers, Warsaw. Also appears in Ref. [3], p. 97.)

FIGURE 11.3
Turbulent flow in a wall boundary layer. A sheet of light illuminates on oil fog. The wall is at the bottom of the photograph. (From Ref. [3], reprinted by permission of Parabolic Press.)

ℓ_λ Taylor microscale
ℓ_K Kolmogorov microscale

In the following sections, we examine each of the above, providing some physical interpretation and expanding our view of turbulence structure.

L, **CHARACTERISTIC WIDTH OF FLOW OR MACROSCALE.** This is the largest length scale in the system and is the upper bound for the largest possible eddies. For example, in a pipe flow, the largest eddy would be equal to the pipe diameter; and for a jet flow, L would be the local width of the jet at any axial location. In a reciprocating internal combustion engine, L might be taken as the time-varying clearance between the piston top and the head, or perhaps the cylinder bore. In general, this length scale is defined by the actual hardware or device being considered. This length scale is frequently used to define a Reynolds number based on the mean flow velocity, but is not used to define a turbulence Reynolds number, as are the other three length scales.

ℓ_0, **INTEGRAL SCALE OR TAYLOR MACROSCALE.** The **integral scale**, ℓ_0, physically represents the mean size of the large eddies in a turbulent flow: those eddies with low frequency and large wavelength. The integral scale is always smaller than L, but is of the same order of magnitude. Operationally, the integral scale can be measured by integrating the correlation coefficient for the fluctuating velocities obtained as a function of the distance between two points, i.e.,

$$\ell_0 = \int_0^\infty R_x(r)dr \qquad (11.4a)$$

where

$$R_x(r) \equiv \frac{\overline{v_x'(0)v_x'(r)}}{v_{x,rms}'(0)v_{x,rms}'(r)} \qquad (11.4b)$$

In less precise terms, ℓ_0 represents the distance between two points in a flow where there ceases to be a correlation between the fluctuating velocities at the two locations. Reference [4] presents physical pictures of ℓ_0 in terms of possible structural models of turbulence: one where ℓ_0 represents the spacing between narrow vortex tubes comprising the fine structure of the flow [5], and another where ℓ_0 is the spacing between thin vortex sheets [6].

ℓ_λ, **TAYLOR MICROSCALE.** The **Taylor microscale** is an intermediate length scale between ℓ_0 and ℓ_K, but is weighted more towards the smaller scales. This scale is related to the mean rate of strain and can be formally expressed [4] as

$$\ell_\lambda = \frac{v_{x,rms}'}{\left[\overline{\left(\frac{\partial v_x}{\partial x}\right)^2}\right]^{1/2}}, \qquad (11.5)$$

where the denominator represents the mean strain rate.

ℓ_K, **KOLMOGOROV MICROSCALE.** The **Kolmogorov microscale** is the smallest length scale associated with a turbulent flow and, as such, is representative of the dimension at which the dissipation of turbulent kinetic energy to fluid internal energy occurs. Thus, the Kolmogorov scale is the scale at which molecular effects (kinematic viscosity) are significant. Dimensional arguments [7,8] show that ℓ_K can be related to the rate of dissipation, ϵ_0 as

$$\ell_K \approx (\nu^3/\epsilon_0)^{1/4} \qquad (11.6)$$

where ν is the molecular kinematic viscosity, and the dissipation rate is approximately expressed as

$$\epsilon_0 \equiv \frac{\delta(ke_{\text{turb}})}{\delta t} \approx \frac{3v_{rms}'^2/2}{\ell_0/v_{rms}'}. \qquad (11.7)$$

Note that the integral length scale, ℓ_0 appears in the approximation for the dissipation rate, thereby linking the two scales. We will shortly show the relationships among the various length scales. As an aside, it is helpful to new students of turbulence to point out that dimensional, and sometimes heuristic, arguments are invoked in discussions of turbulence, the above (Eqns. 11.6 and 11.7) being examples of these.

The final point we wish to make concerning ℓ_K is possible physical interpretations. In Tennekes' [5] model of a turbulent flow, ℓ_K represents the thickness of the smallest vortex tubes or filaments that permeate a turbulent flow, while Ref. [6] suggests that ℓ_K represents the thickness of vortex sheets imbedded in the flow.

Turbulence Reynolds Numbers

Three of the four length scales discussed above are used to define three turbulence Reynolds numbers. In all of the Reynolds numbers, the characteristic velocity is the root-mean-square fluctuating velocity, v'_{rms}. Thus, we define

$$Re_{\ell_0} \equiv v'_{rms}\ell_0/\nu, \tag{11.8a}$$

$$Re_{\ell_\lambda} \equiv v'_{rms}\ell_\lambda/\nu, \tag{11.8b}$$

and

$$Re_{\ell_K} \equiv v'_{rms}\ell_K/\nu, \tag{11.8c}$$

Equations 11.6 and 11.7 defining ℓ_K and the dissipation rate, ε_0, can be used to relate the largest (the integral) and the smallest (the Kolmogorov) turbulence length scales:

$$\ell_0/\ell_K = Re_{\ell_0}^{3/4}. \tag{11.9}$$

The Taylor microscale, ℓ_λ, also can be related to Re_{ℓ_0} as follows [8]:

$$\ell_0/\ell_\lambda = Re_{\ell_0}^{1/2}. \tag{11.10}$$

Equation 11.9 expresses, in a semiquantitative way, the wide separation of length scales in high-Re flows discussed earlier in this chapter. For example, with $Re_{\ell_0} = 1000$, the ratio ℓ_0/ℓ_K is about 178:1; but when Re_{ℓ_0} is increased to 10,000, by increasing the mean flow velocity, say, the ratio becomes 1000:1. Figure 11.4 schematically illustrates this development of increasingly finer small-scale turbulence with increasing Re, while the largest scales in the flow remain unchanged. As we will see in Chapter 12, the size of the scales of turbulence, in relation to the laminar flame thickness, determines the character of the turbulent flame.

Example 11.1. A natural-gas-fired industrial gas turbine rated at 3950 kW has the following specifications:

> Air flowrate = 15.9 kg/s
> $F/A = 0.017$
> Primary/secondary air split = 45/55
> Combustor pressure = 10.2 atm

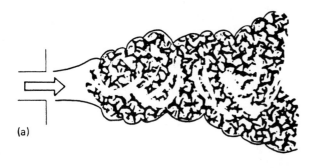

(a)

(b)

FIGURE 11.4
Turbulent jets at low (a) and high (b) Reynolds numbers. The shading pattern illustrates the small-scale turbulence structure. (From Ref. [7], reprinted by permission of MIT Press.)

Combustor inlet temperature = 600 K
Primary zone temperature = 1900 K
Dilution zone temperature = 1300 K.

As shown in Fig. 11.5, gas-turbine combustors can be configured in several ways. The combustor for the turbine specified above is arranged in a can-annular (cannular) configuration with eight cans each of 0.20 m diameter. A single combustor can be seen in Fig. 2.4. The can length-to-diameter ratio is 1.5.

Assuming that the relative turbulence intensity is approximately 10% and that the integral length scale is about 1/10 the can diameter, estimate the Kolmogorov length scales at (i) the combustor inlet, (ii) within the primary zone, and (iii) at the end of the dilution zone.

Solution. We can utilize Eqn. 11.9 to calculate the Kolmogorov length scale ℓ_K. This requires that we first estimate the turbulent Reynolds number based on the integral scale ℓ_0. To get the mean velocity through each can at the desired locations, overall continuity is applied:

$$v_j = \frac{\dot{m}_j}{\rho_j A} \tag{I}$$

where the j subscript denotes the location of interest. The flowrates at the three locations can be calculated:

ANNULAR

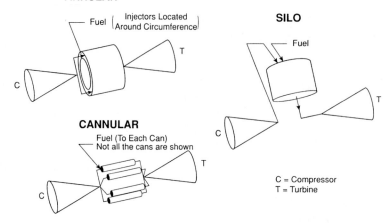

FIGURE 11.5

Schematic representation of the three types of combustor configurations used in large stationary gas turbines. (From Ref. [9], reprinted by permission, ©1992, Gordon & Breach Science Publishers.)

$$\dot{m}_j = \frac{\left(\begin{array}{c}\text{fraction of total}\\\text{air at location } j\end{array}\right)\dot{m}_A + (F/A)\dot{m}_A}{(\text{number of cans})}.$$

Thus, at the combustor inlet and within the primary zone

$$\dot{m}_i = \dot{m}_{ii} = \frac{0.45\,(15.9) + 0.017\,(15.9)}{8} = 0.928\,\text{kg/s}.$$

At the end of the dilution zone, i.e., at the turbine inlet

$$\dot{m}_{iii} = \frac{1.0\,(15.9) + 0.017\,(15.9)}{8} = 2.02\,\text{kg/s}.$$

The flow area is

$$A = \frac{\pi D^2}{4} = \frac{\pi(0.20)^2}{4} = 0.0314\,\text{m}^2$$

and the densities at each location are estimated using the ideal-gas law with properties of air:

$$\rho_j = \frac{P}{(R_u/MW)T_j}.$$

Thus,

$$\rho_i = \frac{10.2\,(101,325)}{(8315/28.85)600} = 5.97\,\text{kg/m}^3$$

$$\rho_{ii} = \rho_i\frac{T_i}{T_{ii}} = 5.97\frac{600}{1900} = 1.89\,\text{kg/m}^3$$

$$\rho_{iii} = \rho_i \frac{T_i}{T_{iii}} = 5.97 \frac{600}{1300} = 2.76 \, \text{kg/m}^3.$$

From Eqn. I, the velocities are determined to be

$$v_i = \frac{\dot{m}_i}{\rho_i A} = \frac{0.928}{5.97 \, (0.0314)} = 4.95 \, \text{m/s}$$

$$v_{ii} = \frac{0.928}{1.89 \, (0.0314)} = 15.6 \, \text{m/s}$$

$$v_{iii} = \frac{2.02}{2.76 \, (0.0314)} = 23.3 \, \text{m/s}.$$

We now calculate Reynolds numbers based on mean flow and turbulence quantities:

$$Re_{L,i} = \frac{\rho_i v_i D}{\mu_i} = \frac{5.97 \, (4.95) \, (0.20)}{305.8 \cdot 10^{-7}} = 1.93 \cdot 10^5$$

$$Re_{L,ii} = \frac{1.89 \, (15.6) \, (0.20)}{663 \cdot 10^{-7}} = 8.89 \cdot 10^4$$

$$Re_{L,iii} = \frac{2.76 \, (23.3) \, (0.20)}{496 \cdot 10^{-7}} = 2.59 \cdot 10^5$$

$$Re_{\ell_0,i} = \frac{\rho_i v'_{rms} \ell_0}{\mu_i} = \frac{5.97 \, (0.1) \, (4.95) \left(\dfrac{0.20}{10}\right)}{305.8 \cdot 10^{-7}} = 1930$$

$$Re_{\ell_0,ii} = \frac{1.89 \, (0.1) \, (15.6) \left(\dfrac{0.20}{10}\right)}{663 \cdot 10^{-7}} = 889$$

$$Re_{\ell_0,iii} = \frac{2.76 \, (0.1) \, (23.3) \left(\dfrac{0.20}{10}\right)}{496 \cdot 10^{-7}} = 2590.$$

In the above, viscosity values are approximated as those of air, $v'_{rms} = 0.1 v$, and $\ell_0 = L/10$. The Kolmogorov scales are now estimated from Eqn. 11.9 as follows:

$$\ell_K = \ell_0 Re_{\ell_0}^{-3/4}$$

$$\ell_{K,i} = \frac{20 \, \text{mm}}{10} (1930)^{-0.75} = 0.069 \, \text{mm}$$

$$\ell_{K,ii} = \frac{20 \, \text{mm}}{10} (889)^{-0.75} = 0.123 \, \text{mm}$$

$$\ell_{K,iii} = \frac{20 \, \text{mm}}{10} (2590)^{-0.75} = 0.055 \, \text{mm}$$

Comment. We see that in this application the Kolmogorov scales are quite small, of the order of 0.1 mm, with the smallest at the turbine inlet.

ANALYZING TURBULENT FLOWS

The basic conservation equations describing fluid motion that we have applied to laminar flows apply equally well to turbulent flows, provided, of course, that the unsteady terms are retained. For example, we can write the continuity (mass conservation) and Navier–Stokes (momentum conservation) equations for unsteady, constant-density, Newtonian fluid as follows (cf. Chapter 7):

MASS CONSERVATION

$$\frac{\partial v_x}{\partial x} + \frac{\partial v_y}{\partial y} + \frac{\partial v_z}{\partial z} = 0 \tag{11.11}$$

x-DIRECTION MOMENTUM CONSERVATION

$$\frac{\partial}{\partial t}\rho v_x + \frac{\partial}{\partial x}\rho v_x v_x + \frac{\partial}{\partial y}\rho v_y v_x + \frac{\partial}{\partial z}\rho v_z v_x$$

$$= \mu\left(\frac{\partial^2 v_x}{\partial x^2} + \frac{\partial^2 v_x}{\partial y^2} + \frac{\partial^2 v_x}{\partial z^2}\right) - \frac{\partial P}{\partial x} + \rho g_x \tag{11.12}$$

The above equations and their companions, the additional two components of momentum, conservation of energy and species, conceptually could be solved for the functions $v_x(t)$, $v_y(t)$, $v_z(t)$, $T(t)$, and $Y_i(t)$ at discrete points in the flow using numerical techniques; however, the number of grid points required to resolve the details of the flow (recall the large range of length scales inherent in turbulent flows) would be huge. For example, Ref. [10] cites that 10^9 grid points would be necessary to deal with a simple plane mixing layer of two adjacent fluids. At present, this overwhelms the best available computers. It should be pointed out, however, that full solutions are being accomplished, provided the Reynolds number is not too large [11].

Reynolds Averaging and Turbulent Stresses

Rather than relying entirely on empirical experimental methods, techniques have been developed that allow turbulent flows to be analyzed to obtain useful information and to allow predictions. One fruitful method of analyzing turbulent flows is to write out the partial differential equations that embody the basic conservation principles—mass, momentum, energy, and species—perform a Reynolds decomposition, and then average the equations over time. The resulting governing equations are called the **Reynolds-averaged** equations. The averaging process has two major consequences: First, it eliminates the fine details of the flow; for example, the complex time-dependent velocity at a point, as illustrated in Fig. 11.1, could not be predicted using time-averaged equations of motion. The second consequence of averaging is the appearance of new terms in the time-averaged governing equations that have no counterpart in the original time-dependent equations. Finding a way to calculate or approximate these new terms is frequently referred to as the **closure problem** of turbulence.

TWO-DIMENSIONAL BOUNDARY LAYER. To develop some feel for the time-averaged approach, we will develop the time-averaged x-momentum equation for a two-dimensional boundary layer flow over a flat plate. For this flow, with x in the flow direction and y perpendicular to the plate, Eqn. 11.12 reduces to

$$\frac{\partial}{\partial t}\rho v_x + \frac{\partial}{\partial x}\rho v_x v_x + \frac{\partial}{\partial y}\rho v_y v_x = \mu \frac{\partial^2 v_x}{\partial y^2}. \tag{11.13}$$

    ①   ②   ③   ④

The first step in the process is to substitute for each fluctuating quantity its representation as a mean and a fluctuating component, i.e., the Reynolds decomposition $v_x = \bar{v}_x + v'_x$ and $v_y = \bar{v}_y + v'_y$. We will then time-average Eqn. 11.13, term by term, using the overbar to signify a time-averaged quantity. Thus, the first term can be averaged:

$$\overline{\frac{\partial}{\partial t}\rho(\bar{v}_x + v'_x)} = \overline{\frac{\partial}{\partial t}\rho\bar{v}_x} + \overline{\frac{\partial}{\partial t}\rho v'_x} = 0, \tag{11.14}$$

where each term on the right-hand-side of Eqn. 11.14 is identically zero; the first because we assume the flow is steady in an overall sense, i.e., $\bar{v}_x$ is a constant, and the second, because the time-derivative of a random function with a zero mean is also a random function with a zero mean.

The third term in Eqn. 11.13 is the most interesting because it yields the dominant additional momentum flux arising from the velocity fluctuations:

$$\overline{\frac{\partial}{\partial y}\rho(\bar{v}_y + v'_y)(\bar{v}_x + v'_x)} =$$

$$\overline{\frac{\partial}{\partial y}\rho(\bar{v}_x\bar{v}_y + \bar{v}_x v'_y + v'_x v'_y + \bar{v}_y v'_x)}. \tag{11.15}$$

Splitting out each term under the large overbar on the right-hand-side and evaluating their individual averages, yields,

$$\overline{\frac{\partial}{\partial y}\rho\bar{v}_x\bar{v}_y} = \frac{\partial}{\partial y}\rho\bar{v}_x\bar{v}_y, \tag{11.16a}$$

$$\overline{\frac{\partial}{\partial y}\rho\bar{v}_x v'_y} = 0, \tag{11.16b}$$

$$\overline{\frac{\partial}{\partial y}\rho v'_x v'_y} = \frac{\partial}{\partial y}\rho\overline{v'_x v'_y}, \tag{11.16c}$$

and

$$\overline{\frac{\partial}{\partial y} \rho \bar{v}_y v'_x} = 0. \tag{11.16d}$$

Similar operations can be performed on the second and fourth terms of Eqn. 11.13 and are left as an exercise for the reader. Reassembling, the now time-averaged Eqn. 11.13 yields

$$\frac{\partial}{\partial x} \rho \bar{v}_x \bar{v}_x + \frac{\partial}{\partial y} \rho \bar{v}_y \bar{v}_x + \boxed{\frac{\partial}{\partial x} \rho \overline{v'_x v'_x}}$$
$$+ \boxed{\frac{\partial}{\partial y} \rho \overline{v'_x v'_y}} = \mu \frac{\partial^2 \bar{v}_x}{\partial y^2}. \tag{11.17}$$

The terms in the dashed boxes are new terms arising from the turbulent nature of the flow. In a laminar flow v'_x and v'_y are zero; thus, Eqn. 11.17 becomes identical with Eqn. 11.13 for a steady flow.

It is common practice to define

$$\tau_{xx}^{\text{turb}} \equiv -\rho \overline{v'_x v'_x}, \tag{11.18a}$$

$$\tau_{xy}^{\text{turb}} \equiv -\rho \overline{v'_x v'_y}, \tag{11.18b}$$

which represent additional momentum fluxes resulting from the turbulent fluctuations. These terms have several designations and are referred to as components of the **turbulent momentum flux** (momentum flow per unit area), **turbulent stresses**, or **Reynolds stresses**. In a general formulation of the Reynolds-averaged momentum equation, a total of nine Reynolds stresses appear, analogous to the nine components of the laminar viscous shear stresses, i.e., $\tau_{ij}^{\text{turb}} = -\rho \overline{v'_i v'_j}$ where i and j represent the coordinate directions.

Rearranging Eqn. 11.17, and applying continuity to the evaluation of the derivatives of the velocity products, yields our final result for a two-dimensional turbulent boundary-layer flow:

$$\rho \left(\bar{v}_x \frac{\partial \bar{v}_x}{\partial x} + \bar{v}_y \frac{\partial \bar{v}_x}{\partial y} \right) = \mu \frac{\partial^2 \bar{v}_x}{\partial y^2} - \frac{\partial}{\partial y} \rho \overline{v'_x v'_y}, \tag{11.19}$$

where we assume that $(\partial/\partial x)\tau_{xx}^{\text{turb}}$ can be neglected.

AXISYMMETRIC JET. The turbulent axisymmetric jet is a particularly important flow in our study of combustion, and in this section, we introduce the Reynolds-averaged form of the momentum equation analogous to the two-dimensional cartesian boundary layer presented in the previous section. For a constant-density jet, the continuity equation and axial momentum equation describing the steady flowfield were given in Chapter 9 (Eqns. 9.3 and 9.4). Performing the same operations of velocity decomposition and time-averaging to the axial momentum equation for an axisymmetric flow, yields, after simplification,

$$\rho\left(\bar{v}_x\frac{\partial \bar{v}_x}{\partial x} + \bar{v}_r\frac{\partial \bar{v}_x}{\partial r}\right) = \mu\frac{1}{r}\frac{\partial}{\partial r}\left(r\frac{\partial \bar{v}_x}{\partial r}\right) - \frac{1}{r}\frac{\partial}{\partial r}(r\rho\overline{v_r'v_x'}). \qquad (11.20)$$

In Eqn. 11.20, we now see the turbulent shear to be related to the fluctuations of the axial and radial velocities, $\tau_{rx}^{\text{turb}} = -\rho\overline{v_r'v_x'}$.

In a subsequent section, we will see how Eqn. 11.20 can be employed to find the velocity distributions in a free (unconfined) turbulent jet.

The Closure Problem

The Reynolds-averaging discussed above introduces new unknowns into the equations of motion, viz., the turbulent stresses, $-\rho\overline{v_i'v_j'}$. Finding a way to evaluate these stresses and solving for any other additional unknowns that may be introduced in the process is termed the **closure problem** of turbulence. Presently, there are many techniques that are used to "close" the system of governing equations, ranging from the very straightforward to the quite sophisticated. A detailed discussion of these methods is beyond the scope of this book and the interested reader is referred to texts devoted to the subject [12–15]. However, we will investigate the simplest ideas that can be employed to achieve closure, and apply these to solving our archetypal flow, the free jet.

EDDY VISCOSITY. The first concept that we wish to explore is that of the **eddy viscosity**. The eddy viscosity is a fiction arising out of our treatment of the turbulent momentum fluxes as turbulent stresses. For example, we can rewrite Eqn. 11.20 explicitly in terms of the laminar (Newtonian) and turbulent (Reynolds) stresses as follows:

$$\rho\left(\bar{v}_x\frac{\partial \bar{v}_x}{\partial x} + \bar{v}_r\frac{\partial \bar{v}_x}{\partial r}\right) = -\frac{1}{r}\frac{\partial}{\partial r}[r(\tau_{\text{lam}} + \tau_{\text{turb}})]. \qquad (11.21)$$

Furthermore, we can define the stresses to be proportional to the mean velocity gradient, i.e.,

$$\tau_{\text{lam}} = -\mu\frac{\partial \bar{v}_x}{\partial r} \qquad (11.22a)$$

and

$$\tau_{\text{turb}} = -\rho\varepsilon\frac{\partial \bar{v}_x}{\partial r} \qquad (11.22b)$$

where μ is the molecular viscosity and ε is the kinematic eddy viscosity ($\varepsilon = \mu_{\text{turb}}/\rho$, where μ_{turb} is the apparent turbulent viscosity). The relationship expressed by Eqn. 11.22a is just the familiar expression derived for a Newtonian fluid for the flow of interest; the relationship expressed by Eqn. 11.22b, however, is the definition of the so-called eddy viscosity. The idea of an eddy viscosity as defined in Eqn. 11.22b was first proposed by Boussinesq [16] in 1877. For our cartesian-coordinate problem (cf. Eqn. 11.19), the stresses are given by

$$\tau_{\text{lam}} = -\mu \frac{\partial \bar{v}_x}{\partial y}, \qquad (11.23a)$$

$$\tau_{\text{turb}} = -\rho\varepsilon \frac{\partial \bar{v}_x}{\partial y}. \qquad (11.23b)$$

An **effective viscosity**, μ_{eff}, is defined as

$$\mu_{\text{eff}} = \mu + \mu_{\text{turb}} = \mu + \rho\varepsilon, \qquad (11.24)$$

so that

$$\tau_{\text{tot}} = -(\mu + \rho\varepsilon) \frac{\partial \bar{v}_x}{\partial y}. \qquad (11.25)$$

For turbulent flows far from a wall, $\rho\varepsilon \gg \mu$, so $\mu_{\text{eff}} \cong \rho\varepsilon$; however, near a wall, both μ and $\rho\varepsilon$ contribute to the total stress in the fluid.

Note that the introduction of the eddy viscosity, *per se*, does not achieve closure; the problem is now transformed into how to determine a value or the functional form of ε. Unlike the molecular viscosity μ, which is a thermophysical property of the fluid itself, the eddy viscosity ε depends on the flow itself. One would not necessarily expect the same value of ε for two distinctly different flows; for example, a swirling confined flow with recirculation, and a free jet, are not likely to have the same values for ε. Moreover, since ε depends on the local flow properties, it will take on different values at different locations within the flow. Therefore, one must be careful not to take too literally the analogy between laminar and turbulent flows implied by Eqns. 11.22a and b and 11.23a and b. Also, in some flows, the turbulent stresses are not proportional to the mean velocity gradients, as is required by Eqns. 11.22b and 11.23b [13].

MIXING-LENGTH HYPOTHESIS. The simplest closure scheme would be to assume the eddy viscosity is a constant throughout the flowfield; unfortunately, experimental evidence shows this not to be a generally useful assumption, as expected. More sophisticated hypotheses, therefore, need to be applied. One of the most useful, and yet simple, hypotheses is that proposed by Prandtl [17]. Prandtl's hypothesis, by analogy with the kinetic theory of gases, states that the eddy viscosity is proportional to the product of the fluid density, a length-scale called the **mixing length**, and a characteristic turbulent velocity, i.e.,

$$\mu_{\text{turb}} = \rho\varepsilon = \rho\ell_m v_{\text{turb}}. \qquad (11.26)$$

Furthermore, Prandtl [17] assumed that the turbulent velocity, v_{turb}, is proportional to the product of the mixing length, ℓ_m, and the magnitude of the mean velocity gradient, $|\partial\bar{v}_x/\partial y|$. Thus,

$$\mu_{\text{turb}} = \rho\varepsilon = \rho\ell_m^2 \left| \frac{\partial \bar{v}_x}{\partial y} \right|. \qquad (11.27)$$

Equation 11.27 is useful in dealing with flows near a wall. For free (unconfined) turbulent flows, Prandtl [18] proposed an alternative hypothesis for the characteristic turbulent velocity in Eqn. 11.26, i.e., $v_{\text{turb}} \propto \bar{v}_{x,\text{max}} - \bar{v}_{x,\text{min}}$. The corresponding turbulent viscosity is then

$$\mu_{\text{turb}} = \rho\varepsilon = 0.1365\rho\ell_m(\bar{v}_{x,\text{max}} - \bar{v}_{x,\text{min}}), \tag{11.28}$$

where the numerical constant is chosen to agree with experimental results. Equation 11.28 is a key relation that we will invoke in our subsequent solution to the jet problem. Note, however, that we have yet to obtain closure since we have introduced yet another unknown! All that has been done so far is to replace the unknown velocity correlation $\overline{v_x' v_y'}$ with an expression involving an unknown eddy viscosity, and, in turn, to relate that eddy viscosity to an unknown mixing length. Our next step finally attains closure by specifying the mixing length. Since the mixing length depends on the flow itself, different specifications generally are required for each kind of flow. Mixing length functions are given for a wide variety of flows in Ref. [13]; we will focus, however, only on the mixing lengths required to solve the jet and wall-flow problems.

For a free axisymmetric jet,

$$\ell_m = 0.075\,\delta_{99\%}, \tag{11.29}$$

where $\delta_{99\%}$ is the half-width of the jet measured from the jet centerline to the radial location where $\bar{v}_x$ has decayed to be only 1% of its centerline value. Note that the mixing length increases with distance from the jet origin since $\delta_{99\%}$ grows with axial distance. Note also that there is no radial dependence specified for the mixing length; hence, Eqn. 11.29 implies that ℓ_m is constant over the jet width at any axial station.

A different ℓ_m obtains for flows near a wall, where a cross-stream dependence is inherent in the mixing length. For a wall boundary layer, the flow is conveniently divided into three zones: the **viscous sublayer** adjacent to the wall, a **buffer layer**, and a **fully developed** turbulent region far from the wall. The mixing length for each of these three regions is given by the following equations [13]: for the laminar sublayer,

$$\ell_m = 0.41y\left[1 - \exp\left(-\frac{y\sqrt{\rho\tau_w}}{26\mu}\right)\right], \tag{11.30a}$$

for the buffer layer,

$$\ell_m = 0.41y \quad \text{for} \quad y \le 0.2195\,\delta_{99\%}, \tag{11.30b}$$

and for the fully developed region,

$$\ell_m = 0.09\,\delta_{99\%}. \tag{11.30c}$$

In the above expressions, τ_w is the local wall shear stress, and $\delta_{99\%}$ is the local boundary-layer thickness, defined as the y-location at which the velocity equals 99% of the freestream value. Note that in Eqn. 11.30a, proposed by van Driest [19], the mixing length vanishes as the distance from the wall y goes to zero; hence, $\mu_{\text{eff}} = \mu$. For sufficiently large y-values, Eqn. 11.30a degenerates to Eqn. 11.30b.

For turbulent flows in a circular pipe or tube, the mixing length distribution given by Nikuradse [20] is frequently invoked:

$$\ell_m/R_0 = 0.14 - 0.08(r/R_0)^2 - 0.06(r/R_0)^4, \tag{11.31}$$

where R_0 is the pipe radius. With the closure problem now solved, i.e., the specification of mixing lengths, we are now in a position to solve the governing equations to yield the velocity fields for our chosen example, the jet. This solution is discussed in the next section.

Example 11.2. Determine a numerical value for the viscosity, μ_{turb}, for a free jet of air at an axial location where the mean centerline velocity has decayed to 60% of the initial velocity, i.e., $\bar{v}_{x,0}/v_e = 0.6$.

The jet width, $\delta_{99\%}$, at this location is 15 cm. The initial jet velocity is 70 m/s. The pressure is 1 atm and the temperature is 300 K. Also, compare the turbulent viscosity with the molecular (laminar) viscosity.

Solution. To evaluate μ_{turb}, we will employ the defining relationship, Eqn. 11.28, together with the expression defining the jet mixing length, Eqn. 11.29. We start by finding the mixing length:

$$\ell_m = 0.075\, \delta_{99\%}$$
$$= 0.075\,(0.15) = 0.01125\,\text{m}.$$

We obtain the density via the ideal-gas law,

$$\rho = \frac{P}{(R_u/MW)T} = \frac{101,325}{(8315/28.85)300} = 1.17\,\text{kg/m}^3.$$

The turbulent viscosity is (Eqn. 11.28)

$$\mu_{turb} = 0.1365\rho\ell_m(\bar{v}_{x,\max} - \bar{v}_{x,\min})$$
$$= 0.1365\,(1.17)\,(0.01125)\,[0.6(70) - 0] = 0.0755.$$

We check units:

$$\mu_{turb}[=]\frac{\text{kg}}{\text{m}^3}\,(\text{m})\left(\frac{\text{m}}{\text{s}}\right) = \frac{\left(\frac{\text{N-s}^2}{\text{m}}\right)}{\text{m}^3}\,(\text{m})\left(\frac{\text{m}}{\text{s}}\right) = \frac{\text{N-s}}{\text{m}^2}$$

$$\boxed{\mu_{turb} = 0.0755\,\text{N-s/m}^2}\,.$$

From Table C.1, the molecular viscosity of air at 300 K is $184.6 \cdot 10^{-7}\,\text{N-s/m}^2$. Thus,

$$\boxed{\frac{\mu_{turb}}{\mu_{lam}} = \frac{0.0755}{184.6 \cdot 10^{-7}} = 4090}\,.$$

Comment. These calculations show indeed that the turbulent viscosity dominates over the molecular viscosity, i.e., $\mu_{eff} \cong \mu_{turb}$. We also note that the width of the jet is approximately 13 ($\delta_{99\%}/\ell_m = 1/0.075$) mixing lengths.

AXISYMMETRIC TURBULENT JET

The fundamental conservation equations (mass and axial momentum) that describe the turbulent jet are essentially the same as those used in Chapter 9 for the laminar jet; however, mean velocities replace instantaneous ones, and the molecular viscosity is replaced by the effective viscosity. For the turbulent jet, the molecular viscosity is negligible in comparison to the eddy viscosity (see Example 11.2). Thus, the axial momentum equation, Eqn. 9.4, becomes

$$\bar{v}_x \frac{\partial \bar{v}_x}{\partial x} + \bar{v}_r \frac{\partial \bar{v}_x}{\partial r} = \frac{1}{r} \frac{\partial}{\partial r} \left(r\varepsilon \frac{\partial \bar{v}_x}{\partial r} \right), \tag{11.32}$$

and mass conservation (cf. Eqn. 9.3),

$$\frac{\partial(\bar{v}_x r)}{\partial x} + \frac{\partial(\bar{v}_r r)}{\partial r} = 0. \tag{11.33}$$

The boundary conditions for the mean velocities are identical to those used to solve the laminar jet problem, Eqns 9.7a, b, and d.

To determine the eddy viscosity, ε, we combine the mixing-length relationships of Eqns. 11.28 and 11.29 to yield

$$\varepsilon = 0.0102 \, \delta_{99\%}(x) \bar{v}_{x,\max}(x), \tag{11.34}$$

where both the jet width, $\delta_{99\%}(x)$, and maximum axial velocity, $\bar{v}_{\max}(x)$, are functions of axial position. The maximum axial velocity occurs on the jet centerline, so $\bar{v}_{\max}(x) = \bar{v}_{x,0}(x)$, and in arriving at Eqn. 11.34, we assume that $\bar{v}_{\min}$ is zero, since the jet is issuing into a quiescent medium. At this juncture, we will employ some empirical information [21]. First, measurements show that for turbulent jets, $\delta_{99\%} \approx 2.5 r_{1/2}$, where $r_{1/2}$ is the jet radius at which the axial velocity has fallen to half its centerline value. Figure 11.6 illustrates measurements of $r_{1/2}$ and $\delta_{99\%}$. The other experimental evidence we wish to employ is that $r_{1/2}$ grows in direct proportion to x, and $\bar{v}_{x,0}$ declines in an inverse manner with x, i.e.,

$$r_{1/2} \propto x^1 \tag{11.35a}$$

$$\bar{v}_{x,0} \propto x^{-1}. \tag{11.35b}$$

Thus, the x-dependencies in Eqn. 11.34 cancel, yielding

$$\varepsilon = 0.0256 r_{1/2}(x) \bar{v}_{x,0}(x) = \text{constant}. \tag{11.36}$$

This is a rather fortunate result in that we can now use the laminar jet solutions (Eqns. 9.8 and 9.9) by simply replacing the constant molecular viscosity with the just-revealed constant eddy viscosity (times density), $\rho\varepsilon$. Thus, the mean velocity components are

$$\bar{v}_x = \frac{3}{8\pi} \frac{J_e}{\rho\varepsilon x} \left[1 + \frac{\xi^2}{4} \right]^{-2}, \tag{11.37}$$

$$\bar{v}_x(r)/\bar{v}_{x,0}$$

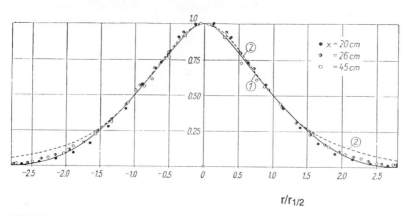

$$r/r_{1/2}$$

FIGURE 11.6
Radial profile of axial velocity for a turbulent jet. (From Ref. [20], reprinted by permission, ©1968, McGraw-Hill.)

$$\bar{v}_r = \left[\frac{3J_e}{16\pi\rho_e}\right]^{1/2}\frac{1}{x}\frac{\xi - \dfrac{\xi^3}{4}}{\left[1 + \dfrac{\xi^2}{4}\right]^2},\tag{11.38}$$

where J_e is the initial jet momentum flow, which for a uniform exit velocity, v_e, is expressed

$$J_e = \rho_e v_e^2 \pi R^2,\tag{11.39}$$

and

$$\xi = \left[\frac{3J_e}{16\rho_e\pi}\right]^{1/2}\frac{1}{\varepsilon}\frac{r}{x}.\tag{11.40}$$

For the time being, let's retain the unknown constant ε, first finding relationships for $r_{1/2}(x)$ and $\bar{v}_{x,0}(x)$. With these relationships and Eqn. 11.37, we can relate $\varepsilon, r_{1/2}(x)$, and $\bar{v}_{x,0}(x)$ solely to known jet parameters, v_e and R, and, thereby, conclude our theoretical development.

The axial velocity, normalized by the assumed uniform exit velocity v_e, is obtained by substituting Eqn. 11.39 into Eqn. 11.37 and rearranging:

$$\bar{v}_x/v_e = 0.375(v_e R/\varepsilon)(x/R)^{-1}[1 + \xi^2/4]^{-2},\tag{11.41}$$

and the dimensionless centerline velocity decay is obtained by setting $r = 0$ $(\xi = 0)$:

$$\bar{v}_{x,0}(x)/v_e = 0.375(v_e R/\varepsilon)(x/R)^{-1}.\tag{11.42}$$

To find an expression for $r_{1/2}$, we divide Eqn. 11.41 by 11.42, set the result equal to 1/2, i.e., $\bar{v}_x/\bar{v}_{x,0} = 1/2$, and solve for $r(= r_{1/2})$. Thus,

$$r_{1/2} = 2.97\left(\frac{v_e R}{\varepsilon x}\right)^{-1}. \tag{11.43}$$

Solving Eqns. 11.36, 11.42, and 11.43 simultaneously, yields our desired final results: The jet velocity decay is

$$\bar{v}_{x,0}/v_e = 13.15(x/R)^{-1}, \tag{11.44}$$

the jet spreading rate,

$$r_{1/2}/x = 0.08468, \tag{11.45}$$

and the eddy viscosity,

$$\varepsilon = 0.0285 v_e R. \tag{11.46}$$

It is interesting to compare the velocity decays and spreading rates of the turbulent jet with those of the laminar axisymmetric jet (Eqns. 9.13 and 9.14). For the turbulent jet, we have the interesting behavior that neither the velocity decay nor the spreading rate depend on the jet Reynolds number, while for the laminar jet, the velocity decay is directly proportional to Re_j (Eqn. 9.13) and the spreading rate is inversely proportional to Re_j (Eqn. 9.14). Thus, the character of a turbulent jet is independent of exit conditions, provided the Reynolds number is sufficiently high to assure fully turbulent flow. This result has interesting implications for turbulent jet flames, which we will discuss in Chapter 13.

SUMMARY

In this chapter, the groundwork is laid for subsequent discussions of premixed (Chapter 12) and nonpremixed (Chapter 13) turbulent combustion. Turbulence was defined and the concepts of mean and fluctuating properties and turbulence intensity introduced. We discussed, albeit superficially, the structure of turbulent flows and defined four length scales that help to characterize turbulent flow structure. You should be familiar with the length scales and how they interrelate through various turbulent Reynolds numbers. In particular, you should be aware of how the range of length scales (the difference between the largest and smallest eddies) increases with Reynolds number. In introducing the mathematical concept of Reynolds-averaging, we saw how turbulent, or Reynolds, stresses arise in the time-averaged conservation equations, which, in turn, brought to light the problem of closure. You should have some appreciation for this issue. An example of closure, Prandtl's mixing-length hypothesis, was presented, with formulae given for free jets and wall-bounded flows. The mixing-length theory was applied to a free jet, and we saw, as a consequence, that the normalized velocity field $(v(r, x)/v_e)$ scales with the initial jet diameter, indicating a universal (i.e., Re-independent) structure of turbulent jets. Thus, the spreading angle is a constant, a finding distinctly different from the laminar case; this difference results in turbulent jet flames (Chapter 13) having properties that are considerably different than those of laminar flames.

NOMENCLATURE

g	Gravitational acceleration (m/s^2)
J	Momentum flow (kg-m/s^2)
ke	Kinetic energy per unit mass (m^2/s^2)
ℓ_0	Integral scale or Taylor macroscale (m)
ℓ_λ	Taylor microscale (m)
ℓ_K	Kolmogorov microscale (m)
ℓ_m	Mixing length (m)
L	Characteristic width of flow or macroscale (m)
p	Arbitrary property
P	Pressure (Pa)
r	Radial coordinate (m)
$r_{1/2}$	Jet half-width at half-height (m)
R	Initial jet radius
R_x	Correlation coefficient, Eqn. 11.4
R_0	Pipe radius (m)
Re	Reynolds number
t	Time (s)
T	Temperature (K)
v	Velocity
v_r, v_x	Radial and axial velocity components, respectively (m/s)
v_x, v_y, v_z	Velocity components in cartesian coordinates (m/s)
x, y, z	Cartesian coordinates (m)
Y	Mass fraction (kg/kg)

Greek symbols

$\delta_{99\%}$	Jet width (m)
ε	Eddy viscosity (m^2/s)
ϵ_0	Dissipation rate, Eqn. 11.7 (m^2/s^3)
μ	Absolute (molecular) viscosity (N-s/m^2)
μ_{eff}	Effective viscosity, Eqn. 11.24 (N-s/m^2)
ν	Kinematic viscosity (m^2/s)
ρ	Density (kg/m^3)
τ	Shear stress (N/m^2)

Subscripts

e	Exit
lam	Laminar
max	Maximum
min	Minimum
rms	Root-mean-square

turb	Turbulent
w	Wall

Other

$\overline{(\ )}$	Time-averaged quantity
$(\ )'$	Fluctuating quantity

REFERENCES

1. Reynolds, O., "An Experimental Investigation of the Circumstances Which Determine Whether the Motion of Water Shall Be Direct or Sinuous, and of the Law of Resistance in Parallel Channels," *Phil. Trans. Royal Society of London*, 174: 935–982, 1883.
2. Dimotakis, P. E., Lye, R. C., and Papantoniou, D. Z., "Structure and Dynamics of Round Turbulent Jets," *Fluid Dynamics Transactions*, 11: 47–76 (1982).
3. Van Dyke, M., *An Album of Fluid Motion*, Parabolic Press, Stanford, CA, p. 95, 1982.
4. Andrews, G. E., Bradley, D., and Lwakabamba, S. B., "Turbulence and Turbulent Flame Propagation—A Critical Appraisal," *Combustion and Flame*, 24: 285–304 (1975).
5. Tennekes, H., "Simple Model for the Small-Scale Structure of Turbulence," *Physics of Fluids*, 11: 669–671 (1968).
6. Townsend, A. A., "On the Fine-Scale Structure of Turbulence," *Proceedings of the Royal Society of London Series A*, 208: 534–542 (1951).
7. Tennekes, H., and Lumley, J. L., *A First Course in Turbulence*, MIT Press, Cambridge, MA, 1972.
8. Libby, P. A., and Williams, F. A., "Fundamental Aspects," in *Turbulent Reacting Flows* (P. A. Libby, and F. A. Williams, eds.), Springer-Verlag, New York, 1980.
9. Correa, S. M., "A Review of NO_x Formation Under Gas-Turbine Combustion Conditions," *Combustion Science and Technology*, 87: 329–362 (1992).
10. Lumley, J. E. (ed.), "Whither Turbulence? Turbulence of the Crossroads," *Lecture Notes in Physics*, Vol. 357, Springer-Verlag, New York, 1990.
11. Moin, P., "Towards Large Eddy and Direct Simulation of Complex Turbulent Flows," *Computer Methods in Applied Mechanics and Engineering*, 87: 329–334 (1991).
12. Patankar, S. V., and Spalding, D. B., *Heat and Mass Transfer in Boundary Layers*, 2nd Ed., International Textbook, London, 1970.
13. Launder, B. E., and Spalding, D. B., *Lectures in Mathematical Models of Turbulence*, Academic Press, New York, 1972.
14. Schetz, J. A., *Injection and Mixing in Turbulent Flow*, Progress in Astronautics and Aeronautics, Vol. 68, American Institute of Aeronautics and Astronautics, New York, 1980.
15. Wilcox, D. C., *Turbulence Modeling for CFD*, DCW Industries, La Cañada, CA, 1993.
16. Boussinesq, T. V., "Théorie de l'écoulement Tourbillonnant," *Mém. prés. Acad. Sci.*, Paris, XXIII, 46 (1877).
17. Prandtl, L., "Über die ausgebildete Turbulenze," *Z.A.M.M.*, 5: 136–139 (1925).
18. Prandtl, L., "Bemerkungen zur Theorie der Freien Turbulenz," *Z.A.M.M.*., 22: 241–243 (1942).
19. van Dreist, E. R., "On Turbulent Flow Near a Wall," *J. Aero. Sci.*, 23: 1007 (1956).
20. Nikuradse, J., "Laws of Flow in Rough Pipes," English Translation in NACA Technical Memorandum 1292, November 1950. (Original published in German, 1933.)
21. Schlichting, H., *Boundary-Layer Theory*, 6th Ed. McGraw-Hill, New York, 1968.

QUESTIONS AND PROBLEMS

11.1 Make a list of all of the bold-faced words appearing in Chapter 11 and define each.

11.2 The axial velocity at a point in a flow is given by

$$v_x(t) = A \sin(\omega_1 t + \phi_1) + B \sin(\omega_2 t + \phi_2) + C.$$

A. Develop an expression for the time-mean velocity, $\bar{v}_x$.

B. Develop an expression for v'_x.

C. Develop an expression for $v'_{x,rms}$.

11.3. Perform the Reynolds-averaging process to the second and fourth terms of Eqn. 11.13. Compare your results with Eqn. 11.17.

11.4 In the realm of turbulence theory, what is meant by closure? Discuss. Illustrate closure concretely using the free jet as an example, citing appropriate equations as necessary.

11.5. In a spark-ignition engine, the integral or Taylor macroscale, ℓ_0, is found to be approximately equal to one-third the clearance height. At top-dead-center (TDC), the residual inlet jet has a velocity of 30 m/s and a relative turbulence intensity of 30%. Estimate the Taylor and Kolmogorov microscales at TDC, in mm, for a motoring (non-firing) engine. Assume isentropic compression of air from $P = 1$ atm and $T = 300$ K with a volumetric compression ratio of 7:1. The TDC clearance height is 10 mm.

11.6. In play, a child blows through a 6-mm-diameter straw aimed at a sibling. If a velocity of 3 m/s is needed for the sibling to feel the jet, and the child can maintain an initial velocity of 35 m/s sufficiently long, how far away can the child stand from the sibling and the jet still be felt? Also, verify that the jet is turbulent.

CHAPTER

12

TURBULENT PREMIXED FLAMES

OVERVIEW

Paradoxically, turbulent premixed flames are of tremendous practical importance, being encountered in many useful devices, as discussed below, while their theoretical description is still a matter of uncertainty, or at least, controversy. Because there is yet no comprehensive, generally accepted theory of turbulent premixed flames, and because many of the descriptions are highly mathematical, we will avoid developing or discussing any particular theory in detail, departing from the approach of previous chapters. Rather, our approach will be more phenomenological and empirical, discussing some of the important issues that complicate a rigorous understanding of premixed combustion. Several reviews of this subject have been presented in the past few decades and are recommended as a starting point for those wishing to explore this complex subject in greater detail [1–8].

SOME APPLICATIONS

Spark-Ignition Engines

The spark-ignition engine is a prime example of the use of premixed combustion. Figure 12.1 shows several spark-ignition, automobile-engine combustion chamber configurations. The fuel–air mixture is produced either by a carburetor system or, now almost universally in the U.S., by a fuel-injection system. Even though the

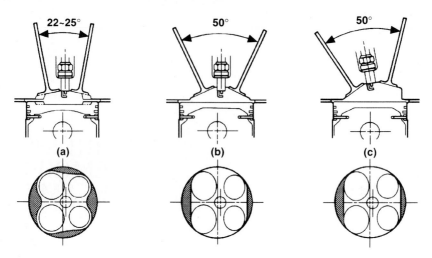

FIGURE 12.1
Various configurations of four-valve, spark-ignition engine combustion chambers. (Courtesy of General Motors Corporation.)

fuel may be introduced as a liquid, spark-ignition engine fuels are highly volatile, and the liquid has time to vaporize and thoroughly mix with the air before the mixture is ignited with a spark. The combustion duration is an important parameter in the operation of spark-ignition engines and is controlled by the turbulent flame speed and the distribution of the combustion volume. Compact combustion chambers, such as shown in Fig. 12.1a, produce short combustion durations. Combustion duration governs, to a large degree, the lean-limit of stable operation, tolerance to exhaust-gas recirculation, thermal efficiency, and the production of oxides of nitrogen (NO_x) emissions. More information directly related to spark-ignition engine combustion can be found in internal combustion engine textbooks, e.g., Refs. [9] and [10].

Gas-Turbine Engines

While gas-turbine engines are primarily used to power aircraft, these engines are being employed more and more in stationary power systems. Current turbine combustor design is greatly influenced by the need to control simultaneously soot, carbon monoxide, and oxides of nitrogen emissions. Older engines employed purely nonpremixed combustion systems, with a near-stoichiometric flame zone integrated with secondary air streams to complete combustion and dilute the products to the proper temperature before entry into the turbine. Some current designs and experimental systems utilize various degrees of premixing to avoid high-temperature, NO_x-forming zones [11,12]. Figure 12.2 illustrates a silo-type combustor (cf. Fig. 11.5) that employs natural-gas burners that can operate in a premixed mode. A low-NO_x gas-turbine combustor can from a premixed cannu-

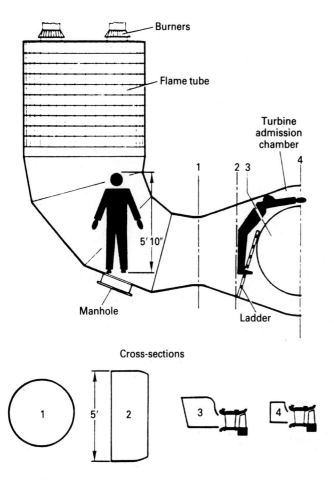

FIGURE 12.2
Schematic of silo-type, gas-turbine combustor with ceramic-tile-lined chamber and access for inspection of the combustion chamber and the turbine inlet. (Reprinted from Ref. [12] by permission of the American Society of Mechanical Engineers.)

lar-type combustor is shown in Fig. 2.4. With the benefit of NO_x control from premixed combustion comes a number of concerns, primary among them are turndown ratio (ratio of maximum to minimum flowrates), flame stability, and carbon monoxide emissions.

Industrial Gas Burners

Premixed flames are used in a large number of industrial applications. Premixing of the fuel gas and air may be accomplished upstream of the burner nozzle using a mixer (see Fig. 12.3), or the fuel gas and air may be mixed within the burner

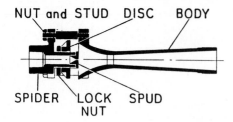

NUT and STUD   DISC   BODY

SPIDER   LOCK   SPUD
          NUT

FIGURE 12.3
Inspirator mixer uses high-pressure gas flow to entrain air. Mixing occurs downstream of the venturi throat as the fuel–air mixture passes to the burner (not shown). (From Ref. [13], reprinted by permission of North American Manufacturing Co.)

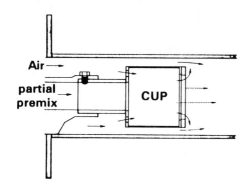

Air →

partial premix →

CUP

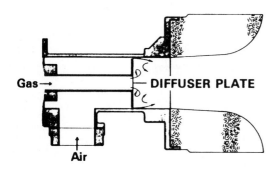

Gas →   DIFFUSER PLATE

Air

FIGURE 12.4
Nozzle-mixing gas burners for industrial applications. (From Ref. [14], reprinted by permission of North American Manufacturing Co.)

nozzle. Figure 12.4 shows two examples of nozzle-mixing burners. Depending upon the degree of premixing achieved in the burner's nozzle, the flame produced by this type of burner may exhibit some nonpremixed or diffusion flame characteristics.

Fully premixed burners are illustrated in Fig. 12.5. Small-port or ported-manifold burners (Fig. 12.5, top) are used in domestic appliances and industrial applications such as make-up air heating, drying ovens, baking ovens, food roasters, and deep-fat vats [14]. The large-port or pressure-type burners (Fig. 12.5, bottom), as well as nozzle-mixing burners, are used in many industrial applications; for example, kilns used in the manufacturing of bricks, porcelain, and tile, and furnaces for heat-treating, forging, and melting [14].

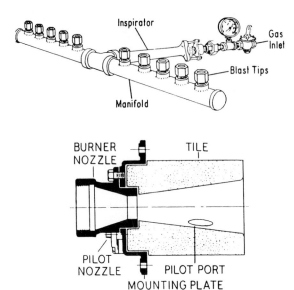

FIGURE 12.5

Examples of premixed burners. Top example includes inspirator mixer illustrated in Fig. 12.3. (From Ref. [13], reprinted by permission of North American Manufacturing Co.)

DEFINITION OF TURBULENT FLAME SPEED

Unlike a laminar flame, which has a propagation velocity that depends uniquely on the thermal and chemical properties of the mixture, a turbulent flame has a propagation velocity that depends on the character of the flow, as well as the mixture properties. This is consistent with the basic nature of turbulent flows as discussed in Chapter 11. For an observer traveling with the flame, we can define a turbulent flame speed, S_t, as the velocity at which unburned mixture enters the flame zone in a direction normal to the flame. In this definition, we assume that the flame surface is represented as some time-mean quantity, recognizing that the instantaneous position of the high-temperature reaction zone may be fluctuating wildly. Since the direct measurement of unburned gas velocities at a point near a turbulent flame is exceedingly difficult, at best, flame velocities usually are determined from measurements of reactant flowrates. Thus, the turbulent flame speed can be expressed as

$$S_t = \frac{\dot{m}}{\overline{A}\rho_u} \tag{12.1}$$

where $\dot{m}$ is the reactant flow rate, ρ_u the unburned gas density, and $\overline{A}$ is the time-smoothed flame area. Experimental determinations of turbulent flame speeds are complicated by determining a suitable flame area, $\overline{A}$, for thick, and frequently curved flames. The ambiguity associated with determining this flame area can result in considerable uncertainty in measurements of turbulent burning velocities.

Example 12.1. Consider the measurement of turbulent flame speeds. An air-fuel mixture passes through a 40 mm by 40 mm flow channel with a flame anchored at the channel exit along the top and bottom walls, as shown in the sketch. Quartz sidewalls contain the flame beyond the exit, while the top and bottom are open to the laboratory. For a mean flow velocity of 68 m/s, the resulting wedge-shaped flame has an included angle of 13.5°, estimated from time-exposure photographs. Estimate the turbulent burning velocity at this condition. The properties of the unburned mixture are $T = 293$ K, $P = 1$ atm, and $MW = 29$ kg/kmol.

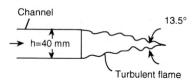

Solution. Equation 12.1 can be applied directly to find the turbulent burning velocity. The reactants' flowrate is

$$\dot{m} = \rho_u A_{\text{duct}} \bar{v}_{\text{duct}}$$
$$= 1.206 \, (0.04)^2 68 = 0.131 \, \text{kg/s}$$

where the reactants' density is estimated using the ideal-gas law, i.e.,

$$\rho_u = \frac{P}{RT} = \frac{101,325}{(8315/29)293} = 1.206 \, \text{kg/m}^3.$$

From the flame geometry (wedge), we estimate the apparent flame area, $\bar{A}$, first by finding the length of the flame sheet, L,

$$\frac{h/2}{L} = \sin\left(\frac{13.5°}{2}\right)$$

or

$$L = \frac{h/2}{\sin 6.75°} = \frac{(0.04)/2}{\sin 6.75°} = 0.17 \, \text{m}.$$

Thus,

$$\bar{A} = 2 \cdot \text{width} \cdot \text{length} = 2(0.04)0.17 = 0.0136 \, \text{m}^2.$$

The turbulent burning velocity is then

$$\boxed{S_t = \frac{\dot{m}}{\bar{A}\rho_u} = \frac{0.131}{0.0136 \, (1.206)} = 8.0 \, \text{m/s}} \, .$$

Comment. Note that we have calculated a mean turbulent burning velocity for the entire flame. The implied assumptions that the flame is perfectly wedge-shaped and that the unburned mixture enters the reaction zone at a uniform velocity are only approximations; thus, local turbulent flame speeds may differ from the calculated mean.

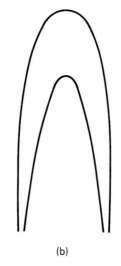

FIGURE 12.6
(a) Superposition of instantaneous reaction fronts obtained at different times. (After Ref. [15] from Ref. [19], reprinted by permission of Academic Press.) (b) Turbulent flame "brush" associated with a time-averaged view of the same flame.

(a)

(b)

STRUCTURE OF TURBULENT PREMIXED FLAMES

Experimental Observations

One particular view of the structure of turbulent flames is illustrated in Fig. 12.6. Here we see (Fig. 12.6a) superimposed instantaneous contours of convoluted thin reaction zones, obtained by visualizing the large temperature gradients in the flame using schlieren photography at different instants. The flow is from bottom to top with the flame stabilized above a tube through which the reactants flow into the open atmosphere. The instantaneous flame front is highly convoluted, with the largest folds near the top of the flame. The positions of the reaction zones move rapidly in space, producing a time-averaged view that gives the appearance of a thick reaction zone (Fig. 12.6b). This apparently thick reaction zone is frequently referred to as a **turbulent flame brush**. The instantaneous view, however, clearly shows the actual reaction front to be relatively thin, as in a laminar premixed flame. These reaction fronts are sometimes referred to as **laminar flamelets**.

As mentioned above, spark-ignition engines operate with turbulent premixed flames. Recent developments in laser-based instrumentation have allowed researchers to explore, in much more detail than previously possible, the hostile environment of the internal combustion engine combustion chamber. Figure 12.7 shows a time sequence of two-dimensional flame visualizations in a spark-ignition engine from a study by zur Loye and Bracco [16]. The flame begins to propagate outward from the spark plug, as shown in the first frame, and moves across the chamber until nearly all the gas is burned. In these flame visualizations, we see that the division between the unburned and burned gases occurs over a very short distance and the flame front is distorted by both relatively large- and small-scale

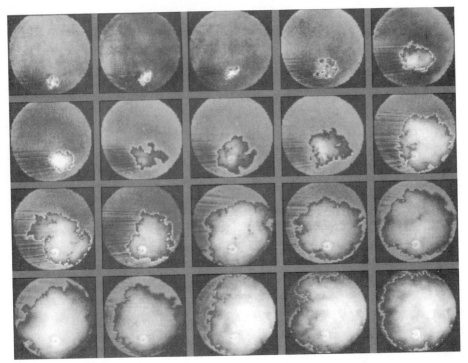

FIGURE 12.7
Visualization of turbulent flame propagation in a spark-ignition engine operating at 1200 rpm. Images represent a planar slice through the combustion chamber with the sequence starting shortly after ignition (upper left) and proceeding until the flame nears the cylinder walls (lower right). (Reprinted with permission from Ref. [16], ©1987 Society of Automotive Engineers, Inc.)

wrinkles. For the specific conditions associated with Fig. 12.7, the burned gas and unburned gas are generally simply connected, i.e., there are very few islands or pockets of burned gas within the burned gas, and vice versa. At higher engine speeds (2400 rpm), however, islands and pockets are seen frequently.

Three Flame Regimes

The visualizations of turbulent flames presented above (Figs. 12.6 and 12.7), suggest that the effect of turbulence is to wrinkle and distort an essentially laminar flame front (Chapter 8). Turbulent flames of this type are referred to as being in the **wrinkled laminar-flame regime**. This is one pole in our classification of turbulent premixed flames. At the other pole is the **distributed-reaction regime**. Falling between these two regimes is a region sometimes referred to as the **flamelets-in-eddies regime**.

REGIME CRITERIA. Before we discuss each regime in more detail, it is helpful to develop a basic understanding of the factors that differentiate these three regimes.

To do this, we appeal to some of the basic concepts of turbulent flow presented in Chapter 11, in particular, the idea that various length scales exist simultaneously in a turbulent flow. Recall that the smallest scale, the Kolmogorov microscale, ℓ_K, represents the smallest eddies in the flow. These eddies rotate rapidly and have high vorticity, resulting in the dissipation of the fluid kinetic energy into internal energy, i.e., fluid friction results in a temperature rise of the fluid. At the other extreme of the length-scale spectrum is the integral scale, ℓ_0, which characterizes the largest eddy sizes. The basic structure of a turbulent flame is governed by the relationships of ℓ_K and ℓ_0 to the laminar flame thickness, δ_L (cf. Chapter 8). The laminar flame thickness characterizes the thickness of a reaction zone controlled by molecular, not turbulent, transport of heat and mass. More explicitly, the three regimes are defined by

$$\text{Wrinkled laminar flames:} \quad \delta_L \leq \ell_K \tag{12.2a}$$

$$\text{Flamelets in eddies:} \quad \ell_0 > \delta_L > \ell_K \tag{12.2b}$$

$$\text{Distributed reactions:} \quad \delta_L > \ell_0 \tag{12.2c}$$

Equations 12.2a and 12.2c have clear physical interpretations; when the flame thickness, δ_L, is much thinner than the smallest scale of turbulence, ℓ_K, the turbulent motion can only wrinkle or distort the thin laminar flame zone (Eqn. 12.2a). The criterion for the existence of a wrinkled laminar flame (Eqn. 12.2a) is sometimes referred to as the **Williams–Klimov criterion** [5]. At the other extreme, if all scales of turbulent motion are smaller than the reaction zone thickness (δ_L), then transport within the reaction zone is no longer governed solely by molecular processes, but is controlled, or at least influenced, by the turbulence. This criterion for the existence of a distributed reaction zone is sometimes referred to as the **Damköhler criterion** [17].

It is convenient to discuss flame structure in terms of dimensionless parameters. The turbulence length scales and laminar flame thickness can be expressed as two dimensionless parameters: ℓ_K/δ_L and ℓ_0/δ_L. Two additional parameters are important to our discussion, the turbulence Reynolds number, Re_{ℓ_0}, defined in Chapter 11, and the Damköhler number, which is introduced below.

DAMKÖHLER NUMBER. An important dimensionless parameter in combustion is the **Damköhler number, Da**. This parameter appears in the description of many combustion problems and is quite important in understanding turbulent premixed flames. The fundamental meaning of the Damköhler number, Da, used here is that it represents the ratio of a characteristic flow or mixing time to a characteristic chemical time; thus,

$$Da \equiv \frac{\text{characteristic flow time}}{\text{characteristic chemical time}} = \frac{\tau_{\text{flow}}}{\tau_{\text{chem}}}. \tag{12.3}$$

The evaluation of Da depends on the situation under study, in the same sense that the Reynolds number has many particular definitions derived from its fundamental meaning as the ratio of inertia to viscous forces. For our study of premixed flames, particularly useful characteristic times are the lifetimes of large eddies in the flow $(\tau_{\text{flow}} \equiv \ell_0/v'_{rms})$ and a chemical time based on a laminar flame $(\tau_{\text{chem}} \equiv \delta_L/S_L)$. Using these characteristic times, we define

$$Da = \frac{\ell_0/v'_{rms}}{\delta_L/S_L} = \left(\frac{\ell_0}{\delta_L}\right)\left(\frac{S_L}{v'_{rms}}\right). \qquad (12.4)$$

When chemical reactions rates are fast in comparison to fluid mixing rates, then $Da \gg 1$, and a **fast-chemistry regime** is defined. Conversely, when reaction rates are slow in comparison to mixing rates, then $Da \ll 1$. Note that the characteristic rates are inversely proportional to their corresponding characteristic times. The definition of Da in Eqn. 12.4 is also instructive in that it represents the product of the length-scale ratio, ℓ_0/δ_L, and the reciprocal of a relative turbulence intensity, v'_{rms}/S_L. Thus, if we fix the length-scale ratio, the Damköhler number falls as turbulence intensity goes up.

Thus far in our discussion, we have identified five dimensionless parameters: ℓ_K/δ_L, ℓ_0/δ_L, Re_{ℓ_0}, Da, and v'_{rms}/S_L. From their fundamental definitions, these five groups can be interrelated, and one such way of viewing these interrelationships is shown in Fig. 12.8 [17]. With such a representation (Fig. 12.8), we can estimate the flame regime that might occur in practical combustion devices, provided we have sufficient information characterizing the turbulent flowfield. The two bold lines in Fig. 12.8 define three separate regions on the graph of Da versus Re_{ℓ_0} corresponding to the three regions defined by Eqns. 12.2a–c. Above the bold line denoted $\ell_K/\delta_L = 1$, reactions can take place in thin sheets, i.e., the wrinkled laminar-flame regime; below the other bold line, denoted $\ell_0/\delta_L = 1$, reactions will take place over a distributed region in space. The region between the two bold lines is our so-called flamelets-in-eddies regime. The boxed region containing the data symbols represents an estimate of the domain associated with spark-ignition engine combustion [17]. Here we see that combustion is predicted to occur with either wrinkled laminar flames or flamelets in eddies, depending on the specific operating conditions.

Example 12.2. Estimate the Damköhler number and the ratio of the Kolmogorov length scale to the laminar flame thickness for conditions prevailing in the combustor of a utility-class gas-turbine engine. What flame regime does this suggest? Assume the unburned gas temperature is 650 K, the burned gas temperature is 2000 K, the pressure is 15 atm, the mean velocity is 100 m/s, equivalence ratio is unity, fuel properties are those of isooctane, and the combustor can diameter is 0.3 m. Assume a relative turbulence intensity of 10% and an integral scale of 1/10 the can diameter. Treat the fuel and air as essentially premixed.

Solution. The Damköhler number is estimated from Eqn. 12.4, where the characteristic flow time is

$$\tau_{\text{flow}} = \frac{\ell_0}{v'_{rms}} = \frac{D/10}{0.10\bar{v}} = \frac{0.30/10}{0.10\,(100)}$$

$$\tau_{\text{flow}} = 0.003\,\text{s} \quad \text{or} \quad 3\,\text{ms}$$

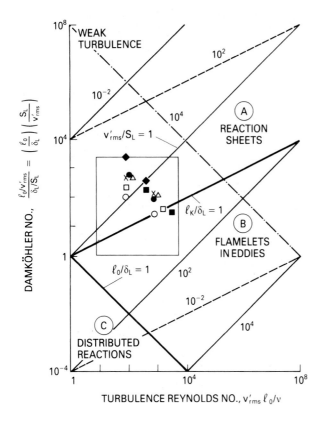

FIGURE 12.8
Important parameters characterizing turbulent premixed combustion. Conditions satisfying the Williams–Klimov criterion for the existence of wrinkled flames lie above the solid line ($\ell_K = \delta_L$), and conditions satisfying the Damköhler criterion for distributed reactions fall below the solid line ($\ell_0 = \delta_L$). (After Ref. [17], reprinted with permission from SAE Paper No. 850345, ©1985 Society of Automotive Engineers, Inc.)

and the characteristic chemical time is δ_L/S_L. To estimate the chemical time, we will use the laminar flame speed correlations of Chapter 8 to find S_L (Eqn. 8.28), and the simple theory result (Eqn. 8.21b) to estimate the laminar flame thickness δ_L. Following the procedures of Example 8.3, we obtain the laminar flame speed, assuming the fuel burns similarly to isooctane:

$$S_L = S_{L,\mathrm{ref}}\left(\frac{T_u}{T_{u,\mathrm{ref}}}\right)^{\gamma}\left(\frac{P}{P_{\mathrm{ref}}}\right)^{\beta}$$

$$S_L = 24.9\left(\frac{650}{298}\right)^{2.18}\left(\frac{15}{1}\right)^{-0.16} = 88.4\,\mathrm{cm/s}.$$

The laminar flame thickness (Eqn. 8.21b) is

$$\delta \cong 2\alpha/S_L.$$

The thermal diffusivity is estimated at the average temperature, $0.5(T_b + T_u) = 1325\,\mathrm{K}$, using air properties (Table C.1) and corrected for the elevated pressure,

$$\alpha = 254 \cdot 10^{-6} \left(\frac{1\,\text{atm}}{15\,\text{atm}}\right) = 1.7 \cdot 10^{-5}\,\text{m}^2/\text{s}.$$

Thus,

$$\delta_L \cong 2(1.7 \cdot 10^{-5})/0.884 = 3.85 \cdot 10^{-5}\,\text{m}$$
$$\delta_L \cong 0.039\,\text{mm}.$$

The characteristic chemical time is then

$$\tau_{chem} = \frac{\delta_L}{S_L} = \frac{3.85 \cdot 10^{-5}}{0.884} = 4.4 \cdot 10^{-5}\,\text{s}$$
$$\tau_{chem} = 0.0435\,\text{ms}.$$

The Damköhler number can now be estimated as

$$\boxed{Da = \frac{\tau_{flow}}{\tau_{chem}} = \frac{3\,\text{ms}}{0.0435\,\text{ms}} = 69}.$$

We can locate a point on Fig. 12.8 after calculating Re_{ℓ_0}:

$$Re_{\ell_0} = \frac{\rho v'_{rms}\ell_0}{\mu} = \frac{(P/RT_b)\,(0.1\bar{v})\,(D/10)}{\mu_b}$$
$$= \frac{15\,(101,325)/[(288.3)\,(2000)](0.1)\,100(0.30/10)}{689 \cdot 10^{-7}} = 11,477.$$

This corresponds to $\ell_K/\delta_L \approx 1$ from Fig. 12.8 and falls on the boundary between the wrinkled flame and the flamelets-in-eddies regimes. More accurately, we can estimate ℓ_K/δ_L by calculating ℓ_K from Eqn. 11.9, as in Example 11.1:

$$\ell_K = \ell_0 Re_{\ell_0}^{-3/4} = \left(\frac{0.30}{10}\right)(11,477)^{-0.75} = 2.7 \cdot 10^{-5}\,\text{m}$$
$$\ell_K/\delta_L = 2.7 \cdot 10^{-5}/3.85 \cdot 10^{-5} = 0.70$$

$$\boxed{\ell_K/\delta_L = 0.7 \approx 1}.$$

This confirms our estimate obtained from the graph.

Comment. In Fig. 12.8, our turbine example conditions fall just to the right of the box representing reciprocating engine conditions. Thus, we see that the turbulent combustion regimes of both devices are not that far apart. We also note that our estimate of the mean thermal diffusivity was based on a density evaluated at the mean temperature, rather than the unburned gas density as employed previously in the theoretical developments in Chapter 8. Using ρ_u instead of $\rho(\bar{T})$ to evaluate $\alpha(\bar{T})$ yields $\alpha = 8.8 \cdot 10^{-6}\,\text{m}^2/\text{s}$, which is about half as large as that calculated above. Regardless of which value is used for $\alpha(\bar{T})$, we still estimate that the conditions are near the boundary between the wrinkled-flame and flamelets-in-eddies regimes.

WRINKLED LAMINAR-FLAME REGIME

In this regime, chemical reactions occur in thin sheets. Referring again to Fig. 12.8, we see that reaction sheets only occur for Damköhler numbers greater than unity, depending on the turbulence Reynolds number, clearly indicating that the reaction sheet regime is characterized by fast chemistry (in comparison to fluid mechanical mixing). For example, typical values for the engine-data Damköhler numbers in the reaction-sheet regime are of the order of 500 for $Re_{\ell_0} \approx 100$. For these conditions, the turbulence intensity v'_{rms} is of the same order of magnitude as the laminar flame speed S_L.

One of the simplest ways of dealing with the wrinkled laminar-flame regime of turbulent combustion is to assume that the flamelets propagate with a velocity consistent with a plane (one-dimensional) laminar flame. In this view, the only effect of turbulence is the wrinkling of the flame, which results in an increase in flame area; therefore, the ratio of the turbulent flame speed to the laminar flame speed is simply a ratio of the wrinkled flamelet area to the time-mean flame area $\overline{A}$ defined in Eqn. 12.1. This can be seen by expressing the turbulent burning rate, $\dot{m}$, in terms of flamelet area and speed, i.e.,

$$\dot{m} = \rho_u \overline{A} S_t = \rho_u A_{\text{flamelets}} S_L. \tag{12.5}$$

Thus,

$$S_t/S_L = A_{\text{flamelets}}/\overline{A}, \tag{12.6}$$

and is illustrated in Fig. 12.9. In reality, S_L will not be a single value but will depend on local flow properties. In particular, flame curvature, velocity gradients in the flow, and recirculation of burned products into the flame, can all alter the local laminar flame velocity [1]. A discussion of these effects is beyond the scope of this book, and the interested reader is referred to the literature and advanced textbooks, e.g., Refs. [4,5,18,19].

Many theories have been developed to relate turbulent flame speeds to flow properties, based on the underlying concept of wrinkled laminar flamelets; for

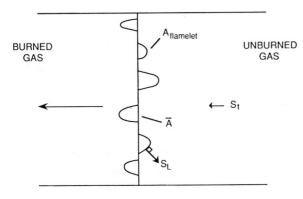

FIGURE 12.9

Sketch of wrinkled laminar flame illustrating instantaneous flamelet area together with the mean area, $\overline{A}$, used to define the turbulent flame speed, S_t.

example, Andrews et al. [1], in 1975, cite 13 different models and more have been developed since. We will not attempt to review the many theories, but, rather, present three models as examples. The first model is by Damköhler [20], and expressed as

$$S_t/S_L = 1 + v'_{rms}/S_L, \qquad (12.7)$$

and the second, a more recent development, by Clavin and Williams [21], given by

$$S_t/S_L = \left\{ 0.5 \left[1 + \left(1 + 8Cv'^2_{rms}/S^2_L \right)^{1/2} \right] \right\}^{1/2}, \qquad (12.8a)$$

where C is a constant with a value of approximately 1. For small values of v'_{rms}/S_L, Eqn. 12.8a reduces to

$$S_t/S_L = 1 + Cv'^2_{rms}/S^2_L. \qquad (12.8b)$$

The third relationship, proposed by Klimov [22], is

$$S_t/S_L = 3.5 \left(v'_{rms}/S_L \right)^{0.7}, \qquad (12.9)$$

for $v'_{rms}/S_L \gg 1$.

The Damköhler model (Eqn 12.7) is based on the fact that for a constant laminar flame speed in a purely laminar flow, the flame area, A_{flame}, is directly proportional to the flow velocity, v_u, i.e., $\dot{m} = \rho_u v_u A = \rho_u S_L A_{flame}$; hence, the area ratio A_{flame}/A is equal to v_u/S_L, where A is the flow area, in accordance with the laminar flame concepts developed in Chapter 8. Analogously, this idea is then extended to the turbulent flow case by assuming that

$$A_{wrinkles}/\overline{A} = v'_{rms}/S_L \qquad (12.10)$$

where the area of the wrinkles is defined as the area in excess of the time-mean flame area, i.e., $A_{wrinkles} \equiv A_{flamelets} - \overline{A}$. So, from our definition of turbulent flame speed (Eqn. 12.5), we recover the Damköhler model (Eqn. 12.7):

$$S_t = \frac{A_{flamelets}}{\overline{A}} S_L = \frac{\overline{A} + A_{wrinkles}}{\overline{A}} S_L = \left(1 + \frac{v'_{rms}}{S_L} \right) S_L. \qquad (12.11)$$

The Clavin and Williams expressions (Eqns. 12.8a and b) are derived from a more rigorous treatment of the dynamics of wrinkled laminar flames for small values of v'_{rms}. Further discussion is beyond the scope of this book, while more information can be found in Refs. [6,7,21]. The functional form of the Klimov relationship (Eqn. 12.9) is based on theoretical grounds; however, the proportionality constant and exponent are based on experimental data in the Russian literature (Ref. [23] and others) cited by Klimov [22].

Figure 12.10 shows experimental data for turbulent flame speeds [23] and the predictions from the wrinkled laminar-flame models of Damköhler (Eqn. 12.7) and Klimov (Eqn. 12.9). Since the Klimov model [22] has constants partially derived from this experimental data set, we expect good agreement. Note, however, that the straight-line form of the Damköhler model does not capture the

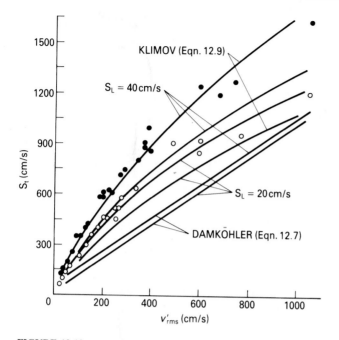

FIGURE 12.10

Experimental data for S_t versus v'_{rms} compared with wrinkled laminar-flame theories of turbulent flame propagation. (Data from Ref. [23].)

experimental trend. Since the Clavin and Williams model (Eqn. 12.8) is based on low levels of v'_{rms}, the predictions of this model are not shown.

Although many different theoretical formulae have been developed to predict S_t for the wrinkled laminar-flame regime, there appears to be general agreement that S_t/S_L depends only on v'_{rms}/S_L and does not involve any other turbulence properties, such as length scales [4]. Figure 12.11 shows experimental results obtained for unconfined flames attached at the end of a channel, where the channel contained turbulence-generating grids of 8-mm (Configuration I) or 4-mm (Configuration II) rods or was smooth. Since the rods affect the turbulence length scales, the lack of any clear differentiation by configuration supports the idea of length-scale independence. Further research is needed before specific recommendations can be made for flame-speed relationships appropriate for engineering design purposes.

Example 12.3. Laser Doppler anemometry is used to measure the mean and fluctuating velocities in a specially instrumented spark-ignition engine. Estimate the turbulent flame speed for the following conditions: $v'_{rms} = 3\,\text{m/s}$, $P = 5\,\text{atm}$, $T_u = 500°\text{C}$, and $\Phi = 1.0$ (propane–air). The mass fraction of the residual burned gases mixed with the fresh charge is 0.09.

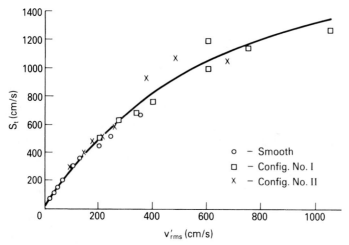

FIGURE 12.11
Turbulent flame speeds for flames anchored downstream of a smooth section or turbulence-generating grids (Config. I, 8-mm rods, Config. II, 4-mm rods). $S_L = 40$ cm/s. (From Ref. [23].)

Solution. We will employ the theoretical relations of Klimov (Eqn. 12.9) and Damköhler (Eqn. 12.7) to provide estimates of the turbulent burning velocity. Both relations require a value for the laminar flame speed S_L to evaluate S_t; thus, we first employ the correlations of Chapter 8 to determine S_L (Eqn. 8.28) as follows:

$$S_{L,\text{ref}} = B_M + B_2(\Phi - 1.08)^2$$
$$= 33.33 - 138.65\,(1 - 1.08)^2 = 32.44\,\text{cm/s}$$

$$S_L = 32.44\left(\frac{T_u}{T_{u,\text{ref}}}\right)^{\gamma}\left(\frac{P}{P_{\text{ref}}}\right)^{\beta}(1 - 2.1Y_{\text{dil}})$$
$$= 32.44\left(\frac{773}{298}\right)^{2.18}\left(\frac{5}{1}\right)^{-0.16}[1 - 2.1(0.09)] = 162.4\,\text{cm/s}.$$

Thus,

$$\frac{v'_{rms}}{S_L} = \frac{3}{1.62} = 1.85.$$

From Eqn. 12.9,

$$S_t = 3.5S_L\left(\frac{v'_{rms}}{S_L}\right)^{0.7}$$
$$= 3.5\,(1.67)\,(1.8)^{0.7}$$

$$\boxed{S_t = 8.8\,\text{m/s}}.$$

Or, from Eqn. 12.7,

$$S_t = S_L + v'_{rms}$$
$$= 1.67 + 3$$
$$\boxed{S_t = 4.7\,\text{m/s}}\,.$$

Comment. We note that the values from the two theories differ by nearly a factor of two. Also, since v'_{rms}/S_L is only 1.8, it is not clear that the condition of $v'_{rms}/S_L \gg 1$ for Eqn. 12.9 has been met.

DISTRIBUTED-REACTION REGIME

One way to enter this regime is to require small integral length scales, $\ell_0/\delta_L < 1$, and small Damköhler numbers ($Da < 1$). This is difficult to achieve in a practical device, since these requirements imply that simultaneously ℓ_0 must be small and v'_{rms} must be large, i.e., small flow passages and very high velocities. (These conditions can be inferred easily from Fig. 12.8.) Pressure losses in such devices surely would be huge, hence, rendering them impractical. Also, it is not clear that a flame can be sustained under such conditions [22]. Nonetheless, it is instructive to look at how chemical reactions and turbulence might interact in this regime, even if it is generally inaccessible for flame reactions, since many pollutant formation reactions are slow and, hence, occur in distributed regions.

Figure 12.12 heuristically illustrates a distributed-reaction zone in which all turbulence length scales are within the reaction zone. Since reaction times are

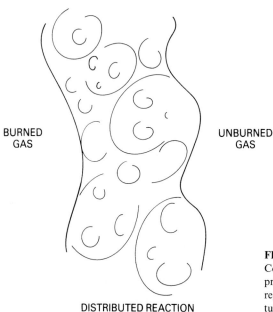

BURNED
GAS

UNBURNED
GAS

DISTRIBUTED REACTION
ZONE

FIGURE 12.12
Conceptual view of turbulent flame propagation in the distributed-reaction regime showing various length scales of turbulence within the reaction zone proper.

longer than eddy lifetimes $(Da < 1)$, fluctuations in velocity, v'_{rms}, temperature, T'_{rms}, and species mass fractions, $Y'_{i,rms}$, all occur simultaneously. Thus, the instantaneous chemical reaction rates depend on the instantaneous values of $T(= \bar{T} + T')$ and $Y_i(= \bar{Y}_i + Y'_i)$, and fluctuate as well. Moreover, the time-average reaction rate is not simply evaluated using mean values, but involves correlations among the fluctuating quantities. (Recall from Chapter 11 that the correlation of velocity components results in the Reynolds stresses.) In the following, we develop a mean reaction rate for a single bimolecular reaction step

$$A + B \overset{k(T)}{\rightarrow} AB.$$

Recall from Chapter 4 that the reaction rate for species A, $\dot{\omega}_A$ (kmol/m^3-s) can be expressed

$$\dot{\omega}_A = -k[X_A][X_B] \tag{12.12}$$

where the brackets denote molar concentrations (kmol/m^3) and k is the temperature-dependent rate coefficient. Expressing Eqn. 12.12 in terms of mass fractions yields

$$\frac{dY_A}{dt} = -kY_A Y_B \frac{\rho}{MW_B}, \tag{12.13}$$

where ρ is the mixture density. Defining the instantaneous values for each variable,

$$k = \bar{k} + k',$$
$$Y_A = \bar{Y}_A + Y'_A,$$
$$Y_B = \bar{Y}_B + Y'_B,$$
$$\rho = \bar{\rho} + \rho',$$

substituting into Eqn. 12.3, and taking the time average, as denoted by the overbar, we arrive at the average reaction rate, $\overline{dY_A/dt}$,

$$\overline{dY_A/dt} = -\overline{k\rho Y_A Y_B} = -\overline{(\bar{k} + k')(\bar{\rho} + \rho')(\bar{Y}_A + Y'_A)(\bar{Y}_B + Y'_B)}, \tag{12.14}$$

where MW_B has been absorbed in the rate coefficient k. The right-hand-side of Eqn. 12.14 can be expanded to yield

$$-\frac{\overline{dY_A}}{dt} = \bar{\rho}\bar{k}\bar{Y}_A\bar{Y}_B$$
$$+ \bar{\rho}\bar{k}\overline{Y'_A Y'_B} + \text{five additional two-variable correlation terms}$$
$$+ \bar{k}\overline{\rho' Y'_A Y'_B} + \text{three additional three-variable correlation terms}$$
$$+ \overline{\rho'k'Y'_A Y'_B}. \tag{12.15}$$

From Eqn. 12.15, the complications caused by turbulent fluctuations are immediately obvious, and multitudinous. The leading term on the right-hand-side of

Eqn. 12.15 is the rate of reaction that would be obtained simply by substituting the mean values of ρ, k, Y_A, and Y_B into Eqn. 12.13. This term is then augmented by six two-variable correlations, four three-variable correlations, and a single four-variable correlation! Obviously, many terms could be eliminated by assuming isothermal ($k = $ constant) and constant-density flow, leaving only the correlations involving Y_A' and Y_B'; however, the problem would still be formidable.

FLAMELETS-IN-EDDIES REGIME

This regime lies in the wedge-shaped region between the wrinkled laminar-flame and distributed-reactions regimes as shown in Fig. 12.8. This region is typified by moderate Damköhler numbers and high turbulence intensities ($v_{rms}'/S_L \gg 1$). This region is of particular interest in that it is likely that some practical combustion devices operate in this regime. For example, we note that a portion of the estimated region of spark-ignition engine combustion [17] lies in the flamelets-in-eddies regime. The experiments of Ballal and Lefebvre [24,25], utilizing premixed propane flames in a confined flow, provide much of the experimental data related to this regime.

Figure 12.13 illustrates, conceptually, how combustion might proceed in this regime and follows the ideas that support the **eddy-breakup model** [4,26]. This concept has met with success in predicting combustion rates in some devices. As illustrated in Fig. 12.13, the burning zone consists of parcels of unburned gas and almost fully burned gas. The intrinsic idea behind the eddy-breakup model is that the rate of combustion is determined by the rate at which parcels of unburned gas are broken down into smaller ones, such that there is sufficient interfacial area between the unburned mixture and hot gases to permit reaction [4]. The implication of this is that chemical reaction rates play no role in determining the burning rates, but, rather, turbulent mixing rates completely control

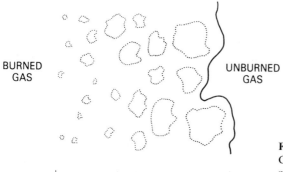

BURNED GAS

UNBURNED GAS

|← FLAME ZONE →|

FIGURE 12.13
Conceptual view of turbulent flame propagation in the flamelets-in-eddies regime.

combustion. Implementing these ideas in mathematical form, the fuel mass burning rate per unit volume, $\bar{m}_F'''$, can be expressed [7]

$$\bar{m}_F''' = -\rho C_F Y_{F,rms}' \epsilon_0 / (3v_{rms}'^2 / 2) \qquad (12.16)$$

where C_F is a constant ($0.1 < C_F < 100$, but typically of the order of unity), $Y_{F,rms}'$ is the root-mean-square fuel mass fraction fluctuation, ϵ_0 is the turbulence dissipation rate (defined in Chapter 11 by Eqn. 11.7) and $3v_{rms}'^2 / 2$ is the turbulence kinetic energy (per unit mass) assuming $v_{rms}' = v_{x,rms}' = v_{y,rms}' = v_{z,rms}'$, i.e., isotropic turbulence. Utilizing the definition of ϵ_0 and pulling all of the constants into C_F, we obtain

$$\bar{m}_F''' = -\rho C_F Y_{F,rms}' v_{rms}' / \ell_0. \qquad (12.17)$$

In Eqn. 12.17, we see that the volumetric mass burning rate depends directly on the characteristic fluctuation of Y, $Y_{F,rms}'$, and the characteristic turn-around time of an eddy, v_{rms}' / ℓ_0. Therefore, unlike the theories describing the wrinkled laminar-flame regime, this model predicts that the turbulence length scale is quite important in determining turbulent burning rates.

FLAME STABILIZATION

As mentioned earlier in this chapter, there are several important practical applications or specific devices that employ essentially turbulent premixed flames: premixed and nozzle-mixed gas burners for industrial or commercial applications, premixing/prevaporizing gas-turbine combustors, turbojet afterburners, and spark-ignition engines. In spark-ignition engines, no provision for flame stabilization is required since the flame freely propagates in a sealed chamber, and the concepts of flashback, liftoff, and blowoff (cf. Chapter 8) have no meaning here. Instability in spark-ignition (SI) engines is characterized, rather, by failure to achieve consistent ignition, or early flame growth, and incomplete propagation of the flame to all reaches of the combustion chamber. Therefore, our attention in this section will be directed toward applications other than SI engines.

In a practical device, a stable flame is one that is anchored at a desired location and is resistant to flashback, liftoff, and blowoff over the device's operating range. Several methods are employed to hold and stabilize flames:

- Low-velocity by-pass ports
- Refractory burner tiles
- Bluff-body flameholders
- Swirl or jet-induced recirculating flows
- Rapid increase in flow area creating recirculating separated flow.

In some applications, several methods may be used simultaneously, and, in general, these same methods are employed in stabilizing turbulent nonpremixed flames, as discussed in Chapter 13.

The essential principle involved in anchoring a flame in a turbulent flow, at conditions sufficiently removed from blowout, is that the local turbulent flame speed matches the local mean flow velocity. This is the same principle that we applied to the stabilization of laminar flames, except that now the turbulent flame speed replaces the laminar flame speed. Criteria establishing blowout, however, are more similar to those associated with ignition, as discussed below.

By-Pass Ports

Figure 12.14 illustrates the application of low-velocity by-pass ports to stabilize an industrial burner flame. The same principle is used in hand-held propane torches and modern laboratory Bunsen burners, so it might be possible for you to get a first-hand look at such a device.

Burner Tiles

Flames are frequently stabilized within a refractory passageway, referred to as a **burner tile**, in industrial burners. Figure 12.5 (bottom) illustrates a typical burner tile for a premixed burner. After startup, the refractory tile represents a nearly adiabatic boundary, reradiating back to the flame and thereby maintaining near-adiabatic flame temperatures. This helps to keep turbulent burning velocities high through the strong temperature dependence of the laminar flame speed (cf. Eqns. 12.7 and 8.24). From Fig. 12.5, we also observe that the specific burner tile shown has been designed with a relatively large divergence angle; therefore, it is possible

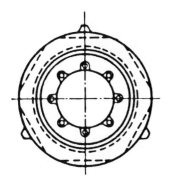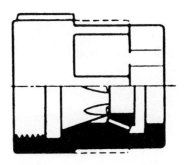

FIGURE 12.14
Flame-retention-type industrial burner. The lower half of this burner nozzle is shown in section to illustrate the by-pass ports which serve to relight the main flame in the event that it is blown out. A gas mixer must be provided upstream. (From Ref. [13], reprinted by permission of North American Manufacturing Co.)

that the boundary layer separates and creates a recirculation zone within the tile. Recirculation of hot combustion products back upstream promotes ignition of the unburned mixture. Swirling flows, discussed below, are also frequently employed in conjunction with burner tiles. Presser *et al.* [27] present results of a numerical study that explored the effects of burner tile geometry and recirculation on flame stability.

Bluff Bodies

Turbulent flames can also be stabilized in the wake of a bluff, i.e., unstreamlined, body, as shown in Fig. 12.15. A considerable amount of research has been conducted on bluff-body stabilization, and a good review can be found in Ref. [29]. Applications utilizing bluff-body stabilizers include ramjets, turbojet afterburners, and nozzle-mixing burners, as shown in Fig. 12.4.

The principal characteristic of bluff-body stabilized flames is the existence of a strong recirculation zone behind the flame-holding device, which is frequently in the form of a "vee gutter" with the point of the vee facing upstream. The recirculation zone consists of burned products of nearly uniform and adiabatic temperature. The flame stabilization point lies close to the edge of the flame holder, as suggested by Fig. 12.15. Blowout is governed by the processes occurring near the recirculation zone [29].

Several theories have been proposed to explain blowout from bluff-body stabilized flames; however, we will confine our discussion to the ideas of Spalding [30] and Zukoski and Marble [28], summarized and expanded by Williams [7,29]. This model is that a critical amount of energy must be released during the time that the initially unburned gases are in contact with the hot gases of the recircula-

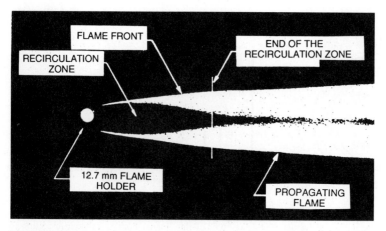

FIGURE 12.15
Turbulent flame stabilized in the wake of a bluff body. (After Ref. [28], reprinted by permission of the authors and Butterworth-Heinemann.)

tion zone. Applying this model results in the following formula for the **blowoff velocity**, i.e., the value of the upstream velocity that causes the flame to blow off the flame holder:

$$v_{\text{blowout}} = 2\rho_0 L \left(\frac{S_L}{\rho \alpha_T} \right)^2, \qquad (12.18)$$

where ρ_0 and ρ are the unburned and burned gas densities, respectively, L is a characteristic length of the recirculation zone, and α_T denotes a so-called **turbulent thermal diffusivity**. If we assume a turbulent Prandtl number of unity, then $\alpha_T = \varepsilon$, where ε is the turbulent diffusivity, or eddy viscosity, as defined in Chapter 11.

Stabilization of flames by a rapid increase in flow area, the most drastic being a step, has much in common with bluff-body stabilization. Again, the presence of a strong recirculation zone of hot products ignites the unburned gases and provides a region where the local turbulent flame speed can match the local flow velocity. Steps for stabilization are used in premixed gas-turbine combustors and premixed industrial burners.

Swirl or Jet-Induced Recirculating Flows

As discussed above, the creation of a recirculation zone using a solid obstruction or a rapid area change can anchor a flame. Recirculation zones also can be created by introducing a swirl component to the incoming gases or by directing jets in an appropriate manner into the combustion space. Figure 12.16 illustrates the recirculation zone created by inlet swirl, while Fig. 12.17 shows several configurations of can combustors with jet-induced recirculation zones [31].

Swirl stabilization is frequently used in industrial burners and gas-turbine combustors for both premixed and nonpremixed modes of combustion. Of course, with nonpremixed flames, the swirl-induced flow patterns not only affect mixing of products and reactants, but also the mixing of fuel and air. Further discussion of this aspect of swirling flows is presented in Chapter 13.

SUMMARY

In this chapter, you were introduced to the many applications of premixed turbulent combustion. The concept of a turbulent flame speed was introduced and defined, and the nature of turbulent premixed flames described. We saw that there were three regimes of turbulent premixed combustion: the wrinkled laminar-flame regime, the flamelets-in-eddies regime, and the distributed-reaction regime. Criteria for combustion occurring in each of these regimes were defined. These criteria are based on the ratio of the laminar flame thickness to various turbulence length scales. The Damköhler number was defined as the ratio of a characteristic flow time to a characteristic chemical time, and the idea of a fast-chemistry regime was presented. We briefly explored wrinkled laminar-flame theories and showed

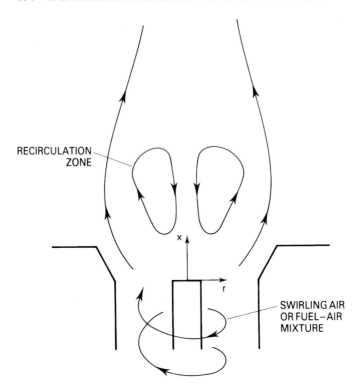

FIGURE 12.16
Flow patterns for a flame with inlet swirl.

that there is no single theory that is generally agreed upon. We also explored the nature of the distributed-reaction regime and saw the tremendous complexity introduced into the species conservation equations as a result of the various turbulent correlations. In dealing with the intermediate flamelet-in-eddies regime, we discussed the eddy-breakup model, which assumes that the combustion rate is dominated by fluid mechanical, rather than chemical, phenomena. The chapter ends with a discussion of the several ways turbulent flames are stabilized in practice. These included low-velocity by-pass ports, burner tiles, bluff bodies, swirl or jet-induced recirculation zones, and recirculation zones created by area-change-induced separation. All told, the understanding of turbulent premixed flames is in a tremendous state of flux. Therefore, our goal in this chapter has been to highlight some applications and to present some of the key theoretical concepts, supplemented by some experimental findings, to introduce this subject, cautioning the reader that, unlike some other mature engineering sciences, definitive answers to many questions are not yet available.

NOMENCLATURE

A	Area (m^2)
Da	Damköhler number

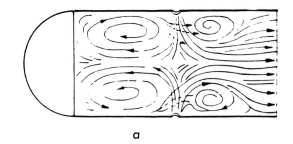

a

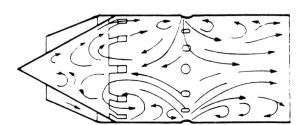

b

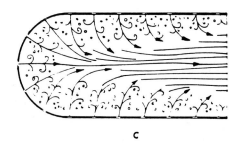

c

FIGURE 12.17
Flow patterns for can combustors with (a) single row of holes with enclosed end, (b) shrouded cone, and (c) multiple rows of holes. (From Ref. [31], reprinted by permission of The Combustion Institute.)

k	Reaction rate coefficient (various units)
ℓ_K	Kolmogorov microscale (m)
ℓ_0	Integral or Taylor macroscale (m)
$\dot{m}$	Mass flowrate (kg/s)
$\bar{\dot{m}}'''$	Volumetric mass production rate (kg/s-m^3)
MW	Molecular weight (kg/kmol)
Re	Reynolds number
S_L	Laminar flame speed (m/s)
S_t	Turbulent flame speed (m/s)
t	Time (s)
T	Temperature (K)
v	Velocity (m/s)
Y	Mass fraction (kg/kg)

Greek symbols

α	Thermal diffusivity (m²/s)
α_T	Turbulent thermal diffusivity (m²/s)
δ_L	Laminar flame thickness (m)
ε	Eddy viscosity (m²/s)
ϵ_0	Dissipation rate, Eqn. 11.7 (m²/s³)
ν	Kinematic viscosity (m²/s)
ρ	Density (kg/m₃)
τ	Time (s)
$\dot{\omega}$	Reaction rate (kmol/m³-s)

Subscripts

b	Burned
chem	Chemical
dil	Diluent
F	Fuel
ref	Reference state
rms	Root-mean-square
u	Unburned

Other symbols

$(\overline{})$	Time-averaged
$()'$	Fluctuating component
$[X]$	Molar concentration of species X (kmol/m³)

REFERENCES

1. Andrews, G. E., Bradley, D., and Lwakabamba, S. B., "Turbulence and Turbulent Flame Propagation—A Critical Appraisal," *Combustion and Flame*, 24: 285–304 (1975).
2. Abdel-Gayed, R. G., and Bradley, D., "Dependence of Turbulent Burning Velocity on Turbulent Reynolds Number and Ratio of Laminar Burning Velocity to R.M.S. Turbulent Velocity," *Sixteenth Symposium (International) on Combustion*, The Combustion Institute, Pittsburgh, pp. 1725–1735, 1976.
3. Libby, P. A., and Williams, F. A., "Turbulent Flows Involving Chemical Reactions," *Annual Review of Fluid Mechanics*, Vol. 8, Annual Reviews, Inc., Palo Alto, pp. 351–376, 1976.
4. Bray, K. N. C., "Turbulent Flows with Premixed Reactants," in *Topics in Applied Physics, Vol. 44, Turbulent Reacting Flows* (P. A. Libby, and F. A. Williams, eds.), Springer-Verlag, New York, pp. 115–183, 1980.
5. Williams, F. A., "Asymptotic Methods in Turbulent Combustion," *AIAA Journal*, 24: 867–875 (1986).
6. Clavin, P., "Dynamic Behavior of Premixed Flame Fronts in Laminar and Turbulent Flows," *Progress in Energy and Combustion Science*, 11: 1–59 (1985).
7. Williams, F. A., *Combustion Theory*, 2nd Ed., Addison-Wesley, Redwood City, CA, 1985.
8. Chomiak, J., *Combustion: A Study in Theory, Fact and Application*, Gordon & Breach, New York, 1990.
9. Heywood, J. B., *Internal Combustion Engine Fundamentals*, McGraw-Hill, New York, 1988.
10. Obert, E. F., *Internal Combustion Engines and Air Pollution*, Harper & Row, New York, 1973.
11. David, L. B., and Washam, R. M., "Development of a Dry Low NOₓ Combustor," ASME 89-GT-255, Gas Turbine and Aeroengine Congress and Exposition, Toronto, ON, 4–8 June, 1988.

12. Maghon, H., Berenbrink, P., Termuehlen, H., and Gartner, G., "Progress in NO_x and CO Emission Reduction of Gas Turbines," ASME 90-JPGC/GT-4, ASME/IEEE Power Generation Conference, Boston, 21–25 October 1990.
13. North American Manufacturing Co., *North American Combustion Handbook*, The North American Manufacturing Co., Cleveland, 1952.
14. North American Manufacturing Co., *North American Combustion Handbook*, 2nd Ed., North American Manufacturing Co., Cleveland, 1978.
15. Fox, M. D., and Weinberg, F. J., "An Experimental Study of Burner Stabilized Turbulent Flames in Premixed Reactants", *Proceedings of the Royal Society of London Series A*, 268: 222–239 (1962).
16. zur Loye, A. O., and Bracco, F. V., "Two-Dimensional Visualization of Premixed-Charge Flame Structure in an IC Engine," Paper 870454, SAE SP-715, Society of Automotive Engineers, Warrendale, PA, 1987.
17. Abraham, J., Williams, F. A., and Bracco, F. V., "A Discussion of Turbulent Flame Structure in Premixed Charges," Paper 850345, SAE P-156, Society of Automotive Engineers, Warrendale, PA, 1985.
18. Kuo, K. K., *Principles of Combustion*, John Wiley & Sons, New York, 1986.
19. Glassman, I., *Combustion*, 2nd Ed., Academic Press, Orlando, 1987.
20. Damköhler, G., "The Effect of Turbulence on the Flame Velocity in Gas Mixtures," *Zeitschrift Electrochem*, 46: 601–626 (1940) (English translation, NACA TM 1112, 1947).
21. Clavin, P., and Williams, F. A., "Effects of Molecular Diffusion and of Thermal Expansion on the Structure and Dynamics of Premixed Flames in Turbulent Flows of Large Scale and Low Intensity," *Journal of Fluid Mechanics*, 116: 251–282 (1982).
22. Klimov, A. M., "Premixed Turbulent Flames—Interplay of Hydrodynamic and Chemical Phenomena," in *Flames, Lasers, and Reactive Systems* (J. R. Bowen, N. Manson, A. K. Oppenheim, and R. I. Soloukhin, eds.), Progress in Astronautics and Aeronautics, Vol. 88, American Institute of Aeronautics and Astronautics, New York, pp. 133–146, 1983.
23. Ill'yashenko, S. M., and Talantov, A. V., *Theory and Analysis of Straight-Through-Flow Combustion Chambers*, Edited Machine Translation, FTD-MT-65-143, Wright-Patterson AFB, 7 April 1966.
24. Ballal, D. R., and Lefebvre, A. H., "The Structure and Propagation of Turbulent Flames," *Proceedings of the Royal Society of London Series A*, 344: 217–234 (1975).
25. Ballal, D. R., and Lefebvre, A. H., "The Structure of a Premixed Turbulent Flame," *Proceedings of the Royal Society of London Series A*, 367: 353–380 (1979).
26. Mason, H. B., and Spalding, D. B., "Prediction of Reaction Rates in Turbulent Premixed Boundary-Layer Flows," *Combustion Institute European Symposium* (F. J. Weinberg, ed.), Academic Press, New York, pp. 601–606, 1973.
27. Presser, C., Greenberg, J. B., Goldman, Y., and Timnat, Y. M., "A Numerical Study of Furnace Flame Root Stabilization Using Conical Burner Tunnels," *Nineteenth Symposium (International) on Combustion*, The Combustion Institute, Pittsburgh, pp. 519–527, 1982.
28. Zukoski, E. E., and Marble, F. E., "The Role of Wake Transition in the Process of Flame Stabilization on Bluff Bodies," in *Combustion Researches and Reviews, 1955*, AGARD, Butterworth, London, pp. 167–180, 1955.
29. Williams, F. A., "Flame Stabilization of Premixed Turbulent Gases," in *Applied Mechanics Surveys* (N. N. Abramson, H. Liebowitz, J. M. Crowley, and S. Juhasz, eds.), Spartan Books, Washington, DC, pp. 1157–1170, 1966.
30. Spalding, D. B., "Theoretical Aspects of Flame Stabilization," *Aircraft Engineering*, 25: 264–268 (1953).
31. Jeffs, R. A., "The Flame Stability and Heat Release Rates of Some Can-Type Combustion Chambers," *Eighth Symposium (International) on Combustion*, Williams & Wilkins, Baltimore, pp. 1014–1027, 1962.

PROBLEMS

12.1. Make a list of all the bold-faced words in Chapter 12 and discuss.

12.2. A turbulent flame is stabilized in a rectangular duct in the wake of a circular rod as shown in the sketch. The included angle of the V-shaped flame is 11.4°. Assuming the approach velocity of the unburned mixture is a uniform 50 m/s, estimate the turbulent flame speed.

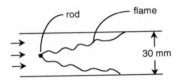

12.3. A turbulent flame is stabilized by a pilot flame at the exit of a 2-mm-diameter pipe coannular with a 25-mm-diameter duct. The flame is in the shape of a truncated cone. Assume that the flame goes all the way to the duct wall and that the unburned mixture velocity is constant. The flowrate through the duct is 0.03 kg/s. The unburned mixture is at 310 K at 1 atm with a molecular weight of 29.6 kg/kmol. Estimate the length of the flame zone, L, if the turbulent burning velocity is 5 m/s.

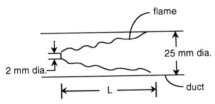

12.4. Estimate the turbulence intensity v'_{rms} and the relative intensity $v'_{rms}/\bar{v}$ for the experiment described in Example 12.1.

12.5. Show that Eqn. 12.8b follows from 12.8a for $v'_{rms}/S_L \ll 1$.

12.6. If v'_{rms} is doubled in the calculations given in Example 12.2, does the estimated combustion regime change? If so, in what way?

12.7. Consider turbulent premixed combustion given the following conditions and parameters:

$$\text{Propane–air mixture}$$
$$\Phi = 0.6$$
$$T_u = 350\,\text{K}$$
$$P = 2\,\text{atm}$$
$$v'_{rms} = 4\,\text{m/s}$$
$$\ell_0 = 5\,\text{mm}.$$

Calculate the characteristic chemical and flow times and determine the value of the Damköhler number. Are these conditions representative of "fast" or "slow" chemistry?

12.8. Reference [17] suggests that turbulence intensities in spark-ignition engines can be estimated as v'_{rms} (at time of spark) $\approx v_P/2$, where v_P is the piston velocity. Also, the integral scale $\ell_0 \approx h/2$, where h is the instantaneous clearance between the top of the piston and the cylinder head in disk-shaped combustion chambers. The instantaneous piston speed in m/s is related to the rotational speed, N (rev/s), the crank angle after top-dead-center (TDC), θ, and the ratio of the connecting rod length to crank radius, R^*, by the following:

$$v_P = 2LN\frac{\pi}{2}\sin\theta\left[1 + \frac{\cos\theta}{(R^{*2} - \sin^2\theta)^{1/2}}\right]$$

where L is the engine stroke in meters. The instantaneous clearance height is expressed as

$$\frac{h}{h_{TDC}} = 1 + \frac{1}{2}(r_c - 1)\left[R^* + 1 - \cos\theta - (R^{*2} - \sin^2\theta)^{1/2}\right]$$

where r_c is the geometric compression ratio.

For the following conditions, estimate the turbulent Reynolds number based on the integral scale, Re_{ℓ_0}, at the time of spark. Also estimate the combustion regime implied by these parameters using Fig. 12.8. Use $R^* = 3.5$. For simplicity, use air properties to evaluate the thermal diffusivity at a mean temperature of $\bar{T} = (T + T_{\text{flame}})/2$. Although the flame temperature is different in each case, assume, again for simplicity, a constant value of $\sim 2200\,\mathrm{K}$.

Parameter	Case i	Case ii	Case iii	Case iv
r_c	8.7	4.8	7.86	8.5
L (mm)	83	114.3	89	95
h_{TDC} (mm)	10.8	30	13	12.5
N (rev/min)	1500	1380	1220	5000
Φ	0.6	1.15	1.13	1.0
P at spark (atm)	4.5	1.75	7.2	6
T at spark (K)	580	450	570	650
Mass fraction of residual burned gases	0.10	0.20	0.20	0.10
Spark timing (° before TDC)	40	55	30	25
Fuel	Propane	Propane	Isooctane	Isooctane

12.9. A turbulent methane–air flame is stabilized in the wake of a circular rod ($d = 3.2\,\mathrm{mm}$) held perpendicular to the flow. For inlet conditions of 1 atm and 298 K, the blowout velocity is 85 m/s when the equivalence ratio is unity. The recirculation zone behind the rod is six diameters long. Estimate the turbulent thermal diffusivity, α_T. How does this value compare with the molecular thermal diffusivity, α? (Use air properties for α.)

TURBULENT NONPREMIXED FLAMES

OVERVIEW

Turbulent nonpremixed flames are employed in the majority of practical combustion systems, principally because of the ease with which such flames can be controlled [1]. With current concern for pollutant emissions, however, this advantage becomes something of a liability in that there is also less ability to control, or tailor, the combustion process for low emissions. For example, current practice for low-NO_x gas-turbine combustors now employs premixed primary zones, rather than the nonpremixed systems used almost exclusively in the past.

Because of the many applications of nonpremixed combustion, there are many types of nonpremixed flames. For example, simple jet flames are employed in glass melting and cement clinker operations, among others; unsteady, liquid-fuel sprays of many shapes are burned in diesel engines (cf. Chapter 10); flames stabilized by strong recirculation zones created by swirling flows or diverging walls are used in many systems, such as utility and industrial boilers; flames stabilized behind bluff bodies are used in turbojet afterburners; and partially premixed flames, created by nozzle-mix burners (cf. Fig. 12.4), are employed in many industrial furnaces. Figure 13.1 shows a radiant-tube burner that employs a confined nonpremixed jet flame with some swirl imparted. In this application, a long flame length is desirable to provide uniform heating of the tube walls. The load is heated indirectly by radiation from the outer tube and, thus, avoids

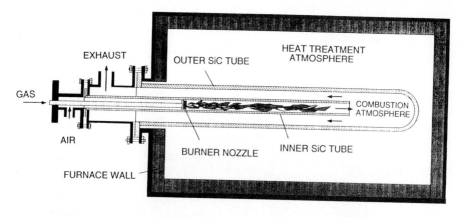

FIGURE 13.1

Radiant-tube burner schematic (top). (Reprinted with permission, the Center for Advanced Materials, Penn State University.) Photograph of two radiant-tube burners in an aluminum holding furnace (bottom). (Courtesy of Eclipse Combustion, Rockford, IL.)

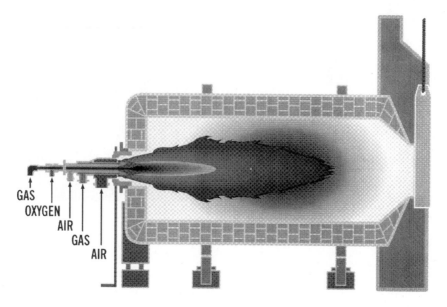

FIGURE 13.2
Both air and pure oxygen are employed as oxidizers in some applications. This oxy-fuel burner is used in aluminum recycling furnaces. (Courtesy of Air Products.)

contact with the combustion products. A nonpremixed, or partially premixed, flame employing pure oxygen is illustrated in Fig. 13.2. Here we see that the mixing among several fluid streams is used to tailor the flame characteristics. Other examples include flaring operations in refineries and oil fields, and pool and other natural fires. As you can see, the list, although incomplete, is long.

The large variety of flame types reflects the wide range of needs in practical devices. For any particular application, the designer is faced with many issues. Foremost among them are the following:

• Flame shape and size
• Flame holding and stability
• Heat transfer
• Pollutant emissions.

The first three of these issues will guide our discussion in this chapter. To achieve a firm grasp of the nature of turbulent nonpremixed combustion, we will use the simple jet flame as our primary example. The jet flame is relatively uncomplicated, and, because of this, it has been the subject of many theoretical and experimental investigations. We will rely on this wealth of information. Also, the limitations of the jet flame in dealing with the design issues listed above provide motivation for looking at other flame systems frequently employed in practice.

JET FLAMES

General Observations

Turbulent nonpremixed jet flames visually have brushy or fuzzy edges, similar to premixed flames; however, the nonpremixed hydrocarbon flames generally are more luminous than their premixed counterparts, since some soot is usually present within the flame. Figure 13.3 illustrates these observations for an ethylene flame burning in air. The last flame in the sequence of photographs shown here is a 4-second time exposure. This image closely resembles the visual perception of a turbulent jet flame. The other photographs shown in Fig. 13.3 are instantaneous views of the flame. From these, we see that the instantaneous visible length of the flame is highly variable, as is the overall flame shape. The character of the flame luminosity can be inferred from Figure 13.3. The luminosity at the base of the flame is quite weak, is blue in color, and characteristic of a soot-free region. At higher levels in the flame, considerable quantities of soot exist, and the flame takes on a bright-yellow appearance. For fuels with less sooting propensity, e.g., methane, the length of the blue-flame region is much longer and the luminosity in the soot-containing region is much less. Spectral radiation measurements by Gore [2] from laboratory methane–air flames showed that, although a flame may have some visible luminosity from soot, the contribution of the soot radiation to the total radiant loss may be insignificant. For more highly sooting fuels, however, soot radiation can be a major contribution to the total radiant heat loss [2]. Later in this chapter, we will discuss flame radiation in greater detail.

Figure 13.4 shows instantaneous planar images of OH radicals in an H_2–air jet flame [3,4]. These images clearly show the convoluted nature of the high-temperature region in which OH radicals are in abundance. We see that the width of the "flame zone", i.e., the OH zone, increases with downstream distance and the appearance of a large high-temperature region at the flame tip. As we will see in Chapter 15, the flame structure implied by these images has important consequences for pollutant emissions.

The second general observation we wish to discuss is the influence of initial jet diameter and fuel flowrate on the size of the flame. Figure 13.5 shows the results from the classical experiments of Wohl *et al.* [5]. Several important features of nonpremixed flames are apparent in this figure. First, at low flowrates, where the flames are laminar, the flame height is independent of the initial jet diameter, and depends only on the flowrate. This characteristic of laminar jet diffusion flames was discussed in Chapter 9. As the flowrate increases, turbulence begins to influence the flame height and a transitional regime can be seen. Over this transitional region, the increasing turbulence levels with flowrate result in the fully turbulent flames being shorter than their laminar counterparts, indicated by the local minimum in each curve. As the flowrate is increased further, flame lengths either remain essentially constant (tube diameters less than 0.133 in.), or increase at decreasing rates (tube diameters of 0.152 in. and greater). This is a consequence of the air entrainment and mixing rates being proportional, more or less, to the fuel flow. Furthermore, we observe a significant dependence of flame length on

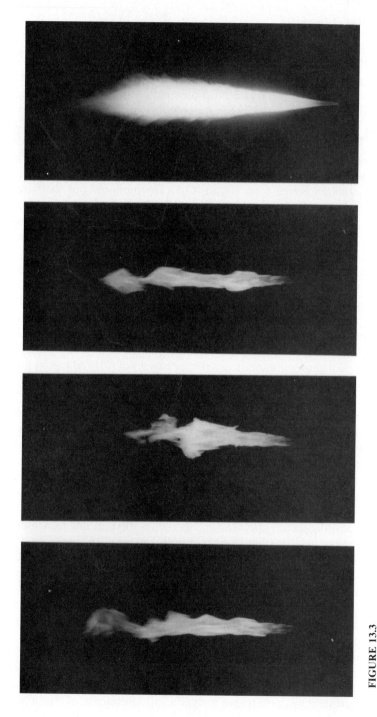

FIGURE 13.3

Instantaneous and time-averaged photographs of turbulent jet diffusion flames (C_2H_4–air, $d_j = 2.18$ mm). Because of the low luminosity at the base of the flame, this region is not visible on the instantaneous images (the first three photographs).

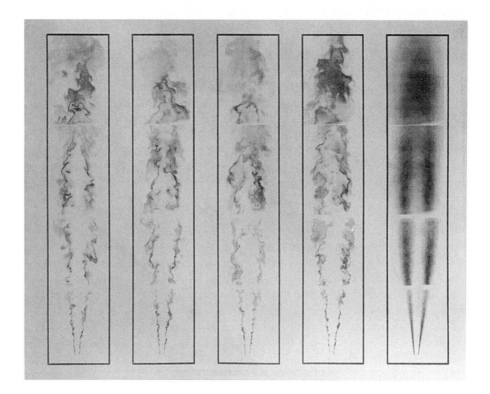

FIGURE 13.4
Instantaneous planar images of OH radicals obtained using laser-induced fluorescence in an H_2–air jet flame at a jet Reynolds number of 25,000. The region shown is from the nozzle exit to 219 nozzle diameters downstream. The image on the right shows the average of the instantaneous images. (Reproduced from Ref. [3] by permission of the author.)

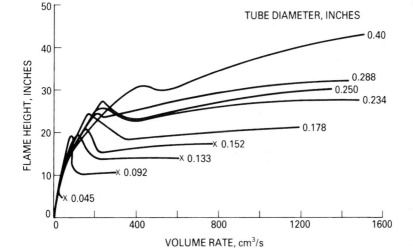

FIGURE 13.5
Effects of flowrate on flame height illustrating behavior in laminar, transitional, and fully turbulent regimes. (Reprinted from Ref. [5] by permission of The Combustion Institute.)

initial jet diameter. These interesting characteristics of turbulent jet flames will be discussed more fully in subsequent sections of this chapter.

Our last general observation concerns flame stability. At sufficiently low flowrates, the base of a jet flame lies quite close to the burner tube outlet (say, within a few millimeters) and is said to be **attached**. As the fuel flowrate is increased, holes begin to form in the flame sheet at the base of the flame, and with further increase in the flowrate, more and more holes form until there is no continuous flame close to the burner port. This condition is called **liftoff**. A lifted jet flame is shown in the photograph in Fig. 13.6. With yet further increases in flowrate, the **liftoff distance**—the distance from the burner port to the flame base—increases. At a sufficiently large flowrate, the flame blows out. Thus, there are two critical flow conditions related to flame stability: liftoff and **blowout**. In Chapter 8, we studied these phenomena as they apply to laminar premixed flames.

Flame stability has many implications for practical applications. For example, liftoff should be avoided so that the flame is close to the burner and its position is independent of the flowrate. This allows for positive ignition by a spark or pilot flame at the burner and assures that the flame position is controlled. Obviously, for reasons of safety, operation near the blowout limit should be avoided. A large furnace filled with a raw fuel–air mixture would be an immense hazard.

FIGURE 13.6
Photograph of lifted ethylene–air jet flame ($d_j = 2.18$ mm). The base of the lifted flame is wide and appears blue. The burner exit is at the bottom of the frame.

Simplified Analysis

Mathematical modeling of turbulent flames is a formidable task. As we saw in Chapter 11, analyzing an isothermal turbulent flow is in itself challenging, while with combustion, variable density and chemical reactions need to be taken into account in some manner. In keeping with the spirit of other chapters in this book, we will develop a very simplified mathematical model, this time for a jet flame, to illuminate some of the essential underlying physics. The modeling of turbulent combustion is a field where the state-of-the-art is changing rapidly. Our intent here is to provide a basic foundation from which a greater understanding can be developed by study at a more advanced level.

COMPARISON WITH NONREACTING JETS. In Chapter 11, we developed a simple mixing-length model of a constant-density turbulent jet and discovered the following three important characteristics: first, the velocity field is a "universal" function when all velocities are scaled by the exit velocity and the spatial coordinates, x and r are scaled by the jet nozzle radius $R(d_j \equiv 2R)$; second, the jet spreading angle is a constant, independent of both jet exit velocity and diameter; and third, the so-called eddy viscosity, ε, is independent of location in the flowfield and is directly proportional to both the nozzle exit velocity, v_e, and diameter, d_j. These simple theoretical results also are in reasonable agreement with experimental findings.

It seems reasonable, at least to a first approximation, to propose that jet flames share some of these characteristics of isothermal jets. If we make this assumption, what implications follow? The primary implications concern flame shape and length. If we make the further assumption that the turbulent diffusivity for mass transfer is the same as that for momentum transfer, then the resulting fuel mass fraction distribution should be equivalent to the dimensionless velocity distribution, i.e., $Y_F(x, r) = v(r, x)/v_e = f(x/d_j$ only). However, this can only be true in the absence of combustion since Y_F is zero outside of the flame boundary, while, obviously, the velocity has not yet decayed to zero. As we saw in Chapter 9, the mixture fraction can be used instead of the fuel mass fraction and has behavior analogous to the dimensionless velocity field. Thus, we expect that, for a given fuel type, the flame length should be independent of jet velocity v_e and proportional to the nozzle diameter d_j, and the spreading angle should be independent of both v_e and d_j. The experimental results in Fig. 13.5 show that, for small diameter tubes, flame lengths are indeed independent of v_e and that the flame lengths are roughly proportional to d_j. As we will see later, buoyancy causes a breakdown of this simple analogy of jet flames to isothermal jets and can be used to explain the nonconstancy of flame lengths for the larger diameter tubes. Nonetheless, it is instructive to see how the underlying physics of simple jets has much in common with jet flames.

CONSERVED SCALARS REVISITED. In our simplified analysis of the jet flame, we wish to use the mixture fraction as a single variable to describe the composition of the flame at any location, rather than employing separate species conservation relations for fuel, oxidizer, and products. The concept of the mixture fraction and its conservation throughout the flowfield was discussed in Chapter 7 and developed for the laminar jet diffusion flame in Chapter 9. Although key definitions and relationships will be repeated here, it is recommended that the sections of Chapter 7 and 9 dealing with the conserved scalar concept be reviewed before proceeding.

From Chapter 7, the definition of the mixture fraction, f, which applies locally for a sufficiently small control volume, is

$$f \equiv \frac{\text{mass of material having its origin in the fuel stream}}{\text{mass of mixture}}. \tag{7.51}$$

This quantity has two particularly important characteristics: first, it can be used to define the flame boundaries, since it is uniquely related to the equivalence ratio as

$$f \equiv \frac{\Phi}{(A/F)_{\text{stoic}} + \Phi}, \tag{13.1}$$

where $(A/F)_{\text{stoic}}$ is the stoichiometric air–fuel ratio for the fuel issuing from the nozzle. Thus, as we did for the laminar diffusion flame in Chapter 9, a flame boundary is defined as the location where $\Phi = 1$; hence, the flame boundary is also defined by the location where the mixture fraction takes on the value f_s, defined as

$$f_s \equiv \frac{1}{(A/F)_{\text{stoic}} + 1}. \tag{13.2}$$

The second important characteristic of the mixture fraction is that it is conserved throughout the flowfield as defined by a "sourceless" governing equation. It is this property that allows us to use f in place of the individual species conservation equations and, as a result, greatly simplifies the mathematical formulation of the problem.

ASSUMPTIONS. The following assumptions are used to construct a simple mathematical model of a nonpremixed turbulent jet flame:

1. The time-average flow is steady and axisymmetric and is produced by a jet of fuel emerging from a circular nozzle of radius R, which burns in a quiescent, infinite reservoir of air.
2. Molecular transport of momentum, species, and thermal energy is unimportant in comparison to turbulent transport.
3. The turbulent momentum diffusivity, or eddy viscosity, $\varepsilon(= \mu_{\text{turb}}/\rho)$, is constant throughout the flowfield and equal to $0.0285 \, v_e R$ (cf. Eqn. 11.46). This is an extension of the mixing-length hypothesis for the constant-density jet

(Chapter 11) to the variable-density reacting jet by neglecting density fluctuations.

4. All correlations involving density fluctuations are neglected.

5. The turbulent transport of momentum, species, and thermal energy are all equal, i.e., the turbulent Schmidt, Prandtl, and Lewis numbers are all unity, $Sc_T = Pr_T = Le_T$. The consequence of this assumption is that the turbulent momentum diffusivity (eddy viscosity, ε) can be substituted for the turbulent mass diffusivity and thermal diffusivity, $\varepsilon = \mathcal{D}_T = \alpha_T$.

6. Buoyancy is neglected.

7. Radiation heat transfer is negligible.

8. Only radial turbulent diffusion of momentum, species, and thermal energy is important; axial turbulent diffusion is neglected.

9. The fuel jet velocity is uniform at the nozzle exit, i.e., a top-hat profile.

10. Mixture properties are defined by three species: fuel, oxidizer, and products. All have equal molecular weights ($MW = 29$ kg/kmol) and specific heats ($c_p = 1200$ J/kg-K), and the fuel heat-of-combustion is $4 \cdot 10^7$ J/kg$_F$. The stoichiometric mass air–fuel ratio is 15:1 ($f_s = 1/16 = 0.0625$).

11. The fluctuations in mixture fraction are ignored in the state relations used to determine the mean density. In a more rigorous analysis, the mean density would be calculated from some assumed mixture fraction probability distribution function characterized by a mean value and a variance.

APPLICATION OF CONSERVATION LAWS. With the above assumptions, the basic conservation equations are identical to those we derived in Chapter 7 and applied to the laminar jet flame in Chapter 9, except that time-averaged variables replace the instantaneous ones, and the turbulent transport properties (momentum, species, and thermal energy diffusivities) replace their molecular counterparts. Defining dimensionless variables using a characteristic length R and a characteristic velocity v_e, overall mass conservation is written (Eqn. 9.36):

$$\frac{\partial}{\partial x^*} \left(\bar{\rho}^* \bar{v}_x^* \right) + \frac{1}{r^*} \frac{\partial}{\partial r^*} \left(r^* \bar{\rho}^* \bar{v}_r^* \right) = 0. \tag{13.3}$$

Axial momentum conservation (Eqn. 9.37) becomes:

$$\frac{\partial}{\partial x^*} \left(r^* \bar{\rho}^* \bar{v}_x^* \bar{v}_x^* \right) + \frac{\partial}{\partial r^*} \left(r^* \bar{\rho}^* \bar{v}_r^* \bar{v}_x^* \right) = \frac{\partial}{\partial r^*} \left[\left(\frac{1}{Re_T} \right) r^* \frac{\partial \bar{v}_x^*}{\partial r^*} \right], \tag{13.4}$$

and the mixture fraction equation (Eqn. 9.38) is given by:

$$\frac{\partial}{\partial x^*} \left(r^* \bar{\rho}^* \bar{v}_x^* \bar{f} \right) + \frac{\partial}{\partial r^*} \left(r^* \bar{\rho}^* \bar{v}_r^* \bar{f} \right) = \frac{\partial}{\partial r^*} \left[\left(\frac{1}{Re_T Sc_T} \right) r^* \frac{\partial \bar{f}}{\partial r^*} \right], \tag{13.5}$$

where the turbulent Reynolds number is defined

$$Re_T \equiv \frac{v_e R}{\varepsilon}. \tag{13.6}$$

With our third assumption, $Re_T = 35$. Note that with a constant Reynolds number, the dimensionless solution to the problem, $\bar{v}_x^*(r^*, x^*)$, $\bar{v}_r^*(r^*, x^*)$, and $\bar{f}(r^*, x^*)$, does not depend on either the initial jet velocity or nozzle diameter.

The boundary conditions are:

$$\bar{v}_r^*(0, x^*) = 0 \tag{13.7a}$$

$$\frac{\partial \bar{v}_x^*}{\partial r^*}(0, x^*) = \frac{\partial \bar{f}}{\partial r^*}(0, x^*) = 0 \quad \text{(symmetry)} \tag{13.7b}$$

$$\bar{v}_x^*(r^* \leqslant 1, 0) = \bar{f}(r^* \leqslant 1, 0) = 1 \qquad \text{(top-hat exit profiles)} \tag{13.7c}$$
$$\bar{v}_x^*(r^* > 1, 0) = \bar{f}(r^* > 1, 0) = 0.$$

Since the boundary conditions on $\bar{v}_x^*$ and $\bar{f}$ are identical, and since the governing equations for $\bar{v}_x^*$ and $\bar{f}$ become identical for $Sc_T = 1$ (assumption 5), we need solve only Eqn. 13.3 and either Eqn. 13.4 or Eqn. 13.5 where $\bar{v}_x^* = \bar{f}$. With assumptions 10 and 11, the state relationship for temperature is a simple, piecewise-linear function of $\bar{f}$ (cf. Chapter 9) as shown in Fig. 13.7. The mean density is then related simply to the mean temperature through the ideal-gas equation of state, $\bar{\rho} = PMW/(R_u \bar{T})$.

SOLUTION. A finite-difference numerical scheme was used to solve the problem posed above, where the mixture fraction was chosen as the primary variable. The results of these calculations are shown in Fig. 13.8 where mixture fraction contours are shown on the left, and mixture fractions are plotted versus radial distance for fixed axial distance on the right. Using the definition of flame length as the axial location where the mixture fraction takes on the stoichiometric value

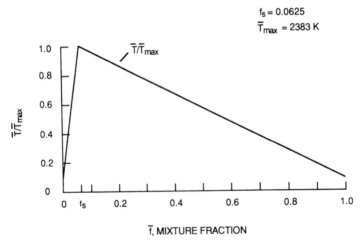

FIGURE 13.7
State relationship for temperature for simplified chemistry.

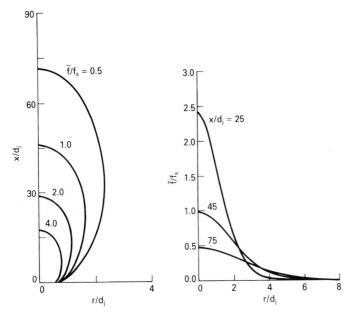

FIGURE 13.8
Calculated mixture fraction distribution using Prandtl's mixing length model applied to jet flame.

$(\bar{f}/f_s = 1)$, we see that the predicted flame length is about 45 nozzle diameters $(L_f/d_j = 45)$. Again using the stochiometric contour to define the flame boundary, the aspect ratio (ratio of flame length to width) is found to be about 11:1. This value is somewhat greater than experimental values of about 7:1 found for hydrocarbon jet flames. In spite of the great simplicity of our turbulent jet flame model, the general features of the flame are well predicted, although accuracy certainly cannot be claimed. Neglecting density fluctuations is probably the most serious oversimplification; for more realistic mathematical models of turbulent jet flames, which explicitly account for density fluctuations, the reader is referred to the literature [6–8].

Flame Length

Interest in being able to explain and predict turbulent jet flame lengths has a long history. The earliest, and now classical, studies are those of Hottel [9], Hawthorne et al. [10], and Wohl et al. [5] reported in the late 1940s and early 1950s. Major reviews of this subject were performed by Becker and Liang [11] and, more recently, by Delichatsios [12] and Blake and McDonald [13].

FLAME LENGTH DEFINITIONS. Many definitions and techniques for measuring flame lengths are found in the literature, and no single definition is accepted as preferred. Therefore, care must be exercised in comparing results of different investigators and in the application of correlation formulae. Common definitions of flame length include visual determinations by a trained observer, averaging a number of individual instantaneous visible flame lengths from photographic records, measuring the axial location of the average peak centerline temperature using thermocouples, and measuring the axial location where the mean mixture fraction on the flame axis is the stoichiometric value using gas sampling. In general, visible flame lengths tend to be larger than those based on temperature or concentration measurements. For example, Ref. [14] reports temperature-based flame lengths to range between approximately 65% to 80% of time-averaged visible flame lengths, depending on fuel type.

FACTORS AFFECTING FLAME LENGTH. For vertical flames created by a fuel jet issuing into a quiescent environment, four primary factors determine flame length:

- Relative importance of initial jet momentum flux and buoyant forces acting on the flame, Fr_f
- Stoichiometry, f_s
- Ratio of nozzle fluid to ambient gas density, ρ_e/ρ_∞
- Initial jet diameter, d_j.

The first of these factors, the relative importance of initial momentum and buoyancy, can be characterized by a flame Froude number, Fr_f. Recall that in Chapter 9, a flame Froude number was defined to establish momentum-controlled and buoyancy-controlled regimes for laminar jet flames (cf. Eqns. 9.68 and 9.69). For turbulent jet flames, the following definition of the flame Froude number is useful [12]:

$$Fr_f = \frac{v_e f_s^{3/2}}{\left(\dfrac{\rho_e}{\rho_\infty}\right)^{1/4} \left[\dfrac{\Delta T_f}{T_\infty} g d_j\right]^{1/2}}, \tag{13.7}$$

where ΔT_f is the characteristic temperature rise resulting from combustion. Other similar definitions are defined in the literature [11,15]. For very small values of Fr_f, flames are dominated by buoyancy, while for very large values, the initial jet momentum controls the mixing and, hence, the velocity field within the flame. For example, the simplified analysis presented above ignores buoyancy and, thus, applies only in the limit of large Fr_f.

The remaining three factors are important regardless of whether or not buoyancy exerts an influence. For example, fuels with small values of stoichio-metric mixture fraction, f_s, require greater quantities of air to be entrained per unit mass of fuel to achieve stoichiometric proportions in comparison to fuels with large values of f_s. This implies longer flames for smaller stoichiometric mixture fractions. As an illustration, the stoichiometric air requirement of propane is about six times that of carbon monoxide, and a propane flame is approximately seven times longer than a carbon monoxide flame [10].

The density ratio, ρ_e/ρ_∞, and initial jet diameter, d_j, can conveniently be combined as a single parameter, frequently referred to as the **momentum diameter**, d_j^*, and defined as

$$d_j^* = d_j(\rho_e/\rho_\infty)^{1/2}, \tag{13.8}$$

where a uniform exit velocity profile has been assumed. The basic idea embodied in this definition is that jets with identical initial jet momentum fluxes should have identical velocity fields. Thus, increasing the density of the nozzle fluid produces the same effect as increasing the nozzle diameter in accordance with Eqn. 13.8. Such a result is predicted by jet theory [16], and experimental evidence [17] shows this to be true.

CORRELATIONS. Experimental results showing the combined influence of the four primary factors affecting flame length, discussed above, are shown in Fig. 13.9. The flame Froude number, Fr_f, appears as the abscissa, while the remaining

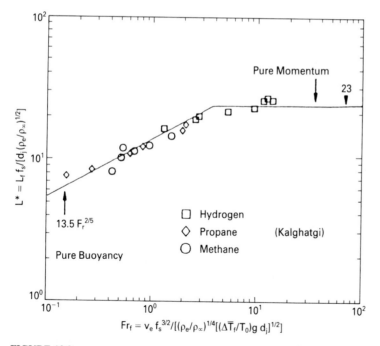

FIGURE 13.9

Flame lengths for jet flames correlated with flame Froude number. (Reprinted by permission of Elsevier Science, Inc., from Ref. [12]. ©1993, The Combustion Institute.)

three factors are used to define a dimensionless flame length, which is plotted on the ordinate, and given by

$$L^* \equiv \frac{L_f f_s}{d_j (\rho_e / \rho_\infty)^{1/2}} \qquad (13.9a)$$

or

$$L^* = \frac{L_f f_s}{d_j^*}. \qquad (13.9b)$$

Two regimes are identified in Fig. 13.9: a buoyancy-dominated regime that is correlated by the expression

$$L^* = \frac{13.5 Fr_f^{2/5}}{\left(1 + 0.07 Fr_f^2\right)^{1/5}} \quad \text{for } Fr_f < 5, \qquad (13.10)$$

and a momentum-dominated regime where the dimensionless flame length L^* is constant, i.e.,

$$L^* = 23 \quad \text{for } Fr_f \geq 5. \qquad (13.11)$$

Other correlations have been proposed [11]; however, the above are easy to use and probably as accurate as others. As previously discussed, various investigators use different definitions and experimental techniques to determine flame lengths; hence, the accuracy of any correlation depends on the consistency of the data base used to establish it. The data points shown in Fig. 13.9 represent averages of measurements taken from individual video frames.

Example 13.1. Estimate the flame length for a propane jet flame in air at ambient conditions ($P = 1$ atm, $T_\infty = 300$ K). The propane mass flowrate is $3.66 \cdot 10^{-3}$ kg/s and the nozzle exit diameter is 6.17 mm. Assume the propane density at the nozzle exit is 1.854 kg/m^3.

Solution. We will use the Delichatsios correlations (Eqns. 13.10 and 13.11) to find the propane flame length. To do so first requires us to determine the flame Froude number Fr_f. The properties required are the following:

$$\rho_\infty = \rho_{\text{air}} = 1.1614 \, \text{kg/m}^3 \qquad \text{(Table C.1)}$$

$$T_f \cong T_{ad} = 2267 \, \text{K} \qquad \text{(Table B.1)}$$

$$f_s = \frac{1}{(A/F)_{\text{stoic}} + 1} = \frac{1}{15.57 + 1} = 0.06035.$$

The stoichiometric air–fuel ratio in the above is calculated from Eqn. 2.32. The nozzle exit velocity is calculated from the mass flowrate:

$$v_e = \frac{\dot{m}_e}{\rho_e \pi d_j^2/4}$$

$$= \frac{3.66 \cdot 10^{-3}}{1.854\pi(0.00617)^2/4} = 66.1 \, \text{m/s}.$$

We now have all the information necessary to evaluate Fr_f (Eqn. 13.7):

$$Fr_f = \frac{v_e f_s^{3/2}}{\left(\dfrac{\rho_e}{\rho_\infty}\right)^{1/4}\left(\dfrac{T_f - T_\infty}{T_\infty}gd_j\right)^{1/2}}$$

$$= \frac{66.1\,(0.06035)^{1.5}}{\left(\dfrac{1.854}{1.1614}\right)^{0.25}\left[\left(\dfrac{2267 - 300}{300}\right)9.81(0.00617)\right]^{0.5}}$$

$$Fr_f = 1.386.$$

Since $Fr_f < 5$, we employ Eqn. 13.10 to find the dimensionless flame length, L^*:

$$L^* = \frac{13.5 Fr_f^{2/5}}{\left(1 + 0.07 Fr_f^2\right)^{1.5}}$$

$$= \frac{13.5\,(1.386)^{0.4}}{\left[1 + 0.07\,(1.386)^2\right]^{0.2}}$$

$$L^* = 15.0.$$

From the definition of L^* (Eqn. 13.9) and d_j^* (Eqn. 13.8), we determine the actual flame length in meters:

$$d_j^* = d_j\left(\frac{\rho_e}{\rho_\infty}\right)^{1/2} = 0.00617\left(\frac{1.854}{1.1614}\right)^{0.5}$$

$$= 0.0078 \, \text{m}$$

and

$$L_f = \frac{L^* d_j^*}{f_s} = \frac{15.0(0.0078)}{0.06035}$$

$$\boxed{L_f = 1.94 \, \text{m}}$$

or

$$\boxed{L_f/d_j = 314}.$$

Comment. From Fig. 13.9, we see that this flame is in the mixed regime where both the initial momentum flow and flame-generated buoyancy are important. It is also interesting to note that the flame length predicted above is somewhat less than, but quite close to, the visible flame length measured ($L_f/d_j = 341$) in Ref. [14]. That the flame length estimated from Eqn. 13.10 is less than that measured is consistent with the different experimental techniques used to determine L_f.

Example 13.2. For the same heat release rate and nozzle exit diameter used in Example 13.1 above, determine the flame length when the fuel is methane and compare with the propane flame length. The density of methane is $0.6565\,\text{kg/m}^3$.

Solution. We can use the same procedures to find L_f as in Example 13.1, but first we must determine the methane flowrate. Since both flames release the same chemical energy,

$$\dot{m}_{CH_4}LHV_{CH_4} = \dot{m}_{C_3H_8}LHV_{C_3H_8}.$$

Using the lower heating values from Table B.1, we can find the CH_4 flowrate:

$$\dot{m}_{CH_4} = \dot{m}_{C_3H_8}\frac{LHV_{C_3H_8}}{LHV_{CH_4}} = 3.66 \cdot 10^{-3}\frac{46,357}{50,016}$$

$$\dot{m}_{CH_4} = 3.39 \cdot 10^{-3}\,\text{kg/s}.$$

Following the approach in Example 13.1, we obtain the following:

$$\rho_\infty = 1.1614\,\text{kg/m}^3,$$
$$T_f = 2226\,\text{K},$$
$$f_s = 0.0552,$$
$$v_e = 172.7\,\text{m/s}.$$

Using the above with Eqns. 13.7–13.10, we obtain the following:

$$Fr_f = 4.154,$$
$$L^* = 20.36,$$
$$d_j^* = 0.0046\,\text{m}.$$

Thus,

$$\boxed{L_f = 1.71\,\text{m}}$$

or

$$\boxed{L_f/d_j = 277}$$

Comparing the methane flame length with that of the propane flame,

$$\frac{L_{f,CH_4}}{L_{f,C_3H_8}} = \frac{1.71}{1.94} = 0.88,$$

we see that the CH_4 flame is only about 12% shorter.

Comment. What factors contribute to the methane flame being shorter? First, we see that the CH_4 flame is more nearly momentum controlled ($Fr_{f,CH_4} > Fr_{f,C_3H_8}$), which implies a greater dimensionless flame length ($L^*_{CH_4} = 20.36$ vs. $L^*_{C_3H_8} = 15.0$). However, the lower density of the methane results in a significantly smaller momentum diameter ($d^*_{j,CH_4} = 0.0046\,\text{m}$ vs. $d^*_{j,C_3H_8} = 0.0078\,\text{m}$). This smaller d_j^* is the controlling factor in producing the shorter CH_4 flame and outweighs the small opposing difference in stoichiometries.

Flame Radiation

Turbulent nonpremixed flames can be highly radiating. In certain practical applications, this radiation is a desired attribute, contributing to heating a load. In other applications, however, radiant losses can contribute to loss of efficiency (e.g., diesel engines) or safety hazards (e.g., flaring operations). In gas-turbine engines, the radiant heat load is a major factor in the durability of the combustor liner. In this section, we will present a brief overview of the radiation characteristics of jet flames to acquaint the reader with this important subject. Review articles [18] and [19] are recommended for readers seeking more information on radiation from combustion systems and applications other than jet flames.

A frequently used term in the combustion literature is the **radiant fraction,** χ_R. The radiant fraction represents the ratio of the radiant heat transfer rate from the flame to the surroundings, $\dot{Q}_{rad}$, to the total heat released by the flame, $\dot{m}_F \Delta h_c$, i.e.,

$$\chi_R \equiv \frac{\dot{Q}_{rad}}{\dot{m}_F \Delta h_c}, \tag{13.12}$$

where $\dot{m}_F$ is the mass flowrate of fuel supplied to the flame and Δh_c is the fuel heat of combustion. Depending on fuel type and flow conditions, radiant fractions for jet flames range from a few percent to more than 50%. Figure 13.10 shows the variation of χ_R with heat release rate, $\dot{Q}(= \dot{m}\Delta h_c)$, for three fuels and various sized burners [20].

Several interesting observations can be made from Fig. 13.10. First, we see that the radiant fractions for the three fuels arrange in the same order as the fuel's sooting propensity. From Table 9.5, the smoke points are $\dot{m}_{sp}$ (mg/s) = 0.51 and 1.12 for C_2H_2 and C_3H_6, respectively, while methane is nonsooting; the corresponding maximum radiant fractions are approximately 0.6, 0.45, and 0.15, respectively. This clearly suggests that the in-flame soot is important in determining a flame's radiant fraction. More will be said about this below. The second observation is that χ_R depends both on flame size (d_j) and heat release rate. The general trend is for χ_R to decrease both as flame size decreases at a fixed firing rate, and as the firing rate increases for a fixed flame size. Although the actual processes involved are quite complicated, especially since soot kinetics is involved, these trends can be interpreted by a simple scaling analysis [15]. If we consider the entire flame to be both a uniform source of heat release and radiation, the rate at which energy is lost from the flame can be approximated as

$$\dot{Q}_{rad} \approx a_p V_f \sigma T_f^4, \tag{13.13}$$

where a_p is an appropriate absorption coefficient for the flame, and V_f and T_f are the flame volume and temperature, respectively. The radiant fraction, from Eqn. 13.12, becomes

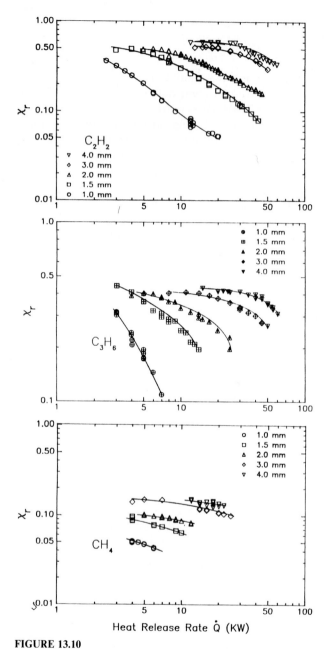

FIGURE 13.10

Jet flame radiant fractions as functions of heat release rate and burner size. (After Ref. [20]. Reprinted by permission of the Gas Research Institute.)

$$\chi_R = \frac{a_p V_f \sigma T_f^4}{\dot{m}_F \Delta h_c}.$$ (13.14)

Now, from our previous discussion of flame lengths, we know that, in the momentum-dominated regime, the flame length is directly proportional to the burner diameter, d_j; hence, we expect the flame volume

$$V_f \propto d_j^3.$$

Furthermore,

$$\dot{m}_F = \rho_F v_e \pi d_j^2 / 4.$$

Combining the V_f and $\dot{m}_F$ scalings above into Eqn. 13.14 yields

$$\chi_R \propto a_p T_f^4 d_j / v_e,$$ (13.15)

which is consistent with the diameter and heat release rate influences on χ_R shown in Fig. 13.10 for the larger $\dot{Q}$ values. Note that $\dot{Q} \propto v_e$ for fixed d_j. The basic idea expressed by Eqn. 13.15 is that χ_R depends directly on the time available for radiant energy to be lost from the flame, where the characteristic time is proportional to d_j / v_e. It should be kept in mind that this simple analysis ignores buoyant effects and the interrelationships among a_p, T_f, and χ_R. More sophisticated approaches to radiation scaling in jet flames are available in the literature [21].

As mentioned above, the sooting propensity of the fuel is a major factor in determining the radiant loss from a flame. There are two sources of radiation in flames: molecular radiation, primarily from CO_2 and H_2O; and essentially blackbody radiation from in-flame soot. The molecular radiation is concentrated in broadened bands of the infrared spectrum. Figures 13.11 and 13.12 show spectral radiation intensities for a methane flame, which contains very little in-flame soot (Fig. 13.11), and an ethylene flame (Fig. 13.12), which produces substantial in-flame soot [19,22]. Comparing Figs. 13.11 and 13.12, we see that both flames exhibit significant intensity peaks in the bands at 2.5–3 μm and 4–5 μm. These correspond to the molecular radiation. In contrast, the ethylene flame (Fig. 13.12) exhibits strong continuum radiation at the short wavelengths, peaking near 1.5 μm. This continuum radiation is absent in the methane flame (Fig. 13.11). We can use Wien's displacement law [23] to estimate the wavelength associated with the maximum intensity of the soot blackbody radiation in the ethylene flame as follows:

$$\lambda_{\max} = \frac{2897.8 \,\mu\text{m-K}}{T_f(\text{K})} \approx 1.22 \,\mu\text{m},$$

where the adiabatic flame temperature for a stoichiometric ethylene–air mixture (2369 K) has been used for T_f. Since the flame is nonadiabatic, the true flame temperature must be less than 2369 K and $\lambda_{\max}$ larger than 1.22 μm. Using a $\lambda_{\max}$ of 1.5 μm, which is consistent with the experimental data of Fig. 13.12, a characteristic flame temperature of about 1930 K is predicted.

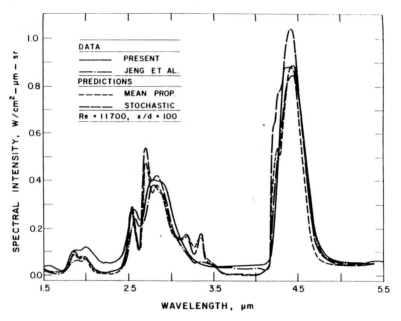

FIGURE 13.11

Spectral measurements of thermal radiation from a nonpremixed methane–air jet flame showing strong peaks associated with molecular band radiation. (From Ref. [19]. Reproduced with permission of Taylor & Francis. All rights reserved.)

Liftoff and Blowout

As mentioned above and illustrated in Fig. 13.6, a jet flame will lift from an attached position at the burner exit if the exit velocity is sufficiently high. The **liftoff height**, the distance between the burner port and the base of the flame, will increase with additional increases in velocity until the flame blows out. The phenomena of liftoff and blowout of jet flames have been the subject of much research, and a good overview of this work can be found in Pitts [24]. Three different theories have been proposed to explain liftoff. The criteria for establishing the liftoff height are different for each theory and can be given as follows:

Theory I   The local flow velocity at the position where the laminar flame speed is a maximum matches the turbulent burning velocity of a premixed flame, i.e., $\bar{v}(S_{L,\max}) = S_T$.

Theory II   The local strain rates in the fluid exceed the extinction strain rate for a laminar diffusion flamelet, i.e., $\epsilon > \epsilon_{\text{crit}}$.

Theory III   The time available for backmixing by large-scale flow structures of hot products with fresh mixture is less than a critical chemical time required for ignition, i.e., $\tau_{\text{local mixing}} < \tau_{\text{chem,crit}}$.

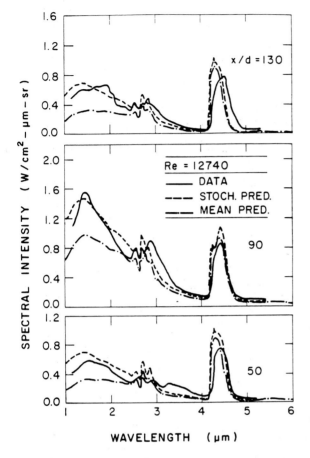

FIGURE 13.12

Spectral measurements of thermal radiation from a nonpremixed ethylene–air jet flame showing both continuum radiation from soot and molecular band radiation. (Reprinted from Ref. [22] with permission of The Combustion Institute.)

The first of these theories has its origins with Wohl *et al.* [5] and was articulated by Vanquickenborne and Van Tiggelen [25], while the other two theories are of more recent origins [26–28].

Figure 13.13 shows liftoff heights, h, for methane, propane, and ethylene jet flames as functions of initial velocity, v_e. It is interesting to note the lack of a burner-diameter dependence and the ordering of the curves with respect to their laminar flame speeds ($S_{L,CH_4} < S_{L,C_3H_8} < S_{L,C_2H_4}$). Kalghatgi [29], interpreting his data in terms of Theory I, developed the following correlation that can be used to describe the liftoff behavior of hydrocarbon–air flames:

$$\frac{\rho_e S_{L,max} h}{\mu_e} = 50 \left(\frac{v_e}{S_{L,max}} \right) \left(\frac{\rho_e}{\rho_\infty} \right)^{1.5}, \tag{13.16}$$

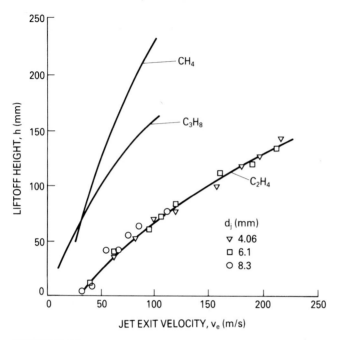

FIGURE 13.13
Liftoff height versus jet exit velocity for methane, propane, and ethylene jet flames. (After Kalghatgi [29].)

where $S_{L,\text{max}}$ is the maximum laminar flame speed, which occurs near stoichiometric ratios for hydrocarbons.

The phenomenon of blowout can also be interpreted in terms of premixed turbulent flame concepts, i.e., Theory I, where it is assumed that the base of the lifted flame is a premixed flame. In this view, blowout occurs at a flowrate where the turbulent burning velocity falls more rapidly with distance downstream than does the local velocity at the position of $S_{L,\text{max}}$. This explains the sudden occurrence of blowout just beyond a critical liftoff height, even though the mixture is still within the flammability limits at the flame base.

Kalghatgi [30] proposes the following correlation to estimate blowout flowrates for jet flames:

$$\frac{v_e}{S_{L,\text{max}}}\left(\frac{\rho_e}{\rho_\infty}\right)^{1.5} = 0.017 Re_H \left(1 - 3.5 \cdot 10^{-6} Re_H\right), \qquad (13.17a)$$

where the Reynolds number, Re_H, is given by

$$Re_H = \frac{\rho_e S_{L,\text{max}} H}{\mu_e}. \qquad (13.17b)$$

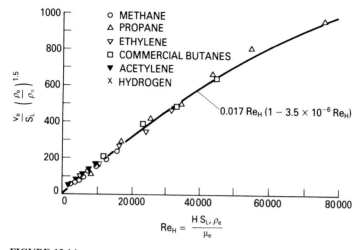

FIGURE 13.14
Universal blowout stability curve from Kalghatgi [30]. (Reprinted with permission. ©1981, Gordon & Breach Publishers.)

The characteristic length, H, is the distance along the burner axis where the mean fuel concentration has fallen to its stoichiometric value and can be estimated by

$$H = 4\left[\frac{Y_{F,e}}{Y_{F,\text{stoic}}}\left(\frac{\rho_e}{\rho_\infty}\right)^{1/2} - 5.8\right]d_j. \qquad (13.17c)$$

Figure 13.14 shows the applicability of Eqn. 13.17 to a wide range of fuels. Note that for a fixed fuel type, blowout velocities increase with jet diameter. This helps to explain the difficulty associated with blowing out oil-well fires.

Example 13.3. Determine the blowoff velocity for a propane jet flame in air for a nozzle diameter of 6.17 mm. Also estimate the liftoff height at the incipient blowoff condition. The ambient conditions are $P = 1$ atm and $T_\infty = 300$ K. The propane temperature at the nozzle exit is also 300 K. The propane density is 1.854 kg/m^3.

Solution. To determine the blowout velocity, we will employ Kalghatgi's correlation, Eqn. 13.17a. We first must determine the characteristic length H (Eqn. 13.17c) to find the Reynolds number Re_H (Eqn. 13.17b) required by the correlation.
  To evaluate H, we note that

$$Y_{F,\text{stoic}} = f_s = 0.06035 \qquad \text{(see Example 13.1)}$$

$$Y_{F,e} = 1 \quad \text{(pure fuel at nozzle exit)}.$$

Thus,

$$
H = 4d_j \left[\frac{Y_{F,e}}{Y_{F,s}} \left(\frac{\rho_e}{\rho_\infty} \right)^{1/2} - 5.8 \right]
$$

$$
= 4\,(0.00617) \left[\frac{1}{0.06035} \left(\frac{1.854}{1.1614} \right)^{0.5} - 5.8 \right]
$$

$$
= 0.3735\,\text{m}.
$$

To evaluate Re_H, we also need to find the maximum laminar flame speed for a propane–air mixture, $S_{L,\max}$, and the propane viscosity, μ, at 300 K:

$$
\mu_e = 8.26 \cdot 10^{-6}\,\text{N-s/m}^2. \qquad \text{(Table B.3 curvefits)}
$$

Using the Metghalchi and Keck flame-speed correlations (Table 8.3):

$$
S_{L,\max} = S_{L,\text{ref}} = 0.3422\,\text{m/s},
$$

noting that $S_{L,\max}$ occurs when $\Phi = \Phi_M = 1.08$.
We can now calculate Re_H:

$$
Re_H = \frac{\rho_e S_{L,\max} H}{\mu_e} = \frac{1.854(0.3422)0.3735}{8.26 \cdot 10^{-6}}
$$

$$
Re_H = 28,688.
$$

Using the blowout velocity correlation (Eqn. 13.17a), we evaluate

$$
\frac{v_e}{S_{L,\max}} \left(\frac{\rho_e}{\rho_\infty} \right)^{1.5} = 0.017 Re_H (1 - 3.5 \cdot 10^{-6} Re_H)
$$

$$
= 0.017\,(28,688)[1 - 3.5 \cdot 10^{-6}(28,688)]
$$

$$
= 439.
$$

Finally, we can use the above to solve for the blowout velocity, v_e:

$$
v_e = 439\,(0.3422) \left(\frac{1.1614}{1.854} \right)^{1.5}
$$

$$
\boxed{v_e = 74.5\,\text{m/s}}.
$$

We can use this velocity to determine the liftoff height at incipient blowout. From Fig. 13.13, we obtain

$$
\boxed{h_{\text{liftoff}} \cong 135\,\text{mm}}.
$$

Comment. Comparing the above results to the conditions in Example 13.1, we see that the Example 13.1 flame is close to the blowout condition and requires stabilization of some sort to prevent lifting. Experimental results corresponding to the Example 13.1 flame [14] show that a hydrogen pilot flame with a flowrate of 1.4% that of the propane was required to prevent lifting.

OTHER CONFIGURATIONS

In most practical devices employing nonpremixed flames, the combustion air is usually introduced in some coflowing arrangement with the fuel, unlike the simple jet flames discussed above where the fuel jet flowed into a reservoir of air. Figure 13.15 illustrates a simple gas burner designed to produce long, luminous flames. In this particular design, the combustion air flows through an annulus surrounding the fuel tube. A burner tile (cf. Chapter 12) is used to anchor the flame to the burner outlet. By minimizing the relative velocity between the fuel and air streams, mixing rates are slow, resulting in long flames. Furthermore, the long residence times within the fuel jet core are favorable for the production of soot (cf. Chapter 9), thus a highly luminous flame is produced. The burner type illustrated in Fig. 13.15 is useful for applications desiring a relatively uniform radiative heating over a large distance. Similarly, slow-mixing designs are used in radiant-tube burners (see Fig. 13.1) where uniform heating over the length of the tube is required.

Nozzle-mix burners, shown previously in Fig. 12.4, partially premix the air and fuel within the nozzle causing the flame to have some attributes of both premixed and nonpremixed combustion, the relative proportions depending upon the degree of mixing achieved at the nozzle.

Swirl is also frequently used in practical nonpremixed burners, particularly those employing sprays of liquid fuel or pulverized coal. Figure 13.16 illustrates an experimental burner arrangement where the degree of swirl is controlled by the relative amounts of air introduced tangentially and axially. In practical applications, vanes are typically used to impart swirl to the air and/or fuel streams. Figure 13.17 shows an adjustable swirl vane arrangement for a furnace burner.

Swirl is useful for two reasons: first, swirl can stabilize a flame by creating a recirculation zone, if the amount of swirl is sufficiently great; and second, the length of the flame can be controlled by the amount of swirl. These two aspects of swirl combustion are illustrated in Figs. 13.18 and 13.19, respectively. In Fig. 13.18, we see the dimensionless swirl number, S, and the tangential velocity

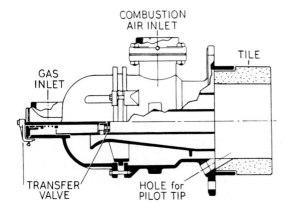

FIGURE 13.15
Nonpremixed-flame burner employing annular flow of air around central fuel jet.

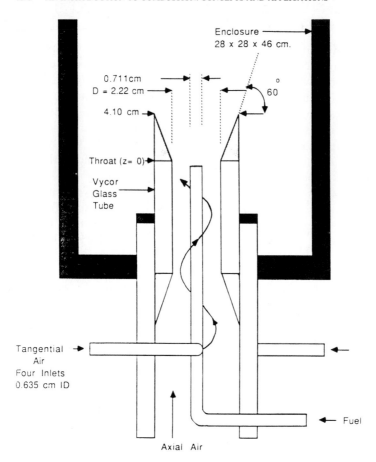

Enclosure
28 x 28 x 46 cm.

0.711cm
D = 2.22 cm
4.10 cm
60°

Throat (z= 0)

Vycor
Glass
Tube

Tangential
Air
Four Inlets
0.635 cm ID

Fuel

Axial Air

FIGURE 13.16
Schematic diagram of experimental swirl-flame burner having both tangential and axial air entries. (Reprinted from Ref. [31] with permission. ©1987, Gordon & Breach Science Publishers.)

component, v_θ, plotted on the vertical axis, and the reciprocal of the overall equivalence ratio, $1/\Phi$, on the horizontal axis. Also shown on the horizontal axis are the corresponding fuel velocity, u_F, and the flame heat-release rate $\dot{Q}$. To understand the influence of swirl on blowout stability, let us consider first the lower boundary of the region labeled stable. Below this line, no flame can be stabilized; however, as swirl is added to the inlet air, a condition is reached where a stable flame is possible. For example, at $\Phi = 1$, a stable flame results when the swirl number reaches approximately 0.4. The length of a horizontal line lying within the stable region gives a measure of the overall stability, expressed as a range of equivalence ratios over which stable flames occur. The maximum overall stability, hence, occurs at about $S = 0.6$, with smaller ranges of stability for swirl numbers both larger and smaller than this value.

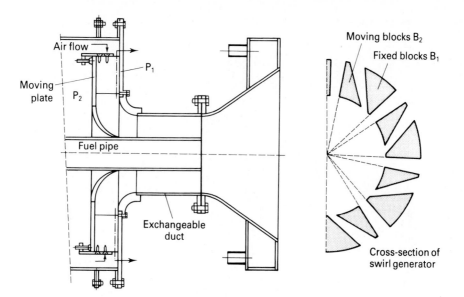

FIGURE 13.17
Movable-block swirl vane arrangement for furnace burner. (From Ref. [32] (Figure 5.3). Reprinted by permission of Krieger Publishing Co.)

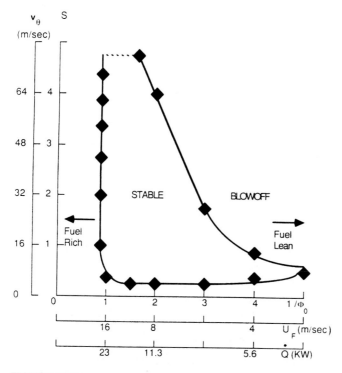

FIGURE 13.18
Rich and lean blowout limits for swirl-stabilized flames for a fixed velocity of air of 19 m/s. Burner geometry corresponds to that of Fig. 13.16. (Reprinted from Ref. [31] with permission. ©1987, Gordon & Breach Science Publishers.)

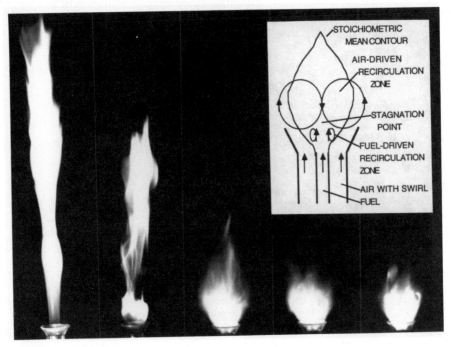

FIGURE 13.19
Effect of swirl on flame length. Photographic sequence showing no swirl (left) progressing to a swirl number of $S = 1.1$. (Reprinted from Ref. [33] with permission of The Combustion Institute.)

The dramatic effect of swirl on flame length is illustrated in the sequence of photographs shown in Fig. 13.19. Here we see that the addition of swirl ($S = 1.1$) reduces the flame length by a factor of about five in comparison to the flame with no swirl. Swirl greatly enhances the mixing of air and fuel streams causing the shorter flame. Chen and Driscoll [33] provide scaling relations that relate flame length to both jet and swirl mixing parameters.

SUMMARY

In this chapter, we explored turbulent nonpremixed combustion, focusing primarily on the simple turbulent jet flame. A simple mathematical analysis was developed that built upon our previous study of laminar nonpremixed jet flames (Chapter 9) and nonreacting turbulent jets (Chapter 11). The usefulness of conserved scalars was again demonstrated. We saw that when buoyancy is unimportant, the turbulent flame length is directly proportional to the nozzle diameter and independent of the initial jet velocity. Empirical correlations for turbulent jet flame lengths, covering a wide range of flow conditions, were presented and applications of their use shown. We also saw that radiation heat transfer is an important aspect of nonpremixed combustion. The concepts of liftoff and blowout were explored and, again, empirical correlations for these phenomena were presented for simple jet flames. Swirling flames, which are often used in practical devices, were introduced, emphasizing the ability of swirl to create a recirculation zone that acts to both stabilize and shorten the flame.

NOMENCLATURE

a_p	Mean absorption coefficient (m^{-1})
A/F	Air–fuel ratio (kg/kg)
d	Diameter (m)
$\mathcal{D}$	Mass diffusivity (m^2/s)
f	Mixture fraction (kg/kg)
Fr	Froude number
g	Gravitational acceleration (m/s^2)
h	Liftoff height (m)
H	Characteristic length (m)
L	Length (m)
Le	Lewis number
LHV	Lower heating value (J/kg)
$\dot{m}$	Mass flowrate (kg/s)
P	Pressure (Pa)
Pr	Prandtl number
$\dot{Q}$	Heat transfer or heat release rate (W)
r	Radial coordinate (m)
R	Nozzle radius (m)
Re	Reynolds number
S	Swirl number
S_L	Laminar flame speed (m/s)
Sc	Schmidt number
T	Temperature (K)
v	Velocity (m/s)
V	Volume (m^3)
x	Axial coordinate (m)
Y	Mass fraction (kg/kg)

Greek symbols

α	Thermal diffusivity (m^2/s)
Δh_c	Heat of combustion
ε	Eddy viscosity (m^2/s)
ϵ	Strain rate (s^{-1})
λ	Wavelength
μ	Absolute viscosity (N-s/m^2)
ν	Kinematic viscosity (m^2/s)
ρ	Density (kg/m^3)

| Φ | Equivalence ratio |
| χ_R | Radiant fraction |

Subscripts

crit	Critical
e	Exit
f	Flame
F	Fuel
j	Jet
max	Maximum
r	Radial
rad	Radiation
s, stoic	Stoichiometric
sp	Smoke point
turb, T	Turbulent
∞	Ambient

Other

| ( )* | Dimensionless variable |
| $\overline{(\ )}$ | Time-averaged quantity |

REFERENCES

1. Weinberg, F. J., "The First Half-Million Years of Combustion Research and Today's Burning Problems," *Progress in Energy and Combustion Science*, 1: 17–31 (1975).
2. Gore, J. P., *A Theoretical and Experimental Study of Turbulent Flame Radiation*, Ph.D. Thesis, The Pennsylvania State University, University Park, PA, p. 119, 1986.
3. Seitzman, J. M., "Quantitative Applications of Fluorescence Imaging in Combustion," Ph.D. Thesis, Stanford University, Stanford, CA, June 1991.
4. Seitzman, J. M., Üngüt, A., Paul, P. H., and Hanson, R. K., "Imaging and Characterization of OH Structures in a Turbulent Nonpremixed Flame," *Twenty-Third Symposium (International) on Combustion*, The Combustion Institute, Pittsburgh, pp. 637–644, 1990.
5. Wohl, K., Gazley, C., and Kapp, N., "Diffusion Flames," *Third Symposium on Combustion and Flame and Explosion Phenomena*, Williams & Wilkins, Baltimore, p. 288, 1949.
6. Chen, J.-Y., Kollmann, W., and Dibble, R. W., "Pdf Modeling of Turbulent Nonpremixed Methane Jet Flames," *Combustion Science and Technology*, 64: 315–346 (1989).
7. Bilger, R. W., "Turbulent Flows with Nonpremixed Reactants," in *Turbulent Reacting Flows* (P. A. Libby, and F. A. Williams, eds.), Springer-Verlag, New York, pp. 65–113, 1980.
8. Bilger, R. W., "Turbulent Jet Diffusion Flames," *Progress in Energy and Combustion Science*, 1: 87–109 (1976).
9. Hottel, H. C., "Burning in Laminar and Turbulent Fuel Jets," *Fourth Symposium (International) on Combustion*, Williams & Wilkins, Baltimore, p. 97, 1953.
10. Hawthorne, W. R., Weddell, D. S., and Hottel, H. C., "Mixing and Combustion in Turbulent Gas Jets," *Third Symposium on Combustion and Flame and Explosion Phenomena*, Williams & Wilkins, Baltimore, p. 266, 1949.
11. Becker, H. A., and Liang, P., "Visible Length of Vertical Free Turbulent Diffusion Flames," *Combustion and Flame*, 32: 115–137 (1978).
12. Delichatsios, M. A., "Transition from Momentum to Buoyancy-Controlled Turbulent Jet Diffusion Flames and Flame Height Relationships," *Combustion and Flame*, 92: 349–364 (1993).

13. Blake, T. R., and McDonald, M., "An Examination of Flame Length Data from Vertical Turbulent Diffusion Flames," *Combustion and Flame*, 94: 426–432 (1993).

14. Turns, S. R., and Bandaru, R. B., "Oxides of Nitrogen Emissions from Turbulent Hydrocarbon/Air Jet Diffusion Flames," Final Report—Phase II, GRI 92/0470, Gas Research Institute, September 1992.

15. Turns, S. R., and Myhr, F. H., "Oxides of Nitrogen Emissions from Turbulent Jet Flames: Part I—Fuel Effects and Flame Radiation," *Combustion and Flame*, 87: 319–335 (1991).

16. Thring, M. W., and Newby, M. P., "Combustion Length of Enclosed Turbulent Jet Flames," *Fourth Symposium (International) on Combustion*, Williams & Wilkins, Baltimore, p. 789, 1953.

17. Ricou, F. P., and Spalding, D. B., "Measurements of Entrainment by Axisymmetrical Turbulent Jets," *Journal of Fluid Mechanics*, 11: 21–32 (1963).

18. Viskanta, R., and Mengüç, M. P., "Radiation Heat Transfer in Combustion Systems," *Progress in Energy and Combustion Science*, 13: 97–160 (1987).

19. Faeth, G. M., Gore, J. P., Chuech, S. G., and Jeng, S.-M., "Radiation from Turbulent Diffusion Flames," in *Annual Review of Numerical Fluid Mechanics and Heat Transfer*, Vol. 2, Hemisphere, Washington, DC, pp. 1–38, 1989.

20. Delichatsios, M. A., Markstein, G. H., Orloff, L., and deRis, J., "Turbulent Flow Characterization and Radiation from Gaseous Fuel Jets," Final Report, GRI 88/0100, Gas Research Institute, 1988.

21. Orloff, L., deRis, J., and Delichatsios, M.A., "Radiation from Buoyant Turbulent Diffusion Flames," *Combustion Science and Technology*, 84: 177–186 (1992).

22. Gore, J. P., and Faeth, G. M., "Structure and Spectral Radiation Properties of Turbulent Ethylene/Air Diffusion Flames," *Twenty-First Symposium (International) on Combustion*, The Combustion Institute, Pittsburgh, p. 1521, 1986.

23. Siegel, R., and Howell, J. R., *Thermal Radiation Heat Transfer*, Second Ed., McGraw-Hill, New York, 1981.

24. Pitts, W. M., "Importance of Isothermal Mixing Processes to the Understanding of Lift-Off and Blowout of Turbulent Jet Diffusion Flames, *Combustion and Flame*, 76: 197–212 (1989).

25. Vanquickenborne, L., and Van Tiggelen, A., "The Stabilization Mechanism of Lifted Diffusion Flames," *Combustion and Flame*, 10: 59–69 (1966).

26. Peters, N., "Local Quenching Due to Flame Stretch and Non-Premixed Turbulent Combustion," *Combustion Science and Technology*, 30: 1–17 (1983).

27. Janicka, J., and Peters, N. "Prediction of Turbulent Jet Diffusion Flame Lift-Off Using a PDF Transport Equation," *Nineteenth Symposium (International) on Combustion*, The Combustion Institute, Pittsburgh, p. 367, 1982.

28. Broadwell, J. E., Dahm, W. J. A., and Mungal, M. G., "Blowout of Turbulent Diffusion Flames," *Twentieth Symposium (International) on Combustion*, The Combustion Institute, Pittsburgh, p. 303, 1984.

29. Kalghatgi, G. T., "Lift-Off Heights and Visible Lengths of Vertical Turbulent Jet Diffusion Flames in Still Air," *Combustion Science and Technology*, 41: 17–29 (1984).

30. Kalghatgi, G. T., "Blow-Out Stability of Gaseous Jet Diffusion Flames. Part I: In Still Air," *Combustion Science and Technology*, 26: 233–239 (1981).

31. Tangirala, V., Chen, R. H., and Driscoll, J. F., "Effect of Heat Release and Swirl on the Recirculation within Swirl-Stabilized Flames," *Combustion Science and Technology*, 51: 75–95 (1987).

32. Beér, J. M., and Chigier, N. A., *Combustion Aerodynamics*, Krieger, Malabar, FL, 1983.

33. Chen, R.-H., and Driscoll, J. F., "The Role of the Recirculation Vortex in Improving Fuel–Air Mixing within Swirling Flames," *Twenty-Second Symposium (International) on Combustion*, The Combustion Institute, Pittsburgh, pp. 531–540, 1988.

REVIEW QUESTIONS

1. Make a list of all of the bold-faced words in Chapter 13 and discuss.
2. Discuss the factors that cause different fuels to produce different jet-flame lengths for identical initial conditions, i.e., equal d_j values and v_e values.
3. Discuss why flame lengths for momentum-dominated jet flames do not depend on initial velocity, but rather are directly proportional to the initial jet diameter. Use the Prandtl mixing-length model applied to jets to support your arguments.
4. What happens to the length of a jet flame when an inert diluent is added to the fuel? Discuss.
5. Discuss the concept of flame stability and the various methods employed to stabilize nonpremixed turbulent flames.
6. Make a list of applications that employ turbulent nonpremixed combustion.
7. Discuss the factors that affect the radiant heat transfer from turbulent, nonpremixed hydrocarbon–air flames.

PROBLEMS

13.1. What nozzle exit velocities are required to achieve momentum-dominated propane and carbon monoxide jet flames for a nozzle diameter of 5 mm? At nozzle exit conditions, the density of propane is $1.854 \, \text{kg/m}^3$ and for carbon monoxide $1.444 \, \text{kg/m}^3$. The adiabatic flame temperature for a CO–air flame is 2400 K. Discuss your results.

13.2. Calculate and compare the flame lengths for momentum-dominated propane–air and hydrogen–air jet flames for a nozzle exit diameter of 5 mm. Assume ambient and fuel temperatures of 300 K. Discuss your results.

13.3. Determine if the flames in problem 13.2 above will require some form of stabilization to prevent them from being blown out. Useful hydrogen properties are: $T_{ad} = 2383 \, \text{K}$, $\mu_{300\text{K}} = 8.96 \cdot 10^{-6} \, \text{N-s/m}^2$, and $S_{L,max} = 3.25 \, \text{m/s}$. Assume that the velocity is the minimum required for a momentum-dominated flame.

13.4. A propane–air jet flame has a nozzle exit velocity of 200 m/s. Determine the minimum nozzle exit diameter required to prevent the flame from being blown out.

13.5. Determine the length of the flame in problem 13.4 above.

13.6. A propene (C_3H_6)–air jet flame is stabilized on a 3-mm-diameter nozzle. The jet exit velocity is 52.7 m/s. Determine the radiant heat-transfer rate (kW) to the cold surroundings. Assume the propene density is approximately $1.76 \, \text{kg/m}^3$ at the jet exit conditions.

13.7. Consider a methane–air jet flame. The nozzle exit diameter is 4 mm and the heat release rate of the flame is 25 kW. The density of the methane at the exit conditions is $0.6565 \, \text{kg/m}^3$.

A. Estimate the liftoff height of the flame.
B. Compare the liftoff length calculated in part A above with the total flame length.

13.8. Estimate the change in flame length in a momentum-dominated ethane–air jet flame when the pure fuel stream is diluted with nitrogen to 50% N_2 by volume. Assume ideal-gas behavior.

CHAPTER
14

BURNING
OF SOLIDS

OVERVIEW

Thus far in our study of combustion, we have considered primarily the burning of gaseous fuels (Chapters 8, 9, 12 and 13), with some attention to liquid fuels (Chapters 3 and 10) where the combustion reactions ultimately involve gaseous species, i.e., the liquid must first vaporize before it can burn. In this chapter, we introduce the subject of burning solids. One of the most important solid fuels is coal, which is typically burned as a pulverized powder in utility boilers, as discussed below. Other applications involving solids combustion include refuse burning, metals combustion, hybrid rocket engines, wood burning, and carbon combustion (coal char or coke), among others.

As suggested by the diversity of the applications and types of fuels listed above, the problem of solids combustion is very complex, with the details depending upon both the nature of the fuel and the specific application. For example, an entire book (or several) would be required to treat coal combustion in detail. Therefore, our approach will be, first, to introduce some of the fundamental concepts that are important to solids combustion, and, second, to apply these concepts to the development of simple models of the burning of a spherical solid carbon particle. The carbon combustion models provide some insight into the general nature of solids combustion and also have relevance to the problem of coal combustion. The chapter concludes with a brief overview of some of the real-world complications associated with the combustion of coal, as well as a few other solids.

COAL-FIRED BOILERS

Figure 14.1 illustrates a typical pulverized-coal-fired boiler. The boiler produces steam for steam-turbine generation of electricity. Utility boilers are huge. The combustion space may be as large as 15 m by 20 m, with total heights reaching over 50 m. Crushed coal is pulverized so that most of the coal particles are smaller than about 75 μm. The coal is blown into the primary zone (lower furnace) by the primary air. The primary air is of the order of 20% of the total air supplied, and the oxygen in the primary air is consumed in the combustion of the volatiles. Secondary air enters through the overfire port at high velocities, mixing with the char and the combustion products from the lower furnace. Heat from the flame gases is transferred through the tubes that line the combustion space to the super-heated steam. Further downstream where the combustion gases are cooler, steam from the turbines is reheated, feedwater heated, and combustion air preheated. The combustion gases are then treated to remove particulate matter and reduce sulfur oxides and, in some cases, nitrogen oxides. A large portion of the boiler-system volume is occupied by the pollution control system(s).

Other configurations are also employed in coal burning. For example, larger coal particles can be burned on fixed or traveling grates. Cyclone combustors, with air and/or fuel streams directed to create a swirling flow, are used in some boilers. Also, fluidized-bed combustors are becoming more popular and development efforts are focused on scale-up for large power outputs [2].

HETEROGENEOUS REACTIONS

Solids combustion differs in a fundamental way from our previous topics in that, now, heterogeneous chemical reactions assume importance. A **heterogeneous reaction** is a reaction involving species existing in different physical states, i.e., gas–liquid or gas–solid reactions. Except for a passing mention of heterogeneous reactions in Chapter 4, and a brief discussion of soot oxidation in Chapter 9, all of our previous discussions assumed chemical reactions occurred as a result of colliding gas–phase molecules, i.e., **homogeneous reactions**. Again, a detailed study of heterogeneous reactions would require several volumes; therefore, our treatment here is but a very brief introduction. As a starting point for further study, basic textbooks on chemical kinetics are suggested, e.g., Ref. [3].

Gardiner [3] subdivides the overall process of gas–solid reactions into the following constituent processes:

1. Transport of the reactant molecule to the surface by convection and/or diffusion.
2. Adsorption of the reactant molecule on the surface.
3. Elementary reaction steps involving various combinations of adsorbed molecules, the surface itself, and gas-phase molecules.
4. Desorption of product molecules from the surface.

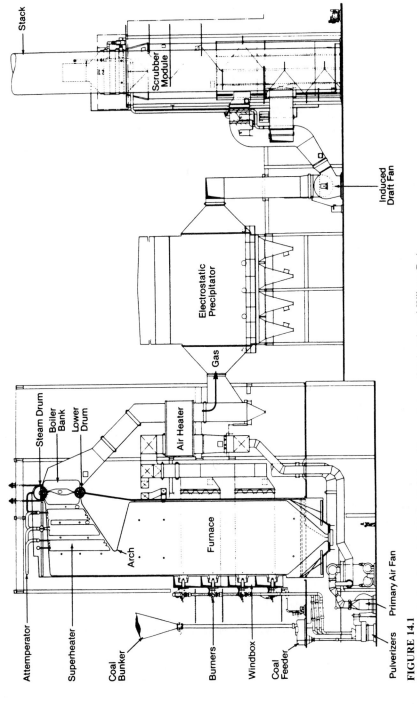

FIGURE 14.1
Pulverized-coal boiler. (Reprinted from Ref. [1] with permission of Babcock and Wilcox Co.)

5. Transport of the product molecules away from the surface by convection and/or diffusion.

The first and fifth steps are familiar to us and can be treated using the mass-transfer concepts developed in Chapter 3. The intervening steps are more complex, especially step 3, and are more properly in the realm of physical chemistry. Rather than elaborate on these steps, we will cite three "rate laws" [3] that arise as a result of how strongly the reactant and/or product molecules are adsorbed on the surface. First, if the reactant molecule A is weakly adsorbed, then the reaction rate, $\Re$, is proportional to the gas-phase concentration of A adjacent to the surface:

$$\Re = k(T)[A], \tag{14.1}$$

where $k(T)$ is the rate coefficient. Second, if A is strongly adsorbed, then the reaction rate is independent of the gas-phase concentration of A, i.e.,

$$\Re = k(T). \tag{14.2}$$

The last case we consider is when the reactant molecule A is weakly adsorbed, while the product molecule B is strongly adsorbed. For this case,

$$\Re = k(T)\frac{[A]}{[B]}, \tag{14.3}$$

where [A] and [B] are the gas-phase concentrations of A and B immediately adjacent to the surface. The point in presenting Eqns. 14.1–14.3 is to illustrate how gas–solid reaction-rate expressions differ from those for elementary homogeneous reactions with which you are familiar (cf. Chapter 4). Furthermore, we will employ expressions of the form of Eqn. 14.1 in the development of our models of carbon combustion below.

BURNING OF CARBON

In addition to providing a nice example illustrating the general nature of solids combustion, carbon combustion is interesting for practical reasons as well. For example, in the combustion of pulverized coal, a carbon char is produced after the volatile matter has been driven from the coal particle and burned. The subsequent burnout of the carbon char is the limiting process establishing the necessary residence time requirements, and hence volume, of the combustion space. Moreover, a substantial amount of heat is radiated to the load from the burning char particles. Even though the real processes involved in coal-char combustion are much more complicated than implied by the models developed here, these models provide insight into the real processes and can serve as order-of-magnitude approximations.

Because of its importance to coal combustion, carbon combustion has a large literature associated with it, for example, Refs. [4–6]; and many models have been developed. Caram and Amundson [7] review and compare twelve models developed between 1924 and 1977. Before beginning our simplified analysis, we first present an overview of the various processes involved.

Overview

Figure 14.2 schematically shows a burning carbon surface within a reacting boundary layer. At the surface, the carbon can be attacked by either O_2, CO_2, or H_2O, depending primarily upon the surface temperature, via the following global reactions:

$$C + O_2 \xrightarrow{k_1} CO_2 \qquad\qquad (R14.4)$$

$$2C + O_2 \xrightarrow{k_2} 2CO \qquad\qquad (R14.5)$$

$$C + CO_2 \xrightarrow{k_3} 2CO \qquad\qquad (R14.6)$$

$$C + H_2O \xrightarrow{k_4} CO + H_2. \qquad\qquad (R14.7)$$

The principal product at the carbon surface is CO. The CO diffuses away from the surface through the boundary layer where it combines with the inward-diffusing O_2 according to the following global homogeneous reaction:

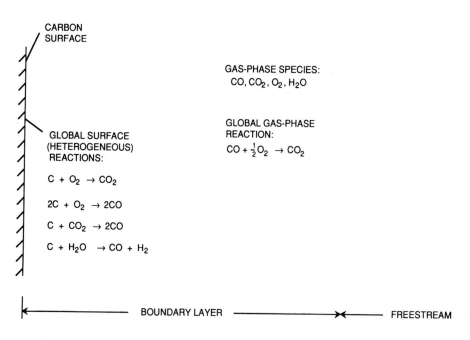

FIGURE 14.2
General scheme for carbon combustion showing global heterogeneous and homogeneous reactions.

$$CO + \tfrac{1}{2}O_2 \rightarrow CO_2. \tag{R14.8}$$

Of course, many elementary reaction steps are involved in R14.8, with one of the most important being $CO + OH \rightarrow CO_2 + H$, as you may recall from Chapter 5.

In principle, the problem of carbon oxidation could be solved by writing the appropriate conservation equations for species, energy, and mass, defining all of the elementary reaction steps, and then solving these equations subject to appropriate boundary conditions at the surface and free stream. A major complication to this scenario, however, is that the carbon surface is porous and the detailed nature of the surface changes as the carbon oxidation proceeds. Thus, the process of **intraparticle diffusion** plays a major role in carbon combustion under certain conditions. A review of this subject can be found in Simons [8].

Simplified models of carbon combustion rely on the global reactions given in Fig. 14.1 and usually assume that the surface is impervious to diffusion. Depending upon the assumptions made for both the surface and gas-phase chemistry, different scenarios emerge which are generally classified as **one-film, two-film**, or **continuous-film** models. In the one-film models, there is no flame in the gas phase and the maximum temperature occurs at the carbon surface. In the two-film models, a flame sheet lies at some distance from the surface, where the CO produced at the surface reacts with incoming O_2. In the continuous-film models, a flame zone is distributed within the boundary layer, rather than occurring in a sheet.

In our analyses below, we will develop both one-film and two-film models. The one-film model is quite simple to conveniently and clearly illustrate the combined effects of heterogeneous kinetics and gas-phase diffusion. The two-film model, although also still quite simplified, is more realistic in that it shows the sequential production and oxidation of CO. We then use these models to obtain estimates of carbon-char burning times.

One-Film Model

The basic approach to the problem of carbon combustion is quite similar to our previous treatment of droplet evaporation in Chapter 3 except that now chemical reaction at the surface replaces evaporation. We consider the burning of a single spherical carbon particle subject to the following assumptions. Because of the similarity of the present analysis to previous ones, we will not elaborate on those assumptions that have been employed and explained previously. If the implications of certain assumptions are not clear, a review of the appropriate sections of Chapters 3 and 10 is recommended.

ASSUMPTIONS

1. The burning process is quasi-steady.
2. The spherical carbon particle burns in a quiescent, infinite ambient medium that contains only oxygen and an inert gas, such as nitrogen. There are no interactions with other particles, and the effects of convection are ignored.

3. At the particle surface, the carbon reacts kinetically with oxygen to produce carbon *dioxide*, i.e., reaction R14.4, $C + O_2 \rightarrow CO_2$, prevails. In general, this reaction choice is not particularly good since carbon *monoxide* is the preferred product at combustion temperatures. Nonetheless, this assumption eliminates the problem of how and where the CO oxidizes, and we will do better in our two-film model.

4. The gas phase consists only of O_2, CO_2, and inert gas. The O_2 diffuses inward, reacts with the surface to form CO_2, which then diffuses outward. The inert gas forms a stagnant layer as in the Stefan problem (cf. Chapter 3).

5. The gas-phase thermal conductivity, k, specific heat, c_p, and the product of the density and mass diffusivity, ρD, are all constants. We furthermore assume that the Lewis number is unity, i.e., $Le = k/(\rho c_p D) = 1$.

6. The carbon particle is impervious to gas-phase species, i.e., intraparticle diffusion is ignored.

7. The particle is of uniform temperature and radiates as a gray body to the surroundings without participation of the intervening medium.

Figure 14.3 illustrates the basic model embodied by the above assumptions, showing how the species mass fraction and temperature profiles vary with the radial

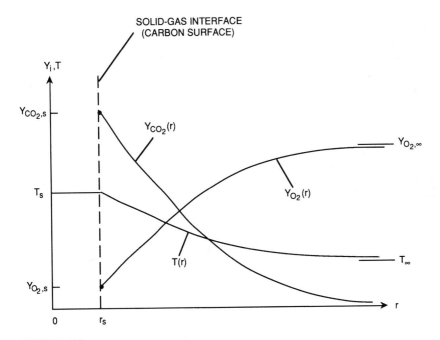

FIGURE 14.3
Species and temperature profiles for one-film model of carbon combustion assuming that CO_2 is the only product of combustion at the carbon surface.

coordinate. Here we see that the CO_2 mass fraction is a maximum at the surface and is zero far from the particle surface. Conversely, the O_2 mass fraction takes on its smallest value at the surface. Later, we will see that if the chemical kinetic rate of O_2 consumption is very fast, the oxygen concentration at the surface, $Y_{O_2,s}$, approaches zero. If the kinetics are slow, there will be an appreciable concentration of O_2 at the surface. Since we assume that there are no reactions occurring in the gas phase and all of the heat release occurs at the surface, the temperature monotonically falls from a maximum at the surface, T_s, to its value far from the surface, T_∞.

PROBLEM STATEMENT. Our primary objective in the following analysis is to determine expressions that allow evaluation of the mass burning rate of the carbon, $\dot{m}_C$, and the surface temperature, T_s. Intermediate variables of interest are the mass fractions of O_2 and CO_2 at the carbon surface. The problem is straightforward and only requires dealing with species and energy conservation.

OVERALL MASS AND SPECIES CONSERVATION. The relationship among the three species mass fluxes, $\dot{m}_C''$, $\dot{m}_{O_2}''$, and $\dot{m}_{CO_2}''$, is illustrated in Fig. 14.4. At the surface, the mass flow of carbon must equal the difference between the outgoing flow of CO_2 and incoming flow of O_2, i.e.,

$$\dot{m}_C'' = \dot{m}_{CO_2}'' - \dot{m}_{O_2}''. \tag{14.9}$$

Similarly, at any arbitrary radial position, r, the net mass flux is the difference between the CO_2 and O_2 fluxes,

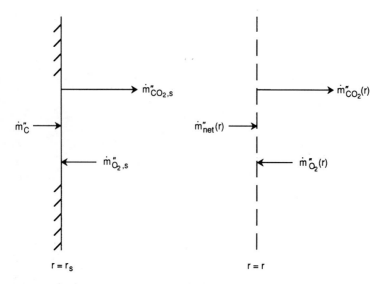

FIGURE 14.4
Species mass fluxes at the carbon surface and at an arbitrary radial location.

$$\dot{m}''_{net} = \dot{m}''_{CO_2} - \dot{m}''_{O_2}. \tag{14.10}$$

Since the mass flowrates of each species are constant with respect to both radial position (no gas-phase reactions) and time (steady state), we have

$$\dot{m}''_C 4\pi r_s^2 = \dot{m}''_{net} 4\pi r^2 \tag{14.11}$$

or

$$\dot{m}''_C = \dot{m}''_{net} = \dot{m}''_{CO_2} - \dot{m}''_{O_2}. \tag{14.12}$$

Thus, we see that the outward flowrate is just the carbon combustion rate, as expected. The CO_2 and O_2 flowrates can be related by the stoichiometry associated with the reaction at the surface:

$$12.01 \, kg \, C + 31.999 \, kg \, O_2 \rightarrow 44.01 \, kg \, CO_2. \tag{14.13a}$$

On a per-kg-of-C basis, we have

$$1 \, kg \, C + \nu_1 \, kg \, O_2 \rightarrow (\nu_1 + 1) \, kg \, CO_2, \tag{14.13b}$$

where the mass stoichiometric coefficient is

$$\nu_1 = \frac{31.999 \, kg \, O_2}{12.01 \, kg \, C} = 2.664. \tag{14.14}$$

The subscript I is used to denote that this coefficient applies to the one-film model. A different value of the stoichiometric coefficient results for the two-film model.

We can now relate the gas-phase species flowrates to the carbon burning rate:

$$\dot{m}_{O_2} = \nu_1 \dot{m}_C, \tag{14.15a}$$

and

$$\dot{m}_{CO_2} = (\nu_1 + 1)\dot{m}_C. \tag{14.15b}$$

Thus, the problem now is to find any one of the species flowrates. To do this, we apply Fick's Law (Eqn. 3.1) to express the conservation of O_2:

$$\dot{m}''_{O_2} = Y_{O_2}(\dot{m}''_{O_2} + \dot{m}''_{CO_2}) - \rho D \frac{d Y_{O_2}}{dr}. \tag{14.16}$$

Recognizing that the mass fluxes are simply related to the mass flows as $\dot{m}_i = 4\pi r^2 \dot{m}''_i$ and substituting Eqns. 14.15a and 14.15b, taking care to account for the direction of the flows (inward flow is negative, outward flow is positive), Eqn. 14.16 becomes, with some additional manipulation,

$$\dot{m}_C = \frac{4\pi r^2 \rho D}{(1 + Y_{O_2}/\nu_1)} \frac{d(Y_{O_2}/\nu_1)}{dr}. \tag{14.17}$$

The boundary conditions that apply to the equation are

$$Y_{O_2}(r_s) = Y_{O_2,s}, \tag{14.18a}$$

$$Y_{O_2}(r \to \infty) = Y_{O_2,\infty}. \tag{14.18b}$$

Having two boundary conditions for our first-order ordinary differential equation allows us to determine an expression for $\dot{m}_C$, the eigenvalue of the problem. Separating Eqn. 14.17 and integrating between the two limits given by Eqns. 14.18a and b yields

$$\dot{m}_C = 4\pi r_s \rho D \ln\left[\frac{1 + Y_{O_2,\infty}/\nu_1}{1 + Y_{O_2,s}/\nu_1}\right]. \tag{14.19}$$

Since $Y_{O_2,\infty}$ is treated as a given quantity, our problem would be solved if we knew the value of $Y_{O_2,s}$, the oxygen mass fraction at the carbon surface. To find this value, we apply our model of the chemical kinetics at the surface.

SURFACE KINETICS. We assume that the reaction $C + O_2 \to CO_2$ is first-order with respect to O_2 and follows the form of Eqn. 14.1. Adopting the conventions of Ref. [7], the carbon reaction rate is expressed

$$\Re_C(\text{kg/s-m}^2) = \dot{m}_{C,s}'' = k_c MW_C[O_{2,s}], \tag{14.20}$$

where $[O_{2,s}]$ is the molar concentration (kmol/m^3) of O_2 at the surface and k_c is the rate coefficient, which is usually expressed in Arrhenius form, i.e., $k_c = A\exp[-E_A/R_u T_s]$. Converting the molar concentration to a mass fraction,

$$[O_{2,s}] = \frac{MW_{\text{mix}}}{MW_{O_2}} \frac{P}{R_u T_s} Y_{O_2,s},$$

and relating the burning rate to the carbon mass flux at the surface ($r = r_s$), Eqn. 14.20 becomes

$$\dot{m}_C = 4\pi r_s^2 k_c \frac{MW_C MW_{\text{mix}}}{MW_{O_2}} \frac{P}{R_u T_s} Y_{O_2,s}, \tag{14.21}$$

or more compactly,

$$\dot{m}_C = K_{\text{kin}} Y_{O_2,s}, \tag{14.22}$$

where all of the kinetic parameters except $Y_{O_2,s}$ have been absorbed into the factor K_{kin}. Note that K_{kin} depends on the pressure, the surface temperature, and the carbon particle radius.

Solving Eqn. 14.22 for $Y_{O_2,s}$ and substituting into Eqn. 14.19 yields a single transcendental (and awkward) equation for the burning rate $\dot{m}_C$. Rather than working with such a result, we will adopt an electrical circuit analogy, similar to those that you may be familiar with for heat transfer, to more conveniently express our solution. Moreover, such an approach yields considerable physical insight.

CIRCUIT ANALOG. To develop our circuit analogy, we need to transform our two expressions for $\dot{m}_C$ (Eqns. 14.19 and 14.22) into forms involving a so-called potential difference, or driving force, and a resistance. For Eqn. 14.22, this is trivial,

$$\dot{m}_C = \frac{(Y_{O_2,s} - 0)}{(1/K_{kin})} \equiv \frac{\Delta Y}{R_{kin}} \tag{14.23}$$

where the zero has been added to indicate a "potential difference," and the "resistance" is the reciprocal of our kinetic factor K_{kin}. Equation 14.23 is thus analogous to Ohm's Law ($i = \Delta V/R$), where $\dot{m}_C$ is the "flow variable" or current analog.

Dealing with Eqn. 14.19 requires a bit of manipulation. First, we rearrange the logarithm term to yield

$$\dot{m}_C = 4\pi r_s \rho D \ln\left[1 + \frac{Y_{O_2,\infty} - Y_{O_2,s}}{\nu_1 + Y_{O_2,s}}\right]. \tag{14.24}$$

As an aside, if we define a transfer number $B_{o,m}$ to be

$$B_{o,m} \equiv \frac{Y_{O_2,\infty} - Y_{O_2,s}}{\nu_1 + Y_{O_2,s}}, \tag{14.25}$$

Eqn. 12.24 becomes

$$\dot{m}_C = 4\pi r_s \rho D \ln(1 + B_{o,m}), \tag{14.26}$$

which is of the same form as the expression developed for liquid droplet evaporation (Eqn. 3.53) and combustion (Eqn. 10.68c). Returning to the problem at hand, Eqn. 14.26 can be linearized, if the numerical value of $B_{o,m}$ is small, by truncating the series

$$\ln(1 + B_{o,m}) = B_{o,m} - \tfrac{1}{2}B_{o,m}^2 + \tfrac{1}{3}B_{o,m}^3 - \cdots \tag{14.27a}$$

after the first term, i.e.,

$$\ln(1 + B_{o,m}) \approx B_{o,m}. \tag{14.27b}$$

Since $\nu_1 = 2.664$, and $Y_{O_2,s}$ must range between zero and $Y_{O_2,\infty}(= 0.233$ for air), it is easy to show that our approximation (Eqn. 14.27b) is reasonable. The desired linearized version of Eqn. 14.19 is written

$$\dot{m}_C = 4\pi r_s \rho D \left[\frac{Y_{O_2,\infty} - Y_{O_2,s}}{\nu_1 + Y_{O_2,s}}\right], \tag{14.28}$$

where, in turn, $\dot{m}_C$ can be expressed as the ratio of a "potential difference" and a "resistance," i.e.,

$$\dot{m}_C = \frac{(Y_{O_2,\infty} - Y_{O_2,s})}{\left(\dfrac{\nu_1 + Y_{O_2,s}}{4\pi r_s \rho D}\right)} \equiv \frac{\Delta Y}{R_{diff}}. \tag{14.29}$$

Note that the appearance of $Y_{O_2,s}$ in R_{diff} being nonconstant, which creates a nonlinear relationship between $\dot{m}_C$ and ΔY.

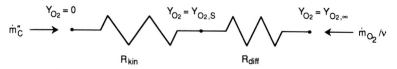

FIGURE 14.5
Electrical circuit analog for a burning carbon particle showing chemical-kinetic and diffusional resistances in series.

Since the burning rate expressed by Eqn. 14.23, derived from chemical kinetics, must be the same as that expressed by Eqn. 14.29, which was derived from mass transfer considerations alone, a two-resistor series circuit results. Figure 14.5 illustrates the resulting circuit analog. Note that, since we chose our potentials to be O_2 mass fractions, the carbon flows from a low potential to a high potential, just the opposite of the electrical analog. Our analogy is perfectly consistent, however, when the flow variable is $\dot{m}_{O_2}/\nu_1\ (=-\dot{m}_C)$, which is also indicated on Fig. 14.5.

We can now determine the burning rate $\dot{m}_C$ with the aid of the circuit analog. Referring to Fig. 14.5, we write

$$\dot{m}_C = \frac{(Y_{O_2,\infty} - 0)}{R_{\text{kin}} + R_{\text{diff}}}, \tag{14.30}$$

where

$$R_{\text{kin}} \equiv 1/K_{\text{kin}} = \frac{\nu_1 R_u T_s}{4\pi r_s^2 M W_{\text{mix}} k_c P} \tag{14.31}$$

and

$$R_{\text{diff}} \equiv \frac{\nu_1 + Y_{O_2,s}}{\rho D 4\pi r_s} \tag{14.32}$$

Since R_{diff} involves the unknown value of $Y_{O_2,s}$, some iteration is still required in this approach. In the following section, we further exploit the circuit analog (Eqns. 14.30–14.32).

LIMITING CASES. Depending on the particle temperature and size, primarily, one of the resistors may be much larger than the other, thus causing $\dot{m}_C$ to depend essentially only on that resistor. For example, let us assume that $R_{\text{kin}}/R_{\text{diff}} \ll 1$. In this case, the burning rate is said to be **diffusionally controlled**. When does this occur? What does this imply? Using the definitions of R_{kin} and R_{diff} (Eqns. 14.31 and 14.32) and taking their ratio, we obtain

$$\frac{R_{\text{kin}}}{R_{\text{diff}}} = \left(\frac{\nu_1}{\nu_1 + Y_{O_2,s}}\right)\left(\frac{R_u T_s}{M W_{\text{mix}} P}\right)\left(\frac{\rho D}{k_c}\right)\left(\frac{1}{r_s}\right), \tag{14.33}$$

TABLE 14.1
Summary of carbon combustion regimes

Regime	R_{kin}/R_{diff}	Burning rate law	Conditions of occurrence
Diffusionally controlled	$\ll 1$	$\dot{m}_C = Y_{O_2,\infty}/R_{diff}$	r_s large, T_s high, P high
Intermediate	~ 1	$\dot{m}_C = Y_{O_2,\infty}/(R_{diff} + R_{kin})$	—
Kinetically controlled	$\gg 1$	$\dot{m}_C = Y_{O_2,\infty}/R_{kin}$	r_s small, T_s low, P low

and can now see how individual parameters affect this quantity. This ratio can be made small in several ways. First, k_c can be very large; this implies a fast surface reaction. We also see that a large particle size, r_s, or high pressure, P, has the same effect. Although the surface temperature appears explicitly in the numerator of Eqn. 14.33, its effect is primarily through the temperature-dependence of k_c, where k_c typically increases rapidly with temperature since $k_c = A \exp(-E_A/R_u T)$. As a result of the burning being diffusionally controlled, we see that none of the chemical kinetic parameters influence the burning rate and that the O_2 concentration at the surface approaches zero.

The other limiting case, **kinetically controlled** combustion, occurs when $R_{kin}/R_{diff} \gg 1$. In this case, the R_{diff} is small and the nodes $Y_{O_2,s}$ and $Y_{O_2,\infty}$ are essentially at the same value, i.e., the concentration of O_2 at the surface is large. Now the chemical kinetic parameters control the burning rate and the mass-transfer parameters are unimportant. Kinetically controlled combustion occurs when particle sizes are small, pressures low, and temperatures low (a low temperature causes k_c to be small).

Table 14.1 summarizes our discussion of the limiting regimes of carbon combustion.

Example 14.1. Estimate the burning rate of a 250-μm-diameter carbon particle burning in still air ($Y_{O_2,\infty} = 0.233$) at 1 atm. The particle temperature is 1800 K, and the kinetic rate constant k_c is 13.9 m/s. Assume the mean molecular weight of the gases at the surface is 30 kg/kmol. Also, what combustion regime prevails?

Solution. We will employ the circuit analogy to find $\dot{m}_C$. The diffusional resistance is calculated from Eqn. 14.32, where the density is estimated from the ideal-gas law at the surface temperature:

$$\rho = \frac{P}{\left(\dfrac{R_u}{MW_{mix}}\right)T_s} = \frac{101,325}{\left(\dfrac{8315}{30}\right)1800} = 0.20\,\text{kg/m}^3$$

and the mass diffusivity is estimated using a value for CO_2 in N_2 from Table D.1, corrected to 1800 K:

$$D = \left(\frac{1800\,\text{K}}{393\,\text{K}}\right)^{1.5} 1.6 \cdot 10^{-5}\frac{\text{m}^2}{\text{s}} = 1.57 \cdot 10^{-4}\,\text{m}^2/\text{s}.$$

Thus, assuming $Y_{O_2,s} \approx 0$ for the time being,

$$R_{\text{diff}} = \frac{\nu_1 + Y_{O_2,s}}{\rho D 4\pi r_s} = \frac{2.664 + 0}{0.2(1.57 \cdot 10^{-4})4\pi(125 \cdot 10^{-6})}$$

$$= 5.41 \cdot 10^7\,\text{s/kg}.$$

The chemical kinetic resistance is calculated from Eqn. 14.31:

$$R_{\text{kin}} = \frac{\nu_1 R_u T_s}{4\pi r_s^2 MW_{\text{mix}} k_c P}$$

$$= \frac{2.664(8315)1800}{4\pi(125 \cdot 10^{-6})^2 30(13.9)101,325}$$

$$= 4.81 \cdot 10^6\,\text{s/kg}.$$

From the above calculations, we see that R_{diff} is slightly more than 10 times the value of R_{kin}; thus, the combustion is **nearly diffusion controlled**. We can now estimate $\dot{m}_C$ using Eqn. 14.30, and then find $Y_{O_2,s}$ to get an improved value for R_{diff}, and iterate if necessary to get an improved value for $\dot{m}_C$.

$$\dot{m}_C = \frac{Y_{O_2,\infty}}{R_{\text{kin}} + R_{\text{diff}}} = \frac{0.233}{4.81 \cdot 10^6 + 5.41 \cdot 10^7}$$

$$\boxed{\dot{m}_C = 3.96 \cdot 10^{-9}\,\text{kg/s}} \quad \text{1st iteration.}$$

From the circuit diagram (Fig. 14.5),

$$Y_{O_2,s} - 0 = \dot{m}_C R_{\text{kin}}$$

$$= 3.96 \cdot 10^{-9}(4.81 \cdot 10^6)$$

$$Y_{O_2,s} = 0.019 \text{ or } 1.9\%.$$

Thus,

$$R_{\text{diff}} = \frac{2.664 + 0.019}{2.664}(R_{\text{diff}})_{\text{1st iter}}$$

$$= 1.007(5.41 \cdot 10^7) = 5.45 \cdot 10^7\,\text{s/kg}.$$

Since R_{diff} changes by less than 1%, no further iteration is required.

Comment. This example shows how the circuit analog provides a simple calculation procedure with easy iteration. We also see that an appreciable O_2 concentration exists at the surface because of the non-negligible kinetic resistance. It should be emphasized that the one-film model, as developed, is not an accurate representation of the actual chemical processes occuring, but, rather, serves as a pedagogical tool to illuminate key concepts with a minimum of complexity.

ENERGY CONSERVATION. So far in our analysis we have treated the surface temperature T_s as a known parameter; however, this temperature cannot be any arbitrary value but is a unique value that depends upon energy conservation at the particle surface. As we will see, the controlling surface energy balance depends strongly on the burning rate, i.e., the energy and mass-transfer processes are coupled.

Figure 14.6 illustrates the various energy fluxes associated with the burning carbon surface. Writing the surface energy balance yields

$$\dot{m}_C h_C + \dot{m}_{O_2} h_{O_2} - \dot{m}_{CO_2} h_{CO_2} = \dot{Q}_{s-i} + \dot{Q}_{s-f} + \dot{Q}_{rad}. \qquad (14.34)$$

Since we assume combustion occurs in a steady state, there is no heat conducted into the particle interior, thus $\dot{Q}_{s-i} = 0$. Following the development of Chapter 10 (Eqns. 10.55–10.60), it is easy to show that the left-hand-side of Eqn. 14.34 is simply $\dot{m}_C \Delta h_c$, where Δh_c is the carbon–oxygen reaction heat of combustion (J/kg-C). Thus, Eqn. 14.34 becomes

$$\dot{m}_C \Delta h_c = -k_g 4\pi r_s^2 \left.\frac{dT}{dr}\right|_{r_s} + \varepsilon_s 4\pi r_s^2 \sigma\left(T_s^4 - T_{sur}^4\right). \qquad (14.35)$$

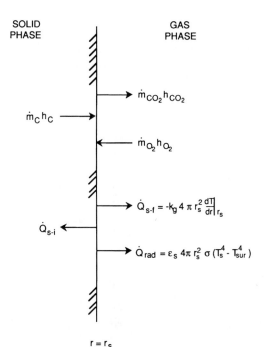

SOLID PHASE

GAS PHASE

$\dot{m}_C h_C$

$\dot{m}_{CO_2} h_{CO_2}$

$\dot{m}_{O_2} h_{O_2}$

$\dot{Q}_{s-i}$

$\dot{Q}_{s-f} = -k_g 4\pi r_s^2 \left.\frac{dT}{dr}\right|_{r_s}$

$\dot{Q}_{rad} = \varepsilon_s 4\pi r_s^2 \sigma\left(T_s^4 - T_{sur}^4\right)$

$r = r_s$

FIGURE 14.6
Energy flows at surface of a spherical carbon particle burning in air.

To obtain an expression for the gas-phase temperature gradient at the surface requires that we write an energy balance within the gas phase and solve for the temperature distribution. Since we have already done this for our droplet evaporation model, we simply use the result from Chapter 10 (Eqn. 10.10) substituting T_s for T_{boil}:

$$\left. \frac{dT}{dr} \right|_{r_s} = \frac{Z\dot{m}_C}{r_s^2} \left[\frac{(T_\infty - T_s) \exp(-Z\dot{m}_C/r_s)}{1 - \exp(-Z\dot{m}_C/r_s)} \right], \tag{14.36}$$

where $Z \equiv c_{pg}/(4\pi k_g)$. Substituting Eqn. 14.36 into Eqn. 14.35 yields, upon rearrangement, our final result,

$$\dot{m}_C \Delta h_c = \dot{m}_C c_{pg} \left[\frac{\exp\left(\dfrac{-\dot{m}_C c_{pg}}{4\pi k_g r_s}\right)}{1 - \exp\left(\dfrac{-\dot{m}_C c_{pg}}{4\pi k_g r_s}\right)} \right] (T_s - T_\infty) + \varepsilon_s 4\pi r_s^2 \sigma \left(T_s^4 - T_{sur}^4\right). \tag{14.37}$$

Note that Eqn. 14.37 contains two unknowns, $\dot{m}_C$ and T_s. To effect the complete solution of the carbon burning problem requires the simultaneous solution of Eqns. 14.37 and 14.30. Since both of these equations are nonlinear, an iterative method is probably the best approach to their solution. Note too that, in the intermediate regime between diffusional and kinetic control, $Y_{O_2,s}$ also becomes an unknown. Thus, Eqn. 14.21 will have to be added to the equation set.

Example 14.2. In the combustion of solid fuels, radiation usually plays a key role. Estimate the gas temperature required to keep a 250-μm-diameter burning carbon particle at 1800 K for (i) when there is no radiation ($T_s = T_{sur}$), and (ii) when the particle radiates as a blackbody to surroundings at 300 K. Conditions are identical to those presented in Example 14.1.

Solution. The surface energy balance (Eqn. 14.37) can be used to determine T_∞ for the two cases. We will estimate the gas-phase properties using those of air at 1800 K:

$$c_{pg}(1800 \text{ K}) = 1286 \text{ J/kg-K} \qquad \text{(Table C.1)}$$

$$k_g(1800 \text{ K}) = 0.12 \text{ W/m-K}. \qquad \text{(Table C.1)}$$

Since the particle is a blackbody, the emissivity, ε_s, is unity, and the heat of combustion for carbon, $\bar{h}_{f,CO_2}^o / MW_C$ is

$$\Delta h_c = 3.2765 \cdot 10^7 \text{ J/kg}. \qquad \text{(Table A.2)}$$

i. In the absence of radiation, Eqn. 14.37 can be rearranged to solve for T_∞, as

$$T_\infty = T_s - \frac{\Delta h_c}{c_{pg}} \frac{\left[1 - \exp\left(\dfrac{-\dot{m}_C c_{pg}}{4\pi k_g r_s}\right) \right]}{\exp\left(\dfrac{-\dot{m}_C c_{pg}}{4\pi k_g r_s}\right)}$$

and evaluated using the burning rate ($\dot{m}_C = 3.96 \cdot 10^{-9}$ kg/s) from Example 14.1:

$$T_\infty = 1800 - \frac{3.2794 \cdot 10^7}{1286} \frac{\left[1 - \exp\left(\dfrac{-3.96 \cdot 10^{-4}(1286)}{4\pi(0.12)125 \cdot 10^{-6}}\right)\right]}{\exp\left(\dfrac{-3.96 \cdot 10^{-4}(1286)}{4\pi(0.12)125 \cdot 10^{-6}}\right)}$$

$$= 1800 - 698$$

$$\boxed{T_\infty = 1102 \,\text{K}} \quad \text{without radiation.}$$

ii. With surroundings at 300 K, the radiation loss is

$$\dot{Q}_{\text{rad}} = \varepsilon_s 4\pi r_s^2 \sigma \left(T_s^4 - T_{\text{sur}}^4\right)$$
$$= (1.0)4\pi(125 \cdot 10^{-6})^2 5.67 \cdot 10^{-8}(1800^4 - 300^4)$$
$$= 0.1168 \,\text{W}.$$

The chemical heat release is

$$\dot{m}_C \Delta h_c = 3.96 \cdot 10^{-4}(3.2765 \cdot 10^7)$$
$$= 0.1299 \,\text{W}.$$

The energy conducted from the particle surface is then

$$\dot{Q}_{\text{cond}} = \dot{m}_C \Delta h_c - \dot{Q}_{\text{rad}} = \dot{m}_C c_{pg} \frac{\exp\left(\dfrac{-\dot{m}_C c_{pg}}{4\pi k_g r_s}\right)}{1 - \exp\left(\dfrac{-\dot{m}_C c_{pg}}{4\pi k_g r_s}\right)} (T_s - T_\infty).$$

Solving for T_∞ using the numerical values given above, yields

$$\boxed{T_\infty = 1730 \,\text{K}} \quad \text{with radiation.}$$

Comment. We see that the gas temperature needs to be quite high to maintain the 1800 K surface temperature in the presence of radiation.

Two-Film Model

As the one-film model developed above was intended to be more instructive than realistic, we now present a model that somewhat more realistically captures the chemical and physical processes involved in carbon combustion, at least for some conditions. In particular, the two-film model has the carbon oxidize to carbon monoxide, rather than carbon dioxide. Since the basic methods employed to develop the two-film model are the same as those for the one-film model, we will be more brief in this section, leaving the gaps to be filled in by the interested reader, or completed as homework assignments.

Figure 14.7 illustrates the species concentration and temperature profiles through the two gas films, one interior to the flame sheet and one exterior. In the two-film model, the carbon surface is attacked by CO_2 according to the global

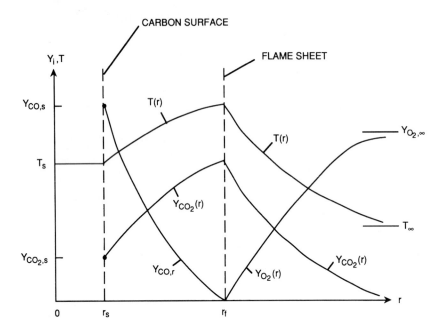

FIGURE 14.7
Species mass fractions and temperature profiles for a two-film model of a burning spherical carbon particle.

reaction R.14.6, $C + CO_2 \rightarrow 2CO$. The CO produced at the surface diffuses outward and is consumed at a flame sheet where it meets an inward-diffusing flow of O_2 in stoichiometric proportions. The global reaction $CO + \frac{1}{2}O_2 \rightarrow CO_2$ is assumed to be infinitely fast; thus, both CO and O_2 are identically zero at the flame sheet. The temperature peaks at the flame sheet. Except for the carbon surface reaction, the scenario illustrated in Fig. 14.7 is identical to our previous treatment of droplet combustion in Chapter 10 (cf. Fig. 10.10). The basic assumptions of the one-film model still hold, except as modified by the preceding discussion. Our specific objective now is to find the burning rate $\dot{m}_C$.

STOICHIOMETRY. The mass flowrates of the various species can be related by simple mass balances at the particle surface and at the flame, as illustrated in Fig. 14.8. These are:

At the surface:	$\dot{m}_C = \dot{m}_{CO} - \dot{m}_{CO_2,i}$	(14.38a)
At the flame:	$\dot{m}_{CO} = \dot{m}_{CO_2,i} - \dot{m}_{CO_2,o} - \dot{m}_{O_2}$	(14.38b)

$$\text{or}$$

$$\dot{m}_C = \dot{m}_{CO_2,o} - \dot{m}_{O_2}. \qquad (14.38c)$$

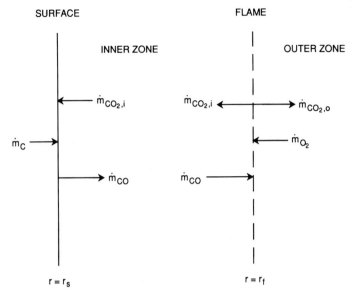

FIGURE 14.8
Species mass flowrates at carbon surface and flame sheet.

Using the stoichiometric relations at the surface and at the flame, all of the flowrates can be related to the burning rate, $\dot{m}_C$:

At the surface: $\quad 1\,\mathrm{kg\,C} + \nu_s\,\mathrm{kg\,CO_2} \rightarrow (\nu_s + 1)\,\mathrm{kg\,CO}$ $\quad\quad$ (14.39a)

At the flame: $\quad\quad 1\,\mathrm{kg\,C} + \nu_f\,\mathrm{kg\,O_2} \rightarrow (\nu_f + 1)\,\mathrm{kg\,CO_2}$ $\quad\quad$ (14.39b)

where

$$\nu_s = \frac{44.01}{12.01} = 3.664 \tag{14.40a}$$

and

$$\nu_f = \nu_s - 1. \tag{14.40b}$$

Thus, the magnitudes of the flowrates are

$$\dot{m}_{CO_2,i} = \nu_s \dot{m}_C \tag{14.41a}$$

$$\dot{m}_{O_2} = \nu_f \dot{m}_C = (\nu_s - 1)\dot{m}_C, \tag{14.41b}$$

$$\dot{m}_{CO_2,o} = (\nu_f + 1)\dot{m}_C = \nu_s \dot{m}_C. \tag{14.41c}$$

SPECIES CONSERVATION. We proceed by applying Fick's Law to obtain differential equations describing the distribution of CO_2 in both the inner and outer zones and, similarly, an equation for the inert species (N_2). These are:

Inner zone CO₂

$$\dot{m}_C = \frac{4\pi r^2 \rho D}{(1 + Y_{CO_2}/\nu_s)} \frac{d(Y_{CO_2}/\nu_s)}{dr},$$ (14.42a)

with boundary conditions

$$Y_{CO_2}(r_s) = Y_{CO_2,s},$$ (14.42b)

$$Y_{CO_2}(r_f) = Y_{CO_2,f}.$$ (14.42c)

Outer zone CO₂

$$\dot{m}_C = \frac{-4\pi r^2 \rho D}{(1 - Y_{CO_2}/\nu_s)} \frac{d(Y_{CO_2}/\nu_s)}{dr},$$ (14.43a)

with boundary conditions

$$Y_{CO_2}(r_f) = Y_{CO_2,f},$$ (14.43b)

$$Y_{CO_2}(r \to \infty) = 0.$$ (14.43c)

Inert (N₂)

$$\dot{m}_C = \frac{4\pi r^2 \rho D}{Y_I} \frac{dY_I}{dr},$$ (14.44a)

with boundary conditions

$$Y_I(r_f) = Y_{I,f},$$ (14.44b)

$$Y_I(r \to \infty) = Y_{I,\infty}.$$ (14.44c)

Integration of these three equations (Eqns. 14.42–14.44) between the limits indicated by the boundary conditions yields the following three algebraic equations involving five unknowns: $\dot{m}_C$, $Y_{CO_2,s}$, $Y_{CO_2,f}$, $Y_{I,f}$, and r_f:

$$\dot{m}_C = 4\pi \left(\frac{r_s r_f}{r_f - r_s}\right) \rho D \ln\left[\frac{1 + Y_{CO_2,f}/\nu_s}{1 + Y_{CO_2,s}/\nu_s}\right],$$ (14.45)

$$\dot{m}_C = -4\pi r_f \rho D \ln(1 - Y_{CO_2,f}/\nu_s),$$ (14.46)

$$Y_{I,f} = Y_{I,\infty} \exp(-\dot{m}_C/(4\pi r_f \rho D)).$$ (14.47)

From $\sum Y_i = 1$, we also know that

$$Y_{CO_2,f} = 1 - Y_{I,f}.$$ (14.48)

The remaining equation for closure results from writing a chemical kinetic expression involving $\dot{m}_C$ and $Y_{CO_2,s}$, which is done in the next section.

SURFACE KINETICS. The reaction $C + CO_2 \rightarrow 2CO$ is first-order in CO_2 concentration [9] and thus the rate is expressed in a form identical to that developed for the one-film model reaction:

$$\dot{m}_C = 4\pi r_s^2 k_c \frac{MW_C MW_{\text{mix}}}{MW_{CO_2}} \frac{P}{R_u T_s} Y_{CO_2,s}, \tag{14.49}$$

where

$$k_c \text{ (m/s)} = 4.016 \cdot 10^8 \exp\left[\frac{-29,790}{T_s \text{ (K)}}\right], \tag{14.50}$$

as given by Mon and Amundson [9]. Equation 14.49 can be written more compactly as

$$\dot{m}_C = K_{\text{kin}} Y_{CO_2,s}, \tag{14.51}$$

where

$$K_{\text{kin}} = 4\pi r_s^2 k_c \frac{MW_C MW_{\text{mix}}}{MW_{CO_2}} \frac{P}{R_u T_s}. \tag{14.52}$$

CLOSURE. To present a tractable solution to our problem, Eqns. 14.45–14.48 can be manipulated to eliminate all variables but $\dot{m}_C$ and $Y_{CO_2,s}$, i.e.,

$$\dot{m}_C = 4\pi r_s \rho D \ln(1 + B_{CO_2,m}), \tag{14.53}$$

where

$$B_{CO_2,m} = \frac{2Y_{O_2,\infty} - [(\nu_s - 1)/\nu_s] Y_{CO_2,s}}{\nu_s - 1 + [(\nu_s - 1)/\nu_s] Y_{CO_2,s}}. \tag{14.54}$$

Equation 14.53 can be solved iteratively with Eqn. 14.51 to find $\dot{m}_C$. For diffusion-controlled burning, $Y_{O_2,s}$ is zero and $\dot{m}_C$ can be evaluated directly from Eqn. 14.53.

To obtain the surface temperature, it is necessary to write and solve energy balances at the surface and at the flame sheet. The procedures are the same as those employed earlier in this chapter and previously in Chapter 10. Determining the surface temperature is left as an exercise.

Example 14.3. Assuming diffusion-controlled combustion and identical conditions ($Y_{O_2,\infty} = 0.233$), compare the burning rates predicted by the one-film and two-film models.

Solution. The burning rates for both the one-film and two-film models are of the form

$$\dot{m}_C = 4\pi r_s \rho D \ln(1 + B_m).$$

For identical conditions, the B_ms are the only parameters having different values; thus,

$$\frac{\dot{m}_C \text{ (two-film)}}{\dot{m}_C \text{ (one-film)}} = \frac{\ln(1 + B_{CO_2,m})}{\ln(1 + B_{o,m})}$$

where the transfer numbers $B_{CO_2,m}$ and $B_{o,m}$ are evaluated from Eqns. 14.54 and 14.25, respectively. For diffusion control, the surface concentrations of CO_2 (two-film model) and O_2 (one-film model) are zero. The transfer numbers are thus evaluated:

$$B_{CO_2,m} = \frac{2Y_{O_2,\infty} - [(\nu_s - 1)/\nu_s] Y_{CO_2,s}}{\nu_s - 1 + [(\nu_s - 1)/\nu_s] Y_{CO_2,s}}$$

$$= \frac{2(0.233) - 0}{3.664 - 1 + 0} = 0.175$$

and

$$B_{o,m} = \frac{Y_{O_2,\infty} - Y_{O_2,s}}{\nu_1 + Y_{O_2,s}} = \frac{0.233 - 0}{2.664 + 0} = 0.0875.$$

The ratio of burning rates is then

$$\boxed{\frac{\dot{m}_C \text{ (two-film)}}{\dot{m}_C \text{ (one-film)}} = \frac{\ln(1 + 0.175)}{\ln(1 + 0.087)} = 1.92} \; .$$

Comment. It is interesting to note that this difference in burning rates is not a result of the type of model, *per se*, but, rather, is a result of the reaction assumed to occur at the gasifying carbon surface. We can show that this is true by assuming that CO, rather than CO_2, is the product formed at the surface in a one-film model. In this case, $\nu_1 = 31.999/24.01 = 1.332$ and B_m then becomes 0.175, which is identical to the two-film model. In this case then, the one-film and two-film models predict identical burning rates independent of the fate of the CO produced at the surface and independent of the surface-attacking species (O_2 or CO_2), as long as the product is CO.

Example 14.4. Use the two-film model to estimate the burning rate of a 70-μm-diameter carbon particle burning in air ($Y_{O_2,\infty} = 0.233$). The surface temperature is 1800 K, and the pressure is 1 atm. Assume the molecular weight of the gaseous mixture at the particle surface is 30 kg/kmol.

Solution. The conditions of this problem are identical to those of Example 14.1, so the gas-phase properties are the same, i.e., $\rho = 0.2 \text{ kg/m}^3$ and $\mathcal{D} = 1.57 \cdot 10^{-4} \text{ m}^2/\text{s}$.
From Eqn. 14.50, the kinetic rate constant for the C–CO_2 reaction is

$$k_c = 4.016 \cdot 10^8 \exp\left[\frac{-29{,}790}{T_s}\right]$$

$$= 4.016 \cdot 10^8 \exp\left[\frac{-29{,}790}{1800}\right] = 26.07 \text{ m/s}.$$

The combustion rate can be expressed in terms of the surface CO_2 concentration (Eqns. 14.49 and 14.51):

$$\dot{m}_C = 4\pi r_s^2 k_c \frac{MW_C MW_{\text{mix}}}{MW_{CO_2}} \frac{P}{R_u T_s} Y_{CO_2,s}$$

$$= \frac{4\pi(35 \cdot 10^{-6})^2 (26.07) 12.01 (30) 101,325}{44.01 (8315) 1800} Y_{CO_2,s} \qquad \text{(I)}$$

$$\dot{m}_C = 2.22 \cdot 10^{-8} Y_{CO_2,s} \quad \text{(kg/s)}.$$

Equations 14.53 and 14.54 also provide an expression for $\dot{m}_C$ in terms of $Y_{CO_2,s}$:

$$\dot{m}_C = 4\pi r_s \rho \mathcal{D} \ln(1 + B)$$

$$= 4\pi(35 \cdot 10^{-6}) 0.20 (1.57 \cdot 10^{-4}) \ln(1 + B) \qquad \text{(II)}$$

$$\dot{m}_C = 1.381 \cdot 10^{-8} \ln(1 + B) \quad \text{(kg/s)}$$

and

$$B = \frac{2 Y_{O_2,\infty} - [(\nu_s - 1)/\nu_s] Y_{CO_2,s}}{\nu_s - 1 + [(\nu_s - 1)/\nu_s] Y_{CO_2,s}}$$

$$B = \frac{2(0.233) - [(3.664 - 1)/3.664] Y_{CO_2,s}}{3.664 - 1 + [(3.664 - 1)/3.664] Y_{CO_2,s}} \qquad \text{(III)}$$

$$= \frac{0.466 - 0.727 Y_{CO_2,s}}{2.664 + 0.727 Y_{CO_2,s}}.$$

We now iteratively solve Eqns. I, II, and III above for $\dot{m}_C$, B, and $Y_{CO_2,s}$. We start the iteration assuming $Y_{CO_2,s}$ is zero, the diffusion-controlled limit:

Iteration	$Y_{CO_2,s}$	B	$\dot{m}_C$ (kg/s)
1	0	0.1749	$2.225 \cdot 10^{-9}$
2	0.1003	0.1436	$1.853 \cdot 10^{-9}$
3	0.0835	0.1488	$1.915 \cdot 10^{-9}$
4	0.0863	0.1479	$1.905 \cdot 10^{-9}$

Given two-significant-figure accuracy, the solution converges to

$$\boxed{\dot{m}_C = 1.9 \cdot 10^{-9} \text{ kg/s}}.$$

Comment. Ignoring chemical kinetics at the surface (cf. Example 14.1) results in overestimating the burning rate by about 16.8% ($= 100\%(22.22 - 1.9)/1.9$). A lower surface temperature (or lower pressure) would make kinetics even more important. Kinetics also becomes increasingly important as the particle diameter decreases as it burns out.

Particle Burning Times

For diffusion-controlled burning, it is a simple matter to find particle burning times. The procedure follows directly from those used in Chapters 3 and 10 to establish the D^2 law and will not be repeated here. The particle diameter can be expressed as a function of time as follows:

$$D^2(t) = D_0^2 - K_B t \tag{14.55}$$

where the burning rate constant, K_B, is given by

$$K_B = \frac{8\rho D}{\rho_C} \ln(1 + B). \tag{14.56}$$

Setting $D = 0$ in Eqn. 14.55 gives the particle lifetime

$$t_C = D_0^2 / K_B. \tag{14.57}$$

Depending whether a one-film or two-film analysis is employed, the transfer number B is either $B_{o,m}$ (Eqn. 14.25) or $B_{CO_2,m}$ (Eqn. 14.54), with the surface mass fractions set to zero. Note the appearance of two densities in Eqn. 14.56, where ρ applies to the gas phase and ρ_C to the solid carbon.

    Thus far, our analyses have assumed a quiescent gaseous medium. To take into account the effects of a convective flow over a burning carbon particle, the *film-theory* analysis of Chapter 10 can be applied. For diffusion-controlled conditions with convection, the mass burning rates are augmented by the factor $Sh/2$, where Sh is the Sherwood number and plays the same role for mass transfer as the Nusselt number does for heat transfer. For unity Lewis number, $Sh = Nu$; thus:

$$(\dot{m}_{C,\text{diff}})_{\substack{\text{with} \\ \text{convection}}} = \frac{Nu}{2} (\dot{m}_{C,\text{diff}})_{\substack{\text{without} \\ \text{convection}}}. \tag{14.58}$$

The Nusselt number can be evaluated using Eqn. 10.78 as a reasonable approximation.

    Example 14.5. Estimate the lifetime of a 70-μm-diameter carbon particle assuming diffusionally controlled combustion at the conditions given in Example 14.4. Assume the carbon density is 1900 kg/m^3.

    Solution. The particle lifetime is straightforwardly calculated from Eqn. 14.57. The burning rate constant (Eqn. 14.56) is evaluated as

$$K_B = \frac{8\rho D}{\rho_C} \ln(1 + B_{CO_2,m})$$

$$= \frac{8(0.20)1.57 \cdot 10^{-4}}{1900} \ln(1 + 0.1749)$$

$$= 2.13 \cdot 10^{-8} \, \text{m}^2/\text{s}$$

where the value for the transfer number $B_{CO_2,m}$ is that for the first iteration in Example 14.4. The lifetime is evaluated as

$$t_C = D_0^2 / K_B = (70 \cdot 10^{-6})^2 / 2.13 \cdot 10^{-8}$$

$$\boxed{t_C = 0.23 \, \text{s}}.$$

Comment. This value seems reasonable in that residence times in coal-fired boilers are of the order of a few seconds and the upper size limit of pulverized coal is about 70 μm. It is important to note that in a real boiler $Y_{O_2,\infty}$ does not remain constant, but decreases as the combustion process runs its course, which tends to increase particle combustion times. Opposing this effect, however, is the augmentation of burning rates by convection, which is present in real combustors. Note also that heterogeneous chemical kinetics controls the latter stages of burnout as the particle diameter decreases. Under these conditions, the particle surface temperature becomes quite important, being greatly influenced by the radiation field within the combustor.

COAL COMBUSTION

As mentioned at the outset of this chapter, the subject of coal combustion has a huge literature associated with it. Our goal here is merely to describe the physical and chemical nature of coal and some of the peculiarities of coal combustion.

A primary factor complicating a description of coal and its combustion is the wide variability of its composition. For example, anthracite coal mined in Pennsylvania has a much different composition than a Montana bituminous coal. Coal is a sedimentary rock formed principally from organic matter, but includes many minerals of different types and in different proportions. Table 14.2 shows the so-called **proximate analysis** of coal where the constituents of the rock are grouped into four categories. From this table, we see that a large portion of the coal may be noncombustible (moisture and mineral matter). The volatiles and char contribute to the useful energy value of the coal, while the mineral matter produces an ash and/or slag, which contributes to operational difficulties (or complexities) and to environmental problems. The mineral matter typically occurs as inclusions in the carbonaceous rock matrix.

The elemental composition of the "useful" portion of the coal, the so-called dry, mineral-matter-free portion (volatiles + char), also has a widely variable composition, as can be seen in Table 14.3. Such a breakdown is referred to as an **ultimate analysis**. The sulfur and nitrogen contribute to air pollution problems and frequently require removal from the stack gases of utility boilers, as you will see in Chapter 15.

TABLE 14.2
Proximate analysis of coal

Constituent class	Mass percentage range (%)[a]
Moisture	10–30
Volatiles	10–30
Mineral matter	10–30
Char	Balance

[a]These ranges are typical. A particular coal may indeed fall outside of these ranges.

TABLE 14.3
Elemental composition of dry, mineral-matter-free coal

Element	Typical range of composition (% by mass)
C	65–95
H	2–6
O	2–25
S	< 10
N	1–2

As might be suggested by the heterogeneous nature of coal and the wide variation in its composition, all coals do not burn in the same manner; however, the general scheme is for the moisture to be driven off, followed by the evolution of the volatiles. The volatiles may burn homogeneously in the gas phase or at the coal-particle surface. The coal may swell and become porous as the volatiles are given off. The material left after devolatilazation is the char and its associated mineral matter. The char then burns and the mineral matter is transformed into ash, slag, and fine particulate fume in various proportions. The combustion of the char proceeds in a manner suggested by our previous discussion of carbon combustion, although the pore structure of the char can be quite important in the actual process.

OTHER SOLIDS

Wood burning has much in common with coal burning in that the evolution of volatiles and char combustion are both important. A review of wood burning can be found in Tillman et al. [10]. Metals which burn heterogeneously include boron, silicon, titanium, and zirconium [11]. Boron has been investigated as a fuel additive for military applications because of its high energy density. The combustion of boron is complicated by the fact that the liquid product of combustion, B_2O_3, can form an inhibiting layer on the surface of the burning boron. A review of boron combustion can be found in King [12].

SUMMARY

In this chapter, the concept of heterogeneous chemical reactions, i.e., those occurring on or at a surface, was introduced, and the importance of these reactions to solids combustion discussed. Simple models of carbon combustion were developed to illustrate certain fundamental aspects common to the combustion of most solids. In particular, the idea of chemical kinetic processes occurring in series with diffusional processes was illustrated by developing an electrical circuit analog. Diffusionally controlled and kinetically controlled combustion are key concepts of this chapter and should be clearly understood. Means of estimating carbon char particle combustion times were presented for diffusionally controlled combustion. The similarities and differences between solid combustion and droplet combustion should be understood by the reader. Finally, ever-so-brief discussions of coal and other solids combustion were presented.

NOMENCLATURE

B_m	Spalding transfer number, Eqns. 14.25 and 14.54
c_p	Specific heat (J/kg-K)
D	Diameter (m)
$\mathcal{D}$	Mass diffusivity (m^2/s)
k	Thermal conductivity (W/m-K) or kinetic rate constant (various units)
K_B	Burning rate constant (m^2/s)
K_{kin}	Parameter defined in Eqns. 14.22 and 14.52
Le	Lewis number
$\dot{m}$	Mass flowrate (kg/s)
$\dot{m}''$	Mass flux (kg/s-m^2)
MW	Molecular weight (kg/kmol)
Nu	Nusselt number
P	Pressure (Pa)
$\dot{Q}$	Heat-transfer rate (W)
r	Radius or radial coordinate (m)
R	Mass-transfer resistance (s/kg)
$\mathfrak{R}$	Reaction rate (kg/s-m^2)
R_u	Universal gas constant (J/kmol-K)
Sh	Sherwood number
t	Time (s)
t_C	Carbon particle lifetime (s)
T	Temperature (K)
Y	Mass fraction (kg/kg)
Z	Parameter in Eqn. 14.36, $c_{pg}/(4\pi k_g)$

Greek symbols

Δh_c	Heat of combustion (J/kg)
ε	Emissivity
ν	Mass stoichiometric coefficient
ρ	Density
σ	Stefan–Boltzmann constant (W/m^2-K^4)

Subscripts

cond	Conduction
diff	Diffusion
f	Flame
g	Gas
i	Interior
I	One-film model or inert

mix	Mixture
o	Outward or exterior
rad	Radiation
s	Surface
sur	Surroundings
∞	Freestream

Other

$[X]$	Molar concentration of X (kmol/m^3)

REFERENCES

1. Stultz, S. C., and Kitto, J. B. (eds.), *Steam: Its Generation and Use*, 40th Ed., Babcock & Wilcox Co., Barberdon, OH, 1992.
2. Radovanovic, M. (ed.), *Fluidized Bed Combustion*, Hemisphere, Washington, DC, 1986.
3. Gardiner, W. C., Jr., *Rates and Mechanisms of Chemical Reactions*, Benjamin, Menlo Park, CA, 1972.
4. Smith, I. W., "The Combustion Rates of Coal Chars: A Review," *Nineteenth Symposium (International) on Combustion*, The Combustion Institute, Pittsburgh, p. 1045, 1983.
5. Laurendeau, N. M., "Heterogeneous Kinetics of Coal Char Gasification and Combustion," *Progress in Energy and Combustion Science*, 4: 221–270 (1978).
6. Mulcahy, M. F. R., and Smith, T. W., "Kinetics of Combustion of Pulverized Fuel: Review of Theory and Experiment," *Reviews of Pure and Applied Chemistry*, 19: 81–108 (1969).
7. Caram, H. S., and Amundson, N. R., "Diffusion and Reaction in a Stagnant Boundary Layer about a Carbon Particle," *Industrial Engineering Chemistry Fundamentals*, 16(2): 171–181 (1977).
8. Simons, G. A., "The Role of Pore Structure in Coal Pyrolysis and Gasification," *Progress in Energy and Combustion Science*, 9: 269–290 (1983).
9. Mon, E., and Amundson, N. R., "Diffusion and Reaction in a Stagnant Boundary Layer about a Carbon Particle. 2. An Extension," *Industrial Engineering Chemistry Fundamentals*, 17(4): 313–321 (1978).
10. Tillman, D. A., Amadeo, J. R., and Kitto, W. D., *Wood Combustion, Principles, Processes, and Economics*, Academic Press, New York, 1981.
11. Glassman, I., *Combustion*, 2nd Ed., Academic Press, Orlando, 1987.
12. King, M. K., "Ignition and Combustion of Boron Particles and Clouds," *Journal of Spacecraft*, 19(4): 294-306 (1982).

QUESTIONS AND PROBLEMS

14.1. List and define all of the bold-faced words in Chapter 14.

14.2. A. Determine the reaction rates in kg$_C$/m^2-s for the following reactions for surface temperatures of 500, 1000, 1500, and 2000 K.

$$2C + O_2 \xrightarrow{k_1} 2CO \tag{R.1}$$

$$C + CO_2 \xrightarrow{k_2} 2CO \tag{R.2}$$

where

$$k_1 = 3.007 \cdot 10^5 \exp(-17,966/T_s)[=] \, m/s$$

$$k_2 = 4.016 \cdot 10^8 \exp(-29,790/T_s)[=]\,\text{m/s}.$$

Assume unity mass fractions for $Y_{O_2,s}$ and $Y_{CO_2,s}$.

B. Determine the ratio $\mathcal{R}_1/\mathcal{R}_2$ for the same temperatures. Discuss.

14.3. Use the one-film model to determine burning fluxes $(= \dot{m}_C/4\pi r_s^2)$ for carbon particles with radii of 500, 50 and 5 μm burning in air at 1 atm. Assume a surface temperature of 1500 K and that the kinetic rate constant, k_c, can be approximated as $3 \cdot 10^5 \exp(-17,966/T_s)$ with units of m/s. Assume the mixture molecular weight at the surface is 29 kg/kmol. In which combustion regime, diffusionally controlled, kinetically controlled, or intermediate, does the burning occur for each particle size?

14.2. Use the one-film model to determine the surface temperature of a 1-mm-diameter carbon particle burning in air $(Y_{O_2,\infty} = 0.233)$. Both the air and the surroundings are at 300 K. Assume diffusional control and $\varepsilon_s = 1$. Is diffusional control a good assumption? Discuss.

14.5. Estimate the lifetime of the carbon particle in problem 14.4 above.

14.6. Explain why Eqns. 14.55 and 14.56 apply only for diffusionally controlled combustion. How would you find the droplet lifetime if diffusionally controlled combustion does not prevail?

14.7. Use the two-film model to determine the burning rate of a 10-μm-diameter carbon particle burning in air $(Y_{O_2,\infty} = 0.233)$. Assume a surface temperature of 2000 K. Is the burning kinetically or diffusionally controlled?

14.8. Determine the influence of the freestream oxygen mole fraction on the burning times of 1-mm-diameter carbon particles. Assume diffusional control. Let $Y_{O_2,\infty} = 0.1165, 0.233$, and 0.466. Assume a surface temperature of 2000 K.

14.9. Fill in the missing steps in the development of the two-film model.

14.10. Rederive the two-film solution treating $Y_{CO_2,\infty}$ as a parameter, rather than setting it equal to zero as was done in the Chapter 14 development.

14.11. Derive an expression to allow evaluation of the surface temperature for the two-film problem. Note that the reaction at the surface is endothermic and that heat will be conducted from the flame to the surface. Use the Chapter 10 development as a guide.

CHAPTER
15

POLLUTANT
EMISSIONS

OVERVIEW

Control of pollutant emissions is a major factor in the design of modern combustion systems. Pollutants of concern include particulate matter, such as soot, fly ash, metal fumes, and various aerosols, etc.; the sulfur oxides, SO_2 and SO_3; unburned and partially burned hydrocarbons, such as aldehydes; oxides of nitrogen, NO_x, which consist of NO and NO_2; carbon monoxide; and greenhouse gases such as N_2O, but particularly CO_2. Early concerns with air pollution focused on the visible particulate emissions from industrial processes and stationary power generation. As was shown in Chapter 1, dramatic reductions in particulate emissions in the United States were achieved, starting in 1950 and leveling out in about 1980. In the 1950s, it became clear that the photochemical smog in the Los Angeles basin was primarily the result of automobile emissions of unburned hydrocarbons and NO_x [1]. Emission controls on vehicles were instituted in California in the 1960s, and national air quality standards were set in the federal Clean Air Act of 1963 for a variety of pollutants. Several amendments to the Clean Air Act in various years have generally imposed stricter standards and have brought more and more sources under scrutiny. In general, California emission standards have been more stringent than federal standards, and California frequently leads the nation in subjecting new sources to control. Other major industrialized nations also have adopted stringent emission standards and implemented emission controls.

472

This chapter takes a somewhat different approach than previous ones, being more descriptive and less theoretical. All of the theoretical concepts necessary to understanding this chapter have been previously developed. Also, much of Chapter 15 is specific to particular devices. We begin our discussion with a brief review of some of the consequences of combustion-generated pollutants, followed by a discussion of the many ways emissions are quantified. The remainder of the chapter is concerned with the origins of pollutants from premixed and nonpremixed systems.

EFFECTS OF POLLUTANTS

Primary air pollutants, those emitted directly from the source, and secondary pollutants, those formed via reactions involving primary pollutants in the atmosphere, affect our environment and human health in many ways. Seinfeld [2] indicates four principal effects of air pollutants in the troposphere:

1. Altered properties of the atmosphere and precipitation.
2. Harm to vegetation.
3. Soiling and deterioration of materials.
4. Potential increase of morbidity (sickness) and mortality in humans.

Each of these effects is briefly discussed below.

Altered properties of the atmosphere affecting local areas include reduced visibility, resulting from the presence of carbon-based particulate matter, sulfates, nitrates, organic compounds, and nitrogen dioxide; increased fog formation and precipitation, resulting from high concentrations of SO_2 that form sulfuric acid droplets, which then serve as condensation nuclei; reduced solar radiation; and altered temperature and wind distributions. On a larger scale, greenhouse gases may alter global climates. Also, acid rain, produced from SO_x and NO_x emissions, affects lakes and susceptible soils.

Vegetation is harmed by the phytotoxicants SO_2, peroxyacetyl nitrate (PAN), C_2H_4, and others. Phytotoxicants destroy chlorophyll and disrupt photosynthesis.

Particulate matter soils clothing, buildings, and other structures, creating not only a reduced aesthetic quality, but also additional cleaning costs over pollution-free environments. Acid and alkaline particles—in particular, those containing sulfur—corrode paint, masonry, electrical contacts, and textiles; while ozone severely deteriorates rubber.

Because of the difficulty of conducting research on human subjects and the large number of uncontrolled variables, controversy exists in assessing the effects of pollution on human health. However, it is well known that pollutants can aggravate pre-existing respiratory ailments. The occurrence of both acute and chronic bronchitis, as well as emphysema, can be correlated with SO_2 and particulate matter. The famous air pollution episodes in Donora, Pennsylvania (1948),

London (1952), and New York (1966), resulted in many excess deaths and other effects. These episodes were all consequences of simultaneously high levels of SO_2 and particles. Secondary pollutants in photochemical smogs cause eye irritation. These pollutants—ozone, organic nitrates, oxygenated hydrocarbons, and photochemical aerosol—are formed primarily by the reactions among nitric oxide and various hydrocarbons. Also, carbon-based particles may contain adsorbed carcinogens. The health effects of carbon monoxide are well documented. Figure 15.1 shows the effects on humans of exposure to various levels of CO.

In addition to the concerns enumerated above, which are all related to pollutants in the troposphere (the lowest layer of the atmosphere), emission of NO_x into the stratosphere by supersonic transport (SST) aircraft is also of interest. Concern here is for the catalytic destruction of stratospheric ozone by NO following the reaction mechanism,

$$NO + O_3 \rightarrow NO_2 + O_2$$
$$NO_2 + O \rightarrow NO + O_2$$

Note that O_3 is destroyed in the first reaction by NO, while NO is regenerated in the second reaction to enter again into the O_3-destruction step. Removal of O_3 from the stratosphere allows more harmful ultraviolet solar radiation to penetrate to the Earth's surface. Development of low-NO_x combustors for supersonic transport aircraft is presently receiving much attention from NASA and engine manufacturers, and is a major factor in determining the future growth of SST operations [3,4].

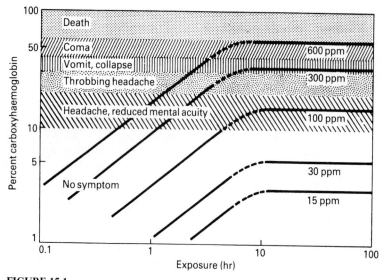

FIGURE 15.1
Effects of CO exposure on humans. (From Ref. [2]. ©1986. Reprinted by permission of John Wiley & Sons, Inc.)

QUANTIFICATION OF EMISSIONS

Emission levels are expressed in many different ways, which can make comparisons difficult and, sometimes, ambiguous. These differences arise from the needs of different technologies; for example, automobile emissions are expressed in grams-per-mile, utility boiler emissions in pounds-per-million BTUs, and many measurements are reported as parts-per-million (by volume) for a stated O_2 concentration. Although the interconversion among various ways of quantifying emissions is not necessarily difficult, we develop some of them here because they are so frequently useful. Reference [5] provides additional information to that given here.

Emission Indices

The **emission index** for species i is the ratio of the mass of species i to the mass of fuel burned by the combustion process,

$$EI_i = \frac{m_{i,\text{emitted}}}{m_{F,\text{burned}}} \tag{15.1}$$

In principle, the emission index is a dimensionless quantity, like the Reynolds number and other dimensionless groups; however, units such as g/kg, g/lb, etc., are used to avoid working with very small numbers, so caution must be exercised. The emission index is particularly useful in that it unambiguously expresses the amount of pollutant formed per mass of fuel, independent of any dilution of the product stream or efficiency of the combustion process. Thus, the emission index can be thought of as a measure of the efficiency of a particular combustion process in producing a particular pollutant, uncoupled from the specific application.

   For the combustion of a hydrocarbon fuel in air, the emission index can be determined from concentration (mole fraction) measurements of the species of interest, together with those of all of the C-containing species. Assuming all of the fuel carbon appears either as CO_2 or CO, the emission index is expressed

$$EI_i = \left(\frac{\chi_i}{\chi_{CO} + \chi_{CO_2}}\right)\left(\frac{x\, MW_i}{MW_F}\right), \tag{15.2}$$

where the χs are mole fractions; x is the number of moles of carbon in a mole of fuel, $C_x H_y$; and MW_i and MW_F are the molecular weights of species i and the fuel, respectively. Physically, the first bracketed term in Eqn. 15.2 represents the number of moles of i per mole of carbon originating in the fuel, while the other term provides the necessary conversion of C moles to fuel moles and their respective conversion to mass units. From Eqn. 15.2, it is obvious that the measurement of an emission index is independent of any dilution by air, for example, since all of the measured concentrations appear as a ratio, with the effect of the diluent canceling.

Example 15.1. A spark-ignition engine is running on a dynamometer test stand and the following measurements of the exhaust products are made:

$$CO_2 = 12.47\%$$
$$CO = 0.12\%$$
$$O_2 = 2.3\%$$
$$C_6H_{14} \text{ (equivalent)} = 367 \text{ ppm}$$
$$NO = 76 \text{ ppm.}$$

All concentrations are by volume on a dry basis. The engine is fueled by isooctane. Determine the emission index of the unburned hydrocarbons expressed as equivalent hexane.

Solution. If we ignore the fact that not all of the fuel appears as CO and CO_2, i.e., unburned hydrocarbons are measured, we can use Eqn. 15.2 directly. The molecular weights of hexane and isooctane are 86.2 and 114.2 kg/kmol, respectively. Thus,

$$EI_{C_6H_{14}} = \left(\frac{\chi_{C_6H_{14}}}{\chi_{CO} + \chi_{CO_2}} \right) \left(\frac{x \, MW_{C_6H_{14}}}{MW_{C_8H_{18}}} \right)$$

$$= \left(\frac{367 \cdot 10^{-6}}{0.0012 + 0.1247} \right) \frac{8(86.2)}{114.2}$$

$$\boxed{EI_{C_6H_{14}} = 0.0176 \text{ kg/kg or } 17.6 \text{ g/kg}}.$$

We can redo this calculation, taking into account the unburned hydrocarbons, by adding $6 \chi_{C_6H_{14}}$ to $\chi_{CO} + \chi_{CO_2}$ in the denominator of Eqn. 15.2:

$$EI_{C_6H_{14}} = \left(\frac{367 \cdot 10^{-6}}{0.0012 + 0.1247 + 6(367 \cdot 10^{-6})} \right) \frac{8(86.2)}{114.2}$$

$$\boxed{EI_{C_6H_{14}} = 17.3 \text{ g/kg}}.$$

This value is lower than the previous value by about 1.7%; thus, the amount of fuel carbon appearing as unburned hydrocarbons has only a small effect on the calculated emission indices.

Corrected Concentrations

Concentrations, corrected to a particular level of O_2 in the product stream, are frequently reported in the literature and used in practice. The purpose of correcting to a specific O_2 level is to remove the effect of various degrees of dilution so that true comparisons of emission levels can be made, while still retaining a familiar mole-fraction-like variable. Before discussing corrected concentrations, we need to define "wet" and "dry" concentrations (mole fractions) of an arbitrary species in a combustion product stream, since corrected concentrations may be expressed either on a **wet** or **dry** basis. Assuming stoichiometric or lean combustion with only trace amounts of CO, H_2, and pollutants, the combustion of one mole of fuel with air (21% O_2, 79% N_2 by volume) can be expressed:

$$C_xH_y + a\,O_2 + 3.76a\,N_2 \rightarrow$$

$$x\,CO_2 + (y/2)\,H_2O + b\,O_2 + 3.76a\,N_2 + \text{trace species.} \qquad (15.3)$$

In many applications, moisture is removed from the exhaust sample prior to analysis, yielding so-called dry concentrations, while sometimes the sample is heated and the moisture retained. Assuming all the moisture is removed, the dry mole fraction for species i is then defined,

$$\chi_{i,\text{dry}} = \frac{N_i}{N_{\text{mix,dry}}} = \frac{N_i}{x + b + 3.76a}, \qquad (15.4a)$$

while the corresponding wet mole fraction is

$$\chi_{i,\text{wet}} = \frac{N_i}{N_{\text{mix,wet}}} = \frac{N_i}{x + y/2 + b + 3.76a}. \qquad (15.4b)$$

Using these definitions (Eqn. 15.4) and an atom balance for O atoms, we can find the ratio of the total number of moles in a wet mixture to the total number of moles in a dry mixture,

$$\frac{N_{\text{mix,wet}}}{N_{\text{mix,dry}}} = 1 + \frac{y}{2(4.76a - y/4)}, \qquad (15.5)$$

where the oxygen coefficient a is defined by the measured O_2 mole fraction as

$$a = \frac{x + (1 + \chi_{O_2,\text{wet}})y/4}{1 - 4.76\chi_{O_2,\text{wet}}} \qquad (15.6a)$$

or

$$a = \frac{x + (1 - \chi_{O_2,\text{dry}})y/4}{1 - 4.76\chi_{O_2,\text{dry}}} \qquad (15.6b)$$

Equation 15.5 can then be used to interconvert wet and dry concentrations, i.e.,

$$\chi_{i,\text{dry}} = \chi_{i,\text{wet}} \frac{N_{\text{mix,wet}}}{N_{\text{mix,dry}}} \qquad (15.7)$$

Remember that the above relations were derived assuming stoichiometric or lean mixtures. For rich mixtures, the situation is more complex since CO and H_2 need to be considered (cf. Chapter 2 and Ref. [5]).

We return now to the concept of corrected concentrations, in which a "raw" measured mole fraction (wet or dry) is expressed as a mole fraction (wet or dry) corrected to a specific O_2 mole fraction. An example of this usage is "200 ppm NO corrected to 3% O_2." To correct a measured concentration or convert from one O_2 level to another, one simply applies

$$\chi_i \begin{pmatrix} \text{corrected to} \\ O_2\text{-level 2} \end{pmatrix} = \chi_i \begin{pmatrix} \text{corrected to} \\ O_2\text{-level 1} \end{pmatrix} \frac{N_{\text{mix},O_2\text{-level 1}}}{N_{\text{mix},O_2\text{-level 2}}}, \qquad (15.8)$$

where, for wet concentrations,

$$N_{mix,wet} = 4.76 \left[\frac{x + (1 + \chi_{O_2,wet})y/4}{1 - 4.76\chi_{O_2,wet}} \right] + y/4, \qquad (15.9a)$$

and for dry concentrations,

$$N_{mix,dry} = 4.76 \left[\frac{x + (1 - \chi_{O_2,dry})y/4}{1 - 4.76\chi_{O_2,dry}} \right] - y/4. \qquad (15.9b)$$

Example 15.2. Using the data provided in Example 15.1, convert the given NO concentration to a wet basis.

Solution. The conversion from wet to dry basis concentrations is accomplished using Eqn. 15.7. We first calculate the ratio of the total number of moles in a wet mixture to the number of moles in a dry mixture using Eqns. 15.5 and 15.6b:

$$a = \frac{x + (1 - \chi_{O_2,dry})y/4}{1 - 4.76\chi_{O_2,dry}}$$

$$= \frac{8 + (1 - 0.023)18/4}{1 - 4.76(0.023)} = 13.92,$$

$$\frac{N_{mix,wet}}{N_{mix,dry}} = 1 + \frac{y}{2(4.76a - y/4)}$$

$$= 1 + \frac{18}{2[(4.76)13.92 - 18/4]} = 1.146.$$

The wet NO concentration can now be found as

$$\chi_{NO,wet} = \chi_{NO,dry} \frac{N_{mix,dry}}{N_{mix,wet}}$$

$$= 76 \text{ ppm} \frac{1}{1.146}$$

$$\boxed{\chi_{NO,wet} = 66.3 \text{ ppm}} .$$

Thus, the wet-basis concentration is about 12.7% less than the dry-basis value.

Comment. From the calculation of the wet-to-dry total moles ratio, we see that the product stream originally contained 14.6% H_2O. Presumably, nearly all of this moisture was removed prior to the gases being analyzed.

Example 15.3. In Example 15.1, 76 ppm (dry) NO was measured in an exhaust stream containing 2.3% O_2. What is the NO concentration corrected to 5% O_2?

Solution. To correct the NO concentration from 2.3% to 5% O_2, we first calculate the total moles associated with each condition (Eqn. 15.9b):

$$N_{mix} @ \chi_{O_2} = 4.76 \left[\frac{x + (1 - \chi_{O_2})y/4}{1 - 4.76\chi_{O_2}} \right] - y/4$$

$$N_{mix} @ 2.3\% \ O_2 = 4.76 \left[\frac{8 + (1 - 0.023)18/4}{1 - 4.76(0.023)} \right] - \frac{18}{4} = 61.76$$

$$N_{mix} @ 5\% \ O_2 = 4.76 \left[\frac{8 + (1 - 0.05)18/4}{1 - 4.76(0.05)} \right] - \frac{18}{4} = 72.18.$$

The corrected concentration is then (Eqn. 15.8):

$$\chi_{NO} @ 5\% \ O_2 = \chi_{NO} @ 2.3\% \ O_2 \ \frac{N_{mix} @ 2.3\% \ O_2}{N_{mix} @ 5\% \ O_2}$$

$$= 76 \text{ ppm } \frac{61.76}{72.18}$$

$$\boxed{\chi_{NO} @ 5\% \ O_2 = 65.0 \text{ ppm}} \ .$$

Comment. Correcting to the 5% level reduces the given concentration by about 15%. When emissions are reported as concentrations, it is essential that the effect of dilution be taken into account when comparisons are made.

Various Specific Emission Measures

In the dynamometer testing of spark-ignition and diesel engines, emissions are frequently expressed as,

$$\text{Mass specific emission} = \frac{\text{Mass flow of pollutant}}{\text{Brake power produced}} \tag{15.10}$$

where the units are typically g/kW-hr, or the mixed units of g/hp-hr. Mass specific emissions (MSE) are conveniently related to the emission index as

$$(\text{MSE})_i = \dot{m}_F \ EI_i/\dot{W} \tag{15.11}$$

where $\dot{m}_F$ is the fuel mass flowrate and $\dot{W}$ is the power delivered.

Another frequently employed specific emission measure is the mass of pollutant emitted per amount of fuel energy supplied, which is expressed as,

$$\frac{\text{Mass of pollutant } i}{\text{Fuel energy supplied}} = \frac{EI_i}{\Delta h_c}, \tag{15.12}$$

where Δh_c is the fuel heat of combustion. Usual units are g/MJ or lb/MMBTU, where MMBTU refers to 10^6 BTU. (Note that confusion can arise in the British units where MBTU refers to 10^3 BTU.)

Other measures of emissions may depend on obtaining a particular weighted average over a specified test cycle. Examples include the use of a driving cycle to determine emissions in grams-per-mile from automobiles [6], and test cycles for aircraft engines to establish emission levels in pounds per thousand pounds thrust per hour per cycle [4]. Such procedures are used to define legislated emission standards. Other emission measures are defined for various industrial processes.

Although all of the quantities discussed above make good sense and are quite useful as measures in specific applications, the emission index is a particularly useful parameter from a combustion point of view.

EMISSIONS FROM PREMIXED COMBUSTION

The primary pollutants that we wish to deal with are oxides of nitrogen, carbon monoxide, unburned and partially burned hydrocarbons, and soot. Sulfur oxides are emitted quantitatively based on the sulfur content of the fuel. Since nearly all premixed combustion deals with very low sulfur-content fuels, SO_x (SO_2 and SO_3) emissions from such systems are usually not of concern. Natural gas contains essentially no sulfur, and gasoline less than 600 ppm S by weight. For non-premixed systems burning coal or low-quality oils, SO_x is a major concern. Our discussion of SO_x emissions, therefore, will be taken up later.

Oxides of Nitrogen

REVIEW OF CHEMICAL MECHANISMS. The chemical kinetics of NO and NO_2 formation and destruction were discussed in Chapter 5, and a review of that material now would be helpful. In Chapter 5, we saw that NO is formed through several mechanisms and variations thereof. Bowman [7] classifies these into the following three categories:

1. The extended Zeldovich (or thermal) mechanism in which O, OH, and N_2 species are at their equilibrium values and N atoms are in steady state (Reactions N.1–N.3 in Chapter 5).
2. Mechanisms whereby NO is formed more rapidly than predicted by the thermal mechanism above, either by (i) the Fenimore CN and HCN pathways (Reactions N.7 and N.8), (ii) the N_2O-intermediate route (Reactions N.4–N.6), or (iii) as a result of superequilibrium concentrations of O and OH radicals in conjunction with the extended Zeldovich scheme.
3. Fuel nitrogen mechanism, in which fuel-bound nitrogen is converted to NO.

The primary nitrogen oxide from combustion systems is NO; although, in some systems, appreciable NO_2 is produced, usually as a result of NO $\rightarrow$ NO_2 conversion in low-temperature mixing regions of nonpremixed systems (cf. Reactions N.12–N.15 in Chapter 5). Therefore, in this section, our discussion focuses on NO.

Calculation of NO formed via the thermal mechanism with equilibrium O and OH radicals is relatively straightforward, following the principles of Chapter

4. In fact, several of the Chapter 4 examples and homework problems are based on this mechanism. Neglecting reverse reactions, we found that

$$\frac{d[NO]}{dt} = 2k_{1f}[O]_e\,[N_2]_e \tag{15.13}$$

where k_{1f} is the forward rate coefficient for the rate-limiting reaction $O + N_2 \rightarrow NO + N$. Of course, reverse reactions need to be included when NO levels become appreciable. The basic premise behind the use of Eqn. 15.13 is that the NO chemistry is much slower than the combustion chemistry; thus, the O- and OH-atom concentrations have had time to equilibrate. This assumption of uncoupled combustion and NO formation chemistry breaks down, however, when O- and OH-atoms are formed in quantities well over equilibrium (up to a factor of 10^3!), which can occur in flame zones. In this case, NO is formed via the Zeldovich reactions much more rapidly than if O atoms were in equilibrium. Calculation of superequilibrium radical concentrations is quite complex and must be coupled to the fuel oxidation kinetics. Also, within the flame zone, the Fenimore prompt-NO pathways can be important. Although workers have had some success in using only the thermal-equilibrium-O mechanism to predict NO emissions in the past, our current understanding of NO production shows that the situation is indeed more complex. Of course, there are applications where the thermal mechanism dominates, and the simple mechanism is thus useful.

Table 15.1 presents calculated relative contributions of the various NO production pathways in premixed combustion [7]. The effect of pressure on NO from laminar flames is given by the first data grouping. Here we see that at low pressures, the NO yield is dominated by the Fenimore (HC–N_2) and super-equilibrium O, OH routes. At 10 atmospheres, the simple thermal mechanism produces a little more than half of the NO_x, with the other three routes making substantial contributions. These data have significance for spark-ignition engines where stoichiometric mixtures are employed and pressures can go up to more than 20 atmospheres.

The second data grouping in Table 15.1 shows the effect of equivalence ratio for rich conditions. The principal observation here is that as the mixture is made increasingly rich, the Fenimore mechanism dominates, yielding 95% of the total NO at $\Phi = 1.32$. At sufficiently rich mixtures, however, this mechanism no longer dominates [11]. Also of interest, but not shown in Table 15.1, is the question of what mechanism(s) dominate at ultralean conditions, which are employed in low-NO_x, premixing, prevaporizing gas-turbine combustors. Although still the subject of research, Correa and Smooke [12] suggest that the N_2O-intermediate route dominates.

The well-stirred reactor data in Table 15.1 show that under conditions of strong backmixing of reactants and products, the superequilibrium O, OH route dominates for lean mixtures, while the Fenimore mechanism controls for stoichiometric and rich mixtures.

The third NO-formation mechanism, the fuel-N route, is not generally important in premixed combustion applications since most fuels used in premixed

TABLE 15.1
Relative contributions of various mechanisms to NO_x formation in premixed combustion[a]

Flame	Φ	P(atm)	Total NO_x (ppm)	Fraction of total NO formation			
				Equilibrium thermal	Superequilibrium	HC–N_2	N_2O
Premixed, laminar, CH_4–air [8]	1	0.1	9 @ 5 ms	0.04	0.22	0.73	0.01
	1	1.0	111	0.50	0.35	0.10	0.05
	1	10.0	315	0.54	0.15	0.21	0.10
Premixed, laminar, CH_4–air [9]	1.05	1	29 @ 5 mm	0.53	0.30	0.17	—
	1.16	1	20	0.30	0.20	0.50	—
	1.27	1	20	0.05	0.05	0.90	—
	1.32	1	23	0.02	0.03	0.95	—
Well-stirred reactor, CH_4–air [9,10]	0.7	1	12 @ 3 ms	≈ 0	0.65	0.05	0.30
	0.8	1	20	—	0.85	0.10	0.05
	1.0	1	70	—	0.30	0.70	—
	1.2	1	110	—	0.10	0.90	—
	1.4	1	55	—	—	1.00	—

[a] From Ref. [7]. Sources of original data are Refs. [8–10].

combustion (natural gas and gasolines) contain little or no bound nitrogen. Pulverized coal and heavy distillate fuels, however, contain significant quantities of fuel nitrogen; thus, we defer our discussion of the fuel-N mechanism until the section on nonpremixed combustion.

NO_x CONTROL STRATEGIES. For processes dominated by thermal NO formation, time, temperature, and oxygen availability are the primary variables affecting NO_x yields. The rate coefficient for the $O + N_2 \rightarrow NO + N$ reaction has a very large activation temperature ($E_A/R_u = 38,370\,K$) and thus increases rapidly at temperatures above about 1800 K. From Fig. 2.14, we see that for adiabatic, constant-pressure combustion, the maximum equilibrium O-atom mole fraction lies near $\Phi = 0.9$. This is also approximately the same equivalence ratio where the maximum kinetically formed NO is found for spark-ignition engines as can be seen in Fig. 15.2. Unfortunately, from the viewpoint of emission control, maximum efficiency also is achieved near this equivalence ratio for many practical devices.

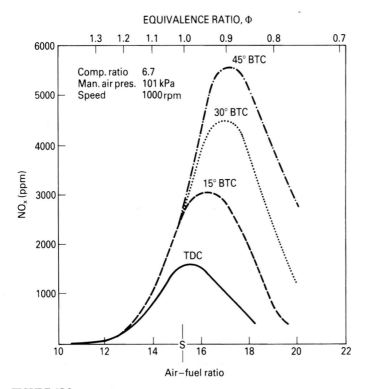

FIGURE 15.2

NO_x concentrations as functions of air–fuel and equivalence ratios for various spark timings. (After Ref. [13]. Reprinted with permission of the Air and Waste Management Association.)

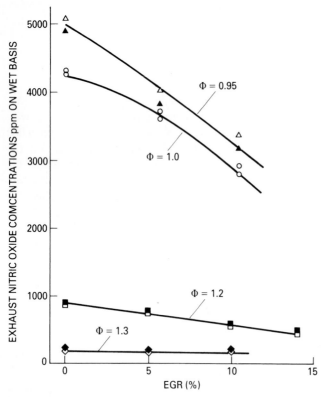

FIGURE 15.3
Effect of exhaust-gas recirculation (EGR) on NO_x emissions from a spark-ignition engine. (Reprinted with permission from Ref. [14], ©1973, Society of Automotive Engineers, Inc.)

Reducing peak temperatures can significantly reduce NO_x emissions. In industrial burners and spark-ignition engines, this can be achieved by mixing flue gases or exhaust gases with the fresh air or fuel. Figure 15.3 shows experimental results for exhaust-gas recirculation, frequently denoted EGR, for a spark-ignition engine. The effect of EGR or FGR (flue-gas recirculation) is to increase the heat capacity of the burned gases for a given quantity of heat release, thus lowering the combustion temperature. Figure 15.4 shows the correlation of NO reduction with diluent heat capacity for an SI engine. The effect of ultralean operation also is to increase the heat capacity of the products and, consequently, reduce temperatures.

Example 15.4. Consider nitric oxide formation in the post-flame gases of a stoichiometric propane–air mixture at atmospheric pressure. Assuming adiabatic conditions, how does the initial rate of NO formation (ppm/s) from the Zeldovich mechanism compare for no dilution and 25% dilution by N_2 (moles N_2 added equals 0.25 the number of moles of air)? The reactants and N_2 diluent are initially at 298 K.

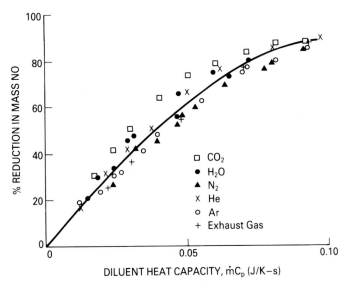

FIGURE 15.4

Correlation of NO reduction with diluent heat capacity $\dot{m}c_p$ for a spark-ignition engine. (Reprinted from Ref. [15], ©1971, Society of Automotive Engineers, Inc.)

Solution. We first calculate the equilibrium adiabatic flame temperature and equilibrium composition for the two cases using an equilibrium routine (cf. Chapter 2 and Appendix F). Results of this computation are:

	No dilution	**25% dilution N_2**
T_{ad} (K)	2267.9	2033.2
$\chi_{O,e}$	$3.12 \cdot 10^{-4}$	$3.59 \cdot 10^{-5}$
$\chi_{N_2,e}$	0.721	0.777

We can use Eqn. 15.13 to evaluate d[NO]/dt,

$$\frac{d[NO]}{dt} = 2k_{1f}[O]_e[N_2]_e,$$

where the rate coefficient k_{1f} from Chapter 5 is

$$k_{1f} = 1.82 \cdot 10^{11} \exp[-38{,}370/T(K)] \, m^3/kmol\text{-}s.$$

For the case of no dilution,

$$k_{1f} = 1.82 \cdot 10^{11} \exp[-38{,}370/2267.9] = 8173 \, m^3/kmol\text{-}s$$

and, converting molar concentrations to mole fractions,

$$\frac{d\,\chi_{NO}}{dt} = 2k_{1f}\,\chi_{O,e}\,\chi_{N_2,e}\,\frac{P}{R_u\,T_{ad}}$$

$$= 2(8173)3.12\cdot10^{-4}(0.721)\frac{101{,}325}{8315(2267.9)}$$

$$\left(\frac{d\,\chi_{NO}}{dt}\right)_{\text{no dil}} = 1.98\cdot10^{-2}\ 1/s \ \text{or}\ 19{,}750\ \text{ppm/s}.$$

With 25% N_2 dilution,

$$k_{1f} = 1.82\cdot10^{11}\exp[-38{,}370/2033.2] = 1159\ \text{m}^3/\text{kmol-s}$$

and

$$\left(\frac{d\,\chi_{NO}}{dt}\right)_{25\%\ N_2} = 2(1159)3.59\cdot10^{-5}(0.777)\frac{101{,}325}{8315(2033.2)}$$

$$= 3.875\cdot10^{-4}\ 1/s\ \text{or}\ 388\ \text{ppm/s}.$$

The ratio of the formation rates with and without dilution is

$$\boxed{\ \frac{\left(\dfrac{d\chi_{NO}}{dt}\right)_{25\%\ N_2}}{\left(\dfrac{d\chi_{NO}}{dt}\right)_{\text{no dil}}} = \frac{388}{19{,}750} = 0.0196\ }.$$

Thus, without dilution the initial NO formation rate is about 50 times greater!

Comment. From this example, we see that thermal NO_x can be greatly reduced by dilution with cold inerts. The two major factors in reducing the formation rates are the decreased value of the rate coefficient (a factor of $\sim$7) and the decreased equilibrium O-atom concentration (a factor of $\sim$9), both of which are controlled by the temperature.

Another means to lower combustion temperatures in spark-ignition engines is to retard the spark timing. Late spark timing shifts the combustion event so that peak pressures occur when the piston is well beyond top-dead-center (minimum volume), resulting in lower pressures and temperatures. This effect can easily be seen in Fig. 15.2 where each curve represents a different spark timing. Significant fuel economy penalties result from retarded spark timings.

The amount of thermal NO_x produced in a device is strongly linked to the time that combustion products spend at high temperatures. For conditions where NO levels are well below their equilibrium values and reverse reactions are unimportant, the NO yield is directly proportional to time (cf. Example 4.4). In the design of a combustion system, therefore, the temperature-versus-time relationship is key to the control of NO emissions; however, drastic alteration of the time–temperature relationship for the gas flow may compromise the useful operation of the device. Obviously, a furnace that fails to properly heat the load, but has low NO_x emissions, is not a useful device.

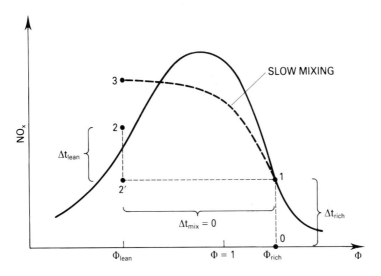

FIGURE 15.5
Schematic representation of staged combustion on NO_x-equivalence ratio coordinates. The path 0–1–2′–2 represents the ideal case of instantaneous secondary air mixing, while 0–1–3 indicates the path for slow secondary mixing.

Staged combustion, in which a rich–lean or lean–rich combustion sequence takes place, is also an NO_x control strategy. The basic concept is illustrated in Fig. 15.5 for a rich–lean sequence. The idea here is first to take advantage of both the good stability and low NO_x emissions associated with rich combustion and, subsequently, complete the combustion of the unburned CO and H_2 in a lean stage where additional NO_x production is also low. For staging to be effective, the mixing of rich products and air must be very rapid, or a substantial amount of heat must be removed between stages. Consider the ideal staged-combustion process in Fig. 15.5 represented by the path 0–1–2′–2 where the bell-shaped curve represents the NO_x yield for a fixed residence time, $\Delta t (= \Delta t_{rich})$. In the rich stage, the amount of NO_x formed in the time Δt_{rich} is represented by the segment 0–1. Secondary air is then instantaneously mixed ($\Delta t_{mix} = 0$) with the rich products (segment 1–2′) with no additional NO_x formed. In the lean stage, the CO and H_2 are oxidized and an additional amount of NO_x is formed (segment 2′–2) in the time associated with the lean stage (Δt_{lean}). If the mixing is not instantaneous, as it must be in any real process, additional NO_x is formed during the mixing process as the stoichiometry passes through the region of high NO_x formation rates (path 1–3). Obviously, the success of staging depends on how well the mixing process can be controlled in practice. Although the ideal staged combustion (0–1–2′–2) is represented as a sequence of two premixed combustion processes, most real processes become nonpremixed because of the in-situ mixing of rich products and secondary air. Siewert and Turns [16] describe the implementation of an ideal staged sequence in which two different cylinders of a spark-ignition engine are employed. The rich products are cooled and mixed with air before combustion is again initiated and completed in the second cylinder. Very low NO_x levels were demonstrated, although CO and unburned hydrocarbon emissions were found to be unacceptably high without aftertreatment.

In automotive applications, combustion system modifications alone are unable to reduce NO_x levels below legislated standards, and, thus, catalytic converters also are employed to reduce NO_x in the exhaust stream. We will discuss catalytic converters later, in conjunction with CO and unburned hydrocarbon control strategies.

Carbon Monoxide

As we saw in Chapter 2, CO is a major species in rich combustion products; thus, substantial CO will be produced whenever rich mixtures are used. In normal operation of most devices, rich conditions are generally avoided; however, spark-ignition engines employ rich mixtures during startup to prevent stalling, and at wide-open-throttle conditions to provide maximum power. For stoichiometric and slightly lean mixtures, CO is found in substantial quantities at typical combustion temperatures as a result of the dissociation of CO_2. The upper curve in Fig. 15.6 shows CO concentrations ranging from 1.2% (by vol.) at $\Phi = 1$ to 830 ppm at $\Phi = 0.8$ in the product gases of adiabatic, atmospheric-pressure, propane-air flames. Carbon monoxide concentrations rapidly fall with temperature, as illustrated by the values shown in Fig. 15.6 for equilibrium at a temperature of 1500 K. Thus, if CO were to remain equilibrated as useful energy is extracted from the combustion products, very low levels of CO would be found in the exhaust system. In furnaces, where residence times are of the order of a second, equilibrium is likely to prevail; however, in spark-ignition engines, temperatures fall very rapidly during the expansion and exhaust processes, CO is not equilibrated and passes into the exhaust stream frozen at levels somewhere between equilibrium at peak temperatures and pressures, and exhaust temperatures and pressures [17,18]. Calculations indicate that the important reaction, $CO + OH \Leftrightarrow CO_2 + H$ (Reaction CO.3 from Chapter 5), is equilibrated during the expansion and blowdown processes; however, the three-body recombination processes, e.g., $H + OH + M \rightarrow H_2O + M$, are not fast enough to maintain equilibrium among all the radicals. This causes the partial-equilibrium CO concentrations to be well above those for full equilibrium [18,19].

Other CO production mechanisms include quenching by cold surfaces, following the ideas presented above, and partial oxidation of unburned fuel. The latter is the subject of the next section.

Unburned Hydrocarbons

In most devices employing premixed reactants, unburned hydrocarbons are usually negligible. An exception to this is the spark-ignition engine. The problem of SI engine hydrocarbon emissions has a large literature, and Heywood's text-

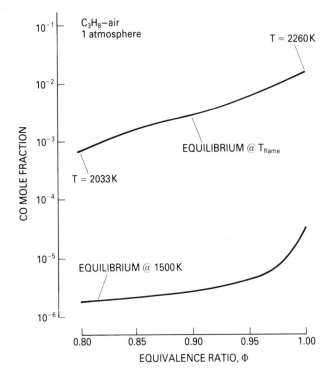

FIGURE 15.6
Equilibrium carbon monoxide mole fractions in propane–air combustion products at adiabatic flame temperatures and at 1500 K.

book [20] provides an excellent review of this subject. In this section, we will briefly discuss some of the most salient aspects of this problem.

In Chapter 8, we discussed the process of flame quenching, whereby a flame is extinguished a short distance from a cold surface. The quenching process leaves a thin layer of unburned fuel–air mixture adjacent to the wall. Whether or not this **quench layer** contributes to unburned hydrocarbon emissions depends upon subsequent diffusion, convection, and oxidation processes. In an SI engine, most of the hydrocarbons from wall quenching ultimately mix with hot gases and are oxidized; however, unburned hydrocarbons can result from flame quenching within and at the entrance to **crevices**, such as those formed by the piston topland and ring pack. The helical spark-plug thread crevice can also be a source of unburned hydrocarbons. Figure 15.7 illustrates this crevice-volume mechanism for unburned hydrocarbons emissions in engines. Other known contributors to unburned hydrocarbon emissions in engines are adsorption and subsequent desorption of fuel into oil layers on the cylinder walls (Fig. 15.7). A similar process can occur for wall deposits, which for unleaded-fuel operations are carbonaceous. Unburned hydrocarbon emissions can also result from incomplete flame propagation in the bulk of the charge. This occurs for lean and/or dilute mixtures approaching the flammability limits [21].

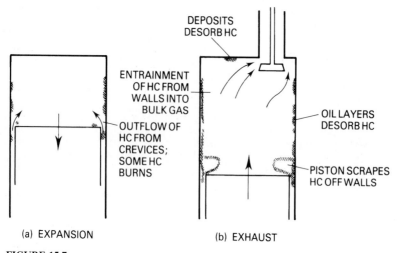

FIGURE 15.7
Schematic representation of unburned hydrocarbon emission mechanism for spark-ignition engines.
(After Ref. [20].)

Only about a third of the unburned hydrocarbons found in the untreated exhaust are fuel molecules [22]. The remainder are fuel pyrolysis and partial oxidation products, as shown in Table 15.2. The partial oxidation of hydrocarbons results in the production of CO, aldehydes, and other particularly undesirable compounds. For lean operation, this partial oxidation of crevice, oil and deposit-layer hydrocarbons is the major source of CO, since the previously discussed CO-mechanisms cannot account for the level of CO found at such conditions.

TABLE 15.2
Typical composition of spark-ignition engine unburned hydrocarbons without aftertreatment[a]

Species	Fraction of total unburned constituents
Ethylene	19.0
Methane	13.8
Propylene	9.1
Toluene	7.9
Acetylene	7.8
1-Butane, i-Butane, 1,3-Butadiene	6.0
p, m, o-Xylene	2.5
i-Pentane	2.4
n-Butane	2.3
Ethane	2.3
TOTAL	73.1

[a] From Ref. [22].

Catalytic Aftertreatment

Catalytic aftertreatment is the primary technique applied to control, simultaneously, nitric oxide, carbon monoxide, and unburned hydrocarbon emissions from spark-ignition engines. Figures 15.8 and 15.9 illustrate the two principal types of catalytic converters currently employed. In both types, noble-metal catalysts, e.g., platinum, palladium, and rhodium, provide active sites for reactions that oxidize carbon monoxide and unburned hydrocarbons while simultaneously reducing nitric oxide. To achieve high conversion efficiencies, i.e. pollutant destruction, requires that the composition of the stream through the converter be maintained in a narrow range near the stoichiometric ratio ($\Phi = 1$). Typical three-way catalyst conversion efficiencies are illustrated in Fig. 15.10. Reference [20] contains more detailed information on three-way catalyst systems and additional references.

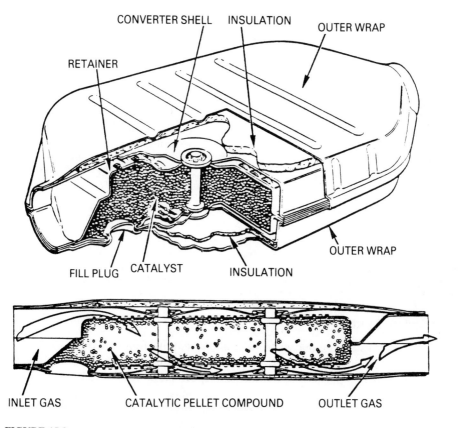

FIGURE 15.8

Pellet bed-type catalytic converter. (Reprinted from Ref. [23] with permission of the American Society of Mechanical Engineers.)

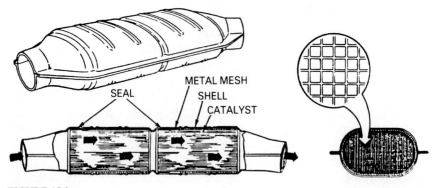

FIGURE 15.9
Monolith catalytic converter. (Reprinted from Ref. [23] with permission of the American Society of Mechanical Engineers.)

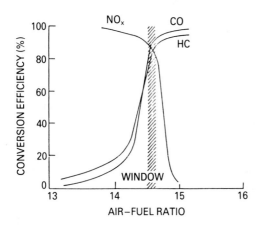

FIGURE 15.10
Conversion efficiencies for a typical three-way automotive catalyst, showing narrow air–fuel ratio window for simultaneous destruction of unburned hydrocarbons, CO, and NO. (Reprinted from Ref. [23] with permission of the American Society of Mechanical Engineers.)

Particulate Matter

Emissions of particulate matter from premixed combustion results only from rich operation or from fuel additives. With the removal of tetraethyl lead from gasolines, this source of particulate matter from spark-ignition engines has been eliminated. Fuel–air mixtures sufficiently rich to produce soot are usually the result of some malfunction, rather than typical operation. Table 15.3 shows limiting equivalence ratios (Φ_c) for the formation of soot in atmospheric-pressure premixed flames for selected fuels with air. Soot forms at equivalence ratios equal to or greater than Φ_c. For premixed combustion, the difference in sooting ten-

TABLE 15.3
Limiting equivalence ratios for the formation of soot in premixed flames[a]

Fuel	Limiting equivalence ratio, Φ_c
Ethane	1.67
Propane	1.56
n-Hexane	1.45
n-Octane	1.39
Isooctane	1.45
Isodecane	1.41
Acetylene	2.08
Ethylene	1.82
Propylene	1.67
Ethanol	1.52
Benzene	1.43
Toluene	1.33

[a] From Ref. [24].

dencies of various fuel types is related not only to fuel structure but also to differences in flame temperature, as discussed by Glassman [25].

EMISSIONS FROM NONPREMIXED COMBUSTION

Although the chemical processes are the same in premixed and nonpremixed combustion, the additional physical processes associated with nonpremixed combustion, e.g., evaporation and mixing, can produce a range of local compositions spanning a wide range of stoichiometries. For example, the overall mixture may be stoichiometric, but within the combustion space there may be regions that are quite rich, while others may be quite lean. This aspect of nonpremixed combustion adds considerable complexity to the problem of pollutant formation in such systems. In some situations, however, combustion can occur essentially in a premixed mode when fuel evaporation and subsequent mixing are sufficiently rapid, even though the fuel and air are introduced separately into the combustion space. For such systems, pollutant production should be interpreted within the premixed framework discussed above. Because of the great complexity involved in pollutant formation in nonpremixed systems, and because emissions in such systems frequently depend on specific details of the system (for example, the droplet size distribution of the fuel spray), we present here only a brief introduction to the subject and point to the literature for further information.

Oxides of Nitrogen

In this section, we first look at the NO_x emission characteristics of a simple nonpremixed system, a vertical jet flame in a quiescent environment. This continues our study of this flame type begun in Chapter 13 and serves as a good introduction to the discussions of the more complex nonpremixed systems which follow.

SIMPLE TURBULENT JET FLAMES. NO_x emissions from turbulent jet flames have been extensively studied, and a recent overview of the issues involved can be found in Refs. [26–28]. The structure of jet flames, indicated by the OH imaging shown previously in Fig. 13.4, suggests that NO is produced in thin laminar-like flamelet regions in the lower-to-mid regions of the flame and in relatively large and broadened reaction zones in the upper regions of the flame. The simple thermal, superequilibrium-O, and Fenimore mechanisms for NO formation are all likely to be active in hydrocarbon jet flames, while the determination of the relative contribution of each mechanisms to the total NO_x yield is yet a subject of research. In applications where flame temperatures are quite high, for example, flames in furnaces with radiating walls or flames using oxygen-enriched air, NO_x emissions are likely to be controlled by Zeldovich kinetics.

As indicated in our discussion of Zeldovich kinetics in premixed systems, temperature, composition, and time are the important variables determining NO_x emissions, and these variables are also controlling in nonpremixed flames. In nonpremixed jet flames, however, the composition varies from point to point in the flow and is governed by fluid mechanical mixing. Likewise, the temperature distribution can be coupled to the composition distribution, as we saw in Chapter 13, through the use of the conserved scalar. Although simple analyses, such as employed in Chapter 13, are useful for predicting global flame properties, such as flame length, more complicated approaches are required to capture kinetic effects associated with pollutant formation. A discussion of these approaches is beyond the scope of this book, and we will have to be content with the generality that thermal NO is produced primarily in flame regions that have simultaneously high temperatures and high concentrations of O and OH atoms, i.e., conditions near stoichiometric. These regions may be the thin laminar-like flame regions low in the jet flame or the broad regions near the flame tip. The detailed temperature and composition distributions within these regions are determined by fluid mechanical, chemical kinetic, and thermal effects. The larger regions with longer residence times are particularly susceptible to radiation heat losses.

Figure 15.11 shows fuel-energy specific NO_x emissions for simple propane–air and ethylene–air jet flames. We observe that the characteristic trend with heat release rate varies with both fuel type and initial jet diameter. These trends are explained by offsetting effects of residence time and temperature [26]. Increasing the fuel flowrate (heat release rate) reduces global and local residence times, which tends to reduce NO formation. Reduced residence times also allow the flames to be more adiabatic since less time is available for radiant losses to occur. Smaller flames (smaller d_j) also yield shorter residence times. Thus, we see that for the more luminous flames and larger flames, temperature effects prevail, causing the increasing trend of NO_x with heat release.

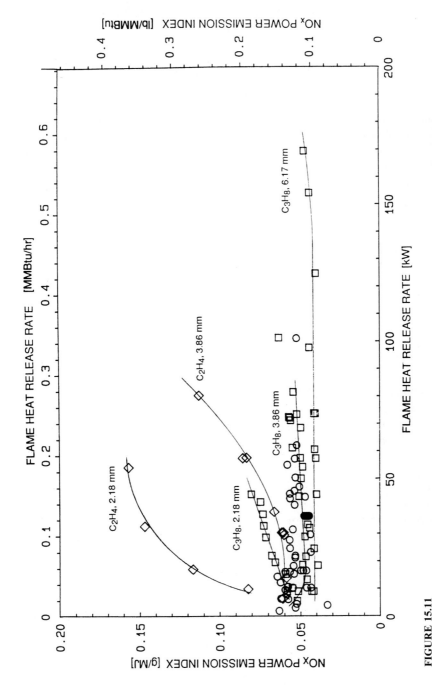

FIGURE 15.11

Oxides of nitrogen emissions from turbulent hydrocarbon–air jet flames for highly luminous (C_2H_4) and less-luminous (C_3H_8) flames of various sizes ($d_j = 2.18$, 3.86, and 6.17 mm). (Reprinted by permission of Elsevier Science, Inc. From Ref. [26]. © 1991, The Combustion Institute.)

   The importance of flame radiation is more clearly delineated in the results shown in Fig. 15.12 where four fuels with different luminosities, and hence radiation characteristics, were employed. As shown at the top of the figure, the ethylene flames had the greatest radiant fractions followed by propane, methane, and a mixture of carbon monoxide and hydrogen. This is consistent with the discussion of sooting tendencies of nonpremixed flames (Chapter 9). The addition of N_2 to the fuel has two effects: first, dilution causes a decrease in adiabatic flame temperature; and, second, N_2 decreases the amount of soot formed in the flame. For the most luminous flames (C_2H_4), the decrease in radiant heat losses more than compensates for the adiabatic flame temperature effect, and characteristic flame temperatures increase (Fig. 15.12, center). For the nonluminous (nonsooting) CO–H_2 flames, the adiabatic flame temperature effect controls. The C_3H_8 and CH_4 flames show intermediate characteristics. At the bottom of Fig. 15.12, we see that the NO_x-versus-N_2-dilution trends all mirror the

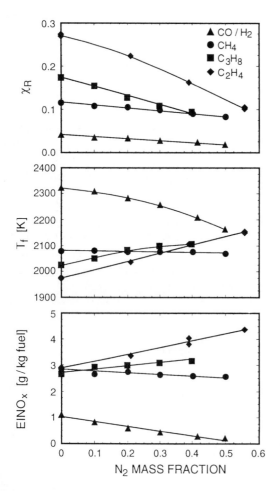

FIGURE 15.12

The influence of N_2 dilution on radiant fractions, characteristic flame temperatures, and NO_x emission indices for jet flames having various luminosities (sooting propensities). (Reprinted by permission of Elsevier Science, Inc. From Ref. [27]. ©1993, The Combustion Institute.)

flame-temperature-versus-dilution trends, clearly showing the importance of heat losses on NO_x emissions [26,27].

For simple hydrocarbon–air turbulent jet flames radiating to room-temperature surroundings, Turns *et al.* [27] correlated NO_x emissions with characteristic flame temperatures T_f (K), and global residence times τ_G (s), as follows:

$$\ln \left[[NO_x]/\tau_G \right] = A + B \ln \tau_G + C/T_f \tag{15.14}$$

where

$$A = 1.1146$$
$$B = -0.7410$$
$$C = -16,347$$

and $[NO_x]$ is defined as gmol of NO_x per cm^3 at stoichiometric conditions at the nonadiabatic flame temperature, T_f. The global residence time is defined by

$$\tau_G \equiv \frac{\rho_f W_f^2 L_f f_{stoic}}{3 \rho_{F,0} d_j^2 v_e} \tag{15.15}$$

where ρ_f, W_f, and L_f are flame density, maximum visible width, and visible length, respectively; $\rho_{F,0}$ is the cold fuel density; and f_{stoic} is the mass fraction of fuel in a stoichiometric mixture.

INDUSTRIAL COMBUSTION EQUIPMENT. In addition to boilers, this class of devices includes process heaters, furnaces, and ovens, all burning, primarily, natural gas. Discussion of oil- and coal-fired devices is limited to the section on utility boilers, which follows. Legislated control of NO_x emissions from industrial combustion devices is much more recent, for example, in comparison to automobiles, and, for that reason, much less information is available concerning their NO_x emissions. Table 15.4 shows the wide range of NO_x levels associated with such equipment, while Table 15.5 shows California South Coast Air Quality Management District standards. For some devices, very large reductions are required in order to be in compliance. The federal Clean Air Act Amendments of 1990 also require reduced emissions from industrial sources.

TABLE 15.4
Typical uncontrolled NO_x levels for industrial processes[a]

Process	Range (ppm at 3% O_2)
High-Temperature direct	
High preheat	500–2000
Low preheat	200–800
High-Temperature indirect	200–600
Low temperature	30–100
Boilers	25–100

[a] Courtesy of Energy and Environmental Research Corp.

TABLE 15.5
NO_x emission regulations for industrial sources[a] (California SCAQMD)[b]

Process	Limit	Rule no.
Industrial boilers (5–40 MMBtu)	40 ppm (3% O_2)	1146
Industrial boilers (> 40 MMBtu)	30 ppm (3% O_2)	1146.1
Refining heaters	30 ppm (3% O_2)	1109
Glass-melting furnaces	4 lb/ton of glass	1117
Gas turbines (no SCR)	15 ppm (15% O_2)	1134
Gas turbines (SCR)	9 ppm (15% O_2)	1134
Others	Best available current technology	

[a] Courtesy of Energy and Environmental Research Corp.
[b] South Coast Air Quality Management District.

Figure 15.13 shows various strategies employed to reduce NO_x emissions from gas-fired equipment [29]. Certain of these techniques also apply to oil-fired devices. NO_x reduction techniques are divided into those involving combustion modifications and those involving post-combustion controls. Within each broad classification there are several specific techniques (Fig. 15.13). Each of these will be briefly discussed here, while more detailed information can be found in Refs. [29] and [30].

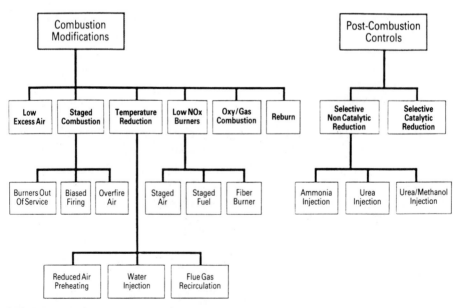

FIGURE 15.13
NO_x control technologies for gas-fired industrial combustion equipment. (Reprinted from Ref. [29] with permission of the Gas Research Institute.)

Low excess air. Thermal NO_x emissions peak at leaner than stoichiometric equivalence ratios (cf. Fig. 15.2). This NO_x reduction technique involves reducing the air supplied to move down the NO_x–Φ curve from the peak toward stoichiometric. Only limited NO_x reductions are possible with this method since CO emissions rise as the amount of excess air is decreased.

Staged combustion. In this method of NO_x control, operation of existing burners in a multi-burner device is modified to create, typically, a rich–lean staging of combustion. This is achieved by having upstream burners operate rich, while adjusting downstream burners to supply air only; or by adjusting some burners to run rich and some lean; or by adjusting all burners to operate rich, with additional air supplied through downstream ports. NO_x reductions attainable with these techniques range from 10 to 40% [29].

Temperature reduction. In many combustion devices, the combustion air is pre-heated by the hot exhaust gases to improve thermal efficiency. Reducing the amount of air preheat reduces combustion temperatures and, consequently, NO_x formation. Injecting water reduces flame temperatures because combustion energy is used to vaporize and superheat the water to combustion temperatures. In concept, water injection is the same as flue-gas recirculation (FGR) in that both act as diluents. The effectiveness of FGR depends on both the quantity and temperature of the recirculated gas. Figure 15.14 shows the effects of FGR on

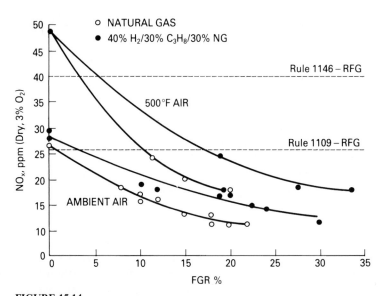

FIGURE 15.14
Effects of flue-gas recirculation (FGR) on NO_x emissions from staged-fuel burners using ambient or preheated air. (Courtesy of John Zink Co., Tulsa, OK.)

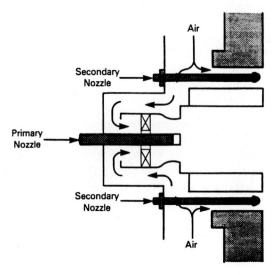

FIGURE 15.15
Low-NO$_x$ burner employing fuel staging (lean–rich combustion). (From Ref. [30].)

NO$_x$ for burners operating with ambient and 500°F (533 K) combustion air [31]. NO$_x$ reductions from approximately 50 to 85% are possible with FGR in gas-fired industrial boilers [29].

Low-NO$_x$ burners. Burners designed for low NO$_x$ emissions employ fuel or air staging. Fuel staging creates a sequential lean–rich (actually, less lean) combustion process (Fig. 15.15), while air staging creates a rich–lean process (Fig. 15.16). Another class of low-NO$_x$ burners are the fiber-matrix burners. These burners employ premixed combustion above or within a metal or ceramic fiber matrix. Because of radiation and convection heat transfer from the matrix, combustion temperatures are quite low, as are NO$_x$ emissions. A fiber burner is illustrated in Fig. 15.17.

Oxy/gas combustion. The concentration of nitrogen in the combustion system can be reduced by supplying additional oxygen to the combustion air. With sufficiently large O$_2$ additions, the decreased N$_2$ concentration outweighs the increased combustion temperatures and NO$_x$ levels can be reduced. If air leaks into the combustion chamber can be prevented, operation with pure O$_2$ ideally eliminates all thermal NO$_x$ production.

Reburn. In this method of NO$_x$ control, about 15% of the total fuel is introduced downstream of the main, fuel-lean combustion zone. Within the reburning zone ($\Phi > 1$), NO is reduced via reactions with hydrocarbons and hydrocarbon intermediates, such HCN, similar to those involved in the Fenimore mechanism. Additional air is then supplied to provide the final burnout of the reburn fuel. NO$_x$ reductions of about 60% are typical for boilers employing reburn technol-

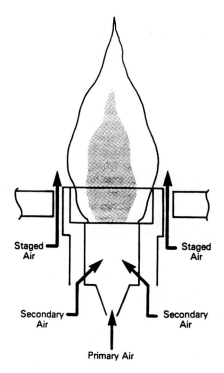

FIGURE 15.16
Low-NO$_x$ burner employing air staging (rich–lean combustion). (From Ref. [30].)

Staged Air

Staged Air

Secondary Air

Secondary Air

Primary Air

ogy [32]. The reburn process is schematically shown in Fig. 15.18, and additional information on reburn chemistry and physical processes can be found in Refs. [7,33,34].

Selective non-catalytic reduction (SNCR). In this post-combustion control technique, a nitrogen-containing additive, either ammonia, urea, or cyanuric acid, is injected and mixed with flue gases to effect chemical reduction of NO to N$_2$ without the aid of a catalyst. Temperature is a critical variable, and operation within a relatively narrow range of temperatures is required to achieve large NO$_x$ reductions. Figure 15.19 illustrates this point [7]. With imperfect mixing and nonuniformity of temperature in an actual exhaust stream, NO$_x$ reductions in practice are somewhat less than the maximum shown in Fig. 15.19 for a laboratory-scale reactor. Additional information on SNCR can be found in Refs. [7,9,35–38].

Selective catalytic reduction (SCR). In this technique, a catalyst is used in conjunction with ammonia injection to reduce NO to N$_2$. The temperature window for effective reduction depends upon the catalyst used, but is contained within the range of about 480 K (400°F) to 780 K (950°F) [29]. The advantage of SCR over SNCR is that greater NO$_x$ reductions are possible, and the operating window is at lower temperatures. Costs of NO$_x$ removal ($/ton) with SCR are generally the

FIGURE 15.17
Ceramic fiber burner being installed in high-pressure steam boiler. (Courtesy of the Gas Research Institute.)

highest of all NO_x control techniques because of both initial high cost and the operating costs associated with catalyst replacement [29]. Sources of additional information on selective catalytic reduction are Refs. [7,39–41].

UTILITY BOILERS. As a class, electric utility boilers produce approximately 34% of the NO_x produced by combustion sources in the U.S. [7], and they are subject to some of the most stringent emission standards worldwide [7]. These boilers are predominantly fired by coal (54.3% in 1972), followed by gas (27%) and oil (18.6%). These fuels are sometimes used in combination.

Burning coal and heavy oils provides an additional source of NO_x over devices burning natural gas and light distillate fuels because of the bound nitrogen in the fuel. Table 15.6 compares the nitrogen content of coal and liquid fuels. Light distillate fuels have small amounts of nitrogen in comparison to both coal and heavy distillate fuels, which can contain up to a few percent nitrogen by weight.

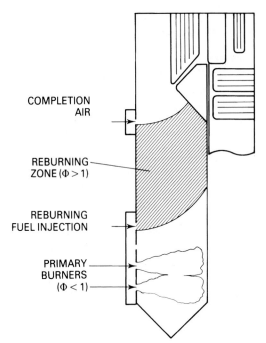

COMPLETION AIR

REBURNING ZONE ($\Phi > 1$)

REBURNING FUEL INJECTION

PRIMARY BURNERS ($\Phi < 1$)

FIGURE 15.18
Industrial boiler equipped with reburn NO_x control. (After Ref. [32].)

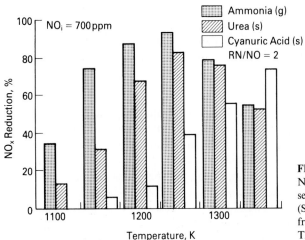

$NO_i = 700\,ppm$

Ammonia (g)
Urea (s)
Cyanuric Acid (s)
$RN/NO = 2$

NO_x Reduction, %

Temperature, K

FIGURE 15.19
NO_x reduction effectiveness for selective non-catalytic reduction (SNCR) techniques. (Reprinted from Ref. [7] by permission of The Combustion Institute.)

TABLE 15.6
Typical bound nitrogen content of coals and distillate fuels

Fuel	Average nitrogen (wt. %)	Range (wt. %)
Coal and coal-derived fuels[a]	1.3	0.5–2.0
Crude oil[b]	0.65	0.2–3.0
Heavy distillates[b]	1.40	0.60–2.15
Light distillates[b]	0.07	0.002–0.60
Natural gas	Nil	—

[a] From Ref. [7].
[b] From Ref. [42].

For gas-fired units, all of the combustion modification techniques and after-treatment methods discussed in the previous section can be employed for NO_x reduction. For oil- and coal-fired boilers, combustion modifications which tend to limit O_2 availability, e.g., low excess air and staged combustion, reduce both thermal and fuel NO_x, while temperature-reduction techniques (e.g., FGR and water injection) have their effect primarily on thermal NO_x [43]. In oil- and coal-fired units, about 20–40% of the fuel-N is converted to NO_x that appears in the flue gases, resulting in as much as half of the total NO_x emitted [42]. Application of post-combustion NO_x reduction techniques (SNCR and SCR) are complicated by the sulfur in coal (cf. Chapter 14) and in residual oils, and by particulate matter [40,41,44]. Ammonia used in either SNCR or SCR reacts with SO_3 to form ammonium bisulfate (NH_4HSO_4), an extremely corrosive substance [40,41,44]. Poisoning of catalysts by SO_3 and plugging of the catalyst surface by particulate matter make application of SCR much more difficult for oil and coal than for natural gas [40,41,44]. Techniques are also being developed that simultaneously remove both NO_x and SO_2 [44].

GAS-TURBINE AND DIESEL ENGINES. Thus far in our discussion of NO_x emissions from nonpremixed combustion systems, we have focused on stationary combustion devices that operate essentially at atmospheric pressure. Gas-turbine and diesel engines, on the other hand, may be mobile or stationary, and combustion occurs at high pressure. For stationary gas turbines, combustion occurs in a range of 10–15 atmospheres, while aircraft-engine combustors operate in a range of 20–40 atmospheres [45]. Diesel engines operate at even higher pressures, up to 100 atmospheres. Compression of air from atmospheric conditions to these high pressures results in the air entering the combustor at temperatures well above atmospheric. For example, adiabatic compression of 300 K air from 1 to 40 atmospheres results in a temperature of 860 K. Peak combustion temperatures are thus high, and, consequently, NO formation rates very rapid. Residence times range over a few milliseconds in aircraft engines and 10–20 ms in stationary applications [45]. In diesel engines [46,47], and turbine engines without emission controls, NO is formed in the high-temperature, near-stoichiometric regions of the flame. Therefore, the combustion modification techniques employed to reduce NO_x are those that lower temperatures. Exhaust-gas recirculation is employed in diesels, and water or steam injection in stationary turbines. Late injection timing in diesels also reduces peak temperatures and, hence, NO_x emissions.

The diesel engine combustion process depends on diffusion burning and, therefore, is inherently less flexible than that of gas turbines. To achieve very low emissions with diesels requires post-combustion controls; selective non-catalytic reduction using cyanuric acid as the reducing agent and selective catalytic reduction with ammonia have been employed to reduce NO_x in stationary diesel installations [7].

For gas turbines, options other than SNCR and SCR are being investigated to achieve so-called ultralow NO_x emissions, the most prominent being lean premixed combustion and rich–lean staging [45]. Both techniques have applicability to both stationary and aircraft engines, although presently there are no operational systems for aircraft [45]. At the time of this writing, lean premixed combustion appears to be the system of choice for ultralow NO_x. There is considerable research and development activity in this area, and some manufacturers currently produce lean premixed engines [48].

Unburned Hydrocarbons and Carbon Monoxide

In nonpremixed combustion systems, there are two sources of unburned hydrocarbons and carbon monoxide that result directly from the nature of nonpremixed combustion. First, overly lean regions are created within the combustion chamber that do not support rapid combustion. Fuel injector characteristics and fuel–air mixing patterns are important parameters in this mechanism. Since a normal flame does not propagate through overlean regions, fuel pyrolysis and partial oxidation products are formed. Among these are oxygenated species, such as aldehydes, and carbon monoxide. The overlean mechanism is particularly important at light loads when the amount of excess air is great.

The second source of incomplete combustion products directly related to nonpremixed combustion is the creation of overly rich regions that subsequently do not mix with sufficient additional air, or, if they do, there is not sufficient time for oxidation reactions to go to completion. Overrich regions are more likely to be a source of unburned and partially burned species at heavy loads, where excess air levels are low.

Additional mechanisms that can result in unburned and partially burned species are the following:

- Wall quenching (diesel engines)
- Quenching by secondary or dilution air jets (gas-turbine engines)
- Fuel dribble from the volume between the injector valve seat and the hole exposed to the combustion space, i.e., the nozzle sac volume (diesel engines)
- Occasional formation of very large rogue fuel droplets (gas-turbine engines).

Whether or not these mechanisms contribute to emissions depends to a large degree on specific details of hardware design, particularly the fuel injection system. For example, fuel issuing from the nozzle sac volume is a major contributor to diesel engine hydrocarbons and can only be affected by changes in nozzle design [49].

In addition to unburned hydrocarbons, partially burned species are emitted from nonpremixed systems without emission controls. These species (aldehydes, ketones, etc.) typically are quite reactive in photochemical smog, act as eye irritants, and are odorous. The wide variety of diesel exhaust odors result from the different compositions of oxygenates produced under various operating conditions [50].

Particulate Matter

Excepting the mineral-matter ash produced by coal burning, which is removed from the effluent stream by electrostatic precipitators, baghouse filters, or other means, the primary particulate matter produced in nonpremixed combustion is soot. Formation of soot can be considered an intrinsic property of most diffusion flames. In Chapter 9, we saw that soot is formed in the rich regions of diffusion flames, and whether or not soot is emitted from a flame depends upon competition between soot formation and soot oxidation processes. Combustion system modifications to minimize soot thus can act to reduce the amount of soot produced prior to oxidation and/or to increase oxidation rates. In diesel engines, particulate traps are used as post-combustion control devices.

Oxides of Sulfur

In combustion processes, all of the sulfur that is present in the fuel appears as SO_2 or SO_3 in the combustion products, the combination of the two being denoted SO_x. Because of this quantitative conversion of fuel sulfur, there are only two possible ways to control SO_x emissions: remove the sulfur from the fuel, or remove the SO_x from the product gases. Both of these techniques are used in varying degrees in practice. Table 15.7 provides estimates of the sulfur content of

TABLE 15.7
Sulfur content of various fuels[a]

Fuel (wt. %)	Range (%)
Coal	≤ 10
Heavy residual oil	0.5–4
Blended residuals and crudes	0.2–3
Diesel fuel (No. 2)	0.1–0.8
Unleaded gasoline	0.015–0.06

[a] Data from Refs. [20] and [51].

various fuels. Coal and residual oils are particularly high in sulfur, while there is very little sulfur in unleaded gasoline.

The amount of SO_3 produced is typically only a few percent of the amount of SO_2, although the SO_3 is usually found in greater than equilibrium concentrations. Sulfur trioxide readily reacts with water to form sulfuric acid ($SO_3 + H_2O \rightarrow H_2SO_4$); thus, sulfuric acid is formed in exhaust streams because of the simultaneous presence of SO_3 and H_2O. In addition to the obvious deleterious effects of producing sulfuric acid, SO_3 also poisons automotive three-way catalysts; thus, sulfur levels are low in gasolines (cf. Table 15.7).

The fate of SO_2 in the atmosphere is for it to be oxidized by, primarily, OH radicals in gas-phase reactions, or after it has been absorbed on a particle or droplet [2]. Subsequent reaction with water then produces sulfuric acid.

The most commonly used method of removing SO_x from flue gases involves reacting SO_2 with limestone ($CaCO_3$) or lime (CaO) [52]. In this control method, an aqueous slurry of limestone or lime is sprayed in a tower through which the flue gases pass. The overall reactions for the process are, for limestone,

$$CaCO_3 + SO_2 + 2H_2O \rightarrow CaSO_3 \cdot 2H_2O + CO_2, \qquad (15.16)$$

and for lime,

$$CaO + SO_2 + 2H_2O \rightarrow CaSO_3 \cdot 2H_2O. \qquad (15.17)$$

The process can be either **wet** or **dry** depending upon whether the reactions occur in solution (wet) or with particles from which the water has evaporated (dry). In a wet process, the final product, calcium sulfite dihydrate ($CaSO_3 \cdot 2H_2O$), precipitates from a retention tank and is disposed of in a pond or landfill, while in a dry process, electrostatic precipitators are used to remove the particular product. Other methods of SO_x control are discussed in Ref. [52].

SUMMARY

In this relatively long chapter, we discussed first the implications of pollutant emissions from combustion systems. You should have a knowledge of the major effects of the primary pollutants, NO_x, CO, unburned and partially burned hydrocarbons, particulate matter, and SO_x; that is, what is it that makes these species pollutants? Next we investigated the various ways used to quantify pollutants. The bases for all of the measures are simple species or atom balances and mass conservation. You should understand why some measures are more useful than others depending on the application, and be able to convert from one measure to another. The next major topics dealt with the formation and control of emissions; first, from premixed systems, and second, from nonpremixed systems. Much of the material concerning pollutant formation relies on previous chapters, particularly sections of Chapters 4, 5, 8 and 9. Review of that material would be appropriate now to consolidate your understanding. Although not comprehensive, many practical applications were also discussed in this chapter. You should be able to discuss the most important pollutant formation and control mechanisms and how they apply to spark-ignition engines, gas-fired industrial combustion equipment, utility boilers, and diesel and gas-turbine engines. Particular emphasis was placed on NO_x emissions because of their current importance.

NOMENCLATURE

c_p	Specific heat (J/kg-K)
d_j	Jet diameter (m)
EI	Emission index (kg/kg or related)
f	Mixture fraction (kg/kg)
L	Length (m)
m	Mass (kg)
$\dot{m}$	Mass flowrate (kg/s)
MW	Molecular weight (kg/kmol)
N	Number of moles (kmol)
P	Pressure (Pa)
R_u	Universal constant (J/kmol-K)
t	Time (s)
T	Temperature (K)
v_e	Exit velocity (m/s)
W	Width (m)
$\dot{W}$	Power (W)
x	Number of carbon atoms in fuel molecule
y	Number of hydrogen atoms in fuel molecule

Greek symbols

Δh_c	Heat of combustion (J/kg)
ρ	Density (kg/m³)
τ_G	Global residence time (s)
Φ	Equivalence ratio
χ	Mole fraction (kmol/kmol)
χ_R	Radiant fraction

Subscripts

ad	Adiabatic
c	Critical for soot production
e	Equilibrium
f	Flame
F	Fuel
i	species i
mix	Mixture
stoic	Stoichiometric

Other symbols

$[X]$ Molar concentration of species X (kmol/m^3)

REFERENCES

1. Haagen-Smit, A. J., "Chemistry and Physiology of Los Angeles Smog," *Industrial Engineering Chemistry*, 44: 1342–1346 (1952).
2. Seinfeld, J. H., *Atmospheric Chemistry and Physics of Air Pollution*, John Wiley & Sons, New York, 1986.
3. Johnson, H. S., Kinnison, D. E., and Wuebbles, D. J., "Nitrogen Oxides from High Altitude Aircraft: An Update of Potential Effects of Ozone," *Journal of Geophysical Research*, 94: 16351–16363 (1989).
4. Jones, R. E., "Gas Turbine Engine Emissions—Problems, Progress and Future," *Progress in Energy and Combustion Science*, 4: 73–113 (1978).
5. Stivender, D. L., "Development of a Fuel-Based Mass Emission Measurement Procedure." SAE Paper 710604, 1971.
6. Federal Register, "Control of Air Pollution from New Motor Vehicles and New Motor Vehicle Engines," U.S. Department of Health, Education, and Welfare, Vol. 35, No. 2, Part II, July 1970.
7. Bowman, C. T., "Control of Combustion-Generated Nitrogen Oxide Emissions: Technology Driven by Regulations," *Twenty-Fourth Symposium (International) on Combustion*, The Combustion Institute, Pittsburgh, pp. 859–878, 1992.
8. Drake, M. C., and Blint, R. J., "Calculations of NO$_x$ Formation Pathways in Propagating Laminar, High Pressure Premixed CH$_4$/Air Flames," *Combustion Science and Technology*, 75: 261–285 (1991).
9. Miller, J. A., and Bowman, C. T., "Mechanism and Modeling of Nitrogen Chemistry in Combustion," *Progress in Energy and Combustion Science*, 15: 287–338 (1989).
10. Glarborg, P., Miller, J. A., and Kee, R. J., "Kinetic Modeling and Sensitivity Analysis of Nitrogen Oxide Formation in Well-Stirred Reactors," *Combustion and Flame*, 65: 177–202 (1986).
11. Bachmeir, F., Eberius, K. H., and Just, Th., "The Formation of Nitric Oxide and the Detection of HCN in Premixed Hydrocarbon–Air Flames at 1 Atmosphere," *Combustion Science and Technology*, 7: 77–84 (1973).
12. Correa, S. M., and Smooke, M. D., "NO$_x$ in Parametrically Varied Methane Flames," *Twenty-Third Symposium (International) on Combustion*, The Combustion Institute, Pittsburgh, pp. 289–295, 1990.
13. Nebel, G. J., and Jackson, M. W., "Some Factors Affecting the Concentration of Oxides of Nitrogen in Exhaust Gases from Spark-Ignition Engines," *Journal of the Air Pollution Control Association*, 8: 213–219 (1958).
14. Komiyama, K., and Heywood, J. B., "Predicting NO$_x$ Emissions and Effects of Exhaust Gas Recirculation in Spark-Ignition Engines," SAE Paper 730475, 1973.
15. Quader, A. A., "Why Intake Charge Dilution Decreases NO Emissions from S. I. Engines," Paper 710009, *SAE Transactions*, 80: 20–30 (1971).
16. Siewert, R. M., and Turns, S. R., "The Staged Combustion Compound Engine (SCCE): Exhaust Emissions and Fuel Economy Potential," Paper 750889, *SAE Transactions*, 84: 2391–2420 (1975).
17. Newhall, H. K., "Kinetics of Engine-Generated Nitrogen Oxides and Carbon Monoxide," *Twelfth Symposium (International) on Combustion*, The Combustion Institute, Pittsburgh, pp. 603–613, 1968.
18. Delichatsios, M. M., "The Kinetics of CO Emissions from an Internal Combustion Engine," S. M. Thesis, Massachusetts Institute of Technology, Cambridge, MA, June 1972.
19. Keck, J. C., and Gillespie, D., "Rate-Controlled Partial-Equilibrium Method for Treating Reacting Gas Mixtures," *Combustion and Flame*, 17: 237–241 (1971).
20. Heywood, J. B., *Internal Combustion Engine Fundamentals*, McGraw-Hill, New York, 1988.

21. Quader, A. A., "Lean Combustion and the Misfire Limit in Spark Ignition Engines," SAE Paper 741055, 1974.

22. Jackson, M. W., "Effects of Some Engine Variables and Control Systems on Composition and Reactivity of Exhaust Hydrocarbons," SAE Paper 660404, 1966.

23. Mondt, J. R., "An Historical Overview of Emission-Control Techniques for Spark Ignition Engines: Part B—Using Catalytic Converters," in *History of the Internal Combustion Engine* (E. F. C. Sommerscales, and A. A. Zagotta, eds.), ICE—Vol. 8, American Society of Mechanical Engineers, New York, 1989.

24. Street, J. C., and Thomas, A., "Carbon Formation in Pre-mixed Flames," *Fuel*, 34: 4–36 (1955).

25. Glassman, I., *Combustion*, 2nd Ed., Academic Press, Orlando, 1987.

26. Turns, S. R., and Myhr, F. H., "Oxides of Nitrogen Emissions from Turbulent Jet Flames: Part I—Fuel Effects and Flame Radiation," *Combustion and Flame*, 87: 319–335 (1991).

27. Turns, S. R., Myhr, F. H., Bandaru, R. V., and Maund, E. R., "Oxides of Nitrogen Emissions from Turbulent Jet Flames: Part II—Fuel Dilution and Partial Premixing Effects," *Combustion and Flame*, 43: 255–269 (1993).

28. Driscoll, J. F., Chen, R.-H., and Yoon, Y., "Nitric Oxide Levels of Turbulent Jet Diffusion Flames: Effects of Residence Time and Damköhler Number," *Combustion and Flame*, 88: 37–49 (1992).

29. Bluestein, J., "NO_x Controls for Gas-Fired Industrial Boilers and Combustion Equipment: A Survey of Current Practices," GRI-92/0374, Gas Research Institute Report, October 1992.

30. U.S. Environmental Protection Agency, "Nitrogen Oxide Control of Stationary Combustion Sources," EPA-625/5-86/020, July 1986.

31. Waibel, R. T., Price, D. N., Tish, P. S., and Halprin, M. L., "Advanced Burner Technology for Stringent NO_x Regulations," API Midyear Refining Meeting, Orlando, 8 May 1990.

32. U.S. Environmental Protection Agency, "Sourcebook: NO_x Control Technology Data," EPA-600/2-91/029, Control Technology Center, July 1991.

33. Lanier, W. S., Mulholland, J. A., and Beard, J. T., "Reburning Thermal and Chemical Processes in a Two-Dimensional Pilot-Scale System," *Twenty-First Symposium (International) on Combustion*, The Combustion Institute, Pittsburgh, pp. 1171–1179, 1986.

34. Chen, S. L., *et al.*, "Bench and Pilot Scale Process Evaluation of Reburning for In-Furnace NO_x Reduction," *Twenty-First Symposium (International) on Combustion*, The Combustion Institute, Pittsburgh, pp. 1159–1169, 1986.

35. Chen, S. L., *et al.*, "Advanced NO_x Reduction Processes Using -NH and -CN Compounds in Conjunction with Staged Air Addition," *Twenty-Second Symposium (International) on Combustion*, The Combustion Institute, Pittsburgh, pp. 1135–1145, 1988.

36. Heap, M. P., Chen, S. L., Kramlick, J. C., McCarthy, J. M., and Pershing, D. W., "Advanced Selective Reduction Processes for NO_x Control," *Nature*, 335: 620–622 (1988).

37. Sarv, H., and Rodgers, L. W., "NO_x Reduction in an Industrial-Scale Boiler by Injecting Cyanuric Acid Powder," Paper WSS/CI 89–87, 1989 Fall Meeting, Western States Section/The Combustion Institute, Livermore, CA, 23–24 October 1989.

38. Muzio, L. J., Montgomery, T. A., Quartucy, G. C., Cole, J. A., and Kramlick, J. C., "N_2O Formation in Selective Non-Catalytic NO_x Reduction Processes," *Proceedings: 1991 Joint Symposium on Stationary Combustion NO_x Control*, Vol. 2, EPRI GS-7447, Electric Power Research Institute, Palo Alto, pp. 5A73-5A96, November 1991.

39. May, P. A., Campbell, L. M., and Johnson, K. L., "Environmental and Economic Evaluation of Gas Turbine SCR NO_x Control," *Proceedings: 1991 Joint Symposium on Stationary Combustion NO_x Control*, Vol. 2, EPRI GS-7447, Electric Power Research Institute, Palo Alto, pp. 5B19–5B36, November 1991.

40. Behrens, E. S., Ikeda, S., Teruo, Y., Mittelbach, G., and Makato, Y., "SCR Operating Experience on Coal-Fired Boilers and Recent Progress," *Proceedings: 1991 Joint Symposium on Stationary Combustion NO_x Control*, Vol. 1, EPRI GS-7447, Electric Power Research Institute, Palo Alto, pp. 4B59–4B77, November 1991.

41. Robie, C. P., Ireland, P. A., and Cichanowicz, J. E., "Technical Feasibility and Cost of SCR for U.S. Utility Application," *Proceedings: 1991 Joint Symposium on Stationary Combustion NO_x*

Control, Vol. 1, EPRI GS-7447, Electric Power Research Institute, Palo Alto, pp. 4B81–4B100, November 1991.

42. Bowman, C. T., "Kinetics of Pollutant Formation and Destruction in Combustion," *Progress in Energy and Combustion Science*, 1: 33–45 (1975).

43. Sarofim, A. F., and Flagan, R. C., "NO_x Control for Stationary Combustion Sources," *Progress in Energy and Combustion Sciences*, 2: 1–25 (1976).

44. Rosenberg, H. S., Curran, L. M., Slack, A. V., Ando, J., and Oxley, J. H., "Post Combustion Methods for Control of NO_x Emissions," *Progress in Energy and Combustion Science*, 6: 287–302 (1980).

45. Correa, S. M., "A Review of NO_x Formation Under Gas-Turbine Combustion Conditions," *Combustion Science and Technology*, 87: 329–362 (1992).

46. Plee, S. L., Ahmad, T., and Myers, J. P., "Diesel NO_x Emissions—A Simple Correlation Technique for Intake Air Effects," *Nineteenth Symposium (International) on Combustion*, The Combustion Institute, Pittsburgh, pp. 1495–1502, 1983.

47. Ahmad, T., and Plee, S. L., "Application of Flame Temperature Correlations to Emissions from a Direct-Injection Diesel Engine," Paper 831734, *SAE Transactions*, 92: 4.910–4.921, (1983).

48. Davis, L. B., and Washam, R. M., "Development of a Dry Low NO_x Combustor," ASME 89-GT-255, Gas Turbine and Aeroengine Congress and Exposition, Toronto, ON, 4–8 June 1988.

49. Greeves, G., Khan, I. M., Wang, C. H. T., and Fenne, I., "Origins of Hydrocarbon Emissions from Diesel Engines," SAE Paper 770259, 1977.

50. Levins, P. C., Kendall, D. A., Caragay, A. B., Leonardos, G., and Oberholter, J. E., "Chemical Analysis of Diesel Exhaust Odor Species," SAE Paper 740216, 1974.

51. Lefebvre, A. H., *Gas Turbine Combustion*, Hemisphere, Washington, DC, 1983.

52. Flagan, R. C., and Seinfeld, J. H., *Fundamentals of Air Pollution Engineering*, Prentice Hall, Englewood Cliffs, NJ, 1988.

QUESTIONS AND PROBLEMS

15.1. Make a list of the bold-faced words in Chapter 15 and discuss their meaning and significance.

15.2. Discuss the implications of each of the following to environmental and human health effects: nitric oxide, sulfur trioxide, unburned hydrocarbons, carbon monoxide, and diesel exhaust particulates.

15.3. A natural gas-fired, stationary, gas-turbine engine is used for electrical power generation. The exhaust emission level of nitric oxide is 20 ppm (by volume), measured in the exhaust with an oxygen concentration of 13% (by volume). No aftertreatment (SNCR or SCR) is used.

   A. What is the nitric oxide concentration corrected to 3% oxygen?

   B. Determine the NO_x emission index in grams of NO_x (NO_2 equivalent) per kilogram of fuel burned. Assume that the natural gas is essentially all methane.

   C. Would this engine meet the California South Coast Air Quality Management District—Rule 1134 emission standards?

15.4. A heavy-duty naturally aspirated diesel engine is being evaluated on a dynamometer test stand. Operating at an air–fuel ratio of 21:1 with a fuel flowrate of $4.89 \cdot 10^{-3}$ kg/s, the engine produces 80 kW of brake power. The multi-component fuel has the equivalent formula $C_{12}H_{22}$ The unburned hydrocarbon concentration measured in the exhaust stream is 120 ppm C_1 (wet basis).

   A. Determine the unburned hydrocarbon concentration of a dry basis.

B. Determine the unburned hydrocarbon emission index (g/kg) for the engine. Assume that the hydrogen–carbon ratio of the unburned C_1 equivalent is the same as the original fuel molecule.

C. Find the brake-specific unburned hydrocarbon emission in g/kW-hr for the engine.

15.5. Consider the idealized combustion of a hydrocarbon fuel (CH_4) and air in stoichiometric proportions. Assume no dissociation and constant and equal specific heats for reactants and products of $1200\,J/kg$-K. Assume a fuel heating value of $4 \cdot 10^7$ J/kg.

A. Calculate the adiabatic constant-pressure flame temperatures for zero, 10 and 20% of the undiluted reactants (by mass) exhaust-gas recycle. Assume that both the reactants and recycled gas are initially at 300 K.

B. Repeat the calculations of part a above, but assume the recycled gas is at 1200 K and the air and fuel are at 300 K.

C. Discuss the implications of your calculations above for NO_x production.

15.6. Explain the differences among the nitric oxide formation mechanisms denoted simple thermal (Zeldovich) mechanism, superequilibrium mechanism, and the prompt Fenimore mechanism. Use information from Chapter 5 as necessary.

15.7. Derive an expression for $d[NO]/dt$ for the thermal NO mechanism assuming equilibrium [O] concentrations and steady-state [N]. Neglect reverse reactions. Eliminate $[O]_e$ as a variable, using $[O_2]_e$ instead from the equilibrium $\frac{1}{2}O_2 \leftrightarrow O$. Hint: Your final result should involve only the forward rate constant k_1 for the reaction $O + N_2 \rightarrow NO + N$, the equilibrium constant K_p, $[O_2]_e$, $[N_2]_e$, and the temperature.

15.8. Starting with the result from problem 15.7 above:

A. Convert your expression involving molar concentrations ($kmol/m^3$) to one involving mole fractions.

B. Calculate the initial rate of NO formation (ppm/s) for $k_1 = 7.6 \cdot 10^{10}$ $\exp(-38{,}000/T(K))$ $m^3/kmol$-s and $K_p = 3.6 \cdot 10^3 \exp(-31{,}090/T(K))$ for the following conditions:

   i. $\chi_{O_2,e} = 0.20$, $\chi_{N_2,e} = 0.67$, $T = 2000$, $P = 1$ atm.
   ii. $\chi_{O_2,e} = 0.10$, with other conditions as part i.
   iii. $\chi_{O_2,e} = 0.05$, with other conditions as part i.
   iv. $\chi_{O_2,e} = 0.20$, $\chi_{N_2,e} = 0.67$, $T = 1800$, $P = 1$ atm.
   v. $T = 2200$, with other conditions same as part iv.

C. Plot your results from part B above to show the effects of $\chi_{O_2,e}$ and T. Use separate graphs. Discuss.

15.9. Discuss the fundamental differences between the origins of unburned hydrocarbons in spark-ignition engines and gas-turbine engines. What source of unburned hydrocarbons occurs with diesel engines that is not present in either SI or gas-turbine engines?

15.10. Use an equilibrium code to determine the equilibrium composition of the products of CH_4/air combustion over a range of equivalence ratios from 1.0 to 1.4 for the following two conditions: (1) $T = 2000\,K$ and $P = 10$ atm; (2) $T = 925\,K$ and $P = 1$ atm.

   A. Plot the CO mole fractions versus Φ for both cases on the same graph.

   B. Assuming condition 1 approximates a point early in the SI engine expansion process, and condition 2 approximates conditions in the exhaust pipe, what are the implications of the plot you made in part A above?

15.11. Discuss why the formation of SO_3 in a combustion system is more undesirable than the formation of SO_2.

15.12. An oil-fired industrial boiler uses No. 2 fuel oil. Estimate the likely range of concentrations of SO_2 in the flue gases for an O_2 level of 3%.

APPENDIX

A

SELECTED THERMODYNAMIC PROPERTIES OF GASES COMPRISING C–H–O–N SYSTEM

TABLES A.1–A.12:

Ideal-gas values for standard reference state ($T = 298.15\,\text{K}$, $P = 1$ atm) for:

$$\bar{c}_p(T), \bar{h}^o(T) - \bar{h}^o_{f,\text{ref}}, \bar{h}^o_f(T), \bar{s}^o(T), \bar{g}^o_f(T) \text{ for}$$

$$CO, CO_2, H_2, H, OH, H_2O, N_2, N, NO, NO_2, O_2, O.$$

Enthalpy of formation and Gibbs function of formation for compounds are calculated from the elements as:

$$\bar{h}^o_{f,i}(T) = \bar{h}^o_i(T) - \sum_{j\,\text{elements}} v'_j \bar{h}^o_j(T)$$

$$\bar{g}^o_{f,i}(T) = \bar{g}^o_i(T) - \sum_{j\,\text{elements}} v'_j \bar{g}^o_j(T)$$

$$= \bar{h}^o_{f,i}(T) - T\bar{s}^o_i(T) - \sum_{j\,\text{elements}} v'_j \left[-T\bar{s}^o_j(T) \right].$$

Source: Tables were generated from curvefit coefficients given in Kee, R. J., Rupley, F. M., and Miller, J. A., "The Chemkin Thermodynamic Data Base," Sandia Report, SAND87-8215B, March 1991.

TABLE A.13

Curvefit coefficients for $c_p(T)$ for the same gases as above.
     Source: Ibid.

TABLE A.1
Carbon monoxide (CO), mol. wt. = 28.010, enthalpy of formation @ 298 K
(kJ/kmol) = −110,541

T(K)	$\bar{c}_p$ (kJ/kmol-K)	$(\bar{h}^o(T) - \bar{h}_f^o(298))$ (kJ/kmol)	$\bar{h}_f^o(T)$ (kJ/kmol)	$\bar{s}^o(T)$ (kJ/kmol-K)	$\bar{g}_f^o(T)$ (kJ/kmol)
200	28.687	−2,835	−111,308	186.018	−128,532
298	29.072	0	−110,541	197.548	−137,163
300	29.078	54	−110,530	197.728	−137,328
400	29.433	2,979	−110,121	206.141	−146,332
500	29.857	5,943	−110,017	212.752	−155,403
600	30.407	8,955	−110,156	218.242	−164,470
700	31.089	12,029	−110,477	222.979	−173,499
800	31.860	15,176	−110,924	227.180	−182,473
900	32.629	18,401	−111,450	230.978	−191,386
1000	33.255	21,697	−112,022	234.450	−200,238
1100	33.725	25,046	−112,619	237.642	−209,030
1200	34.148	28,440	−113,240	240.595	−217,768
1300	34.530	31,874	−113,881	243.344	−226,453
1400	34.872	35,345	−114,543	245.915	−235,087
1500	35.178	38,847	−115,225	248.332	−243,674
1600	35.451	42,379	−115,925	250.611	−252,214
1700	35.694	45,937	−116,644	252.768	−260,711
1800	35.910	49,517	−117,380	254.814	−269,164
1900	36.101	53,118	−118,132	256.761	−277,576
2000	36.271	56,737	−118,902	258.617	−285,948
2100	36.421	60,371	−119,687	260.391	−294,281
2200	36.553	64,020	−120,488	262.088	−302,576
2300	36.670	67,682	−121,305	263.715	−310,835
2400	36.774	71,354	−122,137	265.278	−319,057
2500	36.867	75,036	−122,984	266.781	−327,245
2600	36.950	78,727	−123,847	268.229	−335,399
2700	37.025	82,426	−124,724	269.625	−343,519
2800	37.093	86,132	−125,616	270.973	−351,606
2900	37.155	89,844	−126,523	272.275	−359,661
3000	37.213	93,562	−127,446	273.536	−367,684
3100	37.268	97,287	−128,383	274.757	−375,677
3200	37.321	101,016	−129,335	275.941	−383,639
3300	37.372	104,751	−130,303	277.090	−391,571
3400	37.422	108,490	−131,285	278.207	−399,474
3500	37.471	112,235	−132,283	279.292	−407,347
3600	37.521	115,985	−133,295	280.349	−415,192
3700	37.570	119,739	−134,323	281.377	−423,008
3800	37.619	123,499	−135,366	282.380	−430,796
3900	37.667	127,263	−136,424	283.358	−438,557
4000	37.716	131,032	−137,497	284.312	−446,291
4100	37.764	134,806	−138,585	285.244	−453,997
4200	37.810	138,585	−139,687	286.154	−461,677
4300	37.855	142,368	−140,804	287.045	−469,330
4400	37.897	146,156	−141,935	287.915	−476,957
4500	37.936	149,948	−143,079	288.768	−484,558
4600	37.970	153,743	−144,236	289.602	−492,134
4700	37.998	157,541	−145,407	290.419	−499,684

TABLE A.1 (continued)

T(K)	$\bar{c}_p$ (kJ/kmol-K)	$(\bar{h}^o(T) - \bar{h}_f^o(298))$ (kJ/kmol)	$\bar{h}_f^o(T)$ (kJ/kmol)	$\bar{s}^o(T)$ (kJ/kmol-K)	$\bar{g}_f^o(T)$ (kJ/kmol)
4800	38.019	161,342	−146,589	291.219	−507,210
4900	38.031	165,145	−147,783	292.003	−514,710
5000	38.033	168,948	−148,987	292.771	−522,186

TABLE A.2
Carbon dioxide (CO₂), mol. wt. = 44.011, enthalpy of formation @ 298 K (kJ/kmol) = −393, 546

T(K)	$\bar{c}_p$ (kJ/kmol-K)	$\left(\bar{h}^o(T) - \bar{h}^o_f(298)\right)$ (kJ/kmol)	$\bar{h}^o_f(T)$ (kJ/kmol)	$\bar{s}^o(T)$ (kJ/kmol-K)	$\bar{g}^o_f(T)$ (kJ/kmol)
200	32.387	−3,423	−393,483	199.876	−394,126
298	37.198	0	−393,546	213.736	−394,428
300	37.280	69	−393,547	213.966	−394,433
400	41.276	4,003	−393,617	225.257	−394,718
500	44.569	8,301	−393,712	234.833	−394,983
600	47.313	12,899	−393,844	243.209	−395,226
700	49.617	17,749	−394,013	250.680	−395,443
800	51.550	22,810	−394,213	257.436	−395,635
900	53.136	28,047	−394,433	263.603	−395,799
1000	54.360	33,425	−394,659	269.268	−395,939
1100	55.333	38,911	−394,875	274.495	−396,056
1200	56.205	44,488	−395,083	279.348	−396,155
1300	56.984	50,149	−395,287	283.878	−396,236
1400	57.677	55,882	−395,488	288.127	−396,301
1500	58.292	61,681	−395,691	292.128	−396,352
1600	58.836	67,538	−395,897	295.908	−396,389
1700	59.316	73,446	−396,110	299.489	−396,414
1800	59.738	79,399	−396,332	302.892	−396,425
1900	60.108	85,392	−396,564	306.132	−396,424
2000	60.433	91,420	−396,808	309.223	−396,410
2100	60.717	97,477	−397,065	312.179	−396,384
2200	60.966	103,562	−397,338	315.009	−396,346
2300	61.185	109,670	−397,626	317.724	−396,294
2400	61.378	115,798	−397,931	320.333	−396,230
2500	61.548	121,944	−398,253	322.842	−396,152
2600	61.701	128,107	−398,594	325.259	−396,061
2700	61.839	134,284	−398,952	327.590	−395,957
2800	61.965	140,474	−399,329	329.841	−395,840
2900	62.083	146,677	−399,725	332.018	−395,708
3000	62.194	152,891	−400,140	334.124	−395,562
3100	62.301	159,116	−400,573	336.165	−395,403
3200	62.406	165,351	−401,025	338.145	−395,229
3300	62.510	171,597	−401,495	340.067	−395,041
3400	62.614	177,853	−401,983	341.935	−394,838
3500	62.718	184,120	−402,489	343.751	−394,620
3600	62.825	190,397	−403,013	345.519	−394,388
3700	62.932	196,685	−403,553	347.242	−394,141
3800	63.041	202,983	−404,110	348.922	−393,879
3900	63.151	209,293	−404,684	350.561	−393,602
4000	63.261	215,613	−405,273	352.161	−393,311
4100	63.369	221,945	−405,878	353.725	−393,004
4200	63.474	228,287	−406,499	355.253	−392,683
4300	63.575	234,640	−407,135	356.748	−392,346
4400	63.669	241,002	−407,785	358.210	−391,995
4500	63.753	247,373	−408,451	359.642	−391,629
4600	63.825	253,752	−409,132	361.044	−391,247
4700	63.881	260,138	−409,828	362.417	−390,851

TABLE A.2 (continued)

$T(K)$	$\bar{c}_p$ (kJ/kmol-K)	$(\bar{h}^o(T) - \bar{h}_f^o(298))$ (kJ/kmol)	$\bar{h}_f^o(T)$ (kJ/kmol)	$\bar{s}^o(T)$ (kJ/kmol-K)	$\bar{g}_f^o(T)$ (kJ/kmol)
4800	63.918	266,528	−410,539	363.763	−390,440
4900	63.932	272,920	−411,267	365.081	−390,014
5000	63.919	279,313	−412,010	366.372	−389,572

TABLE A.3
Hydrogen (H_2), mol. wt. = 2.016, enthalpy of formation @ 298 K (kJ/kmol) = 0

T(K)	$\bar{c}_p$ (kJ/kmol-K)	$(\bar{h}^o(T) - \bar{h}_f^o(298))$ (kJ/kmol)	$\bar{h}_f^o(T)$ (kJ/kmol)	$\bar{s}^o(T)$ (kJ/kmol-K)	$\bar{g}_f^o(T)$ (kJ/kmol)
200	28.522	−2,818	0	119.137	0
298	28.871	0	0	130.595	0
300	28.877	53	0	130.773	0
400	29.120	2,954	0	139.116	0
500	29.275	5,874	0	145.632	0
600	29.375	8,807	0	150.979	0
700	29.461	11,749	0	155.514	0
800	29.581	14,701	0	159.455	0
900	29.792	17,668	0	162.950	0
1000	30.160	20,664	0	166.106	0
1100	30.625	23,704	0	169.003	0
1200	31.077	26,789	0	171.687	0
1300	31.516	29,919	0	174.192	0
1400	31.943	33,092	0	176.543	0
1500	32.356	36,307	0	178.761	0
1600	32.758	39,562	0	180.862	0
1700	33.146	42,858	0	182.860	0
1800	33.522	46,191	0	184.765	0
1900	33.885	49,562	0	186.587	0
2000	34.236	52,968	0	188.334	0
2100	34.575	56,408	0	190.013	0
2200	34.901	59,882	0	191.629	0
2300	35.216	63,388	0	193.187	0
2400	35.519	66,925	0	194.692	0
2500	35.811	70,492	0	196.148	0
2600	36.091	74,087	0	197.558	0
2700	36.361	77,710	0	198.926	0
2800	36.621	81,359	0	200.253	0
2900	36.871	85,033	0	201.542	0
3000	37.112	88,733	0	202.796	0
3100	37.343	92,455	0	204.017	0
3200	37.566	96,201	0	205.206	0
3300	37.781	99,968	0	206.365	0
3400	37.989	103,757	0	207.496	0
3500	38.190	107,566	0	208.600	0
3600	38.385	111,395	0	209.679	0
3700	38.574	115,243	0	210.733	0
3800	38.759	119,109	0	211.764	0
3900	38.939	122,994	0	212.774	0
4000	39.116	126,897	0	213.762	0
4100	39.291	130,817	0	214.730	0
4200	39.464	134,755	0	215.679	0
4300	39.636	138,710	0	216.609	0
4400	39.808	142,682	0	217.522	0
4500	39.981	146,672	0	218.419	0
4600	40.156	150,679	0	219.300	0
4700	40.334	154,703	0	220.165	0

TABLE A.3 (continued)

T(K)	$\bar{c}_p$ (kJ/kmol-K)	$(\bar{h}^o(T) - \bar{h}_f^o(298))$ (kJ/kmol)	$\bar{h}o_f(T)$ (kJ/kmol)	$\bar{s}^o(T)$ (kJ/kmol-K)	$\bar{g}_f^o(T)$ (kJ/kmol)
4800	40.516	158,746	0	221.016	0
4900	40.702	162,806	0	221.853	0
5000	40.895	166,886	0	222.678	0

TABLE A.4

H atom (H), mol. wt. = 1.008, enthalpy of formation @ 298 K (kJ/kmol) = 217,977

T(K)	$\bar{c}_p$ (kJ/kmol-K)	$(\bar{h}^o(T) - \bar{h}_f^o(298))$ (kJ/kmol)	$\bar{h}_f^o(T)$ (kJ/kmol)	$\bar{s}^o(T)$ (kJ/kmol-K)	$\bar{g}_f^o(T)$ (kJ/kmol)
200	20.786	−2,040	217,346	106.305	207,999
298	20.786	0	217,977	114.605	203,276
300	20.786	38	217,989	114.733	203,185
400	20.786	2,117	218,617	120.713	198,155
500	20.786	4,196	219,236	125.351	192,968
600	20.786	6,274	219,848	129.141	187,657
700	20.786	8,353	220,456	132.345	182,244
800	20.786	10,431	221,059	135.121	176,744
900	20.786	12,510	221,653	137.569	171,169
1000	20.786	14,589	222,234	139.759	165,528
1100	20.786	16,667	222,793	141.740	159,830
1200	20.786	18,746	223,329	143.549	154,082
1300	20.786	20,824	223,843	145.213	148,291
1400	20.786	22,903	224,335	146.753	142,461
1500	20.786	24,982	224,806	148.187	136,596
1600	20.786	27,060	225,256	149.528	130,700
1700	20.786	29,139	225,687	150.789	124,777
1800	20.786	31,217	226,099	151.977	118,830
1900	20.786	33,296	226,493	153.101	112,859
2000	20.786	35,375	226,868	154.167	106,869
2100	20.786	37,453	227,226	155.181	100,860
2200	20.786	39,532	227,568	156.148	94,834
2300	20.786	41,610	227,894	157.072	88,794
2400	20.786	43,689	228,204	157.956	82,739
2500	20.786	45,768	228,499	158.805	76,672
2600	20.786	47,846	228,780	159.620	70,593
2700	20.786	49,925	229,047	160.405	64,504
2800	20.786	52,003	229,301	161.161	58,405
2900	20.786	54,082	229,543	161.890	52,298
3000	20.786	56,161	229,772	162.595	46,182
3100	20.786	58,239	229,989	163.276	40,058
3200	20.786	60,318	230,195	163.936	33,928
3300	20.786	62,396	230,390	164.576	27,792
3400	20.786	64,475	230,574	165.196	21,650
3500	20.786	66,554	230,748	165.799	15,502
3600	20.786	68,632	230,912	166.384	9,350
3700	20.786	70,711	231,067	166.954	3,194
3800	20.786	72,789	231,212	167.508	−2,967
3900	20.786	74,868	231,348	168.048	−9,132
4000	20.786	76,947	231,475	168.575	−15,299
4100	20.786	79,025	231,594	169.088	−21,470
4200	20.786	81,104	231,704	169.589	−27,644
4300	20.786	83,182	231,805	170.078	−33,820
4400	20.786	85,261	231,897	170.556	−39,998
4500	20.786	87,340	231,981	171.023	−46,179
4600	20.786	89,418	232,056	171.480	−52,361
4700	20.786	91,497	232,123	171.927	−58,545

TABLE A.4 (continued)

T(K)	$\bar{c}_p$ (kJ/kmol-K)	$(\bar{h}^o(T) - \bar{h}_f^o(298))$ (kJ/kmol)	$\bar{h}_f^o(T)$ (kJ/kmol)	$\bar{s}^o(T)$ (kJ/kmol-K)	$\bar{g}_f^o(T)$ (kJ/kmol)
4800	20.786	93,575	232,180	172.364	−64,730
4900	20.786	95,654	232,228	172.793	−70,916
5000	20.786	97,733	232,267	173.213	−77,103

TABLE A.5
Hydroxyl (OH), mol. wt. = 17.007, enthalpy of formation @ 298 K (kJ/kmol)
= 38,985

T(K)	$\bar{c}_p$ (kJ/kmol-K)	$\left(\bar{h}^o(T) - \bar{h}_f^o(298)\right)$ (kJ/kmol)	$\bar{h}_f^o(T)$ (kJ/kmol)	$\bar{s}^o(T)$ (kJ/kmol-K)	$\bar{g}_f^o(T)$ (kJ/kmol)
200	30.140	−2,948	38,864	171.607	35,808
298	29.932	0	38,985	183.604	34,279
300	29.928	55	38,987	183.789	34,250
400	29.718	3,037	39,030	192.369	32,662
500	29.570	6,001	39,000	198.983	31,072
600	29.527	8,955	38,909	204.369	29,494
700	29.615	11,911	38,770	208.925	27,935
800	29.844	14,883	38,599	212.893	26,399
900	30.208	17,884	38,410	216.428	24,885
1000	30.682	20,928	38,220	219.635	23,392
1100	31.186	24,022	38,039	222.583	21,918
1200	31.662	27,164	37,867	225.317	20,460
1300	32.114	30,353	37,704	227.869	19,017
1400	32.540	33,586	37,548	230.265	17,585
1500	32.943	36,860	37,397	232.524	16,164
1600	33.323	40,174	37,252	234.662	14,753
1700	33.682	43,524	37,109	236.693	13,352
1800	34.019	46,910	36,969	238.628	11,958
1900	34.337	50,328	36,831	240.476	10,573
2000	34.635	53,776	36,693	242.245	9,194
2100	34.915	57,254	36,555	243.942	7,823
2200	35.178	60,759	36,416	245.572	6,458
2300	35.425	64,289	36,276	247.141	5,099
2400	35.656	67,843	36,133	248.654	3,746
2500	35.872	71,420	35,986	250.114	2,400
2600	36.074	75,017	35,836	251.525	1,060
2700	36.263	78,634	35,682	252.890	−275
2800	36.439	82,269	35,524	254.212	−1,604
2900	36.604	85,922	35,360	255.493	−2,927
3000	36.759	89,590	35,191	256.737	−4,245
3100	36.903	93,273	35,016	257.945	−5,556
3200	37.039	96,970	34,835	259.118	−6,862
3300	37.166	100,681	34,648	260.260	−8,162
3400	37.285	104,403	34,454	261.371	−9,457
3500	37.398	108,137	34,253	262.454	−10,745
3600	37.504	111,882	34,046	263.509	−12,028
3700	37.605	115,638	33,831	264.538	−13,305
3800	37.701	119,403	33,610	265.542	−14,576
3900	37.793	123,178	33,381	266.522	−15,841
4000	37.882	126,962	33,146	267.480	−17,100
4100	37.968	130,754	32,903	268.417	−18,353
4200	38.052	134,555	32,654	269.333	−19,600
4300	38.135	138,365	32,397	270.229	−20,841
4400	38.217	142,182	32,134	271.107	−22,076
4500	38.300	146,008	31,864	271.967	−23,306
4600	38.382	149,842	31,588	272.809	−24,528
4700	38.466	153,685	31,305	273.636	−25,745

TABLE A.5 (continued)

T(K)	$\bar{c}_p$ (kJ/kmol-K)	$(\bar{h}^o(T) - \bar{h}_f^o(298))$ (kJ/kmol)	$\bar{h}_f^o(T)$ (kJ/kmol)	$\bar{s}^o(T)$ (kJ/kmol-K)	$\bar{g}_f^o(T)$ (kJ/kmol)
4800	38.552	157,536	31,017	274.446	−26,956
4900	38.640	161,395	30,722	275.242	−28,161
5000	38.732	165,264	30,422	276.024	−29,360

TABLE A.6
Water (H$_2$O), mol. wt. = 18.016, enthalpy of formation @ 298 K (kJ/kmol) = 241,845, enthalpy of vaporization (kJ/kmol) = 44,010

T(K)	$\bar{c}_p$ (kJ/kmol-K)	$(\bar{h}^o(T) - \bar{h}_f^o(298))$ (kJ/kmol)	$\bar{h}_f^o(T)$ (kJ/kmol)	$\bar{s}^o(T)$ (kJ/kmol-K)	$\bar{g}_f^o(T)$ (kJ/kmol)
200	32.255	−3,227	−240,838	175.602	−232,779
298	33.448	0	−241,845	188.715	−228,608
300	33.468	62	−241,865	188.922	−228,526
400	34.437	3,458	−242,858	198.686	−223,929
500	35.337	6,947	−243,822	206.467	−219,085
600	36.288	10,528	−244,753	212.992	−214,049
700	37.364	14,209	−245,638	218.665	−208,861
800	38.587	18,005	−246,461	223.733	−203,550
900	39.930	21,930	−247,209	228.354	−198,141
1000	41.315	25,993	−247,879	232.633	−192,652
1100	42.638	30,191	−248,475	236.634	−187,100
1200	43.874	34,518	−249,005	240.397	−181,497
1300	45.027	38,963	−249,477	243.955	−175,852
1400	46.102	43,520	−249,895	247.332	−170,172
1500	47.103	48,181	−250,267	250.547	−164,464
1600	48.035	52,939	−250,597	253.617	−158,733
1700	48.901	57,786	−250,890	256.556	−152,983
1800	49.705	62,717	−251,151	259.374	−147,216
1900	50.451	67,725	−251,384	262.081	−141,435
2000	51.143	72,805	−251,594	264.687	−135,643
2100	51.784	77,952	−251,783	267.198	−129,841
2200	52.378	83,160	−251,955	269.621	−124,030
2300	52.927	88,426	−252,113	271.961	−118,211
2400	53.435	93,744	−252,261	274.225	−112,386
2500	53.905	99,112	−252,399	276.416	−106,555
2600	54.340	104,524	−252,532	278.539	−100,719
2700	54.742	109,979	−252,659	280.597	−94,878
2800	55.115	115,472	−252,785	282.595	−89,031
2900	55.459	121,001	−252,909	284.535	−83,181
3000	55.779	126,563	−253,034	286.420	−77,326
3100	56.076	132,156	−253,161	288.254	−71,467
3200	56.353	137,777	−253,290	290.039	−65,604
3300	56.610	143,426	−253,423	291.777	−59,737
3400	56.851	149,099	−253,561	293.471	−53,865
3500	57.076	154,795	−253,704	295.122	−47,990
3600	57.288	160,514	−253,852	296.733	−42,110
3700	57.488	166,252	−254,007	298.305	−36,226
3800	57.676	172,011	−254,169	299.841	−30,338
3900	57.856	177,787	−254,338	301.341	−24,446
4000	58.026	183,582	−254,515	302.808	−18,549
4100	58.190	189,392	−254,699	304.243	−12,648
4200	58.346	195,219	−254,892	305.647	−6,742
4300	58.496	201,061	−255,093	307.022	−831
4400	58.641	206,918	−255,303	308.368	5,085
4500	58.781	212,790	−255,522	309.688	11,005
4600	58.916	218,674	−255,751	310.981	16,930
4700	59.047	224,573	−255,990	312.250	22,861

TABLE A.6 (continued)

T(K)	$\bar{c}_p$ (kJ/kmol-K)	$(\bar{h}^o(T) - \bar{h}_f^o(298))$ (kJ/kmol)	$\bar{h}_f^o(T)$ (kJ/kmol)	$\bar{s}^o(T)$ (kJ/kmol-K)	$\bar{g}_f^o(T)$ (kJ/kmol)
4800	59.173	230,484	−256,239	313.494	28,796
4900	59.295	236,407	−256,501	314.716	34,737
5000	59.412	242,343	−256,774	315.915	40,684

TABLE A.7
Nitrogen (N$_2$), mol. wt. = 28.013, enthalpy of formation @ 298 K (kJ/kmol) = 0

T(K)	$\bar{c}_p$ (kJ/kmol-K)	$(\bar{h}^o(T) - \bar{h}_f^o(298))$ (kJ/kmol)	$\bar{h}_f^o(T)$ (kJ/kmol)	$\bar{s}^o(T)$ (kJ/kmol-K)	$\bar{g}_f^o(T)$ (kJ/kmol)
200	28.793	−2,841	0	179.959	0
298	29.071	0	0	191.511	0
300	29.075	54	0	191.691	0
400	29.319	2,973	0	200.088	0
500	29.636	5,920	0	206.662	0
600	30.086	8,905	0	212.103	0
700	30.684	11,942	0	216.784	0
800	31.394	15,046	0	220.927	0
900	32.131	18,222	0	224.667	0
1000	32.762	21,468	0	228.087	0
1100	33.258	24,770	0	231.233	0
1200	33.707	28,118	0	234.146	0
1300	34.113	31,510	0	236.861	0
1400	34.477	34,939	0	239.402	0
1500	34.805	38,404	0	241.792	0
1600	35.099	41,899	0	244.048	0
1700	35.361	45,423	0	246.184	0
1800	35.595	48,971	0	248.212	0
1900	35.803	52,541	0	250.142	0
2000	35.988	56,130	0	251.983	0
2100	36.152	59,738	0	253.743	0
2200	36.298	63,360	0	255.429	0
2300	36.428	66,997	0	257.045	0
2400	36.543	70,645	0	258.598	0
2500	36.645	74,305	0	260.092	0
2600	36.737	77,974	0	261.531	0
2700	36.820	81,652	0	262.919	0
2800	36.895	85,338	0	264.259	0
2900	36.964	89,031	0	265.555	0
3000	37.028	92,730	0	266.810	0
3100	37.088	96,436	0	268.025	0
3200	37.144	100,148	0	269.203	0
3300	37.198	103,865	0	270.347	0
3400	37.251	107,587	0	271.458	0
3500	37.302	111,315	0	272.539	0
3600	37.352	115,048	0	273.590	0
3700	37.402	118,786	0	274.614	0
3800	37.452	122,528	0	275.612	0
3900	37.501	126,276	0	276.586	0
4000	37.549	130,028	0	277.536	0
4100	37.597	133,786	0	278.464	0
4200	37.643	137,548	0	279.370	0
4300	37.688	141,314	0	280.257	0
4400	37.730	145,085	0	281.123	0
4500	37.768	148,860	0	281.972	0
4600	37.803	152,639	0	282.802	0
4700	37.832	156,420	0	283.616	0

TABLE A.7 (continued)

T(K)	$\bar{c}_p$ (kJ/kmol-K)	$\left(\bar{h}^o(T) - \bar{h}_f^o(298)\right)$ (kJ/kmol)	$\bar{h}_f^o(T)$ (kJ/kmol)	$\bar{s}^o(T)$ (kJ/kmol-K)	$\bar{g}_f^o(T)$ (kJ/kmol)
4800	37.854	160,205	0	284.412	0
4900	37.868	163,991	0	285.193	0
5000	37.873	167,778	0	285.958	0

TABLE A.8
N atom (N), mol. wt. = 14.007, enthalpy of formation @ 298 K (kJ/kmol)
= 472,629

T(K)	$\bar{c}_p$ (kJ/kmol-K)	$(\bar{h}^o(T) - \bar{h}_f^o(298))$ (kJ/kmol)	$\bar{h}_f^o(T)$ (kJ/kmol)	$\bar{s}^o(T)$ (kJ/kmol-K)	$\bar{g}_f^o(T)$ (kJ/kmol)
200	20.790	−2,040	472,008	144.889	461,026
298	20.786	0	472,629	153.189	455,504
300	20.786	38	472,640	153.317	455,398
400	20.786	2,117	473,258	159.297	449,557
500	20.786	4,196	473,864	163.935	443,562
600	20.786	6,274	474,450	167.725	437,446
700	20.786	8,353	475,010	170.929	431,234
800	20.786	10,431	475,537	173.705	424,944
900	20.786	12,510	476,027	176.153	418,590
1000	20.786	14,589	476,483	178.343	412,183
1100	20.792	16,668	476,911	180.325	405,732
1200	20.795	18,747	477,316	182.134	399,243
1300	20.795	20,826	477,700	183.798	392,721
1400	20.793	22,906	478,064	185.339	386,171
1500	20.790	24,985	478,411	186.774	379,595
1600	20.786	27,064	478,742	188.115	372,996
1700	20.782	29,142	479,059	189.375	366,377
1800	20.779	31,220	479,363	190.563	359,740
1900	20.777	33,298	479,656	191.687	353,086
2000	20.776	35,376	479,939	192.752	346,417
2100	20.778	37,453	480,213	193.766	339,735
2200	20.783	39,531	480,479	194.733	333,039
2300	20.791	41,610	480,740	195.657	326,331
2400	20.802	43,690	480,995	196.542	319,612
2500	20.818	45,771	481,246	197.391	312,883
2600	20.838	47,853	481,494	198.208	306,143
2700	20.864	49,938	481,740	198.995	299,394
2800	20.895	52,026	481,985	199.754	292,636
2900	20.931	54,118	482,230	200.488	285,870
3000	20.974	56,213	482,476	201.199	279,094
3100	21.024	58,313	482,723	201.887	272,311
3200	21.080	60,418	482,972	202.555	265,519
3300	21.143	62,529	483,224	203.205	258,720
3400	21.214	64,647	483,481	203.837	251,913
3500	21.292	66,772	483,742	204.453	245,099
3600	21.378	68,905	484,009	205.054	238,276
3700	21.472	71,048	484,283	205.641	231,447
3800	21.575	73,200	484,564	206.215	224,610
3900	21.686	75,363	484,853	206.777	217,765
4000	21.805	77,537	485,151	207.328	210,913
4100	21.934	79,724	485,459	207.868	204,053
4200	22.071	81,924	485,779	208.398	197,186
4300	22.217	84,139	486,110	208.919	190,310
4400	22.372	86,368	486,453	209.431	183,427
4500	22.536	88,613	486,811	209.936	176,536
4600	22.709	90,875	487,184	210.433	169,637
4700	22.891	93,155	487,573	210.923	162,730

TABLE A.8 (continued)

$T(K)$	$\bar{c}_p$ (kJ/kmol-K)	$(\bar{h}^o(T) - \bar{h}_f^o(298))$ (kJ/kmol)	$\bar{h}_f^o(T)$ (kJ/kmol)	$\bar{s}^o(T)$ (kJ/kmol-K)	$\bar{g}_f^o(T)$ (kJ/kmol)
4800	23.082	95,454	487,979	211.407	155,814
4900	23.282	97,772	488,405	211.885	148,890
5000	23,491	100,111	488,850	212.358	141,956

TABLE A.9
Nitric oxide (NO), mol. wt. = 30.006, enthalpy of formation @ 298 K (kJ/kmol)
= 90,297

T(K)	$\bar{c}_p$ (kJ/kmol-K)	$(\bar{h}^o(T) - \bar{h}_f^o(298))$ (kJ/kmol)	$\bar{h}_f^o(T)$ (kJ/kmol)	$\bar{s}^o(T)$ (kJ/kmol-K)	$\bar{g}_f^o(T)$ (kJ/kmol)
200	29.374	−2,901	90,234	198.856	87,811
298	29.728	0	90,297	210.652	86,607
300	29.735	55	90,298	210.836	86,584
400	30.103	3,046	90,341	219.439	85,340
500	30.570	6,079	90,367	226.204	84,086
600	31.174	9,165	90,382	231.829	82,828
700	31.908	12,318	90,393	236.688	81,568
800	32.715	15,549	90,405	241.001	80,307
900	33.489	18,860	90,421	244.900	79,043
1000	34.076	22,241	90,443	248.462	77,778
1100	34.483	25,669	90,465	251.729	76,510
1200	34.850	29,136	90,486	254.745	75,241
1300	35.180	32,638	90,505	257.548	73,970
1400	35.474	36,171	90,520	260.166	72,697
1500	35.737	39,732	90,532	262.623	71,423
1600	35.972	43,317	90,538	264.937	70,149
1700	36.180	46,925	90,539	267.124	68,875
1800	36.364	50,552	90,534	269.197	67,601
1900	36.527	54,197	90,523	271.168	66,327
2000	36.671	57,857	90,505	273.045	65,054
2100	36.797	61,531	90,479	274.838	63,782
2200	36.909	65,216	90,447	276.552	62,511
2300	37.008	68,912	90,406	278.195	61,243
2400	37.095	72,617	90,358	279.772	59,976
2500	37.173	76,331	90,303	281.288	58,711
2600	37.242	80,052	90,239	282.747	57,448
2700	37.305	83,779	90,168	284.154	56,188
2800	37.362	87,513	90,089	285.512	54,931
2900	37.415	91,251	90,003	286.824	53,677
3000	37.464	94,995	89,909	288.093	52,426
3100	37.511	98,744	89,809	289.322	51,178
3200	37.556	102,498	89,701	290.514	49,934
3300	37.600	106,255	89,586	291.670	48,693
3400	37.643	110,018	89,465	292.793	47,456
3500	37.686	113,784	89,337	293.885	46,222
3600	37.729	117,555	89,203	294.947	44,992
3700	37.771	121,330	89,063	295.981	43,766
3800	37.815	125,109	88,918	296.989	42,543
3900	37.858	128,893	88,767	297.972	41,325
4000	37.900	132,680	88,611	298.931	40,110
4100	37.943	136,473	88,449	299.867	38,900
4200	37.984	140,269	88,283	300.782	37,693
4300	38.023	144,069	88,112	301.677	36,491
4400	38.060	147,873	87,936	302.551	35,292
4500	38.093	151,681	87,755	303.407	34,098
4600	38.122	155,492	87,569	304.244	32,908
4700	38.146	159,305	87,379	305.064	31,721

TABLE A.9 (continued)

T(K)	$\bar{c}_p$ (kJ/kmol-K)	$(\bar{h}^o(T) - \bar{h}^o_f(298))$ (kJ/kmol)	$\bar{h}^o_f(T)$ (kJ/kmol)	$\bar{s}^o(T)$ (kJ/kmol-K)	$\bar{g}^o_f(T)$ (kJ/kmol)
4800	38.162	163,121	87,184	305.868	30,539
4900	38.171	166,938	86,984	306.655	29,361
5000	38.170	170,755	86,779	307.426	28,187

TABLE A.10
Nitrogen dioxide (NO₂), mol. wt. = 46.006, enthalpy of formation @ 298 K
(kJ/kmol) = 33,098

$T(K)$	$\bar{c}_p$ (kJ/kmol-K)	$(\bar{h}^o(T) - \bar{h}^o_f(298))$ (kJ/kmol)	$\bar{h}^o_f(T)$ (kJ/kmol)	$\bar{s}^o(T)$ (kJ/kmol-K)	$\bar{g}^o_f(T)$ (kJ/kmol)
200	32.936	−3,432	33,961	226.016	45,453
298	36.881	0	33,098	239.925	51,291
300	36.949	68	33,085	240.153	51,403
400	40.331	3,937	32,521	251.259	57,602
500	43.227	8,118	32,173	260.578	63,916
600	45.737	12,569	31,974	268.686	70,285
700	47.913	17,255	31,885	275.904	76,679
800	49.762	22,141	31,880	282.427	83,079
900	51.243	27,195	31,938	288.377	89,476
1000	52.271	32,375	32,035	293.834	95,864
1100	52.989	37,638	32,146	298.850	102,242
1200	53.625	42,970	32,267	303.489	108,609
1300	54.186	48,361	32,392	307.804	114,966
1400	54.679	53,805	32,519	311.838	121,313
1500	55.109	59,295	32,643	315.625	127,651
1600	55.483	64,825	32,762	319.194	133,981
1700	55.805	70,390	32,873	322.568	140,303
1800	56.082	75,984	32,973	325.765	146,620
1900	56.318	81,605	33,061	328.804	152,931
2000	56.517	87,247	33,134	331.698	159,238
2100	56.685	92,907	33,192	334.460	165,542
2200	56.826	98,583	32,233	337.100	171,843
2300	56.943	104,271	33,256	339.629	178,143
2400	57.040	109,971	33,262	342.054	184,442
2500	57.121	115,679	33,248	344.384	190,742
2600	57.188	121,394	33,216	346.626	197,042
2700	57.244	127,116	33,165	348.785	203,344
2800	57.291	132,843	33,095	350.868	209,648
2900	57.333	138,574	33,007	352.879	215,955
3000	57.371	144,309	32,900	354.824	222,265
3100	57.406	150,048	32,776	356.705	228,579
3200	57.440	155,791	32,634	358.529	234,898
3300	57.474	161,536	32,476	360.297	241,221
3400	57.509	167,285	32,302	362.013	247,549
3500	57.546	173,038	32,113	363.680	253,883
3600	57.584	178,795	31,908	365.302	260,222
3700	57.624	184,555	31,689	366.880	266,567
3800	57.665	190,319	31,456	368.418	272,918
3900	57.708	196,088	31,210	369.916	279,276
4000	57.750	201,861	30,951	371.378	285,639
4100	57.792	207,638	30,678	372.804	292,010
4200	57.831	213,419	30,393	374.197	298,387
4300	57.866	219,204	30,095	375.559	304,772
4400	57.895	224,992	29,783	376.889	311,163
4500	57.915	230,783	29,457	378.190	317,562
4600	57.925	236,575	29,117	379.464	323,968
4700	57.922	242,367	28,761	380.709	330,381

TABLE A.10 (continued)

T(K)	$\bar{c}_p$ (kJ/kmol-K)	$(\bar{h}^o(T) - \bar{h}^o_f(298))$ (kJ/kmol)	$\bar{h}^o_f(T)$ (kJ/kmol)	$\bar{s}^o(T)$ (kJ/kmol-K)	$\bar{g}^o_f(T)$ (kJ/kmol)
4800	57.902	248,159	28,389	381.929	336,803
4900	57.862	253,947	27,998	383.122	343,232
5000	57.798	259,730	27,586	384.290	349,670

TABLE A.11
Oxygen (O_2), mol. wt. = 31.999, enthalpy of formation @ 298 K (kJ/kmol) = 0

T(K)	$\bar{c}_p$ (kJ/kmol-K)	$(\bar{h}^o(T) - \bar{h}_f^o(298))$ (kJ/kmol)	$\bar{h}_f^o(T)$ (kJ/kmol)	$\bar{s}^o(T)$ (kJ/kmol-K)	$\bar{g}_f^o(T)$ (kJ/kmol)
200	28.473	−2,836	0	193.518	0
298	29.315	0	0	205.043	0
300	29.331	54	0	205.224	0
400	30.210	3,031	0	213.782	0
500	31.114	6,097	0	220.620	0
600	32.030	9,254	0	226.374	0
700	32.927	12,503	0	231.379	0
800	33.757	15,838	0	235.831	0
900	34.454	19,250	0	239.849	0
1000	34.936	22,721	0	243.507	0
1100	35.270	26,232	0	246.852	0
1200	35.593	29,775	0	249.935	0
1300	35.903	33,350	0	252.796	0
1400	36.202	36,955	0	255.468	0
1500	36.490	40,590	0	257.976	0
1600	36.768	44,253	0	260.339	0
1700	37.036	47,943	0	262.577	0
1800	37.296	51,660	0	264.701	0
1900	37.546	55,402	0	266.724	0
2000	37.788	59,169	0	268.656	0
2100	38.023	62,959	0	270.506	0
2200	38.250	66,773	0	272.280	0
2300	38.470	70,609	0	273.985	0
2400	38.684	74,467	0	275.627	0
2500	38.891	78,346	0	277.210	0
2600	39.093	82,245	0	278.739	0
2700	39.289	86,164	0	280.218	0
2800	39.480	90,103	0	281.651	0
2900	39.665	94,060	0	283.039	0
3000	39.846	98,036	0	284.387	0
3100	40.023	102,029	0	285.697	0
3200	40.195	106,040	0	286.970	0
3300	40.362	110,068	0	288.209	0
3400	40.526	114,112	0	289.417	0
3500	40.686	118,173	0	290.594	0
3600	40.842	122,249	0	291.742	0
3700	40.994	126,341	0	292.863	0
3800	41.143	130,448	0	293.959	0
3900	41.287	134,570	0	295.029	0
4000	41.429	138,705	0	296.076	0
4100	41.566	142,855	0	297.101	0
4200	41.700	147,019	0	298.104	0
4300	41.830	151,195	0	299.087	0
4400	41.957	155,384	0	300.050	0
4500	42.079	159,586	0	300.994	0
4600	42.197	163,800	0	301.921	0
4700	42.312	168,026	0	302.829	0

TABLE A.11 (continued)

T(K)	$\bar{c}_p$ (kJ/kmol-K)	$(\bar{h}^o(T) - \bar{h}_f^o(298))$ (kJ/kmol)	$\bar{h}_f^o(T)$ (kJ/kmol)	$\bar{s}^o(T)$ (kJ/kmol-K)	$\bar{g}_f^o(T)$ (kJ/kmol)
4800	42.421	172,262	0	303.721	0
4900	42.527	176,510	0	304.597	0
5000	42.627	180,767	0	305.457	0

TABLE A.12
Oxygen atom (O), mol. wt. = 16.000, enthalpy of formation @ 298 K (kJ/kmol) = 249,197

T(K)	$\bar{c}_p$ (kJ/kmol-K)	$(\bar{h}^o(T) - \bar{h}_f^o(298))$ (kJ/kmol)	$\bar{h}_f^o(T)$ (kJ/kmol)	$\bar{s}^o(T)$ (kJ/kmol-K)	$\bar{g}_f^o(T)$ (kJ/kmol)
200	22.477	−2,176	248,439	152.085	237,374
298	21.899	0	249,197	160.945	231,778
300	21.890	41	249,211	161.080	231,670
400	21.500	2,209	249,890	167.320	225,719
500	21.256	4,345	250,494	172.089	219,605
600	21.113	6,463	251,033	175.951	213,375
700	21.033	8,570	251,516	179.199	207,060
800	20.986	10,671	251,949	182.004	200,679
900	20.952	12,768	252,340	184.474	194,246
1000	20.915	14,861	252,698	186.679	187,772
1100	20.898	16,952	253,033	188.672	181,263
1200	20.882	19,041	253,350	190.490	174,724
1300	20.867	21,128	253,650	192.160	168,159
1400	20.854	23,214	253,934	193.706	161,572
1500	20.843	25,299	254,201	195.145	154,966
1600	20.834	27,383	254,454	196.490	148,342
1700	20.827	29,466	254,692	197.753	141,702
1800	20.822	31,548	254,916	198.943	135,049
1900	20.820	33,630	255,127	200.069	128,384
2000	20.819	35,712	255,325	201.136	121,709
2100	20.821	37,794	255,512	202.152	115,023
2200	20.825	39,877	255,687	203.121	108,329
2300	20.831	41,959	255,852	204.047	101,627
2400	20.840	44,043	256,007	204.933	94,918
2500	20.851	46,127	256,152	205.784	88,203
2600	20.865	48,213	256,288	206.602	81,483
2700	20.881	50,300	256,416	207.390	74,757
2800	20.899	52,389	256,535	208.150	68,027
2900	20.920	54,480	256,648	208.884	61,292
3000	20.944	56,574	256,753	209.593	54,554
3100	20.970	58,669	256,852	210.280	47,812
3200	20.998	60,768	256,945	210.947	41,068
3300	21.028	62,869	257,032	211.593	34,320
3400	21.061	64,973	257,114	212.221	27,570
3500	21.095	67,081	257,192	212.832	20,818
3600	21.132	69,192	257,265	213.427	14,063
3700	21.171	71,308	257,334	214.007	7,307
3800	21.212	73,427	257,400	214.572	548
3900	21.254	75,550	257,462	215.123	−6,212
4000	21.299	77,678	257,522	215.662	−12,974
4100	21.345	79,810	257,579	216.189	−19,737
4200	21.392	81,947	257,635	216.703	−26,501
4300	21.441	84,088	257,688	217.207	−33,267
4400	21.490	86,235	257,740	217.701	−40,034
4500	21.541	88,386	257,790	218.184	−46,802
4600	21.593	90,543	257,840	218.658	−53,571
4700	21.646	92,705	257,889	219.123	−60,342

TABLE A.12 (continued)

$T(K)$	$\bar{c}_p$ (kJ/kmol-K)	$(\bar{h}^o(T) - \bar{h}_f^o(298))$ (kJ/kmol)	$\bar{h}_f^o(T)$ (kJ/kmol)	$\bar{s}^o(T)$ (kJ/kmol-K)	$\bar{g}_f^o(T)$ (kJ/kmol)
4800	21.699	94,872	257,938	219.580	−67,113
4900	21.752	97,045	257,987	220.028	−73,886
5000	21.805	99,223	258,036	220.468	−80,659

TABLE A.13
Curvefit coefficients for thermodynamic properties (C–H–O–N system)

$$\bar{c}_p/R_u = a_1 + a_2 T + a_3 T^2 + a_4 T^3 + a_5 T^4$$

$$\bar{h}^o/R_u T = a_1 + \frac{a_2}{2}T + \frac{a_3}{3}T^2 + \frac{a_4}{4}T^3 + \frac{a_5}{5}T^4 + \frac{a_6}{T}$$

$$\bar{s}^o/R_u = a_1 \ln T + a_2 T + \frac{a_3}{2}T^2 + \frac{a_4}{3}T^3 + \frac{a_5}{4}T^4 + a_7$$

Species	T(K)	a_1	a_2	a_3	a_4	a_5	a_6	a_7
CO	1000–5000	0.03025078E + 02	0.14426885E − 02	−0.05630827E − 05	0.10185813E − 09	−0.06910951E − 13	−0.14268350E + 05	0.06108217E + 02
	300–1000	0.03262451E + 02	0.15119409E − 02	−0.03881755E − 04	0.05581944E − 07	−0.02474951E − 10	−0.14310539E + 05	0.04848897E + 02
CO_2	1000–5000	0.04453623E + 02	0.03140168E − 01	−0.12784105E − 05	0.02393996E − 08	−0.16690333E − 13	−0.04896696E + 06	−0.09553959E + 01
	300–1000	0.02275724E + 02	0.09922072E − 01	−0.10409113E − 04	0.06866686E − 07	−0.02117280E − 10	−0.04837314E + 06	0.1018488E + 02
H_2	1000–5000	0.02991423E + 02	0.07000644E − 02	−0.05633828E − 06	−0.09231578E − 10	0.15827519E − 14	−0.08350340E + 04	−0.13551101E + 01
	300–1000	0.03298124E + 02	0.08249441E − 02	−0.08143015E − 05	−0.09475434E − 09	0.04134872E − 11	−0.10125209E + 04	−0.03294094E + 02
H	1000–5000	0.02500000E + 02	0.00000000E + 00	0.00000000E + 00	0.00000000E + 00	0.00000000E + 00	0.02547162E + 06	−0.04601176E + 01
	300–1000	0.02500000E + 02	0.00000000E + 00	0.00000000E + 00	0.00000000E + 00	0.00000000E + 00	0.02547162E + 06	−0.04601176E + 01
OH	1000–5000	0.02882730E + 02	0.10139743E − 02	−0.02276877E − 05	0.02174683E − 09	−0.05126305E − 14	0.03886888E + 05	0.05595712E + 02
	300–1000	0.03637266E + 02	0.01850910E − 02	−0.16761646E − 05	0.02387202E − 07	−0.08431442E − 11	0.03606781E + 05	0.13588605E + 01
H_2O	1000–5000	0.02672145E + 02	0.03056293E − 01	−0.08730260E − 05	0.12009964E − 09	−0.06391618E − 13	−0.02989921E + 06	0.06862817E + 02
	300–1000	0.03386842E + 02	0.03474982E − 01	−0.06354696E − 04	0.06968581E − 07	−0.02506588E − 10	−0.03020811E + 06	0.02590232E + 02
N_2	1000–5000	0.02926640E + 02	0.14879768E − 02	−0.05684760E − 05	0.10097038E − 09	−0.06753351E − 13	−0.09227977E + 04	0.05980528E + 02
	300–1000	0.03298677E + 02	0.14082404E − 02	−0.03963222E − 04	0.05641515E − 07	−0.02444854E − 10	−0.10208999E + 04	0.03950372E + 02
N	1000–5000	0.02450268E + 02	0.10661458E − 03	−0.07465337E − 06	0.01879652E − 09	−0.10259839E − 14	0.05611604E + 06	0.04448758E + 02
	300–1000	0.02503071E + 02	−0.02180018E − 03	0.05420529E − 06	−0.05647560E − 09	0.02099904E − 12	0.05609890E + 06	0.04167566E + 02
NO	1000–5000	0.03245435E + 02	0.12691383E − 02	−0.05015890E − 05	0.09169283E − 09	−0.06275419E − 13	0.09800840E + 05	0.06417293E + 02
	300–1000	0.03376541E + 02	0.12530634E − 02	−0.03302750E − 04	0.05217810E − 07	−0.02446262E − 10	0.09817961E + 05	0.05829590E + 02
NO_2	1000–5000	0.04682859E + 02	0.02462429E − 01	−0.10422585E − 05	0.01976902E − 08	−0.13917168E − 13	0.02261292E + 05	0.09885985E + 01
	300–1000	0.02670600E + 02	0.07838500E − 01	−0.08063864E − 04	0.06161714E − 07	−0.02320150E − 10	0.02896290E + 05	0.11612071E + 02

TABLE A.13 (continued)

Species	T(K)	a_1	a_2	a_3	a_4	a_5	a_6	a_7
O₂	1000–5000	0.03697578E + 02	0.06135197E − 02	−0.12588420E − 06	0.01775281E − 09	−0.11364354E − 14	−0.12339301E + 04	0.03189165E + 02
	300–1000	0.03212936E + 02	0.11274864E − 02	−0.05756150E − 05	0.13138773E − 08	−0.08768554E − 11	−0.10052490E + 04	0.06034737E + 02
O	1000–5000	0.02542059E + 02	−0.02755061E − 03	−0.03102803E − 07	0.04551067E − 10	−0.04368051E − 14	0.02923080E + 06	0.04920308E + 02
	300–1000	0.02946428E + 02	−0.16381665E − 02	0.02421031E − 04	−0.16028431E − 04	0.03890696E − 08	0.02914764E + 06	0.02963995E + 02

Source: Kee, R. J., Rupley, F. M., and Miller, J. A., "The Chemkin Thermodynamic Data Base," Sandia Report, SAND87-8215B, reprinted March 1991.

APPENDIX
B

FUEL PROPERTIES

TABLE B.1
Selected properties of hydrocarbon fuels: enthalpy of formation,[a] Gibbs function of formation,[a] entropy,[a] and higher and lower heating values all at 298.15 K and 1 atm; boiling points[b] and latent heat of vaporization[c] at 1 atm; constant-pressure adiabatic flame temperature at 1 atm;[c] liquid density[d]

Formula	Fuel	Mol. wt. (kg/kmol)	$\bar{h}_f^o$ (kJ/kmol)	$\bar{g}_f^o$ (kJ/kmol)	s^o (kJ/kmol-K)	HHV[†] (kJ/kg)	LHV[†] (kJ/kg)	Boiling pt. (°C)	h_{fg} (kJ/kg)	$T_{ad}^{‡}$ (K)	ρ_{liq}^* (kg/m³)
CH_4	Methane	16.043	−74,831	−50,794	186.188	55,528	50,016	−164	509	2226	300
C_2H_2	Acetylene	26.038	226,748	209,200	200.819	49,923	48,225	−84	—	2539	—
C_2H_4	Ethene	28.054	52,283	68,124	219.827	50,313	47,161	−103.7	—	2369	—
C_2H_6	Ethane	30.069	−84,667	−32,886	229.492	51,901	47,489	−88.6	488	2259	370
C_3H_6	Propane	42.080	20,414	62,718	266.939	48,936	45,784	−47.4	437	2334	514
C_3H_8	Propane	44.096	−103,847	−23,489	269.910	50,368	46,357	−42.1	425	2267	500
C_4H_8	1-Butene	56.107	1,172	72,036	307.440	48,471	45,319	−63	391	2322	595
C_4H_{10}	n-Butane	58.123	−124,733	−15,707	310.034	49,546	45,742	−0.5	386	2270	579
C_5H_{10}	1-Pentene	70.134	−20,920	78,605	347.607	48,152	45,000	30	358	2314	641
C_5H_{12}	n-Pentane	72.150	−146,440	−8,201	348.402	49,032	45,355	36.1	358	2272	626
C_6H_6	Benzene	78.113	82,927	129,658	269.199	42,277	40,579	80.1	393	2342	879
C_6H_{12}	1-Hexene	84.161	−41,673	87,027	385.974	47,955	44,803	63.4	335	2308	673
C_6H_{14}	n-Hexane	86.177	−167,193	209	386.811	48,696	45,105	69	335	2273	659
C_7H_{14}	1-Heptene	98.188	−62,132	95,563	424.383	47,817	44,665	93.6	—	2305	—
C_7H_{16}	n-Heptane	100.203	−187,820	8,745	425.262	48,456	44,926	98.4	316	2274	684
C_8H_{16}	1-Octene	112.214	−82,927	104,140	462.792	47,712	44,560	121.3	—	2302	—
C_8H_{18}	n-Octane	114.230	−208,447	17,322	463.671	48,275	44,791	125.7	300	2275	703
C_9H_{18}	1-Nonene	126.241	−103,512	112,717	501.243	47,631	44,478	—	—	2300	—
C_9H_{20}	n-Nonane	128.257	−229,032	25,857	502.080	48,134	44,686	150.8	295	2276	718
$C_{10}H_{20}$	1-Decene	140.268	−124,139	121,294	539.652	47,565	44,413	170.6	—	2298	—
$C_{10}H_{22}$	n-Decane	142.284	−249,659	34,434	540.531	48,020	44,602	174.1	277	2277	730
$C_{11}H_{22}$	1-Undecene	154.295	−144,766	129,830	578.061	47,512	44,360	—	—	2296	—
$C_{11}H_{24}$	n-Undecane	156.311	−270,286	43,012	578.940	47,926	44,532	195.9	265	2277	740

TABLE B.1 (continued)

Formula	Fuel	Mol. wt. (kg/kmol)	$\bar{h}_f^o$ (kJ/kmol)	$\bar{g}_f^o$ (kJ/kmol)	$\bar{s}^o$ (kJ/kmol-K)	HHV[†] (kJ/kg)	LHV[†] (kJ/kg)	Boiling pt. (°C)	h_{fg} (kJ/kg)	$T_{ad}^{\ddagger}$ (K)	ρ_{liq}^* (kg/m³)
$C_{12}H_{24}$	1-Dodecene	168.322	−165,352	138,407	616.471	47,468	44,316	213.4	—	2295	—
$C_{12}H_{26}$	n-Dodecane	170.337	−292,162	—	—	47,841	44,467	216.3	256	2277	749

† Based on gaseous fuel.

‡ For stoichiometric combustion with air (79% N_2, 21% O_2).

* For liquids at 20°C or for gases at the boiling point of the liquified gas.

Sources:

[a]Rossini, F. D., et al., *Selected Values of Physical and Thermodynamic Properties of Hydrocarbons and Related Compounds*, Carnegie Press, Pittsburgh, 1953.

[b]Weast, R. C. (ed.), *Handbook of Chemistry and Physics*, 56th Ed., CRC Press, Cleveland, 1976.

[c]Obert, E. F., *Internal Combustion Engines and Air Pollution*, Harper & Row, New York, 1973.

[d]Calculated using HPFLAME (Appendix F).

TABLE B.2
Curvefit coefficients for fuel specific heat and enthalpy[a] for reference state of zero enthalpy of the elements at 298.15 K, 1 atm

$$\bar{c}_p \text{ (kJ/kmol-K)} = 4.184(a_1 + a_2\theta + a_3\theta^2 + a_4\theta^3 + a_5\theta^{-2}),$$

$$\bar{h}^o \text{ (kJ/kmol)} = 4184(a_1\theta + a_2\theta^2/2 + a_3\theta^3/3 + a_4\theta^4/4 - a_5\theta^{-1} + a_6),$$

where $\theta \equiv T(K)/1000$

Fuel	Formula	Mol. wt.	a_1	a_2	a_3	a_4	a_5	a_6	a_8^b
Methane	CH_4	16.043	-0.29149	26.327	-10.610	1.5656	0.16573	-18.331	4.300
Propane	C_3H_8	44.096	-1.4867	74.339	-39.065	8.0543	0.01219	-27.313	8.852
Hexane	C_6H_{14}	86.177	-20.777	210.48	-164.125	52.832	0.56635	-39.836	15.611
Isooctane	C_8H_{18}	114.230	-0.55313	181.62	-97.787	20.402	-0.03095	-60.751	20.232
Methanol	CH_3OH	32.040	-2.7059	44.168	-27.501	7.2193	0.20299	-48.288	5.3375
Ethanol	C_2H_5OH	46.07	6.990	39.741	-11.926	0	0	-60.214	7.6135
Gasoline	$C_{8.26}H_{15.5}$	114.8	-24.078	256.63	-201.68	64.750	0.5808	-27.562	17.792
	$C_{7.76}H_{13.1}$	106.4	-22.501	227.99	-177.26	56.048	0.4845	-17.578	15.232
Diesel	$C_{10.8}H_{18.7}$	148.6	-9.1063	246.97	-143.74	32.329	0.0518	-50.128	23.514

[a]From Heywood, J. B., *Internal Combustion Engine Fundamentals*, McGraw-Hill, New York, 1988, by permission of McGraw-Hill, Inc.
[b]To obtain 0 K reference state for enthalpy, add a_8 to a_6.

TABLE B.3
Curvefit coefficients for fuel vapor thermal conductivity, viscosity, and specific heat[a]

$$\left.\begin{array}{l} k\,(\text{W/m-K}) \\ \mu\,(\text{N-s/m}^2)\cdot 10^6 \\ c_p\,(\text{J/kg-K}) \end{array}\right\} = a_1 + a_2T + a_3T^2 + a_4T^3 + a_5T^4 + a_6T^5 + a_7T^6$$

Formula	Fuel	T-range (K)	Property	a_1	a_2	a_3	a_4	a_5	a_6	a_7
CH_4	Methane	100–1000	k	−1.34014990E − 2	3.66307060E − 4	−1.82248608E − 6	5.93987998E − 9	−9.14055050E − 12	−6.78968890E − 15	−1.95048736E − 18
		70–1000	μ	2.96826700E − 1	3.71120100E − 2	1.21829800E − 5	−7.02426000E − 8	7.54326900E − 11	−2.72371660E − 14	0
			c_p	See Table B.2						
C_3H_8	Propane	200–500	k	−1.07682209E − 2	8.38590325E − 5	4.22059864E − 8	0	0	0	0
		270–600	μ	−3.54371100E − 1	3.08009600E − 2	−6.99723000E − 6	0	0	0	0
			c_p	See Table B.2						
C_6H_{14}	n-Hexane	250–1000	k	1.28775700E − 3	−2.00499443E − 5	2.37858831E − 7	−1.60944555E − 10	7.71027290E − 14	0	0
		270–900	μ	−1.54541200E + 0	1.15080900E − 2	2.72216500E − 5	−3.26900000E − 8	1.24545900E − 11	0	0
			c_p	See Table B.2						
C_7H_{16}	n-Heptane	250–1000	k	−4.60614700E − 2	5.95652224E − 4	−2.98893153E − 6	8.44612876E − 9	−1.22927E − 11	9.0127E − 15	−2.62961E − 18
		270–580	μ	1.54009700E + 0	1.09515700E − 2	1.80066400E − 5	−1.36379000E − 8	0	0	0
		300–755	c_p	9.46260000E + 1	5.86099700E + 0	−1.98231320E − 3	−6.88699300E − 8	−1.93795260E − 10	0	0
		755–1365	c_p	−7.40308000E + 2	1.08935370E + 2	−1.26512400E − 2	9.84376300E − 6	−4.32282960E − 9	7.86366500E − 13	0
C_8H_{18}	n-Octane	250–500	k	−4.01391940E − 3	3.38796092E − 5	8.19291819E − 8	0	0	0	0
		300–650	μ	8.32435400E − 1	1.40045000E − 2	8.79376500E − 6	−6.84030000E − 9	0	0	0
		275–755	c_p	2.14419800E + 2	5.35690500E + 0	−1.17497000E − 3	−6.99115500E − 7	0	0	0
		755–1365	c_p	2.43596860E + 3	−4.46819470E + 0	1.66843290E − 2	−1.78856050E − 5	8.64282020E − 9	−1.61426500E − 12	0
$C_{10}H_{22}$	n-Decane	250–500	k	−5.88274000E − 3	3.72449646E − 5	7.55109624E − 8	0	0	0	0
			μ	Not available						
		300–700	c_p	2.40717800E + 2	5.09965000E + 0	−6.29026000E − 4	−1.07155000E − 6	0	0	0
		700–1365	c_p	−1.35345890E + 4	9.14879000E + 1	−2.20700000E − 1	2.91406000E − 4	−2.15307400E − 7	8.38600000E − 11	−1.34400000E − 14
CH_3OH	Methanol	300–550	k	−2.02986750E − 2	1.21910927E − 4	−2.23748473E − 8	0	0	0	0
		250–650	μ	1.19790000E + 0	2.45028000E − 2	1.86162740E − 5	−1.30674820E − 8	0	0	0
			c_p	See Table B.2						
C_2H_5OH	Ethanol	250–500	k	−2.46663000E − 2	1.55892550E − 4	−8.22954822E − 8	0	0	0	0
		270–600	μ	−6.33595000E − 2	3.20713470E − 2	−6.25079576E − 6	0	0	0	0
			c_p	See Table B.2						

[a]*Source:* Andrews, J. R., and Biblarz, O., "Temperature Dependence of Gas Properties in Polynomial Form," Naval Postgraduate School, NPS67-81-001, January 1981.

APPENDIX
C

TABLE C.1
Selected properties of air[a]

T (K)	ρ (kg/m^3)	c_p (kJ/kg-K)	$\mu \cdot 10^7$ (N-s/m^2)	$\nu \cdot 10^6$ (m^2/s)	$k \cdot 10^3$ (W/m-K)	$\alpha \cdot 10^6$ (m^2/s)	Pr
100	3.5562	1.032	71.1	2.00	9.34	2.54	0.786
150	2.3364	1.012	103.4	4.426	13.8	5.84	0.758
200	1.7458	1.007	132.5	7.590	18.1	10.3	0.737
250	1.3947	1.006	159.6	11.44	22.3	15.9	0.720
300	1.1614	1.007	184.6	15.89	26.3	22.5	0.707
350	0.9950	1.009	208.2	20.92	30.0	29.9	0.700
400	0.8711	1.014	230.1	26.41	33.8	38.3	0.690
450	0.7740	1.021	250.7	32.39	37.3	47.2	0.686
500	0.6964	1.030	270.1	38.79	40.7	56.7	0.684
550	0.6329	1.040	288.4	45.57	43.9	66.7	0.683
600	0.5804	1.051	305.8	52.69	46.9	76.9	0.685
650	0.5356	1.063	322.5	60.21	49.7	87.3	0.690
700	0.4975	1.075	338.8	68.10	52.4	98.0	0.695
750	0.4643	1.087	354.6	76.37	54.9	109	0.702
800	0.4354	1.099	369.8	84.93	57.3	120	0.709
850	0.4097	1.110	384.3	93.80	59.6	131	0.716
900	0.3868	1.121	398.1	102.9	62.0	143	0.720
950	0.3666	1.131	411.3	112.2	64.3	155	0.723
1000	0.3482	1.141	424.4	121.9	66.7	168	0.726
1100	0.3166	1.159	449.0	141.8	71.5	195	0.728
1200	0.2902	1.175	473.0	162.9	76.3	224	0.728
1300	0.2679	1.189	496.0	185.1	82	238	0.719
1400	0.2488	1.207	530	213	91	303	0.703
1500	0.2322	1.230	557	240	100	350	0.685
1600	0.2177	1.248	584	268	106	390	0.688
1700	0.2049	1.267	611	298	113	435	0.685
1800	0.1935	1.286	637	329	120	482	0.683
1900	0.1833	1.307	663	362	128	534	0.677
2000	0.1741	1.337	689	396	137	589	0.672
2100	0.1658	1.372	715	431	147	646	0.667

TABLE C.1 (continued)

T (K)	ρ (kg/m³)	c_p (kJ/kg-K)	$\mu \cdot 10^7$ (N-s/m²)	$\nu \cdot 10^6$ (m²/s)	$k \cdot 10^3$ (W/m-K)	$\alpha \cdot 10^6$ (m²/s)	Pr
2200	0.1582	1.417	740	468	160	714	0.655
2300	0.1513	1.478	766	506	175	783	0.647
2400	0.1448	1.558	792	547	196	869	0.630
2500	0.1389	1.665	818	589	222	960	0.613
3000	0.1135	2.726	955	841	486	1570	0.536

[a]*Source:* Incropera, F. P., and DeWitt, D. P., *Fundamentals of Heat and Mass Transfer*, 3rd Ed. Reprinted by permission, ©1990, John Wiley & Sons, Inc.

TABLE C.2
Selected properties of nitrogen and oxygen[a]

T (K)	ρ (kg/m^3)	c_p (kJ/kg-K)	$\mu \cdot 10^7$ (N-s/m^2)	$\nu \cdot 10^6$ (m^2/s)	$k \cdot 10^3$ (W/m-K)	$\alpha \cdot 10^6$ (m^2/s)	Pr
Nitrogen (N$_2$)							
100	3.4388	1.070	68.8	2.00	9.58	2.60	0.768
150	2.2594	1.050	100.6	4.45	13.9	5.86	0.759
200	1.6883	1.043	129.2	7.65	18.3	10.4	0.736
250	1.3488	1.042	154.9	11.48	22.2	15.8	0.727
300	1.1233	1.041	178.2	15.86	25.9	22.1	0.716
350	0.9625	1.042	200.0	20.78	29.3	29.2	0.711
400	0.8425	1.045	220.4	26.16	32.7	37.1	0.704
450	0.7485	1.050	239.6	32.01	35.8	45.6	0.703
500	0.6739	1.056	257.7	38.24	38.9	54.7	0.700
550	0.6124	1.065	274.7	44.86	41.7	63.9	0.702
600	0.5615	1.075	290.8	51.79	44.6	73.9	0.701
700	0.4812	1.098	321.0	66.71	49.9	94.4	0.706
800	0.4211	1.22	349.1	82.90	54.8	116	0.715
900	0.3743	1.146	375.3	100.3	59.7	139	0.721
1000	0.3368	1.167	399.9	118.7	64.7	165	0.721
1100	0.3062	1.187	423.2	138.2	70.0	193	0.718
1200	0.2807	1.204	445.3	158.6	75.8	224	0.707
1300	0.2591	1.219	466.2	179.9	81.0	256	0.701
Oxygen (O$_2$)							
100	3.945	0.962	76.4	1.94	9.25	2.44	0.796
150	2.585	0.921	114.8	4.44	13.8	5.80	0.766
200	1.930	0.915	147.5	7.64	18.3	10.4	0.737
250	1.542	0.915	178.6	11.58	22.6	16.0	0.723
300	1.284	0.920	207.2	16.14	26.8	22.7	0.711
350	1.100	0.929	233.5	21.23	29.6	29.0	0.733
400	0.9620	0.942	258.2	26.84	33.0	36.4	0.737
450	0.8554	0.956	281.4	32.90	36.3	44.4	0.741
500	0.7698	0.972	303.3	39.40	41.2	55.1	0.716
550	0.6998	0.988	324.0	46.30	44.1	63.8	0.726
600	0.6414	1.003	343.7	53.59	47.3	73.5	0.729
700	0.5498	1.031	380.8	69.26	52.8	93.1	0.744
800	0.4810	1.054	415.2	86.32	58.9	116	0.743
900	0.4275	1.074	447.2	104.6	64.9	141	0.740
1000	0.3848	1.090	477.0	124.0	71.0	169	0.733
1100	0.3498	1.103	505.5	144.5	75.8	196	0.736
1200	0.3206	1.115	532.5	166.1	81.9	229	0.725
1300	0.2960	1.125	588.4	188.6	87.1	262	0.721

[a]*Source:* Incropera, F. P., and DeWitt, D. P., *Fundamentals of Heat and Mass Transfer*, 3rd Ed. Reprinted by permission, © 1990, John Wiley & Sons, Inc.

APPENDIX

D

TABLE D.1
Binary diffusivities at 1 atmosphere[a,b]

Substance A	Substance B	$T(K)$	$D_{AB} \cdot 10^5$ (m²/s)
Benzene	Air	273	0.77
Carbon dioxide	Air	273	1.38
Carbon dioxide	Nitrogen	393	1.6
Cyclohexane	Air	318	0.86
n-Decane	Nitrogen	363	0.84
n-Dodecane	Nitrogen	399	0.81
Ethanol	Air	273	1.02
n-Hexane	Nitrogen	288	0.757
Hydrogen	Air	273	0.611
Methanol	Air	273	1.32
n-Octane	Air	273	0.505
n-Octane	Nitrogen	303	0.71
Toluene	Air	303	0.88
2,2,4-Trimethyl pentane (Isooctane)	Nitrogen	303	0.705
2,2,3-Trimethyl heptane	Nitrogen	363	0.684
Water	Air	273	2.2

[a]*Source:* Perry, R. H., Green, D. W., and Maloney, J. O., *Perry's Chemical Engineers' Handbook*, 6th Ed., McGraw-Hill, New York, 1984.

[b]Assuming ideal-gas behavior, the pressure and temperature dependence of the binary diffusion coefficient can be estimated using $D_{AB} \propto T^{3/2}/P$.

APPENDIX

E

GENERALIZED NEWTON'S METHOD FOR THE SOLUTION OF NONLINEAR EQUATIONS

The Newton–Raphson method can be applied to a system of nonlinear equations:

$$x_{n+1} = x_n - \frac{f(x_n)}{f'(x_n)} = x_n - \frac{f(x_n)}{\dfrac{\mathrm{d}f}{\mathrm{d}x}(x_n)} \tag{E.1}$$

system:

$$f_1(x_1, x_2, x_3, \ldots, x_n) = 0$$
$$f_2(x_1, x_2, x_3, \ldots, x_n) = 0$$
$$\vdots \tag{E.2}$$
$$f_n(x_1, x_2, x_3, \ldots, x_n) = 0.$$

Each of these may be expanded in Taylor's series form (truncating second-order and higher terms) as

$$f_i(\tilde{x} + \tilde{\delta}) = f_i(\tilde{x}) + \frac{\partial f_i}{\partial x_1}\delta_1 + \frac{\partial f_i}{\partial x_2}\delta_2 + \frac{\partial f_i}{\partial x_3}\delta_3 + \ldots + \frac{\partial f_i}{\partial x_n}\delta_n, \tag{E.3}$$

for $i = 1, 2, 3, \ldots, n$, where

$$\tilde{x} \equiv \{x\}.$$

At the solution, $f(\tilde{x} + \tilde{\delta}) \to 0$; the above can be arranged as a set of *linear* equations in the matrix form,

$$\left[\frac{\partial f}{\partial x}\right]\{\delta\} = -\{f\};$$

that is,

$$\begin{bmatrix} \dfrac{\partial f_1}{\partial x_1} & \dfrac{\partial f_1}{\partial x_2} & \cdots & \dfrac{\partial f_1}{\partial x_n} \\ \vdots & \vdots & & \vdots \\ \dfrac{\partial f_n}{\partial x_1} & \dfrac{\partial f_n}{\partial x_2} & \cdots & \dfrac{\partial f_n}{\partial x_n} \end{bmatrix} \begin{Bmatrix} \delta_1 \\ \vdots \\ \delta_n \end{Bmatrix} = \begin{Bmatrix} -f_1 \\ \vdots \\ -f_n \end{Bmatrix} \tag{E.4}$$

where the coefficient matrix on the left-hand-side is called the **Jacobian**.

Equation (E.4) may be solved (for δ) using Gauss elimination; once δ is known, the next (better) approximation is found from the recursion relation,

$$\{x\}_{k+1} = \{x\}_k + \{\delta\}_k.$$

The process of forming the Jacobian, solving Eqn. (E.4), and calculating new values for $\{x\}$ is repeated until a stop criteria is met. The following is suggested by Suh and Radcliffe [1]:

Stop criteria	*Condition*
$\|\delta_j/x_j\| \le 10^{-7}$	$\|x_j\| \ge 10^{-7}$
or	
$\|\delta_j\| \le 10^{-7}$	$\|x_j\| \le 10^{-7}$

for $j = 1, 2, 3, \ldots, n$.

Estimates to the partial derivatives may be formed numerically from:

$$\frac{\partial f_i}{\partial x_j} = \frac{f_i(x_1, x_2, \ldots, x_j + \varepsilon, \ldots, x_n) - f_i(x_1, x_2, x_3, \ldots, x_j, \ldots, x_n)}{\varepsilon}$$

where

$$\varepsilon = 10^{-5}|x_j| \quad \text{for} \quad |x_j| > 1.0$$
$$\varepsilon = 10^{-5} \quad \text{for} \quad |x_j| < 1.0.$$

Instability may (in many cases) be avoided as follows:

1. Compare the norm of the new function vector to the norm of the previous function vector, where

$$\text{norm} = \sum_{i=1}^{n} |f_i(\tilde{x})|.$$

2. If the norm of the new function vector is greater than that of the old, assume that the full step $\{\delta\}$ would not be productive and take a partial step $\{\delta\}/5$; otherwise, take a full step as usual.

The process of comparing norms and dividing $\{\delta\}$ by an arbitrary constant is termed "damping" and has proved successful in obtaining convergence even with very poor initial guesses.

A weakness of the Newton–Raphson method is that the Jacobian must be calculated at every step.

REFERENCE

1. Suh, C. H., and Radcliffe, C. W., *Kinematics and Mechanisms Design*, John Wiley & Sons, New York, pp. 143–144, 1978.

APPENDIX

F

COMPUTER CODES FOR EQUILIBRIUM PRODUCTS OF HYDROCARBON–AIR COMBUSTION

Supplied with this book is a diskette containing the following files:

File	*Purpose*
README	File containing instructions and other information concerning the use of the files listed below
TPEQUIL	Executable module that calculates combustion products' equilibrium composition and properties for specified fuel, equivalence ratio, temperature, and pressure
TPEQUIL.F	Fortran source listing for TPEQUIL
INPUT.TP	Input file read by TPEQUIL containing user specifications for fuel, equivalence ratio, temperature, and pressure
HPFLAME	Executable module that calculates the adiabatic flame temperature, equilibrium composition, and properties of the products of

combustion for **adiabatic constant-pressure combustion** with specified fuel composition, reactant enthalpy, equivalence ratio, and pressure

HPFLAME.F   Fortran source listing for HPFLAME

INPUT.HP   Input file read by HPFLAME containing user specifications for fuel, reactant enthalpy (per kilomole of fuel), equivalence ratio, and pressure

UVFLAME   Executable module that calculates the adiabatic flame temperature, equilibrium composition, and properties of the products of combustion for **adiabatic constant-volume combustion** with specified fuel composition, reactant enthalpy, equivalence ratio, and initial temperature and pressure

UVFLAME.F   Fortran source listing for UVFLAME

INPUT.UV   Input file read by UVFLAME containing user specifications for fuel, reactant enthalpy (per kilomole of fuel), equivalence ratio, moles of reactants per mole of fuel, molecular weight of reactants, and initial temperature and pressure

GPROP.DAT   Thermodynamic property data file

The various codes above all incorporate the Olikara and Borman routines [1] for calculating equilibrium products of combustion for a fuel composed of C, H, O, and N atoms, given by $C_N H_M O_L N_K$ and air.[1] Thus, oxygenated fuels, such as alcohols, and fuels with bound nitrogen can be handled by the code. For simple hydrocarbons, the number of fuel oxygen and nitrogen atoms, L and K, respectively, are set equal to zero in the user-modified input files. The oxidizer is assumed to be air with the simplified composition of 79% N_2, and 21% O_2 and is specified in the subroutine TABLES. A more complex oxidizer composition, including Ar, for example, can be obtained easily by modifying this subroutine and recompiling the source code. Eleven species are considered in the products of combustion: H, O, N, H_2, OH, CO, NO, O_2, H_2O, CO_2, and N_2. The code also considers Ar if it is included in the oxidizer. The Olikara and Borman routines [1] have been modified to deal in SI units. Other modifications to the original code include the way the JANAF thermodynamic data and equilibrium constants are input, as indicated in the source listings.

REFERENCE

1. Olikara, C., and Borman, G. L., "A Computer Program for Calculating Properties of Equilibrium Combustion Products with Some Applications to I. C. Engines," SAE Paper 750468, 1975.

[1]The imbedded codes from Ref. [1], with modifications, are used with permission of the Society of Automotive Engineers, Inc., © 1975.

INDEX